CRIMINAL EVIDENCE AND HUMAN RIGHTS

Criminal procedure in the common law world is being recast in the image of human rights. The cumulative impact of human rights laws, both international and domestic, presages a revolution in common law procedural traditions. Comprising 16 essays plus the editors' thematic introduction, this volume explores various aspects of the 'human rights revolution' in criminal evidence and procedure in Australia, Canada, England and Wales, Hong Kong, Malaysia, New Zealand, Northern Ireland, the Republic of Ireland, Singapore, Scotland, South Africa and the USA. The contributors provide expert evaluations of their own domestic law and practice with frequent reference to comparative experiences in other jurisdictions. Some essays focus on specific topics, such as evidence obtained by torture, the presumption of innocence, hearsay, the privilege against self-incrimination, and 'rape shield' laws. Others seek to draw more general lessons about the context of law reform, the epistemic demands of the right to a fair trial, the domestic impact of supra-national legal standards (especially the ECHR), and the scope for reimagining common law procedures through the medium of human rights.

This edited collection showcases the latest theoretically informed, methodologically astute and doctrinally rigorous scholarship in criminal procedure and evidence, human rights and comparative law, and will be a major addition to the literature in all of these fields.

Criminal Evidence and Human Rights

Reimagining Common Law Procedural Traditions

Edited by

Paul Roberts
and
Jill Hunter

• HART •
PUBLISHING
OXFORD AND PORTLAND, OREGON
2012

Published in the United Kingdom by Hart Publishing Ltd
16C Worcester Place, Oxford, OX1 2JW
Telephone: +44 (0)1865 517530
Fax: +44 (0)1865 510710
E-mail: mail@hartpub.co.uk
Website: http://www.hartpub.co.uk

Published in North America (US and Canada) by
Hart Publishing
c/o International Specialized Book Services
920 NE 58th Avenue, Suite 300
Portland, OR 97213-3786
USA
Tel: +1 503 287 3093 or toll-free: (1) 800 944 6190
Fax: +1 503 280 8832
E-mail: orders@isbs.com
Website: http://www.isbs.com

British Library Cataloguing in Publication Data
Data Available

ISBN: 978-1-84946-172-6

Typeset by Compuscript Ltd, Shannon
Printed and bound in Great Britain by
CPI Group (UK) Ltd, Croydon, CR0 4YY

Acknowledgements

The sixteen new essays comprising this collection were specially commissioned as part of a long-standing collaboration between the editors to develop comparative cosmopolitan perspectives on the law of criminal evidence and procedure. This phase of the project focuses on the expanding influence of human rights in common law criminal trials. In order to promote genuine dialogue and debate around these revolutionary developments in criminal adjudication, and to share comparative experiences, we devised and ran two linked two-day contributors' conferences, the first at UNSW in Sydney in April 2010, with a follow-up meeting in Nottingham that September. With a couple of unavoidable exceptions, all of the essays in this volume were aired in draft form at one or other of our contributors' colloquia. Many evolved through successive drafts presented and debated at both meetings. The proof of this methodology is to be found in the prominent points of continuity and contrast, shared policy dilemmas, and cross-cutting themes featured in the following pages.

The Sydney conference, entitled *Criminal Evidence & Human Rights: Common Law Perspectives,* was organised under the auspices of the UNSW Centre for Interdisciplinary Studies of Law and generously funded by the UNSW Faculty of Law. The Nottingham meeting on *Criminal Evidence & Human Rights* was supported by the award of the Society of Legal Scholars Annual Seminar 2010, with additional benefits-in-kind being contributed by the University of Nottingham School of Law. Without this financial sponsorship—increasingly viewed as a luxury in these straitened times—plus further funding from contributors' own institutions to cover travel costs there would have been no conferences and no book. The support of UNSW, SLS and the University of Nottingham, in particular, is gratefully acknowledged. Christine Brooks (UNSW) and Jane Costa and Anne Crump (Nottingham) helped with conference organisation and administration with consummate efficiency.

Everybody who attended the conferences contributed to the discussion, and therefore to the quality of the essays in this volume. We are grateful to them all. But we must single out for special thanks the seminar participants, including colleagues in the earlier stages of their academic careers, who served as discussants at our two meetings. Theirs was a pivotal role, to introduce each draft paper and kick-start the general discussion with incisive comments, questions, queries and challenges, and this duty was discharged, without exception, with vigour and aplomb. Our locally-resident UNSW discussants were Jill Anderson, David Dixon, Gary Edmond, Rezana

Karim, Tyrone Kirchengast and Mehera San Roque. The Nottingham discussants were: Roderick Bagshaw (Oxford); Louise Ellison (Leeds); Dimitrios Giannoulopoulos (Brunel); Richard Glover (Wolverhampton); Laura Hoyano (Oxford); Imogen Jones (Manchester); Roger Leng (Warwick); Jenny McEwan (Exeter); Hannah Quirk (Manchester); Candida Saunders (Nottingham); and Tony Ward (Hull).

Richard Hart was an enthusiastic supporter of this project from the outset. Rachel Turner, Mel Hamill, Tom Adams and their colleagues at Hart Publishing have seen the manuscript through to publication with their characteristic friendly professionalism, encouragement and sound advice.

Our greatest debt is owed to our contributors. We brought together twenty or so of the most eminent Evidence scholars and criminal proceduralists in the common law world, and asked them to subject their work-in-progress to energetic roundtable debate, with no allowance for title, status or reputation. Every one of our contributors fully entered into the spirit of the enterprise and maintained their collaborative poise to the end, despite serial provocations from demanding editors. The bean-counters who today proliferate in higher education will never be able to put a price on the privilege of working with such an extraordinarily talented and collegial group of legal scholars drawn from all four corners of the globe.

We learnt, at an advanced stage of the editorial process, of the sudden death of Craig Callen on 23 April 2011 after a short illness. Craig never had the opportunity to respond to the editors' suggestions and queries on his draft manuscript. His edited chapter appears here as we hope he would have wanted and intended it. Craig Callen personified the creativity, industry, intellectual generosity and collegiality of truly first-rate scholars, and his friendship no less than his inventive contributions to the discipline will be greatly missed by our research group, as by many others in the legal academy. This volume is dedicated to Craig's memory.

PR
Beeston,
Bonfire Night 2011

JH
Birchgrove,

Dedication

In memory of

Professor Craig R Callen
(1950–2011)

Table of Contents

List of Contributors

Andrew Ashworth, Vinerian Professor of English Law, University of Oxford

Christine Boyle, Professor of Law, University of British Columbia

Craig R Callen was Judge John D O'Hair Professor of Evidence and Procedure, Michigan State University College of Law

Andrew L-T Choo, Professor of English Law, Brunel University; Barrister, Matrix Chambers

Emma Cunliffe, Assistant Professor, University of British Columbia, Faculty of Law

Peter Duff, Professor of Criminal Justice, University of Aberdeen

Salim Farrar, Senior Lecturer, Sydney Law School

Chris Gallavin, Senior Lecturer in Law, University of Canterbury, NZ

Jeremy Gans, Associate Professor, Melbourne Law School

David Hamer, Associate Professor, Sydney Law School

Terese Henning, Senior Lecturer in Law, University of Tasmania

Hock Lai Ho, Professor of Law, National University of Singapore

Jill Hunter, Professor of Law, University of New South Wales

John Jackson, Professor of Criminal Law, University College Dublin

Mike Redmayne, Professor of Law, London School of Economics and Political Science

Paul Roberts, Professor of Criminal Jurisprudence, University of Nottingham; Adjunct Professor, University of New South Wales Faculty of Law

PJ Schwikkard, Dean of the Faculty of Law & Professor of Law, University of Cape Town

Simon NM Young, Associate Professor & Director, Centre for Comparative and Public Law, University of Hong Kong

Table of Cases

Australia

Canada

Caribbean Community & Commonwealth

European Convention on Human Rights

Hong Kong

India

International Criminal Tribunal for the Former Yugoslavia (ICTY)

Malaysia

New Zealand

Republic of Ireland

Singapore

South Africa

United Kingdom

England and Wales

Northern Ireland

Scotland

USA

Table of Legislation

National Legislation

Australia

Singapore

South Africa

Introduction—The Human Rights Revolution in Criminal Evidence and Procedure

PAUL ROBERTS AND JILL HUNTER

1. HUMAN RIGHTS REVOLUTION

THIS VOLUME EXPLORES the impact, in theory and practice, of the on-going 'human rights revolution' on the law of criminal evidence and procedure in a variety of common law jurisdictions. Human rights legislation, case-law and principles are transforming criminal evidence and procedure across the common law world. However, there is marked diversity not only—as one would expect—in the technical doctrinal adaptations improvised by individual legal systems, but also in the pace and extent of human rights-inspired innovation. Some jurisdictions, such as Canada and New Zealand, already have several decades' experience in reviewing and sometimes adjusting their criminal procedures to the dictates of human rights norms, especially the right to a fair trial. Others, for example the State of Victoria and the Australian Capital Territory, are just embarking upon similar legislative experiments.[1] Another group of jurisdictions, notably including the Republic of South Africa and Hong Kong, have embraced international fair trial standards as part of reformed and rededicated constitutional frameworks. In the United Kingdom's criminal law jurisdictions, the Human Rights Act 1998 has now been in force for over a decade. Its impact on criminal procedure and evidence has already been profound, and the process of transformation is by no means complete. A striking feature of these developments has been the growing influence of the Strasbourg-based European Court of Human Rights on the domestic criminal procedure jurisprudence of England and Wales, Scotland and Northern Ireland.

Domestic legal systems, under the tutelage of international legality, have embarked upon what are, in effect, high-stakes practical experiments in criminal procedure reform. Lawyers and judges in practice have been presented

[1] See generally, J Gans, T Henning, J Hunter and K Warner, *Criminal Process and Human Rights* (Sydney, Federation Press, 2011).

with new opportunities and confronted with unfamiliar challenges in criminal adjudication. Legal scholarship can and should play its part in theorising these novel juridical configurations and helping to make sense of them, partly—though by no means exclusively—in order to contribute to rational policy-making, law reform and the administration of criminal justice.

There have, of course, been comparable earlier step-changes and seismic events in the historical evolution of common law criminal procedure, such as the adoption of trial by jury,[2] the creation of modern police forces,[3] the development of adversarial cross-examination[4] and the (surprisingly late) decision to allow the accused to testify under oath in his own defence.[5] But it is fair to say that the advent of human rights arguments and principles in routine criminal litigation is one of the most significant jurisprudential developments affecting common law adjudication for many decades, and calling it a 'revolution' does not seem hyperbolic. Pressing new questions arise, for theorists and practitioners alike, when we are required to re-envision criminal procedure through the lens of human rights law and principles of adjudication,[6] including questions concerning normative sources, hierarchy, scope and content, transmission, adaptation, institutional competence and practical implementation. To formulate some of these questions more precisely:

— What are the source(s) of criminal procedure-related human rights in particular jurisdictions? Supra-national, transnational, indigenous, or some blended mixture? By what legal mechanisms have supra-national and/or transnational and/or foreign law norms been received? How have these migrations been effected and justified in accordance with local conceptions of valid legal sources and constitutional traditions? How effectively have such transmissions and translations been implemented in practice?
— What is the content of pertinent human rights norms, especially the 'right to a fair trial'? How, if at all, does the terminology, conceptual structure or scope of human rights differ from established common law procedural traditions? Have standard definitions and approaches been imported wholesale from outside the jurisdiction, or have adaptations been made to accommodate local conditions? How have different legal systems balanced generality and specificity (with corresponding allocations of institutional responsibility for normative development)?

[2] JB Thayer, *A Preliminary Treatise on Evidence at the Common Law* (Boston, MA, Little, Brown & Co, 1898) Part I; N Vidmar (ed), *World Jury Systems* (Oxford, OUP, 2000).

[3] C Emsley, 'The Birth and Development of the Police' in T Newburn (ed), *Handbook of Policing*, 2nd edn (Cullompton, Willan, 2008).

[4] JH Langbein, *The Origins of Adversary Criminal Trial* (Oxford, OUP, 2003); DJA Cairns, *Advocacy and the Making of the Adversarial Criminal Trial 1800–1865* (Oxford, OUP, 1999).

[5] C Tapper, 'The Meaning of s.1(f)(i) of the Criminal Evidence Act 1898' in CFH Tapper (ed), *Crime, Proof and Punishment* (London, Butterworths, 1981).

[6] C Gearty, *Principles of Human Rights Adjudication* (Oxford, OUP, 2004).

— What have jurisdictions learnt from international or comparative experience, for example, in addressing drafting or interpretative controversies? Why, how, and how effectively were such controversies resolved?
— Which particular issues or topics in criminal procedure and evidence have been, or are likely to be, most affected by the reception of human rights norms? Why have these particular issues and topics (and not others) become notable successes or pressure points?
— Has the advent of human rights considerations achieved any notable successes in the reform or improvement of criminal procedure? In those jurisdictions still contemplating human rights legislation, which improvements are expected or promised by human rights advocates?
— Has human rights legislation created particular problems or difficulties for criminal procedure? Are there identifiable points of normative conflict or institutional resistance to the reception of human rights standards, especially those standards deriving from supra-national, transnational or foreign law influences? How are these conflicts playing out in particular legal systems?
— Are there intrinsic or symbolic dimensions to local debates and institutional developments that manifest in particular ways, or is the impact of human rights norms on criminal evidence and procedure simply a question of instrumental effects?
— How does human rights legislation interact with other primary sources of criminal evidence, including piecemeal legislation addressing evidentiary topics and more systematic codification of procedural law (to the extent that such instruments exist in particular jurisdictions)?
— To what extent has human rights legislation introduced, or facilitated, institutional realignments in the distribution of powers and responsibility for developing and implementing procedural norms (eg from trial to appellate courts, or vice versa; from ordinary law to more-or-less entrenched constitutional law; from domestic to international law, etc)?
— To what extent do any or all of the foregoing questions call for systematic reconsideration of the nature of evidentiary and other procedural norms at the doctrinal or micro-jurisprudential levels, or—by extension—urge fundamental rethinking about the Law of (Criminal) Evidence as a discrete, institutionally-differentiated and coherent discipline (eg as an identifiable module in law school curricula, as an 'essentially common law subject', or as exclusively a matter for regulation by state authorities)?[7]

[7] See further, P Roberts, 'Groundwork for a Jurisprudence of Criminal Procedure' in RA Duff and SP Green (eds), *Philosophical Foundations of Criminal Law* (New York, OUP, 2011); P Roberts and M Redmayne (eds), *Innovations in Evidence and Proof* (Oxford, Hart Publishing, 2007); W Twining, *Rethinking Evidence*, 2nd edn (Cambridge, CUP, 2006).

By exploring these, and related, questions in depth across a number of differently-situated common law jurisdictions, the essays in this volume shed new light on the nature, extent and diverse implications of existing and contemplated interactions between human rights legislation and the law and practice of criminal procedure. A particular brand of distinctively common law comparativism is key to this enterprise, as we conceive it.

2. COMMON LAW COMPARATIVISM

Comparative methodology barely calls for extended justification in an era of globalisation and increasingly cosmopolitan law. Tangible traces of cosmopolitan legality are everywhere to be seen: in the institutions of regional governance, such as the (EU) European Council and Commission[8] and the (Council of Europe's) European Court of Human Rights;[9] in unprecedented efforts to implement international criminal law through novel creations such as the UN ad hoc tribunals for the former Yugoslavia (ICTY) and Rwanda (ICTR), culminating in the historic achievement of a permanent International Criminal Court;[10] and in the pervasive discourses and institutionalised practices of human rights law itself. Small wonder that comparative law specialists are now proclaiming—albeit not for the first time—that their day has truly dawned.[11]

The essays in this volume explore human rights-related developments in criminal procedure law in most of the world's leading common law jurisdictions, including Australia (especially where its uniform Evidence Acts apply), Canada, England and Wales, Hong Kong, Malaysia, New Zealand, Northern Ireland, the Republic of Ireland, Scotland, Singapore, South Africa, and the United States.[12] A project with this geographical coverage cannot fail to be 'comparative' in the literal sense, if only implicitly; just like the common law itself. Extending beyond merely geographical juxtaposition, our aim has been to pioneer an approach to comparative legal analysis which departs from Comparative Law studies in their more conventional mould.

[8] P Craig and G de Búrca, *EU Law: Text, Cases and Materials*, 4th edn (Oxford, OUP, 2008) chs 1, 2 and 11.

[9] A Mowbray, *Cases and Materials on the European Convention on Human Rights*, 2nd edn (Oxford, OUP, 2007) chs 1–2.

[10] A Cassese, *International Criminal Law*, 2nd edn (Oxford, OUP, 2008) Part III; R Cryer, *Prosecuting International Crimes* (Cambridge, CUP, 2005).

[11] See eg E Örücü, 'Developing Comparative Law' in E Örücü and D Nelken (eds), *Comparative Law—A Handbook* (Oxford, Hart Publishing, 2007); G Samuel, 'Comparative Law as a Core Subject' (2001) 21 *Legal Studies* 444; B Markesinis, 'Comparative Law—A Subject in Search of an Audience' (1990) 53 *Modern Law Review* 1.

[12] Significant gaps, which we hope can be filled out in future work, include the Indian subcontinent and sub-Saharan Africa.

In the field of criminal justice, self-consciously 'comparative' perspectives typically compare and contrast common law adversarial systems with their 'inquisitorial' counterparts in western European jurisdictions such as France, Italy and Germany.[13] The approach adopted in this volume is at once narrower than conventional legal comparativism, in being confined to common law jurisdictions, but also broader and deeper, in extending its critical gaze beyond western Europe and North America and, crucially, in tracing the impact of generalised normative standards, such as the right to a fair trial, into the doctrinal details and the practical realities of criminal litigation in different legal systems. We think details matter, in law and life. Even if legal systems within and beyond the common law family are increasingly being shaped by a global law of human rights, each jurisdiction will continue to make its own juridical accommodations between the demands of universal legal standards and local procedural traditions.

Our 'common law comparativism' is a serious attempt to make meaningful and insightful comparisons between the criminal procedure laws and evidentiary practices in a variety of common law jurisdictions, each of which is simultaneously in the process of being transformed—to a greater or lesser extent—by the on-going human rights revolution, alongside other cross-cutting transnational and cosmopolitan influences. Local doctrinal and institutional developments tend to be obscured by the convenient Comparative Law conceit that there is some abstract entity known as *the* adversarial system, which in a few reductive stereotypes and handy generalisations supposedly encapsulates the procedural laws and practices of every English-speaking jurisdiction in the world. In critical—but hopefully productive—engagement with orthodox Comparative Law scholarship, this volume brings together leading academic proceduralists from five continents whose work combines intimate knowledge of criminal evidence and procedure in their own jurisdictions with a keen interest in comparative inquiries and perspectives. In addition to the self-evident importance of its subject-matter, our topical focus on the intersection between human rights law and criminal evidence is intended to showcase common law comparativism as a contribution to the methodological resources of comparative criminal justice scholarship, another tool to help us get to grips with the

[13] See eg R Lempert, 'Anglo-American and Continental Systems: Marsupials and Mammals of the Law' in J Jackson, M Langer and P Tillers (eds), *Crime, Procedure and Evidence in A Comparative and International Context* (Oxford, Hart Publishing, 2008); WT Pizzi, *Trials Without Truth* (New York, NYU Press, 1999); R Vogler and B Huber (eds), *Criminal Procedure in Europe* (Berlin, Duncker and Humblot, 2008); P Fennell, C Harding, N Jörg and B Swart (eds), *Criminal Justice in Europe: A Comparative Study* (Oxford, OUP, 1995); MR Damaška, *The Faces of Justice and State Authority: A Comparative Approach to the Legal Process* (New Haven, CT, Yale UP, 1986). Additional procedural models or 'families' of legal systems are sometimes incorporated into the analysis: cf PL Reichel, *Comparative Criminal Justice Systems*, 3rd edn (Upper Saddle River, NJ, Prentice Hall, 2002); R Vogler, *A World View of Criminal Justice* (Aldershot, Ashgate, 2005).

dynamic, multi-level, cosmopolitan legal environments which constitute today's reality for legal practitioners, commentators and theorists.

In limiting our focus to selected common law jurisdictions we do not mean to imply that similar methodological principles cannot profitably be extended beyond the common law family, for example to Islamic or Asian legal systems, as well as to members of the civilian juristic world. To the contrary, this is precisely how further follow-up studies ideally should proceed. Our restricted focus is unabashedly pragmatic: in order to achieve a level of doctrinal and conceptual sophistication that is frequently missing both from general works on human rights law and from comparative studies of criminal procedure, whilst keeping the present volume at reasonable length, we needed to reduce the number of variables in play—to hold constant much that common law jurisdictions naturally share as a set of baseline assumptions, so that significant contrasts between them can be teased out and apprehended more vividly. Deliberately limiting the geographical scope and legal-cultural variation of our inquiry is a methodological gambit intended to open up fresh perspectives and facilitate lines of inquiry which will hopefully deepen and enrich existing scholarship in criminal procedure, human rights, and comparative law. Far from purporting to be the last word on the subject, this volume will have succeeded best if it generates further critical debate and encourages follow-up studies adapting our methodology to a greater variety of procedural and institutional contexts.

3. REIMAGINING COMMON LAW PROCEDURAL TRADITIONS

Each of the contributions to this volume grapples with the impact of human rights law on criminal evidence and procedure, from a range of doctrinal, institutional, and jurisdictional perspectives. Apart from inviting contributors to address the core theme and outlining some of the basic questions regarding the relationship between criminal procedure and human rights posed in this Introduction, our editorial instructions were sparse and non-prescriptive. Contributors chose their own topics and general approach. Some opted to undertake general surveys of relevant doctrinal or institutional developments in their own jurisdictions, whilst others narrowed their focus to particular procedural or evidentiary topics such as the exclusion of improperly obtained evidence, the privilege against self-incrimination, the presumption of innocence, hearsay, confrontation and witness evidence. The range of topics canvassed is testament to the expansionist ambitions of contemporary human rights legislation. Even in jurisdictions with comparatively limited experience of directly applicable human rights norms, this volume's central themes were recognised as chiming with common law adjudication's familiar epistemic preoccupations and normative aspirations, traditionally expressed in terms of procedural due process, the common law judge's duty to ensure trial fairness, the burden and criminal standard of proof, and the protection of the innocent from wrongful conviction.

Contributors' choices of focus and approach themselves reflect the state of contemporary debates surrounding the impact of human rights principles in particular legal systems, at least as understood by individual contributors. Some essays are highly selective in extracting illustrations from a wealth of local experience. Other essays are more panoptic, generic or speculative in anticipating future developments. Whilst judicial practice in some jurisdictions is acutely conscious of the cosmopolitan character of modern human rights jurisprudence, the case-law of other jurisdictions betrays more insular tendencies and constrained horizons.

The essays that follow have been loosely grouped around five broad themes, to provide a coherent narrative that unfolds logically from one chapter to the next: (a) human rights in constitutional criminal procedure; (b) improperly obtained evidence; (c) human rights and criminal proof; (d) hearsay and confrontation; and (e) fair trials for all. However, the attentive reader will discover many additional parallels and points of contrast operating within and extending beyond this convenient functional division of topics and approaches.

4. HUMAN RIGHTS IN CONSTITUTIONAL CRIMINAL PROCEDURE

PJ Schwikkard in Chapter 1 refracts our central questions through the lens of a constitutional legal framework, in effect reframing the question in terms of whether South African experience supports our hypothesis of a human rights revolution in criminal procedure. As a classic example of a 'mixed' legal system, South African law is fertile and well-trodden ground for the comparativist. It also, at first blush, appears to exemplify the vaunted human rights revolution. Post-Apartheid South Africa adopted a modern Constitution incorporating a justiciable Bill of Rights which, in turn, is supervised by a model Constitutional Court committed to progressively rights-protective principles of interpretation. Schwikkard shows how South Africa's distinctively comprehensive conception of the constitutional right to a fair trial has infused a range of familiar procedural rights and evidentiary doctrines, including the presumption of innocence, the privilege against self-incrimination and the right to silence, the closely related rights to legal representation and to adequate time and facilities to prepare a defence, access to physical samples, confessions, hearsay, equality and dignity in the treatment of sexual assault complainants, and the admissibility of evidence obtained in breach of constitutional rights. The breadth of constitutional oversight in criminal proceedings is impressive, but Schwikkard enters two significant reservations.

First, the courts have not always succeeded in translating broad principles of constitutional interpretation into progressive rulings on the scope of particular procedural rights. Secondly, there is a difference between fine-sounding paper rights and their implementation in practice—the notorious gap between 'the law in the books' and 'the law in action'. Notably, South African law's commitment to fair trials is circumscribed in practice by fiscal constraint, most obviously in the statutory proviso that free legal assistance is available to the accused only 'if substantial injustice would otherwise result'.[14] It is for these reasons that Schwikkard can muster only 'muted celebrations' for an incomplete rights revolution in South African criminal procedure.

There are many striking parallels between Schwikkard's account of constitutional procedural reform in South Africa and Simon Young's review, in Chapter 2, of related developments in the criminal procedure law of Hong Kong SAR. Hong Kong, too, has undergone major constitutional upheaval in recent memory, both preceding and following the British colonial administration's handover to China in 1997. As in South Africa, Hong Kong's principal constitutional instruments have been strongly influenced by international human rights law, originally through the text of the Hong Kong Bill of Rights Ordinance 1991, which borrows heavily from the International Covenant on Civil and Political Rights (ICCPR), as subsequently reinforced by the post-colonial Chinese Basic Law. For over a century, the law of criminal evidence in Hong Kong has developed broadly in line with English common law, under the superintendence of the Privy Council as the final court of appeal, leaving a legacy of common law jurisprudence which, as Young describes, continues to exert significant influence on the reasoning and judgments of the Hong Kong Court of Final Appeal. Yet Hong Kong courts were pioneering the application of human rights principles to criminal proceedings almost a decade in advance of the UK Human Rights Act 1998.

With this distinctively cosmopolitan political history and hybrid legal culture, it should occasion no surprise that Hong Kong courts remain open to a range of international influences on their decision-making. This predisposition is reinforced, as Young explains, by the remarkable institutional innovation of appointing distinguished foreign jurists to sit as Non-Permanent Judges of the Court of Final Appeal. Whilst the broader political context and its evident democratic deficits cannot be discounted, it seems that judicial independence has been preserved and the legacy of the Privy Council in protecting suspects' and the accused's due process rights has been upheld and extended in relation to core procedural issues such as the right to silence, the admissibility of confessions and the presumption

[14] Constitution of South Africa, ss 35(2)(c) and 35(3)(g).

of innocence. Young praises the Hong Kong courts' courageous defence of entrenched procedural rights and their willingness to innovate through comparative example, evident in recent citations of ECHR jurisprudence (notwithstanding the ICCPR pedigree of Hong Kong's indigenous Bill of Rights). At the same time, Young cautions that Hong Kong courts tend to view constitutional remedies as pragmatic tools for mediating between individual rights and broader social interests, and this sometimes precipitates fairly conservative rulings. Viewed from an Australian or British perspective, certain aspects of Hong Kong jurisprudence do seem somewhat old-fashioned. For example, there is an almost exclusive preoccupation with the rights of the accused, apparently un-tempered by the concerns for complainants' fair access to justice and witnesses' humane treatment which have risen to prominence in other common law jurisdictions, and in Strasbourg jurisprudence, over the last several decades.[15]

By most accounts, Canada occupies the more experienced pole on the continuum of common law systems' engagement with constitutional rights in criminal procedure, having adopted its Charter of Rights and Freedoms back in 1982. In Chapter 3, Christine Boyle and Emma Cunliffe fix their sights on one specific procedural right protected by the Charter, the right to counsel during custodial interrogation. Despite the Charter's pivotal status in Canadian law and legal culture, as the source of 'Canada's on-going "human rights revolution"',[16] Boyle and Cunliffe are concerned that Canada might actually have become the poor relation in its failure to 'keep up with the common law Joneses', jurisprudentially speaking, regarding their chosen illustration of a constitutional right central to criminal proceedings. By disavowing any general right to counsel during police interrogation, the Supreme Court of Canada in *R v Sinclair*[17] took a more restrictive view of the right to custodial legal advice than currently prevails in England and Wales, the United States, New Zealand, Australia, and in international criminal proceedings before the ICC. Yet Canada has traditionally prided itself on its robust legal protection of procedural rights. What could have precipitated this apparent reversal of fortune?

Boyle and Cunliffe locate the source of the difficulty in the tension between purposive, rights-promoting approaches to constitutional interpretation and more cramped and conservative styles of judicial reasoning. In other fields of law the Canadian Supreme Court has developed progressive interpretational principles, but it has declined to extend this liberality to the specific Charter

[15] P Roberts and A Zuckerman, *Criminal Evidence*, 2nd edn (Oxford, OUP, 2010) ch 10; L Hoyano and C Keenan, *Child Abuse: Law and Policy Across Boundaries* (Oxford, OUP, 2007) chs 8–9; L Ellison, *The Adversarial Process and the Vulnerable Witness* (Oxford, OUP, 2001).

[16] Boyle and Cunliffe, 79, below.

[17] [2010] 2 SCR 310.

right litigated in *Sinclair*. Boyle and Cunliffe suggest that Canada's existing constitutional framework would support a more prominent role for foreign law precedents, where the weight of common law authority has reached a 'tipping point', provided always that particular norms and remedies are in keeping with Canada's own constitutional principles and traditions. They advocate, not slavish reversion to the common law norm, but active assimilation of best human rights practice 'as an aspect of Canadianness—a "Made in Canada" approach to common law comparativism'.[18] Chapter 3's blend of indigenous principles of constitutional interpretation and wide-ranging survey of promising international precedents itself exemplifies the common law comparativism which Boyle and Cunliffe commend to Canadian courts.

5. IMPROPERLY OBTAINED EVIDENCE

The four chapters in the next cohort all address, in different ways and for a variety of purposes, the admissibility of improperly obtained evidence in the light of human rights instruments and principles.

Salim Farrar's discussion of the Malaysian law of personal searches in Chapter 4 engages with human rights protections at an elementary juridical level. The Malaysian police are a post-colonial force accustomed to extensive operational discretion, minimal legal accountability and widespread popular support. These social, cultural and institutional conditions breed flagrant police abuses, such as the naked squatting exercises—*ketuk ketampi*—imposed on suspected drugs couriers, which eventually became a national scandal. As Farrar explains, procedural law, or rather its absence, is very much implicated in this permissive institutional environment. Malaysia is not a signatory to the main human rights treaties, and its law of evidence remains in a state of arrested development, more or less as JF Stephen conceived it, in the Evidence Act 1950. The well-known Privy Council case of *Kuruma v R*,[19] which is often cited abroad for the proposition that trial judges retain a discretion at common law to exclude improperly obtained evidence where probative value is exceeded by prejudicial effect, has been interpreted in its native Malaysia to mandate the admissibility of all reliable evidence irrespective of the taint of illegality.[20]

Despite this inhospitable environment, the human rights revolution has lately reached Malaysian shores. Systematic reform of criminal procedure has been accompanied by a new political commitment to implementing human rights principles in the conduct of criminal investigations. However,

[18] Boyle and Cunliffe, 102, below.
[19] [1955] AC 197 (PC).
[20] *Public Prosecutor v Seridaran* [1984] 1 *Malayan Law Journal* 141.

the gap between theory and practice remains predictably wide, as revealed by Farrar's pioneering empirical study of the law and conduct of body searches by the Malaysian police, which drafted his IIUM criminal procedure students into a small army of budding criminological researchers. Echoing some of the conclusions of Schwikkard and Young, Farrar's analysis braids together the interweaving strands of doctrine, law reform, institutional culture and broader political context.

All four variables continue as prominent themes in Chapter 5, where John Jackson presents a comparative retrospective on the exclusion of improperly obtained evidence in the two Irelands, north and south. Marked by political upheaval and seething sectarian conflict, Irish criminal procedure has developed the common law tradition in distinctive and sometimes surprising directions. In Northern Ireland, criminal procedure has struggled to extricate itself from the choke-hold of a 'rule *by* law' mentality fostered by the precarious security situation. More recently, Northern Irish law has followed the path of legislative reform previously taken in England and Wales, with its own local version of section 78 of the Police and Criminal Evidence Act 1984. Article 74 of the Police and Criminal Evidence (NI) Order 1988 elevates fairness-based exclusion beyond the fragile common law position described by Farrar, in relation to Malaysia, in the previous chapter. However, as Jackson observes, 'unfairness' is a notoriously malleable criterion by which to regulate the admissibility of improperly obtained evidence.

In addition to our shared common law heritage (including precedents like *Kuruma*), courts in the Republic of Ireland—in striking contrast to their UK counterparts on both sides of the Irish Sea—have also been able to draw on constitutional provisions when assessing the admissibility of tainted evidence. Constitutional authority has enabled the Irish Supreme Court to announce an automatic rule of exclusion for evidence obtained in violation of constitutional rights.[21] But Jackson identifies various obstacles in the way of maintaining a purist line. For one thing, the rule itself recognises exceptions to accommodate 'extraordinary excusing circumstances'. For another, a rule prioritising the constitutional rights of the accused over all other competing considerations has attracted political opposition from those advocating greater 'balance' in the administration of criminal justice.[22] The Balancing Party has even invoked comparative example, in the form of New Zealand's flexible approach to evidentiary exclusion,[23] in support of relaxing the Irish rule. Once again, we encounter the political dynamics of evidentiary reform, and the Irish debates provide instructive

[21] *People (DPP) v Kenny* [1990] 2 IR 110.

[22] L Campbell, 'Criminal Justice and Penal Populism in Ireland' (2008) 28 *Legal Studies* 559.

[23] *R v Shaheed* (2002) 2 NZLR 377. See R Mahoney, 'Abolition of New Zealand's Prima Facie Exclusionary Rule' [2003] *Criminal Law Review* 607.

contrasts with the broader political context of criminal procedure reform in South Africa, Hong Kong and Malaysia discussed in previous chapters.

In conclusion, Jackson brings his largely historical exegesis right up to date by reviewing relevant jurisprudence of the European Court of Human Rights (which Jackson finds problematic in various respects). This sets the scene for the remaining two chapters in this informal grouping. Andrew Ashworth, in Chapter 6, focuses exclusively on European human rights law, situating his discussion of the Strasbourg Court's evidence-related jurisprudence within the framework of the Convention as a whole. Discerning within the text and structure of the ECHR 'the beginnings of a hierarchy' of rights, Ashworth proceeds to show that the predominant tendency of the Strasbourg Court's Article 6 jurisprudence is to reject (often poorly specified) 'public interest' arguments for diluting the right to a fair trial. But he then notes a partial resurgence of public interest arguments, sugar-coated as requirements of 'proportionality', in a raft of recent rulings dealing with the privilege against self-incrimination and the fairness of evidence obtained in breach of Convention rights. Suspicion of inconsistency and backsliding seems to be confirmed by a growing body of dissent within the Court itself; and perhaps these critical voices will form the majority one day soon. For the time being, Ashworth remains dissatisfied with the standard of normative reasoning in the Court's Article 6 jurisprudence, which too often seems to prioritise pragmatic compromises over principled standard-setting.

Paul Roberts takes up the theme of the quality of judicial reasoning in Chapter 7, not only in relation to the merits of particular decisions but also in terms of the broader ramifications of recent appellate court jurisprudence for Evidence scholarship's principal disciplinary concepts, taxonomies and methods. This chapter focuses on coercion and deception in criminal investigations as factors liable to prompt trial judges to exclude relevant evidence. Close examination of a landmark judgment of the House of Lords on the admissibility of 'foreign torture evidence',[24] followed by critical reappraisal of the Strasbourg Court's jurisprudence on police entrapment as a breach of ECHR Article 6, highlights the irreducible roles of moral reasoning and judicial 'discretion' (judgement) in the development and application of procedural law. If modern criminal procedure is an applied field of political morality, argues Roberts,[25] it is difficult to see how the Law of Evidence could be reducible to purely epistemic considerations, in either theory or practice.

A sub-theme of Roberts's chapter is the increasingly 'cosmopolitan' character of common law evidence and criminal adjudication. The remarkable

[24] *A v Secretary of State for the Home Department (No 2)* [2006] 2 AC 221, [2005] UKHL 71.

[25] Also see P Roberts, 'Theorising Procedural Tradition: Subjects, Objects and Values in Criminal Adjudication' in RA Duff, L Farmer, S Marshall and V Tadros (eds), *The Trial on Trial Volume Two: Judgment and Calling to Account* (Oxford, Hart Publishing, 2006).

influence of European human rights law on evidentiary issues, already highlighted by Jackson and Ashworth, is only the most obvious index of how legal norms, concepts, ideas, ideals and institutions today freely cross all kinds of borders and boundaries, geographical, jurisdictional, cultural, social and political. And like all travellers, as they visit new places they are themselves transformed and are sometimes transformative. Further examples can be found in each of the preceding six chapters and throughout the remainder of the volume.

6. HUMAN RIGHTS AND CRIMINAL PROOF

The next segment of the book contains four chapters exploring various epistemological dimensions of evidence and proof and their relationship with procedural rights. At least some of these traditional criminal procedure rights are also 'human rights', but beyond an overlapping normative core there is significant divergence in language, concepts, scope and justificatory rationales.

In Chapter 8, Jeremy Gans presents a detailed case-study of a miscarriage of justice arising from contaminated DNA evidence in the Australian State of Victoria. The problem of enormously powerful scientific evidence, which can also be powerfully misleading when things go wrong, is fundamentally epistemic.[26] Evidence which is often treated in the popular imagination as tantamount to conclusive proof of guilt may be a potent source of wrongful convictions.[27] Gans shows how routine practices of criminal investigation, prosecution, criminal defence and the trial rules of evidence all conspired in his Victorian *cause célèbre* to keep the fatal evidential defect hidden from view, whilst the apparent probative value of a matching DNA profile was allowed to compensate for what were, in retrospect, quite glaring circumstantial weaknesses in the prosecution's case. The accused was convicted of a rape that almost certainly never took place. He was ultimately exonerated, but only by dint of good fortune and after serving a year in gaol.

The right not to be wrongfully convicted of a criminal offence is surely one of the most fundamental procedural rights, more basic even than the vaunted right to a fair trial.[28] However, international human rights law does not attempt to articulate such a right. Nor does Victoria's Charter of Human

[26] AI Goldman, *Pathways to Knowledge: Private and Public* (New York, OUP, 2002) ch 7.

[27] K Roach, 'Forensic Science and Miscarriages of Justice: Some Lessons from Comparative Experience' (2009) 50 *Jurimetrics* 67; J Mnookin, 'Experts and Forensic Evidence' (2008) 37 *Southwestern University Law Review* 1009; C Walker and R Stockdale, 'Forensic Evidence' in C Walker and K Starmer (eds), *Miscarriages of Justice: A Review of Justice in Error* (London, Blackstone Press, 1999); CAG Jones, *Expert Witnesses: Science, Medicine and the Practice of Law* (Oxford, OUP, 1994) ch 10.

[28] Cf Roberts and Zuckerman, above n 15, 18–22.

Rights and Responsibilities Act 2006 figure very prominently in Gans's story. As a public inquiry later concluded, the most effective remedies for wrongful convictions attributable to scientific evidence are as prosaic as their typical causes: more secure procedures for collecting and storing exhibits in contamination-free environments; improved scientific literacy for police, lawyers and judges; willingness to give serious consideration to alternative hypotheses and potentially exculpatory evidence; vigorous criminal defence. Gans notes that traditional doctrines of evidence law sometimes exacerbate the problem, for example by assiduously seeking to exclude extraneous 'bad character' evidence which if properly investigated might, ironically, lead to the accused's acquittal by exposing critical flaws in the prosecution's proof. Human rights law has no ready solutions, either, for these perennial evidentiary conundrums of probative value and prejudicial effect.

David Hamer confronts another acute epistemic dilemma in Chapter 9. What is to be done when crucial evidence may be missing? The problem is an old one for the courts, as Hamer observes, but it has become particularly pronounced in recent decades in relation to (sometimes, long-) delayed allegations of childhood sexual abuse and associated controversies surrounding recovered/implanted memories and the like.[29] The common law's traditional answer is that the accused cannot have a fair trial if the evidence is irremediably stale and incomplete.[30] Hamer challenges this orthodoxy. Drawing on a broad survey of common law authorities, his chapter reconsiders both epistemic and non-epistemic arguments for pro-defendant judicial interventions to halt delayed prosecutions. Hamer finds none of these arguments persuasive. Missing evidence distributes forensic disadvantage indiscriminately and epistemic losses are normally allowed to rest where they fall. Normative reconstructions of fair trial rights identify relevant non-epistemic considerations, but fail to explain—to Hamer's satisfaction—why lost evidence should invariably be the prosecution's bad luck. There is a suspicion that, lurking behind routine invocations of traditional procedural rights and their more recent 'human rights' reinterpretations, are the beguiling martial metaphors of an unreconstructed 'fight theory' of adversarial procedure.[31] Anticipating a theme taken up in later chapters, Hamer insists that the rights and interests of the accused are not the exclusive arbiters of a fair criminal trial.

The second pair of essays comprising the 'human rights and criminal proof' quartet both examine major intersections between the epistemology

[29] See P Lewis, *Delayed Prosecution for Childhood Sexual Abuse* (Oxford, OUP, 2006).

[30] 'The Crown Court has always had the inherent power to stay criminal proceedings on the grounds of abuse of process. One instance of abuse of process is the bringing of a prosecution so long after the events in issue that a fair trial has become impossible': *R* v *F (TB)* [2011] 2 Cr App R 13, [2011] EWCA Crim 726, [24].

[31] EG Thornburg, 'Metaphors Matter: How Images of Battle, Sports and Sex Shape the Adversary System' (1995) 10 *Wisconsin Women's Law Journal* 225.

of judicial fact-finding and the law of criminal procedure. The privilege against self-incrimination and the right to silence are Andrew Choo's focus in Chapter 10. The epistemic legitimacy of drawing adverse inferences from silence has been a long-running preoccupation of the common law.[32] As Choo shows, picking up the threads of a discussion introduced by Andrew Ashworth in Chapter 6, much of the post-human rights revolution debate is framed in terms of the 'right not to incriminate oneself' as one strand of the right to a fair trial. Choo's essay probes the legal and conceptual boundaries of the self-incrimination right by exploring the extent of its application to 'pre-existing' documents and physical samples. Finding the jurisprudence of the European Court of Human Rights lacking in conceptual finesse, Choo seeks enlightenment in a comparative survey of statutory provisions and case-law from New Zealand, the United States, Canada, India and the ICTY. His general approach is reminiscent of Boyle and Cunliffe's methodology for 'keeping up with the common law Joneses' in Chapter 3; but Choo reaches a more sceptical conclusion, doubting the existence of any firm international consensus in relation to self-incrimination and silence. The right (or as common lawyers would tend to say, the 'privilege') against self-incrimination may be ensconced in international human rights law, but the analysis developed in this chapter exposes major limitations in its conceptual elucidation and normative rationalisation. Like Jackson and Ashworth before him, Choo is unimpressed by the Strasbourg Court's evasive retreat into rights 'balancing' as a surrogate for meaningful analysis.

In Chapter 11, Hock Lai Ho revisits one of common law Evidence's great epistemic foundations, the burden and standard of proof. Here, again, the human rights revolution has made its linguistic and conceptual mark, by inviting us now to think in the more comprehensively normative terms of 'the presumption of innocence'.[33] And there is also a significant comparative dimension to this telling evolution of jurisprudential concepts and language. As Ho observes, if the presumption of innocence is to be regarded as a universal human right it can hardly be tied to peculiarly common law conceptions of evidence and procedure. These initial promptings launch Ho into a thorough-going reappraisal of the normative foundations of the presumption of innocence, adopting a distinctively 'jurisprudential' style of analysis (similar to Roberts's approach in Chapter 7) which seeks to integrate legal doctrine with its deeper philosophical rationales.

[32] See eg *Wiedemann v Walpole* [1891] 2 QB 534 (CA).

[33] Also see P Roberts, 'Criminal Procedure, the Presumption of Innocence and Judicial Reasoning under the Human Rights Act' in H Fenwick, G Phillipson and R Masterman (eds), *Judicial Reasoning under the UK Human Rights Act* (Cambridge, CUP, 2007); A Stumer, *The Presumption of Innocence: Evidential and Human Rights Perspectives* (Oxford, Hart Publishing, 2010).

There is an obvious sense in which the criminal trial serves epistemic functions, as a critical inquiry into past events to facilitate just punishment of the guilty—and only them. Yet the criminal standard of proof beyond reasonable doubt clearly implies that at least some of those acquitted will be factually guilty, not truly innocent. Should we infer that the trial has been an epistemic failure every time the guilty escape their just deserts owing to lack of adequate proof? Not at all, insists Ho. We should instead recognise that implicit in our traditions of presuming innocence at trial, in defiance of the probative odds (assuming that the police and the prosecution are honest and professionally competent), is a much richer conception of criminal adjudication reflecting a constitutional balance of state power and individual rights and liberties. So we should not be surprised if authoritarian regimes denounce the presumption of innocence: this takes us back to the broader political context of procedural law highlighted by Schwikkard, Young, Farrar and Jackson in the book's opening chapters. But Ho is also at pains to stress the challenges for liberal polities of a serious commitment to the political morality of criminal adjudication. Political corporatism ('communitarianism') in the 'fight against crime', allied with the insidious logic of 'relative ease of proof', can all too easily lead to the erosion of essential procedural guarantees. Thus, the presumption of innocence becomes peppered with proliferating reverse-onus provisions, like a structural oak beam eaten away by death watch beetle.

7. HEARSAY AND CONFRONTATION

The next trio of essays can be grouped together because they all address aspects of the law of hearsay; though in many ways they simply extend the discussion developed in the previous quartet. The hearsay prohibition is one of the most recognisable and characteristic features of common law evidence, and its traditional rationale is predominantly epistemic. Hearsay evidence has been declared inadmissible in common law criminal trials because it is regarded as unreliable, or at least insufficiently reliable to be placed before the jury.[34] Once again, the advent of human rights in criminal procedure has inflected traditional common law doctrines; and in this context the human rights revolution has been aided and abetted by the rediscovery—or reinvention—of a common law 'right to confrontation',[35] which in the

[34] E Morgan, 'Hearsay Dangers and the Application of the Hearsay Concept' (1948) 62 *Harvard Law Review* 177.

[35] *R v Davis* [2008] 1 AC 1128, [2008] UKHL 36. Cf *R v Smellie* (1919)14 Cr App R 128 (CCA); *R v X, Y and Z* (1990) 91 Cr App R 36 (CA). And see I Dennis, 'The Right to Confront Witnesses: Meanings, Myths and Human Rights' [2010] *Criminal Law Review* 255.

United States enjoys an explicitly constitutional foundation in the Sixth Amendment 'Confrontation Clause'.

Mike Redmayne gets the discussion underway in Chapter 12 with a wide-ranging review of arguments pro and con a right to confrontation. Much turns, of course, on the scope of the mooted right, and also on its asserted rationalisations. Taking his cue from the seemingly interminable '*Al-Khawaja* saga'[36] and the US Supreme Court's vigorous reassertion of an independent constitutional right to confrontation in *Crawford v Washington*,[37] Redmayne methodically works his way through the leading epistemic and non-epistemic rationales thought to justify a strong confrontation right (proceeding much as Hamer did in Chapter 9 in relation to delayed prosecutions). None of these popular rationales stands up particularly well to Redmayne's unflinching close scrutiny. If the Strasbourg Court's conception of confrontation is essentially epistemic, it is hard to see (revisiting the jurisdictional worries expressed by Roberts in Chapter 7) how the Court's institutional position could legitimise an inflexible rule of inadmissibility for 'sole or decisive' evidence on the authority of ECHR Article 6—even if the specific objections raised by the UK Supreme Court in *Horncastle*[38] could be answered satisfactorily, from a purely epistemic point of view. But Redmayne is equally unimpressed by the non-epistemic rationales currently on offer: dignity, tradition, 'something deep in human nature' are all at best, he thinks, over-stated as explanatory rationales for existing doctrinal preferences and, under the pressure of sustained critique, are quickly reduced to rhetorical wishful thinking. Redmayne's rather pessimistic conclusions are sobering. Perhaps human rights 'are largely useless as a protection against false conviction'[39] (as Gans had already warned us in Chapter 8), and the best that can be said for a 'human right' to confrontation is that it is not quite as conceptually vapid or normatively precarious as its related juridical alternatives.

In Chapter 13, Craig Callen revisits the right to confrontation and the presumption of innocence, in direct dialogue with both Redmayne and Ho. Callen argues for a 'right to due deliberation' entailing that fact-finders make appropriately strenuous cognitive efforts to resolve the legal disputes submitted to their determination. In view of the importance of the matters at issue in criminal trials, the cognitive burdens on fact-finders should be commensurately onerous.[40] 'Due deliberation' is not a concept

[36] The long-awaited ECtHR Grand Chamber Judgment, following up on *Al-Khawaja and Tahery v UK* (2009) 49 EHRR 1 and *R v Horncastle* [2010] 2 AC 373, [2009] UKSC 14, was finally handed down on 15 December 2011 (when this book was already in press).

[37] 541 US 36 (2004).

[38] *R v Horncastle* [2010] 2 AC 373, [76]–[108].

[39] Redmayne, 307, below.

[40] Cf JQ Whitman, *The Origins of Reasonable Doubt: Theological Roots of the Criminal Trial* (New Haven, CT, Yale UP, 2008).

known to international human rights law. It derives, instead, from intense reflection on the nature and values of adjudication informed by cognitive science. Developing a distinctive style of analysis pioneered in previous publications,[41] Callen suggests that interdisciplinary studies of human reasoning, cognitive psychology and linguistics can shed new light on the rationality of familiar procedural rules and litigation practices. His method is powerfully comparative, in demonstrating how diverse legal processes and mechanisms (eg common law rules of admissibility versus civilian jurists' standards for judgment-writing) can be regarded as functional equivalents, in terms of their cognitive implications for effective fact-finding.[42]

With the benefit of these interdisciplinary inquiries behind him, Callen reconsiders some of the arguments advanced in previous chapters. Ho's substantive reinterpretation of the presumption of innocence specifies a decisional standard in keeping with the mooted right to due deliberation, since criminal juries must consider and reject all plausible explanations of the evidence consistent with innocence before concluding that the accused is guilty beyond reasonable doubt. It is not enough simply to find the prosecution's story somewhat more plausible than the accused's even less convincing reply to the indictment.[43] By contrast, Callen thinks that Redmayne may have underestimated the cognitive rationality of legal rules excluding un-confronted hearsay from criminal trials. Should we regard the right to due deliberation as a 'human right'? Callen is agnostic on questions of terminology and classification. If one follows Dworkin in grounding all human rights in the more basic 'right to be treated *as* a human being whose dignity fundamentally matters',[44] it is certainly plausible to regard due deliberation as a fundamental human right institutionalised in criminal adjudication. But the important thing, Callen stresses, is that the right to due deliberation is recognised, legislated and respected in practice, irrespective of its formal designation as a 'human', 'constitutional' or garden variety procedural right.

Chris Gallavin's comparative analysis of recent legislative reforms in New Zealand, in Chapter 14, completes the trio of hearsay and

[41] Including CR Callen, 'Interdisciplinary and Comparative Perspectives on Hearsay and Confrontation' in P Roberts and M Redmayne (eds), *Innovations in Evidence and Proof* (Oxford, Hart Publishing, 2007); CR Callen, 'Rationality and Relevancy: Conditional Relevancy and Constrained Resources' [2003] *Michigan State Law Review* 1243; CR Callen, 'Simpson, Fuhrman, Grice, and Character Evidence' (1996) 67 *University of Colorado Law Review* 777.

[42] Also see CR Callen, 'Cognitive Strategies and Models of Fact-finding' in J Jackson, M Langer and P Tillers (eds), *Crime, Procedure and Evidence in A Comparative and International Context* (Oxford, Hart Publishing, 2008); CR Callen, 'Othello Could Not Optimize: Economics, Hearsay and Less Adversary Systems' (2001) 22 *Cardozo Law Review* 1791.

[43] Cf RJ Allen, 'Factual Ambiguity and A Theory of Evidence' (1994) 88 *Northwestern University Law Review* 604.

[44] R Dworkin, *Justice For Hedgehogs* (Cambridge, MA, Harvard UP, 2011) 335.

confrontation-related contributions. The human rights revolution arrived in New Zealand later than in Canada but earlier than in the United Kingdom, with the passage of the New Zealand Bill of Rights Act 1990 (NZBORA). As in South Africa, Hong Kong and Canada, Article 14 of the ICCPR supplied the model for drafting New Zealand's fair trial rights, but the duties and interpretational obligations imposed on New Zealand courts by the NZBORA are considerably weaker than those found in the South African Constitution, the Hong Kong Bill of Rights Ordinance 1991, the Canadian Charter of Rights and Freedoms, or even the UK Human Rights Act 1998. Gallavin consequently soon turns to examine the impact on New Zealand's law of hearsay of other, more discrete, statutory reforms, against the backdrop of the generic right 'to obtain the attendance and examination of witnesses' guaranteed by section 25(f) of the NZBORA.

The law of evidence in New Zealand was systematically modernised and revised by the Evidence Act 2006.[45] Gallavin focuses on those few sections of the 2006 Act which directly regulate the admissibility of hearsay statements by absent witnesses, ostensibly on grounds of reliability and testability. He is critical of some of the drafting choices reflected in the Act's hearsay provisions, questioning their conceptual coherence and capacity, as criteria of admissibility, to differentiate successfully between reliable and unreliable hearsay. A comparative review of comparable legislation and case-law in Canada, England and Wales, Australia, the United States, and European human rights law indicates that similar difficulties are experienced elsewhere, major doctrinal differences notwithstanding.

On reflection, this discovery should not be surprising. Gallavin is concerned with the basic epistemological building-blocks of criminal adjudication—relevance, reliability, probative value, and evidential sufficiency—and these logical requirements of warranted verdicts are relatively impervious to doctrinal variations across legal jurisdictions. This is why the epistemological issues explored by Gans, Hamer, and Callen, amongst others, are so obviously pertinent to criminal adjudication in general, and cannot be confined to particular legal systems.[46] But if legal problems are shared, solutions might be, too. Gallavin's foray into (predominantly) common law comparativism enables him to identify several promising directions for reform in the case-law of Canada, the United States, and the ECtHR. Gallavin's essay also implicitly reinforces a recurring theme of many of the preceding chapters: some of the most fundamental issues in the design and implementation

[45] See C Gallavin, *Evidence* (Wellington, LexisNexis, 2008) esp ch 1.

[46] Also see P Tillers, 'Are There Universal Principles or Forms of Evidential Inference? Of Inference Networks and Onto-Epistemology' in J Jackson, M Langer and P Tillers (eds), *Crime, Procedure and Evidence in a Comparative and International Context* (Oxford, Hart Publishing, 2008); P Tillers, 'Discussion Paper: The Structure and the Logic of Proof in Trials' (2011) 10 *Law, Probability and Risk* 1.

of fair criminal trials will never be encompassed by generic human rights legislation, or even by detailed codifications of procedural law.

8. FAIR TRIALS FOR ALL

We have already adverted to the tendency of human rights in criminal procedure to focus almost exclusively on the rights of suspects and the accused. This bias is arguably built into specifications of the 'right to a fair trial' contained in major international instruments like the ICCPR and the ECHR, which in turn structure human rights adjudication and frame broader policy debates. These instruments were drafted in the shadow of despicable deeds perpetrated by authoritarian regimes in the decades before and after 1945, when nobody needed convincing of the vital importance of robust legal protections for those especially vulnerable to abuses of state power. Whilst the indispensability of procedural rights for suspects and the accused in the administration of criminal justice remains undiminished, contemporary debates have moved on. Today we seek fair trials not only for the accused but, more ambitiously, for *all* the participants in criminal proceedings, including, in particular, complainants and witnesses, who in the past have too often been treated in deplorable ways that betray the ideals of criminal adjudication.

Major procedural reforms have been implemented in many common law jurisdictions over the last several decades designed to assist complainants and witnesses to give their best evidence in a humane procedure which treats them with appropriate concern and respect.[47] Legal conceptions of the 'right to a fair trial' have been adjusted accordingly, and human rights law has been instrumental in effecting this realignment.[48] What might have been a rallying cry for feminist activists in the 1970s is now treated by judges in London, Sydney or Strasbourg as uncontroversial settled law: 'There must be fairness to all sides. In a criminal case this requires the court to consider a triangulation of interests… taking into account the position of the accused, the victim and his or her family, and the public'.[49] However, these long overdue gestures towards a more holistic conception of trial fairness have been accompanied by a darker policy undertow. It is a popular misconception, pedalled in lazy political rhetoric and amplified by certain sections of the media, that rights for victims and witnesses must be secured

[47] See above, n 15.

[48] J Doak, *Victims' Rights, Human Rights and Criminal Justice* (Oxford, Hart Publishing, 2008).

[49] *Attorney General's Reference (No 3 of 1999)* [2001] 2 AC 91, 118, HL (Lord Steyn). Also see *Doorson v Netherlands* (1996) 22 EHHR 330, [70] ('principles of fair trial also require that in appropriate cases the interests of the defence are balanced against those of witnesses or victims called upon to testify').

at the expense of traditional procedural safeguards, as though justice were a kind of commodity that must be taken from some ('criminals') so that others ('victims') can have more. But victims do not truly get justice when offenders are convicted unfairly, still less if flawed procedures lead to the conviction of the innocent. For lawyers, it is trite that the rights and interests of complainants and witnesses must somehow be accommodated, or 'balanced', with the rights of suspects and the accused. The enduring difficulty lies in translating this truism into practice.

The final pair of essays in this volume boldly venture onto this treacherous terrain. In Chapter 15, Terese Henning and Jill Hunter examine recent reforms in Australian criminal evidence and procedure and critically evaluate some of the accumulating case-law interpreting these statutory provisions. Focusing in particular on the admission of hearsay statements from absent witnesses as an exemplar of broader trends, the discussion picks up many of the doctrinal themes introduced by Chris Gallavin in the preceding chapter. Drawing also on historical and socio-legal materials, Henning and Hunter reconsider some of the factors which deter fearful sexual assault complainants, vulnerable witnesses and the accused from entering the witness-box. Echoing Jeremy Gans's conclusions in Chapter 8, Henning and Hunter find that the broad human rights framework, which is gradually becoming more familiar to Australian courts and jurists, seldom drills down to the prosaic institutional realities of criminal litigation.

On the face of it, section 65 read together with the interpretative Dictionary of the uniform Evidence Acts equips Australian courts with a broadly worded statutory basis for admitting the hearsay statements of any witness, and especially an accused, who is unavailable or unwilling to testify. However, the practical scope of this provision pivots on judicial interpretations of 'unavailability', which in turn are influenced by unarticulated (or at any rate indefensible) conceptions of trustworthiness and restrictive entitlements to testimonial status. Neither complainants nor the accused necessarily benefit from each other's misfortune when testimonial voices are silenced. Henning and Hunter argue that traditional common law practices, legal professional habit and judicial culture are at the root of the problem. The persistence of entrenched attitudes, despite major procedural innovation and reform, perpetuates centuries' old mistrust of certain witnesses. Reiterating Schwikkard's admonition from Chapter 1, Henning and Hunter warn against equating—even sweeping and politically vaunted—legislative reform with any tangible revolution in professional culture, attitudes or practices.

In Chapter 16 Peter Duff reconsiders the Scottish 'rape shield', perhaps the procedural issue *par excellence* where the rights and interests of complainants and vulnerable witnesses are thought to clash with the accused's (human) right to a fair trial. Duff begins by explaining the constitutional position of Scots criminal procedure law within the framework of the UK Human

Rights Act 1998. This is a powerful illustration of legal cosmopolitanism at work *within* a national legal jurisdiction that human rights lawyers tend to regard as a single entity. Scots law was apparently even more resistant than the criminal law of England and Wales to the language and concepts of human rights, prior to the Human Rights Act. The challenges of managing revolutionary legal change in Scotland have been exacerbated by a rather surprising, possibly unintended, but certainly widely resented alteration in the institutional structure of appeals on points of criminal procedure and by some of the jurisprudence it has already produced.[50]

Scottish legislation seeking to protect sexual assault complainants from harassing and demeaning cross-examination on their previous sexual history must now be interpreted within the parameters of this 'devolved', human rights-respecting, constitutional framework. Common law comparativism is once again to the fore. Duff notes that Canadian precedents,[51] in particular, have been influential in shaping Scottish rape-shield policy and legislation. However, the tale is not a particularly happy one, from the reformers' perspective. Legislation has not produced the trial outcomes many anticipated, partly because the accused's right to a fair trial under ECHR Article 6 implies (as Redmayne, Callen and Gallavin discuss in Chapters 12–14) a right to cross-examine the prosecution's case. The Scottish courts were obliged to conjure an 'invisible comma' into the Scottish rape-shield provision in order to satisfy Article 6.[52]

However, the core of Duff's critical analysis is not doctrinal. Drawing on significant empirical data, and mirroring the conclusions of Henning and Hunter in the preceding chapter, Duff diagnoses the source of the problem in traditional legal practices and cultural meanings—specifically, in this instance, in relation to the elusive concept of 'relevance'. Previous sexual history evidence is often described as 'irrelevant' to the matters in issue in criminal trials.[53] But irrelevant evidence is *never* admissible in criminal trials: this is an article of faith for common lawyers. And proponents of protective legislation do not generally regard themselves as enemies of fair trials. So it begins to seem puzzling why any dedicated 'rape shield' should be needed at all.

The answer, of course, is that the meaning of 'relevant' evidence is contextual, perspectival, and—applied to this issue—frequently controversial. As Duff puts it, 'a radical feminist or a liberal male academic or a traditional Catholic bishop or a reader of "lads' mags" may have conflicting views about

[50] Also see PR Ferguson, 'Repercussions of the Cadder Case: the ECHR's Fair Trial Provisions and Scottish Criminal Procedure' [2011] *Criminal Law Review* 743.

[51] Especially the 'extremely influential' decision in *R v Seaboyer* [1991] 2 SCR 577.

[52] *DS v HM Advocate* [2007] UKPC 36, 2007 SLT 1026, [48].

[53] See eg A McColgan, 'Common Law and the Relevance of Sexual History Evidence' (1996) 16 *Oxford Journal of Legal Studies* 275.

the relevance of a specific piece of sexual history evidence, in the context of a particular case'.[54] In making admissibility determinations, the trial judge must eschew all partisan perspectives and be guided only by objective considerations that justify the ruling and warrant all parties' rational assent. To be sure, this is a demanding ideal. Beyond comparative legal analysis and broadly framed human rights standards, the matters at issue are irreducibly epistemological. One conclusion, on which all of the essays in this book might be said to converge, is that the human rights revolution in criminal procedure may channel and constrain, but will never displace, the inferential logic of fact-finding and proof in criminal adjudication. It is not hard to imagine, in the light of the analysis and arguments presented in the following chapters, that a progressively expanding and deepening integration of criminal evidence and human rights will continue to play a transformative role in shaping the future of common law procedural traditions.

[54] Duff, 385, below.

1

A Constitutional Revolution in South African Criminal Procedure?

PJ SCHWIKKARD

INTRODUCTION

DURING THE 1990s South African criminal procedure law underwent root-and-branch reform as part of the new post-Apartheid state's radical reconstruction of political institutions. Until 1995 the vast majority of South Africans were—literally—disenfranchised. Legal positivism prevailed, and the only criterion of trial fairness was formal compliance with the rules. Indefinite detention without trial was tolerated and the means of obtaining evidence had little impact on evidentiary issues of admissibility or trial fairness.

The year 1990 marked a profound change in the political climate in South Africa. An intense period of negotiation culminated in the acceptance of the principle of constitutional supremacy and, on 27 April 1995, the country held its first democratic elections with universal adult franchise. The interim Constitution of 1993[1] was superseded in 1996 by a permanent Constitution with a justiciable Bill of Rights. However, a genuine 'revolution' in criminal procedure requires more than just institutional reform and drafting new laws. South Africa has one of the highest income disparities in the world, with a relatively small middle class sandwiched between the substantial majority of the population, which is impoverished, and a super-rich elite. In formal terms, there has been a rights revolution which has made a major impact on the rules of criminal evidence. This chapter considers the extent of that impact, and its limitations.[2]

[1] Constitution of the Republic of South Africa Act 200 of 1993.

[2] Drawing on material previously published in I Currie and J de Waal (eds), *Bill of Rights Handbook*, 5th edn (Cape Town, Juta, 2005); and in S Woolman et al (eds), *Constitutional Law of South Africa*, 2nd edn (Cape Town, Juta, 2008).

1. THE CONSTITUTIONAL REVOLUTION

According to standard comparative law taxonomies, South Africa has a 'mixed' legal system, comprising Roman-Dutch substantive law and procedural law derived from the common law tradition. Modern South African criminal procedure law is essentially statutory,[3] but courts are referred to the English common law as it stood on 30 May 1961 (the day before South Africa became a republic) to fill in any gaps in statutory coverage. Since 1993, statutes and common law precedents must now also be tested against the Constitution and the Bill of Rights. This includes a very detailed specification of the right to a fair trial, which is discussed in the next section. In addition, various other constitutionally-entrenched rights continue to reshape the content and form of the criminal justice system, including the rights to equality,[4] dignity,[5] life,[6] freedom and security of the person,[7] privacy,[8] freedom of religion,[9] freedom of expression,[10] property,[11] and access to information.[12]

Rights declared in the Bill of Rights are subject to the following general limitations clause, contained in section 36 of the Constitution:[13]

> (1) The rights in the Bill of Rights may be limited only in terms of law of general application to the extent that the limitation is reasonable and justifiable in an open and democratic society based on human dignity, equality and freedom, taking into account all relevant factors, including—
> (a) the nature of the right;
> (b) the importance of the purpose of the limitation;
> (c) the nature and extent of the limitation;
> (d) the relation between the limitation and its purpose; and
> (e) less restrictive means to achieve the purpose.

[3] See in particular, Criminal Procedure Act 51 of 1977, as amended.

[4] Eg *S v Ntuli* 1996 (1) SA 1207 (CC); *S v Rens* 1996 (1) SA 1218 (CC); *S v Jordan* 2002 (2) SACR 499 (CC).

[5] Eg *S v Makwanyane* 1995 (3) SA 391 (CC); *S v Williams* 1995 (3) SA 632 (CC).

[6] Eg *S v Makwanyane* 1995 (3) SA 391 (CC).

[7] Eg *Nel v Le Roux* 1996 (3) SA 526 (CC); *S v Makwanyane* 1995 (3) SA 391 (CC); *S v Williams* 1995 (3) SA 632 (CC); *S v Thebus* 2003 (2) SACR 319 (CC).

[8] Eg *Case v Minister of Safety and Security* 1996 (3) SA 165 (CC); *National Coalition of Gay and Lesbian Equality v Minister of Justice* 1999 (1) SA 6 (CC).

[9] Eg *S v Lawrence* 1997 (4) SA 1176 (CC); *Prince v President of the Law Society of the Cape of Good Hope* 2002 (1) SASCR 431 (CC).

[10] Eg *Case v Minister of Safety and Security* 1996 (3) SA 165 (CC); *South African National Defence Force Union v Minister of Defence* 1999 (4) SA 469 (CC); *Phillips v Director of Public Prosecutions*, WLD 2003 (1) SSACR 425 (CC).

[11] Eg *Director of Public Prosecutions: Cape of Good Hope v Bathgate* 2000 (2) SA 535 (C); *National Director of Public Prosecutions v Alexander* 2001 (2) SACR 1 (T); *Mohamed v National Director of Public Prosecutions* 2002 (2) SASCR 93 (W).

[12] Eg *Els v Minister of Safety and Security* 1998 (2) SACR 93 (NC); *Shabalala v Attorney-General of Transvaal* 1995 (2) SACR 761 (CC).

[13] A provision clearly signalling the influence of the Canadian Charter.

(2) Except as provided in subsection (1) or in any other provision of the Constitution, no law may limit any right entrenched in the Bill of Rights.

The limitations clause plays a significant role in balancing the competing interests inherent in any criminal justice system. Section 39 of the Constitution provides courts with further general guidance on the interpretation of substantive rights:

(1) When interpreting the Bill of Rights, a court, tribunal or forum—
  (a) must promote the values that underlie an open and democratic society based on human dignity, equality and freedom;
  (b) must consider international law; and
  (c) may consider foreign law.

(2) When interpreting any legislation, and when developing the common law or customary law, every court, tribunal or forum must promote the spirit, purport and objects of the Bill of Rights.

(3) The Bill of Rights does not deny the existence of any other rights or freedoms that are recognised or conferred by common law, customary law or legislation, to the extent that they are consistent with the Bill.

The Constitutional Court has expounded on the effect of section 39. Although the starting point will always be the text of the Constitution,[14] the court has advocated a generous and purposive interpretation to the text so as to 'give... expression to the underlying values of the Constitution'.[15] The purpose of the right is ascertained by identifying the interests that the right seeks to protect,[16] in the light of South Africa's distinctive political history, as so eloquently explained in *Shabalala v Attorney-General of the Transvaal*:[17]

> [T]he Constitution is not simply some kind of statutory codification of an acceptable or legitimate past. It retains from the past only what is defensible... It constitutes a decisive break from a culture of apartheid and racism to a constitutionally protected culture of openness and democracy and universal human rights for South Africans of all ages, classes and colours. There is a stark and dramatic contrast between the past in which South Africans were trapped and the future on which the Constitution is premised. The past was pervaded by inequality, authoritarianism and repression. The aspiration of the future is based on what is 'justifiable in an open and democratic society based on freedom and equality'. It is premised on a legal culture of accountability and transparency. The relevant provisions of the Constitution must therefore be interpreted so as to give effect to the purposes sought to be advanced by their enactment.

[14] *S v Zuma* 1995 (2) SA 642 (CC).

[15] *S v Makwanyane* 1995 (3) SA 391 (CC), [9].

[16] *S v Zuma* 1995 (2) SA 642 (CC), [15], citing with approval the Canadian Supreme Court in *R v Big M Drug Mart Ltd* (1985) 18 DLR (4th) 321, 395–96.

[17] 1996 (1) SA 725 (CC), [26].

The Constitutional Court stressed the importance of generously interpreting the content of constitutional rights as widely as the text will allow.[18] This should mean that the party bearing the burden of establishing a rights infringement bears a relatively light burden in contrast to the party who seeks to have the right restricted. However, as we will see, there are numerous instances where the courts have elected not to take a generous approach in respect of either the content or the purpose of the right. This cramped approach qualifies the extent to which one may legitimately speak of a constitutional revolution in South African evidence law.

2. THE CONSTITUTIONAL RIGHT TO A FAIR TRIAL

The Apartheid State had used law in general, and the criminal justice system in particular, as powerful tools of political coercion and social control. It was therefore not surprising that the new Bill of Rights made explicit provision, in section 35 of the Constitution, for the protection of the rights of arrested, accused and detained persons. Section 35(1) guarantees to '[e]veryone who is arrested for allegedly committing an offence' the rights to silence and freedom from compelled confession, access to court, and prompt charge or release 'if the interests of justice permit, subject to reasonable conditions'. Section 35(2) contains the rights for all detained persons (including sentenced prisoners) to be informed promptly of the reason for their detention; access to competent legal advice 'at state expense, if substantial injustice would otherwise result'; access to court to challenge the lawfulness of their detention; to conditions of detention that are 'consistent with human dignity, including at least exercise and the provision, at state expense, of adequate accommodation, nutrition, reading material and medical treatment'; and to communicate with family members and doctors and religious counsellors of their own choosing.

Section 35(3) then sets out the following, distinctively South African version of the 'right to a fair trial', adapted from familiar provisions in international human rights law such as ICCPR Article 14 and ECHR Article 6:

> (3) Every accused person has a right to a fair trial, which includes the right—
> (a) to be informed of the charge with sufficient detail to answer it;
> (b) to have adequate time and facilities to prepare a defence;
> (c) to a public trial before an ordinary court;
> (d) to have their trial begin and conclude without unreasonable delay;
> (e) to be present when being tried;
> (f) to choose, and be represented by, a legal practitioner, and to be informed of this right promptly;

[18] See *S v Zuma* 1995 (2) SA 642 (CC), [14]; *S v Mhlungu* 1995 (3) SA 391 (CC).

(g) to have a legal practitioner assigned to the accused person by the state and at state expense, if substantial injustice would otherwise result, and to be informed of this right promptly;
(h) to be presumed innocent, to remain silent, and not to testify during the proceedings;
(i) to adduce and challenge evidence;
(j) not to be compelled to give self-incriminating evidence;
(k) to be tried in a language that the accused person understands or, if that is not practicable, to have the proceedings interpreted in that language;
(l) not to be convicted for an act or omission that was not an offence under either national or international law at the time it was committed or omitted;
(m) not to be tried for an offence in respect of an act or omission for which that person has previously been either acquitted or convicted;
(n) to the benefit of the least severe of the prescribed punishments if the prescribed punishment for the offence has been changed between the time that the offence was committed and the time of sentencing; and
(o) of appeal to, or review by, a higher court.

Section 35(4) stresses that information must be provided in a language that the suspect, accused or detainee understands—a significant proviso in a jurisdiction as linguistically diverse as South Africa. Finally, section 35(5) specifies a generic exclusionary rule pertaining to evidence obtained in violation of the constitution:

Evidence obtained in a manner that violates any right in the Bill of Rights must be excluded if the admission of that evidence would render the trial unfair or otherwise be detrimental to the administration of justice.

Section 35's right to a fair trial is possibly unique in its coverage and detail. This reflects acute consciousness of past abuses and the sterility of positivist definitions. It was only three years before the advent of democracy that the Appellate Division described the concept of trial fairness in the following restrictive terms:

> [A court of appeal] does not enquire whether the trial was fair in accordance with 'notions of fairness and justice', or with 'the ideas underlying ... the concept of justice which are the basis of all civilised systems of criminal administration'. The enquiry is whether there has been an irregularity or illegality that is a departure from the formalities, rules and principles of procedure according to which our law requires a criminal trial to be initiated and conducted. ... What an accused person is entitled to is a trial initiated and conducted in accordance with those formalities, rules and principles of procedure which the law requires. He is not entitled to a trial which is fair when tested against abstract notions of fairness and justice.[19]

[19] *S v Rudman; S v Mthwana* 1992 (1) SACR 70, 100, 109 (A), quoting Didcott J in *S v Khanyile* 1988 (3) SA 795, 802 (N), who reached the opposite conclusion.

In its very first judgment, in *S v Zuma*, the Constitutional Court resoundingly rejected this positivist approach. It held that the constitutional right to a fair trial embraced 'a concept of substantive fairness' that 'required criminal trials to be conducted in accordance with just those 'notions of basic fairness and justice'.[20] The Court also held that the right to a fair trial was not restricted to those rights enumerated in section 35(3).[21] The Constitutional Court again in *S v Dzukuda; S v Tshilo* emphasised the difference in approach between the old and new legal orders:

> [A]n accused's right to a fair trial under s 35(3) of the Constitution is a comprehensive right… Elements of this comprehensive right are specified in paras (a) to (o) of ss (3). The words 'which include the right' preceding this listing indicate that such specification is not exhaustive of what the right to a fair trial comprises. It also does not warrant the conclusion that the right to a fair trial consists merely of a number of discrete sub-rights, some of which have been specified in the subsection and others not. The right to a fair trial is a comprehensive and integrated right, the content of which will be established, on a case by case basis, as our constitutional jurisprudence on s 35(3) develops… At the heart of the right to a fair criminal trial and what infuses its purpose, is for justice to be done and also to be seen to be done. But the concept of justice itself is a broad and protean concept. In considering what, for purposes of this case, lies at the heart of a fair trial in the field of criminal justice, one should bear in mind that dignity, freedom and equality are the foundational values of our Constitution. An important aim of the right to a fair criminal trial is to ensure adequately that innocent people are not wrongly convicted, because of the adverse effects which a wrong conviction has on the liberty, and dignity (and possibly other) interests of the accused. There are, however, other elements of the right to a fair trial such as, for example, the presumption of innocence, the right to free legal representation in given circumstances, a trial in public which is not unreasonably delayed, which cannot be explained exclusively on the basis of averting a wrong conviction, but which arise primarily from considerations of dignity and equality.[22]

The remainder of this chapter examines in more detail some of the most important discrete strands of the constitutional right to a fair trial and their development by the South African courts since the mid-1990s.

3. CONSTITUTIONAL RIGHTS IN CRIMINAL PROCESS

This section explores the impact of South Africa's new constitutional arrangements on some familiar features of criminal procedure law and fair

[20] 1995 (2) SA 642 (CC), [16].

[21] See eg *S v Msithing* 2006 (1) SACR 266 (N); *S v Khumalo* 2006 (1) SACR 477 (N); *S v Muller* 2005 (2) SACR 451 (C).

[22] *S v Dzukuda; S v Tshilo* 2000 (4) SA 1078 (CC), [9], [11]. Also *S v Zuma* 1995 (2) SA 642 (CC), [16]; *S v Ntuli* 1996 (1) SA 1207 (CC); *Key v Attorney-General Cape Provincial Division* 1996 (4) SA 187 (CC); *Sanderson v Attorney-General, Eastern Cape* 1998 (2) SA 38 (CC), [22]; *S v Jaipal* 2005 (4) SA 581 (CC).

trial rights, specifically: (a) the presumption of innocence; (b) discharge where there is no case to answer; (c) the right to legal representation; (d) the right to silence; and (e) the right to adequate time and facilities to prepare a defence.

(a) The Presumption of Innocence

Prior to 1995 the presumption of innocence had the same equivocal status in legal theory and practice as it enjoyed in the country from which it was inherited, as part of the legacy of English common law. That is to say, it was given high rhetorical regard but subjected to the vagaries of legislative will.

From its very first decision,[23] the South African Constitutional Court has consistently struck down any deviation from the presumption of innocence's demand that the state prove each and every element of a crime beyond reasonable doubt.[24] Unlike apex courts in other jurisdictions, the Court has declined to draw distinctions between 'crimes' and 'regulatory offences' or between the defence and offence components in the definition of a criminal prohibition.[25] The sole determinant of constitutional compliance is whether there is the possibility of a conviction despite the existence of a reasonable doubt. However, the scope of the right to be presumed innocent has been restricted to the criminal trial; consequently it does not apply to interrogation procedures outside of the criminal process, nor to post-conviction proceedings.[26]

Although the Constitutional Court has never upheld a limitation on the presumption of innocence it has been careful to distinguish the presumption of innocence from the cluster of rights closely associated with it, such as the right to remain silent and the privilege against self-incrimination.[27] In contrast to Canadian jurisprudence, South African courts have held that the imposition of an evidentiary burden will not infringe the right to remain silent.[28] The decision in *S v Manamela*[29] marked a shift from a more generous approach to interpreting the constitutional presumption of innocence, by effectively equating it to nothing more than a standard of proof. This

[23] *S v Zuma* 1995 (2) SA 642 (CC).

[24] Eg *S v Zuma* 1995 (2) SA 642 (CC); *S v Coetzee* 1997 (3) SA 527 (CC); *S v Bhulwana; S v Gwadiso* 1996 (1) SA 388 (CC); *S v Boesak* 2001 (1) SA 912 (CC).

[25] *S v Coetzee* 1997 (3) SA 527 (CC).

[26] Eg *S v Dzukuda; S v Tshilo* 2000 (4) SA 1078 (CC); *NDPP v Phillips* 2001 (2) SACR 542 (W). Quasi-exceptions concern civil imprisonment of debtors and civil law contempt of court proceedings: *Uncedo Taxi Service Association v Maninjwa* 1998 (2) SACR 166 (E). See generally, *S v Baloyi* 2000 (2) SA 425 (CC); *S v Mamabolo* 2001 (3) SA 409 (CC); *S v Singo* 2002 (4) SA 858 (CC).

[27] *S v Manamela* 2000 (3) SA 1 (CC).

[28] *Scagell v Attorney-General of the Western Cape* 1997 (2) SA 368 (CC).

[29] 2000 (1) SACR 414 (CC).

undermines the rationale of the presumption of innocence, which is directed at reducing the possibility of an erroneous conviction in pursuit of the ideal that only the blameworthy should be punished. If the location of the burden of proof as a component of the presumption of innocence is ignored, the possibility of error increases.

(b) Discharge at the Close of the State's Case

Constitutional norms have influenced the interpretation of section 174 of the Criminal Procedure Act 1977, which provides:

> If at the close of the case for the prosecution at any trial, the court is of the opinion that there is no evidence that the accused committed the offence referred to in the charge or any offence of which he may be convicted on the charge, it may return a verdict of not guilty.

Prior to the new constitutional dispensation there was a significant body of case authority in support of the proposition that the use of the word 'may' in section 174 conferred a discretion on the court to refuse discharge in the absence of evidence supporting a conviction, provided there was a 'reasonable possibility that the defence evidence might supplement the state case'.[30] The correctness of this approach was soon challenged when the Interim Constitution came into force. Claasen J in *S v Mathebula*[31] held that an accused's right to freedom and security of person as well as his rights to be presumed innocent and remain silent severely curtailed the discretion conferred by section 174. Consequently, courts no longer had discretion to refuse discharge when there was no evidence tendered against the accused. However, this approach was not uniformly adopted by the High Court.[32]

The Supreme Court of Appeal's decisions in *S v Legote*[33] and *S v Lubaxa*[34] extend this line of reasoning. In *Legote*, Harms JA held that a court had a duty to ensure that an unrepresented accused against whom the state had not made out a prima facie case was discharged and the principle of equality required that this duty be extended to accused persons with legal representation. In *Lubaxa*, Nugent AJA (as he was then) stated:

> I have no doubt that an accused person (whether or not he is represented) is entitled to be discharged at the close of the case for the prosecution if there is no possibility of a conviction other than if he enters the witness box and incriminates himself.

[30] *S v Shuping* 1983 (2) SA 119 (BSC) 120; *R v Kritzinger* 1952 (2) SA 402 (W); *S v Zimmerie* 1989 (3) SA 484 (C); *S v Campbell* 1991 (1) SACR 435 (Nm).

[31] *S v Mathebula* 1997 (1) BCLR 123 (W).

[32] Cf *S v Makofane* 1998 (1) SACR 603 (T).

[33] *S v Legote* 2001 (2) SACR 179 (SCA).

[34] *S v Lubaxa* 2001 (2) SACR 703 (SCA). See also *S v Zwezwe* 2006 (2) SACR 599 (N).

> The failure to discharge an accused in those circumstances, if necessary *mero motu*, is in my view a breach of the rights that are guaranteed by the Constitution and will ordinarily vitiate a conviction based exclusively upon his self-incriminatory evidence.[35]

The *Lubaxa* court found that the right to be discharged did not necessarily arise from the rights to be presumed innocent, to remain silent or not to testify, but rather from the constitutional rights to dignity and personal freedom which require the existence of a '"reasonable and probable" cause to believe that the accused is guilty'.[36] However, the court did not disentangle the constitutional rights to dignity, personal freedom and a fair trial. It concluded that the protection afforded by the rights to dignity and personal freedom will be 'pre-eminently' eroded 'where the prosecution has exhausted the evidence and a conviction is no longer possible except by self-incrimination'.

Presumably, it is the privilege against self-incrimination which underlies the *Lubaxa* court's finding that '[t]he same considerations do not necessarily arise ... where the prosecution's case against one accused might be supplemented by the evidence of a co-accused'.[37] The *Lubaxa* court reasoned that '[t]he prosecution is ordinarily entitled to rely upon the evidence of an accomplice and it is not self-evident why it should necessarily be precluded from doing so merely because it has chosen to prosecute more than one person jointly'.[38] However, it is equally not self-evident why the rights to privacy and freedom of the person cease to be infringed merely because the prosecution has chosen to prosecute more than one person jointly. One argument that might support this view is that the refusal of discharge is premised, not on the possibility that the accused will incriminate himself, but rather on the likelihood that the co-accused will complete the prosecution's task.[39] We are left with a penumbra of uncertainty surrounding the ambit of several key constitutional rights.

(c) The Right to Legal Representation

Under the old legal order there was no substantive right to legal representation except in capital cases.[40] Except for those arrested under security

[35] *S v Lubaxa* 2001 (2) SACR 703 (SCA), [18]. See also *S v Zwezwe* 2006 (2) SACR 599 (N).

[36] *S v Lubaxa* 2001 (2) SACR 703 (SCA), [19].

[37] Ibid [20]. See also *S v Tusani* 2002 (2) SACR 468 (TD); *S v Tsotetsi (2)* 2003 (2) SACR 638 (W).

[38] *S v Lubaxa* 2001 (2) SACR 703 (SCA), [20].

[39] In *S v Zuma* 2006 (2) SACR 191, 208 (W), Van der Merwe JA refers to *Lubaxa* and then appears to invert the mirror, by refusing discharge on the basis that he was not convinced of the accused's innocence beyond a reasonable doubt. This seems contrary to the presumption of innocence, placing the burden of proof on the prosecution.

[40] *S v Rudman; S v Mthwana* 1992 (1) SA 343 (A).

legislation, suspects had a right to legal representation at their own expense. The importance of legal representation at both trial and pre-trial stages was already well-established in many Anglo-American jurisdictions prior to the 1990s,[41] and this realisation was extended to South Africa by section 35(1)(c) of the new constitution. Thus, the link between the right to counsel and other essential procedural rights was succinctly restated by Froneman J in *S v Melani*:

> The purpose of the right to counsel and its corollary to be informed of that right... is thus to protect the right to remain silent, the right not to incriminate oneself and the right to be presumed innocent until proven guilty.... [T]his protection exists from the inception of the criminal process that is on arrest, until its culmination up to and during the trial itself. This protection has nothing to do with the need to ensure the reliability of evidence adduced at the trial. It has everything to do with the need to ensure that an accused is treated fairly in the entire criminal process: in the 'gatehouse' of the criminal justice system (that is the interrogation process), as well as in its 'mansions' (the trial court).[42]

The Constitution affords detained and accused persons the right to be provided with legal assistance at state expense only 'if substantial injustice would otherwise result'.[43] However, if legal representation is necessary to uphold the privilege against self-incrimination (and associated rights) and the protection of the right not to incriminate oneself is necessary to ensure a fair trial, then a person ought to have access to legal representation in order to secure their basic rights irrespective of financial means. The logical conclusion to this line of reasoning is that if the state finds itself unable to provide legal representation to an arrested, detained or accused person, police interrogation should cease.[44] There can be little doubt that the reason for qualifying the substantive right to legal representation is that the South African state simply does not have the resources to provide legal representation for every indigent accused. An unqualified right to legal representation would paralyse an already overburdened criminal justice system. Factors taken into account in applying the substantial injustice test include: the complexity of the case;[45] the severity of the potential sentence;[46] and the level of education and indigence of the accused.[47] Where the potential for substantial injustice is clear, a trial may not proceed in the absence of legal

[41] See eg *Miranda v Arizona*, 384 US 436 (1966); *Escobedo v Illinois*, 378 US 478 (1964); *Harris v New York*, 401 US 222 (1970); *Rhode Island v Innis*, 446 US 291 (1980); *New York v Quarles*, 467 US 649 (1984).

[42] See *S v Melani* 1996 (1) SACR 335 (E).

[43] Constitution of South Africa, s 35(2)(c) and s 35(3)(g).

[44] But cf *Mgcina v Regional Magistrate Lenasia* 1997 (2) SACR 711 (W).

[45] See generally, *Pennington v The Minister of Justice* 1995 (3) BCLR 270 (C); *Msila v Government of the RSA* 1996 (3) BCLR 362 (C); *S v Khanyile* 1988 (3) SA 795 (N).

[46] *S v Moos* 1998 (1) SACR 372 (C); *S v Du Toit* 2005 (2) SACR 411 (T).

[47] *S v Vermaas; S v Du Plessis* 1995 (3) SA 292 (CC); *S v Ambros* 2005 (2) SACR 211 (C).

representation unless the accused makes an informed waiver of her right to counsel.[48] Whilst legal representation will normally be afforded to indigents at trial,[49] the widespread incidence of pre-trial abuses in South Africa indicates dire need for *pre-trial* access to legal advice and assistance.

Where an accused is unrepresented it is well-established that presiding officers must ensure that the accused is informed of her rights,[50] including the right to legal representation, prior to the commencement of the trial.[51] However, failure to inform an accused of the right to legal representation will result in an unfair trial only if it can be shown 'that the conviction has been tarnished by the irregularity'.[52] The state's fiscal inability to provide legal representation to all those who become embroiled in criminal process undoubtedly undermines the substantive impact of South Africa's constitutional 'rights revolution'.

(d) The Right to Remain Silent

At common law, the prosecution could refer to the accused's silence once a prima facie case had been established. There was clear authority for the proposition that, in certain circumstances, an accused's refusal to testify, when the prosecution had established a prima facie case, could be a factor in assessing guilt.[53] The High Court in *S v Brown*[54] observed that its new constitutional status would affect the application of the common law right to silence. The most obvious change is that any infringement of the right to remain silent must now be justified by reference to the limitations clause in section 36 of the Constitution.

In *Brown* the court ruled that use of silence as an item of evidence amounted to an indirect compulsion to testify and that the drawing of an adverse inference from silence diminished and possibly nullified the right to remain silent. It would therefore be unconstitutional for the court to draw an adverse inference where accused persons elect to exercise their

[48] *S v Manuel* 2001 (4) SA 11351 (W).

[49] See Country Report for Legal Aid South Africa, ILAG Conference, Helsinki, June 2011, www.ilagnet.org/jscripts/tiny_mce/plugins/filemanager/files/Helsinki_2011/national_reports/National_Report_-_South_Africa.pdf.

[50] Including proper explanation of the proceedings and concepts such as 'cross-examination' and 'opportunity to address the court': *S v Lekhetho* 2002 (2) SACR 13 (O).

[51] *S v Radebe, S v Mbonani* 1998 (1) SACR 191 (T); *S v Van Heerden en Ander sake* 2002 (1) SACR 409 (T).

[52] *S v May* 2005 (2) SACR 331 (SCA). See also *Htlantlalala v Dyanti NO* 1999 (2) SACR 541 (SCA).

[53] *S v Mthetwa* 1972 (3) SA 766 (A); *S v Snyman* 1968 (2) SA 582 (A); *S v Letsoko* 1964 (4) SA 768 (A); *R v Ismail* 1952 (1) SA 204 (A).

[54] *S v Brown* 1996 (2) SACR 49 (NC).

constitutional right to remain silent.[55] However, the court went on to say that this conclusion does not imply that reliance on the right to remain silent will never have adverse consequences for the accused.[56] Where the state has established a prima facie case, and the accused fails to testify or to adduce any other evidence to rebut it, the court is obliged to assess the uncontradicted evidence of the state. In this situation it is foreseeable, indeed commonplace, that the prosecution's prima facie case will be sufficient to sustain a conviction. In other words, although the accused's silence may not be treated as an independent item of evidence, he or she will have to accept the risk of conviction on the basis of uncontroverted evidence of guilt (rather than any inference drawn directly from the accused's silence).[57]

Reaching the opposite conclusion (and without reference to *Brown*), the court in *S v Lavhengwa* affirmed that an adverse inference could be permitted in appropriate circumstances:

> It accords, first, with common sense. The inference is permissible only when the accused fails to give evidence despite the fact that the prosecution evidence strongly indicates guilt, an innocent accused would have refuted evidence against him, and there is no other explanation of his failure to do so. In these circumstances common sense demands that an inference be drawn and human nature is such that one would be all but inevitable. It has indeed been suggested that 'no rule of law can effectively legislate against the drawing of an inference from a failure to testify'. Secondly, it is not mere sophistry to reason... that an accused's right to remain silent is not denied or eroded by an inference drawn from his choice to exercise that right in circumstances where an innocent person would not have chosen to do so. It is suggested thirdly that, even if the rule permitting an adverse inference impinged upon the right of the accused to remain silent, it is in any event probably a justifiable limitation.[58]

The Constitutional Court has not expressly ruled on whether drawing an adverse inference from silence at trial would pass constitutional muster. However, in *Thebus*, the Court wrote that 'if there is evidence that requires a response and if no response is forthcoming... the Court may be justified in concluding that the evidence is sufficient, in the absence of an explanation, to prove the guilt of the accused'.[59] This is not the same as treating

[55] Ibid 62.

[56] Ibid 63.

[57] See also *S v Hlongwa* 2002 (3) SACR 37 (T); *S v Scholtz* 1996 (2) SACR 40 (NC). Generally, see SE Van der Merwe 'The Constitutional Passive Defence Right of an Accused versus Prosecutorial and Judicial Comment on Silence: Must we Follow *Griffin v California?*' [1994] *Obiter* 1.

[58] *S v Lavhengwa* 1996 (2) SACR 453, 487 (W): cf *S v Mseleku* 2006 (2) SACR 574 (D), discussed by W Trengove, 'Evidence' in M Chaskalson et al (eds), *Constitutional Law of South Africa* (Cape Town, Juta, 1999) 26-14–26-16.

[59] *S v Thebus* 2003 (6) SA 505 (CC), [58]. See also *S v Boesak* 2001 (1) SA 912 (CC); *S v Mokoena* 2006 (1) SACR 29 (W); *S v Hena* 2006 (2) SACR 33 (SE). Cf *S v Sithole* 2005 (2) SACR 504 (SCA).

silence as an item of evidence. However, more recently the Supreme Court of Appeal handed down judgments that clearly imply that the Court is prepared to expand the ambit of negative consequences to include using silence as independent proof of guilt.[60]

At common law, when an alibi defence was raised for the first time at trial, the court in determining whether a late alibi was possibly true could take into account that there had been no opportunity for the state to investigate it properly.[61] The constitutionality of the common law approach to late alibis was considered by the Constitutional Court in *S v Thebus*.[62] Seven of the ten judges who heard the case held that it was constitutionally impermissible to draw an adverse inference as to guilt from the accused's pre-trial silence. However, four of this seven-strong majority indicated that if the constitutionally mandated warning was rephrased so as to apprise arrested persons of the consequences of remaining silent, an adverse inference from pre-trial silence might be constitutionally acceptable. Three other judges held that although an adverse inference as to guilt was not justifiable, an adverse inference as to credibility was a justifiable limitation on the right to remain silent and that it was permissible to cross-examine the accused on his failure to disclose an alibi timeously. Four justices expressly rejected this conclusion. All eight of the judges dealing with the question of adverse inferences appeared to agree that there may well be acceptable negative consequences that attach to remaining silent. It would seem, therefore, that the common law position remains largely intact and that it is constitutionally permissible to take the late disclosure of an alibi into account in determining what weight should be attached to an alibi defence.

As to the drawing of inferences from pre-trial silence, Moseneke J stated categorically that negative inferences are constitutionally impermissible. On the other hand, the concurring judgment of Goldstone and O'Regan JJ suggests that such inferences might be constitutional if arrested persons are warned of the consequences of their silence. One conclusion that would be consistent with both judgments is that the ambiguity of silence (and the impermissibility of drawing any inference) would remain if an arrested person did not understand the revised warning. This interpretation would make it highly unlikely that a negative inference could ever be drawn from silence at any stage where an arrested person or accused person is not represented by counsel.

[60] *S v Monyane* 2008 (1) SACR 543 (SCA), [19]. See also *S v Mavinini* 2009 (1) SACR 523 (SCA).

[61] *R v Mashele* 1944 AD 571.

[62] *S v Thebus* 2003 (6) SA 505 (CC).

In 2002 the South African Law Commission[63] submitted a report to the Minister of Justice addressing the desirability of drawing adverse inferences from pre-trial and trial silence. The Report canvassed two possible options without making a firm recommendation: (a) expressly permitting inferences from pre-trial and trial silence; or (b) retaining the status quo. The first option was strongly influenced by developments in Northern Ireland and in England and Wales, whilst the second rejected the English approach implemented through section 34 of the Criminal Justice and Public Order Act 1994 on the basis that it was contextually inappropriate[64] and an unjustifiable infringement of the right to remain silent. The Law Commission was unable to provide unequivocal advice on the constitutionality of the first option. A major source of uncertainty is the courts' apparent reluctance (the Constitutional Court excepted) to adopt a generously purposive approach in ascertaining the scope of a right before reaching for the limitations clause to mediate competing interests in the administration of criminal justice. Crime control imperatives loom especially large in societies, such as South Africa, where there is a high incidence of crime.[65]

(e) The Right to Adequate Time and Facilities to Prepare a Defence

Prior to 1995 an accused who sought information contained in the police docket, such as witness statements, or who wished to interview state witnesses would be routinely blocked by a claim of 'blanket docket privilege' made by the prosecution.[66] The central role of access to information in enabling an accused to exercise his or her fair trial rights was recognised by the Constitutional Court in *Shabalala v Attorney-General of Transvaal.*[67] *Shabalala* abolished 'blanket docket privilege' and broadened the accused's access to state witnesses. Where the prosecution resists disclosure, it is for the court to determine whether disclosure is required to satisfy the requirements of the right to a fair trial.[68]

[63] South African Law Commission, Report, Project 73 Simplification of Criminal Procedure (A more inquisitorial approach to criminal procedure—police questioning, defence disclosure, the rule of judicial officers and judicial management of trial) (Pretoria, 2002).

[64] Particularly in the light of limited pre-trial representation and the absence of technology, such as video recording of police station interviews, to provide the necessary safeguards.

[65] Crime statistics for South Africa can be found at www.saps.gov.za/statistics/reports/crimestats/2010/totals.pdf. For comparative statistics see www.nationmaster.com/country/sf-south-africa/cri-crime.

[66] *R v Steyn* 1954 (1) SA 324 (A).

[67] *Shabalala v Attorney-General of Transvaal* 1995 (2) SACR 761 (CC).

[68] *S v Crossberger* 2008 (2) SACR 317 (SCA); *S v Rowand* 2009 (2) SACR 450 (W).

4. CONSTITUTIONAL RIGHTS AND THE LAW OF EVIDENCE

We now turn to aspects of the traditional law of evidence which have been affected by South Africa's new constitutional dispensation. This section's selective survey considers: (a) samples and other physical evidence recovered from the accused; (b) admissions and confessions; (c) hearsay and the right to challenge evidence; (d) aspects of credibility in sexual offence prosecutions; and (e) the constitutional exclusionary rule.

(a) Samples and Other Physical Evidence Recovered From the Accused

Section 37(1) of the Criminal Procedure Act authorises police officials to take the fingerprints, palm prints or footprints of any person who has been arrested or charged. The police may also take such steps as are necessary to ascertain whether any arrested person has any bodily mark, characteristic or distinguishing feature or shows any condition or appearance. Obviously evidence of this nature might incriminate the accused. The question then arises whether section 37 is in conflict with the constitutional right against compelled self-incrimination.

In the old common law case of *R v Maleke,* the court refused to admit evidence of a footprint compelled by force.[69] According to Krause J:

> [I]t compels an accused person to convict himself out of his own mouth; that it might open the door to oppression and persecution of the worst kind; that it is a negation of the liberty of the subject and offends against our sense of natural justice and fair play...[70]

This line of reasoning was firmly rejected by the Appellate Division in a 1941 ruling concerned with the admissibility of evidence of a palm print taken by compulsion.[71] Watermeyer JA explained that the privilege against self-incrimination applies only to testimonial utterances:

> Now, where a palm-print is being taken from an accused person, he is, as pointed out by Innes CJ in *R v Camane* (1925 AD 570, 575), entirely passive. He is not being compelled to give evidence or to confess, any more that he is being compelled to give evidence or confess when his photograph is being taken or when he is put upon an identification parade or when he is made to show a scar in court. In my judgement, therefore, neither the maxim *nemo tenetur se ipsum prodere* nor the confession rule make inadmissible palm-prints compulsorily taken.[72]

[69] *R v Maleke* 1925 TPD 491.
[70] Ibid 534. See also *Gooprushad v R* 1914 35 NLR 87; *R v B* 1933 OPD 139.
[71] *Ex parte Minister of Justice: In re R v Matemba* 1941 AD 75.
[72] Ibid 82–83.

This remains the position under the new Constitution.

In *S v Huma (2)*, Claassen J held that taking fingerprints does not constitute testimonial evidence by the accused and was therefore not in conflict with the privilege against self-incrimination.[73] The *Huma* court relied heavily on *Schmerber v California*,[74] in which a majority of the US Supreme Court held that the Fifth Amendment privilege against self-incrimination relates only to the testimonial or communicative acts of the accused and does not apply to non-communicative acts such as submission to a blood test. This approach was adopted by the South African Supreme Court of Appeal in *Levack*,[75] where compelling an accused to provide a voice sample was found to infringe neither the right to silence nor the privilege against self-incrimination. In *S v Orrie*, the High Court held that taking a blood sample for the purposes of DNA profiling without consent infringed both the right to privacy and the right to bodily security and integrity, but that the infringement was justifiable.[76] Desai J, in *Minister of Safety and Security v Gaqa*,[77] confirmed an order compelling the respondent to submit himself to an operation to remove a bullet from his leg. In so doing, the High Court rejected the respondent's argument that this procedure would infringe his constitutional right not to incriminate himself. The *Gaqa* court held that sections 27 and 37 of the Criminal Procedure Act sanctioned 'the violence necessary to remove the bullet',[78] and that although these procedures constituted a serious infringement of dignity and bodily integrity, they met the requirements of the Constitution's limitation clause. A similar application was made to the High Court in *Minister of Safety and Security v Xaba*.[79] The respondent's arguments were apparently limited to the right to be free from all forms of violence and the right to have bodily security and control, pursuant to section 12 of the Constitution. Southwood AJ held that the conclusion of the court in *Gaqa* was clearly wrong. In the absence of a law of general application authorising the specific constitutional infringements, Southwood AJ reasoned, the requirements of the limitation clause could not be met.

Can a clear distinction be made between forcibly taking physical samples and testimonial or communicative statements? Black and Douglas JJ, dissenting in *Schmerber v California*, thought not:

> [T]he compulsory extraction of a petitioner's blood for analysis so that the person who analysed it could give evidence to convict him had both a 'testimonial' and a 'communicative nature'. The sole purpose of this project which proved to be

[73] *S v Huma (2)* 1995 (2) SACR 411, 419 (W). See also *S v Maphumulo* 1996 (2) SACR 84 (N); *Msomi v Attorney-General of Natal* 1996 (8) BCLR 1109 (W).

[74] *Schmerber v California*, 384 US 757 (1966).

[75] *Levack v Regional Magistrate Wynberg* 2003 (1) SACR 187 (SCA).

[76] *S v Orrie* 2004 (1) SACR 162 (C), [20].

[77] *Minister of Safety and Security v Gaqa* 2002 (1) SACR 654 (C).

[78] Ibid 658.

[79] *Minister of Safety and Secruity v Xaba* 2004 (1) SACR 149 (D).

> successful was to obtain 'testimony' from some person to prove that the petitioner had alcohol in his blood at the time he was arrested. And the purpose of the project was certainly 'communicative' in that the analysis of the blood was to supply information to enable a witness to communicate to the court and jury that the petitioner was more or less drunk.[80]

A formal distinction between 'testimonial' or 'communicative' and non-communicative conduct is perhaps necessary, in the absence of a generic limitations clause in the US Bill of Rights, to preserve the admissibility of DNA swabs, fingerprints and routine physical samples. The inclusion of section 36 in the South African Constitution ought, in theory, to enable South African judges to take a more principled and coherent approach to delineating the content of the right against self-incrimination without compromising the effective administration of criminal justice. But this notional freedom has been under-utilised in practice.

(b) Admissions and Confessions

South African law draws a distinction between admissions and confessions.[81] An admission is simply a statement that is adverse to its maker whereas a confession is not merely adverse to the maker but also amounts to an unequivocal acknowledgement of guilt. The only requirement that needs to be met before an admission will be accepted into evidence is that it must have been made voluntarily.[82] In this context 'voluntary' has a very restricted meaning, excluding only those statements induced by a promise or threat proceeding from a person in authority.[83] Section 217 of the Criminal Procedure Act requires a confession to be made freely and voluntarily whilst the maker is in his sound and sober senses and without undue influence. Section 35(1)(c) of the Constitution, providing that arrested persons shall have the right 'not to be compelled to make any confession or admission that could be used in evidence against' them, may well encourage the courts to abandon the artificial and technical common law interpretation of the requirements of 'voluntariness' and undue influence.

In *S v Agnew*, Foxcroft J questioned the artificial distinction between confessions and admissions.[84] Historically, the distinction was rationalised on the basis that admissions require less stringent procedural safeguards

[80] *Schmerber v California*, 384 US 757, 774 (1966) (Black J). The minority judgment in *Schmerber* was preferred by the Canadian Supreme Court in *R v Stillman* (1997) 42 CRR (2d) 189.

[81] *S v Ralukukwe* 2006 (2) SACR 394 (SCA).

[82] Criminal Procedure Act 51 of 1977, s 219A.

[83] *R v Barlin* 1926 AD 459.

[84] *S v Agnew* 1996 (2) SACR 535 (C).

than full-blown confessions.[85] However, as Foxcroft J observed, in many instances admissions could be just as damaging as confessions.[86] The *Agnew* court held that '[i]f full effect is given to the maxim that no one should be obliged to incriminate himself, then it is difficult to understand how incriminating statements contained in confessions should be treated differently from words amounting to admissions only'.[87]

An analogous situation arises where the accused is required, under legal compulsion,[88] to point out a thing or place that is thought relevant to the investigation. It was sometimes argued that 'pointings out' were akin to collecting fingerprints and other physical evidence, and therefore beyond the scope of the privilege against self-incrimination or rules pertaining to confessions. In *S v Sheehama*, the Appellate Division found this reasoning untenable, holding that 'a pointing out is essentially a communication by conduct and, as such, is a statement by the person pointing out'.[89] Consequently, a pointing out, like any other extra-judicial admission, has to be made voluntarily before it will be admitted into evidence. Although a pointing out may result in the production of physical evidence, it differs materially from fingerprints, blood samples and the like in the degree of active or communicative conduct it entails.[90]

All the reasons for excluding involuntary confessions apply equally to involuntary admissions and legally compelled demonstrations by the accused. Involuntary confessions and admissions are excluded not only because they are potentially unreliable,[91] but also because a conviction based on an involuntary admission or confession is obtained without due process of law.[92] No admission or confession should be the product of abuse.[93] Admitting a forced admission or confession would likewise be contrary to the right not to incriminate oneself.[94] As the South African Law Commission argued, admissions, confessions and the 'pointing out' type of demonstrations, should all be subject to the same unified test of admissibility, namely that they were made freely and voluntarily, in sound and sober senses and without undue influence.[95] A decade later, the Law Commission's recommendations still remain unimplemented. In the meantime, section 35(5) of the Constitution, which is considered in the final part of this section, provides an alternative legal basis for excluding admissions

[85] Ibid 538.
[86] Cf *R v Xulu* 1956 (2) SA 288 (A). See also *S v Orrie* 2005 (1) SASCR 63, 76 (C).
[87] *S v Agnew* 1996 (2) SACR 535 (C).
[88] Criminal Procedure Act 51 of 1977, s 218.
[89] *S v Sheehama* 1991 (2) SA 860 (A).
[90] See *S v Binta* 1993 (3) SACR 553 (C).
[91] *S v Radebe* 1968 (4) SA 410, 418–19 (A).
[92] *Brown v Allen*, 344 US 443 (1953).
[93] *S v January; Prokureu-Generaal, Natal v Khumalo* 1994 (2) SACR 801 (A).
[94] *R v Duetsimi* 1950 (3) SA 674 (A); *S v Sheehama* 1991 (2) SA 860 (A).
[95] South African Law Commission Project 73, above n 63, 6.83.

(including admissions by conduct) and confessions—or indeed, any other evidence—obtained in violation of the Bill of Rights.[96]

(c) Hearsay and the Right to Challenge Evidence

The right to adduce and challenge evidence was well-established at common law. Post-1995, the Constitution has been used as a vehicle for bolstering this common law right. The constitutional right to adduce and challenge evidence[97] affects both the rules governing the admissibility of evidence and the conduct of presiding judges. Trial judges must ensure that unrepresented accused are aware of their right to adduce evidence, and must assist accused in exercising their right to testify.[98] A failure to allow cross-examination will generally be viewed as a serious irregularity that encroaches upon the accused's right to a fair trial.[99] The right to challenge evidence also has potential implications for the common law of hearsay.[100]

In *Ndhlovu*,[101] the Supreme Court of Appeal was required to consider the constitutionality of section 3 of the Law of Evidence Amendment Act,[102] which governs the admissibility of hearsay evidence. The general rule is that hearsay evidence is inadmissible, except where: (a) the party against whom the evidence is adduced consents; (b) the person upon whose credibility the probative value of the evidence depends testifies; or (c) a court determines that it is in the interests of justice that the hearsay be admitted. The court in *Ndhlovu* identified two principal objections to admitting hearsay evidence. First, it is 'not subject to the reliability checks applied to first-hand testimony'; and secondly, 'its reception exposes the party opposing its proof to the procedural unfairness of not being able to counter effectively inferences that may be drawn from it'.[103] Presumably it was on the basis of such potential unfairness that counsel for the accused based the assertion that the accused's constitutional right to challenge evidence was infringed. The court noted that section 3 is primarily an exclusionary rule and that its significant departure from the common law was intended to create 'supple

[96] See, eg, *S v Agnew* 1996 (2) SACR 535 (C); *S v Mphala* 1998 (1) SACR 388 (W); *S v Lottering* 1999 (12) BCLR 1478 (N); *S v Soci* 1998 (2) SACR 275 (E).

[97] Constitution of South Africa, s 35(3)(i).

[98] *S v Matladi* 2002 (2) SACR 447 (T).

[99] *S v Kok* 2005 (2) SACR 240 (NC); *R v Ndawo* 1961 (1) SA 16 (N); *S v Malatji* 1998 (2) SACR 622 (W).

[100] As the European Court of Human Rights' much-discussed decision in *Al-Khawaja and Tahery v UK* (2009) 49 EHRR 1 graphically illustrates. See the contributions to this volume by Ashworth, Redmayne, Callen and Gallavin.

[101] *S v Ndhlovu* 2002 (2) SACR 325 (SCA). Cf *S v Msimango* 2010 (1) SACR 544 (GSJ).

[102] Act 45 of 1988.

[103] *S v Ndhlovu* 2002 (2) SACR 325 (SCA), [13]. See also *Harksen v Attorney General Cape* 1999 (1) SA 718 (C).

standards within which courts may consider whether the interests of justice warrant the admission of hearsay notwithstanding the procedural and substantive disadvantages its reception might entail'.[104] Cameron JA held that the criteria to be taken into account in applying the interests of justice test were 'consonant with the Constitution',[105] and reiterated the court's reluctance to admit or rely 'on hearsay evidence which plays a decisive or even significant part in convicting an accused, unless there are compelling justifications for doing so'.[106] In order to ensure that an accused's fair trial rights are upheld when hearsay evidence is offered, trial judges should: (a) actively guard against the inadvertent admission or 'venting' of hearsay evidence;[107] (b) ensure that the significance of the contents of section 3 are properly explained to an unrepresented accused;[108] and (c) protect an accused from 'the late or unheralded admission of hearsay evidence'.[109] These requirements are creatures of judicial interpretation; they are not enumerated in the 1988 Act itself.

Cameron JA also emphasised the 'rigorous legal framework' created by section 3 for determining the admissibility of hearsay evidence.[110] This is not merely an exercise of judicial discretion, but a decision of law that can be reviewed and possibly overruled by an appeal court.[111] The manner in which section 3 regulates the admission of hearsay evidence was said to be 'in keeping with developments in other democratic societies based on human dignity, equality and freedom'.[112] The court concluded that the constitutional right to challenge evidence will not be infringed where evidence is admitted in the interests of justice in terms of section 3 of the Law of Evidence Amendment Act 1988.[113] The crux of the court's reasoning is contained in the following passage:

> It has correctly been observed that the admission of hearsay evidence 'by definition denies an accused the right to cross-examine', since the declarant is not in court and cannot be cross-examined. I cannot accept, however, that 'use of hearsay evidence by the State violates the accused's right to challenge evidence by cross-examination', if it is meant that the inability to cross-examine the source of

[104] *S v Ndhlovu* 2002 (2) SACR 325 (SCA), [14]. See also *Makhathini v Road Accident Fund* 2002 (1) SA 511 (SCA).

[105] *S v Ndhlovu* 2002 (2) SACR 325 (SCA) 16.

[106] Ibid [16].

[107] See also *S v Zimmerie* 1989 (3) SA 484, 492 (C); *S v Ramavhale* 1996 (1) SACR 639, 651 (A).

[108] See also *S v Ngwani* 1990 (1) SACR 449 (N).

[109] *S v Ndhlovu* 2002 (2) SACR 325 (SCA), [18]. See also *S v Ralukukwe* 2006 (2) SACR 394 (SCA).

[110] *S v Ndhlovu* 2002 (2) SACR 325 (SCA), [22]. See also *S v Molimi* 2008 (3) SA 608 (CC).

[111] *McDonald's Corporation v Joburgers Drive-Inn Restaurant (Pty) Ltd* 1997 (1) SA 1, 27E (A).

[112] *S v Ndhlovu* 2002 (2) SACR 325 (SCA), [23].

[113] Cf *S v Libazi* 2010 (2) SACR 233 (SCA).

> a statement in itself violates the right to 'challenge' evidence. The Bill of Rights does not guarantee an entitlement to subject all evidence to cross-examination. What it contains is the right (subject to limitation in terms of s 36) to 'challenge evidence'. Where that evidence is hearsay, the right entails that the accused is entitled to resist its admission and to scrutinise its probative value, including its reliability. The provisions enshrine these entitlements. But where the interests of justice, constitutionally measured, require that hearsay evidence be admitted, no constitutional right is infringed. Put differently, where the interests of justice require that the hearsay statement be admitted, the right to 'challenge evidence' does not encompass the right to cross-examine the original declarant.

Although not expressly articulated, Cameron JA's interpretation of the right to challenge evidence rejects a generous approach to the interpretation of rights. There can be little doubt that the right to challenge witness evidence must ordinarily include the right to cross-examine. The admission of hearsay evidence, by virtue of the statutory definition of hearsay,[114] precludes cross-examination of the person upon whom its probative value depends. Had the Supreme Court of Appeal taken a more generous interpretative approach to the scope of substantive constitutional rights it would have been forced to engage in the second, justificatory stage of limitations analysis.[115]

A second important testing ground for the scope and application of the right to challenge evidence concerns the testimony of children and other vulnerable witnesses. Section 170A, permitting a witness under the biological or mental age of 18 who would otherwise be exposed to undue mental stress or suffering to give his or her evidence through an intermediary, was inserted[116] into the Criminal Procedure Act prior to the transition to democracy. In due course, the constitutionality of this section was challenged in *K v The Regional Court Magistrate NO*,[117] but the court rejected the argument that section 170A infringed any purported right to cross-examine, without resort to limitations analysis. This ruling accords with the view expressed by the South African Law Commission that '[t]he purpose of "translated" cross-examination is not to weaken intelligent and even sharp cross-examination, but rather to limit aggressiveness and intimidation towards the child witness'.[118]

[114] Section 3(4) of the Law of Evidence Amendment Act 45 of 1988 defines hearsay as 'evidence, whether oral or in writing the probative value of which depends upon the credibility of any person other than the person giving such evidence'.

[115] See further, PJ Schwikkard 'The Challenge to Hearsay' (2003) 120 *South African Law Journal* 63.

[116] Originally, as s 3 of Act 135 of 1991.

[117] 1996 (1) SACR 434 (E).

[118] See further, PJ Schwikkard, 'The Abused Child: A Few Rules of Evidence Considered' (1996) *Acta Juridica* 148; PJ Schwikkard and SE van der Merwe, *Principles of Evidence* (Cape Town, Juta, 2009) 375 et seq.

In 2008 section 170A again came under constitutional scrutiny, in *S v Mokoena; S v Phaswane*,[119] from the very different perspective of protecting children's constitutional rights. The court identified section 28 of the Constitution—which enumerates various specific rights accruing to children[120] and states, in subsection (2), that '[t]he child's best interests are of paramount importance in every matter concerning the child'—as the primary lens through which the constitutionality of criminal procedure legislation[121] had to be viewed. Bertelsmann J held that, by virtue of the application of section 28(2), children's rights will inevitably take precedence over other constitutional rights.[122]

Bertelsmann J referred to the international instruments ratified and adopted by South Africa which are directed at protecting the interests of children.[123] He also referred to the Children's Act 38 of 2005, particularly section 42(8), which emphasises that 'the proceedings of the children's courts should be held in a locality that should be specifically adapted to put children at ease and should be conducive to an informal conduct of proceedings'.[124] Child victims and witnesses are recognised as extremely vulnerable and disadvantaged participants in adversarial criminal procedures. Bertelsmann J held that, within this general framework, the courts should ensure that children 'are protected from further trauma and are treated with proper respect for their dignity and their unique status as vulnerable young human beings'.

The protections afforded to child witnesses by section 170A of the Criminal Procedure Act are dependent on a judicial finding that such a witness would suffer 'undue stress'. This has been interpreted in some High Court cases as requiring something more than the 'ordinary stress' likely to be experienced by a young victim in a sexual offence trial.[125] In *Mokoena*, Bertelsmann J held[126] that the requirement of 'undue stress'

> places a limitation upon the best interests of the child that is neither rational nor justifiable when weighed up against the legitimate concerns of the accused, the court and the public interest. The child is entitled as of right to a procedure that eliminates as much as possible of the anguish that accompanies the necessity of having to relive the horror of abuse, violation, rape, assault or deprivation that the child experienced when he or she became a victim or witness. To demand an

[119] 2008 (2) SACR 216 (T).
[120] Defined as any person under the age of 18: s 28(3).
[121] Specifically, ss 153, 158, 164 and 170A of the Criminal Procedure Act, as amended by the Criminal Law (Sexual Offences and Related Matters) Amendment Act 32 of 2007.
[122] *S v Mokoena; S v Phaswane* 2008 (2) SACR 216 (T), [37].
[123] These included the United Nations Convention on the Rights of the Child, the Hague Convention on the Civil Aspects of International Child Abduction, and the Hague Convention on Protection of Children and Co-operation in Respect of Inter-Country Adoption.
[124] *S v Mokoena; S v Phaswane* 2008 (2) SACR 216 (T), [43].
[125] See *S v Stefaans* 1999 (1) SACR 182 (C); *S v F* 1999 (1) SACR 571 (C).
[126] *S v Mokoena; S v Phaswane* 2008 (2) SACR 216 (T), [79].

> extraordinary measure of stress or anguish before the assistance of an intermediary can be called upon clearly discriminates against the child and is constitutionally untenable.

The court concluded that section 170A(1) was unconstitutional in so far as it made the appointment of intermediaries for child witnesses in criminal proceedings a matter of judicial discretion. Section 170A was deemed presumptively mandatory, 'unless there are cogent reasons not to appoint such intermediary, in which event the court shall place such reasons on record before the commencement of proceedings'.[127] In addition, 'the court may appoint a competent person for a witness under the mental age of eighteen years in order to give his or her evidence through that intermediary'.

Subsection 170A(7) was also found to be unconstitutionally objectionable and irrational, in restricting protection to child *complainants* whilst excluding other child witnesses.[128] No doubt limited resources, again, explain why the National Prosecuting Authority suggested that the compulsory provision of intermediaries should be restricted to children under the age of 14. This limitation, said the *Mokoena* court, had no rational foundation. However, the court did not rule out the possibility of cogent reasons for refusing to appoint an intermediary, one of which may be the unavailability of adequate resources. Section 158(5) of the Criminal Procedure Act requires a court to provide reasons for refusing an application to allow a child complainant under the age of 14 years to testify by means of electronic media or closed circuit television. This provision was also declared unconstitutional in *Mokoena*. Bertelsmann J directed that 'the words "below the age of 14 years" should be regarded as *pro non scripto* and the word "complainant" should be read as "witness"'.[129] Amongst additional constitutionally-inspired refinements to criminal procedure ordered in this important case, old-fashioned competency requirements tied to an understanding of the witness oath[130] were replaced with a functional test requiring only the ability to communicate. This was motivated by a conscious effort to secure more viable testimony for the courts, and brings South African law into line with other Anglo-American jurisdictions.

Bertelsmann J judgment in *Mokoena* echoes recommendations of the South African Law Reform Commission,[131] which the legislature declined to follow when it enacted the Criminal Law (Sexual Offences and Related Matters) Amendment Act 32 of 2007. The judgment is notable for its generous and purposive approach to interpreting the rights specified by section 28 of the Constitution, which at the same time delimits the scope

[127] Ibid [85].
[128] Ibid [83].
[129] Ibid [185].
[130] Criminal Procedure Act 51 of 1977, s 164(1).
[131] See South African Law Commission, Project 107, *Sexual Offences* Report (Pretoria, 2002).

of the accused's constitutional right to challenge evidence through cross-examination, guaranteed by section 35(3)(i). However, this High Court judgment has yet to be confirmed by the Constitutional Court or endorsed by the Supreme Court of Appeal.

(d) Equality and Dignity in Sexual Offence Prosecutions

Prior to the 1988 Supreme Court of Appeal ruling in *S v Jackson*,[132] advocacy groups had achieved little success in their challenges to a misogynist set of legal rules applicable to complaints in sexual offence cases. Strangely, the Supreme Court of Appeal made no reference to the Constitution in its judgment, but there can be no doubt that this ruling—in tandem with the reforms introduced by the Criminal Law (Sexual and Related Matters) Amendment Act 2007 ('the Sexual Offences Act')—was informed by a broader institutional context demanding judicial and legislative compliance with the constitutional values of equality and dignity.[133]

Sections 58 and 59 of the Sexual Offences Act prohibit negative inference as to credibility solely on the basis that the complainant did not make an earlier report of the sexual assault. Section 60 cements the change of judicial approach in *Jackson*, which dispensed with automatic corroboration warnings in relation to any sexual offence complainant. Section 60 is mandatory in effect: 'a court *may not* treat the evidence of a complainant in criminal proceedings involving the alleged commission of a sexual offence pending before that court, with caution, on account of the nature of the offence' (emphasis added).[134] (However, the cautionary rule in respect of children remains intact.) The Sexual Offences Act also amends section 227 of the Criminal Procedure Act so as to severely restrict the use of evidence of the complainant's prior sexual history.[135] However, the normative effect of this legislation on judicial practice is yet to be seen.[136]

(e) Unconstitutionally Obtained Evidence

The dominant approach to the admission of improperly obtained evidence at common law, with the exception of confessions, was that provided the

[132] 1998 (1) SACR 470 (SCA).

[133] See further, PJ Schwikkard, 'Getting Somewhere Slowly: the Revision of a Few Evidence Rules' in L Artz and D Smythe (eds), *Should We Consent?* (Cape Town, Juta, 2008).

[134] Criminal Law (Sexual and Related Matters) Amendment Act 32 of 2007, s 60.

[135] This re-drafted provision was influenced by the Canadian case of *R v Seaboyer* [1991] 2 SCR 577 and the subsequent amendment to s 276 of the Canadian Criminal Code, as well as by s 227A of the Namibian Criminal Procedure Act 1977.

[136] Cf *S v Dyira* 2010 (1) SACR 78 (ECG) (8-year-old complainant could not be regarded as a convincing witness without taking proper account of 17 weeks' delay in reporting the incident).

evidence was relevant the manner in which it was obtained would not render it inadmissible.[137] Despite dicta asserting a judicial discretion to exclude evidence where prejudicial effect outweighed probative value, the courts invariably ruled in favour of admissibility. Section 35(5) of the Constitution has radically altered this position by directing courts to exclude unconstitutionally obtained evidence in specified circumstances. This remedy for a constitutional breach is not restricted to arrested, detained and accused persons.[138] Moreover, its rationale is far broader than providing redress to aggrieved individuals. Evidentiary exclusion is seen as playing an integral role in ensuring constitutional and judicial integrity in the criminal justice system as a whole, as well as promoting constitutional compliance by the police and prosecutorial services.[139]

Once it has been established that evidence was obtained in breach of the Bill of Rights, a trial court must exclude the evidence if its admission would: (a) render the trial unfair; or (b) otherwise be detrimental to the administration of justice. To admit evidence that would render the trial unfair will always be detrimental to the interests of justice. However, particular evidence could still be detrimental to the interests of justice even if its admission would not precipitate an unfair trial. Subsection 35(5) is peremptory, once either of the triggering conditions is found to exist.[140] However, the court must make value judgements in ascertaining whether either of these two conditions is satisfied, and this is where an element of judicial 'discretion' is unavoidable.[141]

The first analytical task is to establish a link between the violation of a right and obtaining evidence. This has received little sustained attention from the South African courts. It would appear that a generously inclusive approach is favoured, unless the accused had an opportunity to re-assert his rights and broke the chain of causation.[142] It makes no difference to the operation of section 35(5) whether the evidence was procured by the state or a private person. Even in the absence of any breach of a discrete constitutional right, evidence may still be excluded employing a constitutional interpretation of the residual common law discretion to exclude evidence improperly obtained.[143]

[137] This seems to have been the default rule across the common law world: cf the chapters by Jackson, Farrar and Roberts, in this volume.

[138] See, eg, *S v Mark* 2001 (1) SACR 572 (C).

[139] See DT Zeffertt, A Paizes and A Skeen, *The South African Law of Evidence* (Durban, LexisNexis Butterworths, 2003) 625–30; Schwikkard and Van der Merwe, above n 118, 68.

[140] *S v Soci* 1998 (2) SACR 275, 394f (E). See Schwikkard and Van der Merwe, above n 118, 201; N Steytler, *Constitutional Criminal Procedure* (Durban, Butterworths, 1998) 36.

[141] *Pillay v S* 2004 (2) BCLR 158 (SCA); *S v Lottering* 1999 (12) BCLR 1478 (N).

[142] *S v Soci* 1998 (2) SACR 275, 293–94 (E). See Zeffertt, Paizes and Skeen, above n 139, 638; Schwikkard and Van der Merwe, above n 118, 206.

[143] See, eg, *S v Mthethwa* 2004 (1) SACR 449 (E); *S v Kidson* 1999 (1) SACR 338 (W); *S v Mansoor* 2002 (1) SACR 629 (W); *S v Hena* 2006 (2) SACR 33 (E).

It is clearly the accused's constitutional right to a fair trial which section 35 seeks to protect, and subsection (5) might be interpreted accordingly. However, fairness to the prosecution may well be a factor to be taken into account in determining whether the admission of evidence would 'otherwise be detrimental to the administration of justice'.[144] Exclusion of evidence that would result in substantial unfairness to the prosecution may well be detrimental to the administration of justice.

It is consistent with the right to a fair trial, as broadly formulated in *S v Zuma*[145] and *S v Dzukuda; S v Tshilo*,[146] that overall trial fairness will not necessarily be compromised even if one of the discrete sub-rights enumerated in section 35(3) is breached. If a rights violation is neither deliberate nor flagrant, and despite the violation the 'police conduct was objectively reasonable having regard to the facts of the case',[147] the admission of evidence might not render the trial unfair.[148] In assessing the impact of rights violations on trial fairness, courts take into account a complex matrix of competing societal interests. The general approach was encapsulated by Lord Cooper over half a century ago in the Scottish case of *Lawrie v Muir*:[149]

> From the standpoint of principle it seems to me that the law must strive to reconcile two highly important interests which are liable to come into conflict—(a) the interest of the citizen to be protected from illegal or irregular invasions of his liberties by the authorities, and (b) the interest of the State to secure that evidence bearing upon the commission of crime and necessary to enable justice to be done shall not be withheld from Courts of law on a merely formal or technical ground.

Other pertinent factors identified by South African courts include: the type and degree of the breach;[150] the type and the degree of potential prejudice to the accused—if any; and general public policy considerations.[151]

Partly owing to the doctrinal distinction between testimonial or communicative acts and non-testimonial conduct resulting in the production of real evidence,[152] plus the fact that real evidence inevitably exists irrespective of the constitutional breach, a court is less likely to find that the admission

144 Cf *S v Madiba* 1998 (1) BCLR 38 (D).

145 1995 (1) SACR 568 (CC).

146 2000 (2) SACR 443 (CC).

147 Schwikkard and Van der Merwe, above n 118, 218.

148 Eg *S v Lottering* 1999 (12) BCLR 1478 (N).

149 *Lawrie v Muir* 1950 SC (J) 16, 26–27. A South Africa application is *S v Soci* 1998 (2) SACR 275 (E).

150 *S v Seseane* 2000 (2) SACR 225 (O); *S v Lottering* 1999 (12) BCLR 1478, 1483 (N) (flagrant and deliberate violation of a constitutional right must inevitably result in exclusion).

151 *S v Soci* 1998 (2) SACR 275 (E); *S v Lottering* 1999 (12) BCLR 1478 (N).

152 Section 218 of the Criminal Procedure Act 51 of 1977 provides for the admission of real evidence discovered as a consequence of an inadmissible admission or confession but is now subject to s 35(5) of the Constitution.

of real evidence will undermine trial fairness.[153] However, the courts may be more cautious in admitting real evidence discovered as a result of a testimonial communication following a breach of the privilege against self-incrimination. In *S v Pillay* the Supreme Court of Appeal, *obiter*, appears to have approved the approach taken by the Canadian Supreme Court in *Burlingham*[154] in terms of which

> evidence derived (real or derived) from conscriptive evidence, ie self-incriminating evidence obtained through a violation of a Charter right, will be excluded on grounds of unfairness if it is found that but for the conscriptive evidence the derivative evidence would not have been discovered.[155]

The Supreme Court of Appeal, finding that the real evidence in this case had been discovered as a consequence of an infringement of the accused's right to privacy (rather than in breach of a fair trial right), held that the admission of the impugned evidence would render the trial unfair and that its admission would be detrimental to the administration of justice.[156]

Judicial inquiry as to whether the admission of evidence would be *otherwise* detrimental to the administration of justice arises when it is determined that the admissibility would not render the trial unfair. In relation to this second component of the section 35(5) test, the Constitutional Court in *S v Mphala* stated:

> So far as the administration of justice is concerned, there must be a balance between, on the one hand, respect (particularly by law enforcement agencies) for the Bill of Rights and, on the other, respect (particularly by the man in the street) for the judicial process. Overemphasis of the former would lead to acquittals on what would be perceived by the public as technicalities whilst overemphasis of the latter would lead at best to a dilution of the Bill of Rights and at worst to its provisions being negated.[157]

Significant weight is accorded to public opinion in determining whether admission would 'otherwise be detrimental to the administration of justice'. Unfortunately, the high crime rate in South Africa, coupled with official concern about retaining public confidence in the criminal justice system, has led some courts[158] and commentators to overlook or ignore the salutary

[153] *S v Mkhize* 1999 (2) SACR 632 (W); *S v R* 2000 (1) SACR 33 (W); *S v M* 2002 (2) SACR 411 (SCA). See Zeffertt et al, above n 139, 639–41; Schwikkard and Van der Merwe, above n 118, 223–29.

[154] *Burlingham v R* (1995) 28 CRR (2d) 244.

[155] *S v Pillay* 2004 (2) SACR 419 (SCA), [89].

[156] Ibid [90]. See also *S v Tandwa* 2008 (1) SACR 613 (SCA).

[157] *S v Mphala* 1988 (1) SACR 388, 657 (W).

[158] Cf *S v Ngcobo* 1998 (10) BCLR 1248, 1254 (W), per Combrinck J: 'At the best of times but particularly in the current state of endemic violent crime in all parts of our country it is unacceptable to the public that such evidence be excluded. Indeed the reaction is one of shock, fury and outrage when a criminal is freed because of the exclusion of such evidence'. See also Schwikkard and van der Merwe, above n 118, 235.

advice issued by the Canadian Supreme Court in *R v Collins*.[159] The *Collins* approach requires a court to take into account the views of the reasonable person, who is usually the average person in the community, 'but only when the community's current mood is reasonable'. However, the court in exercising its discretion must consider 'long-term community values' and not 'render a decision that would be unacceptable to the community when that community is not being wrought with passions or otherwise under passing stress due to current events'.[160] The danger of slighting 'long-term community values' is that the educational role of court decisions in promoting constitutional values is sacrificed to the more expedient demands of placating public outrage. In *S v Naidoo* McCall J admonished:[161]

> There may be those members of the public who will regard the exclusion of the evidence as being evidence of undue leniency towards criminals. The answer to that is that crime in this country cannot be brought under control unless we have an efficient, honest, responsible and respected police force, capable of enforcing the law. One of the mistakes which must be learnt from the past is that illegal methods of investigation are unacceptable and can only bring the administration of justice into disrepute, particularly when they impinge upon the basic human rights which the Constitution seeks to protect.

To date, South African courts have displayed prudence in identifying relevant factors. Evidence should be excluded if its admission would encourage 'police officers to ignore or overlook the constitutional protection afforded to accused persons'.[162] So the absence of good faith and reasonableness in police conduct would constitute a barrier to admission.[163] Conversely, good faith will not be sufficient to condone constitutional breaches where the infringement is a result of systemically poor practices arising from defective training, instruction or departmental directives.[164] Evidence will be excluded if its admission 'might create an incentive for law enforcement agents to disregard an accused person's constitutional rights'.[165] Reasonable good faith conduct has been identified with the need to promote public safety and exigent circumstances.[166]

The nature and extent of the violation will be relevant factors in relation to both limbs of the section 35(5) discretion in regard to both legs of the

[159] *R v Collins* (1987) 28 CCR 122.
[160] Ibid 136.
[161] *S v Naidoo* 1998 (1) SACR 479, 531 (N).
[162] *S v Lottering* 1999 (12) BCLR 1478, 1483 (N).
[163] See, eg, *S v Naidoo* 1998 (1) SACR 479 (N); *S v Mphala* 1998 (1) SACR 388 (W) and *S v Hena* 2006 (2) SACR 33 (E): cf. *S v Madiba* 1998 (1) BCLR 38 (D) (absence of bad faith significant in securing admissibility).
[164] *S v Soci* 1998 (2) SACR 275 (E). Cf *S v Tsotetsi (1)* 2003 (2) SACR 623 (W); *S v Tostetsi (3)* 2003 (2) SACR 648 (W).
[165] *S v Pillay* 2004 (2) SACR 419 (SCA), [94].
[166] *S v Madiba* 1998 (1) BCLR 38 (D); *S v Lottering* 1999 (12) BCLR 1478 (N).

inquiry. If there were alternative lawful means of obtaining the evidence, the breach will be regarded less favourably.[167] If real evidence, which pre-existed the breach, would have been discovered in any event, its admission is less likely to be detrimental to the administration of justice. However, the court will always determine admissibility in relation to all contextually relevant facts. For example, in *S v Pillay*,[168] where the real evidence in question would have been found irrespective of compelled self-incrimination, the court ruled that to admit a statement elicited from a person on a false undertaking that they would not be charged 'would be more harmful to justice than advance it'.[169] In reaching its conclusion, the court noted that in high crime societies the public must be encouraged to assist the police.[170] False undertakings undermine the public's faith in the criminal justice system. Similarly, the court has excluded real evidence obtained as a consequence of torture despite the fact that the evidence existed independently of the breach.[171]

CONCLUSION

The adoption of the principle of constitutional supremacy and a justiciable Bill of Rights in 1995 has had a substantial impact on the South African law of evidence. This chapter has provided a selective overview of the impact of these far-reaching developments on criminal process rights and familiar common law evidentiary doctrines. Section 35(5) of the Constitution has possibly made the single greatest contribution to the ongoing 'rights revolution' in the law of evidence, making it impossible to divorce detailed rules of criminal procedure and evidence from broader considerations of trial fairness.

However, as we have seen, South African courts have not always chosen to interpret constitutional rights in the expansive way contemplated by the new constitutional framework. Moreover, the progress of constitutional rights in criminal proceedings has been inhibited by broader societal and contextual factors, particularly limited resources (eg in providing access to counsel and protections for child witnesses), an exceptionally high crime rate, and the dominance of one political party, the ANC, as a de facto permanent government. Political rhetoric is often anti-due process rights, irrespective of the fact that curtailing these rights will have no impact on

[167] *S v Pillay* 2004 (2) SACR 419 (SCA); *S v Hena* 2006 (2) SACR 33 (E).
[168] *S v Pillay* 2004 (2) SACR 419 (SCA).
[169] Ibid [96]. Cf *Wesso v Director of Public Prosecutions, Western Cape* 2001 (1) SACR 674 (C).
[170] *S v Pillay* 2004 (2) SACR 419 (SCA), [96].
[171] *S v Mthembu* 2008 (2) SACR 407 (SCA); *S v Tandwa* 2008 (1) SACR 613 (SCA).

the crime rate in a society with the most extreme socio-economic inequality in the world.

In light of these social and political realities, it should come as no surprise that the rights of accused, arrested and detained people have exerted very weak normative influence on police behaviour. Five-hundred-and-fifty-six suspects were killed by the police between April 2008 and March 2009.[172] Torture of suspects does not seem altogether unusual.[173] Celebrations of a 'rights revolution' in South African criminal procedure must accordingly be somewhat muted.

[172] S Alcock 'Killing by cops at a 10 year high', *Mail & Guardian* 16–22 October 2009, 3; D Bruce 'Interpreting the Body Count: South African Statistics on Lethal Police Violence' (2005) 36 *South African Review of Sociology* 141.

[173] In its 2007/2008 report, available at www.info.gov.za/view/DownloadFileAction?id=90292, the Independent Complainants Directorate asserted its strong belief that 'it is time that our courts demonstrate that torture will not be tolerated in the South African Police Service. The number of reported cases of alleged torture is alarming especially when perpetrated by some of the police units that are regarded as the "cream of the crop" in the SAPS'.

2

Human Rights in Hong Kong Criminal Trials

SIMON NM YOUNG[1]

INTRODUCTION

HONG KONG OFFERS a unique perspective and makes a distinctive contribution to the dialogue on human rights and criminal evidence. For more than 150 years, Hong Kong was a British colony, with final appeals heard by the Judicial Committee of the Privy Council in London. Criminal trials in the colony were modelled on those in English courts. On 1 July 1997, Hong Kong became the only common law jurisdiction under Chinese sovereignty. Colonial appeals to London were abolished, and Hong Kong established its own Court of Final Appeal (CFA) with a mechanism that allowed visiting foreign judges to hear cases as Hong Kong judges.

This chapter explores the evolution and development of human rights standards in Hong Kong criminal trials post-1997. It will be shown that the Privy Council's legacy continues to live on in the evolving jurisprudence of the CFA, which has assumed the mantle of protector of defendants' rights and interests. Far from rolling back any of the previous human rights standards, the CFA has extended them to other areas by employing traditional common law discourse and initiating new constitutional developments, though its general approach in relation to remedies for constitutional breaches has been pragmatic and cautious.

Even before the handover, defendants could invoke constitutional rights in trial proceedings. The Hong Kong Bill of Rights Ordinance (HKBORO) 1991 contained a set of rights that were taken almost verbatim from

[1] This publication is supported by a grant from the Research Grants Council of the Hong Kong Special Administrative Region, China (Project No HKU 7467/06H) and the University of Hong Kong's Outstanding Young Researcher Award 2008–2009. I thank PY Lo and D Giannoulopoulos for their comments on an earlier draft of this chapter.

the International Covenant on Civil and Political Rights (ICCPR).[2] The HKBORO was introduced by the British to reassure local inhabitants following the 1989 Beijing massacre in Tiananmen Square. When the new constitutional order began there was a pervasive fear of Chinese intervention and erosion of rights and freedoms. However, China allowed the Hong Kong Bill of Rights (HKBOR)[3] to continue after 1997, even though the ICCPR was and continues to be non-binding on the Chinese mainland.[4] Hong Kong's post-1997 constitution, the Basic Law, provided for a rich set of rights, in addition to those in the HKBOR.[5] It also established a local judiciary of final adjudication and promised to maintain the underlying principles and institutions for the administration of criminal justice which were inherited from the British.[6] An additional post-1997 concern, namely the unknown quality and independence of a new cohort of local judicial officers (the main reason for having foreign judges on the final court), proved groundless in large part due to the leadership of the first Chief Justice, Andrew Li, who retired in August 2010.

Hong Kong's law of criminal evidence currently resembles English evidence law in the early 1980s. Hong Kong has not adopted a local version of the Police and Criminal Evidence Act 1984, or any of the statutory interventions that have since transformed criminal procedure in England and Wales.[7] Unlike elsewhere, criminal justice issues have rarely been politicised in Hong Kong, which has yet to become fully democratic.[8] In the absence of legislative erosion of rights, whether arising from political programmes, the demands of special interest groups or other social pressures, common law norms under the stewardship of judges continue to steer the direction of criminal trials. The post-9/11 anti-terrorism legislation enacted in

[2] Hong Kong Bill of Rights Ordinance (Cap 383) (HKBORO), enacted in 1991 and entered into force on 8 June 1991.

[3] The HKBOR is contained in Part II of the HKBORO.

[4] China decided not to adopt ss 2(3), 3 and 4 of the HKBORO but in practice this made no difference to the application of the HKBOR after 1 July 1997. China signed the ICCPR on 5 October 1998, but has not yet ratified it.

[5] See The Basic Law of the Hong Kong Special Administrative Region of the People's Republic of China, adopted on 4 April 1990, by the National People's Congress, Arts 19, 80–93. Article 35 of the Basic Law provides for the right to confidential legal advice, which is one example of a right not found in the HKBOR. The text of the Basic Law is available at www.basiclaw.gov.hk.

[6] Basic Law, Art 87 ('the principles previously applied in Hong Kong and the rights previously enjoyed by parties to proceedings shall be maintained').

[7] Such as the transformation of hearsay law in the Criminal Justice Act 2003, as applied in *R v Z* [2009] 1 Cr App R 34.

[8] While sentencing cases, such as the recent one concerning the niece of a CFA judge, can excite much public and media attention, rarely do these cases result immediately in new criminal offences or police powers.

Hong Kong was mild compared to that in many other jurisdictions.[9] When Hong Kong tried to enact controversial national security legislation in 2003 it was ultimately shelved after large-scale public protests.[10] Another telling illustration is Hong Kong's rape shield legislation,[11] which is still based on the Sexual Offences (Amendment) Act 1976 provisions that were superseded in England and Wales more than a decade ago. In Hong Kong, however, the original legislative scheme enacted in 1978 has not attracted any challenges or calls for reform, probably because it confers sufficient discretion on trial judges to balance the defendant's right to make full answer and defence with the complainant's right to privacy. In these social and political circumstances, human rights in the administration of criminal justice are safeguarded not so much through judicial activism and creative constitutional adjudication as by the absence of serious threats to fair trial rights due to political inertia.

The next Section provides a brief overview of the Privy Council's jurisprudence and impact in Hong Kong, before turning to consider more recent developments.

1. THE PRIVY COUNCIL'S LEGACY

Owing to the prohibitive cost and other barriers to access, the Privy Council decided only some 56 Hong Kong criminal appeals. About half of these cases concerned matters relating to evidence or trial procedure, and each case had the potential to shape and reinforce fundamental criminal justice values in the colony. The Privy Council's Hong Kong criminal evidence decisions articulated legal principles, generally reflecting a humane and liberal approach to criminal justice, that continue to be cited throughout the common law world. These decisions defined the character of criminal trials in Hong Kong. One contributing factor shaping this approach may have been the large number of capital appeals in homicide cases heard by the Privy Council.[12] Judgments in those days did not frame the issues in terms of a defendant's 'human rights', at least not until after the passage of the HKBORO in 1991. They were mostly concerned with common law

[9] See generally SNM Young, 'Security Laws for Hong Kong' in VV Ramraj, M Hor, K Roach and G Williams (eds), *Global Anti-Terrorism Law and Policy*, 2nd edn (Cambridge, CUP, 2012) 357.

[10] See HL Fu, CJ Petersen and SNM Young (eds), *National Security and Fundamental Freedoms: Hong Kong's Article 23 under Scrutiny* (Hong Kong, HKUP, 2005).

[11] Crimes Ordinance (Cap 200), s 154.

[12] The history of the death penalty is described in *Lau Cheong v HKSAR* (2002) 5 HKCFAR 415, 443–44. The death penalty in Hong Kong was abolished in 1993, though the last execution was in 1966.

duties and principles, which, as we would say now, had inherent human rights content.

(a) Law of Confessions

The most important evidence jurisprudence from Hong Kong appeals was that on confession evidence. Sadly, the frequency of confession cases reflected an historical period when suspects in police custody complained bitterly, often for good reasons, about their treatment by the authorities.[13]

The most famous confession case to come from Hong Kong was *Ibrahim*, known throughout the common law world for Lord Sumner's authoritative statement of the prosecution's onus to prove the voluntariness of a confession 'in the sense that it has not been obtained from him either by fear of prejudice or hope of advantage exercised or held out by a person in authority'.[14] Although *Ibrahim* was not a case of official misconduct, it made clear as early as 1914 that Hong Kong law would follow English criminal law in matters of criminal evidence.[15]

Many important legal principles that still contribute to the corpus of the common law of confessions derive from Hong Kong cases. In *Wong Kam-ming* the Privy Council confronted the novel situation of the prosecution—in a desperate attempt to save its case following the judge's ruling to exclude a confession—seeking to adduce in the trial proper the *voir dire* testimony of the accused.[16] Local courts were prepared to allow this but the Privy Council held that the accused should not be asked on the *voir dire* about the truth or falsity of his out-of-court statements, as this might result in improper self-incrimination.[17] In addition, the accused's *voir dire* testimony was declared to be inadmissible in the trial proper if the confession statement is excluded.[18]

The very last Hong Kong criminal case decided by the Privy Council in 1998 was also an important confession case favouring the interests of defendants.[19] Their Lordships held that where there was evidence of possible involuntariness in the making of an oral admission, the trial judge had a duty to rule on voluntariness, and thus the admissibility of the statement,

[13] See generally C Jones and J Vagg, *Criminal Justice in Hong Kong* (Abington, Routledge-Cavendish, 2007) 453, 466, 505; B Downey, 'Confessions to Police Officers' (1971) 1 *Hong Kong Law Journal* 131; P Morrow, 'Police Powers and Individual Liberty' in R Wacks (ed), *Civil Liberties in Hong Kong* (New York, OUP, 1988) 260–61.

[14] *Ibrahim v R* [1914] AC 599, 609.

[15] Ibid.

[16] *Wong Kam-ming v R* [1980] AC 247.

[17] Ibid 258–59.

[18] But admissible to impeach for inconsistency if admitted.

[19] *Thakoen Gwitsa Thaporn Thongjai v R*; *Lee Chun-kong v R* [1998] AC 54.

irrespective of whether the issue was raised by the accused or counsel.[20] The decision overturned a practice in local courts to decline to rule on admissibility on the ground that the sole issue was the jury's factual determination of whether or not the statement had been made.[21]

Another memorable case is *Law Shing-huen* which held that where oppression taints the admissibility of the defendant's first statement, a second statement, even if given under caution, will only be admissible if the prosecution can establish beyond reasonable doubt that the oppression had dissipated when the statement was taken.[22] In *Li Shu-ling*, the Privy Council imposed strict conditions on the admissibility of video-recorded re-enactment evidence involving the accused by requiring that such evidence should be created only with the accused's informed and voluntary consent.[23]

But the high-water mark of protective confession case law was the quashing of the murder convictions in *Lam Chi-ming*.[24] The Privy Council confirmed that physical or other derivative evidence corroborating the truth of a tainted confession statement could not make admissible an otherwise involuntary and inadmissible statement. This was because

> the rejection of an improperly obtained confession was not dependent only upon possible unreliability but also upon the principle that a man cannot be compelled to incriminate himself and upon the importance that attaches in a civilised society to proper behaviour by the police towards those in their custody.[25]

Lam Chi-ming was an illustration of the maxim that the ends do not justify the means irrespective of the seriousness of the offence charged.

The Privy Council, however, did not always adopt the most protective course. The Hong Kong Full Court in *Chan Wei Keung*, having dismissed the murder appeal *ex tempore*, characteristically changed its mind by the time reasons were to be given.[26] The majority concluded that it was necessary for the trial judge to direct the jury 'that if they were not satisfied that [the statements] were voluntarily made they should give them no weight at all and disregard them'.[27] The Privy Council disagreed, on the basis that such a direction would improperly invite the jury to consider an issue of admissibility which was for the judge alone to decide.[28] Forty years later in 2007, the Privy Council said of *Chan Wei Keung* that it did not accord with the principle against self-incrimination and that it was 'a false step in the

[20] Ibid 61, 67.
[21] Ibid 66.
[22] *R v Law Shing-huen* [1989] 1 HKLR 116 (PC).
[23] *Li Shu-ling v R* [1989] 1 AC 270, 279.
[24] *Lam Chi-ming v R* [1991] 2 AC 212.
[25] *Lam Chi-ming v R* [1991] 2 AC 212, 220.
[26] *Chan Wai Keung v R* [1965] HKLR 815, 834–36 (FC).
[27] Ibid 831–32.
[28] *Chan Wei Keung v R* [1967] 2 AC 160, 169 (PC).

development of the common law'.[29] This *volte face* came as a result of the House of Lords' majority decision in *Mushtaq* (which essentially followed the path taken by the Hong Kong Full Court in 1965).[30] Hong Kong courts have yet to revisit the issue.[31]

(b) Presumption of Innocence Taken Seriously

Errors in directions on the burden and standard of proof were never treated lightly in Hong Kong appeals. In *Chan Kau*, *Woolmington v DPP*'s application in Hong Kong was confirmed in no uncertain terms: 'it is clear that the rule with regard to the onus of proof in cases of murder and manslaughter is of general application and permits no exception save only in the case of insanity, which is not strictly a defence'.[32] The Privy Council also made clear that if the evidence disclosed a possible defence, such as self-defence or provocation, the onus remained throughout 'upon the prosecution to establish that the accused is guilty of the crime ... and the onus is never upon the accused to establish' these defences.[33]

In the drug trafficking case of *Kwan Ping Bong* the issue was whether the proviso[34] ought to apply notwithstanding the trial judge's reversal of the burden of proof on the knowledge element.[35] Lord Diplock, disagreeing with the decision of the Court of Appeal, held that it could not apply as there was 'no principle in the criminal law of Hong Kong more fundamental than that the prosecution must prove the existence of all essential elements of the offence with which the accused is charged'.[36] Consequently, a 'misdirection as to the onus of proving an essential fact in issue at the trial seldom provides an appropriate case for the application of the proviso'.[37] Similarly the Privy Council reversed the Court of Appeal's application of the proviso in a murder case in which the trial judge's summing up was seriously flawed, particularly in having 'no clear statement to the jury that

[29] *Barry Wizzard v R* [2007] UKPC 21, [37].
[30] *R v Mushtaq* [2005] 1 WLR 1513, [2005] UKHL 25.
[31] The Hong Kong Judicial Studies Board notes in its *Specimen Directions in Jury Trials* (July 2009) 39.2 that *Chan Wei Keung* pre-dated the HKBORO and thus a recommended direction along the lines of *Mushtaq* and *Wizzard* was now 'much the safer course'.
[32] *Chan Kau v R* [1955] AC 206, 211, referring to *Woolmington v DPP* [1935] AC 462 (HL).
[33] *Chan Kau v R* [1955] AC 206, 211.
[34] Criminal Procedure Ordinance (Cap 221), s 83(1) empowers the Court of Appeal to dismiss an otherwise favourable appeal against conviction 'if it considers that no miscarriage of justice has actually occurred'.
[35] *Kwan Ping Bong v R* [1979] AC 609.
[36] Ibid 615.
[37] Ibid 616.

the onus of proof rested on the prosecution and that it was not for the accused to prove his innocence'.[38]

The Privy Council's only HKBORO decision on criminal evidence concerned challenges to two offences containing 'reverse onus' clauses requiring proof of particular elements by the defence.[39] In *Lee Kwong-kut*, the accused's challenge to the charge of possessing property reasonably suspected of having been stolen or unlawfully obtained succeeded because the burden of proving an essential ingredient of the offence (failure to give a satisfactory account to the magistrate) had been unreasonably imposed on the defendant. In the companion case of *Lo Chak-man*, a parallel challenge failed because it was not unreasonable to require the defendant to establish absence of knowledge or suspicion when charged with a money-laundering offence predicated on reasonable grounds to believe that another person was a drug trafficker or had benefited from drug trafficking.

Critical reaction to *Lee Kwong-kut* was mixed.[40] On the one hand, the Privy Council was prepared to strike down criminal offences that impermissibly reversed the burden of proof. It also held that compliance with the presumption of innocence under the HKBORO turned on the substance of the provision and not its form, eg regardless of whether it was drafted as a legislative 'defence'.[41] On the other hand, Lord Woolf's criticisms of the two-step approach to justification analysis under the Canadian Charter of Rights and Freedoms appeared to signal a closing of the mind to comparative law experience.[42] The Privy Council preferred what appeared to be a less rigorous one-step approach providing limited guidance for application in future cases.[43] According to Lord Woolf:

> [I]ssues involving the [HKBOR] should be approached with realism and good sense, and kept in proportion ... [R]igid and inflexible standards should not be imposed on the legislature's attempts to resolve the difficult and intransigent problems with which society is faced when seeking to deal with serious crime ...[44]

[38] *Lau Sik Chun v R* [1984] 1 HKC 119, 121 (PC).

[39] *Attorney-General of Hong Kong v Lee Kwong-kut; Attorney-General of Hong Kong v Lo Chak-man* [1993] AC 951.

[40] See, eg, Robin Cooke, 'Brass Tacks and Bill of Rights' (1995) 25 *Hong Kong Law Journal* 64, 67–69; A Byrnes and JMM Chan (eds), 'Editorial comment' in *Bill of Rights Bulletin*, vol 2(3) (Hong Kong, Faculty of Law, University of Hong Kong, 1993) 18–22; W Fong, A Byrnes and GE Edwards (eds), *Hong Kong's Bill of Rights: Two Years On* (Hong Kong, Faculty of Law, University of Hong Kong, 1994) 71–86.

[41] *Attorney-General of Hong Kong v Lee Kwong-kut; Attorney-General of Hong Kong v Lo Chak-man* [1993] AC 951, 968–70.

[42] Ibid 974.

[43] Ibid 969–70; criticised by Byrnes and Chan, above n 40.

[44] *Attorney-General of Hong Kong v Lee Kwong-kut; Attorney-General of Hong Kong v Lo Chak-man* [1993] AC 951, 975.

These remarks raised concerns that the Privy Council was proposing to adopt a more deferential and less robust approach to HKBORO challenges.

(c) Procedural Due Process and Fair Trials

Hong Kong's resolve to combat police corruption during the 1970s and 80s produced numerous Privy Council appeals from corruption offence convictions. While their Lordships were well aware of the importance of Hong Kong's struggle against corruption at that time, the Privy Council maintained its independence and kept the prosecution to the highest standards of criminal due process. In quashing the convictions in *Tsang Ping-nam*, the Board stated:

> [H]owever distasteful it may be to allow a self-confessed corrupt police officer to escape conviction for his gravely corrupt activities, it was wholly illegitimate for the Crown to seek to overcome their difficulties of proof by charging attempts to pervert the course of justice upon [inconsistent and unsupported alternative bases].[45]

In this case, the appellant police sergeant had resiled from his previous statements implicating fellow officers, thereby precipitating their acquittals. As no affirmative evidence existed to prove that Tsang had committed perjury or made false statements, it was illegitimate to charge him with attempting to pervert the course of justice without distinguishing between the mutually inconsistent theories that he was either lying in court or in his original police statements (but not on both occasions).[46] The Privy Council also rejected the prosecution's attempt on appeal to justify the conviction on an entirely new basis.[47]

More generally, fair trial interests were safeguarded by the Privy Council's willingness to allow appeals where unduly prejudicial evidence had been admitted at trial or where there were serious errors in the trial judge's conduct of the case. For example, in *Chan Kwok-keung*[48] the trial judge had misdirected the jury that evidence of the defendant's flight, by stowing away on a boat to Macau some 10 months after the offence in question, was capable of corroborating the evidence of an accomplice. The Privy Council allowed the appeal and quashed the accused's conviction of murder. However, complaints of unfairness were considered in their context and without resort to formulaic reasoning. Thus, in *Attorney General v Siu Yuk-shing*[49] the Board said that the risk of unfair prejudice

45 *Tsang Ping-nam v R* [1981] 1 WLR 1462, 1466 (PC).
46 Ibid 1465.
47 Ibid 1466.
48 *R v Chan Kwok-keung* [1990] 1 HKLR 359 (PC).
49 *Attorney General v Siu Yuk-shing* [1989] 2 HKLR 97, 102 (PC).

flowing from evidence of the accused's previous conviction was 'of infinitely less significance' in cases tried by a judge sitting alone without a jury.

One area in which the Privy Council might have done more to protect the interests of defendants was in relation to the prosecution's use of unsavoury witnesses, such as informants and accomplices. A practice had developed, and continues to flourish today, for the prosecution and law enforcement authorities to confer immunity on such witnesses to secure their testimony at trial. The Hong Kong courts were rightly wary of these self-serving witnesses. In *Wong Muk Ping*, the Court of Appeal thought it was necessary to direct the jury to consider whether a suspect witness's credibility was 'so bad' that it should not be relied upon, even if corroborated.[50] The Privy Council, however, deprecated this two-stage approach as it was unusual and even 'dangerous' to assess the credibility of evidence given by a witness in isolation from other evidence in the case.[51]

In *Chan Wai-keung*, the accused was charged with murder and had allegedly confessed to an informant, who was himself awaiting sentence on a serious drug trafficking offence by the time he testified at Chan's murder trial.[52] An immunity agreement implicitly promised a discounted sentence if the informant cooperated by giving testimony consistent with his previous police statements. To complicate matters the prosecutor in the murder trial then took the initiative to have the informant's sentencing hearing adjourned for one month in order to secure his testimony before he was sentenced.[53] Counsel for Chan argued before the Privy Council that to allow the informant to testify while awaiting sentence on an entirely unrelated matter was improper and abusive. Although critical of the prosecutor's strategy, Lord Mustill, writing for the Board, said that it was neither unfair nor abusive for the court to receive the informant's testimony, where the jury was made fully aware of the terms of the informant's immunity arrangement and pending sentencing hearing, and where the informant had given his statements to the authorities prior to his own offending.[54]

2. JUDICIAL INDEPENDENCE IN CRIMINAL APPEALS POST-1997

As mentioned earlier, initial concerns over Chinese intervention affecting the quality or independence of the judiciary have not materialised, at least not during the tenure of the first Chief Justice. Appointments to the bench, mostly from amongst senior members of the local Bar, have been on merit.

[50] *R v Wong Muk Ping* [1985] 2 HKC 711, 718 (CA).
[51] *Attorney-General of Hong Kong v Wong Muk Ping* [1987] 1 AC 501, 510.
[52] *R v Chan Wai-keung* [1995] 1 HKCLR 123 (PC).
[53] Ibid 127.
[54] Ibid 131–34.

The appellate courts have remained independent and protective of rights, although they have been pragmatic and cautious at times. The CFA did not adopt *Lee Kwong-kut*'s attitude of shunning recourse to comparative law, while at the same time its constitutional jurisprudence has not allowed disputes to 'get out of hand'.[55] To stay on firm ground, constitutional ideas are typically borrowed or 'migrated' from other jurisdictions, particularly from the European Court of Human Rights (ECtHR), rather than being entirely novel innovations.[56] In contrast to the Privy Council, the CFA's primary role of addressing points of law of great and general importance has had to give way, at least in the short-term, to a large proportion of cases that called for the correction of errors in lower courts.

Few would dispute that Hong Kong courts have exhibited strong judicial independence since 1997. This has occurred not only because the Basic Law makes independence a constitutional imperative, but also because both the Hong Kong and Chinese authorities have in practice refrained from interfering with the exercise of local judicial power.[57] In contrast to the more closely watched issues of cross-border migration and political reform, the Chinese Government has generally shown little interest in what occurs in Hong Kong's criminal courts (Falun Gong or politicised issues aside).[58]

Independence is perhaps best illustrated in the prosecution's low, 40% success rate in final appeals. This figure must be understood in the context of a leave jurisdiction wholly controlled by the court that sees only a small percentage of convicted persons obtaining leave each year.[59] The institutional mechanism allowing eminent foreign judges to sit as non-permanent judges (NPJs) of the CFA has been instrumental in ensuring judicial independence and leadership in many areas of the law.[60] The Chief Justice has authority to choose one foreign judge to sit on each appeal.[61] In the past decade-and-a-half a foreign judge has sat in more than 95% of all CFA appeals. Sir Anthony Mason, who has been an NPJ since 1997, stands out as the foreign judge who has contributed the most (both time and leadership)

[55] A reference to Lord Woolf's cautionary note in *Attorney-General of Hong Kong v Lee Kwong-kut; Attorney-General of Hong Kong v Lo Chak-man* [1993] AC 951, 975.

[56] For a discussion of constitutional borrowing, migration and dialogic interpretation, see S Choudhry (ed), *The Migration of Constitutional Ideas* (Cambridge, CUP, 2006) 13–25.

[57] Article 19 of the Basic Law provides that the HKSAR shall be 'vested with independent judicial power' and Art 85 provides that the courts of the HKSAR 'shall exercise judicial power independently, free from any interference. Members of the judiciary shall be immune from legal action in the performance of their judicial functions'.

[58] Cf *Yeung May Wan v HKSAR* (2003) 8 HKCFAR 137 (Falun Gong demonstration) and *HKSAR v Ng Kung Siu* (1999) 2 HKCFAR 442 (flag burning).

[59] In the 111 criminal appeals heard in the CFA from 1997 to the end of June 2010, the prosecution lost 67 (60%) appeals. However, from 2001 to 2008 the Court granted leave to appeal in only 17% of all defence applications.

[60] Basic Law, Art 92; HKCFAO, s 9.

[61] HKCFAO, s 16.

to the court's jurisprudence, especially in criminal and constitutional law cases.[62]

Two cases at opposite ends of his tenure on the court illustrate his independence and concern for defendants' rights. In *Chim Hon Man*, Sir Anthony, writing his very first Hong Kong judgment, quashed the conviction of a person charged with child sexual abuse offences.[63] The prosecution's use of a specimen count was rejected for failing to give the defendant sufficient notice of the allegations against him. This decision effectively ended the use of specimen counts in prosecuting sexual offences and set the Department of Justice on a policy mission to try to plug the law-enforcement gap perceived by some to have been created by the Court's decision.[64]

Eleven years after *Chim*, Sir Anthony joined in a judgment that quashed Nancy Kissel's conviction for the murder of her Merrill Lynch banker husband.[65] The case attracted international attention, not only for its salacious details but also for the robust manner in which the final court reversed the Court of Appeal's decision on the merits and refused to follow the appeal court judges' decision to apply the proviso to condone any misdirection or procedural irregularity.[66] The CFA ruled that the prosecution's cross-examination of the defendant and the admission of prejudicial hearsay evidence had resulted in an irreparably unfair trial, precluding any application of the proviso.

The CFA grants leave to appeal on certified points of law of great and general importance or where there may have been a substantial and grave injustice.[67] In early cases, the CFA indicated that leave to appeal on the second limb would be granted only exceptionally, since the Court was not intended to function as a second venue for rehearing criminal appeals.[68] However, a review of CFA practice from 1997 to 2010 reveals that the Court granted leave on the second limb in a significant proportion of cases.[69] It has also widened the ambit of review in appeals from magistrates courts to allow for a rehearing of the evidence.[70]

[62] From 1997 to the end of June 2010, the Chief Justice declined to appoint a foreign judge in only 10 out of 325 appeals (3%). Sir Anthony Mason sat as an NPJ in 91 of these cases, writing 25 majority and 7 concurring judgments.

[63] *Chim Hon Man v HKSAR* (1999) 2 HKCFAR 145.

[64] See A Whitfort, 'The Proposed Offence of Persistent Sexual Abuse of a Child' (2002) 32 *Hong Kong Law Journal* 13. Prosecutorial practices to avoid the problem have not always been successful: cf *HKSAR v Chu Chi-wah* [2010] 4 HKLRD 691 (CA) and [2010] 4 HKLRD 715 (CA) (retrial decision).

[65] *Nancy Ann Kissel v HKSAR* (2010) 13 HKCFAR 27.

[66] *Nancy Ann Kissel v HKSAR*, unreported, CACC 414/2005, 6 October 2008 (CA).

[67] HKCFAO, s 32(2).

[68] See *Kwok Hung Fung v HKSAR* (1998) 1 HKCFAR 78, 82–3 (CFA AC).

[69] Approximately 40% of the 111 criminal appeals decided by the CFA from 1997 to the end of June 2010 were granted leave on the 'substantial and grave injustice' limb.

[70] *Chou Shih Bin v HKSAR* (2005) 8 HKCFAR 70, which has been cited in over 100 authorities.

The CFA has frequently quashed convictions as a result of a glaring miscarriage in the trial process. Fundamental errors made by trial courts and allowed to stand by the Court of Appeal, but subsequently exposed and condemned by the CFA, include: misdirections on the burden of proof; findings of fact without evidence; misapprehension of the evidence; denial of natural justice; and misapplication of the law to the facts of the case.[71] Public controversy in September 2009 over high conviction rates and practitioners' dissatisfaction with the fairness of trials, particularly those in the District Court, reinforce these concerns.[72] In addition to correcting miscarriages of justice in the instant case, the CFA's jurisprudence serves an important educative function for judges and magistrates at all levels of seniority Whilst difficult to quantify, the impact is potentially far-reaching, especially in improving compliance with human rights standards and the overall quality of justice over time. However, these cases do not ordinarily involve any great questions of law and thus do not necessarily contribute to the development of an explicitly 'constitutional' jurisprudence.

3. COMMON LAW PROTECTIONS EXTENDED

The CFA's jurisprudence on criminal evidence since 1997 demonstrates substantial concern for protecting the rights of defendants in criminal trials. Submissions to roll back well-established common law principles have been firmly resisted. A review of the case law in different areas reveals that the Privy Council's legacy in protecting defendants' interests has been preserved, interestingly not so much by the direct application of constitutional instruments or statutory provisions but primarily through application of traditional common law standards and doctrines.

(a) Confession Law and the Right to Silence

In striking contrast to the Privy Council's docket, only a small number of confession cases have reached the CFA in its first 13 years. *Lam Tat Ming*

[71] See eg *Chan Chuen Ho v HKSAR* (1999) 2 HKCFAR 198; *Lam Pui Shan v HKSAR*, unreported, FACC 8/1999, 27 March 2000 (CFA); *Wong Chun Cheong v HKSAR* (2001) 4 HKCFAR 12; *Tsang Wai Man v HKSAR* (2003) 6 HKCFAR 109; *Lau Chi Wai v HKSAR* (2004) 7 HKCFAR 460; *Chau Lin Su-e v HKSAR* (2004) 7 HKCFAR 265; *Lin Ping Keung v HKSAR* (2005) 8 HKCFAR 52; *Chou Shih Bin v HKSAR* (2005) 8 HKCFAR 70; *HKSAR v Tam Lap Fai* (2005) 8 HKCFAR 216; *Ong Chun Ying v HKSAR* (2007) 10 HKCFAR 318; *Ting James Henry v HKSAR* (2007) 10 HKCFAR 730; *Lau Wai Wo v HKSAR* (2003) 6 HKCFAR 624; *Chan Tit Shau v HKSAR* (2004) 7 HKCFAR 492; *Yu Fai Tat v HKSAR* (2004) 7 HKCFAR 293.

[72] See A Wong, 'Courts' 90% conviction rate stirs up row', *South China Morning Post*, 15 September 2009.

provided a useful re-statement of the voluntariness rule, citing many of the earlier Privy Council decisions, but was not itself a case concerning voluntariness.[73] *Nauthum Chau Ching Kay* remains the leading CFA precedent on confessions, specifically addressing confessions made to police officers who ignore the accused's conditional offer to confess.[74] *Nauthum* articulated a new two-stage approach to determining voluntariness, requiring consideration of whether such conduct by interviewing officers was capable of constituting an inducement, and if so whether it was proven not to have influenced the accused's subsequent admissions. Although the case invoked the terminology of inducements, a move deprecated by Lord Hailsham in *Ping Lin*,[75] the *Ibrahim* conception of voluntariness was expressly reaffirmed. In a third case, the CFA recognised the principle that a conviction cannot be supported solely on the basis of an equivocal admission.[76]

Of greater significance are the CFA's judgments that maintain and fortify the defendant's common law right to silence.[77] The decision in *Lam Tat Ming* affords enhanced protection against improper and unfair undercover operations used to gather evidence of a completed offence.[78] By holding that exclusion of the evidence would be warranted if the undercover agent's questioning amounted to an interrogation, the Court's approach seemed to go further than, eg, the right to silence guaranteed under the Canadian Charter of Rights and Freedoms, which is activated only when the defendant is already in police detention.[79]

Lee Fuk Hing held that no adverse inference could be drawn against the defendant for having exercised his pre-trial right to silence, no matter how logically appealing such an inference might seem.[80] This was an important case for Hong Kong, which has not adopted legislative derogations, such as those enacted in England and Wales,[81] permitting adverse inferences from silence during police questioning. In respect of silence in the courtroom, the Court attracted criticism for ruling that judges (but not the prosecutor) may comment adversely on the defendant's failure to testify in certain

[73] *Secretary for Justice v Lam Tat Ming* (2000) 3 HKCFAR 168.

[74] *Nauthum Chau Ching Kay v HKSAR* (2002) 5 HKCFAR 540.

[75] *DPP v Ping Lin* [1976] AC 574, 602 (HL).

[76] *Lau Ka Yee v HKSAR* (2004) 7 HKCFAR 510, 522.

[77] See generally SNM Young, 'A Decade of Self-Incrimination in the Hong Kong Special Administrative Region' (2007) 37 *Hong Kong Law Journal* 475.

[78] *Secretary for Justice v Lam Tat Ming* (2000) 3 HKCFAR 168, 178–82.

[79] In *R v Hebert* [1990] 2 SCR 151, a majority of the Canadian Supreme Court held that the state has control and power over the individual, and as such 'assumes responsibility of ensuring that the detainee's rights are respected', only after a suspect has been formally detained at the conclusion of an undercover operation. But cf *R v Grant* [2009] 2 SCR 353 (indicating a generously broad approach to the definition of 'detention').

[80] *Lee Fuk Hing v HKSAR* (2004) 7 HKCFAR 600. See also *HKSAR v Lam Sze Nga* (2006) 9 HKCFAR 190; *Raymond Chen v HKSAR* [2011] 2 HKLRD 189 (CFA).

[81] Criminal Justice and Public Order Act 1994, s 34.

situations.[82] However, as argued elsewhere,[83] the judgment was in fact attempting to narrow down the permissible scope for such judicial comment, especially having regard to Lord Hoffmann's reminder of 'the importance of not undermining the principle that the accused is not a compellable witness by comments which may give the impression that failure to testify is an admission of guilt'.[84]

(b) Presumption of Innocence

In the same vein as the Privy Council, the CFA has gone out of its way to correct flagrant misapplications of the burden and standard of proof by judges and magistrates.[85] Moreover, the Court has interpreted 'without reasonable excuse' provisions as essential elements of the offence which the prosecution must prove, rather than as statutory negative averments, thereby reducing the incidence of reverse burdens of proof.[86]

These decisions allowed the Court to pre-empt constitutional review of statutory offences (discussed further below), but the result must have come as a surprise to the prosecution, since reasonable excuses have previously been treated as onus-reversing negative averments.[87] Overall, the CFA can be said to have burnished the lustre of *Woolmington*'s golden thread.

(c) Prejudicial Evidence and Fair Trial Procedure

Three murder appeals illustrate the Court's protective approach to prejudicial evidence. In *Kissel*, the deceased told friends that he suspected his wife was trying to kill him by poisoning his drinks.[88] The Court found the hearsay prejudice of this evidence to far outweigh its marginal non-hearsay value of showing the deceased's state of mind regarding the condition of his marriage.[89] Likewise, in *Wong Wai Man*[90] the Court rejected the prosecution's request to allow the jury to compare the confession

[82] *Li Defan v HKSAR* (2002) 5 HKCFAR 320. See M Hor, 'Criminal Due Process in Hong Kong and Singapore: A Mutual Challenge' (2007) 37 *Hong Kong Law Journal* 65, 77–78.

[83] Young, above n 77, 487–88.

[84] *Li Defan v HKSAR* (2002) 5 HKCFAR 320, [18].

[85] See eg *Tsang Wai Man v HKSAR* (2003) 6 HKCFAR 109.

[86] See *Lam Yuk Fai v HKSAR* (2006) 9 HKCFAR 281; *Tong Yiu Wah v HKSAR* (2007) 10 HKCFAR 324. Section 94A(2) of the Criminal Procedure Ordinance (Cap 221) provides that the defence has the burden of proving 'any exception or exemption from or qualification to the operation of the law creating the offence'.

[87] Criminal Procedure Ordinance (Cap 221), s 94A(4).

[88] *Nancy Ann Kissel v HKSAR* (2010) 13 HKCFAR 27.

[89] Ibid [121].

[90] *Wong Wai Man v HKSAR* (2000) 3 HKCFAR 322.

statements of co-accused to determine if they were the product of police concoction. Applying *Mawaz Khan*,[91] the Court held that the comparison exercise was not in itself a breach of the hearsay rule. However, since the prosecution was trying to establish that the statements were actually genuine and true (unlike in *Mawaz Khan*, where the prosecution was trying to expose false alibis), this tactic posed an undue risk of violating the principle that confessions can be admitted only against their maker.[92] A third case, *Zabed Ali*, concerned the admissibility of the defendant's statement, made 10 days before the murder, expressing his intention to avenge his father's political killing in Bangladesh.[93] In the absence of any evidence to suggest that the murder was politically motivated, the only probative value of the accused's out-of-court statement was to establish a general propensity to commit murder, and it was inadmissible for this impermissible purpose.[94]

In *Law Chung Ki*, the trial judge was held to have improperly allowed the prosecutor to cross-examine a defendant on his uncautioned 'antecedent statement', a statement to inform the court of the defendant's criminal record for the purpose of sentence in the event of a guilty plea or verdict.[95] The issue of improper cross-examination was revisited in *Kissel*, where the Court criticised the trial prosecutor for being 'overly zealous and not sufficiently mindful of the prosecutor's duty to conduct the prosecution case fairly as well as fully'.[96] Kissel was cross-examined about documents filed and representations made on her behalf in pre-trial proceedings, in order to show that she 'allowed herself to be presented in the bail application as a normal person with no psychiatric problem'.[97] This seemingly contradicted Kissel's testimony at trial. However, the CFA identified numerous defects in this line of cross-examination, including groundless suggestions of inconsistencies, irrelevant questions that the accused was not qualified to answer, and improper insinuations that the defendant and her legal advisers had misled the court and deliberately obstructed the court's access to the best available evidence.[98]

The Court's active intervention in these two cases stands in contrast to its more conservative approach in *Warren Wong*.[99] The issue in *Wong* was whether it was permissible to ask the defendant in cross-examination whether he knew of any reason why a prosecution witness would lie. Comparative authorities are split: Canadian and Australian courts do not

[91] *Mawaz Khan v R* [1967] 1 AC 454 (PC).
[92] *Wong Wai Man v HKSAR* (2000) 3 HKCFAR 322.
[93] *HKSAR v Zabed Ali* (2003) 6 HKCFAR 192.
[94] Ibid 205–06.
[95] *Law Chung Ki v HKSAR* (2005) 8 HKCFAR 701.
[96] *Nancy Ann Kissel v HKSAR* (2010) 13 HKCFAR 27, [84].
[97] Ibid [66].
[98] Ibid [71]–[88].
[99] *Wong Kwok Wang Warren v HKSAR* (2009) 12 HKCFAR 218.

allow this line of questioning, whilst New Zealand and English judges permit it.[100] Noting that the practice was well-established in Hong Kong, the *Wong* court allowed it to continue, citing New Zealand and English authorities and the dissenting opinion of Justice McHugh in the Australian High Court case of *Palmer*.[101] Though mindful of the risks that the jury might misuse the defendant's answers or perceive a de facto reversal of the burden of proof, the Court held that such dangers could be adequately addressed by appropriate directions to the jury.

It is unclear whether the foreign NPJ, Sir Thomas Gault of New Zealand, influenced the unanimous decision of the court (written by Chan PJ) in *Wong*. One wonders if the result would have been different if Sir Anthony Mason had been the sitting foreign judge. The majority in *Kissel*, decided only nine months later, referred to the 'inadmissibility and impropriety' of inviting a witness to comment on the truthfulness of another witness.[102] It went on to say, '[u]fortunately, the practice is not uncommon but the fact that impropriety is common is no reason why it should be tolerated'.[103] Equally unfortunate is that *Kissel* did not overrule or even cite *Wong*, despite the glaring inconsistency. The CFA will hopefully revisit *Wong* in the not-too-distant future, and disavow it as a 'false step in the development of the common law'.[104]

The CFA's judgment in *Wong Sau Ming* opens with the resounding sentiment that a 'fundamental feature of a fair trial is the right to cross-examine witnesses'.[105] This case concerned the appropriate scope of cross-examination of police witnesses who had lied or been disbelieved in previous criminal proceedings resulting in an acquittal. Declining to apply the restrictive common law approach articulated by the English Court of Appeal in *Edwards*,[106] the Court recognised a new exception to the collateral finality rule to allow independent evidence to rebut the witness's false denials.[107] Full answer and defence also requires that the defendant be given timely adequate notice of the case to meet, as previously mentioned in relation to specimen charges.[108] Non-disclosure of criminal or disciplinary records of police and other prosecution witnesses has been a recurrent

[100] Ibid [16]–[32].

[101] Ibid [34], citing *Palmer v R* (1998) 193 CLR 1, [1998] HCA 2. McHugh NPJ has been a judge of the CFA since 2006.

[102] *Nancy Ann Kissel v HKSAR* (2010) 13 HKCFAR 27, [76].

[103] Ibid.

[104] Borrowing the words of the Privy Council, overruling *Chan Wei Keung*, in *Barry Wizzard v R* [2007] UKPC 21, [37].

[105] *HKSAR v Wong Sau Ming* (2003) 6 HKCFAR 135.

[106] *R v Edwards* [1991] 1 WLR 207 (CA).

[107] *HKSAR v Wong Sau Ming* (2003) 6 HKCFAR 135, [49]–[53].

[108] Above n 64.

problem in Hong Kong, but both the CFA and the Court of Appeal have shown themselves willing to take the issue seriously.[109]

At the same time, it must be acknowledged that there is a pragmatic side to the CFA's protective approach to rights. In its very first criminal appeal, the CFA announced that it would not be straitjacketed by absolute rules or by House of Lords (and now UK Supreme Court) authority in framing common law doctrine suitable for Hong Kong.[110] Thus, *Tang Siu Man* declined to follow the English approach to good character evidence directions, holding that Hong Kong trial judges retained a discretion to give one or both limbs of the *Vye/Aziz*[111] direction, which is mandatory in England and Wales.[112] Writing for the majority, Litton PJ invoked the high quality of Hong Kong's jury panel (arising from the imposition of language requirements) to suggest that jurors had sufficient common sense to make appropriate use of good character evidence irrespective of the judge's directions. Bokhary PJ, dissenting, complained that the majority's approach offered a lower standard of protection for defendants.[113] The majority, however, believed that justice would be best served by enabling trial judges to tailor their summing-up to the needs of individual cases. Consequently, the trial judge's failure in *Tang* to direct the jury on the propensity limb of *Vye*'s good character direction was not a successful ground of appeal. Perhaps *Tang* should be viewed as the CFA tentatively feeling its way in criminal appeals, before the Court had warmed up to its more liberal approach exhibited in later cases.

4. PROCEDURAL RIGHTS AND COMPARATIVE CONSTITUTIONAL LAW

While there is now a sizeable body of CFA jurisprudence on constitutional rights and freedoms, cases on criminal evidence are remarkably few. One explanation for this may be the perception amongst judges and practitioners that invoking a 'constitutional' right to a fair trial does not take the argument further than traditional common law standards; standards which remain vital and robust under the superintendence of the CFA, as we saw in the previous section.[114] However, resort to constitutional arguments

[109] *Ching Kwok Yin v HKSAR* (2000) 3 HKCFAR 387; *HKSAR v Lee Ming Tee* (2003) 6 HKCFAR 336; *HKSAR v Chan Kau Tai* [2006] 1 HKLRD 400 (CA).

[110] *Tang Siu Man v HKSAR (No 2)* (1998) 1 HKCFAR 107.

[111] *R v Vye* [1993] 1 WLR 471 (CA); *R v Aziz* [1996] AC 41 (HL).

[112] *Tang Siu Man v HKSAR (No 2)* (1998) 1 HKCFAR 107.

[113] Ibid 114, 134. See J Brabyn, 'A Defendant's "Good Character" in a Criminal Trial' (2004) 34 *Hong Kong Law Journal* 581.

[114] See eg *HKSAR v Lee Ming Tee* (2003) 6 HKCFAR 336, [157] where the Court noted counsel's acknowledgement that the Basic Law and HKBORO did not take the duty of disclosure further than it is taken by the common law.

becomes necessary in the teeth of statutory inroads. Most of these challenges have failed.[115] The more successful ones have been based on the presumption of innocence and the right to silence, either as a component of the generic right to a fair trial or in the form of the right not to be compelled to testify against oneself.[116] In addition, several cases in which evidence was obtained in breach of privacy rights have required Hong Kong courts to reconsider the admissibility of unconstitutionally obtained evidence.

The CFA has reinvigorated constitutional challenges to reverse burdens of proof. In three separate cases in 2006 and 2008 challenges were lodged against reverse onus provisions in the offences of possessing an imitation firearm,[117] drug trafficking,[118] and failure to comply with a notice to furnish information relating to bribery.[119] The Court found all the relevant provisions to be unjustified restrictions on the presumption of innocence under the HKBOR and the Basic Law.[120] Interestingly, the CFA did not share the Privy Council's expressed unwillingness to draw on comparative experience,[121] and instead opted for an approach (assisted by some local precedent)[122] reminiscent of the Canadian Supreme Court's analysis in *Oakes*.[123] This test considers the legitimacy of the societal aim pursued by an onus-reversing provision and the rationality and proportionality of the measure in achieving its aim.

As well as keeping a refreshingly open mind to comparative jurisprudence, the CFA's treatment of reverse onus clauses demonstrates the Court's willingness to subject legislative incursions on the presumption of innocence to a muscular proportionality test. However, the CFA is generally pragmatic when determining the remedial consequences of violations of constitutionally-protected human rights, preferring to arrive at practical compromises rather than dictating inflexible procedural remedies. It has developed constitutional remedies to either avoid or delay the usual retrospective invalidation that comes with striking down legislation. For the CFA, constitutional remedies are not tools for the strict enforcement of rights but devices that allow for more balanced outcomes having regard

[115] See eg *R v Lam Chi Keung* [1997] HKLRD 421 (CA), leave refused [1998] HKLRD 440 (CFA AC) [HKBOR challenge to the child competency and oath reforms]; *Tse Mui Chun v HKSAR* (2003) 6 HKCFAR 601 [right to examine witness and hearsay exception for proving ownership in copyright cases]. Although not a case challenging legislation, the Court in *Li Defan* rejected a constitutional argument to prevent any adverse comment on a defendant's failure to testify.

[116] Basic Law, Art 87; HKBOR, Arts 10 and 11(2)(g).

[117] *HKSAR v Lam Kwong Wai* (2006) 9 HKCFAR 574.

[118] *HKSAR v Hung Chan Wa* (2006) 9 HKCFAR 614.

[119] *HKSAR v Ng Po On* (2008) 11 HKCFAR 91.

[120] Basic Law, Art 87; HKBOR, Art 11(1).

[121] *HKSAR v Lam Kwong Wai* (2006) 9 HKCFAR 574, [40]; cf *Attorney-General of Hong Kong v Lee Kwong-kut; Attorney-General of Hong Kong v Lo Chak-man* [1993] AC 951, 972.

[122] *Leung Kwok Hung v HKSAR* (2005) 8 HKCFAR 229, 252–53.

[123] *R v Oakes* [1986] 1 SCR 103.

to societal interests. For example, in the reverse onus cases, an implicit remedial jurisdiction has been invoked to 'read down' the relevant provision from a legal burden of proof to a merely evidential burden of production.[124] This outcome represents a middle road, maintaining the validity of the statutory offence whilst minimising the probative burden on the defendant, in accordance with evidentiary principle.

More controversial use of remedial interpretation was made in *Koon Wing Yee*, where the Court struck out a statutory provision that did not itself violate the constitution.[125] The issue was whether proceedings in the Insider Dealing Tribunal (IDT) qualify as 'criminal' proceedings and therefore attract the legal rights guaranteed to accused persons by Articles 10 and 11 of the HKBOR. Contrary to prevailing expectations, the CFA answered affirmatively, pointing to the IDT's jurisdiction to impose a penalty of up to three times the gain made by a person found to have engaged in insider dealing. This meant that Koon and his co-applicants had been subjected to compulsory self-incrimination and denied the right to a fair trial. Ordinarily the relief for the applicants would have been to quash their 'convictions' and order a new HKBOR-compliant trial in the IDT. Instead, the Court acceded to the government party's submission that the penalty provision should be struck out.[126] This pragmatic remedy had the least disruptive effect of quashing penalty orders without compromising the integrity of past findings of insider dealing which may have been based on compelled evidence and proven on the civil standard of proof. In so doing, the Court employed the fiction of legislative intent and took a decision on behalf of the legislature, selecting from a range of policy options to address the unconstitutionality.[127] In essence the Court created a different tribunal which, although immunised from Article 11 scrutiny as a criminal court, could still be challenged under Article 10 (right to a fair hearing) for allowing compelled testimony in IDT hearings. *Koon* did not address the Article 10 implications of its new creation, and any successful challenge along these lines would require the Court to concede that it had created new constitutional problems with its pragmatic remedy. Unsurprisingly, subsequent challenges to the post-*Koon* IDT have failed.[128]

[124] *HKSAR v Lam Kwong Wai* (2006) 9 HKCFAR 574; *HKSAR v Hung Chan Wa* (2006) 9 HKCFAR 614; *HKSAR v Ng Po On* (2008) 11 HKCFAR 91.

[125] *Koon Wing Yee v Insider Dealing Tribunal* (2008) 11 HKCFAR 170.

[126] Ibid [109]–[120].

[127] Ibid [117].

[128] Both the CFA and Court of Appeal rejected new challenges brought by Koon Wing Yee: *Koon Wing Yee v Insider Dealing Tribunal* (2010) 13 HKCFAR 133, refusing leave to appeal from *Koon Wing Yee v Insider Dealing Tribunal*, unreported CACV 358 & 360/2005, 8 June 2009 (CA).

The power to order temporary suspension of a declaration of unconstitutionality was recognised in *Koo Sze Yiu*,[129] a case concerned with covert surveillance and interception of communications. The unconstitutionality of the investigation was not disputed. However, the trial judge made a declaration of temporary validity for a period of six months in order to give the legislature time to pass corrective legislation. The CFA ruled that temporary 'suspension' was warranted, but not temporary 'validity': consequently, there was no immunity from liability for law enforcement agents involved in unconstitutional activities.[130] The pragmatism of temporary suspension, though not beyond criticism, is far less controversial than the *Koon* remedy of excising a non-infringing legislative provision, since suspension still leaves the legislature to determine the appropriate means of compliance with constitutional standards (albeit within judicially-imposed time limits).

Migration Versus Innovation in Human Rights Standards

A remarkable characteristic of Canadian Charter jurisprudence is its originality in developing innovative doctrines and principles rooted in purposive interpretation of legislative enactments.[131] By contrast, Hong Kong constitutional cases—at least those dealing with criminal evidence and procedure—tend towards migrating ideas and principles from other constitutional courts and legal jurisdictions. Indeed, the Basic Law expressly encourages judicial comparativism.[132] A preference for normative borrowings and migration, at least in the Court's early years, possibly signals an element of caution in the development of constitutional law. Reliance on established jurisprudence from familiar jurisdictions helps to foster legitimacy and deflect accusations of unwarranted novelty or judicial activism. Since 1997 Hong Kong courts have been notably receptive to overseas authorities, doubtless reinforced by sitting foreign judges and English QCs admitted to practice ad hoc at the Hong Kong Bar. Hong Kong courts have drawn liberally upon comparative constitutional law and international

[129] *Koo Sze Yiu v Chief Executive of the HKSAR* (2006) 9 HKCFAR 441, reversing *Leung Kwok Hung v Chief Executive of the HKSAR*, unreported, HCAL 107/2005, 9 February 2006 (CFI); affirmed in *Leung Kwok Hung v Chief Executive of the HKSAR*, unreported, CACV 73 & 87/2006, 10 May 2006 (CA).

[130] *Koo Sze Yiu v Chief Executive of the HKSAR* (2006) 9 HKCFAR 441, [49]–[50].

[131] See eg *R v Grant* [2009] 2 SCR 353 (test for excluding evidence); *R v White* [1999] 2 SCR 417 (self-incrimination principle); *R v Bartle* [1994] 3 SCR 173 (right to counsel); and *Hunter v Southam Inc* [1984] 2 SCR 145 (unreasonable searches).

[132] Art 84 of the Basic Law provides that reference may be made by courts 'to precedents of other common law jurisdictions'. For detailed analysis, see AHY Chen, 'International Human Rights Law and Domestic Constitutional Law: Internationalisation of Constitutional Law in Hong Kong' (2009) 4 *National Taiwan University Law Review* 237.

human rights law in applying the HKBOR and Basic Law. Probably the most significant influences have been the jurisprudence of the ECtHR and the decisions of the English courts applying the UK Human Rights Act;[133] notwithstanding the ICCPR pedigree of the HKBOR. In a recent case concerning legal representation in police disciplinary hearings, the CFA preferred the ECtHR's more advanced jurisprudence to the less well developed analysis of the UN Human Rights Committee.[134]

Judicial reference to the ECHR has advanced human rights in Hong Kong in several areas, yet too close an affinity to this jurisprudence also means that its more limiting or restrictive tendencies are likely to be imported as well. For example, ECHR jurisprudence provides limited protection against self-incrimination by derivative evidence and limited guidance on the exclusion of unconstitutionally-obtained evidence. Thus in *Lee Ming Tee*,[135] the CFA, relying upon the broad balancing approach improvised by the Privy Council in *Brown v Stott*,[136] held that the HKBOR did not require derivative use immunity[137] to attach to a company inspector's compulsory powers of investigation where use immunity was stipulated in the controlling legislation. In Australia, the Victorian Supreme Court subsequently declined to follow *Lee Ming Tee*, preferring Canadian cases on derivative use immunity.[138]

Brown, and the parallel ECtHR decision in *O'Halloran*,[139] were also influential in the Hong Kong Court of Appeal's decision in *Latker*,[140] which was likewise concerned with compulsory disclosure of the identity of the driver of a vehicle under investigation by the police. No mention was made of the Canadian approach to self-incrimination under section 7 of the Canadian Charter. Although the Hong Kong provision stipulated imprisonment as a possible penalty for non-compliance, this was not enough to tip the balance in favour of the defendant, who was being prosecuted for failing to comply with a disclosure notice. Justice Stock's separate concurring opinion is noteworthy for its distance from the Chief Judge's preference for balancing the competing interests of crime control and individual rights.[141] Echoing academic criticisms of the simplistic balancing approach adopted

[133] Chen, ibid.

[134] *Lam Siu Po v Commissioner of Police* (2009) 12 HKCFAR 237, [90].

[135] *HKSAR v Lee Ming Tee* (2001) 4 HKCFAR 133.

[136] *Brown v Stott* [2001] 2 WLR 817 (PC).

[137] The immunity from having information or evidence derived from one's compelled statement used against oneself. In this case, the complaint was against the police using the company inspector's compelled statements for further investigation. See also Choo, Chapter 10 in this volume.

[138] See *Re an application under the Major Crime (Investigative Powers) Act 2004* [2009] VSC 381, [117].

[139] *O'Halloran v United Kingdom* (2008) 46 EHRR 21 (ECtHR).

[140] *Secretary for Justice v Latker* [2009] 2 HKC 100 (CA).

[141] Ibid [160].

in *Brown*,[142] Justice Stock highlighted the risk of 'undermining the primacy of fundamental freedoms'.[143]

Chan Kau Tai was the first post-1997 case to consider the exclusion of evidence obtained in breach of the Basic Law.[144] Chan was suspected of receiving bribes, and the police obtained a series of video recordings in violation of his right to privacy. As the Basic Law itself stipulated no remedy for breach, the Court of Appeal was obliged to improvise. Borrowing heavily from the Privy Council's decision in *Mohammed*,[145] the New Zealand Court of Appeal's decision in *Shaheed*[146] and several ECtHR and English cases concerning Article 6 of the European Convention,[147] the Court formulated a discretionary balancing test that favours admission in trials of serious offences.[148] It also adopted *Mohammed*'s hierarchical approach to classifying rights, in preference to emphasising judicial integrity or the rights of the defendant.[149] As a result, few if any accused have yet succeeded in getting evidence excluded under the *Chan* test.[150]

CONCLUSION

This chapter has painted a broad-brush portrait of human rights in criminal trials in Hong Kong. The liberal and protective approach of the Privy Council continues to live on in the post-1997 constitutional order. However, the CFA has developed into a more cosmopolitan court of final appeal receptive to international influence. There is greater uncertainty in the direction of the law, partly exacerbated by the system of foreign judges. But the protective approach is consistent and pronounced, throwing

[142] See eg AJ Ashworth and M Redmayne, *The Criminal Process*, 4th edn (Oxford, OUP, 2010) 42–43.

[143] *Secretary for Justice v Latker* [2009] 2 HKC 100, [160] (CA).

[144] *HKSAR v Chan Kau Tai* [2006] 1 HKLRD 400 (CA).

[145] *Mohammed (Allie) v State of Trinidad and Tobago* [1999] 2 AC 111 (PC).

[146] *R v Shaheed* [2001] 2 NZLR 377 (NZCA).

[147] *Khan v United Kingdom* (2001) 31 EHRR 1016 (ECtHR); *R v Khan (Sultan)* [1997] AC 558 (HL); *R v P* [2002] 1 AC 146 (HL); *R v Looseley* [2001] 1 WLR 2060 (HL). See also Jackson, Chapter 5 in this volume.

[148] *HKSAR v Chan Kau Tai* [2006] 1 HKLRD 400, [116] (CA).

[149] Ibid [116] pt (10).

[150] For example, submissions for exclusion were rejected in *HKSAR v Muhammad Haji*, unreported, CACC 125/2003, 25 June 2007 (CA); *HKSAR v Wong Kwok Hung* [2007] 2 HKLRD 621 (CA); *HKSAR v Lee King Man*, unreported, CACC 96/2005, 27 November 2006 (CA); *HKSAR v So Hoi Chuen*, unreported, HCMA 398/2006, 10 October 2006 (CFI); *HKSAR v Li Man Tak*, unreported, CACC 303/2005, 13 September 2006 (CA). At the time of writing, the CFA has yet to hear the appeal of *Muhammad Riaz Khan v HKSAR*, unreported, FAMC 52/2010, 4 November 2010 (CFA AC). Leave has been granted on the question: where 'evidence has been obtained in breach of a defendant's fundamental rights protected by the Basic Law or the Bill of Rights, does the court have a discretion as to the admission or exclusion of such evidence and, if so, on what principles should such discretion be exercised?'.

anomalous judgments such as *Chan Wei Keung*,[151] *Warren Wong*,[152] *Tang Siu Man*,[153] and *Chan Kau Tai*[154] into sharper relief.

The Privy Council's legacy also implies continued tolerance of unsavoury witnesses in criminal trials. While the CFA has yet to consider this issue directly, it has endorsed sentencing discounts for those who assist the authorities.[155] To change doctrine and judicial attitudes in this area is a great challenge, but perhaps insights gained from growing experience of constitutional adjudication, coupled with the burgeoning international literature exposing wrongful convictions,[156] will prompt judicial or legislative reconsideration.

Many questions remain about the future impact of constitutional law in shaping criminal evidence. Will Hong Kong judges start moving away from normative borrowings and migration and begin developing indigenous principles and doctrines of their own? Can this be done in a way which still preserves the best of the Privy Council's jurisprudential legacy? Another important question is whether the CFA's current pragmatism and cautious approach to constitutional remedies will eventually concede more ground to vindicating rights over 'balancing' public interest considerations. Much balancing of interests in fact already occurs in applying the proportionality test to determine whether restrictions on rights are justified. The Court will hopefully not repeat the mistakes of *Koon Wing Yee*[157] in failing to consider the broader implications of its preferred remedial strategies.

Political inertia will not last forever in Hong Kong, especially with universal suffrage promised for 2017.[158] The true test of the Privy Council's legacy of safeguarding procedural rights in Hong Kong criminal proceedings will ultimately depend on how the CFA and other courts uphold the Basic Law and HKBORO in the context of an evolving political system increasingly responsive to democratic, and potentially populist, demands.

[151] Above n 28 and accompanying text.

[152] Above n 99 and accompanying text.

[153] Above n 110 and accompanying text.

[154] Above n 144 and accompanying text.

[155] *Z v HKSAR* (2007) 10 HKCFAR 183; but cf the more critical approach in *HKSAR v Kevin Egan* (2010) 13 HKCFAR 314, [193]–[210] and the dissenting opinion of Mortimer NPJ in *Peter Gerardus Van Weerdenburg v HKSAR*, unreported, FACC9/2010, 27 July 2011 (CFA).

[156] See K Roach, 'Wrongful Convictions: Adversarial and Inquisitorial Themes' (2010) 35 *North Carolina Journal of International Law and Commercial Regulation* 387, 406–09.

[157] Above n 125 and accompanying text.

[158] See Decision of the Standing Committee of the National People's Congress on Issues Relating to the Methods for Selecting the Chief Executive of the Hong Kong Special Administrative Region and for Forming the Legislative Council of the Hong Kong Special Administrative Region in the Year 2012 and on Issues Relating to Universal Suffrage, adopted 29 December 2007.

3

Right to Counsel During Custodial Interrogation in Canada: Not Keeping Up with the Common Law Joneses

CHRISTINE BOYLE AND EMMA CUNLIFFE

INTRODUCTION

COMPARATIVE ANALYSIS OF criminal evidence, procedure and human rights from a Canadian perspective might begin by noting three distinctive features of Canada's legal landscape. First, while Canada is traditionally seen as a bi-juridical country,[1] its law of criminal evidence and procedure is grounded primarily in the common law. Thus it is well-placed to contribute to, and benefit from, more self-conscious methods of common law comparativism.

Second, Canada has had almost 30 years to develop expertise in the protection of the human rights of persons affected by the criminal justice system, since the adoption in 1982 of the Canadian Charter of Rights and Freedoms.[2] The Charter is Canada's on-going 'human rights revolution'. It includes both great aspirational provisions, such as rights to equality[3] and fair trial,[4] and more focused guarantees, such as the right to counsel.[5] The law relating to evidence-gathering by state officials such as the police must satisfy minimal constitutional standards. This affects, for instance,

[1] Canada could be seen, at least aspirationally, as multi-juridical, by virtue of its attempts to include the indigenous legal systems of its Aboriginal peoples.

[2] Canadian Charter of Rights and Freedoms, Part 1 of the Constitution Act 1982, being Schedule B to the Canada Act 1982 (UK).

[3] Charter, s 15.

[4] Charter, s 7 protects the 'right to life, liberty and security of the person and the right not to be deprived thereof except in accordance with the principles of fundamental justice' and s 11(d) includes the right to a 'fair and public hearing'.

[5] Charter, s 10 states: 'Everyone has the right on arrest or detention … (b) to retain and instruct counsel without delay and to be informed of that right'.

the meaning of the right to counsel during custodial police interrogation. There are thus constitutional, as well as legislative and common law layers to the Canadian legal framework for balancing the rights of suspects and the accused with the protection of individual and societal interests in the effective investigation and prosecution of crime. In Canada, attention to the human rights dimension of criminal evidence and procedure typically means attention to constitutional adjudication.

A third notable feature of the Canadian legal landscape introduces an international dimension. Customary international law is understood to assist in the interpretation of the Charter. In *R v Hape*[6] a majority of the Supreme Court of Canada stated that '[a]bsent an express derogation, courts may look to prohibitive rules of customary international law to aid in the interpretation of Canadian law'.[7] In *United States v Burns*[8] the Court was influenced in its interpretation of the concept of 'fundamental justice', which appears in section 7 of the Charter, by Canada's anti-death penalty initiatives impacting internationally and increasing opposition to the death penalty in most of the world's democracies.[9] Canada has also played a leadership role in the creation of the International Criminal Court (ICC),[10] which notably includes a right to the presence of counsel during interrogation, as discussed below.[11] To the extent, therefore, that common law comparativism may influence the development and interpretation of human rights in the criminal justice system, the Canadian experience reveals that influence may permeate all three primary levels of the legal landscape: case-law; ordinary legislation; and constitutional law. Constitutions set minimum standards which the law must meet. While common law jurisdictions are accustomed to influence each other in terms of common law precedent and legislative policy, drawing on common law comparisons to influence constitutional adjudication is a more radical proposition. Common law is typically subject to constitutional standards, rather than the reverse. Thus common law influence on the constitution might be seen as an inappropriate ratcheting-up of enshrined constitutional standards. A similar point can be made about attention to international rules which

[6] *R v Hape* 2007 SCC 26, [2007] 2 SCR 292.

[7] Ibid [39], per LeBel J.

[8] *US v Burns* 2001 SCC 7, [2001] 1 SCR 283.

[9] Ibid [39].

[10] The ICC was established by international agreement adopting the Rome Statute of the International Criminal Court, 17 July 1998, UN Doc A/Conf 183/9 (as corrected by the procès-verbaux of 10 November 1998 and 12 July 1999, entered into force on 1 July 2002). For information regarding Canada's pivotal role in the framing, development and promotion of this Court, see www.international.gc.ca/court-cour/index.aspx.

[11] See generally, J Jackson, 'Transnational Faces of Justice: Two Attempts to Build Standards Beyond National Boundaries' in J Jackson, M Langer and P Tillers (eds), *Crime, Procedure and Evidence in a Comparative and International Context* (Oxford, Hart Publishing, 2008) 235–48.

are not binding on Canada. Before turning to such arguments, we introduce our case study of the right to counsel.

Access to counsel during custodial interrogation is a Charter issue in Canada and so it presents a possible role for common law comparativism in constitutional adjudication. We argue that Canadian constitutional interpretation should include a 'tipping point' principle.[12] This principle triggers a call for remedial action where analysis of other common law jurisdictions and international aspirations shows that Canada has fallen behind in the protection of human rights.

1. RIGHT OF ACCESS TO COUNSEL DURING CUSTODIAL INTERROGATION?

The Canadian Supreme Court's decision in *R v Sinclair*[13] turned on the meaning of the right to retain and instruct counsel in section 10 of the Charter.[14] These are the material facts, as summarised by the British Columbia Court of Appeal:

> Trent Terrence Sinclair was convicted by a jury of manslaughter in the killing of Garry Grice. After being arrested, Mr Sinclair was advised of his right to counsel, and twice spoke by telephone with a lawyer of his choice. He was later interviewed by a police officer for several hours. Mr Sinclair stated on a number of occasions during the interview, that he did not want to talk to the officer and wished to speak with his lawyer again. However, the officer continued the conversation and, eventually, Mr Sinclair implicated himself in Mr Grice's death. At the end of the interview the police placed Mr Sinclair into a cell with an undercover officer and he made similar incriminating statements to that officer. Later, Mr Sinclair accompanied the police to where Mr Grice had been killed and participated in a re-enactment.[15]

The Supreme Court held that there was no obligation on the police to stop questioning Sinclair to allow him to communicate further with counsel. The Court unanimously rejected a general right to the presence of counsel during custodial interrogation. A majority rejected a right of access to counsel except where changed circumstances justify access to further advice. Thus, in Canada, detained persons have a right of access to counsel on initial

[12] The sociological meaning of tipping point as a build-up of small changes having big effects is probably most famously associated with M Gladwell, *The Tipping Point: How Little Things Can Make a Big Difference* (New York, Little, Brown & Co, 2000).

[13] *R v Sinclair* 2010 SCC 35, (2010) 324 DLR (4th) 385.

[14] Of course, the case could have been analysed in the context of the Judges' Rules, as the common law is not confined to constitutional minima.

[15] 2008 BCCA 127, (2008) 169 CRR (2d) 232, [2].

arrest or detention, but only a limited on-going right to counsel.[16] This is in significant contrast to the law applicable in, for instance, England and Wales, the United States, New Zealand, several Australian States, and several international courts, including the ICC. Can the Supreme Court be legitimately criticised for taking a narrower view of the right to counsel in Canada?

2. CANADIAN PRINCIPLES OF CONSTITUTIONAL INTERPRETATION

As a starting point in exploring this question, there is significant jurisprudential support for the following principles of constitutional adjudication:[17]

— purposive interpretation;
— progressive, or 'living tree', interpretation;
— 'basic tenets' interpretation;
— substantive equality interpretation;
— avoidance of wrongful convictions interpretation; and
— international interpretation.

This section elucidates each principle in turn, with particular reference to the right to counsel and the methodology of common law comparativism.

(a) Purposive Interpretation

Sinclair itself illustrates the established approach of interpreting Charter rights and freedoms in accordance with their purpose. However, the Court was divided on the threshold question of the purpose of the right to retain and instruct counsel following arrest or during detention. The majority took the view that the purpose of section 10(b) was to inform detainees about their legal rights such as the right to remain silent. The dissenting judges saw it as a more general protection of detainees which operates to restore some balance between state agents and individual suspects, for

[16] Two companion cases were decided alongside *R v Sinclair* 2010 SCC 35, (2010) 324 DLR (4th) 385: *R v McCrimmon* 2010 SCC 36; and *R v Willier* 2010 SCC 37. *Sinclair* is the leading case, which establishes the interpretive framework within which *McCrimmon* and *Willier* were decided.

[17] These principles are not articulated within a single case, and receive different emphasis according to context. The list emerges from the totality of Charter jurisprudence: see generally, *Hunter v Southam Inc* [1984] 2 SCR 145; *US v Burns* 2001 SCC 7, [2001] 1 SCR 283; *R v Golden* 2001 SCC 83, [2001] 3 SCR 679; *Reference re Same Sex Marriage* 2004 SCC 79, [2004] 3 SCR 698.

example by safeguarding suspects from feeling compelled to participate in lengthy interrogations without the benefit of informed legal advice.[18] None of the justices turned to other common law jurisdictions to help identify the purpose.

This was in significant contrast to the Court's approach in *Hunter v Southam Inc*,[19] which considered English and US authorities in unanimously establishing the purposive method and applying it to section 8 of the Charter, the right to be secure against unreasonable search or seizure. Having rejected English case-law focusing on the protection of property, the Court was influenced by US case-law in holding that section 8 implies a right of privacy.[20]

(b) Progressive Interpretation

Hunter is one of a series of precedents embedding a progressive approach to constitutional interpretation, conceptualising the constitution as a 'living tree'[21] requiring expert judicial cultivation so that it does not become stunted or grow wild and misshapen. In another well-known example, *Reference re Same-Sex Marriage*,[22] the Supreme Court was asked to determine the constitutionality of federal same-sex marriage legislation, stating that a 'large and liberal, or progressive, interpretation ensures the continued relevance and, indeed, legitimacy of Canada's constituting document'.[23] It is therefore part of Canada's constitutional tradition to be open to the evolution of concepts such as 'person' and 'marriage'. Such openness, as contrasted with narrow doctrinal analysis, is conducive to other common law jurisdictions influencing domestic constitutional adjudication. A striking example of such influence is *R v Golden*,[24] in which one question for the Court was 'whether the common law in Canada authorizes strip searches carried out as an incident to arrest and, if so, whether the common law is consistent with s 8 of the *Charter*'.[25] The majority thought it helpful to 'review the law concerning warrantless personal searches in the United Kingdom and

18 Binnie J, [76], cast the purpose most clearly in a way consistent with the theme of this book, as 'the protection of a detainee's civil liberties'.

19 *Hunter v Southam Inc* [1984] 2 SCR 145.

20 Ibid 154–60.

21 This language dates to *Edwards v AG for Canada* [1930] AC 124 (PC), often called the 'Persons' case because it held that women were persons in the sense that they were not disqualified by gender from being appointed to the Senate.

22 2004 SCC 79, [2004] 3 SCR 698.

23 Ibid [23].

24 *R v Golden* 2001 SCC 83, [2001] 3 SCR 679.

25 Ibid [49].

the United States' in order to interpret the common law power consistently with section 8, and concluded:

> In this connection, we find the guidelines contained in the English legislation, PACE concerning the conduct of strip searches to be in accordance with the constitutional requirements of s 8 of the *Charter*. The following questions [specifying guidelines for the conduct of strip searches], which draw upon the common law principles as well as the statutory requirements set out in the English legislation, provide a framework for the police in deciding how best to conduct a strip search incident to arrest in compliance with the Charter ....[26]

Not only did the Court in *Golden* draw heavily on another common law jurisdiction to create a strikingly detailed common law scheme to satisfy constitutional standards, it did so in a way that reflected the principle of equality, to which we will turn shortly. Yet in *Sinclair*, Justice Binnie, in a somewhat tart dissent, was the only member of the Court to mention the 'liberal and generous interpretation... so often trumpeted in our jurisprudence'.[27]

(c) Basic Tenets

Notwithstanding its commitment to progressive interpretation, the Court has frequently also been influenced by established legal doctrine. This is particularly evident with respect to the concept of 'fundamental justice' in section 7 of the Charter. It is said that the 'principles of fundamental justice are to be found in the basic tenets of our legal system'.[28] The common law of other countries has been understood to be a source of basic tenets. Thus in *R v Seaboyer*,[29] the Court addressed the constitutionality of restrictions on sexual history evidence in sexual assault trials:

> The real issue under s 7 is whether the potential for deprivation of liberty flowing from ss 276 and 277 [of the Criminal Code] takes place in a manner that conforms to the principles of fundamental justice. The principles of fundamental justice are the fundamental tenets upon which our legal system is based. We find them in the legal principles which have historically been reflected in the law of this and other similar states.[30]

Not only does this 'basic tenets' principle[31] provide an interpretational route for the transformation of common law into constitutional law; it also

[26] *R v Golden* 2001 SCC 83, [2001] 3 SCR 679, [101].
[27] *R v Sinclair* 2010 SCC 35, (2010) 324 DLR (4th) 385, [84].
[28] *US v Burns* 2001 SCC 7, [2001] 1 SCR 283 [70]. See also *Re BC Motor Vehicle Act* [1985] 2 SCR 486, [31].
[29] [1991] 2 SCR 577.
[30] Ibid [18].
[31] Sometimes also referred to as the 'fundamental tenets' principle, as in *Seaboyer*, ibid.

supplies a comparativist opportunity for the transformation of the law of other common law jurisdictions into Canadian law.

One might therefore expect argument about the right of access to counsel to include reference to corresponding legal rights in other common law jurisdictions. This did indeed happen in *Sinclair*, although most strikingly in the attention to *lack* of evidence of a uniform right to counsel. The Court was unanimous in rejecting any perceived Americanisation of the right to counsel.[32] The majority rejected the adoption 'in a piecemeal fashion'[33] of procedural protections from other countries. Binnie J left it up to legislators to decide whether Canada should follow foreign examples.[34]

The concept of 'basic' or 'fundamental' tenets leaves much room for debate. Widespread support in the common law world for a right to silence (albeit with jurisdictional variations) means that people who have *not* been arrested or detained are generally free to have their lawyer present during police questioning. It seems counter-intuitive that an undetained person is free to insist on the presence of a lawyer (or indeed to refuse to be questioned at all) while a person under the control of the police may be obliged to submit to questioning, although not, in Canada, obliged to answer, since negative inferences from silence are not permitted. The lack of a right of access to counsel during the 'black hole'[35] of custodial interrogation might be regarded as derogating from the 'basic' rights of all citizens and the equally 'basic' right to counsel during trial proceedings. In addition, the absence of any such procedural 'black hole' in common law countries with similar procedural traditions might be thought to underscore the fundamental importance of access to counsel at all stages of the criminal process.

It is at this level of generality, pre-empting concerns about 'piecemeal' adoption, that the values reflected in other common law jurisdictions are most helpful. A striking contrast to *Sinclair* can be found in *Grant v Torstar*,[36] in which the Court introduced a responsible journalism defence to the tort of defamation to satisfy section 2(b) of the Charter (protecting

[32] Interestingly, reference by the US Supreme Court to foreign precedents is intensely controversial. See for example, the debate focusing on Condorcet's Jury Theorem (in essence that the position taken by a majority of similar states is likely to be correct) see EA Posner and CR Sunstein, 'The Law of Other States' (2006) 59 *Stanford Law Review* 131; EA Posner and CR Sunstein, 'On Learning from Others' (2007) 59 *Stanford Law Review* 1309; and NQ Rosenkranz, 'Condorcet and the Constitution: A Response to the Law of Other States' (2007) 59 *Stanford Law Review* 1281.

[33] *R v Sinclair* 2010 SCC 35, (2010) 324 DLR (4th) 385, [38].

[34] Ibid [103].

[35] The term 'black hole' comes from the dissenting judgment of LeBel, Fish and Abella JJ in *R v Sinclair* 2010 SCC 35, (2010) 324 DLR (4th) 38, [49] where s 10(b) was described as not creating a 'black hole between the time of arrest or detention and the detainee's first appearance before a judge'.

[36] *Grant v Torstar Corp* 2009 SCC 61, [2009] 3 SCR 640.

freedom of expression) and bring Canadian common law into step with other jurisdictions. The Court observed:

> [M]any foreign common law jurisdictions have modified the law of defamation to give more protection to the press, in recognition of the fact that the traditional rules inappropriately chill free speech. While different countries have taken different approaches, the trend is clear.... The time has arrived... for this Court to follow suit.[37]

In contrast with the Supreme Court's more parochial approach in *Sinclair*, in *Grant v Torstar* the balance between expression and reputation struck in the laws of the United States, England, Australia, New Zealand and South Africa influenced Canadian constitutional adjudication at the level of basic values. In finding that the tipping point in favour of introducing a defence of responsible journalism had been reached, the Court simultaneously modified Canadian common law and recalibrated the constitutional weighting of freedom of expression.[38]

(d) Substantive Equality

Section 15 of the Charter grants equality rights. In *R v Kapp*,[39] a unanimous Supreme Court re-emphasised its commitment to *substantive* equality as opposed to merely formal equality with its 'sterile', similarly-situated test. The ideal is that 'all are secure in the knowledge that they are recognized at law as human beings equally deserving of concern, respect and consideration'.[40]

Elaborating the equality precept, the Supreme Court in *R v Golden*[41] invoked what might be characterised as an 'anti-racism principle' in evaluating the harms incidental to strip-searches:

> [E]ven the most sensitively conducted strip search is highly intrusive. Furthermore, we believe it is important to note the submissions of the [African Canadian Legal Clinic and the Aboriginal Legal Services of Toronto, interveners] that African Canadians and Aboriginal people are overrepresented in the criminal justice system and are therefore likely to represent a disproportionate number of those who are arrested by police and subjected to personal searches, including strip searches... As a result, it is necessary to develop an appropriate framework

37 Ibid [40].
38 Ibid [65].
39 2008 SCC 41, [2008] 2 SCR 483.
40 Ibid [15], quoting *Andrews v Law Society of British Columbia* [1989] 1 SCR 143, 171.
41 2001 SCC 83, [2001] 3 SCR 679. This principle is suggested by DM Tanovich, 'Ignoring the Golden Principle of Charter Interpretation' (2009) 42 *Supreme Court Law Review* 441. Also see *R v Mills* [1999] 3 SCR 668, [90], where in relation to sex equality the Court stated: 'Equality concerns must also inform the contextual circumstances in which the rights of full answer and defence and privacy will come into play'.

> governing strip searches in order to prevent unnecessary and unjustified strip searches before they occur ... Women and minorities in particular may have a real fear of strip searches and may experience such a search as equivalent to a sexual assault ... The psychological effects of strip searches may also be particularly traumatic for individuals who have previously been subject to abuse.[42]

The Canadian approach to equality is developing (some might say floundering) in its own distinctive way, without much evident borrowing from other legal jurisdictions. As a principle of constitutional interpretation, critiques are more numerous than direct applications. Thus the Court in *R v Singh*[43] has been criticised for its failure to be more attentive to the 'heightened vulnerability of Aboriginal and racialized individuals in custody not only to violence but to waive their constitutional rights'.[44] Similarly, in *Sinclair*, in spite of counsel's arguments about the impact of incommunicado interrogation on vulnerable individuals, there is precious little discussion of the equality dimensions of the right to counsel.

Attention to equality principles would have significantly enriched the Court's analysis. The protection and promotion of equality requires legal doctrine to be sensitive to the varying social locations and needs of all who may be interrogated by the police in isolation. Some people are particularly susceptible to suggestion, and are thus in heightened danger of making false confessions. Individuals suffering from particular disabilities such as foetal alcohol spectrum disorder spring to mind;[45] as do the particular risks for women of being isolated in police stations. The equality rights of women subjected to police interrogation support effective and on-going access to counsel. It is disturbing, to say the least, that agents of the state should be able to keep women suspects isolated from their legal counsel during interrogation.[46]

A comparative approach might address neglected issues in two ways. First, although comparative legal method brings to mind comparison of laws and legal systems, comparisons of *social realities* could challenge complacent assumptions and draw attention to the scope for enhancing

[42] Ibid [83] and [90] (citations omitted).

[43] 2007 SCC 48, [2007] 3 SCR 405.

[44] See Tanovich, above n 41. See also the Report of the Aboriginal Justice Inquiry of Manitoba (1999), ch 16, which quotes the Australian case of *R v Anunga* (1976) 11 ALR 412. Generally, see AE Taslitz, 'Wrongly Accused: Is Race a Factor in Convicting the Innocent?' (2006) 4 *Ohio State Journal of Criminal Law* 121; DM Tanovich, 'The Charter of Whiteness: Twenty-Five Years of Maintaining Racial Injustice in the Canadian Criminal Justice System' (2008) 40 *Supreme Court Law Review* 655.

[45] There is an extensive literature on false confessions and disability: see eg TE Moore and M Green 'Fetal Alcohol Spectrum Disorder (FASD): A need for Closer Examination by the Criminal Justice System' (2004) 19 *Criminal Reports* (6th) 99.

[46] There is little discussion of this in the literature, but see P Kraska and V Kappeler, 'To Serve and Pursue: Exploring Police Sexual Violence against Women' (1995) 12 *Justice Quarterly* 85.

practical protection of human rights. Thus comparative empirical research revealing the dangers to women and other vulnerable groups in police custody might inform analysis of a right of access to counsel.[47] Secondly, responses adopted in jurisdictions with similar legal cultures can offer reassurance about the feasibility and suitability of adopting new approaches.

(e) The Avoidance of Wrongful Conviction

Heightened judicial awareness of the risks of miscarriages of justice has important implications for the developing right of access to a lawyer. A muscular right to custodial legal advice could help diminish false confessions even where the suspect is not a member of a particularly vulnerable group.[48] The Supreme Court has expressed concern about wrongful convictions linked to false confessions on various occasions. In *R v Oickle*[49] Iacobucci J, for the majority, signalled 'growing understanding of the problem of false confessions':

> [T]he confessions rule is concerned with voluntariness, broadly defined. One of the predominant reasons for this concern is that involuntary confessions are more likely to be unreliable. The confessions rule should recognize which interrogation techniques commonly produce false confessions so as to avoid miscarriages of justice.[50]

A dramatic illustration of judicial attention to both social and legal realities elsewhere, when contemplating the risks of miscarriages of justice, can be found in the Supreme Court's unanimous judgment in *United States v Burns*:

> In recent years… the courts and governments in this country and elsewhere have come to acknowledge a number of instances of wrongful convictions for murder despite all of the careful safeguards put in place for the protection of the innocent. The instances in Canada are few, but if capital punishment had been carried out, the result could have been the killing by the government of innocent individuals. The names of Marshall, Milgaard, Morin, Sophonow and Parsons signal prudence and caution in a murder case. Other countries have also experienced

[47] Sources such as Amnesty Reports might be useful here: see 'Stonewalled': Police Abuse and Misconduct Against Lesbian, Bisexual and Transgender People in the US (New York, Amnesty International USA, 2005); Broken Bodies, Shattered Minds: Torture and Ill-Treatment of Women (London, Amnesty International, 2001). Also see S Ghosh, Torture and Rape in Police Custody: An Analysis (New Delhi, Ashish Publishing House, 1993).

[48] See eg S Kassin 'Confession Evidence Commonplace Myths and Stereotypes' (2008) 35 *Criminal Justice and Behaviour* 1309 (discussing empirical research on police interrogations, including permissible but deceptive interrogation tactics increasing the risk of false confessions).

[49] 2000 SCC 38, [2000] 2 SCR 3.

[50] Ibid [32].

revelations of wrongful convictions, including states of the United States where the death penalty is still imposed and carried into execution.[51]

(f) International Interpretation

Numerous cases illustrate the influence of international law on Charter issues. In addition to the *Burns* Court's discussion of the death penalty, one might mention *Suresh v Canada (Minister of Citizenship and Immigration)*,[52] in which the Court considered the constitutionality of deporting an individual on security grounds who risked torture on their return home:

> The inquiry into the principles of fundamental justice is informed not only by Canadian experience and jurisprudence, but also by international law, including *jus cogens*. This takes into account Canada's international obligations and values as expressed in '[t]he various sources of international human rights law—declarations, covenants, conventions, judicial and quasi-judicial decisions of international tribunals, [and] customary norms'...[53]

The Court was not only referring to binding international law. A 'complete understanding of the [Immigration] Act and the *Charter* requires consideration of the international perspective'.[54] In order to interpret the Canadian constitution in accordance with the dictates of fundamental justice:

> International treaty norms are not, strictly speaking, binding in Canada unless they have been incorporated into Canadian law by enactment. However, in seeking the meaning of the Canadian Constitution, the courts may be informed by international law. Our concern is not with Canada's international obligations qua obligations; rather, our concern is with the principles of fundamental justice. We look to international law as evidence of these principles and not as controlling in itself.[55]

We have already referred to Canada's leadership role in the creation of the ICC, which built on previous Canadian sponsorship of international criminal tribunals. Against this backdrop, *Sinclair* provided a golden opportunity for the further development and application of an internationally

[51] Ibid [1].
[52] 2002 SCC 1, [2002] 1 SCR 3.
[53] Ibid [46].
[54] Ibid [59], quoting *R v Burns* [2001] 1 SCR 283, [79]–[81].
[55] Ibid [60]. As mentioned above, *R v Hape* 2007 SCC 26, [2007] 2 SCR 292, [35], also reflects an internationalist vision of Canadian law: '[C]ertain fundamental rules of customary international law govern what actions a state may legitimately take outside its territory. Those rules are important interpretive aids for determining the jurisdictional scope of s 32(1) of the *Charter*'. See also *Canada (Prime Minister) v Khadr* 2010 SCC 3, [2010] 1 SCR 44, [23], in which the Court wrote that fundamental justice takes into account Canada's 'obligations *and values*, as expressed in the various sources of international human rights law by which Canada is bound' (emphasis added).

recognised right of access to counsel. Alas, in spite of argument from both parties about the implications of a right to the presence of counsel in international criminal investigations, the Court rejected the proposition that a right of access to counsel was a necessary aspect of Canada's constitutional protections. This brings us to the normative heart of our discussion.

3. COMMON LAW COMPARATIVISM: TOWARDS A 'TIPPING POINT' PRINCIPLE?

We have seen that, when Canada interprets its Constitution, it may turn to other common law jurisdictions and international norms for guidance in resolving interpretational controversies, such as whether the right to counsel should include a right of access during custodial interrogation.[56] A comparative approach to interpreting indeterminate constitutional concepts can be helpful in various ways. Bijon Roy suggests that:

> the Supreme Court of Canada's use of foreign jurisprudence and international instruments in its Charter jurisprudence reflects an open-minded approach that remains receptive to new approaches to universal concepts like human rights, even while remaining strongly grounded in the cultural, historical, and political particularities of Canada's domestic law.[57]

Roy discusses the benefits of receptivity to international influences, in terms of: inspiration; reassurance; doctrinal options; support for legitimacy; and promotion of shared human rights and fundamental values, such as human dignity. As *Sinclair* illustrates, however, comparative analysis is merely optional in Canadian constitutional interpretation. A lower court could not be found to be in error simply for failing to consider comparative sources.

Should there instead be a binding norm promoting receptivity? This question can be restated in various ways. Is a lawyer addressing an issue such as a right of access to counsel restricted to mentioning incidental comparative points in the hope that judges will be influenced by them in some diffuse fashion, or is there a way to argue that judges *should* take comparative sources into consideration? Should Canadian courts internalise a sense of shared improvement in the protection of human rights as a principle of constitutional interpretation? Is it possible to identify the point at which Canada has fallen behind common law norms of human rights protection and should renew its efforts to keep up? Should a feeling of normative commitment to keeping up with progressive common law developments

[56] But see AM Dodek, 'Comparative Law at the Supreme Court of Canada in 2008: Limited Engagement and Missed Opportunities' (2009) 47 *Supreme Court Law Review* 445 (including many useful citations on constitutional comparativism).

[57] See B Roy 'An Empirical Survey of Foreign Jurisprudence and International Instruments in Charter Litigation' (2004) 62 *University of Toronto Faculty of Law Review* 99.

animate constitutional adjudication? Should the 'living tree' sprout common law best practice leaves? Of course, it may be that many Canadians would prefer to contribute to a tipping point, rather than simply being tipped by it.

Sticking with the right to counsel as our exemplar, can it be said that a tipping point has been reached in relation to a right to counsel during police interrogation? A brief survey of the relevant law in England and Wales, the United States, Australia and New Zealand, fortified by international support from the ICC system, lends plausibility to the 'tipping point' analysis.

(a) England and Wales

The law governing police interrogations of detained persons in England and Wales grew out of the common law, but now it is governed by a complicated statutory framework, overlaid by the Human Rights Act 1998. The UK Human Rights Act 'strikes a subtle constitutional balance',[58] re-enacting the substantive rights contained in the European Convention on Human Rights and establishing an interpretive presumption that other legislation is consistent with the Human Rights Act unless Parliament plainly intends the contrary. Article 6(3)(c) of the ECHR guarantees the accused's right 'to defend himself in person or through legal assistance of his own choosing [and]... to be given it free when the interests of justice so require'. Thus, for present purposes we can say that criminal procedure law in England and Wales *roughly* approximates the Canadian legal system.[59] Specifically, the Police and Criminal Evidence Act 1984 (PACE) Code of Practice C governs the detention, treatment and questioning of most persons by police officers. If he had been prosecuted in England or Wales, Sinclair[60] would have been informed at the outset, pursuant to section 58 of PACE and paragraph 3.1(ii) of Code C, of his continuing right, exercisable at any stage during his period in custody, to 'consult privately with a solicitor and that free independent legal advice is available'. He then would have had a right to seek legal advice and have a lawyer present during questioning, subject to certain exceptions.

The striking features from a comparative perspective are the legislative source of the right to the presence of counsel, but also the possibility of negative inferences from silence should the accused later rely on a defence that he unreasonably failed to disclose during police interview.[61] Regard must also be had to differences in the legal regulation of pre-trial

[58] P Roberts and A Zuckerman, *Criminal Evidence*, 2nd edn (Oxford, OUP, 2010) 32.
[59] Charter, s 33 gives Canadian legislatures a right to override Charter rights.
[60] *R v Sinclair* 2010 SCC 35, (2010) 324 DLR (4th) 385.
[61] Criminal Justice and Public Order Act 1994, ss 34–39.

disclosure and available remedies for non-disclosure in England and in Canada, respectively. On the other hand, there is a 'constitutional' dimension to some form of right to counsel in England and Wales deriving from the ECHR, with its unequivocal orientation towards human rights protection. Such factors illustrate the commonplace point that comparative method requires attention to context. English law thus provides tangible, if somewhat uneven, support to a 'tipping point' analysis.

(b) United States of America

Stronger endorsement comes from the United States with its similar mixture of common law, legislation and constitution and explicit judicial development of a constitutional right to have counsel present during interrogation. Further, there is no countervailing threat of negative inferences from silence. Indeed, the Fifth Amendment privilege against self-incrimination creates a much broader right to refuse to answer questions, in contrast to Canadian law's preference for use immunity in certain situations under section 13 of the Charter. Had Sinclair been questioned and prosecuted in the United States, *Miranda v Arizona*[62] would have required that he be informed of his rights to consult a lawyer and have his lawyer present during interrogation.[63] Once a detainee has requested a lawyer, 'the interrogation must cease until an attorney is present'.[64]

The protective purpose of *Miranda* is encapsulated in the following powerful passage:

> The current practice of incommunicado interrogation is at odds with one of our Nation's most cherished principles—that the individual may not be compelled to incriminate himself. Unless adequate protective devices are employed to dispel the compulsion inherent in custodial surroundings, no statement obtained from the defendant can truly be the product of his own free choice.[65]

However, *Miranda* is weakened as a tipping-pointer by several significant limitations on its scope, as well as by continuing controversy surrounding its constitutionality and practical effects.[66] *Miranda* prevents the prosecution

[62] *Miranda v Arizona*, 384 US 436 (1966).

[63] Ibid 472.

[64] Ibid 474.

[65] Ibid 457–58.

[66] There is a vast literature debating *Miranda*'s effects, see eg RJ Allen, 'Miranda's Hollow Core' (2006) 100 *Northwestern University Law Review* 71; SB Duke, 'Does Miranda Protect the Innocent or the Guilty?' (2007) 10 *Chapman Law Review* 551; P Shechtman, 'An Essay on Miranda's Fortieth Birthday' (2007) 10 *Chapman Law Review* 655 (usefully summarising the empirical research). For a vigorous defence, see SJ Schulhofer, 'Miranda's Practical Effect: Substantial Benefits and Vanishingly Small Social Costs' (1996) 90 *Northwestern University Law Review* 500.

from adducing non-compliant statements as part of its case in-chief but this does not equate to automatic exclusion of statements obtained in violation of *Miranda* rights. Voluntary statements can be used for impeachment purposes; derivative evidence is not excluded under *Miranda* (although exclusion may be mandated by other evidentiary rules in particular cases); a capacious 'public safety' exception has been created; and there are rather generous (to the prosecution) doctrines of waiver. Indeed, in *Berghuis v Thompkins*[67] the US Supreme Court recently split 5 to 4 in concluding that *Miranda* did not apply to a situation where a suspect neither expressly invoked nor overtly waived his rights to silence and to counsel.

Beyond such local doctrinal details, however, it remains significant for our purposes that the courts of a large common law jurisdiction have constitutionalised a protective right to the presence of counsel during police interrogation. For the time being at least, *Miranda* remains a secure and emblematic feature of US constitutional criminal procedure.[68]

(c) Australia

In Australia, criminal law and process is governed by common law as well as state and Federal legislation bearing on the right to counsel whilst being questioned or held in police custody. This contributes to complex variations across Australia but in broad terms, there is an expectation that a suspect will be permitted to communicate with counsel during questioning. A court will not automatically exclude admissions made by the accused if they are made prior to that communication taking place.[69] In *Driscoll v R*[70] Gibbs J shaped the Australian common law response where a suspect's lawyer is excluded from a police interview:

> The fact that a police officer has attempted to prevent a solicitor from getting in touch with a client who is held for questioning, and has refused to allow the solicitor to be present when the questions are asked, is relevant to the question whether the admissions, alleged by the police to have been made ... were in fact made. It is not of course conclusive.... [F]ailure to allow the solicitor to be present... [would not] in itself render evidence of the interrogation inadmissible,

[67] *Berghuis v Thompkins*, 131 S Ct 33 (2010).

[68] See *Dickerson v US*, 530 US 428, 432 (2000), holding that there was no justification for overruling *Miranda*.

[69] Section 138 of the uniform Evidence Act (Evidence Act 1995 (Cwth); Evidence Act 1995 (NSW); Evidence Act 2001 (Tas); Evidence Act 2004 (Norfolk Island); Evidence Act 2008 (Vic); Evidence Act 2011 (ACT)) provides that evidence obtained improperly is not to be admitted unless the desirability of admitting that evidence outweighs the undesirability of admitting it. Various factors relevant to assessing desirability are set out in s 138(3). These factors parallel the Canadian Supreme Court's interpretation of s 24(2) of the Charter in *R v Grant* 2009 SCC 32, [2009] 2 SCR 353.

[70] *Driscoll v R* [1977] HCA 43, (1977) 137 CLR 517.

> although it might be a ground for the judge to reject the confession in the exercise of his discretion if he regarded it as unfair to allow it to be used.[71]

While the High Court of Australia was reluctant to speak in the language of procedural rights, *Driscoll* is often taken to establish a relatively strong principle that a suspect is entitled to have counsel present while being interviewed.[72] The factual context of *Driscoll* led Gibbs J to predicate his reasoning on the need for a court to satisfy itself that admissions have in fact been made where there is reason to suspect perjury by a police officer. This rationale for requiring the presence of counsel raises the question of whether a videotaped or otherwise reliably recorded statement would provide an adequate substitute.

Australian appeal courts have suggested that a right to the presence of counsel serves additional protective purposes, particularly in relation to Aboriginal suspects (described below). In *Mckinney v R*,[73] a majority of the High Court of Australia held that a warning should be given to a jury when considering whether to convict on the basis of an uncorroborated statement made by an accused to the police. This judgment was predicated on the 'vulnerability of an accused' who is held in custody 'without access to a lawyer or even an independent person'.[74] However, the Court did not suggest that such a statement should be excluded. In *Van Der Meer v R*,[75] the High Court of Australia commented that the purpose of the common law confessions rule is to prevent unfairness to the accused, and that this purpose exceeds reliability concerns.[76]

Sections 86 and 138 of the uniform Evidence Act provide a stronger path to exclusion. Section 86 mandates the exclusion of a document prepared by police to prove the contents of an admission unless the contents are affirmed by the defendant. Section 138 is a general discretion to exclude improperly or illegally obtained evidence. Our research suggests that failure to provide access to a lawyer, without more, does not usually lead to exclusion under section 138; however admissions are excluded in circumstances of compound unfairness and Australian cases support the principle that police should stop questioning a suspect who expresses a desire to remain silent.[77] None of the cases we have found involve active police refusal to

[71] Ibid [25] and [27]; also [9] per Barwick CJ.

[72] See *R v Pollard* [1992] HCA 69, (1992) 176 CLR 177 per McHugh J, 230; and *DPP v MD* [2010] VSCA 233. In *R v Douglas* [2000] NSWCCA 275 [44]–[56] and [61] Mason P appeared to accept that if a denial of access to a solicitor caused a suspect to speak, this would warrant exclusion under s 138 of the uniform Evidence Acts 1995.

[73] [1991] HCA 6, (1991) 171 CLR 468.

[74] Ibid [23], per Mason CJ, Deane, Gaudron and McHugh JJ.

[75] [1988] HCA 56.

[76] Ibid [26], per Mason CJ; [10]–[15] per Wilson, Dawson and Toohey JJ; and [7]–[8] per Deane J.

[77] For example, *R v Helmhout* [2000] NSWSC 208; *R v Lamb and Thurston* [2002] NSWSC 357; *R v Ul-Haque* [2007] NSWSC 1251; *R v Steven Powell* [2010] NSWDC 84.

allow a suspect to speak with a lawyer, and continued interrogation after an expressed wish to obtain legal advice.[78] It is therefore likely that the (video-recorded) admissions made by Sinclair after requesting counsel would be excluded in Australia. A reasonably strong argument for exclusion could be made based on section 138 of the uniform Evidence Acts coupled with the applicable case law.

The common law has played a significant role in its own right. It has also prompted progressive extensive statutory reform. The constitutional dimension of criminal procedure familiar to North Americans is largely absent except to the limited extent that the Victorian Charter and Human Rights Act (ACT) can be described as quasi-constitutional.[79] Section 22 of the Human Rights Act guarantees a charged person the right to legal assistance.[80] Section 25 of the Victorian Charter guarantees the accused's right to be legally aided at trial, to self-representation, or to be represented by counsel of choice. Neither the Charter nor the Human Rights Act contain an express right to counsel for an uncharged suspect. Other statutes do make provision for legal assistance to be offered to suspects.[81]

Australian common law provides additional protections for Aboriginal suspects and these have been reinforced by statute. The so-called *Anunga* Rules[82] recognise the distinctive vulnerability of Aboriginal suspects and establish particular protections, such as an independent 'prisoner's friend' during police interviews and, where requested, the deferral of questioning to allow the attendance of counsel. Any admissions obtained in breach of the *Anunga* Rules are liable to be excluded at trial.[83] Parallel guidelines have been extended to mentally impaired suspects.[84] Legislation in some jurisdictions also makes broader provision for 'vulnerable persons' being questioned by the police.[85] Unfortunately, while these rules usefully illustrate an equality-based response to vulnerability, it cannot be said that the common law world in general has tipped decisively in that direction.[86]

The general expectation that a suspect will be permitted to communicate with counsel during interview is accompanied in Australia by a common law

[78] *R v Steven Powell* [2010] NSWDC 84 is the closest analogue.

[79] Charter of Human Rights and Responsibilities Act 2006 (Vic); Human Rights Act 2004 (ACT).

[80] Human Rights Act 2004 (ACT), s 22.

[81] For example Crimes Act 1914 (Cwth), s 23G.

[82] *R v Anunga* (1976) 11 ALR 412. These common law protocols are also codified in some Australian States: see eg, Law Enforcement (Powers and Responsibilities) Regulations 2005 (LEPR Regs 2005).

[83] See *Anunga* (1976) 11 ALR 412 and LEPR Regs 2005, reg 33; uniform Evidence Acts, s 138.

[84] *R v Narula* (1986) 22 Australian Crim R 409.

[85] For example LEPR Regs 2005 (NSW), reg 24; Crimes Act 1914 (Cwth) Part 1C, Div 3.

[86] Compare the English PACE 1984, s 77.

right to silence.[87] Exercising the right to silence does not authorise adverse inferences at trial.[88] However, where an accused person has answered questions selectively, the whole record of interview, including unanswered questions and the fact of refusal itself, may become admissible at trial.[89] As is the case with England and Wales, limits on the right to silence arguably provide further reason to have counsel present to advise a suspect during a police interview, and suggest a modest contribution to a tipping point.

The development of Australian common law since *Driscoll* has been pre-empted and curtailed by legislative provisions requiring the presence of counsel during police interrogation when reasonably requested by a suspect. New South Wales, being the most populous Australian State and encompassing the Sydney conurbation, exemplifies the statutory reforms that have superseded common law principles in most Australian jurisdictions. The key NSW legislation is the Law Enforcement (Powers and Responsibilities) Act 2002 and its associated regulations. Section 123(5)(b) of the Act establishes a statutory right to have counsel present during questioning. Police questioning must be delayed to allow counsel to attend, but officers may commence an interview if counsel does not arrive within a reasonable time.[90] In addition, LEPR responds to the situation in *Driscoll* by mandating communication assistance between a detained person and a legal representative seeking to make contact.[91]

The NSW Law Reform Commission's report on the right to silence summarise empirical research suggesting that only some 4–9% of suspects remain completely silent during police interrogation and that legal counsel generally advise a suspect to remain silent only when police disclosure is incomplete or counsel has not yet had the opportunity to take full instructions from their client.[92] Aboriginal suspects, women and children appear to be more likely to answer police questions than the population at large.[93] If these empirical finding were broadly generalisable to the Canadian

[87] *Petty v R* [1991] HCA 34, (1991) 173 CLR 95.

[88] Uniform Evidence Acts, s 89. See *Sanchez v R* [2009] NSWCCA 171 for a discussion of the relationship between s 89 and the common law principles. Also see *RPS v The Queen* [2000] HCA 3, (2000) 199 CLR 620, [22] per Gaudron A-CJ, Gummow, Kirby and Hayne JJ; and *Petty v R* (1991) 173 CLR 95, 99, per Mason CJ, Deane, Toohey and McHugh JJ.

[89] *Woon v R* [1964] HCA 23, (1964) 109 CLR 529. See also J White 'Silence is Golden? The Significance of Selective Answers to Police Questioning in NSW' (1998) 72 *Australian Law Journal* 539.

[90] LEPR Act 2002, s 123(3).

[91] LEPR Act 2002, s 127.

[92] Law Reform Commission of NSW, *The Right to Silence* (Final Report No 95, 2000) esp 2.15, 2.69–2.71, 2.124; Law Reform Commission of NSW, *The Right to Silence and Pre-trial Disclosure in New South Wales* (Research Report No 10, 2000) 2.12–2.27: both available via www.lawlink.nsw.gov.au/lawlink/lrc/ll_lrc.nsf/pages/LRC_publications.

[93] Final Report, ibid 2.118. The conclusion in relation to women and children is drawn from English research.

context, Charron J's remarks, speaking for the majority of the Supreme Court of Canada in *R v Singh*,[94] might be viewed as complacent:

> While the fact of detention unquestionably triggers the need for additional checks on police interrogation techniques because of the greater vulnerability of the detainee, the moment of detention does nothing to reduce the suspect's value as an important source of information. Provided that the detainee's rights are adequately protected, including the freedom to choose whether to speak or not, it is in society's interest that the police attempt to tap this valuable source.[95]

The belief that a bright line, *Miranda*-style right to silence will impede the investigation and prosecution of crime is challenged by Australian empirical findings, as well as by US experience. As Fish J observed in his dissenting judgment in *Singh*, 'we have no evidence to support the proposition that requiring the police to respect a detainee's right of silence, once it has been unequivocally asserted, would have a "devastating impact" on criminal investigations anywhere in this country'.[96] Judicial debate over the implications of recognising strong rights during pre-trial investigation, which was renewed in *Sinclair*,[97] nicely illustrates the potential for comparativism to introduce pertinent empirical data into constitutional adjudication.

(d) New Zealand

Section 23 of the New Zealand Bill of Rights Act 1990 provides:

> (1) Everyone who is arrested or who is detained under any enactment…
>   (b) Shall have the right to consult and instruct a lawyer without delay and to be informed of that right;

Section 51 of the Legal Services Act 2000 further provides that a suspect is entitled to the services of a lawyer during the period in which he or she is questioned or detained, and section 52(1)(b) of the Legal Services Act expressly states that a lawyer's duties include attending the place where the suspect is being detained or questioned. These provisions implement a publicly-funded programme to provide legal advice to suspects while they are being questioned or held in police custody.

New Zealand jurisprudence might be viewed as a source of considerable reassurance of common law courts' capacity to strike a balance between suspects' right of access to counsel and the public interest in the effective investigation of crime. New Zealand courts have utilised the concept of a 'reasonable opportunity' to consult counsel as a touchstone for determining

[94] 2007 SCC 48, [2007] 3 SCR 405.
[95] Ibid [45].
[96] Ibid [88].
[97] *R v Sinclair* 2010 SCC 35, (2010) 324 DLR (4th) 38, [61]–[65].

whether the suspect's right has been respected. In *R v Beck*,[98] the New Zealand Court of Appeal dismissed an appeal from an accused who claimed that his section 23(1)(b) right had been breached. The police officer in this case had called two telephone numbers for the suspect's preferred lawyer, offered a list of duty counsel, and invited the suspect to try to call his preferred counsel himself. The Court commented that 'other considerations would arise had the constable prevented the appellant from obtaining counsel of choice or otherwise acted in bad faith, but we agree that this is not such a case'.[99]

In *Ministry of Transport v Noort*,[100] two suspects arrested for offences related to impaired driving were not informed of their right to speak with counsel. Whilst acknowledging minor differences between the New Zealand Bill of Rights and the Canadian Charter, President Cooke drew inspiration from two decisions of the Canadian Supreme Court, *Therens*[101] and *Thomsen*:[102]

> The opportunity [to speak with counsel] is to be limited but reasonable. It is not necessarily restricted to one call, but there must be no unreasonable delay. A driver who cannot immediately contact his own lawyer should normally be allowed to try one or two others.... Hard and fast rules cannot be laid down for all circumstances. Ultimately it must always be a question of fact and common sense whether a reasonable opportunity has been given.[103]

President Cooke held that exclusion of evidence should normally result from a breach of section 23(1)(b), where a court finds that a reasonable opportunity for securing counsel's attendance has not been afforded to a suspect. Read in conjunction with sections 51–52 of the Legal Services Act 2000, New Zealand accordingly supplies substantial evidence for inferring a common law right to the presence of counsel, notably in the context of a constitutionalised set of pre-trial rights which are worded similarly to the Canadian Charter.

In each of the jurisdictions surveyed in this section, the intertwined rights to counsel and to silence are subject to limits which depend on a court's conception of reasonableness. The content of suspects' rights is determined contextually, and in general courts predictably resist inflexible, particularised rules. This review of prominent common law jurisdictions suggests the need for a nuanced yet robust conceptualisation of the right to counsel; and the corresponding utility of considering the principles which underlie the common law right to counsel. Inevitably, the balance of rights and

98 *R v Beck* [2008] NZCA 283.
99 Ibid [15].
100 [1992] 3 NZLR 260.
101 *R v Therens* [1985] 1 SCR 613.
102 *R v Thomsen* [1988] 1 SCR 640.
103 [1992] 3 NZLR 260, 274.

responsibilities, and the implications of exercising those rights, varies from place to place. Nonetheless, the trend towards permitting a suspect to enjoy a broad right of access to counsel is sufficiently clear, even from our whistle-stop survey, to demonstrate that Canadians enjoy a narrower, less protective, right to counsel than their counterparts in broadly similarly-situated common law countries. The lack of any normative principle directing attention to the law and practice of similar democracies means that Canadian courts can decide to follow the comparative lead on freedom of expression, for example, whilst declining to do so in relation to the right to counsel.

(e) The International Criminal Court

Innovations in international criminal adjudication lend additional momentum to developments witnessed in other common law jurisdictions. In particular, Article 55(2) of the ICC's Rome Statute states:[104]

> Where there are grounds to believe that a person has committed a crime within the jurisdiction of the Court and that person is about to be questioned either by the Prosecutor, or by national authorities ... that person shall also have the following rights of which he or she shall be informed prior to being questioned...
>
> (d) To be questioned in the presence of counsel unless the person has voluntarily waived his or her right to counsel.

Article 69 of the Rome Statute contains the following generic provisions regulating the admissibility of evidence in trials before the ICC:

> 4. The Court may rule on the relevance or admissibility of any evidence, taking into account, *inter alia*, the probative value of the evidence and any prejudice that such evidence may cause to a fair trial or to a fair evaluation of the testimony of a witness, in accordance with the Rules of Procedure and Evidence...
>
> 7. Evidence obtained by means of a violation of this Statute or internationally recognized human rights shall not be admissible if:
>
> (a) The violation casts substantial doubt on the reliability of the evidence; or
> (b) The admission of the evidence would be antithetical to and would seriously damage the integrity of the proceedings.[105]

[104] www.icc-cpi.int/library/about/officialjournal/ Rome_Statute_120704-EN.pdf.

[105] It is possible that if the ICC thought that Canadian procedure was fundamentally different from Article 55 it could render statements inadmissible before that court. Turning to the ICTY and the ICTR, Rule 42(B) of both their Rules of Procedure and Evidence states: 'Questioning of a suspect shall not proceed without the presence of counsel unless the suspect has voluntarily waived the right to counsel. In case of waiver, if the suspect subsequently expresses a desire to have counsel, questioning shall thereupon cease, and shall only resume when the suspect has obtained or has been assigned counsel'.

Canada is a State Party to the Rome Statute, which provides a stronger basis for harmonization than diffuse appeals to customary international law. Canada's international treaty obligations should add additional weight in establishing the tipping point.

CONCLUSION: REACHING THE TIPPING POINT

The cogency of comparative analysis in supporting any particular legal proposition is always affected by similarities (and dissimilarities) of social and legal context, level of foreign authority, evidence of the practical impact of a particular rule, breath of judicial and academic support or criticism, and so forth. The perception that a legal jurisdiction is encountering particular difficulties might generate greater interest in looking for alternative solutions. Accordingly, how might comparative research establish that protection for particular human rights norms has become so well-developed and entrenched across the common law world that Canadian courts *ought* to interpret Canadian law to achieve conformity with the international consensus?

We submit that the tipping point is reached when it is possible to say that, on balance, the common law world has pointed the way to a rule more in tune with Canada's own domestic principles of constitutional interpretation than any eligible alternative. Recalling the principles of constitutional adjudication previously summarised, a number of more discrete points can be made. The purposive principle is particularly significant, as it involves comparative method at the higher levels of abstraction employed in *Grant v Torstar*,[106] thus pre-empting objections to piecemeal borrowing. Consideration of whether other common law jurisdictions reflect a more 'protective' rather than merely 'informational' approach to the right to counsel is likely to be more informative and influential than local doctrinal variations. The progressive or living tree principle is less helpful. To be sure, the Constitution is open to change, but the principle itself does not facilitate concrete developments, other than by exhorting the courts to give 'generous and progressive' interpretations to the rights of all people involved in criminal proceedings, whether as suspects or victims of crime. Regarding 'basic tenets', a protective conception of the right to counsel chimes with Canada's distinctive equality principle, since police power to isolate vulnerable individuals provides a setting for inegalitarian behaviour ranging from the discriminatory exercise of discretion to sexist and racist violence. And particular vulnerabilities aside, there is general cause for concern that coercively one-sided police interrogations may contribute to

[106] 2009 SCC 61, [2009] 3 SCR 640.

wrongful convictions. Finally, Canada has agreed that persons suspected of crimes falling within the complementary jurisdiction of the ICC have a right to the presence of counsel, bolstering common law comparisons. Accumulating comparative 'precedents' from other jurisdictions, then viewing them through the lens of Canadian constitutional principles, has the synergistic potential of incorporating foreign legal example into a norm of constitutional adjudication in accordance with the prevailing common law consensus.[107]

There are naturally counter-arguments, both theoretical and normative. It might be said that a tipping point analysis adds nothing to Canada's existing constitutional principles. Appealing to international norms to which Canada has not made a domestic law commitment makes an inference from an omission, which is necessarily equivocal. Canada agreed to procedural rules for the ICC but Parliament has *not* adopted them in Canadian law. International tribunals are generally procedural hybrids, as indeed are some domestic jurisdictions such as Scotland and South Africa, which calls into question the suitability of their models for domestic adoption. The courts should hesitate to ratchet-up the common law rules from other countries to constitutional status. The focus and methods of academic research vary from country to country so it may not be at all clear whether a particular rule would achieve practical improvements in human rights protection. After all, there is a cost to losing evidence of crimes, a cost borne in part by people particularly vulnerable to infringements of their own human rights, such as women vulnerable to domestic violence. Canada's balance might be idiosyncratic and yet still superior to that of other common law jurisdictions. The idea that Canada *ought* to follow improved protection for human rights in other countries is in essence to test Canadian law against a vague external standard. Given the lack of attention, in *Sinclair*, to what we suggest are the principles of constitutional interpretation, a tipping point principle would be just as vulnerable to judicial manipulation as the current approach to comparative sources.

On the other hand, constitutional issues litigated before the Supreme Court of Canada cannot be resolved purely through doctrinal analysis. The principle that Canada should keep up with the common law Joneses, where their laws have tipped in favour of enhanced human rights protection, would be a modest addition to the existing corpus of interpretational principles employed in constitutional adjudication. It would improve on other possible sources of inspiration, such as judicial intuition, unconscious or unexamined leanings, or untested assumptions about the range of possible factual and legal possibilities. A tipping point principle would also foster

[107] In essence this reflects the approach in *Grant v Torstar* [2009] 3 SCR 640, advocating adoption of the laws of similarly-situated democracies where buttressed by Charter principles.

comparative guidance and structure for legal argument, enriching the living tree approach to constitutional interpretation through fertile hybridisation. On what should a 'living tree' constitution draw for its inspiration if not shared common law principles reinforced by international values?[108] Boiled down to its essence, a tipping point principle would reflect a commitment to best human rights practice as an aspect of Canadianness—a 'Made in Canada' approach to common law comparativism.

[108] For discussion of the role of the ICC as a 'standard setter' see B Perrin, 'Making Sense of Complementarity: The Relationship Between the International Criminal Court and National Jurisdictions' (2006) 18 *Sri Lanka Journal of International Law* 301.

4

Degrading Searches and Illegally Obtained Evidence in the Malaysian Criminal Justice System

SALIM FARRAR

INTRODUCTION

UNLIKE MANY MODERN common law jurisdictions, the law of criminal evidence in Malaysia has no constitutional foundations, nor is it influenced directly by human rights concepts, no matter how fundamental.[1] The right not to be subjected to degrading treatment found in Article 7 of the International Covenant on Civil and Political Rights (ICCPR), and Article 3 of the European Convention on Human Rights (ECHR), along with the obligation to take active steps to prevent violations of that right in Article 16 of the UN Convention Against Torture (UNCAT), are legally irrelevant as far as Malaysian law is concerned because Malaysia has not signed these treaties. Moreover, the values underpinning Malaysian evidence law generally reflect the rationalist colonial tradition of James Fitzjames Stephen, the original architect of Malaysia's Evidence Act 1950, more than the libertarian notions and human rights considerations influencing much of the common law world today. Respect for human rights values in Malaysia is a recent *political* phenomenon. It has emerged as a focus for national unity and a key part of the government's strategy for managing tensions between competing ethnicities whose sectarian affiliations might otherwise split the country. The politics of human rights have manifested themselves in different ways across the government's legislative agenda and internationally,[2] with particular salience for criminal justice reform.

[1] See *Mohamad Ezam bin Mohd Noor v Ketua Polis Negara* [2002] 4 MLJ 449, 513–14, in which the Federal C ourt rejected the contention that Malaysian law is subject to the UN Universal Declaration of Human Rights.

[2] Malaysia's formal election to the United Nations Human Rights Council by the UN General Assembly (64th Session) on 13 May 2010 is indicative of recent efforts to embrace human rights treaties.

This chapter critically reconsiders the law relating to body searches in the light of human rights concerns and in the context of a traditionally non-interventionist Malaysian judiciary. The Criminal Procedure (Amendment) Act 2006[3] introduced sweeping reform of many aspects of criminal procedure in Malaysia including the right to legal advice, the abolition of caution statements, amendments to bail, and a new pre-trial disclosure regime.[4] Each reform, in its own way, reflects human rights concerns. The new measures relating to body searches, however, bear directly on the notion of human dignity, and the events which precipitated them usefully illustrate the importance of political and cultural context in the implementation of human rights.

Section 1 describes the historical and political background to the reforms, emphasising the deference traditionally extended to the Royal Malaysian Police Force, the *Polis Di Raja Malaysia* (PDRM), and the almost entrenched 'law and order' orientation of the courts. Section 2 sets out the reforms themselves and explains how they purported to address the problems and scandals that had lately enveloped the PDRM. Of particular interest is the restricted role afforded to the courts, as we shall see. Section 3 summarises the findings of an empirical study of body searches covering a period of one year after the reforms came into effect. In conclusion, this essay questions the wisdom of the government's lack of faith in judicial supervision of police investigations.

1. ABUSE OF POLICE POWER IN A CLIMATE OF LEGAL UNCERTAINTY

Since Independence in 1957, the PDRM have enjoyed almost unfettered de facto powers to implement their policing mandate. In formal legal terms, police investigations are subject to the Federal Constitution and regulated by the Criminal Procedure Code, various Dangerous Drugs enactments, the Evidence Act 1950, and the Police Act 1967. There is additional administrative guidance in the Lock-up Rules 1953 and Standard Operating Procedures (official police protocols). But in practice, police officers have largely been left to police themselves unhindered by judicial or other impartial external scrutiny. They have not been bothered, harried or kept in check by that normal irritant in the adversarial process, the defence lawyer, because suspects can rarely afford legal representation. There is no legal

[3] Act A 1274 2006, the principal amending legislation was itself amended by Act A 1304 2007. A further amendment was introduced in 2008 pertaining to electronic recording.

[4] Generally, see SA Farrar, 'The "New" Malaysian Criminal Procedure: Criminal Procedure (Amendment) Act 2006' (2009) 4 *Asian Criminology* 129–44.

aid available for pre-trial proceedings or on a plea of not guilty.[5] Moreover, even if the accused can afford to hire his own lawyer or is lucky enough to have the voluntary assistance of a barrister,[6] lawyers have been generally excluded from police interview rooms, with the explicit sanction of the Federal Court.[7]

In the absence of effective independent scrutiny, the PDRM has been free to adopt practices more readily associated with a military rather than a civilian police force. A Malaysian Royal Commission on the operation and management of the police, set up in 2005, found that PDRM officers were engaged in de facto torture and frequent physical abuse of suspects.[8] Emblematic of these degrading practices was the procedure known as *ketuk ketampi*, which made national and international headlines. *Ketuk ketampi* was applied to detainees arrested on suspicion of drugs or immigration offences, and involved the suspect being stripped naked, placed against a wall, and ordered to squat and stand repeatedly—in the dubious expectation that drugs secreted anally or vaginally would simply drop out. The frequency and prevalence of its occurrence was disputed in a subsequent commission of enquiry, before whom the police actually defended the practice.[9] However, the commission concluded that *ketuk ketampi* had been used 'indiscriminately' and without any legal authority.[10]

Yet this conclusion begs a vital question: accepting that no law explicitly authorised *ketuk ketampi*, were the police therefore acting beyond their legal authority or could they claim that their conduct was implicitly authorised? The Police Act 1967 conferred upon the police a power to take 'such lawful measures and do such lawful acts as may be necessary'.[11] This would seemingly cover the conduct of body searches and road-side frisks and pat-downs,[12] but could a generic power to do what is 'necessary' extend as far as *ketuk ketampi*? The Police Act's references to 'lawful measures' and

[5] Legal Aid Act 1971, s 10 and sch 2.

[6] In practice, all contested criminal cases (with the exception of murder trials) are handled by the Bar Council's legal aid centres (BLACs), subject to a means test, or defended pro bono. BLACs receive approximately $340,000 per annum from mandatory contributions provided by Bar Council members. See further, R Nekoo, 'Legal Aid in Malaysia: The Need for Greater Government Commitment', 23 November 2009, www.malaysianbar.org.

[7] *Ooi Ah Phua v Officer in Charge Criminal Investigation, Kedah/Perlis* [1975] 2 MLJ 198 (Suffian, LP).

[8] *Report of the Royal Commission to Enhance the Operation and Management of the Royal Police Force* (Kuala Lumpur, Government of Malaysia, 2005).

[9] YY Poh, 'Will the people win in this tussle?', *New Straits Times*, 21 December 2005.

[10] *Report of the Commission to Enquire into the Standard Operating Procedural Rules and Regulations in the Conduct of Body Search in Respect of an Arrest and Detention by the Police* (Kuala Lumpur, Government of Malaysia, 2006).

[11] Police Act 1967, ss 3 and 20(3).

[12] See MK Majid, *Criminal Procedure in Malaysia*, 3rd edn (Kuala Lumpur, University of Malaya Press, 1999) 82.

'lawful acts' suggested that supplementary legislation and regulations might clarify the scope of this power in specific operational contexts.

Prior to its reform, the Criminal Procedure Code (CPC) gave further direction on the scope of lawful searches, but not without ambiguity. Section 17 permitted a body search for concealed articles incidental to a lawful search of premises. Section 20 authorised a police officer to search a person placed under arrest if the officer had any reason to believe that he might discover the fruits of crime or other relevant evidence. The only further stipulation was that a female detainee could be searched only by a female police officer 'with strict regard to decency'.[13] Did this imply that there were *no* further restrictions in relation to male suspects? How 'strict' or 'decent' must searches of female detainees be? And what were the female officer's particular responsibilities when carrying out such a search? Most importantly, what were the legal consequences, if any, of non-compliance? Unfortunately, the CPC provided no further clarification.

The Dangerous Drugs Act 1952 and the Dangerous Drugs (Forfeiture of Property) Act 1988 are also potentially relevant, given that the *ketuk ketampi* seems to have often been incidental to drugs-related crime. The former, however, does not specify any power to conduct body searches. Filling this apparent gap in the legislative framework, section 16 of the 1988 Act legislation states:

> (1) Whenever it appears to any senior police officer that there is reasonable cause to suspect that in or on any premises there is concealed or deposited any property liable to forfeiture ... he may, at any time, by day or by night—
> (a) enter such premises...
> (b) search any person who is in or on such premises, and for the purposes of such search, detain such person and remove him to such place as may be necessary to facilitate such search.

Section 17 further provided:

> (1) A senior police officer may search, or cause to be searched, any person whom he has reason to believe has on his person any property liable to seizure or forfeiture under this Act, or any article whatsoever necessary for the purpose of any investigation under this Act ... and may remove him in custody to such place as may be necessary to facilitate such search.
> (2) A search of a person under this section or under section 16 may extend to a medical examination of his body, both externally and internally, by a medical officer.
> (3) No female person shall be searched under this section or under section 16 except by another female.

[13] Police Act 1967, s 19(ii).

The fact that section 17 specifically mentions both 'external' and 'internal' body searches might be taken to imply that section 16 does not empower a police officer to conduct the more intrusive 'strip search'. Section 17 authorises a medical officer to conduct such a search only on the authority of a senior police officer who has 'reason to believe' (arguably a higher evidential threshold than 'reasonable cause to suspect') that the detainee is concealing an article 'necessary' for the investigation. The additional protection of an examination by a medical examiner might explain why the need for 'decency' (as provided in the CPC) is omitted. Reading both provisions together suggests the illegality of *ketuk ketampi*, since it is a form of 'strip search' conducted by a police officer rather than by a medical examiner. However, the impracticality of having to call out a doctor every time they wanted to conduct a 'strip search' may have encouraged abusive practices to continue, with the police possibly interpreting the absence of public criticism as implicit approval for abusive practices, irrespective of their formal illegality. In addition, section 49 of the Dangerous Drugs Act 1952 stipulates that: 'Nothing done by any officer of the Government in the course of his duties shall be deemed an offence under this Act'.

The Dangerous Drugs Acts and CPC are also silent in relation to any evidential sanction for breach,[14] and the Evidence Act 1950 is equally unilluminating. Sections 24–26 of the Evidence Act exclude statements amounting to confessions procured by threats, promises or inducements, etc, but say nothing about the admissibility of evidence obtained illegally. As in England and Wales before the Police and Criminal Evidence Act (PACE) 1984, these matters are left to be determined by the judges at common law.[15] Malaysian courts have followed the Privy Council ruling in *Kuruma v R*[16] declaring that relevant evidence is admissible irrespective of the manner by which it is obtained. The notion that the civil liberties of the citizen could be protected and the police disciplined through application of an exclusionary *rule*, akin to the US Supreme Court's 'fruit of the poison tree' doctrine,[17] or through exercise of a common law *discretion* to exclude in instances of serious impropriety or unfairness, has never been seriously entertained. Although the Malaysian Government abolished criminal appeals to the Privy Council in 1978,[18] Malaysian courts appear unable or unwilling to modify colonial precedent by adopting the more liberal approaches being developed in other Commonwealth jurisdictions,[19] including those which, like Malaysia,

[14] Section 36 of the 1988 Act may have legitimated such searches in the form of a 'special law'. It stated that evidence gathered pursuant to the Dangerous Drugs Acts 'shall be admissible ... notwithstanding anything to the contrary in any written law'.

[15] There was no equivalent to the English 'Judges' Rules' in Malaysia.

[16] *Kuruma v R* [1955] AC 197; applied in *Saw Kim Hai* [1956] MLJ 21.

[17] *Mapp v Ohio*, 367 US 643 (1961).

[18] Courts of Judicature (Amendment) Act 1976, s 13.

[19] See eg *Collins v R* (1987) 38 DLR 508 (Canada).

have neither a constitutional document entrenching a Bill of Rights nor any well-developed tradition of rights discourse in criminal procedure.[20]

In *Seridaran*,[21] the Public Prosecutor appealed to the Criminal Appeal Court of Seremban against a decision of a magistrate acquitting the accused on the ground that the police had failed to obtain an order to investigate from the Public Prosecutor, contrary to section 108(ii) of the CPC. The question for the court, notwithstanding the patent illegality of the investigation, was whether it still had jurisdiction to hear the case and evidence on which to base its verdict. Setting aside the acquittal, Peh Swee Chin J stated:

> I am bound by, and I do certainly subscribe to the view that if such illegally obtained evidence is relevant to the matters in issue it is admissible in evidence on the authority of the judgment of the Privy Council in *Kuruma*... I am unable to accede to counsel's argument that it would cause a miscarriage of justice, not only because the decision of *Kuruma* is against it but also that the court would have to consider the broader interest of the public to prevent such evidence on crimes or for doing justice, from being withheld.[22]

The illegality in *Seridaran* arose from police negligence rather than deliberate impropriety. It is difficult to say whether the court would have decided differently had the police behaved as they did in some of the more notorious confession cases,[23] but Peh Swee Chin J's expressed preference for 'doing justice' to secure convictions suggests a negative answer. Similarly, in *Kah Wai Video*,[24] another case concerning magisterial supervision, *Kuruma* was applied to validate the seizure and admissibility of items not listed on a search warrant. The seizure was found to be lawful by virtue of an implied common law power, but the court added that, even if their seizure had been unlawful, the items would still have been admissible under the authority of *Kuruma*—a decision which was by now part of Malaysian legal heritage.[25] The more recent and factually similar case of *Public Prosecutor v Then Mee Kom*,[26] in which the court had invalidated an arrest and all subsequent proceedings following an illegal seizure of items subject to Malaysian copyright law, was rejected on the basis that it would 'drain the principle in *Kuruma*'s

[20] See eg *Bunning v Cross* (1978) 19 ALR 641; and *Ridgeway v R* (1995) 129 ALR 41, in which the High Court of Australia held a trial judge had a discretion to exclude evidence on public policy grounds where the evidence had been obtained by the police unlawfully. The former case also laid down guidelines to assist the court in the exercise of its discretion.

[21] *Public Prosecutor v Seridaran* [1984] 1 MLJ 141.

[22] Ibid 142.

[23] Cf *Dato' Mokhtar Bin Hashim v Public Prosecutor* [1983] 2 MLJ 232, in which the police fabricated entries in the suspect's diaries, deprived him of sleep, food and drink, prevented him from praying, and generally treated the suspect inhumanely in their endeavours to obtain a confession.

[24] *Re Kah Wai Video (Ipoh) Sdn Bhd* [1987] 2 MLJ 459.

[25] Ibid 464.

[26] [1983] 2 MLJ 344.

case of all its vitality'.[27] To press home the importance of supporting the police, the court also cited pre-PACE English authorities[28] and endorsed Lord Denning's admonition to keep in check 'the ever-increasing wickedness there is about' whilst urging 'honest citizens' to help the police and 'not hinder them in their efforts to track down criminals'.[29] Clearly, the need to deter police impropriety and illegality through the exclusion of apparently reliable evidence was not uppermost in the judges' minds.

It is notable that the High Court of Singapore in *SM Summit Holdings*,[30] having carefully reviewed relevant authorities across the common law world and the policy considerations underpinning them, subsequently followed the House of Lords' decision in *Sang*[31] in recognising that police impropriety could render evidence inadmissible, especially if there had been a violation of the suspect's privilege against self-incrimination. However, *SM Summit Holdings* has never been applied directly in a Malaysian court and remains merely a persuasive authority. Moreover, the fact that there are no reported appellate decisions since in which defence lawyers have successfully challenged the admissibility of evidence based upon police illegality[32] indicates that relevance, irrespective of the propriety of investigative methods, remains the only test of admissibility. Just as in England and Wales prior to PACE,[33] the courtroom was not regarded as an appropriate venue for disciplining the police. If the police engaged in illegal behaviour, aggrieved persons could, in theory, pursue civil law remedies or complain to the policing authorities and seek administrative sanctions against the offending officer.[34] Yet unlike in England, where dissatisfaction with both political oversight at the local level and internal police investigations of complaints against their own officers precipitated large numbers of successful civil actions for damages,[35] there was no such external check on the powers of the Malaysian police. While there were copious reports of police

[27] *Re Kah Wai Video (Ipoh) Sdn Bhd* [1987] 2 MLJ 459, 464.

[28] *Ghani v Jones* [1970] 1 QB 693; *Truman Export v Metropolitan Police Commissioner* [1977] 3 All ER 431; *Chic Fashions (West Wales) Ltd v Jones* [1968] 2 QB 299.

[29] *Re Kah Wai Video (Ipoh) Sdn Bhd* [1987] 2 MLJ 459, 464, citing Lord Denning in *Chic Fashions (West Wales) Ltd v Jones* [1968] 2 QB 299, 313.

[30] *SM Summit Holdings Ltd v Public Prosecutor* [1997] 3 SLR 922.

[31] *R v Sang* [1980] AC 402.

[32] Section 27 of the Evidence Act 1950 empowers courts to admit real evidence 'discovered' as a result of information supplied by an inadmissible confession and to prove the provenance of the evidence by virtue of that information. The Malaysian Supreme and Federal Courts have vacillated on the application of a 'prejudicial effect versus probative value' balancing exercise: see *Md Desa Bin Hashim v Public Prosecutor* [1995] 3 MLJ 350; *Goi Ching Ang v Public Prosecutor* [1999] 1 MLJ 507; *Francis Antonysamy* [2005] 3 MLJ 389.

[33] See R Clayton and H Tomlinson, *Civil Actions Against the Police* (London, Sweet & Maxwell, 1992) 10.

[34] Police Act 1967, ss 74–78.

[35] Clayton and Tomlinson, above n 33, 13.

malpractice, few citizens were prepared to take official action, apparently for fear of police victimisation.[36]

In short, Malaysian statute and common law had generated its own 'untouchables'. In practice, the police could stop, search, frisk, and subject suspects to body searches with impunity and without even breaching the letter of the law. In this area of criminal procedure at least, both legal rhetoric and the substance of legal rules converged in supporting agendas of crime reduction and social control.

The historical roots of this approach might be traced back to post-Independence local politics and judicial attitudes which were forged at a time when there was a strong perceived need to support the police in their struggles against Communist (CPM) insurgents. Although the Malaysian government had secured victory well before the CPM's official abandonment of armed struggle in 1989,[37] the police enjoyed continued popular support because of their sacrifices in a war that had cost 10,000 Malaysian lives (including many civilian). The perceived need for muscular policing unimpeded by due process obstacles or human rights concerns was reinforced by the race riots of May 1969, and then again following the political crisis and constitutional upheavals of 1987–88; interestingly, the same period in which *Kah Wai Video* was decided. The detailed events of 'Operation Lalang' (lit. 'weeding out') in October 1987 need not concern us, but what is significant for present purposes is the role played by the PDRM as the Malaysian Government's executive arm. The PDRM arrested and detained 106 social activists and opposition leaders under the Internal Security Act. Although this was designed to prevent further social unrest, and was thus justified on law and order grounds, it was also a political act carried out at the behest of the Mahathir Government, which feared that popular protest would lead to its downfall.

In the mid-1980s, an independent Supreme Court became concerned at the extent of the executive powers exercised by the Mahathir administration, and gradually expanded the grounds for judicial review.[38] Government decisions were struck down,[39] much to the annoyance of the Prime Minister. Government policies were thwarted and some of the politicians detained under the ISA in the wake of 'Operation Lalang' were released.[40] The *coup*

[36] See the Report of the Royal Commission, above n 8.

[37] KS Nathan, 'Malaysia in 1989: Communists End Armed Struggle' (1990) 30 *Asian Survey* 210 (February).

[38] *Berthelsen v Director General of Immigration, Malaysia* [1987] 1 MLJ 134 (developing principles of natural justice); *Government of Malaysia v Lim Kit Siang* [1988] 2 MLJ 12 (progressive extension of standing rules); *Persatuan Aliran Kesederan Negara v Minister of Home Affairs* [1988] 1 MLJ 440 (refusal of a licence to publish a reform group's magazine in Bahasa Malaysia struck down).

[39] *Public Prosecutor v Dato' Yap Peng* [1987] 2 MLJ 316; *Berthelsen v Director General of Immigration, Malaysia* [1987] 1 MLJ 134.

[40] *Karpal Singh v Minister for Home Affairs* [1988] 1 MLJ 468; *Inspector-General of Police v Tan Sri Raja Khalid* [1988] 1 MLJ 182.

de grace was Prime Minister Mahathir's own party, UMNO—the dominant member of the ruling Barisan Nasional (National Front) coalition—being declared an illegal organisation by the Supreme Court.[41]

But this victory for the rule of law was short-lived. Article 121(1) of the Federal Constitution which 'vested' judicial power of the Federation with the courts (implying an inherent jurisdiction) was excised by the Constitution (Amendment) Act 1988. Henceforth, the courts would only have such jurisdiction and powers 'as may be conferred by or under federal law'. The Supreme Court was effectively sacked later the same year and substituted by judges thought to be more inclined towards the establishment.[42] One such appointee was Dato' Edgar Joseph, Jr, who had previously decided *Kah Wai Video* and now sat on the special High Court tribunal empanelled to try five members of the deposed Supreme Court. The prospect of robust judicial supervision of police illegality disappeared along with the original Supreme Court.

De facto police untouchability continued through the 1990s. Although the era of human rights had now arrived, in Malaysia this was understood to mean economic rights to development as opposed to civil and political rights.[43] Police disdain for procedural rights and due process reached its symbolic nadir when former Deputy Prime Minister Anwar Ibrahim suffered a black eye at the hands of the Chief of Police, Tan Sri Rahim Noor.[44]

2. REFORM: THE CRIMINAL PROCEDURE (AMENDMENT) ACT 2006

Prime Minister Mahathir Mohamed stepped down in 2003 to be succeeded by Dato' Seri Abdullah Ahmad Badawi, marking the end of an era. Anwar Ibrahim was subsequently released from custody and the accountability of the PDRM now became a matter of political concern. One of the first measures taken by the new Prime Minister was to announce a Royal

41 *Mohamed Noor bin Othman v Haji Mohamed Ismail* [1988] 3 MLJ 82, (Supreme Court) upholding *Mohamed Noor bin Othman v Mohamed Yusoff Jaafar* [1988] 2 MLJ 129 (Harun, J).

42 M Mohamad, 'Legal Coercion, Meanings and UMNO's Legitimacy' in ET Gomez (ed), *Politics in Malaysia—The Malay Dimension* (London, Routledge, 2007) 34. See further regarding the 1988 constitutional crisis, HP Lee, *Constitutional Conflicts in Contemporary Malaysia* (Kuala Lumpur, OUP, 1995) 52–76; A Harding, *Law, Government and the Constitution in Malaysia* (The Hague, Kluwer Law International, 1996) 142–48.

43 For a good illustration of the Malaysian government's attitude towards human rights during the 1990s, see the 1997 speech of Finance Minister Daim Zainuddin, as reported by the Asian Institute for Development and Communication, *Human Rights Handbook for ASEAN Journalists* (Kuala Lumpur, Dynamic Business Press, 1999) 19–21.

44 See C Lopez, 'Globalisation, State and G/local Human Rights Actors: Contestations between Institutions and Civil Society' in Gomez (ed), above n 42, 59–62.

Commission on the PDRM to investigate, amongst other matters, alleged abuses of human rights.[45] The 2005 report of the Royal Commission announced that the PDRM no longer enjoyed the popular support it once took for granted, and that fundamental reform, giving prominence to human rights principles, was necessary.[46]

The impetus for reform was given an additional boost at the end of 2005 when a video clip from a mobile phone was circulated around the world showing a naked woman being forced to do the *ketuk ketampi*. A full-blown diplomatic incident with the Chinese government was narrowly averted when it was realised that the detainee in question was a local Malay woman, and not a Chinese national as had originally been thought.[47] With the woman's faith and ethnicity now clarified, concern was expressed that her Islamic rights of honour and privacy had been denied. Reform of policing methods to take better account of religious sensitivities became a popular demand.[48]

The Criminal Procedure (Amendment) Act 2006 was the government's response to mounting internal and external political pressures for the introduction of new mechanisms of police governance and legal accountability. This legislation represented the most radical reform of Malaysian criminal justice and procedure for more than 20 years. In relation to body searches, it seemed that the right not to be subjected to degrading treatment was at last receiving formal recognition in Malaysian law. Section 20A of the CPC, as inserted by the 2006 Act, states that all personal searches must now conform to the procedures set out in a new fourth schedule to the CPC. Schedule 4 comprises 15 long paragraphs specifying in detail how, in what circumstances, and for which purposes the police or any other law enforcement agency with powers of arrest, may carry out pat-downs, strip searches, intimate searches and intrusive searches. The *ketuk ketampi* in drugs cases has now officially gone, and been replaced by a 'coughing mirror squat' (deemed an 'intimate search' under paragraph 12), to be conducted only when 'necessary'[49] and with authorisation from an Assistant

[45] 'Royal Commission on Police Duties to be set up, says Abdullah', *Bernama Daily Malaysian News*, 29 December 2003; 'Malaysia to probe allegations of police brutality', *Wall Street Journal Asia*, 30 December 2003.

[46] See Farrar, above n 4, 130.

[47] AR Ahmad, 'Dark episode may become a turning point', *New Sunday Times*, 4 December 2005; 'Kit Siang and Teresa ready to face the consequences', *Bernama Daily Malaysian News*, 16 December 2005.

[48] See SA Farrar, above n 4, 133.

[49] Paragraph 12 states that '(a) if necessary, the person arrested may be instructed to remove all clothes covering the bottom half, from the navel downwards; (b) if necessary, the person arrested may be instructed to squat over a mirror placed on the floor and made to cough deeply not more than ten times; (c) when nothing is recovered after the squat and coughing deeply until ten times the intimate search shall stop and the person arrested shall be allowed to put on his clothes; (d) where the officer considers that the person arrested is incapable of doing

Superintendant of Police. In order to forestall another worldwide media circus, paragraph 9 stipulates[50] that no phones, cameras, recording or communicating devices are to be taken into the private room where the search is conducted.

In stark contrast to the pre-existing legal position, Schedule 4 as a whole leaves very little to the personal discretion of the officer carrying out the search and is unequivocal in its stipulations. In demanding that '[a]n officer conducting a body search shall do so in a professional manner and have the highest regard for the dignity of the person arrested', paragraph 3 is a model of liberal legality, human rights and respect for personal dignity. Law enforcement officers are enjoined *by law* to respect religious, cultural, gender and transgender issues and sensitivities. The language of section 20A is mandatory ('Any search of a person *shall comply* with the procedure on body search as specified in the fourth schedule') and, unlike the English PACE Codes of Practice for example, the procedures for conducting searches are set out in primary legislation rather than delegated soft law. However, these provisions do not translate directly into procedural 'rights' for the accused, nor is there any mention of a new exclusionary principle that defence lawyers could invoke to argue for excluding evidence obtained in violation of these provisions. Although public confidence in the police had declined, it seems the government was not prepared to countenance the possibility of guilty persons going free on 'technical' procedural grounds or the accused obtaining an evidential windfall. There remains the theoretical possibility of judges applying the residual common law discretion to exclude evidence where prejudicial effect outweighs probative value. But as we have already seen, there are no examples of this discretion being exercised in favour of the accused in Malaysian criminal proceedings. The courts effectively continue to refuse to regulate the conduct of police investigations (other than through the law of confessions).[51]

If the Malaysian government were sincere in its wish to transform police behaviour and to inculcate respect for human rights in criminal investigations, one might question the wisdom of omitting any procedural remedy for illegal searches. This omission seems even more questionable in light of the fact that most suspects do not have legal representation. The idea seems to have been that legislative force would give the Attorney General

the squat due to the health, physical conditions or appears to be or claims to be pregnant, the squat shall not be performed…'.

[50] Although para 9 refers to strip searches, intimate searches are subject to the same requirements by virtue of para 12(f).

[51] See *Hanafi bin Mat Hassan v Public Prosecutor* [2006] 4 MLJ 134, in which the court, reaffirming *Kuruma*, refused to exclude DNA evidence obtained from the accused without his consent and whilst handcuffed. The residual common law exclusionary discretion was limited to case where the accused could demonstrate that he was the victim of a trick, deception or oppressive behaviour on the part of the police.

leverage over senior police officers in implementing training and education programmes to promote better compliance with the reformed CPC on the ground. In other words, the assumption was that working through existing hierarchical structures within the police force would be a more effective method of enforcing human rights than relying upon adversarial criminal process and a conservative, if not timid, judiciary.

3. AN EMPIRICAL STUDY OF THE REFORMS IN PRACTICE

The author, in collaboration with a former colleague from the International Islamic University Malaysia (IIUM), devised a limited empirical study to test the impact of the 2006 reforms.[52] The project was implemented in two stages. A first round of data-collection was conducted in March 2008, six months after the provisions had come into force in September 2007. Follow-up interviews were then conducted in November 2008, approximately one year after the new procedures for searches had been introduced. Bearing in mind that the Criminal Procedure (Amendment) Act was gazetted and passed into law on 5 October 2006, the Malaysian Government had had plenty of time to devise and implement relevant training programmes.

The project enlisted the assistance of approximately 650 IIUM undergraduate students enrolled in criminal procedure courses.[53] Over two-week periods in March and November 2008, students working mostly in groups of two, three or four interviewed police officers, defence lawyers, prosecutors and magistrates on conditions of complete confidentiality and anonymity. Equipped with letters of introduction from the researchers, students used their own contacts and initiative to identify potential interviewees. The majority of those interviewed were based in the Klang Valley, a metropolitan area with high crime rates and pressure on resources. But some were based in non-metropolitan areas like Perak, Kedah and Kelantan, where police officers, in particular, would not be subject to quite the same operational pressures. The questions ranged over the entire gamut of reforms of pre-trial criminal process, including the conduct of body searches. Our intention was to take a panoramic snapshot of professionals' attitudes towards the amendments and to gauge compliance with the new laws over time. By interviewing these three distinct professional groups, we hoped to access a

[52] S Farrar and STD Rafique, *Amendments of 2006–07: An Empirical Study of their Effects on the Criminal Justice System* (Kuala Lumpur, IIUM Research Centre, 2009).

[53] In the first study, 350 students conducted interviews with between 50 and 60 police officers, magistrates and lawyers. In the second study, approximately 300 students conducted separate interviews of between 50 and 60 police officers and lawyers only. It is impossible to give precise numbers of interviewees because of possible duplication, but a minimum of 50 interviews was conducted for each professional body in both studies.

range of perspectives on the reforms and provide a measure of control for the distorting effects of occupational biases and vested interests.

As can be appreciated, this methodology is not without its weaknesses. Unsupervised student interviews will not always go according to plan. Some questions might be left unasked, and relevant answers unrecorded. Student interviewers sometimes failed to realise that police officers were being deliberately evasive and were unable to re-phrase questions that might have elicited fuller information. Moreover, not all of the students were as meticulous or honest as one might hope. For example, there were some who took short-cuts by interviewing the same police officers, defence lawyers and magistrates as their colleagues. While we endeavoured to filter out rogue results, our data inevitably portray only an imprecise outline or sketch of the real picture. Nevertheless, we felt that the advantages of having a large number of interviews conducted almost contemporaneously during a limited time-frame in different locations outweighed the unavoidable drawbacks in utilising amateur, though enthusiastic, interviewers. In carrying out the process a second time, we were able to refine our questions, better target potential interviewees, and spot rogue results; as well as accounting for periods of operational adjustment that predictably occur when such dramatic changes are introduced into a criminal justice system.

Here, in brief summary, is what we learnt from our interviewees[54] about the practical implementation of the new provisions regulating body searches.

— First, in relation to police training in the reformed procedure, a significant proportion (40%, n = 20) of the officers had not received any training after six months, but this had improved somewhat over the year, as one might expect, to 65% (n = 40) having received some training. It appears that it was primarily the new recruits and the officers in the lower ranks who were being trained in the new procedures as opposed to more experienced officers who were supposed to learn and understand how to apply these quite complex provisions 'on the job'. This is rather disturbing, especially considering the low education levels of many of the officers.
— Secondly, in both sets of interviews the pat-down search was carried out most frequently, whilst strip searches were performed only very rarely. A substantial number of police officers (50%, n = 27, in the first study) admitted to carrying out pat-downs before making an arrest, which is contrary to section 20A. Seventeen officers also admitted

[54] The questions asked in the November follow-up survey were not dissimilar to the first round of interviews, but this time magistrates were excluded and substituted with prosecutors, largely for the purposes of determining adequacy of disclosure under the new amendments. However, prosecutors were not asked about body searches under section 20A and the fourth schedule.

to having employed the *ketuk ketampi* in the past, but there was no indication that the practice was still on-going after the reforms had been implemented.

— Thirdly, as for general police compliance with Schedule 4, a substantial minority of police officers (30%, *n* = 16) interviewed in the first study admitted to not following the new procedure. Most magistrates (68%, *n* = 41) reported that the police were in full compliance, but a minority (17%, *n* = 10) said that the police were not strictly abiding by the letter of Schedule 4 and the remainder were unsure whether the police searchers were fully compliant or not. Defence lawyers, by contrast, reported far lower levels of police compliance. In the first round of interviews 80% (*n* = 35) of defence lawyer respondents said that the police were failing to comply with Schedule 4, falling to 55% (*n* = 30) in the follow-up study. However, respondents added that the police often appeared confused about the requirements of the new provisions, and some of those who answered 'Yes' to the basic question qualified their answer by saying that the police 'sometimes' complied. When asked whether they had complained about police violations of Schedule 4, most lawyers had not done so. Only 26% (*n* = 11) had complained in the first study, and 23% (*n* = 12) in the second. Defence lawyers said there was no point in complaining because the magistrate had no power to intervene in any event. Those who did complain did not achieve what they regarded as a satisfactory outcome at trial. Lawyers were, however, particularly vigilant to detect any recurrence of the *ketuk ketampi* in drugs-related investigations. Overall, a clear majority of defence lawyers (83%, *n* = 44) thought Schedule 4 was an improvement on the prior position, and added that police officers should now be required to comply. But the remainder believed that the provisions were too ambiguous and that there had been no real change in practice.

CONCLUSION

It is still early days and perhaps too soon to judge the Malaysian government's commitment to implementing human rights in the law regulating body searches. Human rights awareness through training programmes is clearly taking place[55] and some of the more undignified and humiliating

[55] Officers learn about human rights in the criminal process as part of their continuing education run by the National University of Malaysia at Bangi (UKM). The author participated in one of these programmes at the Police Training College in Cheras, Kuala Lumpur, in 2008.

practices, including the notorious *ketuk ketampi*, have been halted. But in view of the widespread adverse publicity this infamous practice attracted, it is quite probable that it would have been stopped anyway. The empirical data reported in Section 3 of this chapter, rough and ready as they are, pose more troubling questions. Is there adequate investment in training, at all levels of experience and seniority, to ensure that police officers are able to follow the new search provisions and implement them effectively and conscientiously? Perhaps the only reasons why the courts are not being flooded with claims of illegality are that there are few paid criminal defence lawyers to argue the case and no effective judicial sanctions for police violations. This diagnosis certainly fits with the Malaysian judiciary's longstanding lack of interest in excluding relevant evidence on grounds of illegality, under the baleful influence of *Kuruma*, as described in Section 1 of this chapter.

In the light of this discussion, one wonders whether the response of the Malaysian government in introducing the 2006 reforms of criminal procedure was more symbolic than practical, a reaction to the outrage of the international community rather than a genuine commitment to reorientate its criminal justice system to promote compliance with human rights. Successive governments have seen law as a tool to facilitate social and economic development, rather than as a limitation on state power and a check upon the executive.[56] This is not to deny that symbols can have important societal and communitarian purposes. Indeed, the new Malaysian Prime Minister, Dato' Seri Mohd Najib, has been trying to rally the people behind his 'One Malaysia' concept in order to minimise ethnic rivalries and discontent. If national symbols become devoid of any real content, however, they forfeit their political efficacy.

It is hoped that, as part of its process of institutional reform, the Malaysian government will see the wisdom in fostering a healthy and independent judiciary with the mandate and confidence to exercise effective supervision over police investigations.[57] Even if no further legislative amendments are made to section 20A or Schedule 4 of the CPC, there is nothing to prevent the judges from taking a more robust approach to their discretionary powers of trial management. It is open to the judiciary to develop the common law discretion to exclude illegally obtained evidence, for example where there

[56] Mohamad, above n 42, 27.

[57] As this chapter was being written, a new regulatory body, the Enforcement Agency Integrity Commission was set up by the Enforcement Agency Integrity Commission Act 2009 to supervise the activities of the law enforcement authorities in general, including the police. This represents a watering-down of the recommendations of the Royal Commission for a dedicated Independent Police Complaints Commission. For immediate critical reaction see: A Khoo, 'Who Guards the Guardian? The Rakyat Must Police the Police', 6 May 2010; and R Kesavan, 'Set up oversight mechanism without delay', 5 May 2010, www.malaysianbar.org.my.

are significant and substantial breaches of Schedule 4 in relation to body searches or police conduct tantamount to a violation of the accused's privilege against self-incrimination. Whether they are prepared to do this, we will have to wait and see. But if history is any guide, one should not expect that Malaysian courts will seize the initiative in the absence of express legislative authorisation and direction.

5

Human Rights, Constitutional Law and Exclusionary Safeguards in Ireland

JOHN JACKSON

INTRODUCTION—DEBATING THE EXCLUSIONARY REMEDY

THIS CHAPTER RECONSIDERS the rationale for excluding evidence obtained improperly by state officials in a criminal trial, with particular reference to the two jurisdictions in Ireland. Each of these jurisdictions has had its fair share of state officials prepared to flout the law in order to obtain evidence against those who are regarded not merely as criminals but as enemies of the state. The age-old forensic question of whether a court should be prepared to act upon evidence that has been procured by unlawful or immoral means reaches deeper into broader political issues concerning the aims of criminal justice and the moral basis for the criminal sanction.[1] The question is often presented as a litmus test for differentiating between advocates of 'crime control' and 'due process' in the long-running debate between Packer's two models of criminal process.[2]

Ireland provides an interesting test case for re-examining this question for a number of reasons. First of all, its recent history has posed the dilemma facing judges in a very stark form. During its recent troubled past[3] there has

The author would like to thank participants at the Nottingham conference for their comments on an earlier draft of this paper. Special thanks are owed to Laura Hoyano for her written comments on the paper.

[1] Zuckerman was one of the first writers to argue that it was misconceived to see the problem solely in evidentiary terms: AAS Zuckerman, *Principles of Criminal Evidence* (Oxford, OUP, 1989) 343–44.

[2] H Packer, *The Limits of the Criminal Sanction* (Stanford, CA, Stanford UP, 1968).

[3] Historians refer to two particular periods in Irish history as 'the Troubles': the first period (1916–1923) covering the final stages of British administration in Ireland and the second period covering the serious violence that was concentrated principally in Northern Ireland from 1969 until the ceasefires of the 1990s. See B Lalor (ed), *The Encyclopedia of Ireland* (Dublin, Gill & Macmillan, 2003) 1080.

been an unfortunate number of instances when security forces have flouted basic international human rights norms, most notably in Northern Ireland during a period of acute conflict in the 1970s, and the question of what the judiciary should do when faced with such disregard for basic standards is an important one. Twining reminds us that, despite the considerable academic literature on the question, there is a striking consensus that the judiciary and the law of evidence can make only a marginal contribution to what he considers to be the underlying problem often neglected by Evidence scholars.[4] According to Twining, the key challenge lies in designing a system for ensuring that official behaviour in the pre-trial process conforms to general principles of decent and fair treatment for those who come into contact with the criminal justice system without hampering officials in carrying out their necessary tasks. Addressing this problem involves detailed consideration of issues that go far beyond the exclusion of evidence obtained in breach of recognised standards of decency and fairness. Excluding evidence is an imperfect means of controlling illegality by the executive and potentially diverts attention from what may be more effective means of controlling illegal or improper investigatory behaviour. For this reason the possible exclusion of evidence should be viewed as just one of a basket of measures that includes promulgating clear procedural rules, providing criminal, civil and disciplinary remedies and establishing training programmes, resources and incentives to motivate officials to establish best-practice investigative protocols.

Twining's argument for looking at the broader picture pertains as much, if not more, in times of emergency as in more peaceful times, for it is at points of gravest crisis that security forces may be most tempted to flout standards of decent treatment. Nonetheless, judicial responses to improperly obtained evidence in times of crisis can be of immense symbolic significance, certainly in terms of promoting public confidence or the lack of it in state institutions, whether or not officials' behaviour is directly affected. During the last century of Irish history, there has at times been considerable hostility displayed by large sections of the community on both sides of the border towards fledgling state institutions struggling to establish their legitimacy. As we shall see in this chapter's case study of the two neighbouring Irish jurisdictions, the judiciary can play a key role in shaping public perceptions of the state's institutions, including, of course, the courts. On the one hand, there is a risk of alienating large sections of the community if criminal courts admit and act upon tainted evidence obtained in breach of the most basic human rights. On the other hand, there is a risk that failing to act on

[4] W Twining, *Rethinking Evidence: Exploratory Essays*, 2nd edn (Cambridge, CUP, 2006) 259–61.

such evidence will result in the release of dangerous individuals back into the community to wreak more havoc. The stakes could not be higher.

Within each of the two Irish jurisdictions, north and south, very different approaches have been taken to the problem, facilitating comparative analysis of the impact of different approaches on issues of compliance and legitimacy. The traditional common law rule, harking back to the eighteenth century, held that the manner in which evidence was obtained is irrelevant to the question of its admissibility. This attitude is immortalised in the famous dictum of Crompton J that '[i]t matters not how you get it: if you steal it even, it would be admissible'.[5] In reply, various rationales have been advanced in common law jurisdictions over the years for the exclusion of improperly obtained evidence.[6] First of all, the reliability rationale contends that exclusion is required to preclude the fact-finder acting on unreliable evidence. Another argument often advanced is that the prohibition on the use of evidence serves as a deterrent to investigators and prosecutors from repeating their improper conduct in the future.[7] A third rationale argues that prohibiting the use of evidence obtained in breach of the accused's fundamental rights, by excluding it from the trial, is necessary to vindicate the accused's rights.[8] A fourth rationale, which has acquired considerable following in recent times and which has particular salience for the legitimacy of state institutions, is that the use of improperly obtained evidence endangers judicial integrity as well as the moral authority of the verdict.[9]

[5] *R v Leatham* (1861) 8 Cox 498, 501, per Crompton J. See also *Kuruma v R* [1955] AC 197 where the Privy Council held that courts are not concerned with how relevant evidence was obtained in determining its admissibility.

[6] For reviews of the various rationales, see P Mirfield, *Silence, Confessions and Improperly Obtained Evidence* (Oxford, Clarendon Press, 1997) chs 2 and 6; D McGrath, *Evidence* (Dublin, Thomson Round Hall, 2005) 335–38; I Dennis, *The Law of Evidence*, 4th edn (London, Sweet & Maxwell, 2010) 3.42–3.46, P Roberts and A Zuckerman, *Criminal Evidence*, 2nd edn (Oxford, OUP, 2010) ch 5.

[7] LT Perrin, HM Caldwell, CA Chase and RW Fagan, 'If It's Broken, Fix It: Moving Beyond the Exclusionary Rule' (1998) 83 *Iowa Law Review* 669. The US Supreme Court has endorsed this theory in several cases: see eg, *Mapp v Ohio*, 367 US 643 (1961); and *Elkins v United States*, 364 US 206 (1960) in which the Court held that the purpose of the exclusionary rule was 'to deter—to compel respect for the constitutional guaranty in the only effectively available way—by removing the incentive to disregard it'.

[8] See especially A Ashworth, 'Excluding Evidence as Protecting Rights' [1977] *Criminal Law Review* 723.

[9] See notably Roberts and Zuckerman, above n 6, 188–91; Dennis, above n 6, 3.45, 108. See also *R v Grant* 2009 SCC 32, [2009] 2 SCR 353, [107] in which s 24(2) of the Canadian Charter was interpreted as requiring that admissibility 'be determined by inquiring into the effect admission may have on the repute of the justice system, having regard to the seriousness of the police conduct, the impact of the *Charter* breach on the protected interests of the accused, and the value of the trial on the merits'; *R v Ngai* [2010] AJ No 96 (QL) (CA). A judicial integrity rationale was propounded by Justice Ginsburg in her dissenting opinion in *Herring v US*, 129 S Ct 695, 707 (2009). See RM Bloom and DH Fentin, '"A More Majestic Conception": The Importance of Judicial Integrity in Preserving the Exclusionary Rule' (2010) 13 *University of Pennsylvania Journal of Constitutional Law* 47. Also see Rome Statute of the International Criminal Court, Art 69(7)(b): 'Evidence obtained by means of a violation

An inflexible rule mandating exclusion of all improperly obtained evidence would be unlikely to further any of these rationales in every case. Much evidence that is obtained improperly seems highly reliable. Exclusion may not deter police misconduct, especially in cases where the evidence was obtained improperly but in good faith. Equally, not all improperly obtained evidence necessarily breaches the fundamental rights of the accused. Finally, the routine exclusion of all improperly obtained evidence might undermine rather than promote confidence in the authority of the verdict if it results in the spectre of criminals being 'let off on a technicality'.[10] Commentators have cogently argued that, rather than relying upon inflexible rules, it is better to proceed by way of guiding principles to assist courts in exercising their discretion in particular cases.[11] What is interesting about the Irish experience, viewed against the backdrop of broader common law debates, is the prominence of rule-centred approaches.

In Northern Ireland, during the period when the Troubles were at their most acute in the 1970s and 1980s, the courts' approach to admissibility tended to adopt the traditional common law approach of disregarding the way in which evidence was obtained (although, as we shall see, they made an exception for confessions and were able to develop the common law discretion permitting judges to exclude unfairly obtained evidence). In the south, the Republic of Ireland courts, by contrast, have relied on the Irish Constitution to elaborate one of the strictest exclusionary rules to be seen in the common law world when evidence has been obtained in breach of constitutional rights; albeit that, in recent years, more discretionary approaches have been advocated.

In more peaceful times, the two systems, north and south, are being required to develop an approach towards exclusion which is closely aligned to the dictates of human rights law. As a result of the Good Friday/Belfast Agreement both jurisdictions committed themselves to human rights protection and the human rights legislation that has been put in place in both jurisdictions has required courts to take account of the jurisprudence of the European Court of Human Rights (ECtHR). Under the Agreement the Irish government committed itself to bringing forward measures that would ensure at least an equivalent level of protection of human rights as will pertain in Northern Ireland, and it was envisaged that a joint committee of representatives of the two Human Rights Commissions which the governments agreed to establish would consider the possibility of establishing a charter reflecting and endorsing agreed measures for the protection of fundamental rights of

of this Statute or internationally recognized human rights shall not be admissible if… [t]he admission of the evidence would be antithetical to and would seriously damage the integrity of the proceedings'.

[10] Roberts and Zuckerman, above n 6, 190.

[11] Zuckerman, above n 1, 6–13.

everyone living in the island of Ireland.[12] Section 2(1)(a) of the UK Human Rights Act 1998, which applies in Northern Ireland, provides that a court or tribunal determining a question which has arisen in connection with a right under the European Convention *must* take into account any judgment, decision, declaration or advisory opinion of the ECtHR, so far as, in the opinion of the court, it is relevant to the proceedings. In the Republic of Ireland a parallel but somewhat differently worded provision is found in section 4 of the European Convention on Human Rights Act 2003, which provides that judicial notice shall be taken of the Convention provisions and of any advisory opinion, declaration or judgment of the ECtHR and the court shall, when interpreting and applying the Convention provisions, take *due* account of the principles laid down by those declarations, judgments and advisory opinions.[13] Although this suggests a somewhat more attenuated relationship with Strasbourg jurisprudence than that required under the UK Human Rights Act, there is little doubt that, as in the United Kingdom, Strasbourg cases are increasingly being cited in arguments before the Irish courts.[14] Whilst this jurisprudence does not strictly speaking mandate evidentiary exclusion in relation to all breaches of human rights (as Section 5 of this chapter explores), it does require that the courts retain a discretion to exclude evidence in the interests of a fair trial. This has been used by critics of the strict traditional exclusionary approach in the south to argue for a more discretionary judicial approach towards evidence obtained in breach of constitutional rights.

1. THE IRISH CONTEXT

Ever since the partition of Ireland in 1920, live or dormant emergency legislation has spilled over into the criminal justice systems of both parts of the island. As soon as the Irish Republican Army proclaimed that it did not accept partition, the new Irish Free State responded by a series of draconian emergency laws which gave military tribunals the power to preside over capital crimes. The Irish Constitution which replaced the Constitution of the Irish Free State in 1937 provided for more entrenched systems of judicial review but nevertheless enabled special non-jury courts

[12] See Agreement reached in the multi-party negotiations (1998), *Rights, Safeguards and Equality of Opportunity*, paras 9, 10. On the charter of rights, see S Egan and R Murray, 'A Charter of Rights for the Island of Ireland: An Unknown Quantity in the Good Friday/Belfast Agreement' (2007) 56 *International and Comparative Law Quarterly* 297.

[13] For commentary on the differing degrees of commitment which Member States have given towards taking account of the Strasbourg jurisprudence, see Lord Kerr, 'The Conversation between Strasbourg and National Courts—Dialogue or Dictation?' (2009) 44 *Irish Jurist* 1.

[14] See generally U Kilkenny (ed), *ECHR and Irish Law* (Bristol, Jordans, 2004); F De Londras and C Kelly, *The European Convention on Human Rights Act: Operation, Impact and Analysis* (Dublin, Round Hall, 2010).

to be established by legislation. The Offences Against the State Act 1939 made provision for a Special Criminal Court to come into operation when the government deemed the ordinary courts inadequate to secure the effective administration of justice. Proclamations to this effect were duly made for prolonged periods of time—1939–46, 1961–62 and 1972 to the present day.[15] In the north, the old Stormont government's response to security threats was to resort to detention without any form of trial at all under the infamous Special Powers legislation. After direct rule was imposed by the British government in 1972 non-jury Diplock courts were introduced into the criminal justice system. These remain in existence.[16]

The result of security legislation spill-over into the Irish criminal justice systems was that for many years law was, as Kilcommins and Vaughan have put it, 'in the shadow of the gunman'.[17] Powers designed purely for security were invested in the ordinary criminal justice agencies, which were given the responsibility for countering the security threat in a process known in the north as 'criminalisation'.[18] The 'rule of law' was replaced all too often by 'rule by law'.[19] For example, robberies entirely unconnected with political violence were dealt with in Northern Ireland's non-jury Diplock courts.[20] As well as ordinary criminal cases being brought into the emergency fold, powers justified by the emergency came to be used throughout the criminal justice system. Curtailment of the right of silence, for example, was justified by the need to break 'the wall of silence' confronting the police when questioning paramilitary suspects, but it was applied across the board in all criminal cases.[21] Kilcommins and Vaughan remark that similar trends were to be seen in the south. Confronted with rising crime, authorities in the 1980s turned to legislation and practices intended for use against terrorist activity, such as emergency arrest powers for ordinary crime, the retention of the non-jury Special Criminal Court for non-paramilitary activities, seizing

[15] F Davis, *The History and Development of the Special Criminal Court, 1922–2005* (Dublin, Four Courts Press, 2007).

[16] For a comprehensive analysis of the procedures adopted by the Diplock courts, see J Jackson and S Doran, *Judge without Jury: Diplock Trials in the Adversary System* (Oxford, OUP, 1995).

[17] S Kilcommins and B Vaughan, *Terrorism, Rights and the Rule of Law* (Cullompton, Willan, 2008).

[18] For accounts of the 'criminalisation' strategy, see K Boyle, T Hadden and P Hillyard, *Ten Years On in Northern Ireland: The legal control of political violence* (London, Cobden Trust, 1980) 78–9; T Hadden, K Boyle and Campbell, 'Emergency Law in Northern Ireland: The Context' in A Jennings (ed), *Justice under Fire: The Abuse of Civil Liberties in Northern Ireland* (London, Pluto, 1988) 8–10.

[19] Kilcommins and Vaughan, above n 17.

[20] J Jackson and S Doran, 'Diplock and the Presumption Against Jury Trial' [1992] *Criminal Law Review* 755.

[21] See Arts 3–6 of the Criminal Evidence (NI) Order 1988. For detailed analysis of these provisions, see J Jackson, 'Recent Developments in Criminal Evidence' (1989) 40 *Northern Ireland Legal Quarterly* 105.

criminal assets without requiring a conviction, and use of 'super-grass' testimony in the ordinary courts.

Another consequence of this security seepage into the criminal justice system was a deliberate flouting of the rule of law by security forces at critical times when the state was most under threat. This was most evident in the period during the 1970s in Northern Ireland when security forces resorted to heavy-handed interrogation techniques against suspects in order to obtain confessions,[22] but in the Republic of Ireland there is also evidence of malpractice by the Garda Siochána[23] in the course of criminal investigations, especially into organised crime. Cases have come to light involving threats made and inducements offered to suspects, false information being inserted into interview notes, and allegations of ill-treatment reported by the European Committee for the Prevention of Torture (CPT) after its visits to Ireland in 1993, 1998 and 2002.[24]

2. THE COMMON LAW APPROACH TOWARDS EXCLUSION OF EVIDENCE IN IRELAND

Reflecting the familiar common law approach towards improperly obtained evidence, Irish courts have traditionally excluded involuntary confessions but have otherwise adopted the inclusionary policy, encapsulated in Crompton J's dictum, that relevant evidence would still be admissible even if it had been stolen.[25] The voluntariness rule for confessions can be traced back to the eighteenth century, although it does not appear to have made its mark in Ireland until the beginning of the 1800s. There was considerable uncertainty at first about its application.[26] The exclusionary rule was originally justified on the ground of reliability, since an involuntary confession may not be true. It is only in more recent years that other rationales have been accepted, most noticeably that the rule is necessary to buttress

22 *Ireland v UK* (1978–80) 2 EHRR 25.

23 The national police force of Ireland, known as An Garda Siochána (Guard of the Peace), was established in 1922. See Lawlor, above n 3, 428–29.

24 See I O'Donnell, 'Preventing the Ill-Treatment of Detainees' (2003) 13 *Irish Criminal Law Journal* 2. In its latest report the CPT noted progress in reducing ill-treatment by police officers but also observed that allegations of ill-treatment nevertheless persist: *Report to the Government of Ireland on the visit to Ireland carried out by the European Committee for the Prevention of Torture and Inhuman or Degrading Treatment or Punishment (CPT) from 25 January to 5 February 2010*.

25 See also *Kuruma v R* [1955] AC 197 (PC).

26 This uncertainty ended in 1864 when a majority of 7 out of 11 judges of the Court for Crown Cases Reserved applied the test that had been applied in England, namely whether a confession has been obtained by a threat or promises held out or excited by a person in authority: see *R v Johnston* (1864) 15 ICLR 60, discussed in JD Jackson, 'In Defence of a Voluntariness Doctrine for Confessions: *The Queen* v *Johnston* Revisited' (1986) 21 *Irish Jurist* 208.

the privilege against self-incrimination, which requires that accused persons have a right to choose not to answer questions put by those in authority.[27] This rationale comes close to embracing the 'vindication of rights' rationale for excluding evidence (in this context, the right not to be compelled to answer questions). But reliability concerns better account for the more inclusionary approach adopted towards other evidence, proceeding on the assumption that criminal trials should focus on the probative value of the evidence against the accused. If it is relevant and reliable, probative evidence should be admitted.

Alongside the voluntariness rule, the Irish judges developed a number of rules, known as the 'Judges' Rules', governing the circumstances in which police officers could question a person and requiring cautions to be administered to suspects at particular stages of the criminal process. It is not entirely clear when exactly these Rules came to be applied in Ireland[28] and notably they did not have the force of law. The Irish courts followed the English practice of holding that a breach of the Rules does not result in the automatic exclusion of any subsequently obtained statement. Also like their English counterparts, the Irish judges insisted that they retained a discretion to exclude such evidence. Quite what the basis was for exercising this discretion remained obscure, however. It does not appear to have been invoked on any regular basis in favour of exclusion.[29]

In addition, the Irish courts on both sides of the border have from time to time recognised a general discretion to exclude evidence on grounds of unfairness,[30] although it is difficult to find examples outside the area of testimonial evidence where it has been exercised in favour of an accused.[31] A major stumbling-block has again been the lack of authoritative guidance as to how this discretion should be exercised.[32] We return to the concept of fairness below in the discussion of constitutional law and human rights in Sections 4 and 5 of this chapter.

The broadly inclusionary approach that the Irish courts have traditionally taken towards improperly obtained evidence was indicative of a 'hands

[27] See, eg, *State (McCarthy) v Lennon* [1936] IR 485.

[28] They have their origin in a request by the British Home Secretary to the judges of the King's Bench to draw up rules to clarify the circumstances as to when a caution was required when persons were being questioned by the police.

[29] McGrath comments that despite the statement of O'Higgins CJ in *People (DPP) v Farrell* [1978] IR 13, 21 that statements taken in breach of the Judges' Rules may only be admitted in 'exceptional circumstances' many cases appear to have been decided by reference to the test of whether the accused has suffered any prejudice by reason of the breach. See above n 6, 413.

[30] *AG v Durnan (No 2)* [1934] IR 540, 547, *R v Murphy* [1965] NI 138, 142–43.

[31] McGrath, above n 6, 362.

[32] Cf *R v Murphy* [1965] NI 138 (suggesting that a trial judge has a discretion to exclude unfairly obtained evidence) with the statement of Lowry LCJ in *R v Corey* [1979] NI 49, 50, implying that the discretion is limited to situations where the probative value of the evidence is limited.

off' attitude by judges in criminal trials towards lapses in proper pre-trial procedures, even when officials' misconduct breached the judges' own rules. It is an example of what Ashworth has described as the 'separation thesis'[33] whereby, according to Lord Diplock in *R v Sang*,[34] trial judges are concerned only with how evidence is used by the prosecution at the trial, not with the 'separate' question of how the evidence was procured in the first place. The House of Lords in *Sang* appeared to limit discretionary exclusion to confessions or other incriminating evidence obtained from the accused, apparently a concession to the voluntariness principle and the privilege against self-incrimination. But with this limited exception, the general view was that redress for pre-trial wrongs done to the accused must be sought elsewhere than in the criminal trial. Linked to this is the view that it is not the court's function to supervise the conduct of the police, a proposition somewhat contradicted by the fact that earlier in the century the judges were asked to promulgate Judges' Rules which appeared to do precisely that.

3. EVOLUTION OF A LEGISLATIVE FRAMEWORK IN NORTHERN IRELAND

Lord Diplock played his own part in reinforcing the separation thesis in the Northern Ireland context after direct rule was imposed in 1972 when he led a commission of inquiry proposing changes to the administration of justice in order to deal more effectively with terrorism without using internment under the Special Powers Act.[35] Whilst the Diplock Commission is best known for inaugurating a system of non-jury trial (known colloquially as the 'Diplock courts'), it was also particularly concerned that the Northern Irish courts' strict application of the voluntariness rule was hampering the course of justice and pressurising the authorities to resort to administrative detention in preference to trial.

Throughout the course of the twentieth century the Irish courts had extended the meaning of voluntariness beyond its core common law meaning of the absence of threats or promises, so that the category of 'involuntary' statements now included confessions obtained under oppression where the accused's free will had been sapped.[36] This extension had particular salience

[33] See Ashworth, Chapter 6 in this volume; A Ashworth, 'Exploring the Integrity Principle in Evidence and Procedure' in P Mirfield and R Smith (eds), *Essays for Colin Tapper* (London, LexisNexis, 2003) 107, 112–13.

[34] [1980] AC 402, 437.

[35] Report of the Commission to Consider Legal Procedures to Deal with Terrorist Activities in Northern Ireland, Cmnd 5185 (London, HMSO, 1972).

[36] See *People (DPP) v Madden* [1977] IR 336 following developments in England and Wales such as *R v Priestley* (1966) 51 Cr App R 1.

for the conditions under which questioning was conducted in the detention centres set up to obtain information from terrorist suspects at the height of the Northern Ireland Troubles. In one case in 1972 an accused's confession was excluded specifically on the ground of 'oppression' when an accused had been made to sit on a chair in a cubicle for long periods between questioning in circumstances that sapped 'that free will which must exist before a confession is voluntary'.[37] Shortly afterwards the courts went further in excluding confessions where the conduct of the officers who questioned the accused was not in itself oppressive, but the entire interrogation set-up was regarded as operating oppressively, in the sense that it was systematically intended to obtain information from persons who would otherwise have been unwilling to give it.[38] Though in *Sang* Lord Diplock was later to concede that the privilege against self-incrimination should qualify the general separation thesis, in the Northern Ireland context he appeared to criticise the Northern Irish courts for taking such a strict approach towards the admissibility of confessions in the prevailing emergency situation.

The solution recommended by the Commission was to lower the 'voluntariness' threshold for the admissibility of confessions in cases scheduled to be tried without a jury under the emergency legislation to the minimal standard of an absence of torture, inhuman or degrading treatment (tracking ECHR Article 3). The Diplock Commission reasoned that, while courts could not act upon evidence obtained by unconscionable means such as torture, inhuman or degrading treatment, they should be much less solicitous in regulating how evidence was obtained in the emergency situation that existed at the time. This recommendation was enacted in section 6 of the Northern Ireland (Emergency Provisions) Act 1973. Section 6 immediately posed a dilemma for the courts when confronted with confessions that would have been involuntary at common law but did not fall foul of the Article 3 baseline. The courts responded to the new admissibility regime by re-affirming that there is always a discretion to exclude admissible evidence in the interests of justice and by suggesting that the involuntariness of the confession at common law could be a ground for the exercise of the discretion to exclude confessions.[39] At the same time the courts recognised that they must not subvert the will of Parliament by re-introducing the voluntariness standard by the backdoor, and consequently felt constrained about excluding confessions just because they would have been inadmissible at common law.[40] This sent a clear signal that only the gravest forms of ill-treatment would be likely to result in exclusion, effectively giving a green light to more coercive interrogation than was acceptable at common law.

[37] *R v Gargan* [1972] NIJB (May).
[38] *R v Flynn and Leonard* [1972] NIJB (May).
[39] *R v Tohill* [1974] NIJB (March).
[40] See *R v McCormick and others* [1977] NI 105; *R v Milne* [1978] NI 110.

Much damage was done to the reputation of the Diplock courts when they convicted large numbers of accused on the basis of confessions obtained through dubious means.[41]

In recent years, a more robust attitude has been taken by the Northern Irish courts towards the exclusion of evidence. Although the Diplock courts have remained on the statute book,[42] increasingly cases now proceed under the Police and Criminal Evidence Act regime, known (as in England and Wales) as PACE, which was introduced in Northern Ireland for ordinary criminal cases in 1989. Article 74 of the Police and Criminal Evidence (NI) Order 1988 replaced the voluntariness standard with a rule which requires confessions to be excluded where they have been obtained by oppression or in circumstances which might make them unreliable. But it was Article 76 of the 1988 Order that was to have a more profound effect on the discretionary exclusion of evidence. Paralleling section 78 of PACE in England and Wales, Article 76 directs that courts may reject evidence on which the prosecution proposes to rely

> if it appears to the court that, having regard to all the circumstances, including the circumstances in which the evidence was obtained, the admission of the evidence would have such an adverse effect on the fairness of the proceedings that the court ought not to admit it.

This approach was extended to Diplock cases in 2003, after the ECHR Article 3-derived standard for the admissibility of confessions was finally abandoned.[43]

Article 76 of PACE appeared to disavow the 'separation' thesis in accepting that the circumstances in which evidence was obtained were relevant to the fairness of the proceedings as a whole. One of the difficulties with such a test, however, is that the Northern Irish courts, like their English counterparts, have been unable to provide a clear and convincing rationale to explain when evidence should be excluded where there has been some unfairness or impropriety in the investigative process. Where there have been 'significant or substantial' breaches of the Codes of Practice under PACE (which replaced the old Judges' Rules), the courts have indicated that this should trigger exclusion.[44] Yet this begs the question as to which breaches are 'significant and substantial'. Dennis suggests that the concept of 'fairness' has not been analysed in any depth in any of the cases. The

[41] See Jackson and Doran, above n 16, ch 2.

[42] Justice and Security (NI) Act 2007, ss 1–9. On 5 April 2011 the Secretary of State for Northern Ireland announced that the non-jury trial provisions of the Act would be extended for a further two years: www.nio.gov.uk\\written-ministerial-statement-two-year-extension-to-non-jury-trial-system\\media-detail.htm%3fnewsID=17705.

[43] Terrorism Act 2000 (Cessation of Effect of Section 76) Order 2002.

[44] See eg *R v Absolam* (1988) 88 Cr App R 332; *R v Keenan* [1990] 2 QB 54; *R v Walsh* (1990) 91 Cr App R 161.

concept of 'fairness' would seem wide enough to accommodate any of the goals commonly advanced for the exclusionary rule, including reliability, eliminating prejudice, vindicating the accused's rights, promoting police propriety and protecting the integrity of the criminal process.[45]

4. THE IRISH REPUBLIC'S CONSTITUTIONAL APPROACH TO EXCLUDING EVIDENCE

Although the courts in the Republic of Ireland continue to apply the common law rule of voluntariness in relation to confessions, they have increasingly developed an explicitly constitutional approach towards the exclusion of evidence. An exclusionary rule in relation to improperly obtained evidence was first established in *People (AG) v O'Brien*[46] in the mid-1960s. The Court of Criminal Appeal followed the traditional common law approach, citing *Kuruma v R*,[47] that evidence which is relevant and admissible should not be excluded because of some technical defect in a search warrant. The Supreme Court, however, made a distinction between illegally obtained evidence which could be excluded by the court considering all the circumstances of the case, including the nature and extent of illegality, and *unconstitutionally* obtained evidence which must be automatically excluded where there has been a 'deliberate and conscious violation' of the constitutional rights of the accused. The only occasion when such evidence could be admitted, at the discretion of the trial judge, was if extraordinary, excusing circumstances existed. Examples given by Walsh J of such circumstances were the imminent destruction of vital evidence, the need to rescue a victim in peril or a search without a warrant incidental to and contemporaneous with a lawful arrest. In *O'Brien*, the District Court issued a search warrant that mistakenly included the wrong address. It was argued that a search of a dwelling under the supposed authority of this warrant breached Article 40.5 of the Irish Constitution, which guarantees the inviolability of residential premises, and that evidence produced from this unconstitutional search ought consequently to be excluded. But the Court held that the mistake was a pure oversight. There had been no 'deliberate and conscious violation' of the accused's rights and the trial judge had rightly exercised his discretion in favour of admitting the evidence.

Reference to a 'deliberate and conscious' breach of the rights of the accused is suggestive of a deterrence rationale for exclusion. However, Walsh J distinguished between (mere) illegally obtained evidence and unconstitutionally obtained evidence on the express ground that the vindication

[45] Dennis, above n 6, 8.14, 317–18.
[46] [1965] IR 142.
[47] [1955] AC 197 (PC).

and protection of constitutional rights was of fundamental importance for all courts established under the Irish Constitution.[48] An exclusionary rule based on vindication of rights should logically be applied once the breach has occurred, and should not be dependent on the state of mind of the person who breached the rights.[49] This discrepancy came to light in later cases where there was considerable judicial disagreement as to whether a deliberate and conscious violation need relate only to investigative misconduct, objectively assessed, or whether the official in question had to be *consciously* and *deliberately* violating a constitutional right.[50]

The issue fell for authoritative determination in *People (DPP) v Kenny*,[51] where a majority of the Irish Supreme Court considered that the knowledge of the actor who breaches the constitutional rights of the suspect is irrelevant to the question of admission or exclusion of the evidence. In this case the accused was charged with possession of drugs found during a search of his home. The search warrant was invalidly issued (due to insufficient information) but the police officer executing the warrant had no knowledge that it was invalid and indeed could not have known that it was invalid. For the majority of the Supreme Court, however, it was enough that the officer had nevertheless acted consciously and deliberately in violating a constitutional right, namely Article 40.5 of the Constitution. The Court took a strongly protectionist stance towards constitutional rights. According to Chief Justice Finlay CJ, a rule of absolute protection would provide far more security for the personal, constitutional rights of citizens than would an exclusionary rule based solely on the concept of deterrence. The Chief Justice accepted that such a rule could create problems in the criminal trial, since it meant that evidence of immense probative value may have to be excluded. However:

> the detection of crime and the conviction of the guilty, no matter how important they may be to the ordering of society, cannot ... outweigh the unambiguously expressed constitutional obligation 'as far as practicable to defend and vindicate the personal rights of the citizen'.[52]

It followed that evidence obtained by invasion of the constitutional personal rights of a citizen must be excluded unless the act constituting the breach was committed unintentionally or accidentally, or the court is satisfied that there

[48] [1965] IR 142, 170.

[49] See McGrath, above n 6, 339, 340.

[50] See eg, *People v Madden* [1977] IR 336; *People (DPP) v Shaw* [1982] IR 1 (Griffin J and Walsh J disagreeing) and *People (DDP) v Healy* [1990] 2 IR 73 (Griffin J and Finlay CJ disagreeing with McCarthy J). For further discussion of *O'Brien* and its progeny, see P O'Connor, 'The Admissibility of Unconstitutionally Obtained Evidence' (1982) 17 *Irish Jurist* 257.

[51] [1990] 2 IR 110.

[52] [1990] 2 IR 131, quoting Art 40.3.1 of the Irish Constitution.

were extraordinary, excusing circumstances which justify the admission of evidence at the court's discretion. The court held that the evidence should not have been admitted because the officer's ignorance that he was invading a constitutional right did not alter the fact that his actions in obtaining the warrant and forcibly entering the dwelling were neither unintentional nor accidental.

This strict exclusionary approach has generally been followed by the Irish courts in the years since *Kenny*.[53] Although there must be a causal link between the breach of constitutional rights and subsequently obtained evidence, the rule has had an expanding remit over the years. It has extended to include confessional evidence as well as real evidence,[54] and it has grown in practical significance as the accused's constitutional rights in the pre-trial process have themselves expanded to include not only the right to bodily integrity, the right to inviolability of the dwelling, the right to privacy and the right to liberty but also most recently the right to legal advice and the right to silence.[55] Numerous Irish commentators have supported the vindication principle as the most defensible basis for the exclusionary rule, given the state's obligation to vindicate the constitutional rights of the accused.[56] The rule also sends out a powerful message to police investigators to be more respectful of constitutional rights.[57] However, the rule has attracted criticism in recent years.

In 2006 the Minister for Justice set up the Balance in the Criminal Law Review Group to consider various criminal justice issues, including the operation and extent of the exclusionary rule. Consistent with the theme of 'balance' prevalent in many current criminal justice debates, a majority of Group members considered that one of the central problems of the exclusionary rule was that it did not allow for the trial judge to weigh the public interest in ensuring that constitutional rights are protected by agents of the state as against the public interest in ensuring both that crime is detected and punished and that victims' constitutional rights are vindicated by the courts.[58] The Group quoted approvingly from the New Zealand Court of Appeal in *R v Shaheed*,[59] which concluded that the proper approach based

[53] For commentary see F Martin, 'The Rationale of the Exclusionary Rule of Evidence Revisited' (1992) 2 *Irish Criminal Law Journal* 1; D McGrath, 'The Exclusionary Rule in Respect of Unconstitutionally Obtained Evidence' (2004) 11 *Dublin University Law Journal* 108; Y Daly, 'Unconstitutionally Obtained Evidence in Ireland: Protectionism, Deterrence and the Winds of Change' (2009) 19 *Irish Criminal Law Journal* 40; T O'Malley, *The Criminal Process* (Dublin, Round Hall, 2009) 744–51.

[54] See *People (DPP) v Lynch* [1982] IR 64 rejecting views expressed in *Shaw* that the ratio in *O'Brien* extended only to illegally obtained real evidence. For discussion see O'Connor, above n 50, 276–78.

[55] *People (DPP) v Healy* [1990] 2 IR 73.

[56] See, eg, McGrath, above n 6, 343. See also O'Connor, above n 50.

[57] O'Malley, above n 53, 756, 758.

[58] See *Final Report of the Balance in the Criminal Law Review Group*, 15 March 2007, 155: www.justice.ie/en/JELR/BalanceRpt.pdf/Files/BalanceRpt.pdf.

[59] *R v Shaheed* [2002] 2 NZLR 377.

on the experience of other jurisdictions is to conduct a balancing exercise in which the fact that there has been a breach of the accused's guaranteed right is an important but not determinative factor. This, it was said, still does justice to the purpose of the exclusionary rule, which is to ensure that the fundamental rights of the citizen are vindicated, that the courts are not seen to condone breaches of such rights, and that the police and other state agencies respect them. These aims could be achieved without adopting an absolute rule, which is unable to cater for situations where the breach is outside the control of state officials.

The chairman of the Group (now a High Court judge, Hogan J) expressed a dissenting view. He argued that only mandatory exclusion could do justice to the need to respect the rule of law and vindicate the fundamental freedoms enshrined in the constitution. As soon as one admits that evidence obtained in breach of rights is the subject of an exclusionary discretion rather than an absolute rule of exclusion, one moves away from a pure vindication rationale.[60] The balancing approach applied in *Shaheed* and followed also by the Canadian Supreme Court in relation to evidence whose admission would 'bring the administration of justice into disrepute' under section 24(2) of the Canadian Charter of Rights and Freedoms, is grounded in the judicial integrity rationale rather than in the vindication of rights.[61]

The Group considered that the Irish Supreme Court should be given an opportunity to revisit its jurisprudence by invoking the provisions of the Criminal Justice Act 2006 enabling the prosecution to mount appeals on points of law. The opportunity almost arose in *DPP (Walsh) v Cash*,[62] where the High Court reluctantly accepted the authority of the rule stated in *Kenny*, whilst contrasting it with the more flexible balancing approach previously approved in *O'Brien*. In any event, the rule did not extend to the facts of the instant case, since the evidence that the defendant sought to have excluded in *Cash*—incriminating fingerprints taken from the accused following his arrest—was not itself unlawfully obtained, although the defendant's initial arrest was based on another set of prints whose lawful provenance could not be established. The Supreme Court restricted itself to upholding the trial judge's conclusion that the rule in *Kenny* was not concerned with the lawful provenance of evidence used to ground suspicion, and expressed no view on the merits of the exclusionary rule itself.

One of the difficulties with the strict approach taken in *Kenny* is that it does not fully explain why the accused's constitutional rights need to be vindicated by means of exclusion of evidence. Commentators have been critical of the vindication rationale on the ground that the discovery of cogent evidence, albeit it by unconstitutional or illegal means, engages the

[60] Dennis, above n 6, 3.44, 105–06.
[61] See *R v Grant* [2009] 2 SCR 353.
[62] [2007] IEHC 108, [2010] IESC 1.

state's crime control responsibilities in new ways and the harm created by the violation should not be assuaged by a refusal to act upon these responsibilities.[63] Other avenues of redress are available for remedying the violation, including traditional tortious remedies. The fact that these remedies have not proved particularly effective is an argument for strengthening them or finding alternative, more effective remedies which do not interfere with the adjudicative function of the criminal trial. In recent times much greater effort has been devoted to improving police complaints mechanisms. Both north and south of the border bodies such as the Police Ombudsman and Police Ombudsman Commission have been established to investigate complaints much more effectively. These other remedies do not answer the argument that the overriding obligation on the state to vindicate rights imposes a mandatory constitutional duty on criminal courts to exclude evidence obtained in violation of the accused's procedural rights.[64] But one might still ask: why does vindication of the accused's constitutional rights have to take pride of place over the constitutional rights of others?

It is not entirely accurate to characterise the exclusionary rule developed by the Irish courts as 'absolute'. In *O'Brien* the Supreme Court acknowledged that evidence could be admitted on a discretionary basis where the trial judge is satisfied that there are 'extraordinary excusing circumstances' condoning violation of the accused's rights. Recall that the examples given by Walsh J were: preventing imminent destruction of vital evidence; rescuing a victim in peril; and warrantless searches incidental to, but not justified by, a lawful arrest. Although these examples were meant to be illustrative and not exhaustive, the courts have been reluctant to expand Walsh J's categories and have specifically ruled out any general public interest excuse such as the need to investigate criminal offences expeditiously. It has been pointed out that, with the exception of the imminent destruction of evidence, the examples do not cover circumstances truly *excusing* breaches of constitutional rights, but rather pre-empt breaches occurring in the first place. The distinction is exemplified by *People (DPP) v Shaw*,[65] where the question arose whether it was reasonable to delay bringing the appellant promptly before the District Court to be charged in order to question him about the disappearance of two girls, given that the police were under a duty to protect the constitutional right to life of the missing girls. Similarly it may be argued that police entry into an occupied dwelling in order to prevent a mob burning down the house and imperilling the lives of its occupants forecloses any question of their breaching the constitutional inviolability of the dwelling.[66] Whether the need to rescue a victim in peril

[63] Roberts and Zuckerman, above n 6.
[64] O'Connor, above n 50, 290.
[65] [1982] 1 IR 1.
[66] *DPP v Delaney* [1997] 3 IR 453.

is considered an excusing or justifying circumstance, in each of these cases the threat to life was considered imminent and it would seem that the courts will not lightly balance away the constitutional rights of the accused in the interests of saving life.

What about the need to protect the constitutional rights of persons other than the accused in non-life-threatening situations? What if as a result of a breach of the accused's constitutional rights, entering his house unconstitutionally for example, the prosecution is prevented from using physical evidence found in his house indicating that he was the perpetrator of domestic violence? Should the abuser be allowed to go free, perhaps to perpetrate further acts of violence against a victim who was too afraid to testify against him? And what should happen where state officials have breached the constitutional rights of third parties in order to obtain evidence against the accused? Is evidentiary exclusion only appropriate where *the accused's* constitutional rights have been violated? Furthermore, although constitutional rights are often broadly framed, what if deplorable treatment fails to engage any constitutional rights—where, for example, the accused has been entrapped by state officials into committing an offence?[67] Why, in other words, must exclusion always be the approach when an accused's constitutional rights are breached but not where the accused has been treated in a fashion which might be regarded as legally or morally more egregious?

These questions raise doubts about a principle that elevates the need to vindicate the constitutional rights of the accused above all other considerations. The difficulty with the balancing approach favoured by the Balance in the Criminal Law Group, on the other hand, is that it does not indicate how exactly the different interests are to be balanced. The Irish Supreme Court has adopted a balancing approach towards dealing with evidence that has been obtained improperly but without constitutional defect. In *O'Brien*, for example, Kingsmill Moore J observed that it is desirable in the public interest that crime should be detected and punished and it is also desirable that individuals should not be subjected to 'illegal or inquisitorial' methods of investigation. In every case a determination has to be made by the trial judge as to 'whether the public interest is best served by the admission or exclusion of the evidence'.[68] The various factors to be taken into account, according to Kingsmill Moore J, included the nature and extent of the illegality, whether it was intentional or unintentional, and if intentional whether it was the result of an ad hoc decision or a settled and deliberate policy.[69] Another factor again was whether there were circumstances of urgency or emergency which provided some excuse for the violation.

[67] See A Duff, L Farmer, S Marshall and V Tadros, *The Trial on Trial: Volume 3* (Oxford, Hart Publishing, 2007) 232.

[68] *People v O'Brien* [1965] IR 142, 160.

[69] Ibid.

All these factors go towards assessing the seriousness of the breach. But what if strong probative prosecution evidence is obtained in consequence of a grave breach where a serious crime is under investigation and there is a clear public interest in the guilty being convicted? The difficulty here is that whatever the judge does may appear to flout the public interest: exclusion may lead to the acquittal of a potentially dangerous offender; admission may encourage the perception that the courts do not take official illegality seriously enough.[70]

A third approach that has been suggested by the Irish Supreme Court, but rarely relied on in view of the available alternatives, is to invoke the general constitutional commitment to fairness as a ground for exclusion. Once again, the Court has not indicated how exactly constitutional fairness should operate in this context. In *People (DPP) v Shaw* Griffin J said that a technically voluntary confession might nonetheless be excluded if it was obtained in circumstances falling below the required standards of fairness.[71] This takes us back to the threshold difficulty with the PACE exclusionary discretion now applied by courts in Northern Ireland: how is such an indeterminate and open-ended standard to be applied in practice? The concept of fairness assumes centre stage in relation to the 'right to a fair trial' guaranteed by ECHR Article 6. Yet as we shall see in the next Section, the ECtHR has been neither entirely clear nor consistent in explaining how domestic courts should respond to evidence obtained in breach of a Convention right or otherwise improperly obtained.

5. THE EUROPEAN COURT'S HUMAN RIGHTS APPROACH

Irish courts north and south are now required to take account of relevant ECHR jurisprudence. In its early decisions, the ECtHR appeared to treat issues of admissibility as matters for national courts. In *Schenk v Switzerland*,[72] for example, the Court disavowed any authority to determine, as a matter of principle, whether particular types of evidence—for example, unlawfully obtained evidence—may be admissible. Subsequent decisions have sometimes been more overtly interventionist.[73] In attempting to unravel the ECtHR's approach toward questions of evidence, common

[70] See Ashworth, above n 33, 107, 120.

[71] [1982] IR 1, 61.

[72] (1991) 13 EHRR 242.

[73] In respect of unlawfully obtained evidence, see, eg, *Jalloh v Germany* (2007) 44 EHRR 32 discussed below, evidence obtained under powers of compulsory questioning, see, eg, *Saunders v United Kingdom* (1977) 23 EHRR 313, evidence obtained by entrapment, see, eg, *Teixeira de Castro v Portugal* (1999) 28 EHRR 101, anonymous witnesses, see, eg, *Van Mechelen v Netherlands* (1998) 25 EHRR 647 and hearsay see, eg, *Unterpertinger v Austria* (1991) 13 EHRR 175. Also see the contributions to this volume by Ashworth and Roberts.

lawyers need to rid themselves of common law concepts such as admissibility which have never been invoked by the ECtHR and focus instead, as the ECtHR has done, on what types of evidence can legitimately be used as a foundation for conviction.[74] Here we can see in some of its recent case law that the use of evidence obtained in breach of certain ECHR standards, particularly breaches of Article 3, is considered to violate the ECHR, not because its use would breach these standards per se but because they would breach the accused's right to a fair trial.

The ECtHR has stated in several recent judgments that the use in criminal proceedings of evidence obtained by torture will automatically violate the right to a fair trial, irrespective of the probative value of such evidence (although the Court has been more equivocal about whether evidence obtained by inhuman and degrading treatment automatically breaches Article 6).[75] The linkage between a breach of Article 3 and Article 6 suggests that the rationale for not using such evidence does not rest on vindicating the right under Article 3 not to be subjected to torture or to inhuman or degrading treatment, but rather on some Article 6-derived notion of trial unfairness, although the Court has been less than clear about the precise nature of this putative connection.

According to the ECtHR in *Levinta v Moldova*, 'incriminating evidence—whether in the form of a confession or real evidence—obtained as a result of acts of violence or brutality or other forms of conduct which can be characterised as torture—should never be relied on as proof of the victim's guilt, irrespective of its probative value'.[76] Any other conclusion would only serve to legitimate indirectly morally reprehensible conduct which the authors of Article 3 of the ECHR sought to proscribe. This line of argument suggests that the judicial legitimacy or integrity rationale was being invoked to justify exclusion. An appeal to the legitimacy or integrity of the proceedings was central to Judge Bratza's concurring judgment in *Jalloh v Germany*, as the following passage demonstrates:

> [T]he use of evidence obtained by treatment violating the fundamental values enshrined in Article 3 appears to me to offend against the whole concept of a fair trial, even if the admission of such evidence is not—as it was in the present case—decisive in securing a conviction. As in the case of coerced confessions, it is the offensiveness to civilised values of fairness and the detrimental effect on the integrity of the judicial process, as much as the unreliability of any evidence which may be obtained, which lies at the heart of the objection to its use.[77]

[74] For comprehensive analysis, see J Jackson and S Summers, *The Internationalisation of Criminal Evidence* (Cambridge, CUP, 2012) ch 6.

[75] See *Jalloh v Germany* (2007) 44 EHRR 32; *Harutyunyan v Armenia* (2009) 49 EHRR 9; *Levinta v Moldova* (2011) 52 EHRR 40.

[76] *Levinta v Moldova* (2011) 52 EHRR 40, [63].

[77] (2007) 44 EHRR 32, [O-I8].

Judge Bratza was here distancing himself from the majority's apparent suggestion that, where evidence was obtained by ill-treatment falling short of torture (such as forcible regurgitation of drugs from the applicant's stomach in the instant case), it would not automatically be excluded. Rather, contextual factors such as the seriousness of the offence, the weight of the evidence and the opportunity to challenge its admission at trial could all be taken into account, according to the majority in *Jalloh*.

In relation to breaches of Article 8 of the Convention, the Strasbourg Court has categorically rejected the proposition that the use of evidence obtained in violation of an accused's privacy rights will necessarily result in a violation of Article 6. The view expressed by some dissenting judges, that fairness presupposes respect for lawfulness and thus, *a fortiori*, respect for the rights guaranteed by the Convention which it is the Court's task to supervise,[78] has failed to persuade the majority. The Court has also refused to use the language of 'morally reprehensible conduct' in relation to such breaches, no doubt because it is hard to view all breaches of Article 8 in this light. Article 8(2) permits public authorities to interfere with the right to respect for private life, providing such interference is in accordance with law, proportionate and carried out in pursuit of a legitimate aim—one of which is the prevention of crime and disorder. Where, as in *Khan v United Kingdom*,[79] the authorities resort to surveillance techniques in order to prevent crime and the sole ground for the Article 8 breach is the absence of statutory authority for the interference with the applicant's right to respect for privacy, it seems excessive, if not perverse, to castigate police conduct as 'morally reprehensible.'

Given its express rejection of the 'rights thesis' and its implicit rejection of the 'moral legitimacy' thesis, however, the ECtHR has been less than helpful in indicating how domestic courts should relate breaches of Article 8 to the right to a fair trial. In *Khan*, where admissions obtained by means of a covert listening device constituted the only evidence against the applicant, the Court found no violation of Article 6 because, in particular, the applicant had had the opportunity to challenge the evidence in domestic criminal proceedings and the national court had a discretion to exclude it on grounds of unfairness. The unwillingness of the ECtHR to prescribe how domestic courts should exercise their discretion is understandable, but insofar as *Khan* suggests that the opportunity to challenge the evidence at trial is enough to withstand any breach of Article 6, it may be argued that the Strasbourg Court came too close to embracing the discredited 'separation thesis', implying that how the evidence was obtained is immaterial to its admissibility.

[78] See the opinions of the dissenting judges in *Bykov v Russia* App No 4378/02 (2009). Also see Ashworth, Chapter 6 in this volume.

[79] (2001) 31 EHRR 45.

One factor that the Court has emphasised is the need for investigative methods to respect the privilege against self-incrimination. In a number of decisions the Court has considered that the right of silence and the right not to incriminate oneself are primarily designed to protect against the obtaining of evidence through methods of coercion or oppression in defiance of the will of the accused.[80] In *Allan v United Kingdom* the Court held that the application of these principles 'is not confined to cases where duress has been brought to bear on the accused' but also included cases where 'the will of the accused has been directly overborne in some way'.[81] In this case the applicant's freedom to choose whether to speak to the police or not had been effectively undermined by subterfuge after he had unequivocally invoked his right to silence. Bugging the applicant's cell in breach of Article 8 and adducing covert recordings of the applicant's conversations would not have violated Article 6: the decisive factor was that the police had also planted an informant in the applicant's cell in a blatant attempt to undermine his privilege against self-incrimination. The Court's emphasis on the applicant's freedom of choice is reminiscent of the common law's voluntariness standard for the admissibility of confessions, yet in this case the applicant had not been physically coerced or induced into making damaging admissions but had instead been tricked into self-incrimination. It is hard to see why the use of an informant was deemed to defy the applicant's free will, whilst the use of a covert recording device to trick him into making statements was apparently regarded as consistent with the voluntary exercise of his ECHR rights.

Allan v UK can be compared with the more recent case of *Bykov v Russia*,[82] where the applicant was also tricked into making a confession as a result of a covert operation. The ECtHR distinguished this case from *Allan* on the ground that the applicant had not been officially questioned or charged with a criminal offence. But how does a suspect's formal procedural status affect the voluntariness of his statements? The difficulty in appealing to concepts such as 'voluntariness' or the privilege against self-incrimination as benchmarks for determining the admissibility of evidence is that these concepts are themselves barely less vague, 'fuzzy' or contested than general standards of 'fairness'. Arguably, any statement made in a custodial setting in response to police questioning techniques is coercive and saps the suspect's free will, but is this to say that such statements should never be used against an accused?

[80] See, eg, *John Murray v United Kingdom* (1996) 22 EHRR 29, [45]; *Saunders v United Kingdom* (1997) 23 EHRR 313, [68]–[69]; *Serves v France* (1999) 28 EHRR 265, [46]; *Heaney and McGuinness v Ireland* (2001) 33 EHRR 12, [40].

[81] (2003) 36 EHRR 143, [50].

[82] Application No 4378/02 (2009) ECtHR.

In this way, the Strasbourg Court's human rights-orientated approach to improperly obtained evidence seems to replicate the indeterminacy of the PACE exclusionary discretion in Northern Ireland, discussed in Section 3 of this chapter. It would be possible for the Court to adopt an overtly protectionist stance, linking fairness to the need to vindicate the accused's substantive rights, as the Irish courts have done in interpreting constitutional rights. But the ECtHR has declined to go down this road. As we noted in Section 4's discussion of the Irish constitutional context, this kind of protectionism tends indiscriminately to prioritise the accused's rights over other substantive rights, not least victims' constitutional rights to personal security. The ECtHR has inclined towards theories of judicial legitimacy as a basis for refusing to act on evidence obtained in breach of the Convention. When courts act on evidence obtained by torture, inhuman or degrading treatment, they may appear to legitimise the use of such methods and damage their own moral integrity. This judicial integrity rationale can be reinforced by disciplinary or deterrence considerations, especially if exclusion is linked to bad faith or intentional breaches of procedural standards.

Ultimately, however, cases such as *Jalloh v Germany* fail to send out a clear signal in relation to inhuman and degrading treatment, implying instead that reliance on evidence obtained by such impermissible methods may not be enough to render a criminal trial automatically unfair. This grates against the absolute terms in which the ECtHR has prohibited the use of torture, inhuman or degrading treatment whatever the justification. Thus, in *Gäfgen v Germany*,[83] the Court reaffirmed that the prohibition on ill-treatment of a person in order to extract information from him applies even in the event of a public emergency threatening the life of the nation and irrespective of the authorities' motivations, be it to save a person's life or to further criminal investigations. But the Court immediately clouded its strong moral message by drawing a distinction between real evidence obtained directly from ill-treatment violating Article 3 and the *indirect* evidential fruits of such violations. Whilst recognising a strong presumption favouring exclusion in either scenario, the Court found no violation on the facts of *Gäfgen* because the applicant had made a fresh confession at trial and the impugned items of evidence were merely incidental in securing the applicant's conviction. However, if the impugned evidence was instrumental in leading to other evidence which was used to convict the accused, one might think that the decisive evidence was tainted by its direct association with the impugned evidence; and that reliance on the decisive evidence consequently polluted the moral legitimacy of the trial.

[83] (2009) 48 EHRR 13; affirmed by the Grand Chamber of the ECtHR in *Gäfgen v Germany* (2011) 52 EHRR 1.

CONCLUSION—LINKING IMPROPRIETY, EXCLUSION AND THE RIGHT TO A FAIR TRIAL

Through contextual analysis of Irish legal experiences, north and south, this chapter has endeavoured to shed fresh comparative light on common law approaches to improperly obtained evidence. The traditional disinclination of courts in Northern Ireland to exclude improperly obtained evidence appeared at times to license a disregard for human rights in a period of acute political and social conflict. However, neither the constitutional approach adopted in the Republic of Ireland nor the human rights approach required by Strasbourg provides an entirely convincing rationale for excluding evidence. The constitutional approach does not explain why vindication of the accused's constitutional rights has to be found by means of excluding evidence at the accused's trial or, indeed, why a fair trial demands such exclusion. But neither does the discretionary approach favoured by Strasbourg explain in what circumstances the exclusion of evidence would be justified and why a court's reliance on improperly obtained evidence violates the fairness of the proceedings.

Gäfgen exposes the limitations of appeals to moral legitimacy as the animating rationale for excluding tainted evidence, when this is tied to an elastic notion of 'reprehensible conduct'. Even in relation to evidence obtained through inhuman or degrading treatment there is disagreement within the Court as to whether its use automatically violates the accused's fair trial right. We have seen that neither violations of Article 8 nor police deception are necessarily so morally reprehensible as to lead to a breach of Article 6. Are we then to say that evidence obtained improperly or unlawfully or in breach of an ECHR right should be admissible at trial provided there has been no morally reprehensible conduct on the part of the authorities? This might give a green light to breaches of the Convention and other acts of illegality. But once the force of the moral legitimacy rationale is blunted, we are once more bereft of any determinate criterion for distinguishing between forms of illegality or impropriety that should trigger evidentiary exclusion and procedural irregularities that are more appropriately remedied in other ways. Progress towards greater clarity will require more sustained focus on the principles of fairness that underlie a fair trial and a clearer link between the use of such evidence at trial and the fairness of the proceedings. How, in other words, does the impropriety or the breach of the right impact on the fair trial rights of the accused?

Summers argues that the fair trial rights should be seen as institutional rather than personal in nature, in that they provide institutional support for accused persons to challenge the case against them.[84] The ECtHR

[84] S Summers, *Fair Trials: The European Criminal Procedural Tradition and the European Court of Human Rights* (Oxford, Hart Publishing, 2007).

has arguably embraced this notion in its development of the principles of adversarial procedure and the equality of arms.[85] But instead of limiting the application of such principles to the trial stage, it is important that these principles are elucidated and upheld in the pre-trial phase of proceedings as well. The Court has begun to do this in certain recent decisions such as *Salduz v Turkey*,[86] where the importance of access to legal advice when a suspect is first questioned by the police was asserted. This example illustrates a more general proposition. Instead of focusing exclusively on whether the accused was able to challenge improperly obtained evidence at his or her trial, courts should also consider whether the impugned evidence has undermined the ability of the accused to challenge evidence in the pre-trial phases of investigation. Resort to torture or to inhuman or degrading treatment in order to obtain evidence necessarily undermines the opportunity of those charged with a criminal offence to make a properly informed answer to the allegations against them. Any ill-treatment that is used to obtain evidence—whether it be real evidence (as in *Jalloh*) or testimonial statements—arguably undermines the defence right to answer charges in a fair, adversarial setting. Equally, the improper denial of legal advice or deliberately misleading accused persons about the evidence against them undermines their opportunity to make an informed answer to allegations. When the prosecuting authorities attempt to use evidence obtained by these improper means, and irrespective of its reliability, they impinge on the defence's right to answer allegations in an informed manner. It is no use saying that the defence can always challenge the probative value of the evidence at trial; by using the evidence against the accused to build the prosecution case the damage to the accused's adversarial rights in the pre-trial phase of the proceedings has already been done.

The ECtHR's decision in *Allan v United Kingdom* might be reassessed in this light. Ignoring the Court's own preoccupation with the suspect's freedom of choice, the conclusion reached in *Allan* might be justified not so much because the authorities violated the privilege against self-incrimination but more because the suspect was not afforded the institutional safeguards designed to facilitate his informed participation in the criminal process. Similarly, in evaluating the fairness of evidence obtained by covert surveillance (as in *Khan*), the focus might shift from analysing the quality of any breaches of an applicant's substantive rights to privacy to asking whether the prosecution's reliance on evidence obtained by such methods has deprived the accused of a fair opportunity to answer allegations promptly and effectively.

[85] See also JD Jackson, 'The Effect of Human Rights on Criminal Evidentiary Processes: Towards Convergence, Divergence or Realignment?' (2005) 68 *Modern Law Review* 737.

[86] (2009) 49 EHRR 19.

We saw in Section 3 of this chapter how the strict 'separatist' philosophy embraced by the Northern Ireland courts in the 1970s undermined the legitimacy of verdicts resulting from overtly coercive interrogation techniques. Beyond condemning police violence, however, there is room for argument as to how far the admission of improperly obtained evidence undermines the legitimacy of criminal adjudication. The strict exclusionary approach towards evidence obtained in breach of the accused's constitutional rights adopted by the Irish courts appears to overcompensate. Without doubting for one moment the importance of vindicating the accused's constitutional rights, the public interest arguably demands that probative evidence should still be admissible in a criminal trial, even if rights were violated to obtain it. The remedy of evidentiary exclusion should be reserved for cases in which investigative techniques have undermined the accused's rights to participate effectively in the proceedings; in other words, to evidence which is incompatible with the accused's right to a fair trial. All other rights violations should also be redressed, but not necessarily within the context of criminal trial proceedings and not by excluding probative evidence.

6

The Exclusion of Evidence Obtained by Violating a Fundamental Right: Pragmatism Before Principle in the Strasbourg Jurisprudence

ANDREW ASHWORTH

INTRODUCTION

EVIDENCE SCHOLARS HAVE long discussed the normative (and empirical) arguments relating to the admissibility of improperly obtained evidence. This chapter focuses on two aspects of this debate—the narrower issue of the admissibility of evidence obtained by the violation of a fundamental or human right, and the contribution of the European Court of Human Rights in Strasbourg on this issue. It will be argued that the Court has begun to move away from some basic doctrines of European human rights law, and that some of its recent pronouncements in criminal cases raise questions about the fundamental structure of the European Convention on Human Rights, notably in relation to the fair trial right in Article 6. Two particular aspects of the interpretation of Article 6 are questioned: first, to what extent should 'public interest' factors be relevant in determining whether the right to a fair trial under Article 6 has been violated? Secondly, under what circumstances, if any, should the use of evidence obtained through violation of another Convention right render a trial unfair under Article 6?

Section 1 of this chapter prepares the ground for this enquiry, by setting out the overarching structure of the ECHR. Section 2 considers the general approach to the fair trial right in Article 6 and summarises some of the 'public interest' arguments that were advanced in the late 1990s. Section 3 examines the way in which, in more recent cases, the Court has begun to cite the public interest in prosecutions for serious crime as a reason for taking a different approach. In Section 4 the Court's approach to Article 3 (prohibiting torture and inhuman or degrading treatment) is set out as a basis for Section 5's examination of the Court's approach to the interaction between Articles 3 and 6. Finally, Section 6 turns to the question of the interaction between Article 8 (right to respect for private life) and Article 6, and exposes weaknesses in the Court's judgments, both in terms of their internal coherence and in relation to the normative structure of the Convention.

1. THE STRUCTURE OF THE CONVENTION

Although there is no official ranking of the rights set out in the ECHR, there are two reasons for concluding that the Convention does establish a hierarchy of rights. The first reason derives from Article 15 of the Convention, which singles out certain rights for special treatment:

Article 15

1. In time of war or other public emergency threatening the life of the nation any High Contracting Party may take measures derogating from its obligations under this Convention to the extent strictly required by the exigencies of the situation, provided that such measures are not inconsistent with its other obligations under international law.
2. No derogation from Article 2, except in relation to deaths resulting from lawful acts of war, or from Article 3, 4 (paragraph 1) and 7 shall be made under this provision.

The thrust of Article 15 is that it is permissible for states to derogate from various Convention rights if the conditions for doing so are satisfied, but that no derogation at all is allowed from four rights:

— the right to life (Article 2);
— the right not to be subjected to torture or inhuman or degrading treatment (Article 3);
— the right not to be subjected to forced labour (Article 4.1); and
— the right not to be subjected to retrospective criminal laws or penalties (Article 7).[1]

The fact that these provisions are singled out as non-derogable may be taken to indicate that they are the most basic of the fundamental rights in the Convention. Of course, their meaning and reach are subject to interpretation, and in that sense they are not *absolute* rights[2]—at least, not

[1] Other rights created by the Protocols also fall into this category, notably Protocol No 6, Article 1 (abolition of the death penalty) and Protocol No 7, Article 4 (right not to be tried or punished twice).

[2] The European Court of Human Rights has, however, sometimes expressed itself in such terms: eg 'the Court cannot but take note of the fact that Article 3 of the Convention enshrines an absolute right. Being absolute, there can be no weighing of other interests against it, such as the seriousness of the offence under investigation or the public interest in effective prosecution': *Gäfgen v Germany* (2011) 52 EHRR 1, [176].

until the scope of their application has been finally determined. It could be argued, *per contra*, that rights placed in the non-derogable category are not more fundamental than other rights, but are simply open to fewer weighty countervailing interests than other Convention rights. But, even if that were so, the effect of Article 15 is to place these rights in a specially protected category and, it is submitted, to indicate the beginnings of a hierarchy.

The second reason for discerning a hierarchy of rights in the Convention is the differing degree to which the Convention admits qualifications upon its rights. This is most evident in those Convention rights which might be termed qualified or prima facie rights—the right is declared, but with the rider that it may be interfered with on certain grounds, to the minimum extent possible. Such qualifications circumscribe the right to respect for private life (Article 8), the right to freedom of thought and religion (Article 9), the right to freedom of expression (Article 10), and the right to freedom of assembly and association (Article 11). All these qualified rights appear in the Convention with a second paragraph, which states that each right may be subject to interference if it can be established that this is 'necessary in a democratic society' on one of the stated grounds. The jurisprudence of the Strasbourg Court interprets the second paragraphs of these Articles in such a way as to impose meaningful limitations on state interference with the rights, chiefly through the doctrine of proportionality. This is a major point of differentiation between these qualified rights and the non-derogable rights mentioned earlier, since the latter leave no room for the operation of the proportionality doctrine.

Situated between non-derogable rights and qualified rights is an intermediate category, which is less easy to label and more difficult to assess. In the European Convention this category includes the right to liberty and security of the person (Article 5) and the right to a fair trial (Article 6). One might refer to the rights in this intermediate category as 'strong rights', to demonstrate that their strength is not qualified in the way that the rights in Articles 8–11 are qualified. Indeed, the rights in Articles 5 and 6 are not subject to any explicit qualification on the face of the Convention text. In the internal logic of the ECHR, this is a significant distinction. What it suggests is that, although strong rights are less fundamental than the non-derogable rights, any rationale for curtailing a strong right must, at a minimum, be more powerful than the kind of 'necessary in a democratic society' argument that is needed to establish the acceptability of interference with one of the qualified rights. Identifying the features and evaluating the cogency of arguments for curtailing the fair trial right in Article 6 are amongst this chapter's central objectives.

The analysis thus far points up a significant difference between the European Convention and some other statements of basic rights such as the Canadian Charter of Rights and Freedoms, section 1 of which states that the rights and freedoms are guaranteed 'subject only to such reasonable limits prescribed by law as can be demonstrably justified in a free and democratic society'. The presence of section 1 has engendered a nuanced Supreme Court jurisprudence on when and for what precise reasons various rights can be curtailed.[3] The important difference in the structure of the European Convention is that the equivalent of the 'free and democratic society' exception is found only in qualified rights such as those declared by Articles 8–11, and does not apply to all rights. Occasionally the Strasbourg Court has expressed itself as if the Canadian position also obtained under the ECHR. Consider, for example, the Strasbourg Court's much-cited statement in *Sporrong and Lönnroth v Sweden*:[4]

> [T]he Court must determine whether a fair balance was struck between the demands of the general interest of the community and the requirements of the protection of the individual's fundamental rights. The search for this balance is inherent in the whole of the Convention and is also reflected in the structure of Article 1.[5]

The first part of the final sentence is an exaggeration. It cannot seriously be suggested that when determining whether there has been a breach of Article 2 (right to life) or Article 3 (no torture etc) it is relevant to weigh the public interest against the individual's right. That kind of balancing has never formed part of Article 2 decisions, and we will see later in the chapter that it would be most unusual in relation to Article 3. The first part of the final sentence was clearly not intended as an authoritative pronouncement on the proper approach to all questions under the Convention, despite its unguarded terms. More accurate is the second part of the final sentence, which brings the issue specifically to the matter before the Court, the correct interpretation of Article 1 of Protocol 1's right to peaceful enjoyment of possessions. Indeed, it could be argued that the two sentences are commonly cited out of context, since the words immediately preceding the quoted passage are 'for the purposes of the latter provision', which is a direct reference to Article 1 of Protocol 1. It is submitted that *Sporrong and Lönnroth v Sweden* cannot be relied on as a basis for the argument that a court must balance the individual's right against the general interests of the community in any case arising under the Convention.

2. ESTABLISHING THE BASELINE APPROACH TO INTERPRETING ARTICLE 6

The preceding Section addressed the structure of the Convention and its logical implications for the broad 'public interest' arguments on which

[3] See eg DR Stuart, *Charter Justice in Canadian Criminal Law*, 3rd edn (Toronto, Carswell, 2001) ch 1.

[4] (1983) 5 EHRR 35.

[5] Ibid [69].

governments often wish to rely. We must now look more closely at how the Strasbourg Court has reacted to 'public interest' arguments when they have been advanced as possible limitations on rights that form part of the general right to a fair trial in criminal cases, safeguarded by Article 6. Three examples of the approach taken by the Court in the late 1990s may be offered to illustrate baseline interpretational principles.

First, in *Saunders v United Kingdom*[6] the question was whether the privilege against self-incrimination was an implied right, falling within the general right to a fair trial under Article 6. If so, did it apply in this case? And if it was in fact applicable, should it be upheld notwithstanding the pressing social importance of combating serious fraud? Having answered the first two questions in the affirmative, the Court squarely addressed the third question:

> [The Court] does not accept the Government's argument that the complexity of corporate fraud and the vital public interest in the investigation of such fraud and the punishment of those responsible could justify such a marked departure as that which occurred in the present case from one of the basic principles of a fair procedure... The general requirements of fairness contained in Article 6, including the right not to incriminate oneself, apply to criminal proceedings in respect of all types of criminal offences without distinction, from the most simple to the most complex. The public interest cannot be invoked to justify the use of answers compulsorily obtained in a non-judicial investigation to incriminate the accused during criminal proceedings.[7]

This is a broad statement of principle. It is not entirely unambiguous, since the Court did not offer a concluded opinion on 'whether the right not to incriminate oneself is absolute or whether infringements of it may be justified in particular circumstances'.[8] But its emphatic rejection of the government's 'public interest' argument is noteworthy.

Two years later the Court had to deal with its first case of entrapment in the context of attempts to bring drug-traffickers to justice. In *Teixeira de Castro v Portugal*[9] the Court found that the applicant had been entrapped by police officers into committing the offence of supplying drugs. One of the government's arguments was that proactive methods of law enforcement were vital in order to combat drug-trafficking. The Court's reply reaffirmed the primacy of fair trial rights:

> The use of undercover agents must be restricted and safeguards put in place even in cases concerning the fight against drug-trafficking. While the rise in organized crime undoubtedly requires that appropriate measures be taken, the right to a

[6] (1997) 23 EHRR 313.
[7] Ibid [74].
[8] Ibid.
[9] (1999) 28 EHRR 101. See also the Grand Chamber in *Ramanuaskas v Lithuania* (2010) 51 EHRR 303, discussed by Roberts, Chapter 7 in this volume.

> fair administration of justice nevertheless holds such a prominent place that it cannot be sacrificed for the sake of expedience. The general requirements of fairness embodied in Article 6 apply to proceedings concerning all types of criminal offence from the most straightforward to the most complex. The public interest cannot justify the use of evidence obtained as a result of police incitement.[10]

This is a clear and unqualified statement of the relationship between Article 6 and 'public interest' arguments. Fairness cannot be sacrificed to the public interest.

Perhaps the high-water mark of this approach was reached in *Heaney and McGuinness v Ireland*,[11] where the Court held that the applicants' convictions for the offence of failing to give an account of their movements at a particular time violated their privilege against self-incrimination. The offences formed part of Irish anti-terrorist law, and the government relied on this strong 'public interest' argument to claim that curtailment of the privilege against self-incrimination was justified in order to protect the public from terrorist attack. The Court's response was uncompromising:

> The Court... finds that the security and public order concerns of the Government cannot justify a provision which extinguishes the very essence of the applicants' right to silence and their right not to incriminate themselves guaranteed by Article 6(1) of the Convention.[12]

Once again, the Court re-affirmed the priority of the guarantees of a fair trial in Article 6 over arguments based on some asserted[13] public interest.

3. THE RESURGENCE OF 'PUBLIC INTEREST' ARGUMENTS?

In recent years the Court has been confronted with a range of different situations in which governments have pressed arguments based on the 'public interest'. Sometimes these arguments are phrased in terms of proportionality, a term with several applications in ECHR jurisprudence. As previously noted, the doctrine of proportionality is mostly relevant when determining the justification for interferences with qualified rights such as those in Articles 8–11.[14] Very few judgments on Articles 5 or 6 regard it as relevant.

[10] (1999) 28 EHRR 101, [36].
[11] (2000) 33 EHRR 12.
[12] Ibid [58].
[13] The word 'asserted' is interposed here, to make the point that any argument advanced under the title 'public interest' must be examined carefully, rather than simply accepted. For example, should a court require evidence that the existence of a particular law does advance the 'fight against terrorism', rather than simply accepting the government's assertion that it is necessary? Does the importance of preventing arbitrary uses of power by officials against citizens form part of the 'public interest' too?
[14] See further B Goold, L Lazarus and G Swiney, *Public Protection, Proportionality and the Search for Balance*, Ministry of Justice Research Series 10/07 (London, Ministry of Justice, 2007).

When the notion of proportionality is introduced into discussions of the limits of Article 6 rights, the purpose is typically to repackage 'public interest' arguments in a form cognisable to the Court. The very same arguments that were dismissed in the three judgments quoted in the previous Section are now being regarded by the Court as relevant in certain circumstances.

In *O'Halloran and Francis v United Kingdom*[15] the question was whether the offence in English law committed by a motorist who fails to comply with a police officer's request to identify the driver of a vehicle at a particular time is compatible with the privilege against self-incrimination guaranteed by Article 6. The Grand Chamber of the European Court of Human Rights answered affirmatively, concluding:

> Having regard to all the circumstances of the case, including the special nature of the regulatory regime at issue and the limited nature of the information sought by a notice under section 172 of the Road Traffic Act 1988, the Court considers that the essence of the applicants' right to remain silent and their privilege against self-incrimination has not been destroyed.[16]

This ruling marked a momentous departure in the Court's decision-making. In every previous case in which the applicant had been subjected to compulsion, the Court found that the privilege against self-incrimination had been violated. On this occasion, however, the Court felt that the circumstantial factors, taken in conjunction with the relatively low level of compulsion involved, were insufficient to 'destroy the very essence' of the privilege against self-incrimination. The facts taken to be significant were: (i) official compulsion was part of a regulatory scheme that fairly imposed obligations on vehicle owners and drivers in order to promote safety on the roads; (ii) the information required was simple, specific and restricted to naming the driver on a particular occasion, rather than demanding answers to wide-ranging questions; and (iii) the statutory offence in question was tempered by the safeguard of a due diligence defence, enabling a conscientious vehicle owner to avoid criminal liability. Enumeration of these factors implies a kind of proportionality judgement; and indeed the Court quoted extensively from the leading United Kingdom decision determining the compatibility of this offence with human rights principles, which emphasises the importance of achieving proportionality in balancing competing considerations.[17] The Court itself did not explicitly undertake a proportionality assessment, but its approach was redolent of proportionality balancing and its conclusion that the particular features of this offence did not destroy the essence of the applicants' rights is, in any event, difficult to accept. Legalised coercion was

[15] (2008) 46 EHRR 407.

[16] Ibid [62].

[17] *Brown v Stott* [2003] 1 AC 681 (PC). Lord Bingham's leading speech is quoted extensively by the Strasbourg Court in *O'Halloran and Francis v United Kingdom* (2008) 46 EHRR 407.

undoubtedly applied to the applicants, as the Court fully recognised. Rather than suggesting that the essence of the privilege against self-incrimination was preserved in this case, the Court ought to have admitted that its ultimate decision could only be defended as a pragmatic exception to the general principle.

More explicit resort to proportionality reasoning is evident in a second judgment of the Grand Chamber in *Jalloh v Germany*.[18] The police had been observing a drug dealer operating on the street. When they attempted to arrest him, the suspect swallowed the 'bubble' of drugs he had in his mouth. Later, at the police station, four police officers held Jalloh down while a doctor administered an emetic, after which he regurgitated one bubble of cocaine. The Grand Chamber considered the case under both Article 3 (torture and inhuman or degrading treatment) and Article 6 (privilege against self-incrimination). In relation to the second ground of complaint, the Court announced:

> In order to determine whether the applicant's right not to incriminate himself has been violated, the Court will have regard, in turn, to the following factors: the nature and degree of compulsion used to obtain the evidence; the weight of the public interest in the investigation and punishment of the offence at issue; and the use to which any material so obtained is put... As regards the weight of the public interest in using the evidence to secure the applicant's conviction, the Court observes that... the impugned measure targeted a street dealer who was offering drugs for sale on a comparably small scale and was finally given a six months' suspended prison sentence and probation. In the circumstances of the instant case, the public interest in securing the applicant's conviction could not justify recourse to such a grave interference with his physical and mental integrity.[19]

In this passage the Grand Chamber clearly stated that the weight of the public interest in prosecuting an offence is a relevant consideration. There was no reference to *Saunders v United Kingdom* or to any of the other judgments discussed in Section 2 of this chapter, which indicate that the seriousness of the crime has no bearing on whether or not there has been a violation of the privilege against self-incrimination. The implication of the Court's *Jalloh* ruling is apparently that, in cases where the offence is very serious (unlike small-time drug dealing), official compulsion might be permissible without violating the privilege against self-incrimination. If expressly adopted, this interpretation would mark a significant step away from the Court's older jurisprudence.

[18] (2007) 44 EHRR 32.
[19] Ibid [117] and [119].

4. THE INTERPRETATION OF ARTICLE 3

It would be an even greater divergence from previous jurisprudence if the Court applied similar reasoning to Article 3, the non-derogable right not to be subjected to torture or inhuman or degrading treatment. Yet the Grand Chamber in *Jalloh v Germany* held both that the actions of the police subjected the applicant to inhuman and degrading treatment, and that in some circumstances this might be justifiable on public interest grounds:

> The Court notes that drug trafficking is a serious offence. It is acutely aware of the problem confronting contracting states in their efforts to combat the harm caused to their societies through the supply of drugs. However, in the present case it was clear before the impugned measure was ordered that the street dealer on whom it was imposed had been storing drugs in his mouth and could not, therefore, have been offering drugs for sale on a large scale.[20]

In this passage the Court acknowledges, as it did in *Teixeira de Castro v Portugal*,[21] that states face real difficulties in combating drug-trafficking. But whereas in *Teixeira* the Court followed up with a robust affirmation of the importance of vindicating Convention rights, in *Jalloh* the Court seemed to accept that in a case (unlike the present) involving large-scale drug-trafficking, methods of law enforcement that would normally be regarded as amounting to inhuman or degrading treatment might be justifiable.

Subsequent judgments of the Court appear to have moved away from the *Jalloh* approach, albeit without overt explanation of the apparent change of tack. Thus, in *Saadi v Italy*[22] the Grand Chamber re-asserted the proposition that in determining whether Article 3 has been violated 'the conduct of the person concerned, however undesirable or dangerous, cannot be taken into account'.[23] In *Gäfgen v Germany*[24] the Grand Chamber was even more emphatic, holding that it was 'necessary to underline that... the prohibition on ill-treatment of a person applies irrespective of the conduct of the victim or the motivation of the authorities'. But in neither case was the conflicting analysis propounded in *Jalloh* even mentioned, much less disavowed.

[20] Ibid [71] and [77]. However, the Court's subsequent summary of the effect of Article 3, ibid [99], states that 'the Convention prohibits in absolute terms torture and inhuman or degrading treatment or punishment, irrespective of the victim's conduct', which seems inconsistent with its earlier treatment of the 'public interest' in this context.

[21] (1999) 28 EHRR 101.

[22] (2009) 49 EHRR 30.

[23] Ibid [138].

[24] (2011) 52 EHRR 1.

5. THE RELATIONSHIP BETWEEN ARTICLE 3 AND ARTICLE 6

If evidence obtained through a violation of Article 3 is relied upon by the prosecution in a subsequent criminal trial, does this have a bearing on whether or not the trial is 'fair' in accordance with Article 6? Only in recent years has this question been confronted by the Court, and the answer remains somewhat unclear. The Grand Chamber in *Jalloh v Germany* adopted a strong, though not unwavering, stance on the proper approach. Its general pronouncement was limited to cases of torture:

> Incriminating evidence—whether in the form of a confession or real evidence—obtained as a result of acts of violence or brutality or other forms of treatment which can be characterised as torture—should never be relied on as proof of the victim's guilt, irrespective of its probative value. Any other conclusion would only serve to legitimate indirectly the sort of morally reprehensible conduct which the authors of Article 3 of the Convention sought to proscribe or, as it was so well put in the US Supreme Court's judgment in the *Rochin* case, to 'afford brutality the cloak of law'.[25]

However, this statement of principle was carefully differentiated from the Court's subsequent assessment of the proper approach where official misconduct rises only to the level of inhuman and degrading treatment, which is also prohibited by Article 3. Thus, the Court stated:

> Although the treatment to which the applicant was subjected did not attract the special stigma reserved to acts of torture, it did attain in the circumstances the minimum level of severity covered by the ambit of the Article 3 prohibition. It cannot be excluded that on the facts of a particular case the use of evidence obtained by intentional acts of ill-treatment not amounting to torture will render the trial against the victim unfair irrespective of the seriousness of the offence allegedly committed, the weight attached to the evidence and the opportunities which the victim had to challenge its admission and use at his trial.[26]

The Court followed the 'it cannot be excluded that…' formulation with a statement that the relationship between Articles 3 and 6 is left open when the mistreatment does not attain the level of torture. Having ruled that to allow a court to act on evidence obtained by torture would indirectly legitimise morally reprehensible behaviour, the Strasbourg Court evidently did not think that the same reasoning applied to mere inhuman and degrading treatment, despite the fact that all these forms of mistreatment are encompassed in an Article that is often described as fundamental and enshrining 'one of the most fundamental values of democratic societies'.[27] Not only

[25] (2007) 44 EHRR 32, [105], quoting *Rochin v California*, 342 US 165 (1952).

[26] Ibid [106].

[27] Ibid [99]; cf the Court's judgment in *Ashot Harutyunyan v Armenia*, App No 34334/04, Judgment of 10 June 2010, which found a violation of Article 3 on the ground that keeping the applicant confined in a metal cage during his trial was 'degrading treatment', but which

that, but the Court envisaged that the question whether a trial is fair when the prosecution relies on evidence obtained through a violation of Article 3 depends to some extent on the seriousness of the offence charged. In this case the Court found that Jalloh's fair trial right was violated because he had been subjected to inhuman and degrading treatment and there was insufficient public interest in doing so when he was merely a street dealer. Again, this implies (contrary to the authorities reviewed in Section 4) that if the applicant had been charged with a serious offence the Court might have held that 'the public interest' justified reliance on evidence obtained through a breach of Article 3.

Most recently, in *Gäfgen v Germany*[28] the Grand Chamber noted that the Court's previous case-law had not authoritatively settled the question whether the prosecution's resort to evidence obtained through a violation of Article 3 rendered a trial unfair under Article 6. There was also said to be no clear consensus among Member States or other human rights monitoring institutions. The Grand Chamber continued:

> The Court is further aware of the different competing rights and interests at stake. On the one hand, the exclusion of—often reliable and compelling—real evidence at a criminal trial will hamper the effective prosecution of crime. There is no doubt that the victims of crime and their families as well as the public have an interest in the prosecution and punishment of criminals, and in the present case that interest was of high importance ... On the other hand, a defendant in criminal proceedings has the right to a fair trial, which may be called into question if domestic courts use evidence obtained as a result of a violation of the prohibition of inhuman treatment under Art. 3, one of the core and absolute rights guaranteed by the Convention. Indeed, there is also a vital public interest in preserving the integrity of the judicial process and thus the values of civilised societies founded upon the rule of law.[29]

As the first discussion of these issues by the Court, this analysis is welcome, albeit inconclusive on the facts of the instant case. The Grand Chamber went on to state that Article 6 is not an 'absolute right' (in contrast to Article 3, in the Court's terminology), and that in any event the issue would arise only if the infringing evidence 'had a bearing on the outcome of the

held that this (though 'unacceptable') did not render the trial unfair because it did not prevent him from communicating with his legal representatives and mounting a proper defence. The *Jalloh* approach accords with the special treatment of torture that is evident in Article 15 of the United Nations Convention against Torture and Other Cruel, Inhuman or Degrading Treatment or Punishment, and does so without giving a clear reason that applies to torture and not to inhuman and degrading treatment. See, to the same effect, *A v Secretary of State for the Home Department (No 2)* [2006] 2 AC 221, [2005] UKHL 71, [53] (Lord Bingham), discussed by Roberts, Chapter 7 in this volume.

[28] (2011) 52 EHRR 1.

[29] Ibid.

proceedings against the defendant',[30] which in *Gäfgen*, the majority held, it did not.

6. THE RELATIONSHIP BETWEEN ARTICLE 8 AND ARTICLE 6

Our focus now shifts from Article 3 issues to the related question of the relationship between Article 8 (the right to respect for private life) and Article 6. In this context the Strasbourg Court often repeats the assertion that the admissibility of evidence 'is primarily a matter for regulation under national law'.[31] The Court's invariable position has been that reliance by the prosecution on evidence obtained through a breach of the right to respect for private life in Article 8 does not automatically render a trial unfair under Article 6. Thus in *Khan v United Kingdom*[32] the Court found a violation of Article 8, because the use of listening devices by the British police was not sufficiently governed by a legal framework at that time,[33] but went on to hold that the prosecution's use of evidence obtained by this listening device as the central plank of its case did not infringe Article 6. So long as the defendant has the possibility of challenging the authenticity of the evidence, and so long as the trial court has a discretion to exclude unfair evidence, Article 6 may be satisfied. In a strong dissent, Judge Loucaides argued that such reasoning defies the structure of the Convention:

> This is the first case which comes before the Court where the only evidence against an accused in a criminal case, which also led to his conviction, was evidence secured in a manner contrary to the provisions of Article 8 of the Convention… I cannot accept that a trial can be fair, as required by Article 6, if a person's guilt for any offence is established through evidence obtained in breach of the human rights guaranteed by the Convention.

However, the Court has continued to adopt the same approach. It did so, for example, in *PG and JH v United Kingdom*,[34] but in her dissenting opinion Judge Tulkens again drew attention to wider questions of the structure of the Convention:

> I do not think that a trial can be described as 'fair' where evidence obtained in breach of a fundamental right guaranteed by the Convention has been admitted during that trial. As the Court has already had occasion to stress, the Convention

[30] Ibid [178].

[31] The most frequently cited judgment on this point is *Schenk v Switzerland* (1991) 13 EHRR 242. More recently, see *Heglas v Czech Republic* (2008) 48 EHRR 1018.

[32] (2000) 31 EHRR 1016.

[33] The legal framework put in place by the Regulation of Investigatory Powers Act 2000 (UK) has recently been held compatible with Article 8: *Kennedy v United Kingdom* (2011) 52 EHRR 207.

[34] [2002] *Criminal Law Review* 308.

> must be interpreted as a coherent whole... In concluding that there has not been a violation of Article 6, the Court renders Article 8 completely ineffective. The rights enshrined in the Convention cannot remain purely theoretical or virtual.

Recalling the obligation of Member States under Article 1 of the ECHR to ensure that all Articles of the Convention are safeguarded, both dissenting judges contended that the Convention's structure is undermined if a trial is conducted on the basis of evidence obtained through violation of any right enshrined in the Convention. Judge Tulkens went too far in asserting that Article 8 is rendered 'completely ineffective' if evidence stemming from its violation is subsequently admitted in a criminal trial. But it can surely be maintained that the admission of such evidence inevitably compromises the integrity of the judicial process. Thus it may be said that the dissentients base their preference for exclusion on a mixture of what Roberts and Zuckerman term the 'remedial theory' and the moral integrity principle.[35]

Assessing the merits of these competing arguments is complicated by the fact that the majority's position is so poorly reasoned. Whereas constitutional courts across the world have discussed the principles that should govern evidentiary exclusion,[36] often drawing upon an extensive academic literature, the majority judgments in the Strasbourg Court have failed to elaborate a principled foundation for their position. Those judgments are characterised by two features. First, there is implicit support for what I have elsewhere termed 'the separation thesis';[37] and secondly, the Court explicitly relies on a number of subsidiary arguments that seem ill-suited to the task at hand. Let us examine each of these features in turn.

The Court's prevailing view seems to be that violations of Article 8 and the requirements of Article 6 are two entirely separate matters. The appropriate way to deal with Article 8 breaches is to provide a remedy to the person whose right was infringed, a remedy that might be found in an award of damages or perhaps a reduction in sentence. But the criminal trial is something separate, with its own fairness criteria, and the questionable provenance of the prosecution's evidence will not compromise trial fairness just because other substantive human rights have been breached.

One immediate problem with the separation thesis is the Court's inconsistent adherence to it. Plainly the Court does not support the separation thesis in cases of torture contrary to Article 3. *Jalloh* held that reliance on evidence obtained by torture renders a trial unfair, on reasoning compatible

[35] P Roberts and A Zuckerman, *Criminal Evidence*, 2nd edn (Oxford, OUP, 2010) 181–91.

[36] For surveys, see C Bradley, 'The Emerging International Consensus as to Criminal Procedure Rules' (1993) 14 *Michigan Journal of International Law* 171; B Emmerson, A Ashworth and A Macdonald (eds), *Human Rights and Criminal Justice*, 2nd edn (London, Sweet & Maxwell, 2007) 587–97.

[37] A Ashworth, 'Exploring the Integrity Principle in Evidence and Procedure' in P Mirfield and R Smith (eds), *Essays for Colin Tapper* (London, Butterworths, 2003).

with the 'moral integrity' principle. However, the Court does not regard that reasoning as invariably applicable to inhuman and degrading treatment, nor does it apply that reasoning to evidence obtained through a breach of Article 8. For these Convention rights, the separation thesis prevails. Breaches of Article 8 or the 'inhuman or degrading treatment' limb of Article 3 are regarded as separate matters, calling for discrete remedies divorced from trial fairness. Thus in *Gäfgen v Germany* the Grand Chamber reasoned that the applicant would no longer be classified as a 'victim' for the purposes of ECHR Article 34 if the police officers who mistreated him had been punished appropriately (in fact the Grand Chamber regarded their sentences as 'almost token'), and if the applicant's Article 8-based action for damages against the police had been determined without delay.[38]

The two lines of argument that have been this chapter's central preoccupation came together in *Heglas v Czech Republic*,[39] where the unlawful recording of a conversation between the applicant and another person constituted a breach of Article 8. The Court then had to decide whether the prosecution's reliance on evidence obtained by that violation rendered unfair the applicant's subsequent trial for robbery with violence. Developing its previous case-law, the Court stated:

> The general requirements of fairness provided in Article 6 apply to all criminal proceedings, whatever the type of offence involved. It remains that, in order to determine whether the proceedings as a whole have been fair, the weight of the public interest in the prosecution of a particular offence and the sanction of its author may be taken into consideration and put in the balance with the interest of the individual that the incriminating evidence be gathered lawfully. However, the considerations of public interest cannot justify measures emptying the applicant's rights of defence of their very substance, including that of not contributing to its own incrimination guaranteed by Article 6 of the Convention.[40]

The Court went on to hold that the evidence obtained in violation of Article 8 was not crucial to the applicant's conviction on the facts of the instant case, adding, tellingly for our purposes:

> As regards the weight of the public interest in the use of that evidence to find the applicant guilty, the Court observes that the measure was aimed at the author of a serious offence which caused injuries to a third party, and who was finally imposed a nine-year sentence.[41]

These remarks expose the Court's position with clarity. They echo the finding in *Jalloh* that, torture excepted, the requirements of a fair trial are

[38] (2011) 52 EHRR 1.
[39] (2008) 48 EHRR 1018.
[40] Ibid [87], referring to *Heaney v Ireland* (2000) 33 EHRR 12.
[41] Ibid [91].

held to vary according to the seriousness of the offence with which the defendant is charged.

The key passage from *Heglas* was subsequently repeated by the Grand Chamber in *Bykov v Russia*.[42] The Court in *Bykov* was not called upon to interpret or apply *Heglas*, which raised a different issue, but the Grand Chamber cited the quoted passage without qualification.[43] However, as the majority position hardens, so the dissenting minority appears to grow in strength. In *Bykov* the Court was split 11 votes to 7 on this point,[44] with four other judges signing up to Judge Spielmann's forceful dissent, which in turn extended the reasoning of the dissents of Judge Loucaides in *Khan* and Judge Tulkens in *PG*. Two points in particular were emphasised. First, there is the substantive objection that a trial cannot be fair if evidence has been obtained by methods incompatible with the rule of law—a version of the integrity principle (albeit supported in the dissenting judgment on the basis of deterrent reasoning).[45] Secondly, there is the question of the Court's jurisdiction and authority within the Convention system. The Court has an obligation under ECHR Article 19 to ensure that Member States abide by the terms of the Convention, and judgments that allow a criminal court to proceed on the basis of evidence obtained by violating the Convention seemingly abdicate this responsibility. Both points, severally and in tandem, constitute a direct challenge to the majority's implicit 'separation thesis'. It is a challenge which the leading Strasbourg authorities have yet to grapple with directly,[46] let alone successfully.

What the majority judgments have done instead is to rely on two or three subsidiary arguments, none of which appears persuasive. First, ever since its tone-setting judgment in *Schenk v Switzerland*[47] the Court has maintained that Article 6 does not prescribe detailed rules governing the admissibility of evidence, which is primarily a matter for regulation by national law and not a question for the Court.[48] Whatever the accuracy of that statement (and it is qualified by the adverb 'primarily'), it should not be understood as suggesting that the Court has never found that the admission of certain

[42] [2010] *Criminal Law Review* 413. For critical assessment, see H Jung, 'Faires Verfahrung und menschenrechtswidrige Beweiserhebung Zugleich Besprechung von EGMR' (2009) 156 *Goltdammer's Archiv fur Strafrecht* 651.

[43] *Bykov v Russia*, [100].

[44] Cf *Gäfgen v Germany* (2011) 52 EHRR 1, where the vote was 11:6 on this issue.

[45] Judge Spielmann's main reason for holding the trial unfair contrary to Article 6 was a version of the integrity argument, stemming from the rule of law and respect for human rights; but he also mentioned the danger that, if such evidence was admissible at trial, the police may not be deterred from repeating their misconduct.

[46] Except in the context of Article 3, where the opposing positions were set out in *Gäfgen v Germany* (2011) 52 EHRR 1. Also see *Khan v United Kingdom* (2000) 31 EHRR 1016, [34], where the point is stated in relation to Article 8 but not pursued.

[47] (1991) 13 EHRR 242, [46].

[48] Repeated in most of the cases cited above, eg *Bykov v Russia* [2010] *Criminal Law Review* 413, [88].

evidence was inconsistent with the right to a fair trial under Article 6. This it has certainly done in entrapment cases,[49] and also, as we saw in Section 5 of this chapter, in cases where evidence has been obtained in breach of Article 3. So there is no general prohibition on the Court's finding that the admission of certain evidence breaches the right to a fair trial.

Secondly, the Court is fond of repeating that it is a central tenet of trial fairness that a defendant should have a full opportunity to challenge the authenticity of any evidence obtained through rights violations.[50] This may be true, but it is largely irrelevant in the present context, since Strasbourg applicants are not generally challenging the authenticity of evidence (which is often highly reliable) but the propriety of allowing a criminal conviction to rest on violations of human rights. Which brings us back to the dissentients' arguments, which remain unanswered by the majority.

Thirdly, the Court has occasionally mentioned that a trial may be fair overall if impugned evidence 'played a limited role in a complex body of evidence assessed by the court'.[51] However, it is debateable how much reliance the Court actually places on this consideration, since there are other cases where the impugned evidence has been the centrepiece of the prosecution's case and yet the Court has nevertheless found no breach of Article 6 in admitting it.[52] At any rate, all three reasons—viewed in isolation or taken together—plainly fall short of justifying the position adopted by the majority of the Strasbourg Court. Combined with the absence of any real discussion of the principles which ought to govern the admissibility of evidence obtained in violation of Convention rights, they mark out this line of cases as one of the least impressive areas of the Court's jurisprudence.

CONCLUSIONS AND QUESTIONS

Close reading of recent Strasbourg judgments demonstrates that the Court has failed to develop a consistent or persuasive position on the relationship between violations of Article 3 or Article 8 and the right to a fair trial guaranteed by Article 6. A Court that should shine as a beacon in international human rights litigation has lost its way. Strasbourg judgments in the first decade of the new century call into question the structure of the Convention and some of its hitherto established doctrines, and yet fail to offer convincing reasons—or, sometimes, any reasons—for doing so.

[49] Notably *Teixeira de Castro v Portugal* (1998) 28 EHRR 101, and *Ramanauskas v Lithuania* (2010) 51 EHRR 303.

[50] See *Khan v United Kingdom* (2000) 31 EHRR 1016, [38], citing *Schenk v Switzerland* (1991) 13 EHRR 242; also *Heglas v Czech Republic* (2008) 44 EHRR 1018, [86].

[51] *Bykov v Russia* [2010] *Criminal Law Review* 413, [103].

[52] *Khan v United Kingdom* (2000) 31 EHRR 1016, [37]; cf the puzzled observations in *Heglas v Czech Republic* (2008) 44 EHRR 1018, [86].

Article 3 of the ECHR has been hailed as enshrining 'one of the most fundamental values of democratic societies',[53] but can it really be so fundamental if Article 3 is severable down the middle, so that torture on the one hand, and inhuman or degrading treatment on the other, may have different implications for the fairness of trials? Or if there are circumstances in which the application of Article 3 depends on the seriousness of the offence allegedly committed by the defendant? Or if the prosecution's reliance on evidence obtained through violation of Article 3 is sometimes compatible with the right to a fair trial? The last point also carries over to the relationship between Article 8 and Article 6: if the prosecution adduces evidence obtained through a breach of the Article 8 right to respect for private life, does this have any implications for the fairness of the trial? Can the two issues really be treated as separate, as the Court implies (without spelling out the justifications), or should the Convention be read as a unified whole? Is the privilege against self-incrimination implicit in ECHR Article 6 applicable to all criminal cases, from trivial misdemeanours to the most heinous crimes, as the judgments of the 1990s maintained? Or is it a right that may give way to 'the public interest', ie to the seriousness of the offence being investigated?

The answers to these questions have immense implications for the future of human rights guarantees in criminal cases, and yet the Strasbourg Court has repeatedly failed to support its conclusions with adequate reasons, and inconsistencies have infiltrated its judgments. The absence of any sustained attention to underlying principles is thrown into sharp relief when set against a quite sophisticated scholarly debate, focused on reliability, rights protection, deterrence, and moral integrity as the four most prominent and elaborated rationales for excluding evidence. Dissenting voices in the Court have made some progress in that direction, but the overwhelming poverty of Strasbourg precedents breeds doubts about the structure of the Convention and enfeebles further jurisprudential development.

[53] *Jalloh v Germany* (2007) 44 EHRR 667, [99].

7

Normative Evolution in Evidentiary Exclusion: Coercion, Deception and the Right to a Fair Trial

PAUL ROBERTS*

INTRODUCTION: EVIDENCE BEYOND EPISTEMOLOGY

THE DISCIPLINARY FIELD traditionally known to common lawyers as the Law of Evidence is often regarded as essentially, if not exclusively, preoccupied with epistemic considerations. Nowadays the Law of Evidence is routinely associated with proof and truth, accurate fact-finding, convicting the guilty and acquitting the innocent. Bentham was the genius and pioneering advocate of an epistemic approach to English legal process, and his great project has been revived and extended by modern legal scholars, notably William Twining,[1] and contemporary neo-Benthamites like the philosopher Larry Laudan.[2] Echoes of Bentham's insistence on rational fact-finding uncluttered by doctrinal baroque regularly issue from the mouths of experienced judges and apex courts, including the House of

* Portions of this chapter were originally prepared for the Third Mini-Foro on *Exclusionary Rules in a Comparative Context*, hosted by the Instituto de Investigaciones Filosóficas, UNAM, in Mexico City in June 2008, with thanks to Larry Laudan for his invitation and generous hospitality; and something more closely resembling the final version was aired at the UNSW conference in April 2010. I received much helpful feedback from participants on both occasions. For incisive comments on successive drafts, I am particularly grateful to Ian Dennis, Dimitrios Giannoulopoulos, David Hamer, Jill Hunter, Alastair Mowbray and Mike Redmayne.

[1] W Twining, *Theories of Evidence: Bentham & Wigmore* (London, Weidenfeld & Nicolson, 1985); W Twining, *Rethinking Evidence*, 2nd edn (Cambridge, CUP, 2006).

[2] L Laudan, *Truth, Error and Criminal Law: An Essay in Legal Epistemology* (Cambridge, CUP, 2006).

Lords[3] and the UK Supreme Court.[4] 'Freedom of proof' is the order of the day.[5]

From an epistemic perspective, fairness-based exclusionary rules immediately appear problematic because they authorise, or possibly even require, that ex hypothesi relevant information should be withheld from the trier of fact. This is prima facie irrational: in Bentham's succinct aphorism, to exclude evidence is to exclude justice.[6] There are essentially two strategies for reclaiming fairness-based exclusionary rules for orthodox evidentiary theory. First, one might demonstrate that fairness-based exclusions, on closer analysis, actually serve epistemic objectives, thereby dissolving their apparent irrationality. Alternatively, one might treat fairness-based exclusions as exceptional deviations from the law's epistemological priorities, leaving the question of their contextual legitimacy to ad hoc rationalisations. This approach is reflected, for example, in Wigmore's designation of 'rules of extrinsic probative policy'[7] and in *Cross and Tapper*'s expanding discussion of 'judicial discretion' as the slightly shady alter-ego of authentic rules of evidence.[8]

Both strategies for coping with fairness-based exclusions, together with their associated conceptual taxonomies, involve distancing and silencing. Judicial 'discretion' is presumptively inferior to 'proper rules' in mainstream evidentiary analysis, and frequently attracts direct criticism.[9] If you believe that discretionary decision-making is euphemistic code for rulings by instinct and whim, more sophisticated jurisprudential reconstruction is pre-empted. Meanwhile, evidentiary rules characterised as 'extrinsic' are by express conceptual fiat banished from the core of legal analysis; at best a

[3] See, eg, *R v H* [1995] 2 AC 596, 613, per Lord Griffiths: 'Today with better educated and more literate juries the value of those old restrictive rules of evidence is being re-evaluated and many are being discarded or modified.... This seems to me to be a wholly desirable development of law'.

[4] Cf *R v Horncastle* [2010] 2 AC 373, [2009] UKSC 14, [18], [20], per Lord Phillips PSC: 'There are two principal objectives of a fair criminal trial. The first is that a defendant who is innocent should be acquitted. The second is that a defendant who is guilty should be convicted.... The basic principle is that only the "best" evidence is placed before the jury, that is, the evidence that is most likely to be reliable'.

[5] Theorists' questions, clarifications and objections notwithstanding: cf P Murphy, 'No Free Lunch, No Free Proof' (2010) 8 *Journal of International Criminal Justice* 539; W Twining, 'Freedom of Proof and the Reform of Criminal Evidence' (1997) 31 *Israel Law Review* 439; M Damaška, 'Free Proof and its Detractors' (1995) 43 *American Journal of Comparative Law* 343.

[6] *Rationale of Judicial Evidence* (1827), quoted by T Anderson, D Schum and W Twining, *Analysis of Evidence*, 2nd edn (Cambridge, CUP, 2005) 1.

[7] JH Wigmore, *A Treatise on the System of Evidence in Trials at Common Law* (Boston, Little, Brown & Co, 1904), §11, §1171 and §2175.

[8] C Tapper, *Cross & Tapper on Evidence*, 12th edn (Oxford, OUP, 2010) 191–215.

[9] Cf C Tapper, 'The Law of Evidence and the Rule of Law' (2009) 68 *Cambridge Law Journal* 67.

sideshow to the main event.[10] Predominantly epistemic conceptions of the Law of Evidence also tend to reinforce the awkward and often misleading conventional dichotomy in English criminal jurisprudence between 'evidence' and 'procedure'.[11]

This essay challenges these widespread disciplinary assumptions, extending an argument expounded by Adrian Zuckerman several decades ago. Zuckerman proposed 'an explanation of the existing law in terms of [judicial] discretion' and general principles.[12] Once we recognise evidence law for what it really is, Zuckerman insisted, we can grapple with the essential job of articulating normative standards to guide the exercise of judicial decision-making, mindful that 'the judicial task is a demanding one and that the trial judge is often called upon to make difficult assessments of competing considerations'.[13] Terminological confusions may be partly responsible for a certain amount of unfocused initial hostility towards Zuckerman's thesis. As English courts observe from time to time,[14] what we are really concerned with is wise and well-informed judicial *judgement* rather than free-floating 'discretion'.[15]

This chapter develops the thrust of Zuckerman's insight along three dimensions, using detailed illustrations of evidence obtained by coercion or deception. First, it highlights the importance of moral reasoning in the development and application of evidentiary principles, and—picking up on Zuckerman's remark about the demands of judging—illustrates some of the complexities[16] involved in translating moral reasoning at-large into its applied institutional derivative, criminal jurisprudence.[17] This is not to deny the centrality of epistemic considerations in criminal adjudication,

[10] Cf A Stein, *Foundations of Evidence Law* (Oxford, OUP, 2005) 1: '[R]ules that promote objectives intrinsic to fact-finding are the only ones that classify as genuinely evidential; rules furthering other objectives and values are evidence-related, but situated outside the domains of evidence law'.

[11] An argument developed in P Roberts, 'Groundwork for a Jurisprudence of Criminal Procedure' in RA Duff and SP Green (eds), *Philosophical Foundations of Criminal Law* (New York, OUP, 2011).

[12] AAS Zuckerman, *The Principles of Criminal Evidence* (Oxford, OUP, 1989) 11.

[13] Ibid 15.

[14] See, eg, *R v Millard* [2003] EWCA Crim 3629, [15], per Judge LJ: 'what is loosely described as the discretion… is in fact the judgment of the trial judge'; *R v Davis* [2009] 2 Cr App R 17, [2008] EWCA Crim 1156, [40]: 'The admission of evidence was not a matter of judicial discretion, but more properly an exercise of judgment'.

[15] For theoretical elucidation, see R Dworkin, *Taking Rights Seriously* (London, Duckworth, 1978) 31–9; R Pattenden, *Judicial Discretion and Criminal Litigation*, 2nd edn (Oxford, OUP, 1990); DJ Galligan, *Discretionary Powers: A Legal Study of Official Discretion* (Oxford, OUP, 1986) chs 1–2.

[16] The complexity theme is developed in P Roberts, 'Excluding Evidence as Protecting Constitutional or Human Rights' in J Roberts and L Zedner (eds), *Principles and Values in Criminal Law and Criminal Justice: Essays in Honour of Andrew Ashworth* (Oxford, OUP, 2012).

[17] For systematic application, see P Roberts and A Zuckerman, *Criminal Evidence*, 2nd edn (Oxford, OUP, 2010).

but rather to put them in their rightful place: they are neither the exclusive concern of criminal procedure law nor its overriding preoccupation.[18]

Secondly, this chapter takes up the book's central theme by exploring the growing impact of human rights norms on common law evidence, a development that was barely conceivable 20 years ago but which turns out to be highly congruent with Zuckerman's argument. The 'human rights revolution' has catalysed a strand of British Evidence scholarship, originally also pioneered by Andrew Ashworth[19] and Ian Dennis,[20] which places greater emphasis on normative moral reasoning, utilising—much debated—intermediary concepts such as 'judicial integrity' and the 'legitimacy of the verdict'.[21] What began as a subsidiary and somewhat submerged theme in British Evidence scholarship is now rapidly gaining recognition and new adherents, contributing powerful restatements of distinctive normative visions.[22]

Finally, a third dimension of my analysis is comparative and rather more tentative. The following pages contain further examples of migrating norms, transnational judicial 'conversations', and institutional pluralism and diversification (driven in particular by the expanding influence of the European Court of Human Rights), intimating another major shift in disciplinary thinking.[23] The Law of Evidence as common lawyers have traditionally conceived it is gradually evolving into an increasingly cosmopolitan jurisprudence of criminal procedure, in which overt moral reasoning and a diverse multiplicity of normative sources will become defining characteristics.

[18] This must be English law's worst kept secret, since it is hidden in plain sight: cf CrimPR 2010 (SI 2010/60), Rule 1.1. And see Roberts and Zuckerman, above n 17, 9–22.

[19] AJ Ashworth, 'Excluding Evidence as Protecting Rights' [1977] *Criminal Law Review* 723.

[20] IH Dennis, 'Reconstructing the Law of Criminal Evidence' [1989] *Current Legal Problems* 21; I Dennis, *The Law of Evidence*, 4th edn (London, Sweet & Maxwell, 2010).

[21] For further discussion, see Dennis, *The Law of Evidence*, above n 20, 49–59; A Ashworth, 'Exploring the Integrity Principle in Evidence and Procedure' in P Mirfield and R Smith (eds), *Essays for Colin Tapper* (Oxford, OUP, 2003); P Mirfield, *Silence, Confessions and Improperly Obtained Evidence* (Oxford, OUP, 1997) 23–28; AAS Zuckerman 'Illegally-Obtained Evidence—Discretion as a Guardian of Legitimacy' [1987] *Current Legal Problems* 55.

[22] See, eg, A Duff, L Farmer, S Marshall and V Tadros, *The Trial on Trial Volume Three: Towards a Normative Theory of the Criminal Trial* (Oxford, Hart Publishing, 2007); HL Ho, *A Philosophy of Evidence Law—Justice in the Search for Truth* (Oxford, OUP, 2008).

[23] Building on P Roberts, 'Rethinking the Law of Evidence: A Twenty-first Century Agenda for Teaching and Research' (2002) 55 *Current Legal Problems* 297; P Roberts, 'Faces of Justice Adrift? Damaska's Comparative Method and the Future of Common Law Evidence' in J Jackson, M Langer and P Tillers (eds), *Crime, Procedure and Evidence in A Comparative and International Context* (Oxford, Hart Publishing, 2008); and P Roberts and M Redmayne (eds), *Innovations in Evidence and Proof* (Oxford, Hart Publishing, 2007).

1. COERCION, DECEPTION, AND CRIMINAL ADJUDICATION'S EPISTEMIC ASPIRATIONS

Deception and coercion both relate to the criminal trial's epistemic aspirations in complex ways. People can be tricked into revealing the truth or caught out in a probative lie, such as a false alibi.[24] Deception is *sometimes* an effective investigative strategy for truth-finding. On other occasions, however, it may undermine trust in the veracity of a confession if it was procured through deception or coercion. This elementary point is most obvious in relation to confessions obtained by physical violence or extreme psychological pressure. Everyone is familiar with the idea that people can be tortured or frightened into making a false confession, and psychologists have documented the phenomenon.[25] Solzhenitsyn observes that prisoners' wills can be broken, and rapidly, through the use of entirely prosaic techniques such as sleep deprivation or being made to sit in a chair for days on end.[26] These truisms are well-entrenched in English law as a basis for excluding presumptively unreliable admissions and confessions.[27]

The epistemic connection between coercion and *truthful* revelations cannot be discounted, however. Many police forces and security services around the world are thought to employ torture routinely[28] and for a variety of purposes, some of which certainly include procuring reliable information. Judicial torture has been employed as an epistemic instrument in the past,[29] and the intelligence-gathering potential of coercive interrogation continues to be advocated on a cost/benefit analysis by certain governments and commentators.[30] There are conceivably limiting cases in which coercion—over and above that already implicit in custodial police detention—does not imperil truthfulness.[31] But there are always contingent

[24] See, eg, *Mawaz Khan and Amanat Khan v R* [1967] AC 454 (PC).

[25] GH Gudjonsson, *The Psychology of Interrogations and Confessions: A Handbook* (Chichester, Wiley, 2003); SM Kassin et al, 'Police-induced Confessions: Risk Factors and Recommendations' (2010) 34 *Law & Human Behavior* 3.

[26] AI Solzhenitsyn, *The Gulag Archipelago 1918–1956: An Experiment in Literary Investigation*, trans TP Whitney (New York, HarperCollins, 1973) Part 1, ch 3.

[27] Police and Criminal Evidence Act (PACE) 1984, s 76, superseded the common law voluntariness rule crystallised in its mature form by the Privy Council in *Ibrahim v R* [1914] AC 599. On the pre-PACE common law, see P Mirfield, *Confessions* (London, Sweet & Maxwell, 1985).

[28] See, eg, Amnesty International, *Take A Step to Stamp Out Torture* (London, AI Publications, 2000).

[29] JH Langbein, *Torture and the Law of Proof* (Chicago, University of Chicago Press, 1977); M Damaška, 'The Death of Legal Torture' (1978) 87 *Yale Law Journal* 860.

[30] See P Sands, *Torture Team* (London, Allen Lane, 2008); M Bagaric and J Clarke, 'Not Enough Official Torture in the World? The Circumstances in Which Torture is Morally Justifiable' (2005) 39 *University of San Francisco Law Review* 581.

[31] Consider the Russian police tactic of demanding suspects to confess their guilt before religious icons (an example I owe to my doctoral student, Olga Pleshkova). Cf the infamous 'Christian burial' speech in *Brewer v Williams*, 430 US 387 (1977).

complications. At some level, the intensity of pain or its fearful anticipation will outweigh competing motivations, including moral or religious scruple, for most people. Victims of extreme torture describe the experience in terms of complete loss of autonomy, personality and self.[32] A person can presumably be terrorised into saying just about anything, like Orwell's Winston Smith in Room 101.

The epistemic implications of deception are even denser and more contorted. Deception might be a good way of tricking offenders into giving themselves away and procuring reliable evidence of their guilt. In the classic police sting or eavesdropping operation, for example, the offender is blissfully ignorant of official involvement and neglects additional precautions to cover their tracks. The sting works best just insofar as the coercive pressures liable to undermine the epistemic integrity of custodial confessions are absent. English case-law offers memorable illustrations.[33] However, police deception might equally imperil the reliability of evidence.

Around the world, police officers resort to the same tried-and-tested ruses, unless required to abandon them by robust legal regulation. Suspects are told that it will be better for them to confess early and get it off their chests (a tactic also noted by Solzhenitsyn), which is a snare for those whose overwhelming immediate desire is to be released from police custody.[34] Incriminating evidence is manufactured, or its strength greatly exaggerated, extracting false confessions from fatalistic suspects.[35] In this way, deception may have epistemic consequences similar to physical and mental coercion—producing false positives as well as true positives. Other deceptive investigative tactics, such as encouraging rape complainants to 'text' their alleged assailants in hopes of eliciting admissions or incriminating guilty knowledge in reply,[36] may have somewhat unpredictable epistemic implications.[37] Outright police 'entrapment' raises further, more substantive issues. The burning question here is why the accused did what he did, not—or not only—whether there is reliable evidence to prove it. The legitimacy of entrapment, in other words, concerns the moral limits of the

[32] G Schwab, *Haunting Legacies: Violent Histories and Transgenerational Trauma* (New York, Columbia UP, 2010) ch 6.

[33] *R v Christou and Wright* (1992) 95 Cr App R 264 (CA); *R v Smurthwaite; R v Gill* (1994) 98 Cr App R 437, CA; *R v Bailey and Smith* (1993) 97 Cr App R 365 (CA).

[34] Cf 'The Out' dramatised by D Simon, *Homicide: A Year on the Killing Streets* (London, Hodder & Stoughton, 1992) 206–16.

[35] A Ashworth and M Redmayne, *The Criminal Process*, 4th edn (Oxford, OUP, 2010) 111. Cf *R v Mason* [1988] 1 WLR 139, 144 (CA).

[36] K Beaumont, 'Text Tactics in Rape Investigation—An Interview with Fred Ferguson' (2008) 172 *Justice of the Peace* 112. Also see *R v Jones (Ian)* [2008] QB 460, [2007] EWCA Crim 1118 (police officer posed as 12-year old girl in text-messages sent to a suspected paedophile).

[37] Another dubious scheme was exposed in *R v Colin Stagg*, ruling of Ognall J, Central Criminal Court, 14 September 1994, discussed by Roberts and Zuckerman, above n 17, 211–13.

criminal law and the political morality of policing; though, as we explore later in the chapter, it may also be conceptualised doctrinally as a consideration bearing on the fairness of trials.

It is tempting to imagine that the accused is either guilty or innocent, and knows it, so that the only real issue in criminal adjudication boils down to whether the accused decides to tell the truth, or not. But even if we focus reductively on exclusively epistemic considerations, the reality of criminal evidence and proof is far more complex, and precarious, than popular wisdom can conceive. Evidence is a constructive product and active achievement of criminal investigations and prosecutions.[38] Any information that a suspect divulges—or is said to have divulged—at any stage of the process will be interpreted in the light of investigators' stock of other knowledge and objectives and fitted into an appealing theory of the case. To the extent that coercion or deception is involved in these investigative processes, such tactics inevitably increase the ubiquitous institutional risks that information extracted from a suspect will be false, incomplete or prone to interpretative distortion.

2. COERCION BY TORTURE

Torture involves the most extreme variants of 'coercive' investigative measures. Whereas discussions in the past have featured hypothetical terrorists and 'ticking bomb' scenarios, post 9/11, real terrorists and exploded bombs have brought the evidentiary status of torture evidence into English courts.

A v Home Secretary (No 2)[39] involved conjoined appeals by 10 individuals who had been certified as threats to national security by the Home Secretary and detained without charge pursuant to (since repealed) provisions of the Anti-Terrorism, Crime and Security Act 2001. A person so certified could appeal to 'SIAC'—the Special Immigration Appeals Commission.[40] Lord Bingham formulated the precise question falling for determination by the appellate courts: '[M]ay the Special Immigration Appeals Commission... receive evidence which has or may have been procured by torture inflicted, in order to obtain

[38] See, eg, M McConville, A Sanders and R Leng, *The Case for the Prosecution* (London, Routledge, 1991); P Roberts, 'Science in the Criminal Process' (1994) 14 *Oxford Journal of Legal Studies* 469; A Sanders, 'Constructing the Case for the Prosecution' (1987) 14 *Journal of Law and Society* 229.

[39] *A v Secretary of State for the Home Department (No 2)* [2006] 2 AC 221, [2005] UKHL 71.

[40] Established by the Special Immigration Appeals Commission Act 1997. SIAC has special rules of evidence and operates in secret when dealing with particularly sensitive material. The 'open' parts of SIAC rulings can be accessed at the Commission's website, www.siac.tribunals.gov.uk/.

evidence, by officials of a foreign state without the complicity of the British authorities?'[41]

SIAC itself was prepared to hear such evidence, and this inclusionary approach was upheld by a 2-1 majority of the Court of Appeal.[42] But the House of Lords unanimously ruled that SIAC, as a court of law, could not receive foreign torture evidence, even if the Home Secretary was justified in taking such information into account in making the initial decision to certify a particular individual as a terrorist threat to national security. The Law Lords then split on the further issue of the burden and standard of proof. By four votes to three, the majority[43] held that alleged foreign torture evidence could be received by SIAC unless it had been established, on the balance of probabilities, that the information was tainted by torture. The minority, comprising the three most senior Law Lords, Lord Bingham, Lord Nicholls and Lord Hoffmann, insisted that SIAC should reject information alleged to be the fruits of torture unless the suspicion of torture could be rebutted on the balance of probabilities.[44]

(a) Rationalising Exclusion, Beyond Reliability

Arguments for excluding evidence obtained by torture grounded exclusively in considerations of reliability are instrumental and epistemic. Competing arguments appeal to intrinsic moral values, either as comprehensive alternative rationalisations for excluding torture evidence or as side-constraints on epistemic objectives. Appeals to intrinsic values are not self-evidently compelling—a point lost on some of their proponents. Critics might challenge the salience or weight of the values said to mandate exclusion, in light

[41] [2006] 2 AC 221, [1]. The extent of the British authorities' direct involvement or connivance in extraordinary rendition and systematic torture has since become a hotly debated issue: cf I Cobain, 'UK's Secret Policy on Torture Revealed', *The Guardian*, 5 August 2011. But it was accepted for the purposes of this litigation that the Home Secretary came to court with clean hands.

[42] [2005] 1 WLR 414, [2004] EWCA Civ 1123, discussed by R Pattenden, 'Admissibility in Criminal Proceedings of Third Party and Real Evidence Obtained by Methods Prohibited by UNCAT' (2006) 10 E & P 1.

[43] Lords Hope, Rodger, Carswell and Brown.

[44] Some commentators consider that the House of Lords' majority ruling on the burden and standard of proof effectively undid most of the good work achieved by their Lordships' unanimous condemnation of torture evidence: see, eg, MD Evans, '"All the Perfumes of Arabia": The House of Lords and "Foreign Torture Evidence"' (2006) 19 *Leiden Journal of International Law* 1125. Such criticisms, to my mind, fail to take into account the extent to which SIAC is an inquisitorial tribunal with its own probative responsibilities: cf *Othman (Jordan) v Secretary of State for the Home Department* [2008] EWCA Civ 290, [60]–[61]; *RB (Algeria) v Secretary of State for the Home Department* [2010] 2 AC 110, [260] (Lord Brown). But I cannot develop this argument here.

of their deeper philosophical commitments.[45] A more common reaction is that torture, though contrary to binding standards of humanity and decency, may still be *the lesser evil* all things considered, especially if the alternative might imply leaving dangerous individuals at large and unpunished for their crimes. Such arguments do not necessarily collapse into consequentialism, as is often mistakenly believed. Indeed, the possibility of genuine conflicts of values, rights or duties is categorically denied by classical Utilitarianism. Value-conflict is perforce a problem for deontologists.[46]

Articulated rationales for evidentiary exclusion often blend (and sometimes confuse) instrumental and intrinsic considerations, but it always promotes analytical clarity to try to distinguish between them and to assess their respective cogency and implications. In the context of criminal adjudication, clarity in articulating exclusionary rationales is a vital ingredient of transparency in first instance rulings, and essential for appellate tribunals laying down general guidance for trial judges to apply in future cases. Considerations of reliability, deterrence and intrinsic moral values were all canvassed in their Lordships' speeches in *A v Home Secretary (No 2)* as potential rationales for evidentiary exclusion.

The argument that torture evidence should be excluded because it is unreliable was propounded by Lord Carswell:

> The unreliability of such evidence is notorious: in most cases one cannot tell whether correct information has been wrung out of the victim of torture—which undoubtedly occurred distressingly often in Gestapo interrogations in occupied territories in the Second World War—or whether, as is frequently suspected, the victim has told the torturers what they want to hear in the hope of relieving his suffering. Reliable testimony of the latter comes from Senator John McCain of Arizona, who when tortured in Vietnam to provide the names of the members of his flight squadron, listed to his interrogators the offensive line of the Green Bay Packers football team, in his own words, 'knowing that providing them false information was sufficient to suspend the abuse': *Newsweek*, 2 November 2005.[47]

The contrary position, inferring a different lesson from mid-century experiences, was put by Lord Rodger:

> Information obtained by torture may be unreliable. But all too often it will be reliable and of value to the torturer and his masters. That is why torturers ply

[45] Classical utilitarians, for example, would subordinate considerations of humanity and decency to their overriding imperative of maximising aggregate social welfare ('utility'): see M Bagaric and J Clarke, 'Not Enough Official Torture in the World? The Circumstances in Which Torture is Morally Justifiable' (2005) 39 *University of San Francisco Law Review* 581; R Morgan, 'The Utilitarian Justification of Torture: Denial, Desert and Disinformation' (2000) 2 *Punishment & Society* 181; WL Twining and PE Twining, 'Bentham on Torture' (1973) 24 *Northern Ireland Legal Quarterly* 305.

[46] See, eg, M Stocker, *Plural and Conflicting Values* (Oxford, OUP, 1990); and specifically in relation to torture, MS Moore, 'Torture and the Balance of Evils' (1989) 23 *Israel Law Review* 280.

[47] [2006] 2 AC 221, [147].

> their trade. Sadly, the Gestapo rolled up resistance networks and wiped out their members on the basis of information extracted under torture. Hence operatives sent to occupied countries were given suicide pills to prevent them from succumbing to torture and revealing valuable information about their mission and their contacts.[48]

In the event, the empirical question of the reliability of information procured by torture did not need to be settled, because none of their Lordships regarded reliability as the controlling factor. As Lord Rodger continued, 'the torturer is abhorred as a *hostis humani generis* not because the information he produces may be unreliable but because of the barbaric means he uses to extract it'.[49]

The 'deterrence' rationale for evidentiary exclusion, which is influential in modern US criminal jurisprudence,[50] is instrumental and future-orientated, but predominantly non-epistemic. It posits that improperly obtained evidence must be rejected by the courts, irrespective of its reliability, in order to disincentivise officials from further law-breaking in future cases. A blanket policy of inadmissibility supposedly sends an unequivocal message to law enforcement officers that violating or 'bending' the rules to procure evidence is futile, and might even result in the loss of crucial information that could have been obtained through lawful means. Regrettably, some criminals must be allowed to go free when the constable misbehaves or 'blunders',[51] because the deterrent effect of evidentiary exclusion would be jeopardised if the courts started making ad hoc exceptions in individual cases.

Whatever the (doubtful) merits of deterrence as a general justification for excluding improperly obtained evidence, the scenario confronting the House of Lords in *A* exposes some of its limitations. As Lord Hoffmann observed, the English judiciary, 'cannot aspire to discipline the agents of foreign governments. Their torturers would probably accept with indifference the possibility that the work of their hands might be rejected by an English court'.[52] Lord Rodger added, somewhat testily:

> [I]t is no part of the function of British courts to attempt to discipline officials of a friendly country. Besides anything else, the idea that foreign torturers would

[48] Ibid [130].

[49] Ibid. The *hostis humani generis*, a description traditionally applied to pirates operating on the high seas, is the enemy of all humankind: cf *In Re Piracy Jure Gentium* [1934] AC 586 (PC).

[50] See DA Dripps, 'The "New" Exclusionary Rule Debate: From "Still Preoccupied With 1985" to "Virtual Deterrence"' (2010) 37 *Fordham Urban Law Journal* 743.

[51] Echoing Cardozo J's celebrated remark in *People v Defore*, 242 NY 13, 21, 24–25 (1926): 'There has been no blinking the consequences. The criminal is to go free because the constable has blundered'.

[52] [2006] 2 AC 221, [91].

> pause for a moment because of a decision by SIAC to reject a statement which they had extracted verges on the absurd.[53]

Lord Bingham was not quite so dismissive of instrumental rationales. He thought it 'very likely that the unreliability of a statement or confession procured by torture and a desire to discourage torture by devaluing its product' had influenced the international community to include Article 15, stipulating an exclusionary rule, into the UN Convention Against Torture (UNCAT). However, all seven Law Lords delivering speeches in *A* unequivocally invested intrinsic moral values with primary significance. In the words of Lord Bingham, torture evidence is 'offensive to ordinary standards of humanity and decency and incompatible with the principles which should animate a tribunal seeking to administer justice'.[54]

The intrinsic moral argument for exclusion begins with the opprobrium attaching to the practice of torture itself. Their Lordships did not mince their words. Lord Nicholls simply stated, 'torture is not acceptable. This is a bedrock moral principle in this country'.[55] Lord Hope branded torture 'one of the most evil practices known to man'.[56] Taking his cue from Blackstone, Lord Hoffmann spoke of dishonour, corruption, degradation and the censure of enlightened opinion:

> The use of torture is dishonourable. It corrupts and degrades the state which uses it and the legal system which accepts it. When judicial torture was routine all over Europe, its rejection by the common law was a source of national pride and the admiration of enlightened foreign writers such as Voltaire and Beccaria.[57]

Lord Brown called torture 'an unqualified evil. It can never be justified. Rather it must always be punished'.[58]

Once it is appreciated that torture is the ultimate jurisprudential pariah, universally condemned on imperative moral grounds, judicial exclusion of evidence tainted by torture follows almost by necessary implication. The judicial process cannot allow itself to be 'dishonoured', 'demeaned', 'corrupted' etc, through any association with a practice as morally decrepit as official torture. Lord Hope found institutional support for this conclusion in a passage in Hume's *Commentaries* condemning the barbarity of torture.[59] Lord Bingham thought it embedded in English common law, adding that the categorical rejection of evidence tainted by torture 'is more

[53] Ibid [136].
[54] Ibid [52].
[55] Ibid [64].
[56] Ibid [101].
[57] Ibid [82].
[58] Ibid [160].
[59] Baron Hume, *Commentaries on the Law of Scotland respecting Crimes* (Edinburgh, 1844), vol ii, 324, paraphrased by Lord Hope, [2006] 2 AC 221, [108].

aptly categorised as a constitutional principle than as a rule of evidence'.[60] Lord Bingham then embarked on an extensive review of relevant international law sources, linking Article 15 of UNCAT to 'the wider principle expressed in Article 69(7) of the Rome Statute of the International Criminal Court', which states that evidence obtained in breach of the ICC Statute or 'internationally recognised human rights' must be excluded if 'the admission of the evidence would be antithetical to and would seriously damage the integrity of the proceedings'.[61] Finally, Lord Carswell summarised the conclusion that all of their Lordships, with the possible exception of Lord Rodger,[62] shared:

> [T]he duty not to countenance the use of torture by admission of evidence so obtained in judicial proceedings must be regarded as paramount and that to allow its admission would shock the conscience, abuse or degrade the proceedings and involve the state in moral defilement... In following this [exclusionary] course our state will... retain the moral high ground which an open democratic society enjoys.[63]

(b) The Institutional Morality of Ticking Bombs

None of their Lordships' speeches in *A* ventures beyond the 'bedrock moral principle' that torture is abhorrent, to trace the deeper normative significance of procedural law as an expression of human dignity and democratic political values.[64] Several of their Lordships did, however, seek to explain why reliance on torture evidence is especially inappropriate in *judicial*

[60] [2006] 2 AC 221, [12]. See further, D Friedman, 'Torture and the Common Law' [2006] *European Human Rights Law Review* 180.

[61] [2006] 2 AC 221, [39]. See further, K Ambos, 'The Transnational Use of Torture Evidence' (2009) 42 *Israel Law Review* 362.

[62] Lord Rodger, [2006] 2 AC 221, [128], was noticeably more sympathetic to the Court of Appeal's decision than any of his colleagues, and did not regard it as obvious that Parliament had intended to restrict SIAC's access to relevant information, even if that information was possibly tainted by torture abroad: ibid [134]. Confining his analysis to a somewhat narrower point of statutory interpretation, Lord Rodger nonetheless concluded that 'the revulsion against torture is so deeply ingrained in our law that, in my view, a court could receive statements obtained by its use only where this was authorised by express words, or perhaps the plainest possible implication, in a statute': ibid [137].

[63] Ibid [150].

[64] Unanswered questions include: What, precisely, is meant by 'human dignity'? How should human dignity be served by law in general, and by procedural law in particular? How does human dignity relate to the concept of human rights? Or to institutionalised systems of human rights law, such as the ECHR? What are the epistemological credentials of appeals to human dignity? Can a commitment to human dignity be sustained purely on the basis of a secular rationalism? Or does human dignity only make sense within a broader framework of religious conviction? Is a commitment to human dignity excessively individualistic and 'atomist', in the sense intended by communitarians in their critiques of liberalism? Is it ethnocentrically Western European or Northern Hemisphere? Does it discriminate improperly against

proceedings, as opposed to executive decision-making. Bringing the 'ticking bomb' scenario out of the classroom and into the courtroom, Lord Brown revisited the moral dilemma posed by information obtained by torture which 'may on occasion yield up information capable of saving... perhaps many lives': [65]

> Unswerving logic might suggest that no use whatever should be made of it... the ticking bomb must be allowed to tick on. But there are powerful countervailing arguments too: torture cannot be undone and the greater public good thus lies in making some use at least of the information obtained, whether to avert public danger or to bring the guilty to justice.

The question for decision in these appeals, Lord Rodger reminded counsel, was not whether the Home Secretary acted improperly in seeking to adduce the contested evidence before SIAC, but rather whether SIAC should have agreed to receive in evidence what the Home Secretary legitimately took into account in certifying the applicants as suspected terrorists. It had been 'perfectly proper for him to rely on the statement when issuing his certificate'.[66] The courts had no basis, observed Lord Hoffmann, for interfering with executive intelligence-gathering and analysis conducted to safeguard national security:

> Provided that he acts lawfully, [the Home Secretary] may read whatever he likes. In his dealings with foreign governments, the type of information that he is willing to receive and the questions that he asks or refrains from asking are his own affair.[67]

The key to this distinction was pinpointed by Lord Brown: 'the functions and responsibilities of the executive and the judiciary are entirely different'.[68] The government of the day must have such powers as it needs to keep its citizens safe, within the limits of a democratic constitution. It follows, said Lord Brown, 'that the executive may make use of all information it acquires: both coerced statements and whatever fruits they are found to bear'.[69] Indeed, the government 'would be failing in its duty if it ignores whatever it may learn or fails to follow it up'.[70] But the judicial role is quite different: 'Generally speaking the court will shut its face against the admission in evidence of any coerced statement'.[71]

non-human interests, in the manner condemned as 'speciesism' by Peter Singer? (See P Singer, *Practical Ethics*, 3rd edn (Cambridge, CUP, 2011) ch 3.)

[65] [2006] 2 AC 221, [160].
[66] Ibid [136].
[67] Ibid [93].
[68] Ibid [162].
[69] Ibid [161].
[70] Ibid.
[71] Ibid.

Lord Hoffmann was inclined to believe that ticking bomb dilemmas are 'less common in practice than in seminars on moral philosophy',[72] but Lord Nicholls thought it worthwhile to restate the classic moral poser:[73]

> The context is cross-border terrorism. Countering international terrorism calls for a flow of information between the security services of many countries. Fragments of information, acquired from various sources, can be pieced together to form a valuable picture, enabling governments of threatened countries to take preventative steps. What should the security services and the police and other executive agencies of this country do if they know or suspect information received by them from overseas is the product of torture? Should they discard this information as 'tainted', and decline to use it lest its use by them be regarded as condoning the horrific means by which the information was obtained? The intuitive response to these questions is that if use of such information might save lives it would be absurd to reject it. If the police were to learn of the whereabouts of a ticking bomb it would be ludicrous for them to disregard this information if it had been procured by torture. No one suggests the police should act in this way. Similarly, if tainted information points a finger of suspicion at a particular individual: depending on the circumstances, this information is a matter the police may properly take into account when considering, for example, whether to make an arrest.[74]

Lord Nicholls was prepared to concede that *any* use of torture-derived information by state officials regrettably lends an air of legitimacy to the practice of torture and diminishes its universal prohibition:

> [T]he executive arm of the state is open to the charge that it is condoning the use of torture. So, in a sense, it is. The government is using information obtained by torture. But in cases such as these the government cannot be expected to close its eyes to this information at the price of endangering the lives of its own citizens. Moral repugnance to torture does not require this.[75]

Executive reliance on torture evidence to defuse the ticking bomb is sometimes justified, on this account, as the lesser of two evils, not because such uses are morally unproblematic or free from deleterious side-effects. However, Lord Nicholls went on to insist it would be,

> an altogether different matter for the judicial arm of the state to admit such information as evidence when adjudicating definitively upon the guilt or innocence of a person charged with a criminal offence. In the latter case repugnance to torture demands that proof of facts should be found in more acceptable sources than information extracted by torture.[76]

[72] Ibid.

[73] Generally, see B Brecher, *Torture and the Ticking Bomb* (Oxford, Blackwell, 2007); D Luban, 'Liberalism, Torture, and the Ticking Bomb' (2005) 91 *Virginia Law Review* 1425.

[74] [2006] 2 AC 221, [67]–[68].

[75] Ibid [69].

[76] Ibid [70].

This nuanced analysis should not be confused with the simplistic 'separation thesis' criticised by Andrew Ashworth.[77] Differentiation, not separation, of institutional duties, roles and values is the motor driving Lord Nicholls' train of argument to its ultimate destination: 'torture is torture whoever does it, judicial proceedings are judicial proceedings, whatever their purpose—the former can never be admissible in the latter'.[78]

3. DECEPTION BY 'ENTRAPMENT'

Police 'entrapment' is a useful, if conceptually protean, topic for exploring the implications of deception for the admissibility of evidence in criminal trials.[79] Since the Human Rights Act 1998 fully entered into force in England and Wales on 2 October 2000, an important dimension of English courts' approach to allegations of entrapment is the need to ensure that applications of PACE 1984, section 78,[80] and common law principles of exclusion and abuse of process satisfy the fair trial standards of ECHR Article 6.[81] The following discussion focuses on relevant jurisprudence of the European Court of Human Rights, partly because it is relatively unfamiliar to common lawyers.

On the face of it, the specific fair trial rights enumerated by Article 6 are focused on the trial stage of criminal proceedings. There is no explicit reference to criminal investigations in general, or to police entrapment (or related ideas like undercover operations or covert surveillance) in particular. However, the Strasbourg Court adopts an avowedly flexible and non-formalistic approach to textual interpretation. The Convention is treated as a 'living instrument' that must move with the times and adapt to meet the challenges of securing practical rights protection across the 47 Council of Europe states. The ECtHR is not hidebound by its own past pronouncements, especially if, on later reflection, they appear dated or have been

[77] Chapter 6, in this volume; and Ashworth, above n 21.

[78] Alvaro Gil-Robles, the Council of Europe's former Commissioner for Human Rights, quoted with approval in *A v Home Secretary (No 2)* [2006] 2 AC 221, [35] (Lord Bingham), [150] (Lord Carswell). Now also see *Gäfgen v Germany* (2011) 52 EHRR 1.

[79] Generally, see A Ashworth, 'Should the Police be Allowed to Use Deceptive Practices?' (1998) 114 *Law Quarterly Review* 108; J Kleinig, *The Ethics of Policing* (Cambridge, CUP, 1996) chs 7–8.

[80] Section 78 provides: 'In any proceedings the court may refuse to allow evidence on which the prosecution proposes to rely to be given if it appears to the court that, having regard to all the circumstances, including the circumstances in which the evidence was obtained, the admission of the evidence would have such an adverse effect on the fairness of the proceedings that the court ought not to admit it'.

[81] *R v Looseley; Attorney-General's Reference (No 3 of 2000)* [2001] 1 WLR 2060, [2001] UKHL 53. See A Ashworth, 'Re-drawing the Boundaries of Entrapment' [2002] *Criminal Law Review* 161.

overtaken by events.[82] The prevailing assumption is diametrically opposite to what the common lawyer would expect: authorities (decidedly *not* formal precedents) tend to become less pertinent, not more venerable, with the passage of time. When presented with an obliging set of facts, the ECtHR found little difficulty in extending the scope of Article 6 to protect applicants against 'entrapment' by police investigators.

(a) Evidence of Entrapment in Strasbourg

In *Teixeira de Castro*[83] Portuguese undercover police officers invited VS, a known hashish user and small-time dealer, to put them in touch with somebody who could supply heroin. After much inconclusive negotiation, VS introduced the officers to the accused, who duly procured heroin from an acquaintance and sold it on to the officers. The accused's conviction and six-year sentence for drug-dealing were upheld by the Portuguese Supreme Court, which took the view that sacrifices of individual freedom are sometimes justified in order to pursue legitimate law enforcement objectives like tackling the scourge of illegal drug distribution and its associated misery.

The Strasbourg Court, however, upheld the accused's complaint that he had been denied a fair trial in contravention of Article 6, characterising the undercover officers' conduct as impermissible 'incitement' tantamount to official crime-creation. The operation was further compromised, in the ECtHR's eyes, because it was not properly authorised or supervised by a magistrate. The Court concluded:

> [T]he two police officers did not confine themselves to investigating Mr Teixeira de Castro's criminal activity in an essentially passive manner, but exercised an influence such as to incite the commission of the offence... [Their] actions went beyond those of undercover agents because they instigated the offence and there is nothing to suggest that without their intervention it would have been committed. That intervention and its use in the impugned criminal proceedings meant that, *right from the outset, the applicant was definitively deprived of a fair trial.*[84]

In spite of its technical defects and omissions,[85] *Teixeira* was a pivotal judgment, establishing beyond any doubt that Article 6 fairness encompasses

[82] Albeit that a range of institutional factors tends to promote consistency in decision-making. For further discussion, see A Mowbray, 'An Examination of the European Court of Human Rights' Approach to Overruling its Previous Case Law' (2009) 9 *Human Rights Law Review* 179.

[83] *Teixeira de Castro v Portugal* (1998) 28 EHRR 101.

[84] Ibid [38]–[39] (emphasis supplied).

[85] The respondent Government maintained that there was additional evidence suggesting that Teixeira was already dealing in heroin, or was prepared to do so, albeit that on the occasion in question he was obliged to arrange for the undercover officers to be supplied from a third party: see ibid [32]. Furthermore, the Portuguese courts had found as a fact that the undercover officers did *not* behave as agents provocateurs. For sustained criticism, see

the propriety of *pre*-trial proceedings, including police investigations. Just as in England and Wales section 78 of PACE is concerned with how evidence was obtained,[86] as well as with its proposed use as prosecution evidence at trial, under the European Convention system an accused may be deprived of a fair trial 'right from the outset' if law enforcement officers have violated his rights during the course of their investigations.

Strasbourg judgments often lack what common lawyers would regard as a clear or determinate *ratio decidendi*. The ECtHR generally arrives at holistic judgments of compliance or breach of the Convention. It does not usually parse its findings, or deign to indicate which factors were decisive, where more than one consideration supports a particular conclusion. The Strasbourg Court has contributed to legal literature a style of judgment-writing which is formulaic, repetitive, peppered with leaden boiler-plate, question-begging and inelegant; yet, for all that, commendably effective within its own constrained terms of reference. At least part of the difficulty is attributable to the Strasbourg Court's multinational collegiate composition, political vulnerability and attenuated structural position within a supra-national system of human rights protection.

The primary role of the ECtHR is to hold states parties to their international obligations by determining whether an applicant has suffered a breach of Convention-protected rights.[87] This is usually[88] a distinct and quite different question to the one originally before the national courts in the litigation giving rise to a Strasbourg application. In criminal proceedings, for example, whereas the national court must adjudicate on guilt or innocence, the ECtHR states only whether the trial was fair in accordance with Article 6. The fairness of the trial is obviously not synonymous with the accused's criminal responsibility, and the ECtHR, sensibly, does not allow itself to be drawn on questions of factual guilt or innocence. According to another favourite piece of Euro-boilerplate, 'the admissibility of evidence is primarily a matter for regulation by national law and as a general rule it is for the national courts to assess the evidence before them'.[89]

D Ormerod and A Roberts, 'The Trouble with *Teixeira*: Developing a Principled Approach to Entrapment' (2002) 6 E & P 38.

[86] In applying section 78, trial judges must consider 'all the circumstances, including the circumstances in which the evidence was obtained'.

[87] ECHR Articles 19, 35 and 41.

[88] Compliance with the ECHR may have been litigated directly at the national level, for example by way of judicial review proceedings before the English High Court, rather than as an incidental aspect of domestic legal questions.

[89] *Van Mechelen v Netherlands* (1997) 25 EHRR 647, [50]. Also see, eg, *Vanyan* v *Russia*, App No 53203/99, ECtHR Judgment 15 December 2005, [45]: 'While Article 6 guarantees the right to a fair hearing, it does not lay down any rules on the admissibility of evidence as such, which is therefore primarily a matter for regulation under national law... The question which must be answered is whether the proceedings as a whole, including the way in which the evidence was obtained, were fair'.

> It is therefore not the role of the Court to determine, as a matter of principle, whether particular types of evidence—for example, evidence obtained unlawfully in terms of domestic law—may be admissible or, indeed, whether the applicant was guilty or not. The question which must be answered is whether the proceedings as a whole, including the way in which the evidence was obtained, were fair.[90]

Such declarations of jurisdictional modesty should not be taken to imply that Strasbourg judges *never* rule on what common lawyers would call points of evidence: *Teixeira* itself, together with a host of other important judgments on the right to silence,[91] the privilege against self-incrimination,[92] the admissibility of hearsay,[93] and the use of anonymous witnesses,[94] demonstrates otherwise. However, the ECtHR will generally refrain from commenting on national rules of evidence unless there appears to be a direct clash with a Convention-protected right, in which case the Court is obliged to resolve the conflict in order to promote compliance with the Convention.

These institutional factors conspire to leave the relationship between the ECHR, as interpreted by the Strasbourg Court, and the domestic procedural law of states parties, including evidentiary rules of admissibility, somewhat uncertain, fluid, unpredictable, question-begging, and a potential source of conflict.[95] Compounding these background uncertainties, the ECtHR in *Teixeira* did not really explain why it was objectionable to convict T of drug-dealing on apparently compelling evidence, even if the police *had* put him up to it. Proceeding as though the issue were self-explanatory, the Court peremptorily announced:

> The use of undercover agents must be restricted and safeguards put in place even in cases concerning the fight against drug trafficking.... The general requirements of fairness embodied in Article 6 apply to proceedings concerning all types of criminal offence, from the most straightforward to the most complex. The public interest cannot justify the use of evidence obtained as a result of police incitement.[96]

Judge Butkevych, dissenting, took a rather different view of the facts, in which T ceased to attract any sympathy as a victim whose fundamental rights had supposedly been breached: '[T]he applicant knew that he was committing a criminal offence. The fact that he did not know that those

[90] *Bykov v Russia*, App No 4378/02, ECtHR Grand Chamber Judgment, 10 March 2009, [89].
[91] *Condron v UK* (2001) 31 EHRR 1.
[92] *Jalloh v Germany* (2007) 44 EHRR 32.
[93] *Al-Khawaja and Tahery v UK* (2009) 49 EHRR 1.
[94] *Doorson v The Netherlands* (1996) 22 EHRR 330.
[95] Most obviously reflected, for English lawyers, in the long-running '*Al-Khawaja* saga', dissected by Mike Redmayne, Chapter 12 in this volume. For another illustration, see P Roberts, 'Does Article 6 of the European Convention on Human Rights Require Reasoned Verdicts in Criminal Trials?' (2011) 11 *Human Rights Law Review* 213.
[96] (1998) 28 EHRR 101, [36].

offering to buy the heroin from him were police officers does not change the essence of the case'.

The morality and legality of what transpired in *Teixeira* are evidently open to argument. If one is inclined to maintain, with Judge Butkevych, that T knew perfectly well what he was doing and should have resisted the officers' blandishments, it is difficult to deduce that 'right from the outset' T was 'definitively deprived of a fair trial' under Article 6. One might well think that the officers should be disciplined for failing to follow protocol, but why should that let T off the hook? Evidentiary exclusion is not the only available remedy for police misconduct. Judge Butkevych insisted that he was 'ready to share the fear that unsanctioned acts of the police, even if inspired by noble intentions, may result in gross infringements of human rights'.

Behind the majority's conclusion lurks an unarticulated supposition that T should not be held legally responsible for an offence which police officers had 'incited', perhaps because the conduct of the authorities had fatally undermined the legitimacy of the proceedings or possibly because T was not morally culpable in committing the offence. T was consequently 'definitively deprived of a fair trial', because how could a trial that should never have been brought in the first place ever be considered 'fair'? But notice the significant twist in this tale. What began as an argument about the scope of (presumptively procedural) fair trial rights, appears now to support something closely resembling a substantive criminal law defence of entrapment. This is a remarkable feat of judicial reasoning, with broad and potentially troubling implications for the jurisdiction of the Strasbourg Court and the scope of Article 6.[97]

(b) The Morality of Entrapment after *Teixeira*

Teixeira paved the way for a slew of further applications, originating from various countries, alleging police entrapment in breach of Article 6. Whilst this body of jurisprudence—which the ECtHR itself characterises as 'extensive'[98]—has clarified the *Teixeira* ruling, important questions going to the heart of the rationale for condemning 'entrapment' as a human rights violation are still awaiting clear and convincing answers.

From the earliest days, the Strasbourg Court has accepted that proactive policing is a legitimate weapon in the armoury of law enforcement, especially in responding to organised crime, international fraud, drug-trafficking, people smuggling and terrorism. However, the Court has insisted on drawing a

[97] This criticism is developed in P Roberts, 'The Presumption of Innocence Brought Home? *Kebilene* Deconstructed' (2002) 117 *Law Quarterly Review* 40.

[98] *Bannikova v Russia*, App No 18757/06, ECtHR Judgment 4 November 2010, [35].

distinction—reminiscent of Lord Nicholls' analysis in *A v Home Secretary (No 2)*—between the use of investigative methods to procure intelligence and the use of such information as a basis for criminal convictions. As the Court recently affirmed in *Ramanauskas v Lithuania*, 'the use of special investigative methods—in particular, undercover techniques—cannot in itself infringe the right to a fair trial' provided that they are 'kept within clear limits' in view of 'the risk of police incitement entailed by such techniques':[99]

> However, the subsequent use of such sources by the trial court to found a conviction is a different matter and is acceptable only if adequate and sufficient safeguards against abuse are in place, in particular a clear and foreseeable procedure for authorising, implementing and supervising the investigative measures in question…

Thus, resort to 'special investigative methods' must be counterbalanced by procedural measures to preserve the integrity of the evidence and safeguard the accused's rights. This balancing approach, sometimes (though in my opinion not very helpfully) characterised as 'equality of arms', lies at the heart of the ECHR conception of a fair trial, as interpreted by the Strasbourg Court.[100] Notably, the Court has stressed that the seriousness of the offence(s) with which the accused is charged cannot pre-empt the imperative of balancing: 'the right to a fair trial, from which the requirement of the proper administration of justice is to be inferred… applies to all types of criminal offence, from the most straightforward to the most complex'.[101]

Strasbourg jurisprudence consistently demands some pre-existing objective basis for believing that a suspect is already engaged in particularised criminality before condoning resort to proactive methods. Random virtue-testing by the authorities is not permitted under the Convention, even in relation to serious crimes. This threshold criterion was not satisfied in *Teixeira*, where the Court could find 'no evidence to support the Government's argument that the applicant was predisposed to commit offences'.[102] Reliance was placed on the fact that T apparently did not already have the heroin in his possession when approached by the undercover officers: 'the drugs were not at the applicant's home; he obtained them from a third party who had in turn obtained them from another person'.[103] Moreover, the ECtHR could not discern any basis in the domestic legal record for inferring that 'at the

[99] *Ramanauskas v Lithuania* (2010) 51 EHRR 11, [51], [53].

[100] Eg *Brandstetter v Austria* (1993) 15 EHRR 378, [66]–[67].

[101] *Ramanauskas v Lithuania* (2010) 51 EHRR 11, [53]. Also see, eg, *Sequeira v Portugal*, App No 73557/01, ECtHR Admissibility Decision, 6 May 2003, 5: 'The use of undercover agents must be restricted and safeguards put in place even in cases concerning the fight against drug trafficking'.

[102] (1998) 28 EHRR 101, [38].

[103] Ibid.

time of his arrest, the applicant had more drugs in his possession than the quantity the police officers had requested thereby going beyond what he had been incited to do by the police'.[104]

The authorities likewise failed to produce adequate evidence of pre-existing criminal intent in *Vanyan v Russia*.[105] Moscow police suspected V of being involved in drug-dealing, and in order to secure evidence against him arranged a 'test purchase' using a co-operating informant, OZ, who was supplied with money to buy drugs from V. The operation misfired, and V initially escaped but was later apprehended. In due course, V was convicted of possessing narcotics and of aiding and abetting OZ to procure heroin for her own personal consumption. The ECtHR found,

> no evidence to suggest that before the intervention by OZ the police had reason to suspect that the applicant was a drug dealer. A mere claim at the trial by the police to the effect that they possessed information concerning the applicant's involvement in drug-dealing, a statement which does not seem to have been scrutinised by the court, cannot be taken into account.[106]

As in *Teixeira*, the ECtHR refused to accept police officers' assertions of their pre-existing suspicions of V's drug-dealing, in the absence of explicit judicial confirmation from the domestic Russian courts. To be sure, in the mouth of a respondent Government at Strasbourg, reported assertions by police officials are effectively self-serving. On the other hand, the Russian courts were addressing different legal questions[107] and had ruled that the undercover operation had been conducted entirely in accordance with domestic criminal procedure law.[108] There is no indication in the Strasbourg Court's judgment that the domestic Russian courts had *consciously rejected* the police statements alleging V's prior involvement in drug dealing.[109]

The facts of *Sequeira v Portugal*[110] resemble *Vanyan*, in again featuring an undercover operation employing co-operating informants. Crucially, however, this time the police did not become involved until S's drug smuggling operation was already well advanced. S had met A in prison, where both were serving sentences for drug-related offences, and together they conspired to import cocaine from Brazil to Portugal. It was only when A approached C, a boat owner (and, as it turned out, long-standing police

[104] Ibid.

[105] *Vanyan v Russia*, App No 53203/99, ECtHR Judgment 15 December 2005.

[106] Ibid [49].

[107] As the Strasbourg Court itself observed, ibid [40]: 'there is nothing in the Presidium of the Moscow City Court's decision to suggest that it examined the issue of police incitement in the applicant's case and considered whether and to what extent such incitement could have impaired the fairness of the proceedings'.

[108] Ibid [18].

[109] Also see *V v Finland*, App No 40412/98, ECtHR Judgment, 24 April 2007; *Khudobin v Russia* (2009) 48 EHRR 22.

[110] *Sequeira v Portugal*, App No 73557/01, ECtHR Admissibility Decision, 6 May 2003.

informant), to facilitate the importation of a major cocaine shipment that the plan came to the notice of the authorities. Together with an undercover Portuguese police officer, A and C orchestrated a controlled delivery to S, who was duly arrested in possession of 1,833 kg of cocaine and convicted of drug smuggling. Neither A nor C were charged. The ECtHR distinguished this scenario from the facts of *Teixeira* on the basis of the domestic courts' finding that 'A and C began to collaborate with the criminal-investigation department at a point when the applicant had already contacted A with a view to organising the shipment of cocaine to Portugal', so that 'the authorities had good reasons for suspecting the applicant of wishing to mount a drug-trafficking operation'. These arrangements demonstrated that 'A and C cannot be described as *agents provocateurs*... their activities did not exceed those of undercover agents'.[111]

Compliance with Article 6 is a function not only of what the authorities knew, but also of what investigators and their civilian helpers actually did. In *Eurofinacom v France*, the Court declared that 'the fact that the authorities have "good reason to suspect" the defendant of having a propensity to commit an offence would tend to suggest that an operation... was more akin to "infiltration" than "instigation"...'.[112] 'Instigation' is apparently equated with 'incitement' of an offence, which in turn is said to involve conduct which 'goes beyond that of an undercover agent'.[113] In *Sequeira* the Court contrasted legitimate activities which do not 'exceed those of undercover agents' with the illegitimate conduct of agents provocateurs.[114] These formulations need to be cross-referenced against a further juridical distinction between appropriately 'passive' undercover investigation, and illegitimately active incitement. As the ECtHR summarised in *Ramanauskas*:

> Police incitement occurs where the officers involved—whether members of the security forces or persons acting on their instructions—do not confine themselves to investigating criminal activity in an essentially passive manner, but exert such an influence on the subject as to incite the commission of an offence that would

[111] Also see *Stoimenov v The Former Yugoslav Republic of Macedonia*, App No 17995/02, ECtHR Judgment, 5 April 2007, where a conspiracy to sell WWII poppy-tar was already well advanced before the alleged police informant, NN, came on the scene. 'Nor could [NN] have exercised an influence such as to incite the commission of the offence, as the applicant had already been involved at an earlier stage. In addition, the applicant did not even contact Mr NN: his role was over before the poppy-tar finally reached the alleged *agent provocateur*': ibid [44].

[112] *Eurofinacom v France*, App No 58753/00, ECtHR Admissibility Decision, 7 September 2004. Also see *Sequeira*, above n 110, 5; *Vanyan*, above n 89, [47].

[113] This broadly equates to the English law notion, endorsed by the House of Lords in *R v Looseley; Attorney-General's Reference (No 3 of 2000)* [2001] 1 WLR 2060, of providing suspects with 'an unexceptional opportunity' to 'apply the trick to themselves'. The application of this test is highly context-specific: see, eg, *Jenkins v USA*; *Benbow v USA* [2005] EWHC 1051 (Admin); cf *R v Moon* [2004] EWCA Crim 2872.

[114] *Sequeira*, above n 110, 6.

otherwise not have been committed, in order to ... provide evidence and institute a prosecution...[115]

We observe here a series of rhetorical contrasts, but no settled or serviceable functional test of investigative impropriety. The ECtHR's express or implicit dichotomies—passive/active, infiltration/instigation, investigation/incitement, undercover police/agent provocateur—are categories for expressing conclusions which still owe us a justificatory rationale. The only substantive criterion, to which the Court constantly returns, is an apparently straightforward 'but-for' test of causation: did the officers' conduct 'incite the commission of an offence that would otherwise not have been committed'? However, an unvarnished but-for test is radically over-inclusive for these purposes. For example, *any* police-orchestrated 'test purchase' would clearly not result *in that particular offence* 'but for' the conduct of the police in setting up a dummy transaction. Test purchases are conducted routinely in England and Wales in order, for example, to catch shopkeepers who sell alcohol, cigarettes or 18-rated videos to under-age customers,[116] or to expose mini-cab drivers operating without a licence.[117] Absent any contingent procedural defect undermining the legality or fairness of a particular undercover operation, evidence procured through test purchases would not be excluded, either at common law or under section 78 of PACE 1984, in English criminal proceedings. Does the ECtHR mean to imply that such routine investigative activity is incompatible with the right to a fair trial under Article 6?

Probably not. Yet an unqualified but-for causal test of police 'incitement' is hostage to doubtful applications. In *Eurofinacom v France*,[118] for example, the defendants operated a 'Minitel' electronic mailbox and messaging system. There was ample circumstantial evidence that the service was being used by prostitutes to recruit clients. Users' aliases ('pseudos') listed on the system included 'Lola massage', 'Claire 37 years old', 'Spanker', Bunny rabbit', 'Katy the First' and 'Male slave'. Police officers went on the system using the alias 'AAA', and received responses quoting prices for 'sublime massage of the entire body', 'moments of togetherness', etc. Eurofinacom and its manager were both convicted of living on immoral earnings by the Paris Criminal Court and awarded hefty fines. They argued before the Strasbourg Court that the police had instigated these offences contrary to Article 6, as interpreted in *Teixeira*. Remarkably, the Court agreed that the

[115] *Ramanauskas v Lithuania* (2010) 51 EHRR 11, [55].

[116] *DPP v Marshall* [1988] 3 All ER 683 (DC); *Ealing LBC v Woolworths plc* [1995] *Criminal Law Review* 58 (Woolworths employee sold 18-rated video to 11-year-old son of a trading standards officer, posing as a regular customer).

[117] *Nottingham City Council v Amin* [2000] 1 Cr App R 426 (DC).

[118] *Eurofinacom v France*, App No 58753/00, ECtHR Admissibility Decision, 7 September 2004.

police officers' ruse in this case had incited the 'test purchase' offences. By posting messages 'requesting the "terms" and "cost" in order to obtain a positive identification of any prostitutes from among the replies received', the Court concluded, 'the police officers themselves incited the offers of prostitution that were made to them personally'.[119] Unfortunately for the applicants, the ECtHR went on to say that Eurofinacom had been convicted of an on-going course of criminality, of which the police-incited offences were merely (in English terminology) specimen charges. To cap it all, the Court then appeared to take back what it had just found in the applicants' favour:

> In sum, while *it is true that the investigating officers instigated the offers* of prostitution-related services which were made to them personally on 36-15 ALINE on 30 December 1996, *they did not in the true sense incite the commission of the offence of living on immoral earnings of which the applicant company was convicted*; that offence was a continuing offence which was necessarily committed by the applicant company, not the prostitutes. The applicant company cannot therefore complain of a violation of Article 6(1) of the Convention on that account.[120]

As well as spawning the slippery concept of incitement 'in the true sense', *Eurofinacom* leaves national courts and judges to conjure with the intriguing notion of investigating officers who '*to some extent* contributed to the commission of the offences'.[121] This is an obvious, though presumably unintentional, abdication of the but-for causal standard, which permits of no 'to some extent'. If the ECtHR was floundering here (and in fairness it should be recalled that *Eurofinacom* was only a ruling on admissibility, not a fully reasoned judgment), the root cause might well be the Court's surprisingly anaemic conceptions of 'instigation' and 'incitement'; assuming, *pace Eurofinacom*, that 'instigation' and 'incitement' are roughly equivalent terms in post-*Teixeira* Strasbourg jurisprudence.

Incitement generally requires more (or less) than mere but-for causation, and instigation often does, too. Incitement (unlike instigation) is possibly always pejorative. To incite somebody to behave in a certain way is 'to put them up to it', to 'put ideas into their head', possibly to exert pressure of various sorts upon them to do one's bidding. Incitement generally involves affecting the targeted individual's 'motivational set' by cultivating certain desires and promoting interests and goals that were not already on the incitee's agenda. *Teixeira* itself might well have involved such activity on the part of undercover officers, who did appear to be quite persistent in demanding to be supplied with heroin. Drugs 'test purchase' or 'buy and

[119] Ibid 15.
[120] Ibid 16 (emphasis supplied).
[121] Ibid (emphasis supplied).

bust' scenarios, like those producing Strasbourg applications in *Vanyan* and a string of similar cases,[122] are more equivocal. In each scenario, the participating informant was certainly 'put up to it' by the police, and may effectively have been blackmailed into cooperating with the authorities. It does not necessarily follow that in every case *the accused* was 'put up to it' by the informant, since the idea might well already have been fully formed in his head, awaiting an opportunity for theory to become practice.

Only fine-grained factual investigation could hope to resolve such issues in particular cases. But it is difficult to see, on any analysis other than the ECtHR's naïve causal test, how the police officers in *Eurofinacom* could truly be said to have incited or instigated offers of sexual services from working prostitutes simply by texting the word 'terms' to selected service users. As 'Coco' explained in evidence to the Paris Criminal Court, whilst expressly advertising sexual services was not permitted, 'this was nevertheless understood, as people are not stupid'. Another regular user, 'Eva 93—pretty blonde 38 years old, naughty underwear, 95 bust' added that even explicit pseudos like 'Whore' were not removed from Eurofinacom's Minitel service.

An important further clue to the Court's implicit morality of entrapment may be gleaned from *Shannon v UK*.[123] John James Shannon was a TV actor who starred in a popular 1990s drama series about firemen called *London's Burning*. He was targeted by a tabloid journalist, M, who, posing as a wealthy Arab sheik, offered to pay Shannon to attend the opening of a new nightclub in Dubai as a celebrity guest. A meeting was arranged at the Savoy Hotel in London. The room, naturally, was bugged and the meeting secretly video-recorded. During the course of the conversation the 'sheik' expressed an interest in drugs, and Shannon subsequently agreed to supply the 'sheik' and his entourage (other undercover journalists) with cocaine and cannabis, which he did. The following week the *News of the World* broke the front-page scoop '*London's Burning* Star is Cocaine Dealer'. Worse for Shannon, M (who turned out to be a seasoned exponent of the undercover sting)[124] handed over all his evidence to the police, and Shannon was duly convicted of supplying controlled drugs and sentenced to nine months' imprisonment. M was not charged with any offence.

Shannon argued, unsuccessfully, that he was the victim of entrapment by M's elaborate charade. The domestic English courts could find no reason to exclude the (damning) taped evidence of Shannon offering to buy drugs

[122] *Khudobin v Russia* (2009) 48 EHRR 22; *V v Finland*, App No 40412/98, ECtHR Judgment, 24 April 2007; *Lalas v Lithuania*, App No 13109/04, ECtHR Judgment 1 March 2011: cf *Bannikova v Russia*, App No 18757/06, ECtHR Judgment 4 November 2010.

[123] *Shannon v UK*, App No 67537/01, ECtHR Admissibility Decision, 6 April 2004.

[124] During Shannon's ensuing trial M claimed to have already provided evidence for 89 successful criminal prosecutions.

for the 'sheik', either at common law or under PACE 1984, section 78. The electronic recordings showed that Shannon, although enticed at various points in the conversation, had risen to the challenge with gusto. There was no element of coercion; he could have disengaged at any time. In the unflinching judgment of the Court of Appeal, Shannon had 'voluntarily and readily applied himself to the trick'. Shannon, in other words, had stung himself. On further application to Strasbourg, the ECtHR laid primary emphasis on the fact that Shannon had been entrapped by a journalist acting at his own initiative and in a private capacity. The ruling in *Teixeira* was said to be 'principally directed to the use in a criminal trial of evidence gained by means of an entrapment operation *carried out by or on behalf of the State or its agents*'.[125] In this case, however,

> the State's role was limited to prosecuting the applicant on the basis of information handed to it by a third party… who was not an agent of the State: he was not acting for the police on their instructions or otherwise under their control.

Furthermore, '[t]he police had no prior knowledge of M's operation, being presented with the audio and video recordings after the event'. The ECtHR did not say that evidence procured by 'private' entrapment could *never* result in an unfair trial. However, the Strasbourg judges were satisfied in this case that the domestic English courts had scrutinised the applicant's claims sufficiently carefully, and were justified in rejecting them. S's complaint of a breach of Article 6 was declared 'manifestly unfounded'.

This decision bucks the general trend of Strasbourg jurisprudence on entrapment. State responsibility, of course, is paramount under the Convention system. Thus, as the ECtHR rightly said, the issue in *Shannon* was whether the UK authorities breached Article 6 by relying on arguably tainted evidence to convict S at his criminal trial. S had not been the target of an official police undercover operation. Yet two further considerations cry out for moral appraisal. First, the sting perpetrated against S was far more elaborate and possibly corrupting than most of the simple deceptions challenged in other cases. It is not hard to imagine that S, intoxicated in more ways than one, was acting out of character and against his better judgement in seeking to impress his new friends, the wealthy phony sheikh and his attractive female companions. Whether such temptations are sufficiently intense to be at all exculpatory, as opposed to merely supplying motivation for criminality, poses questions of criminal responsibility and the moral limits of the criminal law meriting further analysis.[126]

[125] *Shannon*, above n 123, 11 (emphasis supplied).

[126] Useful entry points into a voluminous literature include: Ashworth, above n 79; Kleinig, above n 79, ch 8; PM Hughes, 'What is Wrong with Entrapment?' (2004) 42 *Southern Journal of Philosophy* 45; G Dworkin, 'The Serpent Beguiled Me and I did Eat: Entrapment and the Creation of Crime' (1985) 4 *Law and Philosophy* 17; AL-T Choo, *Abuse of Process and Judicial Stays of Criminal Proceedings*, 2nd edn (Oxford, OUP, 2008) ch 5. And

A second troubling aspect of this scenario is that M was a repeat-player, time and again conning celebrities into criminal indiscretions, and then exposing them in the national press and handing over incriminating information to the police. On no occasion was M himself prosecuted, although he was plainly committing criminal offences—incitement to supply narcotics; aiding and abetting their possession, etc.—and there is no general good-faith immunity in English law covering criminality perpetrated in the service of law enforcement.[127] It is obvious, in other words, that M had some kind of on-going relationship with the police, and one may wonder whether, at some point in this developing relationship, M had not become a de facto police informant, notwithstanding his notionally private status.[128] Considered in the round, it seems hard to square the ECtHR's peremptory rejection of S's eminently plausible complaint with the simplistic but-for causal test applied to denounce police entrapment in other cases.

The Lithuanian authorities attempted to reprise the 'private entrapment' argument in *Ramanauskas*, bizarrely one might think, since the sting in that case had been orchestrated by an undercover police officer working in an anti-corruption unit of the Ministry of the Interior. The officer, AZ, approached R, a prosecutor, and offered him a bribe of $3,000 to engineer the acquittal of a third party currently facing criminal charges. The charges against the third party were dropped, and R received $2,500. R was duly exposed, and later pleaded guilty to receiving a corrupt payment and served 10 months in prison. Before the Strasbourg Court, the Lithuanian government argued that AZ had been acting in a private capacity when he first approached R, because at that point AZ's operation had not been properly authorised in accordance with domestic procedural law. Rejecting this topsy-turvy contention out of hand, the ECtHR replied that it was 'particularly important that the authorities should assume responsibility' precisely *because* 'the initial phase of the operation... took place in the absence of any legal framework or judicial authorisation'.[129] The Lithuanian authorities were unable to suggest any personal motivation for AZ's conduct, proffering only the lame excuse that relevant documentation had been

specifically in relation to 'private entrapment', G Yaffe, '"The *Government* Beguiled Me": The Entrapment Defense and the Problem of Private Entrapment' (2005) 1 *Journal of Ethics and Social Philosophy* 1; K Hofmeyr, 'The Problem of Private Entrapment' [2006] *Criminal Law Review* 319.

[127] *R v Latif* [1996] 1 WLR 104 (HL). For penetrating normative analysis, see A Ashworth, 'Testing Fidelity to Legal Values: Official Involvement and Criminal Justice' in S Shute and AP Simester (eds), *Criminal Law Theory: Doctrines of the General Part* (Oxford, OUP, 2002).

[128] The UK's on-going 'phone hacking scandal, which has already seen off *The News of the World* and the Metropolitan Police Commissioner, is revealing the extent to which some British journalists and police officers may have been in cahoots: see P Lewis, 'Phone Hacking: Met Police to Investigate Mobile Tracking Claims', www.guardian.co.uk, 21 July 2011.

[129] (2010) 51 EHRR 11, [63]–[65].

destroyed. Permitting states parties to evade responsibility in such circumstances, admonished the Strasbourg judges, 'would open the way to abuses and arbitrariness by allowing the applicable principles to be circumvented through the "privatisation" of police incitement'. Whatever loophole for 'private' entrapment might have been opened up by *Shannon*, the ECtHR plainly had no intention of letting police officers slip through it, irrespective of an investigation's technical status in domestic law.

The Strasbourg judges also disagreed with the Lithuanian courts' analysis of R's substantive complaint; but here the merits of the issue seem far less cut-and-tried. The Lithuanian judges could find no warrant for R's behaviour. As a lawyer himself, R must have been fully aware of the seriousness of his corruption. There was no evidence of his being threatened or blackmailed by AZ. R freely accepted the bribe and therefore, in the estimation of the domestic courts, deserved to be held accountable for his criminal actions, even if AZ put temptation in his way. The ECtHR saw matters quite differently. For the Strasbourg judges, the scenario presented by *Ramanauskas* was another clear instance of active police incitement falling four-square within *Teixeira*'s strictures:

> [T]he actions of the individuals in question went beyond the mere passive investigation of existing criminal activity.... [They] had the effect of inciting the applicant to commit the offence of which he was convicted and... there is no indication that the offence would have been committed without their intervention. In view of such intervention and its use in the impugned criminal proceedings, the applicant's trial was deprived of the fairness required by Article 6 of the Convention.[130]

In arriving at this conclusion, the Strasbourg judges stressed the absence of any adequate proof that R was predisposed to behave corruptly:

> [T]hrough the contact established on the initiative of AZ and VS [an informant working under AZ's direction], the applicant seems to have been subjected to blatant prompting on their part to perform criminal acts, although there was no objective evidence—other than rumours—to suggest that he had been intending to engage in such activity.[131]

The ECtHR also pointedly observed that 'the domestic authorities denied that there had been any police incitement and took no steps at judicial level to carry out a serious examination of the applicant's allegations to that effect'.[132]

One should not be dogmatic in criticising the judgment in *Ramanauskas*, not least because the facts relied on are, quite typically, scanty and incomplete. But it is perplexing that the Court does not even acknowledge the potential significance of the fact that R himself was a public official, and a lawyer

[130] Ibid [68], [73].
[131] Ibid [67]–[68].
[132] Ibid [72].

to boot. As a general standard for initiating targeted policing methods, the requirement of pre-existing evidence or, at a minimum, well-founded suspicion of on-going or imminent criminality, appropriately precludes random virtue-testing, which is objectionable for many reasons.[133] However, covert virtue-testing—or competency assessment—may be acceptable in certain contexts. Random testing of public officials to ensure that they are not behaving corruptly is not obviously outrageous, especially if those public officials know what they are signing up to when they take the job. But let me emphasise one last time, context is crucial to ethical appraisal. For example, $3,000 might be an enormous amount of money to a Lithuanian prosecutor, like Judas's 30 pieces of silver.[134] Moral appraisal must be sensitive to the offer 'you can't refuse'. My point is only this: for as long as the ECtHR is unwilling, or unable, to engage seriously with the political morality of particular investigative techniques, retreating instead into vacuous rhetorical contrasts and simplistic causal criteria, its conclusions on the application of Article 6 to cases of alleged entrapment are bound to appear inadequately reasoned and, on occasion, unpersuasive.

CONCLUSION: COMMON LAW EVIDENCE, PROCEDURAL MORALITY, AND COSMOPOLITAN JURISPRUDENCE

This chapter has drawn attention to significant normative influences on English law's evolving approach to the admissibility of evidence procured through coercion or deception. The House of Lords' landmark judgment in *A v Home Secretary (No 2)*, declaring foreign torture evidence universally inadmissible, together with the Strasbourg Court's Article 6 jurisprudence on entrapment, in their different ways exemplify the irreducible role of moral reasoning in the development and application of procedural law. In so doing, they implicitly refute the argument for conceiving the Law of Evidence as an exclusively epistemological enterprise.

Evidence procured by torture is to be rejected, the House of Lords said in *A*, because torture is abhorrent. It makes no difference if information obtained by torture is reliable (although it often isn't); this rationale for inadmissibility appeals to intrinsic moral values, not to the predicted

[133] Including the following: random virtue-testing constrains liberty, extends official surveillance, invites police corruption or other abuses of official power, often requires law enforcers to participate in demeaning behaviour or to place themselves in danger, puts temptation in people's way, and is not a sensible or cost-effective use of limited policing resources. Some of these deficiencies also afflict legitimate undercover operations. The point is that proactive policing methods require special justification precisely because they imply greater risks than routine investigations. Cf *Williams and O'Hare v DPP* [1993] 3 All ER 365, DC; *Jacobson v US*, 503 US 540, 112 S Ct 1535 (1992).

[134] Matthew, 26 xiv–xv (King James Version).

consequences or comparative epistemic advantages of receiving or rejecting the evidence. From its very different institutional position at the apex of the Council of Europe's human rights law enforcement machinery, the ECtHR has effectively reached a similar conclusion regarding the impermissibility of relying on evidence obtained by official entrapment, albeit that its reasoning has been more circuitous, tentative and opaque. In broad terms, such evidence is deemed incapable of supporting a legitimate criminal conviction because it is incompatible with basic human rights in a modern democracy for the police to incite criminality or behave as agents provocateurs. The Strasbourg Court has subsequently applied a similar analysis in holding that Article 6 implies the inadmissibility of evidence obtained by torture.[135]

If criminal adjudication is an applied branch of political morality (as I believe it is), it is only to be expected that criminal procedure will generate institutionalised versions of moral dilemmas and conflicting political priorities. In a democracy, conflicts of political morality are best acknowledged and debated openly and tackled head-on. Should courts receive torture evidence? What are the appropriate limits of pro-active policing methods? These are moral and political, as well as legal, questions, and their practical answers demand nuanced judgements tailored to the facts of the instant case within a broad framework of principle. A rejuvenated law of criminal procedure, infused by modern human rights principles, must naturally take the lead in structuring institutional decision-making, but there remains an irreducible role for fine-grained judicial discretion in interpreting, and where necessary adapting, general principles at the point of application.

The growing influence of international human rights law on criminal procedure underscores the timeliness of comparative legal method.[136] No common lawyer can fail to be struck by the broadly cosmopolitan flavour of the case-law discussed in this essay. It was not so long ago that Strasbourg cases were invoked in English legal proceedings—and then only very rarely—merely as a perfunctory gesture, so that an applicant could claim that domestic remedies had finally been exhausted and no further procedural obstacle could bar her path to Strasbourg.[137] The position has been transformed beyond recognition within a decade. English lawyers must now regard pertinent ECtHR jurisprudence, such as Article 6 cases on entrapment, as formal sources of English law, which English courts are bound to take into account (not necessarily *follow*) whenever analogous

[135] *Gäfgen v Germany* (2011) 52 EHRR 1.

[136] Generally, see D Nelken, *Comparative Criminal Justice* (London, Sage, 2010); E Örücü, 'Developing Comparative Law' in Esin Örücü and David Nelken (eds), *Comparative Law—A Handbook* (Oxford, Hart Publishing, 2007); P Roberts, 'On Method: The Ascent of Comparative Criminal Justice' (2002) 22 *Oxford Journal of Legal Studies* 539; G Samuel, 'Comparative Law as a Core Subject' (2001) 21 *Legal Studies* 444.

[137] See, eg, *R v Brown* [1994] 1 AC 212 (HL) 237 (Lord Templeman), 256 (Lord Lowry), 271 (Lord Mustill).

issues arise in domestic criminal litigation.[138] English law is actively being shaped not only by a supra-national European court comprising judges of 47 nationalities, the vast majority of whom are civilian jurists, but also, albeit indirectly and remotely, by the criminal procedure law and practice of each of the 47 Council of Europe national states. Strasbourg jurisprudence on entrapment is a reflection of the activities of Portuguese undercover police officers, Russian drug squad 'buy-bust' operations, and corrupt Lithuanian prosecutors, amongst a multinational cast of thousands. And when the ECtHR has ruled on the compliance, or otherwise, of these investigative practices with Article 6 of the European Convention, English lawyers and judges must decide how, if at all, the Strasbourg Court's analysis and conclusions bear upon the criminal procedure law of England and Wales. Some of the challenges of fulfilling this brief have featured in the preceding discussion.

This is a time of rapid change, daunting prospects and unprecedented opportunity for normative and institutional development. English law is uniquely placed to be the leading common law system in Europe, and the leading European system in the common law world. But in order to realise its full potential, the methodological demands of international human rights, comparative law and legal reasoning are going to have to be taken much more seriously than English common lawyers have generally appreciated in the past. Successfully integrating cosmopolitan human rights into richly-articulated local procedural traditions calls for a methodologically astute common law comparativism in combination with jurisprudentially sophisticated normative reasoning.

[138] Human Rights Act 1998, s 2.

8

Ozymandias on Trial: Wrongs and Rights in DNA Cases

JEREMY GANS

INTRODUCTION

I met a traveller from an antique land
Who said: Two vast and trunkless legs of stone
Stand in the desert.[1]

THE STARTLING RISE and rapid expansion of DNA evidence in the criminal justice system has always been driven by dual narratives. The first time it was used in a criminal investigation, over 25 years ago, Alec Jeffreys' nascent science of 'DNA fingerprinting' not only exonerated a disturbed teenager who falsely confessed to one of a pair of murders in a village near Leicester but also flushed out the previously unsuspected culprit, who was undone by his efforts to side-step the first ever mass DNA screening.[2] The two stories of DNA profiling's power, to expose lies and truths alike, are retold in lengthy lists: hundreds of exonerations of the innocent and thousands of 'cold hit' links between unsolved crimes and unsuspected defendants. These narratives have been punctuated by modest developments in human rights law, including halting steps towards enforcing access to potentially exonerating evidence and towards addressing the retention of the DNA of the unconvicted.[3]

This chapter is concerned with an emerging third strand of the narrative: DNA's potential to conceal truths and create falsehoods. Recently this dark side of DNA has become prominent in the Australian state of Victoria, where it is now associated with one name. Farah Jama was convicted solely on the basis of a matching DNA profile, with tragic repercussions.

[1] P Shelley, 'Ozimandias' in *Rosalind and Helen: A Modern Eclogue; With Other Poems* (London, C & J Ollier, 1819) 72.
[2] See J Wambaugh, *The Blooding* (Bantam, USA, 1989).
[3] See *Skinner v Switzer* (United States Supreme Court Docket 09-9000); *S and Marper v UK* (2009) 48 EHRR 50, [2008] ECHR 1581.

Reporting to the Victorian government on the case, retired Supreme Court judge Frank Vincent observed:

> [T]he DNA evidence was, like Ozymandias' broken statue in the poem by Shelley, found isolated in a vast desert. And like the inscription on the statue's pedestal, everything around it belied the truth of its assertion. The statue, of course, would be seen by any reasonably perceptive observer, and viewed in its surroundings, as a shattered monument to an arrogance that now mocked itself. By contrast, the DNA evidence appears to have been viewed as possessing an almost mystical infallibility that enabled its surroundings to be disregarded.[4]

This chapter explores the *Jama* case and its aftermath in order to argue that this third element of the DNA story demands a fresh response from both evidence law and human rights law. It first describes the miscarriage of justice and its dual victims and then examines the technological and human failings that lay behind Jama's wrongful conviction. Finally, it draws attention to an additional flaw in the process, overlooked by Vincent: the ordinary operation of the law of evidence. To avoid complicity in DNA's potential for harm, evidence law must reinvent the way it seeks to uphold defendants' right to a fair hearing.

1. DNA'S HUMAN VICTIMS

Near them, on the sand,
Half sunk, a shattered visage lies, whose frown,
And wrinkled lip, and sneer of cold command,
Tell that its sculptor well those passions read
Which yet survive, stamped on these lifeless things,
The hand that mocked them and the heart that fed.

She awoke to a woman's voice saying, 'pull up her pants'. The floor underneath her was black. There were male voices too. They told her that she had been found in a cubicle in the women's toilets next to Bar 3 of the Venue Nightclub, in the Melbourne suburb of Doncaster. She recalled having drunk two Franjelicos with her sister-in-law and her partner in the car park and another two inside and speaking with or being spoken to by a few men, one of whom she didn't like because he was 'sleazy'. Her next memory was waking up on the toilet floor in pain, nauseous and unable

[4] F Vincent, *Report: Inquiry Into the Circumstances That Led to the Conviction of Mr Farah Abdulkadir Jama*, Victorian Government Printer, Melbourne, May 2010, available at www.justice.vic.gov.au/wps/wcm/connect/5a103e804263c8da810e832b0760a79a/VincentReportFinal6May2010.pdf?MOD=AJPERES ('Vincent Report') 11.

to move. The security staff told her the time. She had been in the club for only half an hour.[5]

Lapsing in and out of consciousness and vomiting repeatedly, she was taken to the Austin Hospital. Her arms and upper body were bruised, and further bruises later developed on her upper thighs. When she expressed concern that she had been drugged and assaulted, the local rape crisis centre was contacted. Toxicology registered a 0.13 blood/alcohol content and only her own prescription medication. The next morning, in the hospital's Crisis Care Unit, she was examined by Dr Nicola Cunningham, a forensic medical practitioner, who gave her the good news that her genitals were normal and uninjured, and that her bruises were almost certainly caused when security dragged her across the floor of the nightclub. Later came the bad news: a routine swab from her upper cervix found spermatozoa.[6] But she 'had not had sexual intercourse for some considerable time'.[7] At Farah Jama's sentencing for her rape, she told the court: 'I was violated in a most reprehensible way and preyed upon by another individual. Since that night I have tried to recall the events. I have felt shame, rage and unrelenting guilt that I do not think will ever leave me'.[8]

These days, it is possible for police to solve 'stranger rape' cases swiftly—even ones that feature a dark, crowded, anonymous crime scene and an intoxicated, amnesiac complainant. Exactly four months after the nightclub incident, Jama, a teenager living 10km away from Doncaster, was arrested for the rape. Victoria's DNA database had reported a match between his DNA and the sperm on the cervical swab. In his police interview, Jama denied not only the rape, but also having been to the club that night or indeed ever having been in any nightclub or even having heard of the suburb of Doncaster. He consented to give a fresh buccal swab, which also matched the cervical swab and became the centrepiece of his trial two years later.[9]

At the trial, Jama's father, brother and friend Abdul all testified that the 19 year-old had been at home that night, reciting the Koran and listening to his ailing father delivering his last will, details that were later highlighted in racist corners of the internet.[10] Abdul was a problem witness. The two friends had earlier denied seeing each other that night. As well, Abdul admitted in cross-examination that he and Jama had been nightclubbing on two occasions. Trial judge Paul Lacava noted that the alibi evidence 'was most unsatisfactory in many respects' and that he was 'not at all surprised

[5] *R v Jama* [2008] VCC 0886, [4]–[8].
[6] Ibid [9]–[11].
[7] Ibid [17].
[8] Ibid [38].
[9] Ibid [19].
[10] Eg http://abandonskip.blogspot.com/2008/07/i-didnt-rape-her-i-was-reading-koran-to.html.

that the jury rejected that evidence'.[11] After the jury convicted him, Jama pled his youth and clean record, but Judge Lacava found that his prospect of rehabilitation was reduced by his and his family's continued denials of his guilt.[12] Jama was given a four-year minimum gaol sentence, with Judge Lacava emphasising the importance of both general deterrence, to 'reflect the community's disgust with this type of offending and send a clear message to like offenders', and individual deterrence, telling Jama that the sentence would 'encourage you to see the error of your ways, and to take proper steps to do something about it'.[13]

Judge Lacava had not been willing to leave the case on the sole basis of the DNA match. Ignoring objections from both the prosecution and the defence, he told the jurors that they were entitled to view Jama's contradicted denial of ever having been to any nightclub as evidence of 'consciousness of guilt'. That is, the jury could infer not only that Jama lied to the police (and, therefore, that he lacked credibility and was not as naïve as he claimed) but also that he deliberately tried to mislead them about the likelihood of his guilt.[14] The judge's direction contravened Australia's strict (but subtle) common law on evidence of a defendant's lies.[15] So, a year into Jama's sentence, the prosecution conceded that his conviction could not stand.[16] The remaining issue was whether the appeal court should order a new trial or enter an acquittal, a question that squarely raised the issue of whether a defendant can be convicted solely on the basis of DNA evidence.[17]

The prosecution now considered afresh how Jama's DNA came to be matched to the Doncaster rape in the first place.[18] DNA had been taken in a 'separate and entirely unrelated investigation ... related to events that occurred in Reservoir', 16km from Doncaster, for which Jama had not been charged and which was recited in Judge Lacava's sentencing remarks for 'the purposes of setting out in full the chronology'. But the chronology was curious. As Judge Lacava casually observed, the event in Reservoir (without which Jama would never have been identified) actually occurred the 'night before' the alleged rape in Doncaster.[19]

The police and prosecutors knew that the coincidences did not end there. The Reservoir event was also a rape allegation, this time by a complainant who knew and clearly identified Jama and with whom Jama admitted

11 *R v Jama* [2008] VCC 0886, [23].
12 Ibid [37].
13 Ibid [42]–[43].
14 Vincent Report, above n 4, 44–45.
15 *Edwards v R* (1993) 178 CLR 193; *Zoneff v R* (2000) 200 CLR 234.
16 Vincent Report, above n 4, 44.
17 Ibid 45–47.
18 Ibid 46.
19 *R v Jama* [2008] VCC 0886, [18].

engaging in sexual activity.[20] What was not known, until it was reported by a member of the prosecution's appeal team exactly three years after Jama volunteered the vital buccal swab to the police, was that there was a third coincidence: the Reservoir complainant's forensic medical practitioner was Dr Nicola Cunningham, the same doctor who examined the Doncaster complainant the next day.[21] Within two weeks, Jama was a free man and the complainant was told that the rape she had struggled to both remember and forget had almost certainly never taken place.

2. DNA'S HUMAN FAILINGS

And on the pedestal these words appear:
'My name is Ozymandias, king of kings:
Look on my Works ye Mighty, and despair!'

International human rights law makes express provision for the wrongly convicted:[22]

> When a person has by a final decision been convicted of a criminal offence and when subsequently his conviction has been reversed or he has been pardoned on the ground that a new or newly discovered fact shows conclusively that there has been a miscarriage of justice, the person who has suffered punishment as a result of such conviction shall be compensated according to law, unless it is proved that the non-disclosure of the unknown fact in time is wholly or partly attributable to him.

This provision bristles with caveats. It excludes non-defendant victims of miscarriages of justice (such as the complainant in Jama's case) and people whose convictions were reversed in a regular appeal (such as Jama himself). It is limited to mistakes revealed by 'new or newly discovered facts', as opposed to known facts that were inadequately considered, and to errors that are 'conclusively' shown. More importantly, the only requirement that the provision imposes on the state in the aftermath of a miscarriage of justice is to compensate. There is no obligation to try to identify the causes of the mistake or to take steps to prevent a recurrence. Indeed, the provision lists only one potential cause of the mistake: that it may be 'wholly or partly attributable to' the person who was wrongly convicted. Yet this heavily-qualified right proved too much for the Victorian Parliament, which omitted it altogether from the State of Victoria's Charter of Human Rights and Responsibilities Act 2006, enacted the same month as the nightclub

[20] Vincent Report, above n 4, 13, 22, 35.
[21] Ibid 46–47.
[22] International Covenant on Civil and Political Rights, Article 14(6).

incident. However, Jama received over half a million Australian dollars in ex gratia compensation.[23]

Miscarriages of justice are vital teachable moments in criminal law, simultaneously revealing the gravity of the law's mistakes, the potential for further errors and the prospect of uncovering or preventing similar ones. In 2001, when belated DNA analysis revealed that a Queensland man had been wrongly convicted of rape, the state's Court of Appeal declared 'a black day in the history of the administration of criminal justice', pilloried police for focusing solely upon DNA evidence's power to convict and neglecting its power to exonerate, and, pending further findings 'with a view to ensuring that this sort of incident does not occur in the future', called for adequate staffing and financing of the state's major forensic lab.[24] By contrast, nine years later, Victoria's Court of Appeal marked Jama's reversal of fortune with a bland, one sentence ruling noting the submissions before it and entering a verdict of acquittal.[25] While the contrast might be attributed to differences in judicial style, it may also reflect the much more unsettling nature of the error in Jama's case. Not only was DNA evidence the culprit this time, rather than the saviour, but the error's discovery was serendipitous, the mistakes (both technical and human) were obscure and multi-faceted, and—as the following pages recount—the incident was the third such in Victoria's recent history.[26]

The discovery and reversal of Jama's wrongful conviction deviated from the Hollywood script of a triumph by feisty defence lawyers or quirky scientists in the face of stone-walling prosecutors. Instead, it was Detective Karen Porter, one of the police officers investigating Jama, who not long after the rape charge was laid made the first inquiries of the DNA lab, with the following request:

> On 24 November ... I discussed with you an offender identified through a DNA sample allegedly responsible for a rape. Briefly, he has denied all knowledge and the victim has little or no recollection of the night ... In the current climate I need to be able to discount the possibility of cross-contamination. Perhaps a report is all that is required. I have every faith in the process but no doubt the subject will be raised at any subsequent trial so we may as well be armed with suitable answers to the inevitable questions.[27]

[23] R Sexton, 'Man paid $525,000 for wrong conviction', *The Age*, 30 June 2010.

[24] *R v Button* [2001] QCA 133, [4].

[25] *R v Jama*, unreported, VicSCCA, 7 December 2009 (Warren CJ, Redlich and Bongiorno JJA). The judgment simply stated: 'The Court, having read the materials filed by the parties and having considered the submissions and concessions of the Crown, is satisfied that it is appropriate to order that the conviction relating to the applicant be set aside and a verdict of acquittal be entered'.

[26] For a potential fourth DNA-induced wrongful conviction, see *Alecu v R; Theoharethes v R* [2010] VSCA 208, [7]–[11].

[27] Vincent Report, above n 4, 25.

The 'current climate' was almost certainly a reference to the first of the two previous DNA errors in Victoria.

The four-month period between the nightclub incident and Jama's arrest saw the publication of a long-awaited coronial report into the notorious death of toddler Jaidyn Leskie in 1997 in the eastern Victorian town of Moe.[28] A side issue in that case was an obviously spurious DNA match between the toddler's clothing and the victim of a rape 150km away in the Melbourne suburb of Altona.[29] Items from both cases were dealt with by the same police analyst in a single week in early 1998, but Victoria's government forensics lab firmly rejected any connection, citing the separation of the relevant samples by a number of days and the lab's 'second nature' quality assurance procedures. [30] Instead, the lab relied on the very argument typically raised by criminal defendants (including Jama) to explain away suspicious DNA evidence: that the match must be the result of an 'adventitious' shared profile between the rape victim and a mystery woman associated with Leskie's death.[31] The Coroner was troubled that the lab would be willing to rely on a double coincidence—the adventitious match and the relevant samples being in the lab within days of each other—rather than concede even the possibility of a flaw in its processes:

> It is of potential concern for the criminal justice system and its investigatory processes that, in the event that it is possible that a laboratory process error or contamination occurs within the State's forensic laboratory, it has become necessary for international experts to be obtained by an external inquiry process (like a coroner) and a lengthy hearing to occur in order to determine the likely answer. Fortunately, these incidents appear to be relatively rare.[32]

The Coroner endorsed the unanimous view of the external experts that the match was the result of contamination, possibly via a pair of scissors which had been used on all the exhibits.[33] And yet, a month after the Coroner's report was released, a case manager in Victoria's lab responded to the request by Jama's investigator about possible contamination with a similar dismissal of any risk:

> In my opinion I do not think contamination between the two cases could have occurred as items from the two cases and the relevant reference samples were examined at different times, at different areas and by different people. Also,

[28] State Coroner of Victoria, *Inquest into the Death of Jaidyn Raymond Leskie*, Coroner's Case No 0007/98, October 2006.

[29] Ibid 64–85.

[30] Maxwell Jones, the analyst who handled the exhibits, co-authored an early paper on 'trace DNA': R van Oorschot and M Jones, 'DNA fingerprints from fingerprints' (1997) 387 *Nature* 767.

[31] Counsel for VPFSC relied on a 1 in 11 million chance that the profile would be shared by one of the rape victim's 16 half-sisters. See Leskie Report, above n 28, 82.

[32] Ibid 99.

[33] Ibid 85.

> the DNA processes were done at different times such that the samples were not processed together in the same batch.[34]

Vincent later condemned this response as 'incomplete'.[35] It lacked a chronology, which would have shown that the various samples were received and analysed within days of each other, sometimes in adjacent rooms, and contained material inaccuracies. Some of the samples were in fact received or analysed by the same person. Most importantly, it failed to disclose the limited scope of the case manager's internal review and inquiries.

Unfortunately, the Vincent Report made no mention of either the earlier *Leskie* case or of a subsequent revelation of DNA contamination in Victoria's forensic lab. The day after Jama was convicted, Victoria Police proudly announced that their DNA database had solved another notorious cold case, connecting a current prisoner, Russell Gesah, with the 'Tapp murders' in Melbourne's north in 1982.[36] Just two weeks later, the police withdrew the murder charges laid against Gesah, after they realised that clothing from the Tapp case had been analysed in the Victorian lab on the same day in 1999 as clothing from an unrelated case connected to Gesah.[37] This time there was no denying the lab's culpability. The embarrassed Deputy Police Commissioner, Simon Overland, announced a review of 6,000 cases involving DNA evidence to detect any 'similar issue of cross-contamination'.[38] Three months later, the police proudly announced that the review had uncovered just one other problem case, an incorrect link between a theft and cannabis possession where the suspect had not been charged.[39] Although the police's review was unpublished, it seems safe to infer that Jama's was one of the cases examined and cleared. Vincent made no mention of the Gesah case, the failure of the police's review and the apparent missed opportunity to save Jama a year's unnecessary imprisonment.

In one sense, contamination is the very essence of forensic science, epitomised in Locard's aphorism that 'every contact leaves a trace'. But contamination can occur, not only during crimes, but also during the investigation of crimes. Indeed, several aspects of the criminal justice system routinely bring evidence from different cases into 'contact'. Victoria's forensics lab, based in a single building in the Melbourne suburb of MacLeod (coincidentally midway between Doncaster and Reservoir) posed a particular risk. A further independent review conducted in 2010 found that the lab's results

[34] Vincent Report, above n 4, 25.

[35] Ibid 26.

[36] K Moor, 'Russell John Gesah charged over murders of Margaret Tapp and daughter', *Herald Sun*, 22 July 2008.

[37] 'Charges withdrawn over murder of Margaret Tapp and daughter', *Herald Sun*, 6 August 2008.

[38] Ibid.

[39] Victoria Police, 'DNA Review finalised', Media Release, 24 September 2008, available via www.police.vic.gov.au/.

'appear to have a higher proportion of mixed samples than would normally be anticipated', indicating the likelihood of poor contamination management procedures either in the lab or at Victorian crime scenes.[40]

Victoria Police at all levels failed to recognise other forensic magnets in the system. A second set of contamination risks, the police's non-forensic operations, which may link disparate crimes via common officers, cars, equipment or police stations, was unlikely to be the operative factor in Jama's case, since the two alleged rapes were investigated at separate police stations.[41] Rather, the answer lay in a third centripetal force in criminal justice: crisis treatment facilities and, in particular, the specialised services for rape complainants. As the (chance) commonality of forensic medical practitioners in the two cases eventually revealed to the prosecution, the Reservoir and Doncaster complainants were examined in the same rape crisis facility one day apart. That facility was a suite of rooms, including a single examination room at Heidelberg's Austin Hospital (also midway between the two suburbs), which was utilised by about 10% of the state's 300 or so annual rape victims. The tawdry details of the Reservoir event included a major contamination risk factor: the complainant had Jama's semen in her hair.

The inquiry into Jama's wrongful conviction found that the likely pathway from the Reservoir complainant's hair to the Doncaster complainant's cervical swab was not via Dr Cunningham (who had naturally showered and changed clothes when she went home between the two examinations) or the crisis care room's comfortable but uncleanable furniture. The most likely contamination site was a medical trolley positioned to ensure that rape examinations proceed quickly and smoothly. It appeared to have been used as a combined storage spot for fresh (and, in a quirk of Victorian forensic process, unpackaged) swabs and for temporary placement of used ones and associated slides. In the rare circumstance that the facility was used twice in a row, this complainant-friendly system was just one inadequate clean away from cross-contamination.[42] According to Vincent:[43]

> It is almost incredible that, in consequence of a minute particle, so small that it was invisible to the naked eye, being released into the environment and then by some mechanism settling on a swab, slide or trolley surface, a chain of events

[40] S Fraser, J Buckleton and P Gill, *Review of DNA Reporting Practices by Victoria Police Forensic Sciences Division* (April 2010) 3, on-line via www.vicpolicenews.com.au/. The report continues: 'A contributory factor to the situation may be that VPFSD DNA analyses appear to have a higher proportion of mixed samples than would normally be anticipated. This may be a consequence of the scenes of crime collection or item selection policies. A detailed review of laboratory facilities, environment and practices is required in order to ensure good practice and minimise potential contamination incidents'.

[41] Vincent Report, above n 4, 52.

[42] Ibid 18–24.

[43] Ibid 48.

> could be started that culminated in the conviction of an individual for a crime that had never been committed by him or anyone else, created immense personal distress for many people and exposed a number of deficiencies in our criminal justice system. But that, I believe, is what happened.

The Vincent inquiry report naturally included many, sometimes controversial, recommendations aimed at preventing contamination in rape crisis rooms and elsewhere.[44] In notable contrast to the aftermath of Victoria's two previous known contamination cases, Vincent appreciated that the broader system had failed, too, in Jama's case. What he found especially striking (and inspired his poetical reference to Shelley) was that the case was, at least in hindsight, pregnant with danger signs in the form of the inherent unlikelihood of the prosecution's theory of Jama's guilt. These contradictory signs included: the extreme time and space limitations of the alleged nightclub rape; the absence of any other forensic or evidentiary links to Jama; the complainant's prescription drugs and alcohol use as an explanation of her condition when found; and the failure of the complainant, the security cameras and literally hundreds of witnesses to notice a black teenager in a venue full of Caucasian mature adults at an 'over 28s' night club.[45] According to Vincent, the result was that the prosecution's explanation of the presence of Jama's DNA on the complainant's vaginal swab—ejaculation during her rape—was not just unlikely, bold and awful, but 'patently absurd'.[46]

Vincent's explanation for this breathtaking systemic failure was the presence of equally astonishing across-the-board ignorance of scientific evidence:

> After following the history of the proceedings against the unfortunate Mr Jama from their origins through to their disastrous conclusion with his conviction, I have been left with the deep impression that at virtually every point, and by almost everyone involved, it was handled with so little insight into the issues which it presented that no need was seen to explore further or conduct research into them.[47]

The inquiry report details specific failings of particular institutions. The police seemed unaware of the particular contamination risk-factors posed by the two cases.[48] Forensic medical practice was aimed at hygiene and care

[44] Ibid 48–52. The recommendations included adopting 'sexual assault examination kits' used in all other Australian jurisdictions and reducing Melbourne's six rape crisis care units to just two, located in hospitals, to ensure that high forensic standards are maintained. The downsides of this suggestion include both more temporal proximity of unrelated cases (hence contamination risks) and an increased demand on rape complainants to travel across Melbourne to large hospitals in the aftermath of an alleged assault.

[45] Ibid 33–35.

[46] Ibid 11.

[47] Ibid.

[48] Ibid 25.

and neglected the 'special requirements of DNA collection'.[49] The forensics lab took a narrow view not only of the sources of risk but of its own role in addressing them proactively.[50] However, the report's strongest critique was of 'those involved in the legal process', whose lack of insight was deemed to be 'particularly' glaring.[51]

Given the apparent novelty of a DNA-only trial and the particular features of this one, the lawyers, Vincent declared, should have researched the existing case-law on DNA evidence. This critique of the lawyers is curious, because the case-law Vincent detailed was concerned with the dangers of probabilistic calculations, which court experts use to quantify the risk of a coincidental match in the DNA profiles of unrelated people.[52] No one thinks that Jama's wrongful conviction was the result of such a coincidence. Instead, Vincent's looser suggestion was that legal research about this unrelated risk might have led prosecutors to consider the potential weaknesses of their own evidence more carefully.

While Vincent deserves praise for recognising that the problems of DNA evidence go well beyond the particular error in Jama's case, his report is lacking in strong recommendations other than those related to the specific contamination risk he uncovered. Although he clearly believed that DNA-only cases should never proceed to trial, his recommendations were limited to training about the 'nature and appropriate use' of DNA evidence for legal professionals and the police, with only the latter prompted to focus on 'cases where there is minimal corroborative evidence to support proposed or pending charges'.[53] Nevertheless, the Victorian DPP had already pre-empted Vincent's report by inserting the following proviso into its guidelines on the exercise of prosecutorial discretion:

> In any matter in which the prosecution case is wholly or substantially reliant upon DNA evidence, the prosecution should not be instituted or continued until specific instructions have been sought from the Director or in his absence, the Chief Crown Prosecutor. The purpose of this requirement is to ensure that very close scrutiny is given to this category of cases, to ensure that they proceed only if the DNA evidence is clearly reliable and highly probative, and/or where there is sufficient non-DNA evidence available to support the prosecution case.[54]

[49] Ibid 21–23, 49–50.

[50] Ibid 25–26.

[51] Ibid 11, 46.

[52] Ibid 45–46, referring to *R v Green* (unreported, NSWCCA, 26 March 1991) and *R v Pantoja* (1996) 88 A Crim R 534.

[53] Ibid 55–56.

[54] Office of Public Prosecutions Victoria, 'Prosecution Polices and Guidelines', available via www.opp.vic.gov.au/, 2.1.13.

Despite government claims to the contrary,[55] this new rule does not change the decision to prosecute, but only the decision-maker. The rule's 'purpose' clause neither precludes DNA-only prosecutions nor gives any guidance as to when that evidence will be deemed 'clearly reliable and highly probative' or what non-DNA evidence will be 'sufficient' where the first standard is not met. Indeed, the rule's scope, covering any matter *substantially* reliant upon DNA evidence, is so broad that it is inconceivable that the state's two most senior prosecutors will actually give every such case comprehensive individualised attention.

3. THE LAW'S FAILINGS

Nothing beside remains.

International human rights law offers a suite of criminal process guarantees that aims, in part, to pre-empt miscarriages of justice. Particular rights of significance to forensic science evidence include criminal defendants' rights to a competent and independent tribunal, to the benefit of the presumption of innocence, to prompt information about the charge, to adequate defence facilities and to call and cross-examine witnesses.[56] However, as Jama's case demonstrates, these rights are impotent in a case where nobody fully understands the evidence of guilt. Notably, the party best placed to utilise the process guarantees available to Jama—his trial counsel—engaged in what appears to have been a scattergun cross-examination of the prosecution's DNA expert, suggesting weaknesses in the lab analysis[57] and a failure to look hard enough for other, exonerating DNA. However, no DNA expert was called by the defence to challenge the prosecution's evidence. Jama's defence instead relied upon the presumption of innocence and the family alibi. Crucially, the defence accepted the lab's assurance about contamination. Detective Porter's 'inevitable questions' were never put to the prosecution forensic expert.[58]

The Caribbean Court of Justice recently held that human rights law demands more than the list of minimum guarantees where the prosecution case is solely dependent on a single item of scientific evidence. In early

[55] Media Release, 'Hulls discusses report by former Supreme Court judge Frank Vincent', 6 May 2010, www.premier.vic.gov.au/component/content/article/10362.html.

[56] International Covenant on Civil and Political Rights, Article 14(2) and (3).

[57] Pending the appeal, Jama's new defence team queried the procedures at the testing laboratory, and, according to the Vincent Report, above n 4, 45, '[f]urther tests were conducted, one by an independent laboratory *which was unable to replicate the findings* and another at the Forensic Science Centre itself which confirmed them to their satisfaction' (emphasis added).

[58] Ibid 29.

2002, Barbados police charged Frank Gibson with the murder of Francine Bolden, whose crushed body was found on a hillside.[59] The sole prosecution evidence was a wound on Gibson's upper arm, which Dr Victor Edmond, a dentist who had 'some training' in forensic odontology, said was a bite-mark that 'only' Bolden 'could have made'. Gibson maintained that the wound, and other scratches on his body, resulted from falling out of a tree. In 2006, still awaiting his murder trial, Gibson petitioned the Barbados government, and then the courts, for funding for an international forensic odontologist to assist the defence. At his appeal from the rejection of that request in Barbados, the Court of Justice expressed 'serious reservations' about Gibson's argument that a state-funded expert was a 'facility' that Gibson was guaranteed by the Barbados Constitution;[60] however, it nevertheless held that his particular claim was supported by the general right to a fair hearing:[61]

> It is accepted by the parties before us that the only evidence positively linking him to the crime is of a highly scientific kind and that without this evidence there is no viable case against him. That evidence is to be given in court by a doctor who is not himself in regular practice in the particular scientific field. That field is, in the words of the Court of Appeal, of a 'complex and controversial' nature … There is another reason why it is important that Gibson be provided with such assistance. As far as it is possible to do so, we must ensure that at his trial the truth is established especially bearing in mind that if Gibson is convicted the judge has no option but to impose a death sentence.

The Court's ruling is a novel repudiation of avoidable ignorance in criminal trials; albeit one that could easily be limited to its particular facts, involving an especially dire field of forensics, a particularly dubious expert, an impoverished nation and a punishment allowing no room for error. Anyway, the information deficit in Gibson's trial was raised proactively by his own lawyers and allowed for a relatively straightforward solution in the form of government funding for defence experts. By contrast, as Vincent found, ignorance of DNA evidence was endemic to all sides in Jama's case, despite the generous resources available in Victoria's criminal justice system.

Australia's media were quick to lay the blame for Jama's miscarriage of justice on a TV show.[62] The so-called 'CSI effect' is routinely blamed for heightening jurors' expectations of scientific evidence, to the detriment of trials with little or no forensic science content. It is also said to encourage exaggerated reliance on whatever scientific evidence is presented. Vincent's report duly name-checked the supposed effect, quoting a Victorian deputy police commissioner's regret that cases that 'debunked' the CSI effect

[59] *Gibson v Attorney-General* [2010] CCJ 3 (AJ).
[60] Ibid [28].
[61] Ibid [37]–[38].
[62] M Pelly, 'CSI effect on juries confounds scientists', *The Australian*, 21 May 2010.

(including Jama's, it seems) may mean that DNA evidence's 'real value may be seriously diminished'.[63] However, Vincent failed to note that his report's bleak conclusion—that DNA evidence had beguiled and bewildered the entire Victorian criminal justice system—was subject to a significant exception. Jama's jury turned out to be the one institution in the case that asked all the right questions at the right time.

In response to the defence's blunderbuss assault on the quality of the DNA evidence implicating Jama, the prosecution's forensic scientist, Debra Scott, outlined her lab's 'quality control procedures'. Perhaps anticipating that this line of questioning might cause the jury to dwell on the fallibility of DNA evidence, the prosecutor suggested that such matters had no bearing in 'the particular case', to which Scott duly replied that 'there was no evidence of any contamination occurring'. Apparently unimpressed, the jury promptly submitted a question of its own inquiring 'whether there were any statistics relating to detected incidents of contamination'. The prosecutor's response was to instruct Scott to 'forget other cases' and get her to reaffirm that 'there was no evidence of any contamination in this case', an exchange that Vincent's review later criticised as a mutual failure of both scientific experts' and lawyers' obligations when it comes to presenting expert evidence.[64] However, the jury soon appreciated that more was being kept from them than just the general risks of contaminated DNA evidence. How, they enquired, had it come about that the police were in possession of Jama's DNA profile in the first place? Judge Lacava's reply adopted the time-honoured judicial formula for avoiding irregular disclosure of the accused's extraneous bad character: '[T]here was no evidence on that aspect, which was irrelevant to their deliberations'.[65]

In short, the jury asked exactly the right questions that would ultimately solve the case, but were given precisely the wrong answers. This suggests a cause of Jama's wrongful conviction that Vincent overlooked: the law of evidence. The non-answer to the jury's question about error-rate statistics appears to be an instance of a well-known and much lamented phenomenon: the common law's reluctance to permit generalised expert evidence about the reliability of other evidence.[66] This chapter's focus is on a phenomenon that has received less attention to date in the literature on expert evidence: the law's connivance in (if not insistence upon) the concealment of the investigative origins of forensic matches between a defendant and a crime. The impact of this stratagem in Jama's case was dramatic, as it prevented the jury from

[63] Vincent Report, above n 4, 30.

[64] Ibid 28.

[65] Ibid 37. See also *R v Jama* [2008] VCC 0866, [18].

[66] For a recent example, see A Roberts, 'Eyewitness Identification and Expert Insight' (2010) 14 *International Journal of Evidence & Proof* 57.

learning about the very events which, once they became known during Jama's appeal, led to his almost immediate exoneration.

In Jama's case, this concealment was never formally debated and there was no actual ruling on the admissibility of the Reservoir event. Rather, the prosecutors themselves took the lead in ensuring that the jury would not learn about what happened in Reservoir. An early memo to Crown counsel stated:

> There is no other evidence that implicates the defendant other than DNA evidence. The difficulty the prosecution will have is how to lead this evidence without disclosing that the defendant was arrested in relation to another rape that occurred the night before the current offence, for which he was profiled.[67]

Likewise, the defence, having received the lab's assurance that there was no contamination, made no effort to find out about what happened in Reservoir, presumably because it was assumed that further inquiries would not assist their case.[68] It is possible that their (otherwise unexplained) decision not to call Jama as a witness for the defence was based on the fear that their client might reveal something about the earlier case or put his character in issue, potentially freeing the prosecution to adduce evidence about the Reservoir event by way of rebuttal or cross-examination as to credit.[69]

The legal conspiracy to keep the jury from learning about the Reservoir allegations was not limited to the trial. When the police arrested Jama for the nightclub rape, they asked him for a new buccal swab, even though they already had his DNA from the Reservoir incident.[70] A collateral purpose of this step, routine in DNA investigations, is to enable the true origins of the match to be kept from the jury. As Judge Lacava explained in his sentencing remarks: '[A]nalysis of that sample and the DNA profile of you obtained from it, was given in evidence before the jury. The jury were not told of the earlier buccal swab, which alerted the investigators to you…'.[71] But this sleight of hand did not fool Jama's jury,[72] which is why Judge Lacava was forced into actively participating in the cover-up. He responded to the jury's specific and highly pertinent inquiry with the cultivated evasion that the source of police intelligence was irrelevant and that there was no evidence about it.

[67] Vincent Report, above n 4, 33.

[68] Ibid 39: 'no request was made to the OPP to secure access to the file relating to the earlier incident'.

[69] Crimes Act 1958 (Vic), s 399(5) (now repealed). See now Evidence Act 2008 (Vic), ss 104 and 110.

[70] *R v Jama* [2008] VCC 0866, [21].

[71] Ibid.

[72] For another illustration, see J Gans, 'Much Repented: Consent to DNA Sampling' (2007) 30 *University of New South Wales Law Journal* 579, 603.

The purpose of all these half-truths and misinformation is, of course, to reduce the risk of 'prejudice' to Jama.[73] Like most common law systems of evidence, Victoria's courts wholeheartedly adopt the widespread assumption that jurors, once they know that a defendant is linked to other crimes (especially heinous or similar ones, as in this case), will be more inclined to convict regardless of the merits of the case. It is this rule, therefore, that is a proximate cause of the miscarriage of justice in this case. And yet the Vincent inquiry merely noted that Judge Lacava's answer was unlikely to have alleviated jurors' suspicions; to the contrary '[i]t could be seen as akin to an indication that an individual had prior convictions that they were not to know about'.[74] Despite the implicit suggestion that the law not only kept relevant evidence from Jama's jury but created a new and entirely false risk of prejudice, Vincent's report ventured no criticisms of the rules of evidence.

Instead, the inquiry laid the blame for the jury's ignorance of the Reservoir events at the trial lawyers' door:

> Although the DNA evidence had become available because of the investigation of Mr Jama's possible involvement in the commission of a separate offence of a sexual character very shortly prior to the night in question, no attempt was made until well after the trial by the prosecution to secure detailed information concerning that matter or to investigate what had taken place.[75]

Defence lawyers were equally derelict in failing to appreciate the potential evidential implications of the Reservoir incident:

> The material gathered in relation to it may have been useful for any one of a number of purposes, including what might be learned about Mr Jama himself, and, as it ultimately transpired, the likelihood that he may have committed the offence in the circumstances alleged, when, on the previous night, he had not availed himself of the opportunity to engage in consensual penile intercourse with an apparently enthusiastic young woman.[76]

Vincent suggests that the post-trial events that led to the discovery of the miscarriage of justice should have occurred, and in future should be made to occur, pre-trial.[77] This conceit fails to confront the reality that the post-trial revelations in *Jama* arose from prosecutorial scrambling in the face of Judge

[73] *R v Christie* [1914] AC 545. See now Evidence Act 2008 (Vic), ss 101 and 135–37.

[74] Vincent Report, above n 4, 37.

[75] Ibid 35.

[76] Ibid 3.

[77] An obvious, but little discussed, flaw of this approach is that it assumes that professionals in the criminal justice system, be they police, lawyers or judges, are immune to the distorting effects that knowledge of prior, heinous and similar allegations is assumed to have on jurors. Vincent's exclusive focus on everyone's beguilement by DNA sidelines any inquiry into the potential role played by this prejudice, not to mention other varieties related to Jama's origins, against a backdrop of media stories blaming new African arrivals for a Melbourne crime wave. See, eg, R Kerbaj, 'Police say Sudanese a gang threat', *The Australian*, 5 January 2007; B Roberts, 'Rapist refugee gets 17 years', *Herald Sun*, 31 January 2007.

Lacava's erroneous direction regarding Jama's lies. The case is no poster child for systematic or comprehensive risk management. Moreover, but for the—as it turned out, spurious—coincidence of the same doctor examining both complainants, the story's conclusion could have been very different, for the complainant (who would have remained the victim of a rape that did not happen) as well as for Jama. A change in personnel, or a prosecutorial focus on other details, could have left Jama's position unchanged, or even worsened if doubts persisted about the Reservoir allegations and Jama was treated as a potential double rapist.

Indeed, the Vincent inquiry's reasons why Jama's own lawyers should have looked into the Reservoir incident actually demonstrate why criminal justice professionals typically ignore 'unrelated' events and the law routinely excludes them. Maybe Jama's chaste demur to 'consensual penile intercourse' (but not, it seems, ejaculating on someone's hair) made him an unlikely candidate for a rape the next evening. On the other hand, perhaps being falsely accused of one sexual crime was enough to provoke him to assault a stranger. The better view is that Jama's supposed behavioural traits and motivations simply did not explain the Doncaster 'assault', since bare tendency and coincidence reasoning are rarely genuinely probative. Indeed, if Jama had still been under suspicion of the alleged Reservoir rape, and if anything about that rape had shared some commonalities with the nightclub incident, then it would almost certainly have been admitted in his Doncaster trial and most likely would have guaranteed the miscarriage of justice.

Vincent's focus on the prosecution and defence lawyers' failure to comprehensively research the law and the facts in their trial preparations draws an incomplete and misleading lesson from Jama's case. Alongside legal and criminal justice professionals' widespread ignorance of DNA evidence, the law of evidence itself—reflexively enforced by those same professionals—ensured that the jury, in spite of its imperviousness to legal flummery, remained ignorant of the key evidence of Jama's innocence. In short, it was the law's efforts to ensure Jama his right to a fair trial that guaranteed his wrongful conviction.

CONCLUSION

Round the decay
Of that colossal Wreck, boundless and bare
The lone and level sands stretch far away.

Shelley's poem was not an ode to the obtuseness of travellers who come across statues in the desert, but rather a reflection upon the hubris of rulers, both ancient and modern, who commission such monuments. But we can perhaps allow Vincent some poetic licence in developing his analogy:

> [T]he DNA evidence was, like Ozymandias' broken statue in the poem by Shelley, found isolated in a vast desert. And like the inscription on the statue's pedestal,

> everything around it belied the truth of its assertion. The statue, of course, would be seen by any reasonably perceptive observer, and viewed in its surroundings, as a shattered monument to an arrogance that now mocked itself.[78]

As can be seen, Ozymandias's monument has two features that contradict each other: the 'inscription on the statue's pedestal' and the 'broken statue'. The former declares Ozymandias's continuing might, whereas the 'colossal Wreck' of its remains shows that his might had passed. The DNA evidence in Jama's case (and, indeed, all DNA evidence) likewise has two components: the match itself, inviting an inference of guilt, and the investigative origins of that match. In Jama's case, the latter contradicted the former, by showing that an alternative innocent explanation of the match was not only possible, but overwhelmingly likely. So, the wrecked statue (in the form of the alternative link between Jama and the cervical swab) belied the words of the inscription (suggesting a connection between the two) and gave new meaning to the 'vast desert' (the prosecution's absurd case theory.)

What do we learn from this analogy? The Vincent inquiry concluded that 'DNA evidence appears to have been viewed as possessing an almost mystical infallibility that enabled its surroundings to be disregarded'.[79] In other words, people trusted the inscription even though it was uncorroborated.[80] But Vincent does not address why, prior to Jama's appeal, nobody noticed the significance of the origins of the DNA match, even though, just like the self-mocking statue, its significance 'would be seen by any reasonably perceptive observer'. The pertinent question raised is, why did everyone keep their eyes averted from the statue itself? That is, why did they ignore the origins of Jama's DNA match? Evidence law's approach to 'unrelated' events wilfully distracts attention from the investigative origins of DNA evidence. It is like saying, in the analogy, that the condition of a statue is untrustworthy as a source of historical fact, since its appearance may reflect only the skill of its maker. Moreover, statues pose a danger to considered historians, because Ozymandias's 'frown, and wrinkled lip, and sneer of cold command … [w]hich yet survive, stamped on these lifeless things' might shock or entrance or mislead anyone who looks upon them.

The problem posed by evidence of the origins of DNA matches is entirely familiar. On the one hand, those origins are potentially highly probative in supporting (indeed revealing) innocence in DNA-only cases. On the other hand, because current DNA sampling regimes mainly allow police to gather DNA samples from people who are suspected or convicted of crimes, they also typically carry a high risk of prejudice. Further examples of evidence which often confounds probative value with prejudicial effects include not

[78] Vincent Report, above n 4, 11.

[79] Ibid.

[80] Alas, Vincent muddies the analogy by declaring '[t]he fact that the DNA evidence, like Ozymandias' statue, was at odds with all around it': ibid 44.

only classic 'similar fact' evidence, but also other types of 'origin' evidence like eyewitness identifications and confessions. Common law systems of criminal procedure traditionally manage risks of prejudice by inviting trial judges to make contextual evaluations balancing the prejudicial effect against probative value. Probative value is the law's characterisation of rational inference; prejudicial effect is legal shorthand for irrationality in fact-finding. However, the investigative origins of DNA evidence will often (as in *Jama*) fall into an exceedingly boggy middle ground, in which prejudicial details are themselves highly probative. Striking any balance in these circumstances is, to put it mildly, difficult.

By far the most important of Vincent's recommendations is the least likely to be implemented:

> In cases where DNA testing is carried out for forensic purposes, a full report [must] be provided as a matter of course to the investigating police members and, where [the Victorian Institute of Forensic Medicine] is involved, to them, setting out,
>
> 1. The history of the samples as known to the laboratory, both before and after their arrival.
> 2. A statement identifying all items examined, when where and by whom the examination was performed and indicating the findings, whether or not a DNA profile is obtained.
> 3. A clear statement setting out the basis upon which any opinion rests and limitations within which it is expressed.[81]

This recommendation envisages the generation of a paper trail setting out the investigative origins of every DNA match. Its implementation clearly raises practical, cost and logistical issues. However, a greater problem still is that its utility in revealing errors depends entirely on the various institutions that failed in the Jama case. Indeed, Vincent requires that lab workers disclose the report to prosecutors and defendants only 'in any case where a question concerning possible contamination can be seen to arise'.[82] Threshold issues of detection and disclosure are ignored.

If one were seriously minded to detect mismatches between statues and their inscriptions, a rule requiring the inscription's translator to keep a sketch of the statue on file to be passed on at her discretion seems half-baked, at best. Rather, at the very least, the burden should be on anyone seeking to rely on only one part of the statue (the inscription on its pedestal) to justify why it was both unnecessary and dangerous to examine the remainder. Likewise, full evidence of the origins of a DNA match should routinely be admitted in DNA trials. At the very least, the presumption should be that it will be admitted alongside any DNA evidence, with the burden on those opposing disclosure to establish good cause. The problem

[81] Vincent Report, above n 4, 54, Recommendation 6.
[82] Ibid 54, Recommendation 7.

of prejudice should primarily be dealt with, not by complete exclusion or the fiction of a 'fresh buccal swab', but through judicious selective editing to keep out irrelevant or highly prejudicial details and by careful, honest jury directions to manage the risk.[83] Only in this way might the true significance of evidential provenance be appreciated by an astute jury, even if it has been overlooked by blinkered criminal justice professionals.

Although it is admittedly just a single case-study, the story of Jama's erroneous conviction and serendipitous exoneration chimes with many of the broader themes of this book. Human rights law has lately become more prominent in Victoria, and well-known provisions of international human rights law are addressed to miscarriages of justice, directly or indirectly. However, it was the common law conception of 'fair trial' which took centre-stage in *Jama*. In particular, as we saw, traditional doctrines of evidence law, which were supposedly designed to promote fair trials, operated in *Jama* to conceal vital evidence of innocence from the jury. The Vincent inquiry identified many routine features of criminal procedure that need to change if DNA evidence is to be utilised fairly and effectively, and without generating unacceptable and quite avoidable additional risks of wrongful conviction.

It was argued in this chapter that Vincent's analysis actually needs to be pushed further in order to respond to the systemic risks of wrongful conviction arising from the faulty collection, storage and presentation of DNA evidence in Victorian criminal trials. Victoria's then Attorney-General, Rob Hulls, offered an alternative diagnosis when proposing a national response to the *Jama* debacle:

> This was an isolated incident—believed to be the first case in Victoria in which a person was wrongly convicted on DNA evidence alone. It should not happen again.... The community should continue to have confidence in the science of DNA.[84]

If a monument is ever built to DNA evidence, these words would make a fine inscription for its pedestal.

[83] See J Gans and A Palmer, *Uniform Evidence* (OUP, Melbourne, 2010) 246–47.

[84] R Hulls, 'Working group to consider national approach to DNA', Media release, 7 May 2010, www.premier.vic.gov.au/component/content/article/10323.html.

9

Delayed Complaint, Lost Evidence and Fair Trial: Epistemic and Non-epistemic Concerns

DAVID HAMER

INTRODUCTION

JUDICIAL CONCERN ABOUT the impact of delayed complaints on the fairness of trials and the safety of convictions is not a recent phenomenon. As long ago as 1844 Baron Alderson declared:

> It is monstrous to put a man on his trial after such a lapse of time. How can he account for his conduct so far back? If you accuse a man of a crime the next day, he may be enabled to bring forward his servants and family to say where he was and what he was about at the time; but if the charge be not preferred for a year or more, how can he clear himself? No man's life would be safe if such a prosecution were permitted. It would be very unjust to put him on his trial.[1]

In recent decades courts have expressed similar concerns as they have faced increasing numbers of delayed child sexual assault prosecutions. English juries should be directed to:

> [C]onsider the effect which the passage of time has had upon the defendant's ability to respond. He did not know, until recently, that he would have to meet the case now brought against him.... If, having considered the defendant's position, you accept that he has, as a result of the delay, been placed at a material disadvantage, you should consider carefully to what extent that concern might influence your conclusion.[2]

In Australia, at common law, the jury should be instructed:

> [A]s the evidence of the complainant could not be adequately tested after the passage of [however many] years, it would be dangerous to convict on that evidence alone unless the jury, scrutinising the evidence with great care, considering

[1] *R v Robins* (1844) 1 Cox's CC 114.
[2] Judicial Studies Board, *Crown Court Bench Book: Directing the Jury* (March 2010) 34.

> the circumstances relevant to its evaluation and paying heed to the warning, were satisfied of its truth and accuracy.[3]

The Australian direction has been described as 'a not too subtle encouragement by the trial judge to acquit'[4] and has been toned down in recent legislation.[5] In these and other jurisdictions the trial judge may take the view that the effects of delay are so severe that the trial should be stayed altogether.[6]

This chapter examines the justification for these pro-defendant interventions. On first impression they appear to have an epistemic basis. Evidence has been lost through delay, and it is difficult to test properly the little evidence that remains. But as I explore below, it is not clear why this should elicit a pro-defendant response. Missing evidence appears to be just as great a problem for the prosecution, possibly greater in view of the presumption of innocence. Pro-defendant interventions seem to distort the proper inferential processes. Epistemically, the best way to resolve these cases is to simply assess the strength of the available evidence.

If pro-defendant interventions lack an epistemic basis, they may instead have a non-epistemic foundation. The defendant's position is certainly troubling: accused many years after the alleged assault, unable to gather evidence owing to the delay, his defence reduced to one of a bare denial. Perhaps the underlying concern is the defendant's objectification and lack of opportunity to participate in the trial. This non-epistemic rationale does not suffer the logical flaws of the epistemic arguments, but it does not appear strong enough to justify judicial interventions. The primary justification for the defendant's right to present a defence is not the non-epistemic value of autonomy, but rather to assist the court's epistemic, fact-finding endeavour. Where the defendant's participatory rights clash with the epistemic goal, the latter generally prevails.

1. EPISTEMIC CONCERNS

Specifically epistemic objections to criminal prosecutions arising from delayed complaints can be divided into the following three categories: (a) weakness of the prosecution case; (b) defendants' forensic disadvantage;

[3] *R v Longman* (1989) 168 CLR 79, 91 (Brennan, Dawson and Toohey JJ).

[4] *R v BWT* (2002) 54 NSWLR 241, [35] (Wood CJ) and [118] (Sully J).

[5] Section 165B(4) of the Uniform Evidence Law: Evidence Act 1995 (Cth); Evidence Act 1995 (NSW); Evidence Act 2001 (Tas); Evidence Act 2008 (Vic); Evidence Act 2011 (ACT) (collectively known as the uniform Evidence Acts); see also Evidence Act 1929 (SA) s 34CB(3)(b).

[6] Eg *R v Joynson* [2009] All ER (D) 214; *R v Littler* (2001) 120 A Crim R 512. In Ireland the court may order a prohibition: eg *PL v DPP* [2004] 4 IR 494. The issue manifests differently in the US where criminal offences are generally subject to limitations periods: eg, BL Porto, 'New Hampshire's New Statute of Limitations for Child Sexual Assault: Is It Constitutional and Is it Good Public Policy?' (1991) 26 *New England Law Review* 141.

and (c) lack of evidential weight. This section examines each strand of argument in turn.

(a) Weakness of the Prosecution Case

In many delayed complaint cases, the prosecution evidence is little more than the complainant's testimony. Perhaps the most obvious explanation for a pro-defendant intervention is that, given the prosecution's heavy burden of proof, a conviction would be untenable.

At an earlier stage in the law's development this view would have had greater force. The absence of a prompt complaint was considered to weaken the complainant's credibility. The law assumed that, had the offence actually taken place as alleged, the complainant would have raised an immediate hue and cry.[7] There may also have been an element of best evidence reasoning at play. To block delayed prosecutions may motivate prompter complaint, avoiding the loss of evidence.[8] Today, however, it is recognised that there are many reasons for a child sexual assault victim to delay complaint, such as 'embarrassment, fear, guilt, or a lack of understanding and knowledge'.[9] And, of course, to discount the complainant's credibility would hardly motivate a victim to come forward more promptly. The opposite is more likely. In the modern law, reflecting this increased understanding,

> the timing of the complaint is simply one circumstance to consider in the factual mosaic of a particular case. A delay in disclosure, standing alone, will never give rise to an adverse inference against the credibility of the complainant.[10]

Even without any adverse inference working against the complainant, delay will often weaken the prosecution case. It is not only that the complainant's evidence is uncorroborated. As a result of the delay the complainant's account will often lack persuasive detail. This in turn makes it difficult for the defendant to test the complainant's evidence through cross-examination directed at revealing inconsistencies and contradictions.[11] Uncorroborated, undetailed, untested complainant testimony will generally struggle to satisfy a jury beyond reasonable doubt of the defendant's guilt. Hardiman J of the Supreme Court of Ireland stated:

> It would be quite wrong to convict a person of a serious offence, likely to lead to prolonged imprisonment, social, familial and often financial destruction, and

[7] Eg *R v DD* [2000] 2 SCR 275 [60]; *R v Johnston* (1998) 45 NSWLR 362, 367.

[8] See generally, Dale Nance, 'The Best Evidence Principle' (1988) 73 *Iowa Law Review* 227.

[9] *R v DD* [2000] 2 SCR 275, [64] (Major J); see also *R v MM* [2007] EWCA Crim 1558; Crimes Act 1958 (Vic) s 61(1)(b)(i).

[10] *R v DD* [2000] 2 SCR 275, [64] (Major J).

[11] Eg *R v WRC* (2002) 130 A Crim R 89, [100] (Greg James J), [143] (Kirby J).

> lifelong stigmatisation as a sex offender, purely on the basis of impression, as opposed to reason.[12]

According to Hardiman J, prosecutions that are 'pure contest[s] of credibility' with 'no island of facts' should not be allowed to proceed.[13]

Hardiman J's 'island of fact' principle was rightly rejected by a majority of the Irish Supreme Court.[14] It would, in effect, reinstate the much criticised corroboration requirement. Sexual assault complainants—mostly women and children—would be treated as inherently suspect witnesses, a classification which has previously been said to reflect 'the limitations on the experience of judges, who were almost invariably male'[15] and to reveal 'the law itself rather than the witness or her evidence [as] distinctly suspect'.[16] Such a requirement would render many sexual assault prosecutions 'impossible'.[17] Not only in delay cases, but also in acquaintance rape prosecutions, it is not uncommon for there to be no eyewitnesses and no incriminating scientific or medical evidence.[18]

An inflexible demand for corroboration of the complainant's allegations would be over-inclusive. While, as a generalisation, delayed prosecutions may lack sufficient strength to secure conviction, there will inevitably be exceptions. In *Longman*,[19] for example, Deane J observed that

> the evidence of the complainant reads convincingly. It is not surprising that the jury accepted her as an honest witness. The same could not be said of the evidence of the applicant... It is not surprising that the jury plainly rejected the applicant as a witness.[20]

Complainants will often gain an advantage in the credibility stakes on the basis that there is no apparent reason for them to lie, whereas defendants have a clear interest in proclaiming their innocence whether true or not. Of course, care must be taken in this kind of reasoning not to infringe the presumption of innocence.[21] Defendants bear no burden of proof with

[12] *PL v DPP* [2004] 4 IR 494, 506.
[13] Ibid 510.
[14] Ibid 515 (Geoghegan J) and 531–32 (Fennelly J).
[15] *R v Johnston* (1998) 45 NSWLR 362, 367 (Spigelman CJ).
[16] P Roberts and A Zuckerman, *Criminal Evidence*, 2nd edn (Oxford, OUP, 2010) 665.
[17] *R v AG* [2000] 1 SCR 439 (Arbour J).
[18] *R v Johnston* (1998) 45 NSWLR 362, 370 (Spigelman CJ); *PL v DPP* [2004] 4 IR 494, 531–32 (Fennelly J).
[19] *R v Longman* (1989) 168 CLR 79.
[20] Ibid 98; but see n 52 below and accompanying text.
[21] With reference to the complainant's credibility, see: *R v Palmer* (1998) 193 CLR 1, [9] (Brennan CJ, Gaudron and Gummow JJ). However, the majority overstates the dangers, holding that 'a complainant's account gains no legitimate credibility from the absence of evidence of motive'. As McHugh J points out, dissenting, this is inconsistent with the importance generally attached to motive evidence in determining whether a person has committed serious misconduct: [58]–[59]. Cf *R v B* [2003] 1 WLR 2809 [25], [41], preferring McHugh J's reasoning. The court in *R v Batte* (2000) 145 CCC(3d) 449, [120], stated: 'It is difficult to think

respect to the truthfulness or motivations of complainants. The question is not merely who, between the defendant and complainant, is more believable. The prosecution bears the burden of eliminating all reasonable doubt about the defendant's guilt. And the defendant should not be treated as an inherently suspect witness requiring heightened scrutiny.[22] But this does not alter the fact that the defendant generally has the greatest stake in the outcome of a criminal trial. That is why the presumption of innocence demands such a high level of certainty for conviction.[23] Another consequence is that the defendant's interest in the outcome tends to swamp the probative value of other evidence going to his credibility.[24] Having regard to the parties' relative motivations for lying, it is not impossible that the complainant's credibility will sufficiently outweigh the defendant's credibility for a conviction to be secured.

A further question that Hardiman J's proposal raises is why judicial intervention should be necessary. He assumes not only that the prosecution's case has been fatally weakened as a result of the delay and consequent loss of evidence, but also that a jury would fail to appreciate the salience of these evidential infirmities. Hardiman J suggests that '[a] purely impressionistic decision is as likely to be wrong as right, and one cannot hope to justify it objectively'.[25] There is certainly a wealth of empirical data supporting the view that credibility assessments resting on demeanour alone are of dubious reliability,[26] but it does not follow that the defendant's position 'is indeed perilous'[27] or that '[t]he possibilities of success of either side [are] haphazard'.[28] The presumption of innocence stacks the odds against the prosecution and, despite Hardiman J's claims[29] empirical data does not show that juries' credibility assessments are biased in favour of complainants. If anything, there appears to be a bias *against* complainants. Credibility

of a factor which, as a matter of common sense and life experience, would be more germane to a witness' credibility than the existence of a motive to fabricate evidence'. And see *Warren v HKSAR* (2009) 12 HKCFAR 218.

[22] In *R v Robinson* (1991) 180 CLR 531, 535, the High Court of Australia held that it was wrong for the trial judge, having invited the jury to consider witnesses's interests in assessing their credibility, to add that the defendant may be considered to have the greatest interest of all.

[23] *Re Winship*, 397 US 358, 363–64 (Brennan J), 372 (Harlan J) (1970).

[24] *R v Campbell* [2007] 1 WLR 2798, [30].

[25] *PL v DPP* [2004] 4 IR 494, 506.

[26] See Roberts and Zuckerman, above n 16, 297–301; T Lindholm, 'Who Can Judge the Accuracy of Eyewitness Statements? A Comparison of Professional and Lay-Persons' (2008) 22 *Applied Cognitive Psychology* 1301.

[27] *J O'C v DPP* [2000] 3 IR 478, 504 (Hardiman J).

[28] *PL v DPP* [2004] 4 IR 494, 504 (quoting from *O'Reilly v Coras Iompair Eireann* [1973] IR 278, 282).

[29] Eg Hardiman J asserts that 'a complainant may resile from his or her position about a matter of detail… quite easily, but if a defendant were to do so it would, in practice, be gravely prejudicial to his or her credibility', citing only anecdotal support for his position: *PL v DPP* [2004] 4 IR 494, 506.

assessments are mediated by cultural stereotypes and misconceptions that work against complainants.[30] The complainant's passivity during the alleged assault, subsequent delay in complaint, or maintenance of a relatively normal relationship with the alleged perpetrator following the alleged assault may reduce the complainant's credibility with a jury, notwithstanding that these are relatively common features of such acquaintance rape. The subjectivities and vagaries of credibility assessments in sexual assault cases tend to add to the difficulties of enforcement,[31] not to the risk of wrongful conviction.

(b) Defendants' Forensic Disadvantage

Delay will often weaken the prosecution's case, but not necessarily fatally. Furthermore, there is no general tendency for juries to overvalue complainant testimony. If pro-defendant judicial intervention in delayed complaint trials is justified, it must appeal to some specific rationale other than the inherent and unappreciated weakness of prosecution evidence.

Many courts and commentators suggest that the defendant suffers forensic disadvantage from delay and the associated loss of evidence. The Judicial Studies Board direction quoted above,[32] for example, refers to 'the effect which the passage of time has had upon the defendant's ability to respond' to the charges, the possibility that the defendant has 'been placed at a material disadvantage', and the need for the jury to 'consider carefully to what extent that concern might influence [its] conclusion'. The defendant, for example, may have been deprived of the opportunity to advance an alibi,[33] or to obtain exculpatory scientific evidence.[34]

[30] A Cossins, J Goodman-Delahunty and K O'Brien, 'Uncertainty and Misconceptions About Child Sexual Abuse: Implications for the Criminal Justice System' (2009) 16 *Psychiatry, Psychology and Law* 435; R Shackel, 'The Beliefs Commonly Held by Adults about Children's Behavioral Responses to Sexual Victimization' (2008) 32 *Child Abuse and Neglect* 485. More generally, see eg *R v Seaboyer* [1991] 2 SCR 577, [28] (McLachlin J), [147]–[173] (L'Heureux-Dubé J); *R v A (No 2)* [2002] 1 AC 45, [27] (Lord Steyn), [76], [147]–[149] (Lord Hutton); Jennifer Temkin, 'And Always Keep A-hold of Nurse, for Fear of Finding Something Worse: Challenging Rape Myths in the Courtroom' (2010) 13 *New Criminal Law Review* 710; Judicial Studies Board, above n 2, 356.

[31] See eg, A Cossins, *Alternative Models for Prosecuting Child Sex Offences in Australia* (Report of the National Child Sexual Assault Reform Committee) 2010, ch 1; R Ackland, 'Getting Away with Child Abuse', *Sydney Morning Herald*, 17 December 2010, www.smh.com.au.

[32] Above n 2.

[33] Eg *R v Taylor (No 2)* (2008) 18 VR 613.

[34] Eg *R v AM* (2008) 188 A Crim R 457.

There is a tension between this view and the argument considered in the previous section.[35] To suggest that delay weakens the prosecution case is to highlight *missing prosecution evidence*. The present forensic disadvantage argument draws attention to *missing defence evidence*. Given this rough symmetry, how can both considerations favour *pro-defendant* intervention? There is no sensible answer to this question. On examination, as I have explained elsewhere,[36] the forensic disadvantage argument suffers from a fatal logical flaw.

Evidence has been lost because of the delay. Because the evidence is lost its content is unknown.[37] Would the missing witnesses have confirmed the defendant's alibi, or demonstrated the defendant's opportunity? Would forensic science examinations of the alleged scene of abuse have revealed semen stains or clean sheets? The answers remain unknown. Logically, the loss of evidence can cause only *possible* prejudice to the defendant. However, from the court's point of view, this possibility is balanced by the opposite possibility that the loss prejudiced the prosecution.

It might be argued that a corollary of the presumption of innocence is that the lost evidence must be assumed to be exculpatory.[38] But this would give the presumption too much force.[39] The presumption demands a high level of proof for conviction, but it clearly allows for the possibility of the defendant's guilt. It is not contrary to the presumption to accommodate the possibility of the defendant's guilt in measuring the strength of the prosecution evidence. To reject this possibility would defeat the purpose of the trial.

Occasionally judges recognise the balance in risks of forensic disadvantage. Hardiman J asserted that 'long delay prejudices the defendant disproportionately, and may actually assist the prosecution',[40] but his fellow judges retorted that 'delay is damaging to both parties'.[41] In *R v M*[42] the defendant objected that the delayed complaint had deprived him of the opportunity to have the complainant undergo a medical examination, proving that she was a virgin following the alleged sexual assault. The English Court of Appeal responded: '[t]he reality is that, had there been a medical examination ... it might have provided the most damaging evidence against the defendant'.[43] Justice Vanstone in the South Australian

[35] D Hamer, 'Trying Delays: Forensic Disadvantage in Child Sexual Assault Trials' [2010] *Criminal Law Review* 671, 683–85.
[36] Ibid.
[37] '[W]hat has been forgotten can rarely be shown': *Barker v Wingo*, 407 US 514, 532 (1972).
[38] P Lewis, *Delayed Prosecution for Childhood Sexual Abuse* (Oxford, OUP, 2006) 84–85, 148; *PC v DPP* [1999] 2 IR 25, 78 (Lynch J).
[39] Hamer, above n 35, 685.
[40] *PL v DPP* [2004] 4 IR 494, 513.
[41] Ibid 532 (Fennelly J), quoting from *PC v DPP* [1999] 2 IR 25, 63 (Denham J).
[42] [2000] 1 Cr App R 49.
[43] Ibid 58.

Court of Criminal Appeal pointed out that 'since [the defendant's] forensic difficulties were to be assumed... then as a matter of logic, similar difficulties could be assumed to have faced the complainants'.[44] In a New South Wales decision, Chief Justice at Common Law Wood noted that 'the impact of the delay is double edged, since it is just as likely to occasion practical difficulty for the prosecution'.[45]

But these observations are exceptions to the prevailing forensic illogic. Wood CJ at CL was bound by High Court authority to hold that 'the absence of contemporaneity between the alleged offence and complaint, or trial has *in fact* (not "might have") denied to the accused a proper opportunity to meet the charge or charges brought'.[46] And the English Court of Appeal criticised a trial judge who had 'even-handedly draw[n] attention [to the] potential impact [of delay] upon the Crown evidence' for having 'wrongly equated the problems confronting both Crown and Defence'.[47] Illogical though it is, the assumption that only the defendant suffers forensic disadvantage is presented as a key justification for judicial intervention in delayed complaint trials.

(c) Lack of Evidential Weight

We have so far considered two epistemic concerns with delayed sexual assault prosecutions. A third interpretation of the epistemic concerns arising from delay proposes that the prosecution standard of proof requires not only that evidence have sufficient strength, but that it also have sufficient weight.

The distinction between strength and weight was noted by John Maynard Keynes. The strength of a body of evidence, Keynes said, 'depends upon a balance between the favourable and the unfavourable evidence'.[48] The weight of a body of evidence, however, 'turns upon a balance ... between the absolute amount of relevant knowledge and of relevant ignorance respectively'.[49] In delayed complaint cases, evidence may appear sufficiently *strong* for conviction. As noted above, in *Longman* Deane J considered that the complainant was far more credible than the defendant.[50] The balance of *available evidence* strongly favoured the prosecution. Deane J then added: 'All that having been said however, the fact remains that the only evidence

44 *R v Inston* (2009) 103 SASR 265, [112] (Vanstone J).
45 *R v BWT* (2002) 54 NSWLR 241, [23].
46 Ibid [13].
47 *R v Percival*, CA Transcript 97/6746/X4, 19 June 1998.
48 JM Keynes, *A Treatise on Probability* (London, MacMillan and Co, 1921) 71.
49 Ibid.
50 *R v Longman* (1989) 168 CLR 79, 98.

of the applicant's guilt ... was the oral evidence of the complainant'.[51] Deane J was concerned that the evidence lacked sufficient *weight*. Because of the delay there were no corroborating witnesses and no forensic or medical evidence. The weight of the *available evidence* was too slight; too much evidence had been lost. The balance was tipped too far towards ignorance rather than knowledge.

The clearest illustrations of a divergence between weight and strength of evidence, far removed from delayed complaint cases, are the 'naked statistical evidence'[52] (NSE) hypotheticals, much discussed by evidence theorists. In the *Blue Bus case*, having been hit by an unidentified bus, the plaintiff sues the Blue Bus Co, as they own 80 per cent of the buses in town.[53] In the *Prisoners case*, 999 out of 1000 prisoners are involved in the killing of another prisoner. The defendant is charged purely on the basis that he is one of the 1000.[54] In each case the statistical evidence generates a probability figure that appears to satisfy the applicable standard of proof—0.80 and 0.999 respectively. The evidence appears to possess sufficient strength. However, most commentators consider that both the plaintiff and the prosecution would fail.[55] Although probabilistically strong, the evidence lacks sufficient 'weight',[56] 'completeness'[57] or 'comprehensiveness'.[58]

[51] Ibid 98–99.

[52] See, eg, D Kaye, 'Naked Statistical Evidence' (1980) 89 *Yale Law Journal* 601; M Redmayne, 'Exploring the Proof Paradoxes' (2008) 14 *Legal Theory* 281.

[53] LH Tribe, 'Trial by Mathematics: Precision and Ritual in the Legal Process' (1971) 84 *Harvard Law Review* 1329, 1340–41, 1346–50.

[54] C Nesson, 'Reasonable Doubt and Permissive Inferences: The Value of Complexity' (1979) 92 *Harvard Law Review* 1187, 1192–93.

[55] But see J Brook, 'The Use of Statistical Evidence of Identification in Civil Litigation: Well-worn Hypotheticals, Real Cases, and Controversy' (1984) 29 *St Louis University Law Journal* 293, 299.

[56] D Nance, 'The Weights of Evidence' [2008] *Episteme* 267, 268; A Stein, *Foundations of Evidence Law* (Oxford, OUP, 2005) 47–48; LJ Cohen, *The Probable and the Provable* (Oxford, Clarendon Press, 1977). KJ Heller, 'The Cognitive Psychology of Circumstantial Evidence' (2006) 105 *Michigan Law Review* 241, 269, presents an alternative explanation in terms of the distinction between 'vivid' direct evidence and 'pallid' circumstantial evidence. However, as the delayed complaint cases demonstrate, direct evidence can lack detail, weight and persuasive power. Conversely, circumstantial case can accumulate considerable detail and persuasive power; too much on occasions. 'The mind [can be too] apt to take a pleasure in adapting circumstances to one another, and even straining them a little, if need be, to force them to form parts of one connected whole': Baron Alderson in *Hodges Case* (1838) 2 Lewin 228; 168 ER 1136. '[P]eople have a psychological propensity to weave theories from circumstantial evidence': *Hankins v State*, 646 SW 2d 191 (1983), 204–05 (Onions J). Heller generalises inappropriately from relatively atypical circumstantial cases—NSE cases and ones relying heavily on a DNA match—where the evidence is both highly probative, and very abstract and probabilistic.

[57] R Friedman, 'Assessing Evidence' (1996) 94 *Michigan Law Review* 1810, 1819; Nance, above n 56, 268.

[58] HL Ho, *A Philosophy of Evidence Law—Justice in the Search for Truth* (Oxford, OUP, 2008) 166.

The weight concept plausibly explains our resistance to making a positive finding in both NSE and delayed complaint cases. But its normative status is more ambiguous. Clearly a greater weight of evidence is preferable to a lesser weight. To question this would imply scepticism about the viability of the fact-finding venture.[59] Fact-finding presupposes the value of evidence. Where uncertainty exists, fresh evidence will be welcomed in the expectation that it will produce a better decision.[60] Losing evidence through delay reduces the 'chances of the Courts being able to find out what really happened';[61] 'the likelihood of error increases'.[62] But what implications does this carry for low weight cases? In many contexts it will be sensible for a decision-maker to resist committing herself on the basis of a slight weight of evidence. Such reluctance may be a useful heuristic,[63] prompting the search for further evidence and consequently generating a better-informed decision. Imposing an evidential weight requirement on a litigant with access to additional evidence may have the benefit of increasing the overall quantity of evidence available to the fact-finder and improving the accuracy of the verdict.[64]

But these evidential weight requirements will create positive incentives only where further evidence is available to be found and taken into account.[65] This will rarely be the case in delayed complaint cases. A weight requirement will not motivate child sexual assault complainants to come forward earlier. The prosecution will not miraculously unearth lost evidence. A weight requirement, in short, would serve no useful purpose here. From an epistemic point of view, the fact-finder should proceed on the evidence that is available. If the complainant's evidence is sufficiently strong, conviction is the most appropriate result. Lack of weight should pose no obstacle. The 'wait for further evidence' heuristic is counterproductive, potentially producing a 'severe and systematic bias',[66] increasing mistaken acquittals, and undermining the prohibition against sexual assault.

[59] Stein, above n 56, 123; R Allen and M Pardo, 'The Problematic Value of Mathematical Models of Evidence' (2007) 36 *Journal of Legal Studies* 107, 113–15.

[60] IJ Good, *Good Thinking: The Foundations of Probability and Its Applications* (Minneapolis, MN, University of Minnesota Press, 1983) 178; B Skyrms, *The Dynamics of Rational Deliberation* (Cambridge, MA, Harvard University Press, 1990) ch 4.

[61] *Allen v Sir Alfred McAlpine & Sons Limited* [1968] 2 QB 229, 255 (Diplock LJ); quoted in *J O'C v DPP* [2000] 3 IR 478, 497 (Hardiman J).

[62] *R v Longman* (1989) 168 CLR 79, 108 (McHugh J).

[63] See generally, D Kahneman, P Slovic and A Tversky (eds), *Judgement under Uncertainty: Heuristics and Biases* (Cambridge, CUP, 1982).

[64] D Nance, 'Missing Evidence' (1991) 13 *Cardozo Law Review* 831.

[65] As Lord Mansfield observed in *Blatch v Archer* (1774) 1 Cowp 63, 65, 'all evidence is to be weighed according to the proof which it was in the power of one side to have produced, and in the power of the other to have contradicted'.

[66] A Tversky and D Kahneman, 'Judgment under Uncertainty: Heuristics and Biases' in Kahneman, Slovic and Tversky, above n 63, 3. Also see MJ Saks and RF Kidd, 'Human

2. THE RIGHT TO PARTICIPATE AND PRESENT A DEFENCE

Epistemically, delayed sexual assault prosecutions do not threaten the fairness of a trial. There is no heightened risk of wrongful conviction. Evidence that has been lost could have gone either way. The court should not be distracted by the possibility of missing evidence but should decide on the basis of the strength of the evidence that is available. To do otherwise will just add further to the enforcement difficulties in this area. From the point of view of factual accuracy, pro-defendant interventions are unjustified.

However, the loss of evidence in delayed complaint trials may raise non-epistemic concerns beyond any implications for the accuracy of the final verdict. According to Hardiman J, such cases lack 'the fundamental nature of a trial':[67] '[A] forensic inquiry proceeds as far as possible upon evidence... [E]ach of the protagonists in such a trial seeks to offer *reasons* why the result it urges should be arrived at'.[68] Where a complaint has been delayed, evidence and reasons may be in short supply. A trial consisting of a bare allegation and a bare denial is 'scarcely a forensic contest at all'.[69] Indeed, 'the lapse of time may be so great as to deprive the party against whom an allegation is made of his "capacity ... to be effectively heard"'.[70] Hardiman J suggests that, in this respect, delayed complaint trials cannot possibly be fair trials.

The US Supreme Court has observed on numerous occasions that 'an essential component of procedural fairness is an opportunity to be heard'.[71] And in Canada, '[t]he right to make full answer and defence is... one of the principles of fundamental justice'.[72] Others have not drawn the connection as explicitly as Hardiman J, but the defendant responding to a delayed complaint resembles other types of defendant who have been deprived of this right: the defendant lacking adequate notice of the prosecution's case, and thereby denied 'a reasonable opportunity to meet [the charges against him] by way of defense or explanation';[73] the defendant deprived of competent representation through counsel's '(1) failing to investigate

Information Processing and Adjudication: Trial By Heuristics' (1981) 15 *Law and Society Review* 123; D Hamer, 'The Civil Standard of Proof Uncertainty: Probability, Belief and Justice' (1994) 16 *Sydney Law Review* 506, 521; DL Sykes and JT Johnson 'Probabilistic Evidence' (1999) 21 *Basic and Applied Social Psychology* 199; Heller, above n 56, 260–61, 302–5.

[67] *PL v DPP* [2004] 4 IR 494, 506.

[68] Ibid.

[69] *J O'C v DPP* [2000] 3 IR 478, 533.

[70] Ibid 498, quoting from the unreported case of *O'Keeffe v Commissioners of Public Works*, Supreme Court of Ireland, 24 March 1980.

[71] Eg *US v Scheffer*, 523 US 303 (1998), 327; *Powell v Alabama*, 287 US 45, 67 (1932).

[72] *R v Rose* [1998] 3 SCR 262, [98].

[73] *In re Oliver*, 333 US 257, 275 (1948).

[a] potential defence; (2) failing to present crucial evidence; [or] (3) failing to impeach a prosecution witness';[74] the incompetent defendant 'whose capacity for self-determination is compromised to such a degree and in such a way that she could not be anything more than an object of inquiry that passively undergoes processing and eventual labelling'.[75]

On this view, delayed complaint trials may not create a heightened risk of wrongful conviction, but they objectify the defendant and 'convictions ... may be obtained at too high a price'.[76] However, this argument faces a significant obstacle. While it is possible to identify a non-epistemic basis for the right to present a defence, the right also has a strong epistemic basis. The defendant's participation generally assists the court in arriving at the truth. Where the two rationales diverge, allowing less defendant participation may appear preferable to increasing the risk of factual error. To privilege participation over accuracy may reflect not respect for the defendant's autonomy, but an attachment to a dubious sporting or 'fight theory' of the trial.

(a) Non-epistemic Value of Participation

A potential non-epistemic basis for the right to present a defence may be found in the notion of autonomy. This is a central concept in liberal theory,[77] and underlies the notion of responsibility in the substantive criminal law: 'We prosecute and condemn only those who have committed crimes as subjects, as responsible actors'.[78] Clearly autonomy has value independently of the trial's goal of factual accuracy.

Autonomy plays a central role in the normative account of the criminal trial recently developed by Duff, Farmer, Marshall and Tadros. In defining

[74] See B Gershman, *Trial Error and Misconduct*, 2nd edn (Virginia, Lexis Law Publishing, 2007) 3–3(b) (enumerating eight substantive violations of a defence counsel's duty of competent representation).

[75] MD Dubber, 'The Criminal Trial and the Legitimation of Punishment' in A Duff, L Farmer, S Marshall and V Tadros (eds), *The Trial on Trial Vol 1: Truth and Due Process* (Oxford, Hart Publishing, 2004) 85, 92.

[76] *A v Home Secretary (No 2)* [2006] 2 AC 221, [17] (Lord Bingham); quoting from *R v Ireland* (1970) 126 CLR 321, 335 (Barwick CJ). The 'too high a price' was torture in *A*—see Roberts, Chapter 7, in this volume—and the continuation of police questioning after the suspect had invoked the right to silence in *Ireland*.

[77] Eg G Dworkin, *The Theory and Practice of Autonomy* (Cambridge, CUP, 1988) 3ff.

[78] GP Fletcher, *Basic Concepts of Criminal Law* (New York, OUP, 1998) 53–54. See also P Roberts, 'Theorising Procedural Tradition: Subjects, Objects and Values in Criminal Adjudication' in A Duff, L Farmer, S Marshall and V Tadros (eds), *The Trial on Trial Vol 2: Judgment and Calling to Account* (Oxford, Hart Publishing, 2006) 37, 40; Dubber, above n 75, 86.

the criminal trial, they expressly privilege the defendant's active participation in the proceedings over the trial as an epistemic endeavour:

> the trial is not simply ... an attempt to establish the truth *about* the defendant, but ... an attempt to call the defendant to answer the charge against her, and to answer *for* any criminal conduct that she is proved to have committed.[79]

The 'right to be heard ... [has] a non-instrumental grounding in the demands of respect for persons, whether or not it would serve the aim of establishing the truth'.[80]

The imperative of defendant participation generates constraints on the reception of evidence, and the verdicts that may be reached. 'A criminal conviction is warranted... only if knowledge that the defendant is criminally liable has been established through the legitimate communicative process of the criminal trial'.[81] Evidence 'of a type that is in principle incapable of being presented in a communicative forum of reciprocal responsibility... does not constitute evidence'.[82] While not specifically discussed by Duff, Farmer, Marshall and Tadros, delayed complaint trials do not measure up to their model. Where the prosecution case consists of a complainant's testimony, lacking corroboration and detail and providing limited opportunities for probing and testing through cross-examination, the trial will fail as a communicative forum of reciprocal responsibility. This theory of the trial provides a potential rationale for pro-defendant judicial interventions in cases of delayed complaints.

It should be noted, however, that Duff and colleagues shy away from the more stringent implications of their theory. For example, to use evidence of a defendant's prior misconduct to prove the current charge is said to be inconsistent with the imperative to treat the defendant as an autonomous subject. It 'treat[s] her as if her past conduct determines her present conduct'.[83] But despite an exclusionary rule, the courts have long admitted such evidence where its exclusion would be an affront to common sense,[84] and the admissibility gateway in England and Wales has recently widened considerably.[85] Duff and colleagues try to accommodate this reality: 'we are not arguing that evidence of bad character must *never* be admitted; only that there are always good reasons to exclude it... [S]ometimes what matters is more simply to

[79] A Duff, L Farmer, S Marshall and V Tadros, *Trial on Trial Vol 3: Toward a Normative Theory of the Criminal Trial* (Oxford, Hart Publishing, 2007) 101.

[80] Ibid 101.

[81] Ibid 225.

[82] Ibid 253.

[83] Ibid 113–14. See also Ho, above n 58, 300–1.

[84] Eg, *DPP v Boardman* [1975] AC 421, 456 (Lord Cross).

[85] Criminal Justice Act 2003, ss 101, 103. But see D Hamer, 'Similar Fact Reasoning in *Phillips*: Artificial, Disjointed and Pernicious' (2007) 30 *University of New South Wales LJ* 609 (criticising the High Court's narrow approach to admissibility in *R v Phillips* (2006) 225 CLR 303).

establish the guilt of the guilty'.[86] Having established a non-epistemic vision of the trial as a communicative process, they then concede that the epistemic goal may prevail.

These authors recognise that their participatory theory is challenged by other key aspects of the trial. Defence counsel are seen as crucial to a fair trial,[87] but they can also marginalise defendants,[88] resulting in 'the defendant being treated as the mere object of the trial rather than as a participant'.[89] The right to silence is also perceived as central to a fair trial.[90] Can the trial really be viewed as a communicative forum of reciprocal responsibility 'when there is no requirement on [the defendant] to *provide* any answers to the prosecution's case, or… to provide an account of her actions'?[91]

Duff, Farmer, Marshall and Tadros accommodate these features of the trial, but only through a shift in emphasis from process to outcome. Counsel's voice may legitimately replace the defendant's because '[e] ncouraging the defendant to speak in his own voice carries with it the risk that he will not do himself justice, or will not present his case in the best light'.[92] Despite the right to silence, 'the trial is treated as a forum where the defendant can be *expected* to provide an answer'.[93] But this expectation stems, not from an appreciation of the defendant's autonomy, but from the recognition that 'convincing the jury… involves the defendant constructing a plausible alternative story to the one constructed by the prosecution'.[94]

In the *Trial on Trial*, Duff and colleagues sought to construct an integrated account of the trial as a communicative forum of reciprocal responsibility that is 'both normatively attractive and practically plausible'.[95] This is presented as superior to a truth-plus-side-constraints model,[96] which, they say, 'quickly fragments into theorising… about whether the contribution that a practice or rule makes to the probative values of the trial is outweighed either by its prejudicial potential or by particular rights of the defendant'.[97] Ultimately, however, even on their own account, the communicative aspect of the trial sometimes appears secondary to extrinsic concerns—the state's interest in convicting the guilty, and the defendant's desire to avoid conviction.

[86] Duff et al, above n 79, 115.
[87] *Dietrich v R* (1992) 177 CLR 192; *Powell v Alabama*, 287 US 45 (1932); ECHR Article 6(3)(c). Also see Boyle and Cunliffe, Chapter 3 in this volume.
[88] J Hodgson, 'Conceptions of the Trial in Inquisitorial and Adversarial Procedure' in Duff et al (eds), above n 78, 223, 239.
[89] Duff et al, above n 79, 207.
[90] Cf the Fifth Amendment to the US Constitution; *Saunders v UK* (1997) 23 EHRR 313.
[91] Duff et al, above n 79, 149.
[92] Ibid 208.
[93] Ibid 150.
[94] Ibid 149–50.
[95] Duff et al, above n 79, 14.
[96] Ibid 63–64, 95, 127.
[97] Ibid 5.

(b) Epistemic Importance of an Active Defence

The non-epistemic rationale for judicial intervention in delayed complaint cases is weakened further by indications that the defendant's right to present a defence may be valued more for epistemic than non-epistemic reasons. The Canadian Supreme Court has said that, '[t]he right to make full answer and defence is one of the pillars of criminal justice on which we heavily depend to ensure that the innocent are not convicted'.[98] And a US court declared: 'The very premise of our adversary system of criminal justice is that partisan advocacy on both sides of a case will best promote the ultimate objective that the guilty be convicted and the innocent go free'.[99]

The strong epistemic justification for the right to present a defence is apparent in two recent British decisions. *Home Secretary v AF (No 3)*[100] was concerned with the procedure by which courts issue control orders against suspected terrorists under the Prevention of Terrorism Act 2005. For reasons of national security the Home Secretary had disclosed little of the basis for applying these exceptional measures to the intended controlees, and the House of Lords was required to determine whether this satisfied the fair trial requirements of Article 6 of the ECHR. While the facts of *AF* are far removed from the delayed complaint trials, in an important respect the sexual assault defendant and the suspected terrorist are similarly placed. Both may experience 'feelings of resentment [from being] a party to legal proceedings... placed in a position where it is impossible for him to influence the result'.[101] As Lord Hope put it, 'a denunciation on grounds that are not disclosed is the stuff of nightmares'.[102]

The House of Lords held that '[t]he fundamental principle is that everyone is entitled to the disclosure of sufficient material to enable him to answer effectively the case that is made against him'.[103] This principle is easier to state than to apply.[104] A central issue in *AF* was the 'degree of overlap between the question of whether the procedure has been fair and the question of whether the outcome of the hearing has been fair'.[105] The appellants submitted that whether or not disclosure would make any difference to the outcome was beside the point. 'What was in issue', they said,

98 *R v Stinchcombe* [1991] 3 SCR 326, [17].
99 *Herring v NY*, 422 US 853, 862 (1975).
100 [2010] 2 AC 269, [2009] UKHL 28.
101 Ibid [63] (Lord Phillips).
102 Ibid [83] (Lord Hope), citing *A v Home Secretary* [2005] 2 AC 68, [155] (Lord Scott).
103 [2010] 2 AC 269, [83] (Lord Hope); [59] (Lord Phillips) following *A v UK* (2009) 49 EHRR 625 (GC), [220] and reconsidering *Home Secretary v MB* [2008] AC 440.
104 [2010] 2 AC 269, [85] (Lord Hope), [106] (Baroness Hale).
105 Ibid [34].

'was not the fairness of the result, but procedural fairness'.[106] However, Lord Phillips endorsed the 'makes no difference' principle:[107]

> I do not believe that it is possible to draw a clear distinction between a fair procedure and a procedure that produces a fair result. The object of the procedure is to ensure, in so far as this is possible, that the outcome of the process is a result that accords with the law. Why then should disclosure to the controlee of the case against him be essential if, on the particular facts, this cannot affect the result?[108]

In spite of this, the appeals were upheld. Inadequate disclosure could well have made a difference to the outcome in these hearings.

A second recent case shedding light on the epistemic basis for the right to present a defence is *R v Horncastle*.[109] The Court of Appeal and, on further appeal, the UK Supreme Court were required to determine whether convictions could rest to a sole or decisive degree on hearsay evidence—such as a statement of a deceased witness, or one who is too afraid to testify.[110] Recent ECtHR authority[111] held that this would be contrary to Article 6 of the ECHR. Again, despite considerable factual differences, this issue resembles that arising in delayed complaint trials. The Court of Appeal observed that

> [t]he obvious potential weakness of hearsay evidence is that the fact finder never sees the person who gives evidence which he must evaluate, and the parties cannot ask supplementary or testing questions which are likely to help judge the truthfulness or accuracy of the evidence.[112]

In delayed complaint cases, the complainant often presents the sole or decisive evidence. While he or she is available for cross-examination, the defendant may face a similar problem to that presented by hearsay evidence. The complainant's evidence is 'likely to be more vague, bereft of… detail', weakening the defendant's opportunity for 'cross-examination… exposing contradictions and unreliability'.[113]

Evidence that cannot be properly tested through cross-examination may raise epistemic doubts about its reliability. However, Duff, and colleagues identify an alternative, non-epistemic concern. According to them: 'The entitlement to challenge witnesses face to face is best understood as contributing to the participatory forum that the criminal justice process ought to

[106] Ibid [56].
[107] Ibid [62]. Also see [72] (Lord Hoffmann); but cf [85] (Lord Hope).
[108] Ibid [60].
[109] [2010] 2 AC 373, [2009] UKSC 14.
[110] See Redmayne, Chapter 12 in this volume.
[111] *Al-Khawaja v UK* (2009) 49 EHRR 1.
[112] [2010] 2 AC 373, [8] (CA).
[113] *R v WRC* (2002) 130 A Crim R 89, [143] (Kirby J).

aspire to be'.[114] Prosecution hearsay evidence will always be objectionable from the non-epistemic point of view. It deprives the defendant of the opportunity to confront his accuser and detracts from the trial as 'a communicative forum of reciprocal responsibility'.[115] However, from the epistemic point of view, exclusion will not always be the best solution. As the Court of Appeal pointed out in *Horncastle*, rejecting hearsay would

> deprive the fact finder of evidence which may well help him to arrive at the correct answer in the case, and in many instances will eliminate evidence of whose truthfulness and/or accuracy there is little room for real doubt.[116]

In effect, the courts in *Horncastle* came down on the side of the epistemic theory. The Court of Appeal held that '[w]here the hearsay evidence is demonstrably reliable, or its reliability can properly be tested and assessed, the rights of the defence are respected … and the trial is fair'.[117] In a unanimous judgment the Supreme Court agreed. Lord Phillips emphasised that the 'two principal objectives of a fair criminal trial' are to acquit the innocent and convict the guilty.[118] Rejecting the ECtHR's 'sole and decisive test', he held that the English legislation's[119] reliability safeguards 'strike the right balance between the imperative that a trial must be fair and the interests of victims in particular and society in general that a criminal should not be immune from conviction'.[120]

The appellants in both *AF* and *Horncastle* complained of foreshortened opportunities for participation affecting the fairness of the proceedings against them. In both cases the value of the parties' participation was assessed by reference to its implications for the factual accuracy of the result. The defendants in delayed sexual assault trials likewise have reduced opportunities for active participation. But when this does not disadvantage the defendant epistemically, the case for pro-defendant judicial intervention is weak.

(c) Fair Trial as Fair Game?

Common law jurisdictions have taken divergent approaches to the hearsay/confrontation issue, reflecting different conceptualisations of the criminal

114 Duff et al, above n 79, 151.

115 Ibid 253 (putting to one side those rare situations where the defendant had the opportunity to confront the witness in earlier proceedings).

116 [2010] 2 AC 373, [8] (CA).

117 Ibid [80] (CA).

118 Ibid [18] (SC), echoing *R v A (No 2)* [2002] 1 AC 45, [142] (Lord Hutton).

119 Criminal Justice Act 2003, Pt 11, ch 2.

120 [2010] 2 AC 373, [108] (SC).

trial.[121] The Canadian Supreme Court over a series of cases has recognised exceptions to the exclusionary rule based upon principles of necessity and reliability. In a passage quoted in *Horncastle*, the Canadian court described this approach 'as the triumph of a principled analysis over a set of ossified judicially created categories'.[122] It reflects an epistemic vision similar to that expressed in *Horncastle*: 'the rule against hearsay is intended to enhance the accuracy of the court's findings of fact, not impede its truth-seeking function'.[123]

However, in *Crawford v Washington*[124] the US Supreme Court adopted a stringent procedural interpretation of the right of confrontation. The court acknowledged that the 'ultimate goal is to ensure reliability of evidence', but immediately added: '[I]t is a procedural rather than a substantive guarantee. It commands, not that evidence be reliable, but that reliability be assessed in a particular manner: by testing in the crucible of cross-examination'.[125]

If this means that reliable evidence may be excluded and a guilty defendant freed, so be it. The focus of the confrontation right is means, not ends: 'Dispensing with confrontation because testimony is obviously reliable is akin to dispensing with jury trial because a defendant is obviously guilty. This is not what the Sixth Amendment prescribes'.[126]

Dissenting, Chief Justice Rehnquist argued for a stronger focus on outcomes: 'cross-examination is a tool used to flesh out the truth, not an empty procedure'.[127] But is the procedure empty? Duff and colleagues argue that confrontation furthers the participation of the parties and is inherently valuable. But there is another perspective.

Josephine Ross objects that *Crawford* 'treats confrontation rights as a game rather than as a search for truth'.[128] Other commentators have also criticised features of the trial that seem better designed to actuate the contest than to advance factual accuracy. Jenny McEwan suggests that the English adversarial system sometimes works by 'a handicapping system more redolent of the Cheltenham Gold cup than doing justice'. This 'rough and ready balance of disadvantages', McEwan argues, has 'little to do with ascertaining the truth'.[129] Almost 60 years earlier Jerome Frank contrasted the 'fight theory' of the trial with the 'truth theory'. The fight theory features 'players on the one side the attorneys for the defence, and on the other side the attorneys for the State. The defendant figures in it merely

[121] Also see the contributions to this volume by Redmayne, Callen and Gallavin.
[122] *R v Smith* [1992] 2 SCR 915, 930; *R v Horncastle* [2010] 2 AC 373, Annex 1, [2] (SC).
[123] *R v Khelawon* [2006] 2 SCR 787, [2].
[124] 541 US 36 (2004).
[125] Ibid 61 (Justice Scalia).
[126] Ibid 62.
[127] Ibid 74.
[128] J Ross, 'What's Reliability Got to do with the Confrontation Clause after *Crawford*?' (2009) 14 *Widener Law Review* 383, 424.
[129] J McEwan, 'Ritual, Fairness and Truth: The Adversarial and Inquisitorial Models of Criminal Trial' in Duff et al (eds), above n 75, 51, 68.

as the prize'.[130] Alternatively, 'a trial is a battle and the lawyer the client's champion'.[131] Either way, Frank argued that '[i]mprovement in fact-finding will necessitate some considerable diminution of the martial spirit'.[132]

One of Frank's key illustrations of the fight theory is cross-examination.[133] Wigmore famously described cross-examination as the 'greatest legal engine ever invented for the discovery of the truth',[134] and we have seen that both delayed complaint trials and absence of confrontation may hamper cross-examination and raise concerns about the reliability of evidence. However, other commentators echo Frank's objection that cross-examination may be fashioned more for victory than truth-seeking. Mirjan Damaška describes it as 'a two-edged sword': '[I]t is "to a considerable degree ... like other potent weapons, equally lethal for heroes and villains".... [R]eliable testimony may easily be made to look debatable, and clear information may become obfuscated'.[135] Constraints on cross-examination have recently been justified on the basis that 'requirements of a fair trial ... do not involve treating the criminal justice system as if it were a forensic game in which every accused is entitled to some kind of sporting chance'.[136]

As noted above, Duff and colleagues have trouble reconciling the right to silence with their vision of the criminal trial as a communicative process.[137] They also point out its inconsistency with the truth-seeking model of the trial.[138] As Bentham suggests, this principle of evidence law may also reflect the notion of trial as sport:[139] '[T]he accused, innocent or guilty, must, like the fox when it is hunted by gentlemen, be given a fair chance to escape'.[140]

As Frank observed, there is an area of overlap between 'contest' and 'truth' theories of the trial. A traditional justification of the adversarial system is that truth is best served by having 'each side strive as hard as it can, in a keenly partisan spirit, to bring to the court's attention the evidence

130 J Frank, *Courts on Trial* (Mass, Atheneum Reprint, 1963) 91, quoting Damon Runyan.

131 EG Thornburg, 'Metaphors Matter: How Images of Battle, Sports and Sex Shape the Adversary System' (1995) 10 *Wisconsin Women's Law Journal* 225.

132 Above n 130, 102.

133 Ibid 81–85.

134 JH Wigmore, *Evidence in Trials at Common Law*, Peter Tillers (ed) (Boston, Little Brown & Co, 1983) § 1367.

135 M Damaška, 'Presentation of Evidence and Fact-finding Precision' (1975) 123 *University of Pennsylvania LR* 1083, 1094, quoting from ME Frankel, 'The Search for Truth: An Umpireal View' (1975) 123 *University of Pennsylvania Law Review* 1031, 1039.

136 *R v TA* (2003) 57 NSWLR 444, 446 (Spigelman CJ).

137 Above n 79, 149.

138 Ibid 98.

139 *Works of Jeremy Bentham* VII (Bowring ed 1838–43) 454.

140 HLA Hart, 'The Demystification of the Law', in *Essays on Bentham: Studies in Jurisprudence and Political Theory* (Oxford, OUP, 1982) 21, 37.

favorable to that side'.[141] It may be objected that 'the adversaries wage their contest upon a tilted playing field',[142] the poorly-resourced criminal defendant facing an uphill battle. More fundamental, however, is the inconsistency between the games on the one hand, and the pursuit of truth and justice on the other. 'By definition, the opponents in a "fair game" are *a priori* both entitled to win.... Justice, however, again by definition, belongs to one side or another *a priori*, hence, independently of the outcome'.[143] Criminal Procedure should reflect what law and justice require, not just whether the game has been played fairly.[144] Early in the twentieth century, Roscoe Pound described the 'sporting theory of justice, the "instinct of giving the game fair play"' as one of the prime causes of 'popular dissatisfaction with the administration of justice'[145] and confidently anticipated its demise.[146] But the contest theory persists. While judges occasionally suggest, somewhat defensively, 'a judge is not a mere umpire to answer the question "How's that?" His object, above all, is to find out the truth, and to do justice according to law',[147] they continue to talk of 'equality of arms',[148] 'the existence of contestants who are more or less equally matched',[149] and the imperative of holding the 'balance between the contending parties'.[150]

It has been suggested that the fight/sporting theory of the trial originated with 'primitive systems of trial by battle and trial by ordeal'[151] and the use of trials to replace anarchic systems of dispute resolution through private revenge.[152] Its tenacity has been attributed to the ongoing popularity of sporting contests[153] in many common law jurisdictions, along with strong cultural and political attachment to 'personal choice, laissez-faire values'.[154]

[141] Frank, above n 130, 80, citing TB Macaulay, *A History of England* vol 4 (London, Longman, Brown, Green and Longmans, 1855) 84–85. Also see M Hale, *History and Analysis of the Common Law of England* (Stafford, J Nutt, 1713), 258.

[142] D Givelber, 'Meaningless Acquittals, Meaningful Convictions' (1997) 49 *Rutgers Law Review* 1317, 1360; Thornburg, above n 131, 259.

[143] A Rapoport, *Fights, Games and Debates* (Ann Arbor, MI, University of Michigan Press, 1960) 263. Also see Thornburg, above n 131, 259.

[144] R Pound, 'The Causes of Popular Dissatisfaction with the Administration of Justice' (1906) 29 *American Bar Association Reporter* 395, 405–06.

[145] Ibid 404, quoting JH Wigmore, *Evidence in Trials at Common Law* vol 1 (Boston, Little, Brown & Co, 1904) 127.

[146] Above n 144, 417.

[147] *Jones v National Coal Board* [1957] 2 QB 55, 63. Also see *US v McCord*, 509 F 2d 334 (1975), 347.

[148] Eg *R v Horncastle* [2010] 2 AC 373, [26] (SC).

[149] Eg *Dietrich v R* (1992) 177 CLR 192, 354.

[150] Eg *R v Libke* (2007) 230 CLR 559, [72].

[151] M Asimow, 'Popular Culture and the Adversary System' (2007) 46 *Loyola of Los Angeles Law Review* 653, 667–68.

[152] Frank, above n 130, 91, 102.

[153] Ibid. Also see D Abrams, 'Sports in the Courts: The Role of Sports References in Judicial Opinions' (2010) 17 *Villanova Sports and Entertainment Law Journal* 1.

[154] Asimow, above n 151, 658; also Frank, above n 130, 92; Thornburg, above n 131, 248–49.

The implication that a love of sport and individual liberty is limited to the common law world appears dubious, to say the least. But, whatever its supposed attractions, the fight theory of criminal adjudication is potentially inconsistent with promoting accurate fact-finding. In the event of conflict, the latter should prevail. Delayed complaint trials may make poor contests, but this should not distract courts from their central epistemic objectives—convicting the guilty and acquitting the innocent.

CONCLUSION

Victims of child sexual assault may understandably delay their allegations, sometimes for many years, resulting in the loss of important evidence. The court may be presented with little more than the complainant's uncorroborated undetailed allegation, set against the defendant's bare denial. This situation creates a variety of difficulties.

Most obvious is the prosecution's predicament. With such limited evidence the prosecution may struggle to prove guilt to the requisite standard, beyond reasonable doubt. The prosecution's proof difficulties further hamper effective enforcement of criminal prohibitions on sexual assault.[155] Indeed, it might have been thought that, if there was judicial intervention, it would be on the prosecution's side. Courts today routinely acknowledge that 'principles of fair trial ... require that in appropriate cases the interests of the defence are balanced against those of witnesses or victims'.[156] One might argue that, as in other sexual assault cases, 'the balance between the rights of the defendant and those of the complainant is in need of adjustment' if vulnerable complainants 'are to be given the protection under law to which they are entitled'.[157] Such statements may spark concerns about 'a criminal justice system that is increasingly oriented towards the securing of convictions'.[158] But we need not enter this broader debate. The loss of evidence in delayed complaint trials has prompted only pro-defendant judicial interventions. These may be construed as responding to various

[155] Above n 31.

[156] *R v Horncastle* [2010] 2 AC 373, [67] (SC), quoting from *Doorson v Netherlands* (1996) 22 EHRR 330, [70]. See also *Dietrich v R* (1992) 177 CLR 192, 335 (Deane J), quoting from *R v Barton* (1980) 147 CLR 75, 101 (Gibbs ACJ and Mason J); *R v E(AW)* [1993] 3 SCR 155, [84].

[157] *R v A (No 2)* [2002] 1 AC 45, [55] (Lord Hope). See also ibid [92]–[94] (Lord Hope); *PL v DPP* [2004] 4 IR 494, 533, where Fennelly J suggested that sexual assault cases receive a 'special jurisprudence' in which the defendant 'may be required to accept the risk of an unfair trial'; cf 507 (Hardiman J), 520 (Geoghegan J). The more orthodox view is that, whilst 'the guarantee of a fair trial... is absolute', in determining 'what the concept of a fair trial entails... account may be taken of the familiar triangulation of interests of the accused, the victim and society': *R v A (No 2)* [2002] 1 AC 45, [38] (Lord Steyn).

[158] Duff et al, above n 79, 1.

concerns about the position of the defendant in the delayed trial. However, as I have explored in this chapter, these concerns, whether epistemic or non-epistemic, lack any solid foundation.

The epistemic claim that the loss of evidence disproportionately disadvantages the defendant is illogical. Since the evidence is lost, its content is simply unknown. The evidential deficit might just as easily help or hinder the defence. Nor is there any systematic reason to resolve the slightness of the evidence against the prosecution. If a complainant's testimony is sufficiently persuasive, its understandable lack of comprehensiveness should not be an obstacle to conviction.

The lack of evidence in delayed complaint trials has also given rise to non-epistemic concerns. It seems unfair to prosecute on the basis of allegations made years after the event when the defendant has reduced opportunity to gather evidence in rebuttal. The defendant's active participation in the trial is compromised, and his autonomy and subjectivity are inhibited. Although palpable, this apparent source of potential unfairness quickly recedes on closer examination. Of course, it would be horrific if an *innocent* defendant were reduced by the delay and loss of evidence to a bare denial, which the jury rejected. But the injustice of a wrongful conviction is epistemic. As we have seen, delay tends to increase the risk of mistaken acquittal, not wrongful conviction.

Suppose the defendant were actually guilty, and the delay and loss of detail in the complainant's testimony merely blunted the defendant's weapon of obfuscatory cross-examination.[159] Should this cause concern?[160] The reduction in the *defendant's* participation would be minimal. Almost invariably defence counsel would have planned and carried out the cross-examination, not the defendant.[161] The real concern in such a case may be the impression that the trial would not constitute a fair fight. The prosecution has struck a blow with the complainant's allegation, but the defendant appears to have his hands tied behind his back. Admittedly, it would be preferable if the defendant were not limited to a bare denial. But despite the arresting image, the defendant's constraints do not bias the result. To the extent that the defendant's participation is limited, this does not increase the risk of wrongful conviction.

It must be remembered that courts are engaged in practical exercises. They do not demand 'the fairest of all possible trials'.[162] A fair trial does

[159] See A Cossins, 'Cross-Examination in Child Sexual Assault Trials: Evidentiary Safeguard or an Opportunity to Confuse?' (2009) 33 *Melbourne University Law Review* 68.

[160] But see Lewis, above n 38, 148; criticised by Hamer, above n 35, 686.

[161] Even where the defendant is unrepresented, legislation in most jurisdictions prevents the defendant from conducting cross-examination of the complainant in person: eg Criminal Procedure Act 1986 (NSW) s 294A; Youth Justice and Criminal Evidence Act 1999 (UK), ss 34, 36.

[162] *R v O'Connor* [1995] 4 SCR 411, [193].

not imply, for example, that 'all possible witnesses are available to give evidence'.[163] Justice requires only 'as fair a trial as practicable in the circumstances'.[164] While a defendant responding to delayed complaints may have limited opportunity to participate or present a defence at trial, it cannot be said that the defendant has been *silenced* or *actively denied* or *deprived* of such opportunity. The defendant has been placed in that position not by the police, prosecution or court, but by fate and circumstances. There appears therefore, insufficient reason to depart from the law's 'strong preference for a verdict on the merits'.[165] And to stay the prosecution or distort the trial with a pro-defendant direction would disappoint the 'legitimate expectation of a true verdict based on the merits'.[166]

[163] *R v Polyukhovich*, South Australia Supreme Court, 22 December 1992, 10 (Cox J). See also *R v McCarthy*, NSW Court of Criminal Appeal, 12 August 1994 (Gleeson CJ,); *R v WRC* (2002) 130 A Crim R 89, [80] (Hodgson JA); *Holt v Wynter* (2000) 49 NSWLR 128, [79] (Priestley JA, dissenting); *Batistatos v RTA* (2006) 226 CLR 256, [163] (Kirby J, dissenting), [233] (Callinan J, dissenting).

[164] *Dietrich v R* (1992) 177 CLR 192, 324 (Brennan J, dissenting).

[165] *R v Larsen* [2001] BCSC 404, [43] (Romilly J).

[166] Ibid.

10

'Give Us What You Have'—Information, Compulsion and the Privilege Against Self-Incrimination as a Human Right

ANDREW L-T CHOO

1. ON 'SELF-INCRIMINATION'

THIS CHAPTER EXPLORES aspects of the privilege against self-incrimination and its underpinning rationales.[1] In particular, it focuses on the extent of a person's legal obligation to surrender pre-existing documents and bodily samples, in the light of the European Court of Human Rights' insistence that the privilege does not extend to material which 'has an existence independent of the will of the suspect'.

The privilege against self-incrimination is often invoked as a fundamental principle of criminal procedure. Its operation in England and Wales provides excellent fodder for examining the influence of human rights norms on evidentiary principles, since the starting point for analysis is now Article 6 of the ECHR, one of the Articles 'incorporated' into the domestic law of the United Kingdom by the Human Rights Act 1998. Although Article 6 does not contain any express guarantee of the privilege, it is settled Strasbourg law[2] that the privilege is implicit in Article 6(1)'s general guarantee that, '[i]n the determination of his civil rights and obligations or of any criminal charge against him, everyone is entitled to a fair ... hearing'.

Simply expressed, in the words of New Zealand's Evidence Act 2006, 'self-incrimination' may be regarded as 'the provision by a person of information that could reasonably lead to, or increase the likelihood of, the prosecution of that person for a criminal offence'.[3] By extrapolation, recognition

[1] This chapter draws on A L-T Choo, *Evidence*, 2nd edn (Oxford, OUP, 2009) 144–51, and explores ideas and themes developed in a forthcoming monograph to be published by Hart Publishing. I am grateful to Simon Young for sharing his insights into the Canadian position.

[2] *Saunders v UK* (1996) 23 EHRR 313, [68]; *Funke v France* (1993) 16 EHRR 297.

[3] Evidence Act 2006 (NZ), s 4.

of a privilege against self-incrimination should mean that a person cannot be compelled, on pain of a criminal sanction, to provide information that could reasonably lead to, or increase the likelihood of, that person's prosecution for a criminal offence. Yet there are many statutory provisions in England and Wales allowing demands for information that, if provided, could be used in a criminal prosecution, and, if not provided, could result in a criminal prosecution for non-compliance with the demand.

While self-incrimination also occurs in court, this chapter will focus exclusively on the implications of out-of-court demands for information. There is extensive learning on the extent to which cautioning a suspect in England and Wales that 'it may harm your defence if you do not mention when questioned something which you later rely on in Court'[4] constitutes *indirect* compulsion to speak, and on the parallel issue of the appropriateness of drawing adverse inferences[5] from silence which the suspect was legally entitled to maintain. In concentrating on *direct* compulsion to provide information, where failure to do so would constitute a criminal offence, this chapter obviously tells only part of a more complex story.

A simple illustration is afforded by the statutory provisions at issue in the judgment of the Grand Chamber of the European Court of Human Rights in *O'Halloran and Francis v UK*.[6] This case considered section 172(2)(a) of the Road Traffic Act 1988 which requires the registered keeper, on demand, to identify the driver of a vehicle suspected of being implicated in an offence. Both O'Halloran and Francis were served with requests under section 172(2)(a) after their vehicles were 'caught' speeding by roadside cameras. O'Halloran admitted to being the driver and was prosecuted for speeding. Francis refused to provide the information and was prosecuted under the Act for failing to comply with a section 172 request. How does this sit with the recognition of a privilege against self-incrimination? The Grand Chamber's answer will be scrutinised later in the chapter.

2. AN 'IMPLIED' RIGHT

Section 2(1)(a) of the Human Rights Act 1998 provides that

> [a] court or tribunal determining a question which has arisen in connection with a Convention right must take into account any ... judgment, decision, declaration or advisory opinion of the European Court of Human Rights.

[4] PACE Code C, 10.5, issued pursuant to the Police and Criminal Evidence Act 1984, s 66.

[5] Under the Criminal Justice and Public Order Act 1994, s 34.

[6] (2007) 46 EHRR 21 (p 397). Generally, see M Birdling, 'Self-Incrimination Goes to Strasbourg: *O'Halloran and Francis v United Kingdom*' (2008) 12 *International Journal of Evidence and Proof* 58; S Burns, 'Good to Talk?' (2007) 157 *New Law Journal* 1454; JR Spencer, 'Curbing Speed and Limiting the Right of Silence' [2007] *Cambridge Law Journal* 531.

The classic statement of the privilege against self-incrimination as an implied right in the ECHR system is found in *Saunders v UK*.[7] In the following key paragraphs, the Court sought to justify the status of the privilege as an implied right, and as an aspect of the wider right to silence:

> The Court recalls that, although not specifically mentioned in Article 6 of the Convention, the right to silence and the right not to incriminate oneself, are generally recognised international standards which lie at the heart of the notion of a fair procedure under Article 6. Their rationale lies, *inter alia*, in the protection of the accused against improper compulsion by the authorities thereby contributing to the avoidance of miscarriages of justice and to the fulfilment of the aims of Article 6. The right not to incriminate oneself, in particular, presupposes that the prosecution in a criminal case seek to prove their case against the accused without resort to evidence obtained through methods of coercion or oppression in defiance of the will of the accused. In this sense the right is closely linked to the presumption of innocence contained in Article 6(2) of the Convention.
>
> The right not to incriminate oneself is primarily concerned, however, with respecting the will of an accused person to remain silent. As commonly understood in the legal systems of the Contracting Parties to the Convention and elsewhere, it does not extend to the use in criminal proceedings of material which may be obtained from the accused through the use of compulsory powers but which has an existence independent of the will of the suspect such as, *inter alia*, documents acquired pursuant to a warrant, breath, blood and urine samples and bodily tissue for the purpose of DNA testing.[8]

The Court, it can be seen, regards material having an existence *independent of the will of the suspect* as not being subject to the privilege. This idea will now be subjected to further analysis, as it provides a good vehicle for testing the adequacy of the Court's views of the potential scope of the privilege.

3. 'PRE-EXISTING' DOCUMENTS AND PHYSICAL EVIDENCE

To what extent does the privilege against self-incrimination cover 'pre-existing' documents and physical evidence, that is (in the Strasbourg Court's terminology) 'material which has an existence independent of the will of the suspect'? It might be thought, in light of the Court's analysis in *Saunders*, that such material cannot engage the privilege. However, Strasbourg case-law does not appear to speak with one voice on this issue.

In *Funke v France*,[9] the ECtHR considered a prosecution for refusing to produce bank statements to French customs authorities to be in breach

[7] (1996) 23 EHRR 313.

[8] Ibid [68]–[69].

[9] (1993) 16 EHRR 297. Generally, see AS Butler, '*Funke v France* and the Right against Self-Incrimination: A Critical Analysis' (2000) 11 *Criminal Law Forum* 461.

of Article 6. Again, in *JB v Switzerland*,[10] the Court found a violation of Article 6 where 'the authorities were attempting to compel the applicant to submit documents which would have provided information as to his income with a view to the assessment of his taxes' and the applicant had been prosecuted for failing to produce the documents.[11] The judgments in *Funke* and *JB* suggest that, contrary to expectation, there will be circumstances in which the Strasbourg Court considers pre-existing documents to be protected by the privilege against self-incrimination. This point was recognised very recently by Roth J, who noted that 'the approach to the question of pre-existing documents by the ECtHR in some of its decisions is not entirely easy to reconcile'.[12]

A clue to the ECtHR's reasoning may be found in one of its examples of material *not* subject to the privilege, namely, documents acquired pursuant to a *warrant*. A document acquired pursuant to a warrant is effectively acquired through force, without any requirement for co-operation on the part of the suspect. This suggests the possibility, mooted by Redmayne,[13] that it is compulsion to co-operate which lies at the heart of the Strasbourg Court's concerns about self-incrimination, so that freedom from such compulsion represents the essence of the privilege. This reasoning does not condone the use of force where coerced cooperation is not at issue: it merely regards compulsion in these circumstances, unjustified or otherwise, as lying outside the scope of the privilege against self-incrimination.

This rationalisation fails, however, to explain all the relevant case-law. In *A-G's Reference (No 7 of 2000)*[14] the English Court of Appeal said that the prosecution's use of pre-existing documents produced under compulsion did not violate Article 6. The Court was asked to rule on the following question:

> Does the use by the Crown in the prosecution of a bankrupt for an offence under Chapter VI of Part IX of the Insolvency Act 1986 ... of documents which (a) were delivered up to the Official Receiver ... under compulsion (pursuant to the duty imposed on the bankrupt by section 291 of the 1986 Act, which is backed by the contempt sanction in section 291(6) of the 1986 Act) and (b) do not contain statements made by the bankrupt under compulsion violate the bankrupt's rights under Article 6 of the European Convention on Human Rights ...?

[10] Application No 31827/96, 3 May 2001 (ECtHR).

[11] The quality of the Court's reasoning in this case has been subjected to some criticism: AJ Ashworth, 'The Self-Incrimination Saga' [2001] 5 *Archbold News* 5; IH Dennis, *The Law of Evidence*, 4th edn (London, Sweet & Maxwell, 2010) 169.

[12] *Milsom v Ablyazov* [2011] EWHC 1846 (Ch), [19].

[13] M Redmayne, 'Rethinking the Privilege against Self-Incrimination' (2007) 27 *Oxford Journal of Legal Studies* 209.

[14] [2001] EWCA Crim 888, [2001] 1 WLR 1879. Generally, see A Henderson, 'Defining the Limits of Silence' (2001) 145 *Solicitors' Journal* 432.

The Court of Appeal found no violation in these circumstances. The Grand Chamber of the ECtHR adopted parallel reasoning in *Jalloh v Germany*,[15] where the defendant was forced to regurgitate a bag of cocaine by the administration of an emetic without his consent. The ECtHR held that this procedure constituted inhuman and degrading treatment contrary to Article 3 of the ECHR *and* that it breached the privilege against self-incrimination. In other words, the Grand Chamber found that the privilege was engaged even though the evidence in question was 'pre-existing' and obtained by force without the suspect's voluntary co-operation. Neither of these decisions is reconcilable with the 'compelled co-operation' rationalisation for the privilege.

In *Saunders v UK*, as we have seen, the ECtHR excluded breath samples, blood samples, urine samples and bodily tissue from the scope of the privilege against self-incrimination. In *Jalloh v Germany*, the Grand Chamber sought to distinguish the Court's previous analysis from the instant facts:

> [T]he administration of emetics was used to retrieve *real evidence* ... Conversely, the bodily material listed in the *Saunders* case concerned material obtained by coercion for forensic examination *with a view to detecting*, for example, the presence of alcohol or drugs (emphasis added).[16]

The suggestion appears to be that the bag of cocaine regurgitated by Jalloh was per se incriminating, in and of itself, whereas the examples advanced in *Saunder*s concerned material that might only become incriminating in the light of further tests or inferences. A similar distinction between per se incriminating and 'neutral' information appears to underlie the decision, in a different factual context, of the English Court of Appeal in *R v S (F)*.[17] Here, the Court held that knowledge of an encryption key is per se neutral, so that an official demand to divulge the key will engage the privilege only if the protected data turns out to be incriminating. The Court reasoned:

> In much the same way that a blood or urine sample provided by a car driver is a fact independent of the driver, which may or may not reveal that his alcohol level exceeds the permitted maximum, whether the defendants' computers contain incriminating material or not, the keys to them are and remain an independent fact.... [A]lthough the defendants' knowledge of the means of access to the data may engage the privilege against self-incrimination, it would only do so if the data itself ... contains incriminating material. If that data was neutral or innocent, the knowledge of the means of access to it would similarly be either neutral or innocent.[18]

[15] (2006) 44 EHRR 32 (p 667).
[16] Ibid [113].
[17] [2008] EWCA Crim 2177, [2009] 1 WLR 1489.
[18] Ibid [21], [24].

4. COMPARATIVE PERSPECTIVES

The discussion so far suggests that the statement of principle advanced by the ECtHR in *Saunders v UK* is misleading or at least incomplete. It must be read subject to further principles embedded in relevant European and English case-law. With a view to gaining comparative insights, as well as testing the Strasbourg Court's suggestion of an emergent 'international consensus' on the scope of the privilege against self-incrimination (implicit in the Court's description, in the quotation from *Saunders* above, of the privilege as a 'generally recognised international standard' that is in place 'in the legal systems of the Contracting Parties to the Convention and elsewhere'), this section briefly examines the approaches adopted by several other legal systems to these problems of conceptual definition.

(a) New Zealand

The privilege against self-incrimination in New Zealand attaches only to 'a statement of fact or opinion given, or to be given, (a) orally; or (b) in a document that is prepared or created ... after and in response to a requirement to [provide specific information]'.[19] Excluded from the operation of the privilege are all pre-existing documents, as well as all bodily samples and other pre-existing material extractable from the suspect.[20] As the New Zealand Supreme Court observed:

> [T]he privilege against self-incrimination ... does not justify an individual refusing to supply physical evidence which exists and can be found independently of any testimony of the individual, such as bodily samples.... A refusal to produce real evidence emanating from a person in the form of a urine sample does not engage the privilege.[21]

This represents a very narrow view of the potential scope of the privilege.

(b) US Constitutional Law

In *Schmerber v California*[22] the US Supreme Court confirmed that the privilege against self-incrimination protected by the Fifth Amendment to the US Constitution attaches only to 'testimonial communications'. A blood sample was therefore not within the scope of the privilege:

> Not even a shadow of testimonial compulsion upon or enforced communication by the accused was involved either in the extraction or in the chemical

[19] This is the definition of 'information' contained in the Evidence Act 2006 (NZ), s 51(3).
[20] *Cropp v Judicial Committee and McKenzie* [2008] NZSC 46, [47].
[21] Ibid.
[22] 384 US 757 (1966).

> analysis. Petitioner's testimonial capacities were in no way implicated; indeed, his participation, except as a donor, was irrelevant to the results of the test, which depend on chemical analysis and on that alone. Since the blood test evidence, although an incriminating product of compulsion, was neither petitioner's testimony nor evidence relating to some communicative act or writing by the petitioner, it was not inadmissible on privilege grounds.[23]

More recently, in *US v Hubbell*,[24] the US Supreme Court reconsidered the Fifth Amendment status of pre-existing documents. The demand for compulsory disclosure in *Hubbell* was couched in very general terms. The authorities wanted documents that fell within any of 11 very broadly worded categories, resulting in the production of some 13,120 pages of material.[25] The Court held that 'the act of producing documents in response to a subpoena *may* have a testimonial aspect (emphasis added)'[26] in the context of a particular case, and that it did so here:

> Given the breadth of the description of the 11 categories of documents called for by the subpoena, the collection and production of the materials demanded was tantamount to answering a series of interrogatories asking a witness to disclose the existence and location of particular documents fitting certain broad descriptions. The assembly of literally hundreds of pages of material in response to a request for 'any and all documents reflecting, referring, or relating to any direct or indirect sources of money or other things of value received by or provided to' an individual or members of his family during a 3-year period ... is the functional equivalent of the preparation of an answer to either a detailed written interrogatory or a series of oral questions at a discovery deposition.... [R]espondent ... took the mental and physical steps necessary to provide the prosecutor with an accurate inventory of the many sources of potentially incriminating evidence sought by the subpoena. It was only through respondent's truthful reply to the subpoena that the Government received the incriminating documents ...[27]

In arriving at the conclusion that the Fifth Amendment privilege was engaged on these facts, the Supreme Court emphasised the mental effort

[23] Ibid 765.

[24] 530 US 27 (2000).

[25] By way of illustration, the 11 categories listed in an Appendix to the Court's opinion included: 'Any and all documents reflecting, referring, or relating to any direct or indirect sources of money or other things of value received by or provided to Webster Hubbell, his wife, or children from January 1, 1993 to the present, including but not limited to the identity of employers or clients of legal or any other type of work'; and 'Any and all documents reflecting, referring, or relating to work performed or to be performed or on behalf of the City of Los Angeles, California, the Los Angeles Department of Airports or any other Los Angeles municipal Governmental entity, Mary Leslie, and/or Alan S Arkatov, including but not limited to correspondence, retainer agreements, contracts, time sheets, appointment calendars, activity calendars, diaries, billing statements, billing memoranda, telephone records, telephone message slips, telephone credit card statements, itineraries, tickets for transportation, payment records, expense receipts, ledgers, check registers, notes, memoranda, electronic mail, bank deposit items, cashier's checks, traveler's checks, wire transfer records and/or other records of financial transactions'.

[26] 530 US 27, 36 (2000).

[27] Ibid 41–43.

expended by Hubbell in complying with the subpoena, and drew an instructive contrast between surrendering the key to a strongbox (outside the scope of the privilege) and divulging the secret combination of a wall safe (covered by it):

> It was unquestionably necessary for respondent to make extensive use of 'the contents of his own mind' in identifying the hundreds of documents responsive to the requests in the subpoena.... The assembly of those documents was like telling an inquisitor the combination to a wall safe, not like being forced to surrender the key to a strongbox.... The Government's anemic view of respondent's act of production as a mere physical act that is principally nontestimonial in character ... simply fails to account for these realities.[28]

The Court sought to rationalise its decision by reference to previous case-law rather than broader considerations of principle. *Hubbell* consequently failed to state a clear test for identifying the classes of documents covered by the privilege,[29] and there have been many subsequent attempts by commentators to fill in the gaps. For example, Allen and Mace consider the crucial factor to be that 'the government may not compel disclosure of the incriminating substantive results of cognition that themselves (the substantive results) are the product of state action'.[30] For Pardo, on the other hand, the privilege against self-incrimination was implicated in this case because the defendant was being relied upon as an 'epistemic authority' in relation to compelled information: 'In other words, fact-finders could potentially justify their decisions by citing the defendant's own epistemic authority, by claiming that the defendant (and not they) are the ones with direct epistemic support justifying the fact-finders' conclusions'.[31] One thing, though, seems clear: on a narrow interpretation, it is possible to rationalise the decision in *Hubbell* purely on grounds of evidential reliability. In other words, even on the assumption that there is nothing wrong with compelling the provision of information unless the compulsion will potentially generate false or unreliable information, the decision in *Hubbell* can be justified. On this view, a demand for the production of a specific pre-existing document

[28] Ibid 43.

[29] WR LaFave, JH Israel, NJ King and OS Kerr, *Criminal Procedure*, 3rd edn (St Paul, MN, Thomson/West, 2007, updated 2010) vol 3, § 8.13(a): '*Hubbell* leaves unanswered the question of how precisely the government must identify the documents, by reference to its prior knowledge'. It is therefore unclear whether the government must 'identify a specific document as one known to be in the subpoenaed party's possession (eg, an airline ticket for a known trip on a particular day)', or whether it is sufficient to 'refer to a somewhat broader grouping of documents upon showing that the party engaged in a particular type of activity which involved receipt of such documents (eg, airline tickets from a specific airline which the subpoenaed party regularly used)'.

[30] RJ Allen and MK Mace, 'The Self-Incrimination Clause Explained and its Future Predicted' (2004) 94 *Journal of Criminal Law and Criminology* 243, 247.

[31] MS Pardo, 'Self-Incrimination and the Epistemology of Testimony' (2008) 30 *Cardozo Law Review* 1023, 1040.

is unproblematic because the suspect is accorded no leeway to lie, either deliberately or unwittingly. But where, as in *Hubbell*, the demand was sweeping and open-ended, there is a danger that the suspect may, in the process of responding, falsely incriminate himself, just as he might do in the course of a police interrogation.

In short, it is possible to define a 'testimonial communication' as a communication the truthfulness of which is capable of being manipulated. This might be a more appropriate criterion for defining the scope of the privilege against self-incrimination.

(c) Canada

The Supreme Court of Canada would appear to take an expansive view of the potential scope of the privilege against self-incrimination. It indicated in *R v SAB* that no distinction is to be drawn 'between products of the mind and products of the body with respect to the principle against self-incrimination'.[32] The privilege is not expressly provided for in the Canadian Charter of Rights and Freedoms, but is considered to be a 'principle of fundamental justice' under section 7 of the Charter (rather than an implicit feature of section 11(d)'s right to a fair trial). Section 7 provides that: 'Everyone has the right to life, liberty and security of the person and the right not to be deprived thereof except in accordance with the principles of fundamental justice'.

It is notable that, notwithstanding its expansive view of the potential scope of the privilege, the Supreme Court of Canada adopts a 'balancing' approach to applying the privilege in the case at hand. Indeed, the Court openly acknowledges that, ultimately, 'the principle against self-incrimination ... has a limited scope, and requires different things at different times'.[33] The implications of treating the privilege against self-incrimination as a matter of balancing competing interests are explored in the next section.

(d) India

The Supreme Court of India considered the privilege against self-incrimination in *Selvi v State of Karnataka*.[34] Among the issues addressed by the Court was whether the privilege was engaged by polygraph testing or by Brain Electrical Activation Profile ('BEAP') testing, the latter

[32] *R v SAB* 2003 SCC 60, [2003] 2 SCR 678, [34].
[33] Ibid [57].
[34] [2010] INSC 340.

being 'a process of detecting whether an individual is familiar with certain information by way of measuring activity in the brain that is triggered by exposure to selected stimuli'.[35] The Court held:

> Even though the actual process of undergoing a polygraph examination or a BEAP test is not the same as that of making an oral or written statement, the consequences are similar. By making inferences from the results of these tests, the examiner is able to derive knowledge from the subject's mind which otherwise would not have become available to the investigators. These two tests are different from medical examination and the analysis of bodily substances such as blood, semen and hair samples, since the test subject's physiological responses are directly correlated to mental faculties. Through lie-detection or gauging a subject's familiarity with the stimuli, personal knowledge is conveyed in respect of a relevant fact. It is also significant that unlike the case of documents, the investigators cannot possibly have any prior knowledge of the test subject's thoughts and memories, either in the actual or constructive sense. Therefore, even if a highly-strained analogy were to be made between the results obtained from the impugned tests and the production of documents, the weight of precedents leans towards restrictions on the extraction of 'personal knowledge' through such means.[36]

The Court's decision provides an illustration of a carefully considered approach to determining the potential scope of the privilege. While the Court acknowledges that being subjected to polygraph testing or BEAP testing cannot be straightforwardly equated with undergoing police interrogation, evidence generated in all three cases ultimately raises similar concerns, making it distinguishable from evidence of bodily samples.

(e) International Law: The ICTY

The advent of international criminal trials, pioneered from the mid-1990s by the International Criminal Tribunal for the Former Yugoslavia (ICTY), has required new configurations of international courts and judges to grapple with fundamental concepts of criminal procedure. In *Prosecutor v Delalic*, where the authorship of a particular letter was at issue, a Trial Chamber of the ICTY held that a handwriting sample could not be demanded for comparison purposes. The ICTY rejected the contention that 'the privilege from self-incrimination [should be] restricted to testimonial evidence',[37] stating:

> The fact that the handwriting sample *per se* is neutral evidence is not the issue. If the handwriting sample taken together with other evidence will constitute

[35] Ibid [67].
[36] Ibid [160].
[37] Trial Chamber of the ICTY, 19 January 1998, [58].

> material evidence to prove the charge against the accused, then the Order of the Trial Chamber would have compelled the production of self-incriminating evidence.[38]

This ruling implies a notably expansive conception of the privilege against self-incrimination, capable of extending to physical ('real') evidence created under compulsion.

5. A QUESTION OF BALANCE?

Despite the strong statements made in *Saunders v UK*, comparative analysis reveals that the ECtHR has not exactly taken an expansive view of the potential scope of the privilege against self-incrimination. In this, the Court is certainly not alone, since national jurisdictions such as New Zealand have been no less conservative. However, there are additional features of ECtHR jurisprudence which are liable to reduce the scope of the privilege still further.

In *Weh v Austria*,[39] the applicant had been required to state who had been driving his car at a particular time. He responded that a named individual living in 'USA/University of Texas' was the driver. This resulted in Weh being fined for providing inadequate information. The ECtHR decided that his privilege against self-incrimination was not engaged on these facts because, in the absence of formal charges, the prospect of 'possible criminal proceedings for speeding against him remains remote and hypothetical'.[40] According to the Court,

> without a sufficiently concrete link with these criminal proceedings the use of compulsory powers (ie the imposition of a fine) to obtain information does not raise an issue with regard to the applicant's right to remain silent and the privilege against self-incrimination.[41]

A particularly noteworthy feature of the Strasbourg jurisprudence, and one that is potentially far-reaching in its effects, is the endorsement of an approach involving 'balancing all the relevant circumstances' to determine

[38] Ibid [48].

[39] (2004) 40 EHRR 37 (p 890).

[40] Ibid [56]. Also see *Rieg v Austria*, Application No 63207/00, 24 March 2005 (ECtHR). In *Singh v R* [2010] NZSC 161, [31], the New Zealand Supreme Court observed (quoting *Busby v Thorn EMI Video Programmes Ltd* [1984] 1 NZLR 461, 469 per Cooke J): 'Under s 60(1)(b) of the Evidence Act 2006, the privilege against self-incrimination can only be invoked in relation to information which, if provided, would be "likely" to incriminate the person claiming the privilege. The use by the legislature of the word "likely" shows that it intended to confine the privilege to circumstances where the potential for incrimination is "real and appreciable" and not "merely imaginary and fanciful". This means that the claim can only be invoked where later prosecution is itself likely'.

[41] (2004) 40 EHRR 37 (p 890), [56].

whether the right to a fair trial under Article 6 has been violated in the case at hand.[42] The judgment of the ECtHR Grand Chamber in *O'Halloran and Francis v UK* represents the high-water mark of this approach. The Grand Chamber held, in effect, that a number of factors should be 'balanced' in assessing whether Article 6 had been violated.

First, '[t]hose who choose to keep and drive motor cars can be taken to have accepted certain responsibilities and obligations as part of the regulatory regime relating to motor vehicles'.[43] A second factor is the extent of the police compulsion involved. The police power under review in the instant applications was triggered 'only where the driver of the vehicle is alleged to have committed a relevant offence' and authorised the police to require information only 'as to the identity of the driver'.[44] Thirdly, this power did not sanction 'prolonged questioning about facts alleged to give rise to criminal offences'. And the penalty for declining to answer was moderate and non-custodial.[45] Fourthly, the relevant offence was not one of strict liability because 'no offence is committed under s 172(2)(a) if the keeper of the vehicle shows that he did not know and could not with reasonable diligence have known who the driver of the vehicle was'.[46] This implied, said the Court, that 'the risk of unreliable admissions is negligible'.[47] Fifthly, in the case of O'Halloran,

> the identity of the driver is only one element in the offence of speeding, and there is no question of a conviction arising in the underlying proceedings in respect solely of the information obtained as a result of s 172(2)(a).[48]

In the light of these considerations, the Grand Chamber concluded that Article 6 of the Convention had not been violated in relation to either applicant:

> Having regard to all the circumstances of the case, including the special nature of the regulatory regime at issue and the limited nature of the information sought by a notice under s 172 of the Road Traffic Act 1988, the Court considers that the essence of the applicants' right to remain silent and their privilege against self-incrimination has not been destroyed.[49]

The key criterion for the Strasbourg Court, then, is to identify on a case-by-case basis whether the 'essence' of the privilege has been destroyed: it is only in cases where it has been so destroyed that there will be a violation of Article 6. A common criticism of *O'Halloran and Francis* is that, even

[42] Also see Andrew Ashworth, Chapter 6 in this volume.
[43] (2007) 46 EHRR 21 (p 397), [57].
[44] Ibid [58].
[45] Ibid.
[46] Ibid [59].
[47] Ibid.
[48] Ibid [60].
[49] Ibid [62].

if the ultimate result may be justifiable, the Grand Chamber's judgment[50] relies too heavily on a vague 'balancing' of competing considerations.[51] A threshold objection is practical: one might 'question whether there is now *any* coherent guidance'[52] to aid the determination of whether Article 6 has been violated in a particular case. A more comprehensive principled objection is that a right might lose its symbolic significance, and in time actually become devalued, if it can simply be 'balanced away' on an apparently ad hoc basis. A preferable approach to generalised balancing insists that 'in weighing rights and public interests the fulcrum should be comprehensively set closer to the "public interest" than "rights" so that much stronger leverage is required from considerations of the collective good in order to tilt the scales'.[53] The premise of such an approach is that,

> [t]hough rights do not necessarily conclude a matter, they should not be viewed as merely one factor to be taken into account in a global consideration of all relevant factors, but as a factor which presumptively excludes consideration of factors that would otherwise be relevant.[54]

Judges would be required

> not to exercise their own judgement as to what the balance of reasons requires, but rather to assign a greater weight to rights and a lesser weight to the public interest than they would ordinarily think they deserve.[55]

Accordingly, 'courts should not weigh the harm to the right-holder against the gains to the public, but should rather give substantial ... priority to the right-holder's claims'.[56] Meyerson draws an informative analogy to an individual's deliberations on promise-keeping:

> [A]lthough we do not regard a promise as *absolutely* binding, we do not in the *normal course of events* weigh the effects of breaking a promise against the potential countervailing considerations with a view to assessing whether they tip the balance. This kind of reasoning is different from that involved in 'weighing' or 'balancing'. We keep our promises as a matter of principle—based on the kind of

[50] In its approach the judgment of the Grand Chamber would appear wholly consistent with earlier domestic jurisprudence, most notably the decision of the Privy Council in *Brown v Stott* [2003] 1 AC 681. Generally, see P Mirfield, 'Silence, Innocence and Human Rights' in P Mirfield and R Smith (eds), *Essays for Colin Tapper* (London, LexisNexis UK, 2003) 135–37; R Pillay, 'Self-Incrimination and Article 6: The Decision of the Privy Council in *Procurator Fiscal v Brown*' [2001] *European Human Rights Law Review* 78.

[51] Also see J Rivers, 'Proportionality and Variable Intensity of Review' [2006] *Cambridge Law Journal* 174, 186–87.

[52] Birdling, above n 6, 61.

[53] S Greer, *The European Convention on Human Rights: Achievements, Problems and Prospects* (Cambridge, CUP, 2006) 227.

[54] D Meyerson, 'Why Courts Should not Balance Rights against the Public Interest' (2007) 31 *Melbourne University Law Review* 873, 902.

[55] Ibid 883.

[56] Ibid 886.

> person we wish to be—rather than by reference to their practical value or overall beneficial effects, and we break them only when it is glaringly obvious that that is the right thing to do.[57]

If it is accepted that the privilege against self-incrimination is not absolute, then the need to assign different weights or priorities to different considerations is inevitable. The practical difference between the 'balancing' approach and that just described may not be vast. In this respect it is instructive to consider the decision of the Hong Kong Court of Appeal in *Secretary for Justice v Latker*,[58] which concerned the Hong Kong equivalent of the compulsory disclosure provisions considered in *O'Halloran and Francis*. Latker's prosecution for failing to provide the details of the driver of his vehicle (which had been photographed by a digital red-light camera) was unanimously held to be compatible with his right to a fair trial. Chief Justice Ma, adopting the approach in *O'Halloran and Francis*, considered the critical question to be: 'what is the fair balance to be struck between, on the one hand, the demands and interests of the general community and, on the other, the fundamental rights of the individual?'[59] He concluded that the legislation 'provide[d] an acceptable balance struck between the public interest and the fundamental rights of the individual',[60] the public interest in having such legislation being 'overwhelming'.[61] The fact that the Hong Kong legislation provided for the possibility of a custodial penalty for non-compliance was not regarded as a sufficient basis on which to distinguish *O'Halloran and Francis* and tilt the balance in favour of upholding the privilege. Chief Justice Ma observed that 'a custodial sentence will be imposed ... only in the more serious situations', adding: 'Hong Kong is not in any event unique in providing for the possibility of a custodial sentence for this type of offence'.[62]

However, whilst concurring in the result, Stock JA expressly disassociated himself from the Chief Justice's analysis. Stock JA perceived 'the danger ... of undermining the primacy of fundamental freedoms which, after all, reflect the interests of the general community'. In his view, 'the starting point is always the freedom and any derogation from it must, both as to the need for derogation and its extent, be fully justified, albeit on societal grounds, by he who seeks to derogate'.[63] Still, Stock JA's alternative analysis

[57] Ibid 886–87. But cf A Barak, 'Proportionality and Principled Balancing' (2010) 4 *Law & Ethics of Human Rights* Art 1; and S Gardbaum, 'A Democratic Defense of Constitutional Balancing' (2010) 4 *Law & Ethics of Human Rights* Art 5, both available via www.bepress.com/lehr/vol4/iss1.

[58] [2009] 2 HKC 100.

[59] Ibid [37].

[60] Ibid [40].

[61] Ibid [60].

[62] Ibid [54].

[63] Ibid [165].

arrived at the same conclusion on the instant facts (notwithstanding the possibility of imprisonment for non-compliance with the Hong Kong legislation). However, whilst both approaches might produce the same outcome in many, if not most, cases, the 'balancing' approach is deficient in providing limited practical guidance for its application. In the context of European human rights law, it presents the risk that domestic courts will fail to take a Convention right, albeit an 'implied' one like the privilege against self-incrimination, sufficiently seriously. As Ashworth summaries the implications of *O'Halloran and Francis*:

> Although the outcome of the case may be regarded as inevitable, the route by which the Grand Chamber reached its conclusion is unsatisfactory. Rather than recognising a limited exception to the privilege against self-incrimination, based on an emerging European consensus and on an assessment that the exception would not be too damaging to the privilege overall, it has ... suggest[ed] that a wider range of factors should be considered in deciding whether a particular instance of self-incrimination constitutes a violation of the privilege. Some may think that the difference between the two routes is not great ... But the fear is that ... it will come to regard this and other Article 6 rights as capable of being traded off against the public interest.[64]

At the same time, the possibility that 'balancing' may come down in favour of upholding the privilege in particular circumstances should not be overlooked. Thus, in a recent decision of the English Court of Appeal concerning tax evasion charges, the balance of considerations was found to favour the appellant's right to withhold information:

> The social purpose for which the Crown seeks to adduce the evidence in criminal proceedings is the suppression of tax evasion. No doubt the protection of the public revenue is an important social objective, but the question is whether the admission of evidence obtained from the accused under threat of imprisonment is a reasonable and proportionate response to that social need. In our view it is not.... [W]e do not think that the need to punish and deter tax evasion is sufficient to justify such an infringement of the right of the accused not to incriminate himself.[65]

In this situation, the Court regarded compulsory disclosure as incompatible with the appellant's right to a fair trial.[66] Of course, the balance might have tipped the other way if the circumstances had been materially different, for example if the scope of compulsory disclosure had been more limited or if the offence in question had been more serious.

[64] AJ Ashworth, Commentary on *O'Halloran and Francis* at [2007] *Criminal Law Review* 900.

[65] *R v K (A)* [2010] QB 343, [2009] EWCA Crim 1640, [42].

[66] Ibid [43].

It is true that the legislative strategy at issue in *O'Halloran and Francis* might have been achieved by other means. In his dissenting opinion in *O'Halloran and Francis*, Judge Myjer noted that

> a number of contracting states ... have, for example, chosen to draw adverse inferences from a failure to answer questions, or established a statutory but rebuttable presumption of fact that the registered owner of the motor vehicle was the driver in question.[67]

The two legislative techniques mentioned, however, may themselves potentially violate human rights—the right to silence in the case of the former, and the presumption of innocence in the case of the latter. As Ashworth's commentary on *O'Halloran and Francis* observes: 'This points to the conclusion that, if it is thought practically necessary to compel car owners to disclose who was driving, all methods create problems for human rights law'.[68]

6. CONCLUSION: WHAT NOW FOR THE PRIVILEGE?

Despite the supposed importance of the privilege against self-incrimination, there is little agreement on its content or effect. The ECtHR may proclaim optimistically that its conception of the privilege is consistent with doctrinal analysis in other jurisdictions, but the brief comparative survey undertaken in this chapter casts substantial doubt on the existence of any international consensus. For example, in comparison with Canada, New Zealand appears to place far more into the category of material that the privilege definitely does not cover. In any event, the Strasbourg jurisprudence itself cannot easily be rationalised. The following three general themes have emerged from our analysis as a possible basis for rational reconstruction:

(1) the privilege may apply only to material considered in itself incriminating rather than merely 'neutral';
(2) the key concern of the privilege may be with compulsion to co-operate rather than with the use of force; but
(3) the use of a particularly severe form of force may engage the privilege even if the facts simultaneously justify a finding that Article 3 has been violated.

Beyond these rather indeterminate generalisations, we must wait to see how the ECtHR's 'balancing' approach is applied to determine compliance with Article 6 in particular cases. It is true that such case-by-case approaches are not uncommon in the law of criminal evidence of England and Wales,

[67] (2007) 46 EHRR 21 (p 397), [O-III4].
[68] [2007] *Criminal Law Review* 898.

with a similar approach being employed, for example, to determine the human rights-compatibility of reverse-onus statutory provisions.[69] As Roberts and Zuckerman observe,

> [a]s with the domestic reception of Article 6(2)'s presumption of innocence, there is scope for proliferating litigation in relation to each individual statutory provision requiring the accused to provide information to the authorities under threat of a legal penalty for non-compliance.[70]

At present, too, domestic jurisprudence on the privilege against self-incrimination lacks an authoritative recent decision of the House of Lords or Supreme Court that, in the style of the Supreme Court's hearsay decision in *R v Horncastle*,[71] might make a determined effort to integrate comparative perspectives.[72]

Possible rationales or philosophical foundations for the privilege against self-incrimination have been canvassed extensively in the academic literature.[73] In essence, the rationales put forward are either epistemic or non-epistemic in nature. This division of rationales, while not without its limitations, is widely accepted to be a useful heuristic device. Epistemic justifications are instrumental, focusing on the promotion of accurate fact-finding and, hence, the protection of the innocent from wrongful conviction.[74] Their concern is that the compulsion to provide information may produce unreliable evidence.[75] This eventuality is dependent on whether the respondent 'has it within his power to alter the evidence so as to affect its probative value on the issues of guilt or innocence';[76] more simply, dependent on 'the existence of an opportunity to be truthful or not'.[77] The crucial question is whether the respondent's subjective thoughts or

[69] *Sheldrake v DPP* [2005] 1 AC 264, [2004] UKHL 43. Generally, see A Stumer, *The Presumption of Innocence: Evidential and Human Rights Perspectives* (Oxford, Hart Publishing, 2010) ch 5.

[70] P Roberts and A Zuckerman, *Criminal Evidence*, 2nd edn (Oxford, OUP, 2010) 569.

[71] [2010] 2 AC 373, [2009] UKSC 14. See Mike Redmayne, Chapter 12 in this volume.

[72] As in *Re an Application under the Major Crime (Investigative Powers) Act 2004* [2009] VSC 381.

[73] For a US perspective, see AM Dershowitz, *Is There a Right to Remain Silent? Coercive Interrogation and the Fifth Amendment after 9/11* (New York, OUP, 2008) ch 6.

[74] *Murphy v Waterfront Commission*, 378 US 52, 55 (1964): 'the privilege, while sometimes "a shelter to the guilty," is often "a protection to the innocent"' (quoting *Quinn v US*, 349 US 155, 162 (1955)).

[75] Cf DJ Seidmann and A Stein, 'The Right to Silence Helps the Innocent: A Game-Theoretic Analysis of the Fifth Amendment Privilege' (2000) 114 *Harvard Law Review* 430, who argue that removing the privilege against self-incrimination would result in more guilty suspects telling lies in order to exculpate themselves, which in turn could lead triers of fact to discount all exculpatory statements, including those advanced by innocent suspects. Amongst numerous critiques of Seidmann and Stein's thesis, see Roberts and Zuckerman, above n 70, 561–63.

[76] BM Dann, 'The Fifth Amendment Privilege against Self-Incrimination: Extorting Physical Evidence from a Suspect' (1970) 43 *Southern California Law Review* 597, 612.

[77] RS Gerstein, 'The Demise of *Boyd*: Self-Incrimination and Private Papers in the Burger Court' (1979) 27 *UCLA Law Review* 343, 346 fn 17.

knowledge would be implicated in any information that is provided in response to the demand. The ECtHR may have had epistemic considerations in mind when it referred to the privilege's role in preventing miscarriages of justice, and suggested a close relationship between the privilege and the presumption of innocence. It is possible to view the New Zealand approach, which rules out the applicability of the privilege to any pre-existing material, as being focused exclusively on epistemic concerns. The decision of the US Supreme Court in *US v Hubbell* is explicable on a similar basis.

Non-epistemic justifications for the privilege against self-incrimination are varied, but have in common deontological concerns with intrinsic values unrelated to the promotion of accurate fact-finding. One non-epistemic justification that has gained currency is the notion that compelling the provision of potentially incriminatory information is an affront to individual dignity. As an American judge put it in the nineteenth century:

> The reprobation of compulsory self-incrimination is an established doctrine of our civilized society.... The essential and inherent cruelty of compelling a man to expose his own guilt is obvious to everyone, and needs no illustration. It is plain to every person who gives the subject a moment's thought. A sense of personal degradation in being compelled to incriminate one's self must create a feeling of abhorrence in the community at its attempted enforcement.[78]

A related non-epistemic justification posits that respect for personal autonomy[79] demands that those at risk of prosecution must be given a fair opportunity to formulate a response to allegations of criminal wrongdoing. This includes being accorded control over the time and circumstances for disclosing information, and such control may be facilitated by the recognition of a privilege against self-incrimination.[80]

In taking the view expressed in *Funke v France* and *JB v Switzerland* that the privilege attached to pre-existing documents which had been specified with relative precision in official demands for their production, the Strasbourg Court implicitly relied on non-epistemic justifications such as these, albeit without explicit elucidation. In discharging its essentially supervisory functions, the Court sees itself as performing an essentially reactive role, reiterating time and time again, for example, that, '[w]hile Article 6 of the Convention guarantees the right to a fair trial, it does not lay down any rules on the admissibility of evidence as such, which is therefore primarily a matter for regulation under national law'.[81] Perhaps it is therefore unsurprising that the Court exploits imprecise concepts such as the privilege against self-incrimination as expediency dictates.

[78] *Brown v Walker*, 161 US 591, 637 (1896) per Field J (dissenting).

[79] Generally, see HL Ho, 'Liberalism and the Criminal Trial' [2010] *Singapore Journal of Legal Studies* 87.

[80] I have benefited here from the views of Roger Leng.

[81] *Schenk v Switzerland* (1988) 13 EHRR 242, [46].

Summers argues that the ECtHR 'has chosen to rely on the privilege against self-incrimination rather than afford the defence a true adversarial role in the investigation phase'[82] such that '[t]here is a danger ... that the importance of the privilege against self-incrimination is exaggerated precisely in order to obscure the deficiencies of the institutional position of the defence during the investigative phases of the proceedings'.[83] It is obviously unsatisfactory if the privilege is effectively being deployed, ex post facto, as partial compensation for inadequately regulated evidence-gathering. This might help to explain why in England and Wales, where procedures for obtaining statements from suspects in police stations have been tightly regulated for some years,[84] discussion of the privilege against self-incrimination is not prominent in confession case-law.

As a mechanism for regulating evidence-gathering in criminal investigations, the privilege against self-incrimination is flanked by substantive ECHR rights, notably the right to privacy guaranteed by Article 8 and the right to freedom from torture and inhuman or degrading treatment guaranteed by Article 3. These are unarguably important protections for (amongst others) suspects in criminal proceedings. But the Strasbourg Court 'reverse-engineered' the privilege from the general right to a fair trial without really confronting the threshold question of why compelled self-incrimination is inherently objectionable. Indeed, one might argue that, in an inherently coercive criminal justice system, the privilege against self-incrimination runs counter to the idea that there are general moral duties imposed on citizens to assist and co-operate with the authorities in their investigation of crime. After all, 'every citizen has a moral duty to assist the law in achieving its proper purposes, as an aspect of his duty to be concerned for the common good of his community'.[85] Roberts and Zuckerman also comment on the complex of moral and legal rights in this context:

> Broadly speaking, it is perfectly proper to respond to the promptings of conscience by co-operating with such inquiries, even though there is no general legal duty to be a model citizen when the policeman comes knocking. There are, after all, many legal rights which, from a broader moral perspective, one ought not to insist on exercising at every opportunity, and which one sometimes ought to waive. It is a

[82] SJ Summers, *Fair Trials: The European Criminal Procedural Tradition and the European Court of Human Rights* (Oxford, Hart Publishing, 2007) 155.

[83] Ibid 163.

[84] In particular, by relevant provisions of the Police and Criminal Evidence Act 1984 and PACE Codes C and E.

[85] RA Duff, *Trials and Punishments* (Cambridge, CUP, 1986) 132. Also see R Schwartz, 'A Call for Reform: Compelled Questioning of Witnesses in Criminal Securities Fraud Cases' (2009) 54 *Criminal Law Quarterly* 341, 352–54.

> moral failing, and in this context also a derogation of civic responsibility, always to stand on the strict letter of one's legal rights.[86]

One can find judicial comments to similar effect across the common law world.[87] Finally, the privilege has no application at all where there is a guarantee that the compelled information will not be used in any subsequent prosecution of the information-provider ('use immunity'),[88] or where, as the ECtHR found in *Weh v Austria*,[89] the threat of criminal prosecution is insufficiently proximate.

It is therefore misguided to expect the privilege to perform a major role in regulating pre-trial criminal process. What is required is more careful, contextual evaluation of the types of information which might justifiably be demanded from suspects on pain of criminal sanction for non-compliance.[90] In precisely what circumstances should this be permitted? What protections should be available? How should the relevant procedures be regulated? The existence of robust pre-trial regulation would enable courts to get on with the job of assessing the fairness of trials in the round, whilst deflecting the criticism that they are failing to define with greater precision the scope and contours of the privilege against self-incrimination.[91] To the extent that dedicated pre-trial protections are in place, and are routinely supervised and enforced, perhaps not much would be lost if the status of the privilege against self-incrimination as an implied right were abandoned altogether or at least downplayed. As Adrian Zuckerman argued decades ago, '[w]hat the suspect needs is not a lofty and impractical right [against self-incrimination] but a meaningful and effective protection from abuse and distortion'.[92]

[86] Roberts and Zuckerman, above n 70, 543. AJ Ashworth and M Redmayne, *The Criminal Process*, 4th edn (Oxford, OUP, 2010) 154–55 also draw attention to the Terrorism Act 2000, s 38B, which makes it an offence for a person not to disclose, as soon as reasonably practicable, information which he or she knows or believes might be of material assistance in preventing the commission by *another person* of an act of terrorism, or in securing the apprehension, prosecution or conviction of *another person* for a terrorism-related offence.

[87] See, eg, *Thomson Newspapers Ltd v Canada* [1990] 1 SCR 425, [244], where L'Heureux-Dubé J remarked: 'The general freedom to do as one pleases … is not absolute' but rather is subject, 'in particular, to the necessary cooperation of citizens in eradicating crime and other illegal activities. This is sometimes expressed as a "social" or "moral" duty to cooperate with law enforcement agents'. Also see *Rice v Connolly* [1966] 2 QB 414, 419; *R v Grant* 2009 SCC 32, [2009] 2 SCR 353, [37]; *In re Quarles and Butler*, 158 US 532, 535 (1895).

[88] See, eg, Youth Justice and Criminal Evidence Act 1999, s 59.

[89] (2004) 40 EHRR 37 (p 890), discussed above n 39 and associated text.

[90] To similar effect, see LM Seidman, *Silence and Freedom* (Stanford, CA, Stanford UP, 2007) 116.

[91] Cf CM Bradley, 'The Emerging International Consensus as to Criminal Procedure Rules' (1993) 14 *Michigan Journal of International Law* 171 (arguing that robust pre-trial regulation justifies more flexible supervision of criminal investigations by trial judges).

[92] AAS Zuckerman, 'The Right against Self-Incrimination: An Obstacle to the Supervision of Interrogation' (1986) 102 *Law Quarterly Review* 43, 70.

11

The Presumption of Innocence as a Human Right

HOCK LAI HO*

1. TWO WAYS OF LOOKING AT THE PRESUMPTION OF INNOCENCE

THE PRESUMPTION OF innocence is a common law rule of evidence. It is also a human right.[1] This chapter identifies three respects in which one is different from the other. A secondary thesis, which emerges from the human rights angle, is that the presumption of innocence reflects a central purpose of the criminal trial. That purpose is to hold the prosecution, as part of the executive arm of government, to account in its quest to enforce the criminal law.[2]

* I am indebted to the participants in the Nottingham workshop, Sydney conference and Singapore seminar at which earlier versions of this paper were presented. Special thanks to my commentators, Richard Glover and Stanley Yeo and to the editors, Paul Roberts and Jill Hunter. James Franklin and Ian Dennis gave me valuable written comments. I am grateful also for the help received from George Wei, Chin Tet Yung and Jean Ho. Funding was received from the Academic Research Fund Tier 1 provided by the Singapore Ministry of Education (WBS No: R-241-000-063-112).

[1] I assume that it is. This should not be controversial. After all, the presumption is widely recognised in national constitutions and bills of rights, and in regional and international human rights documents.

[2] For convenience, I will sometimes refer to this simply as 'holding the executive to account'. Criminal law is enforced variously by divisions within the executive branch of government, principally, the Police Force and the public prosecutorial office (called the Attorney-General's Chambers in Singapore). While independent of one another, they work as a system. On one theory, the function of the criminal courts is only to hold the prosecution to account on the charge that has been brought against the accused; on a stronger theory, it is also to hold other aspects of the system to account through the prosecutor. It matters which theory is adopted. Whereas the stronger theory allows for criminal proceedings to be stayed where there has been police impropriety, this form of judicial intervention is less easy to defend on the weaker theory.

(a) The Presumption as a Common Law Rule of Evidence

In referring to the presumption of innocence as a common law rule of evidence, I mean the 'golden thread' that runs 'throughout the web of English Criminal Law' as it was famously proclaimed by Lord Sankey in *Woolmington v DPP*.[3] The general conception can be briefly elucidated. The presumption assigns to the prosecution the burden of proving every element of the crime with which the accused is charged, and, subject to certain exceptions,[4] of disproving any defence that has been put in issue. The prosecution will secure a guilty verdict only if it discharges this burden beyond reasonable doubt on all the evidence adduced at the trial.

On this view, the presumption is a rule that regulates the criminal trial. It puts the risk of non-persuasion on the prosecution, sets out what each side must do in order to get the verdict that it wants and tells the judge (or the jury where there is one) of the preconditions that must be met to warrant a conviction and of the 'default' decision in verdict deliberation. Less directly, the presumption influences the selection of evidence to present before (or withhold from) the court, informs the approach counsel take to the examination of witnesses, and, more generally, shapes trial strategies and argumentation.

There are many rules regulating the criminal trial, and only some of them are so important that their absence renders a trial fundamentally unfair. The presumption of innocence is one such rule. It is a standard of fair trial, and it is independent of other standards. A trial is fundamentally unfair where the court is biased or the accused is denied the opportunity to examine the witnesses against her; but—so it is said—these aspects of unfairness, taken separately or together, do not amount to a violation of the right to be presumed innocent.

These then are three salient features of the common law understanding of the presumption of innocence: first, the presumption is described in terms of the burden and standard of proof, as a general rule that places on the prosecution the burden of proving guilt to the standard of beyond reasonable doubt; secondly, this rule regulates verdict deliberation and shapes the conduct of the trial; thirdly, it is free-standing, a standard of fair trial that is conceptually separate from other such standards. As I will now argue, none of these features applies to the presumption as a human right.

[3] [1935] 1 AC 462, 481–82 (HL).

[4] Namely, insanity and statutory exceptions: *Woolmington*, ibid 481.

(b) The Presumption as a Minimal and Universal Human Right[5]

To understand the presumption as a human right, we must begin with the nature of human rights in general. Human rights in general are basic in two senses: their demands are *minimal* and *fundamental*. They are minimal in that they set the 'lower limits on tolerable human conduct'[6] as opposed to envisioning standards of excellence. They are fundamental in the sense that they protect essential aspects of human dignity and secure crucial human interests. The norms of human rights are also *universal*; they are of international application, even if their interpretation needs to be culturally sensitive. If this is too controversial for you, then let us say that human rights conceptually aspire to be universal. I will argue later that the presumption of innocence as a human right is fundamental in protecting our freedoms. Here I want to consider the minimalist and universal dimensions of human rights as they apply to our understanding of the presumption of innocence.

If the presumption of innocence is or aspires to be of universal application, it cannot be defined in common law terms unfamiliar to lawyers of other legal traditions and formulated in a manner which ill fits the structure of non-adversarial systems.[7] As noted above, the common law uses the concepts of 'burden of proof' and 'proof beyond reasonable doubt' in its articulation of the presumption. But the 'burden of proof', with its adversarial presuppositions, is not naturally at home in legal systems of the inquisitorial family, where the court plays a first and active role in ascertaining the facts.[8] And not every legal system recognises the standard of proof beyond reasonable doubt. To capture the presumption as a universal right, a more general statement of its content is needed. An exemplar of such generality can be found in the judgment of Lord Diplock in *Ong Ah Chuan v PP*.[9] According to him, natural justice requires that there must be 'material before the court

[5] The importance of the human rights dimension is stressed by P Roberts and A Zuckerman, *Criminal Evidence* (Oxford, OUP, 2010) 221: 'Only by exploring the political morality of the presumption of innocence can its true jurisprudential significance be appreciated'. Much of what I address in this chapter is also discussed by them in Chapter 6.

[6] H Shue, *Basic Rights—Subsistence, Affluence, and US Foreign Policy* (Princeton, NJ, Princeton UP, 1980) ix.

[7] Indeed, the presumption was not a common law creation. The common law borrowed the concept from the *Ius commune*: Pennington below n 27. On the history, see also: J Franklin, *The Science of Conjecture* (Baltimore, ML, John Hopkins UP, 2001) 5, 7, 9 and A Stumer, *The Presumption of Innocence* (Oxford, Hart Publishing, 2010) 1–2.

[8] Fawcett, for example, argues that 'the presumption of innocence does not imply where lies the burden of proof at the trial of the charge, that is to say, upon the prosecution to prove the guilty of the accused beyond reasonable doubt. The presumption does not necessarily have this function; for example, in Germany there is no such distribution of the burden of proof, since it is the duty to the court to do all that is necessary to discover the truth': JES Fawcett, *The Application of the European Convention on Human Rights* (Oxford, Clarendon Press, 1987) 180; cf J Safferling, *Towards an International Criminal Procedure* (New York, OUP, 2001) 257.

[9] [1979–1980] SLR(R) 710.

that is logically probative of facts sufficient to constitute the offence with which the accused is charged'. I do not think that this formulation captures completely the content of the presumption as a human right; I am only suggesting that broad language must be used in describing the presumption if we are to capture its universal demands, that is, demands that we would make in any country, whatever its legal tradition and whether or not it recognises the concepts of 'burden of proof' and 'proof beyond reasonable doubt'.

To be universal, human rights have to be basic. The basic dimension of the presumption as a human right means that it cannot demand all and everything that the common law rule requires. A level of abstraction is necessary, a search for the minimum standard that must universally hold. So long as the basic demand is met, local variations in interpretation and implementation are permissible. Searching for the basic core is not an empirical matter of finding the lowest common denominator in existing legal systems. Human rights have normative and transformative dimensions.[10]

What the presumption of innocence requires, among other things, is that the state proves guilt as a condition to getting a person convicted of a crime and punished for it. There are different conceptions of the concept of proof. For instance, English law pegs proof to the standard of beyond reasonable doubt whereas French law treats it as a matter of *intime conviction*.[11] Both are compatible with the presumption of innocence as a human right. This is not to say that anything goes. There is an internal constraint in the concept of proof. You have not proved anything if all that you have established is a suspicion.[12] It is a violation of a human right to convict a person on a mere suspicion. This is true everywhere and at all times.[13]

(c) The Presumption as a Complex of Rights Against the State

The second feature of the common law way of understanding the presumption of innocence is to see it as a rule that regulates verdict deliberation and that shapes the conduct of the criminal trial. On this view, the addressees of the rule are the various trial participants. The presumption as a human right must be seen in different terms. Human rights are held primarily against the state, their main function being to constrain and obligate

[10] On the 'realignment' effect of human rights on proof processes in Europe, see JD Jackson, 'The Effect of Human Rights on Criminal Evidentiary Processes: Towards Convergence, Divergence or Realignment?' (2005) 68 *Modern Law Review* 737.

[11] According to M Taruffo, 'Rethinking the Standards of Proof' (2003) 51 *American Journal of Comparative Law* 659, 666–67, they are not equivalent concepts.

[12] 'Suspicion in its ordinary meaning is a state of conjecture or surmise where proof is lacking: "I suspect but I cannot prove"': *Shaaban v Chong Fook Kam* [1969] 2 MLJ 219, 221, per Lord Devlin.

[13] This principle was long accepted, even in Roman law: Franklin, above n 7, 7.

governments in their treatment of persons through institutions, laws and policies. As a human right, the presumption of innocence consists of a complex of rights held against the state. As we will see in the next section, an important corpus of those rights pertains to due process or, equivalently, a fair trial. But these rights do not exhaust the presumption of innocence; as a human right, its domain of operation is wider. The presumption is also the source of other rights against the state, rights that operate outside the confines of the courtroom.[14]

A public controversy arose in Singapore recently over the reach of the presumption. William Ding was convicted after a highly publicised 80-day trial of outraging the modesty of some of his students. He appealed successfully against his conviction. Following his acquittal, there was a call for the law to be changed to allow acquitted persons, such as Ding, to seek compensation from the state for what they have been put through. It was in the context of resisting this call for compensation that the spokesperson for the Attorney-General's Chambers issued the following statement which was reported in *The Straits Times* on 8 May 2008:

> There is often confusion in the public mind regarding what an acquittal means. The prosecution is obliged to prove the case beyond reasonable doubt. This means that if there is any reasonable doubt, the accused gets the benefit of it. It does not mean that the accused was innocent in the sense that he did not do the deed.... Where a case turns on one person's word against another's, very often the trial judge or the appeal court may consider that it is unsafe to convict. This does not mean that the judge is convinced that the accused did not do the act in question. As long as a reasonable doubt remains, the accused is entitled to be acquitted, even if the judge thinks he is probably guilty.[15]

Although this statement was not targeted specifically at Ding, some have read it as questioning his innocence. In his judgment allowing Ding's appeal, which was delivered on 11 July 2008, VK Rajah JA made the following remarks which were widely seen as an implicit response to the views aired by the Attorney-General's Chambers:

> If the evidence is insufficient to support the Prosecution's theory of guilt, and if the weaknesses in the Prosecution's case reveal a deficiency in what is necessary for a conviction, the judge must acquit the accused, and with good reason: it simply has not been proved to the satisfaction of the law that the accused is guilty, and the presumption of innocence stands unrebutted. It is not helpful, therefore,

[14] An analogy may be drawn with legal professional privilege, which was once seen as a mere rule of evidence: *Parry-Jones v Law Society* [1969] 1 Ch 1, 9. It is now widely accepted as a fundamental human right that applies outside the curial context. Andrew Ashworth distinguishes between the presumption in the narrow, trial-centred sense and the presumption in the wider sense that 'concerns the State's duty to recognize the defendant's legal status of innocence at all stages prior to conviction': 'Four Threats to the Presumption of Innocence' (2006) 10 *International Journal of Evidence and Proof* 241, 244.

[15] KC Vijayan, 'When Acquittal is Bitter-Sweet', *The Straits Times*, 8 May 2008.

> for suggestions to be subsequently raised about the accused's 'factual guilt' once he has been acquitted. To do so would be to undermine the court's finding of not guilty and would also stand the presumption of innocence on its head, replacing it with an insidious and open-ended suspicion of guilt that an accused person would be hard-pressed to ever shed, even upon vindication in a court of law. I have no doubt that prosecutions are only commenced after careful investigation and prosecutorial discretion is never lightly exercised, but the decision of guilt or innocence is constitutionally for the court and the court alone to make. The court cannot convict if a reasonable doubt remains to prevent the presumption of innocence from being rebutted. In that result, there is no room for second guessing or nice distinctions; there is only one meaning to 'not proved' and that is that it has not been established in the eyes of the law that the accused has committed the offence with which he has been charged.[16]

The Minister for Law stepped into the fray with a speech in Parliament reaffirming the Government's commitment to the presumption of innocence as a 'core principle' of the 'rule of law' while defending the position taken by the Attorney-General's Chambers and noting that it was 'possible for a person who has committed the offence to walk away free'.[17]

If the presumption of innocence is only a rule of evidence that regulates proof at the trial (as it is regarded in the United States),[18] the views expressed by the Attorney-General's Chambers and the Minister of Law are impeccably logical.[19] But it seems me that they missed the thrust of the concerns expressed by Rajah JA. Justice Rajah took a larger view of the presumption (one that resonates with French and European law),[20] according to which it is not only a rule that regulates the criminal trial. It also reaches beyond the trial and constrains the state in other ways. As a human right, the presumption has what Stefan Trechsel calls a 'reputation-related aspect'. This, according to him:

> aims to protect the image of the person concerned as 'innocent', i.e. not guilty of a specific offence. In other words, it protects the good reputation of the suspect. This means, for example, that a person who has not been convicted in criminal proceedings must not be treated or referred to by persons acting for the state as guilty of an offence.[21]

[16] *XP v PP* [2008] 4 SLR(R) 686, [94].

[17] (2008) 84 *Parliamentary Debates*, col 2981 (25 August 2008, Oral Answers to Questions).

[18] See L Laudan, 'The Presumption of Innocence: Material or Probatory?' (2005) 11 *Legal Theory* 333, 336–39 and F Quintard-Morénas, 'The Presumption of Innocence in the French and Anglo-American Legal Traditions' (2010) 58 *American Journal of Comparative Law* 107, 141–49.

[19] The same position was taken by the United States Supreme Court in *US v One Assortment of 89 Firearms* 465 US 354, 361 (1984): 'an acquittal on criminal charges does not prove that the defendant is innocent; it merely proves the existence of a reasonable doubt as to his guilt'.

[20] Quintard-Morénas, above n 18, 134–41.

[21] S Trechsel, *Human Rights in Criminal Proceedings* (Oxford, OUP, 2005) 164.

In *Allenet de Ribemont v France*, the European Court of Human Rights held that 'the presumption of innocence may be infringed not only by a judge or court but also by other public authorities'.[22] The French Interior Minister and two senior police officers were found to have violated the presumption when they publicly named the applicant as an instigator of a murder while the case was under investigation. In Singapore there occurred, one-and-a-half years after the Ding affair, a high-profile 'hit and run' accident where it served the Government's interest to endorse this aspect of the presumption. A Romanian diplomat was suspected of having knocked down a number of pedestrians with his car, causing death to one and serious injuries to two others. He left the country soon after this incident. Public disquiet grew from the perception that the Government had not done enough to bring the wrongdoer to justice. In reply to a question put to him at a public meeting as to why 'the authorities had been very quiet about the matter', the Minister of Law stressed that 'it was the role of the courts—not the Government—to determine guilt in a criminal case'. To drive the message home, he asked: 'Let's take a situation where a Singaporean is suspected as the driver. Let's say you are the Singaporean. Would you like the Government to come out and say, "we think he's guilty"? Is that fair?'[23]

That would indeed be unfair, and surely even more so where the subject of the comment has been acquitted by the court; the present aspect of the presumption should have greater force in that situation. Here is Trechsel again: 'Once an acquittal has become final, the person concerned is protected... from any official statement which insinuates that he or she is guilty, and from any such statement which says that he or she is still under suspicion'.[24]

In the Ding controversy, as I have noted, the statements issued by the Attorney-General's Chambers were not targeted specifically at him and they were made in the context of resisting calls for legislation to allow compensation in suitable cases where an accused person has been acquitted. So far as I know, the only statement concerning the dispute which referred specifically to Ding appeared in the Chinese daily, *Lianhe Zaobao*, dated 20 September 2008. When asked about Ding's case, the serving Attorney-General was quoted as saying that certain information held by the Attorney-General's Chambers was not disclosed to the public and would not be released:

> In general, when we charge someone, we do not wait for the trial to start before looking for the evidence to convict … . The evidence is already there. Perhaps the judge does not want to accept the evidence. Perhaps the judge does not believe the testimony of the witnesses. However, this does not mean that the decision to bring

[22] (1995) 20 EHRR 557, [36]. See also *Daktaras v Lithuania* (2002) 34 EHRR 60; *Bukevičius v Lithuania*, Application No 48297/99, ECHR 2002-II, 349.

[23] 'Role of courts, not Govt, to determine guilt', *The Straits Times*, 18 January 2010.

[24] Above n 21, 182. See *Sekanina v Austria*, ECtHR (Application No 13126/87) 25 August 1993, [30]; *Rushiti v Austria* (2001) 33 EHRR 56, [31]–[32].

> charges against the defendant is wrong .... Therefore, I do not wish to comment further as to whether justice was done in Ding's case because we have information that cannot be disclosed to the public. I shall not say any more.[25]

If this report is accurate, the Attorney-General, by hinting that there was more to this case than met the public eye, came near to insinuating that Ding might in fact be guilty even though he had been acquitted by the court. While his remarks would be unobjectionable under American law, given the narrow view it takes of the presumption, it is debatable whether they would amount to a violation of the presumption of innocence under European human rights law. Of course, Singapore is not bound by European law. But many human rights are not given legal force in many places. The non-existence of legal recognition should not stop conversation about human rights. Is there not scope for comparative analysis and an interest in global conversation?[26]

(d) The Presumption as the Right to Due Process

Contrary to the third feature of the common law understanding described earlier, the presumption as a human right is not a discrete standard of fair trial, conceptually separate from all other standards of fair trial; it is not merely one of many other qualities that a trial must have to be considered fair. The presumption is the general right to due process: it mandates that the state cannot convict someone of a crime unless and until the prosecution demonstrates her guilt in a process that bears the defining features, including rights and protections, of a fair trial.

This expansive reading of the presumption is unconventional today, at least among lawyers trained in the common law. But it has some historical support. As Kenneth Pennington tells us:

> The maxim, innocent until proven guilty was born in the late thirteenth century, preserved in the universal jurisprudence of the *Ius commune*, employed in the defense of marginalized defendants, Jews, heretics, and witches, in the early modern period, and finally deployed as a powerful argument against torture in the sixteenth, seventeenth and eighteenth centuries. By this last route it entered the jurisprudence of the common law ... . [B]ecause it was a transplant from the *Ius commune*, it entered the world of American law in a very different form. It no longer was a maxim that signified the bundle of rights that was due to every

[25] English translation obtained from www.lawnet.com.sg.

[26] Invoking memories of the 'Asian values' debate of the 1990s, the same Attorney-General has warned Singaporeans (but not in relation to this dispute) to be on guard against 'human rights fanatics' who 'think that their opinion is the standard to which the rest of humanity must conform' and who 'believe that they and their values represent the apex of human moral development': W Woon, 'Human Rights Key to Good Governance but ...', letter to *The Straits Times*, 9 June 2008.

> defendant … . In the jurisprudence of the *Ius commune*, the maxim summarized the procedural rights that every human being should have no matter what the person's status, religion, or citizenship. The maxim protected defendants from being coerced to give testimony and to incriminate themselves. It granted them the absolute right to be summoned, to have their case heard in an open court, to have legal counsel, to have their sentence pronounced publicly, and to present evidence in their defense …. [T]he maxim meant 'no one, absolutely no one, can be denied a trial under any circumstances'. And that everyone, absolutely everyone, had the right to conduct a vigorous, thorough defense.[27]

The original meaning of the presumption is mostly lost, at least to common lawyers. One of the remaining vestiges can be found in the Singapore case of *Ong Ah Chuan v Public Prosecutor*.[28] Constitutional challenges were made to certain provisions of the Misuse of Drugs Act 1973. Under one of the challenged provisions, a person who was shown to be in possession of a certain quantity of proscribed drug was presumed to have it for the purpose of trafficking. It was then for that person to prove, on the balance of probabilities, that he did not have the drug for the said purpose. The defence argued that, by effectively requiring the accused to prove his innocence, the provision violated the presumption of innocence and was therefore unconstitutional. Article 9(1) of the Singapore Constitution states simply, and without mentioning the presumption by name, that 'no person shall be deprived of his life or personal liberty save in accordance with law'. The Privy Council held that the term 'law' includes fundamental rules of natural justice. It further held that the contested statutory provisions did not offend those rules. The opinion of the Board was delivered by Lord Diplock. Rather than defining the presumption in the familiar language of *Woolmington*, as a rule imposing on the prosecution the general burden of proving guilt beyond reasonable doubt, Lord Diplock stated:

> One of the fundamental rules of natural justice in the field of criminal law is that a person should not be punished for an offence unless it has been established to the satisfaction of an independent and unbiased tribunal that he committed it … . To describe this fundamental rule as the 'presumption of innocence' may, however, be misleading to those familiar only with English criminal procedure.[29]

The claim that the accused must be presumed innocent *until proved guilty* begs the question: how is guilt to be proved? Contrary to conventional wisdom, it cannot be enough that the prosecution has adduced evidence before the court capable of meeting the standard of proof beyond reasonable doubt. It is vitally important who controls the evidence to which the standard is applied. The trial is unfair and due process is denied where the

[27] K Pennington, 'Innocent Until Proven Guilty: The Origins of a Legal Maxim' (2003) 63 *The Jurist* 106, 124.

[28] [1979–1980] SLR(R) 710.

[29] Ibid [27].

prosecution alone determines what evidence is presented at the trial and the accused has neither the right to challenge the witnesses against her nor the right to adduce exculpatory evidence. Without those rights, the presumption of innocence is a charade.[30]

As a human right, the presumption is defeated only when guilt is proved *in a manner that satisfies certain minimum requirements.* These requirements are succinctly encapsulated in the phrase 'proved *according to law*'. As Lord Diplock noted, 'law' must include fundamental rules of natural justice, one of which insists that guilt be determined by an independent and unbiased tribunal. Many other basic requirements are widely recognised. Two examples will suffice for present purposes. Article 11(1) of the UN Universal Declaration of Human Rights states that everyone charged with a penal offence has a right to be presumed innocent until proved guilty *in a particular fashion*, to wit, 'in a public trial' at which the accused 'has had all the guarantees necessary for his defence'. Article 6(2) of the European Convention on Human Rights provides that 'everyone charged with a criminal offence shall be presumed innocent until proved guilty according to law'. This is followed by Article 6(3) which elaborates on what the law requires and preceded by a general provision on the right to a fair trial.[31] The former states that guilt must be proved in a process that affords the accused numerous 'minimum' rights: the right to be informed promptly of the accusation, to defend himself in person or through legal assistance, to examine or have examined witnesses against him, and so forth.[32] That the presumption of innocence is contained in a separate paragraph of its own in the European Convention might suggest that it is a distinct principle. But the Strasbourg Court has not interpreted it in that way. The three limbs of Article 6 form an integrated and inter-dependent set. According to Stumer, the Court 'equates the presumption of innocence with a range of fair trial rights'[33] and has treated it as 'an equivalent to the general principle of fair trial'.[34]

The presumption of innocence insists on proper *proof* of guilt as a pre-condition for criminal conviction, which in turn is a pre-requisite of state punishment. 'Proof' can be conceptualised in different ways. One may think

30 See SJ Summers, 'Presumption of Innocence' [2001] *Juridical Review* 37, 52–53.

31 ECHR Art 6(1).

32 Similarly, see Art 14 of the United Nations' International Covenant on Civil and Political Rights and Arts 8(1) and (2) of the American Convention on Human Rights. Equally notable is section 11(d) of the Canadian Charter of Rights and Freedoms which states that anyone charged with an offence has the right 'to be presumed innocent until proven guilty *according to law in a fair and public hearing by an independent and impartial tribunal*'. In *R v Oakes* [1986] 1 SCR 103, 121 the Canadian Supreme Court held that this provision requires not only that the State bear the burden of proving guilt beyond reasonable doubt but also that 'criminal prosecutions must be carried out in accordance with lawful procedures and fairness'.

33 Above n 7, 96.

34 Ibid 95. (Stumer criticises this approach).

of proof as the production of evidence for the purpose of persuading the court to accept an allegation of fact, an outward activity of argumentation that is aimed at influencing the mental activity of deliberation and the analysis of evidence. One may also view proof from the epistemic angle and focus on the relationship between evidence and conclusions. That this relationship lies at the foundation of many disciplines (such as science and history) has fuelled the ambition to construct a general science of proof.[35] We can speak of the sufficiency of evidence to support a finding of guilt just as we can speak of the sufficiency of evidence to support a scientific claim or a historical narrative. What all these disciplines have in common is the goal of finding the truth even though the specification of this goal, and the types and range of evidence, will depend on the particular context. So far as the criminal trial is concerned, the primary goal is to find the truth relating to the charges brought against the accused. And since the end does not always justify the means, we have rules that express standards of fair trial and they act as side constraints on the main enterprise.

However, the 'proof' that we associate with the criminal trial might also be regarded as a distinctive practice, one that is distinguishable from conducting scientific research or historical investigation. There are obvious differences: judging a criminal case involves neither working with test-tubes nor studying ancient scripts; and scientists and historians do not have as their research question whether to take away a person's liberty or life. But it does not follow from such differences, and I do not claim, that the disciplines lack a shared foundation in the logic of inference. But more than logic is at play.

To capture the fullness of 'proof' in the context of a criminal trial, it is not just the logical relation between evidence and conclusions that we need to consider. We must look at the trial process as a whole, the proceeding in and by which the verdict (as a morally-laden declaration that carries social meaning and political force) comes to be authoritatively delivered. 'Proof' in this broader sense has important extra-epistemic functions. And it is these extra-epistemic functions that explain the presumption of innocence. The presumption is defeated only when guilt is established in accordance with rules and procedures that satisfy minimum conditions of legality: in short, due process.[36] In its highest sense, the presumption is the right to basic standards of fair trial. Many of the standards are not side-constraints; they are intrinsic to the nature or function of the criminal trial as an exercise of holding the executive to account on its enforcement of the criminal law.

[35] See eg DA Schum, *Evidential Foundations of Probabilistic Reasoning* (New York, Wiley-Interscience, 1994).

[36] The United States Constitution does not speak explicitly of the presumption of innocence but 'due process' is mentioned in the Fifth and Fourteenth Amendments. Cf PJ Schwikkard, *Presumption of Innocence* (Cape Town, Juta & Co, 1999) 35 *et seq*; Trechsel, above n 21, 165.

A full exegesis of this theory is beyond the scope of this chapter, but the next part will indicate some general lines of thought upon which it rests.

2. TWO THEORIES OF THE CRIMINAL TRIAL

Rawls famously took the criminal trial as an exemplification of imperfect procedural justice:

> The desired outcome is that the defendant should be declared guilty if and only if he has committed the offense with which he is charged. The trial procedure is framed to search for and to establish the truth in this regard.[37]

For sure, the court should only convict those who are truly guilty, and certain features of the trial system serve or help to expose inaccuracies and falsehoods. In a number of important senses, the trial is indeed a search for the truth. Nevertheless, this description is not strictly accurate. We can get at the sense in which it falls short by contrasting a criminal trial with a coroner's inquiry.

Unlike the criminal court, the coroner is not bound by the law of evidence and may conduct the inquiry in any manner she reasonably thinks fit.[38] One explanation for the evidential and procedural differences is that the coroner's inquiry is much closer than the criminal trial to a pure fact-finding enterprise. The purpose of the inquiry is to examine 'the cause of and circumstances connected with' a person's death, in particular, to ascertain 'the identity of the deceased' and 'how, when and where the deceased came by his death'.[39] These are open-ended questions of fact and the coroner is prohibited from framing a finding 'in such a way as to determine any question of criminal … liability'.[40] In contrast, at a criminal trial, the prosecutor does not pose general questions of fact for the court to investigate ('how did this person come to die?' etc); she claims to have the answers and is urging the court to accept them ('the accused killed the victim' etc). The trial is driven by a specific and categorical accusation of criminal wrongdoing levelled against a particular accused, and it is the gravity and consequences of a criminal conviction that generate demands for due process. As Lord Lane noted in *R v South London Coroner, Ex parte Thompson*:

> [A]n inquest is a fact-finding exercise and not a method of apportioning guilt. The procedure and rules of evidence which are suitable for one are unsuitable for the other. In an inquest it should never be forgotten that there are no parties, there is no indictment, there is no prosecution, there is no defence, there is no

37 S Rawls, *A Theory of Justice* (Oxford, OUP, 1999 rev edn) 74.
38 Coroners Act 2010, s 37.
39 Ibid s 28(1).
40 Ibid s 27(2).

> trial, simply an attempt to establish facts. It is an inquisitorial process, a process of investigation quite unlike a criminal trial where the prosecutor accuses and the accused defends, the judge holding the balance or the ring, whichever metaphor one chooses to use.[41]

In *R v Davis*,[42] Lord Bingham specified the following crucial difference: at a criminal trial, but not in a coroner's inquiry, there is an 'accused liable to be convicted and punished in that proceeding'. It is because a person stands to be officially condemned and punished that the law accords him certain rights. They include a right to 'a clear statement in writing of the alleged wrongdoing, a right to call any relevant and admissible evidence, and a right to address factual submissions to the tribunal of fact'.[43] These rights have no place at an inquiry precisely because it is not a trial and a finding of guilt is not at stake.

The presumption of innocence is a central feature of a criminal trial but not of a coronial inquiry. One who doubts that the accused is guilty does not necessarily believe that she is truly innocent. One may be unsure where the truth lies. In that event, if the trial were an enterprise exclusively orientated to fact-finding, one would simply have to declare the mission a failure and confess one's ignorance as to whether the accused is guilty or not. But the court does not have the option available to a coroner of returning an open verdict. Nor can it suspend the proceedings and refer the case back to the police for further investigation.[44] So long as it finds reasonable doubt, the court must acquit. If a 'not guilty' verdict is construed as capable of meaning either that guilt is 'disproved' or that it is merely 'not proved', and so long as the second disjunctive remains open,[45] an acquittal is logically compatible with factual guilt. As we saw, this was the position taken in Singapore by both the Attorney-General's Chambers and the Minister of Law.

This view is incompatible with the presumption as a human right, a right which is foundational for the theory of the trial that I am proposing. As a human right, the presumption is directed against the state; and on the proposed theory, the trial is the political process of holding the executive to account on its quest to get a person officially condemned and punished for

[41] (1982) 126 SJ 625 (HL).

[42] [2008] 1 AC 1128, [21] (HL).

[43] *R (O'Connor) v Avon Coroner* [2010] 2 WLR 1299, [19].

[44] This option used to be available in the Soviet Union but was declared unconstitutional in Russia in 1999: W Burnham and J Kahn, 'Russia's Criminal Procedure Code Five Years Out' (2008) 33 *Review of Central and East European Law* 1, 4, fn 6, and 58.

[45] The Singapore Evidence Act (cap 97, 1997 rev edn) defines 'proof' (s 3(3)), 'disproved' (s 3(4)) and 'not proved' (s 3(5)); on these terms in the civil context where, importantly, there is no presumption of innocence, see *Loo Chay Sit v Estate of Loo Chay Loo* [2010] 1 SLR 286, [22]; and *Cooperatieve Centrale Raiffeisen-Boerenleenbank BA v Motorola Electronics Pte Ltd* [2010] SGCA 47, [35].

a crime. If the trial were aimed simply at finding the truth, every acquittal on the basis of reasonable doubt must be considered a failure to achieve its objective. If the court remains in doubt, it does not know where the truth lies. Yet, in acquitting the accused, the court is in an important sense living up to its purpose. The task of the criminal court is to hold the prosecution's case up to scrutiny and challenge, and it can perform this task successfully and well even where it does not, in the end, believe that it has found the truth and even where it has failed to find the truth.

The task of searching for the truth falls in the first place on the police. Their search should be over by the time the accused is charged.[46] The prosecutor should not bring the case before the court if she does not think the police have caught the real culprit or judges the evidence to be insufficient to support the charge.[47] By the time of the trial, the moment has come when the prosecution must produce the evidential basis for, and publicly explain and defend, the charge and its 'theory of the case' against the accused; it must establish in accordance with due process that she is guilty and thus deserving of punishment.

The practical importance of the presumption of innocence lies in the instruction not to assume that the police have probably caught the right person or that the public prosecutor was probably right in concurring with the police in their investigative conclusion. According to the US Supreme Court, '[t]he presumption of innocence … serve[s] as an admonishment to the jury [not] to judge an accused's guilt … on the basis of suspicions that may arise from the fact of his arrest, indictment, or custody'.[48] Why should it be required that the accused start the trial, as it were, with a clean probatory slate? The very fact that the accused is being tried, that the person is standing in the dock, indicates significant probability that she is guilty as charged.[49] In presuming the accused innocent, we are presuming against

[46] 'Suspicion arises at or near the starting-point of an investigation of which the obtaining of *prima facie* proof is the end. When such proof has been obtained, the police case is complete; it is ready for trial and passes on to its next stage': *Shaaban v Chong Fook Kam* [1969] 2 MLJ 219, 221, per Lord Devlin.

[47] The Attorney-General of Singapore has said that prosecutors have first to 'make sure that they, themselves, are convinced of the guilt of the suspect. They then consider if there is enough evidence to secure a conviction and whether that would be in the public interest': 'A-G answers criticisms over recent cases involving the rich', *The Straits Times*, 12 December 2008. As Lord Ritchie-Calder noted during a Westminster parliamentary debate on the Criminal Law Revision Committee 11th report, 'every innocent person who is brought to trial represents a failure of the police to do their preliminary work properly … [E]very acquittal is itself a miscarriage of justice': HL Debs, 14 February 1973, vol 338, col 1619.

[48] *Bell v Wolfish*, 441 US 520, 533 (1979). See also L Laudan, above n 18, 358; and L Laudan, *Truth, Error and Criminal Law* (Cambridge, CUP, 2006) 104.

[49] See eg DA Nance, 'Civility and the Burden of Proof' (1994) 17 *Harvard Journal of Law and Public Policy* 647, 658: 'the system of police investigation and prosecutorial oversight in place in our system indicate a high probability that the defendant is guilty before any evidence is actually presented at trial'.

the objective probabilities. This is difficult to square with the strict logic of factual inquiry.[50]

But the trial is not strictly speaking a factual inquiry. The presumption of innocence coheres perfectly with the theory of the criminal court as a check on the executive at a critical stage of criminal law enforcement. The accused cannot be convicted unless the prosecutor can properly justify to the satisfaction of the court as an independent and unbiased tribunal, and in an open proceeding that grants the accused the right of participation, its claim that the accused is guilty as charged.[51] This is the substance of the maxim that justice must not only be done (in the outcome of convicting the truly guilty) but must also be seen to be done (by conducting a trial, essentially a public process of holding the executive to account). The principle is that a person is presumed innocent unless *the prosecution succeeds in proving that* she is guilty. It is not that she is presumed innocent unless she *is* guilty. The accused must be treated as innocent so long as the prosecution fails to prove that she committed the alleged crime. It is secondary whether the accused did commit it.[52]

The presumption of innocence is not an epistemic rule but a normative principle, a central pillar of the rule of law that puts protective distance between government and citizens. The presumption of innocence is not a statement of probability but a statement of political conviction. If the criminal trial is to stay true to its function as a check on the executive, the starting point cannot be one of prima facie credence to the prosecutor's allegations. All that was said earlier about the probabilities that the accused

[50] It may be argued that there is double-counting if weight is given to the mere fact that a person is being prosecuted and, on top of this, weight is given to the evidence that the prosecution presents before the court since the decision to prosecute will have been made (substantially) on the basis of that evidence already: I thank Tony Ward for this point; see also LH Tribe, 'Trial by Mathematics: Precision and Ritual in the Legal Process' (1971) 84 *Harvard Law Review* 1329, 1369. However, I doubt that there must be double-counting. The probability of guilt arising from the fact of being prosecuted is grounded in the track record of reliability of the police and prosecutorial machinery in past cases and it is difficult to see why it is illogical to use this information in fixing the prior odds of guilt: cf P Rawling, 'Reasonable Doubt and the Presumption of Innocence: The Case of the Bayesian Juror' (1999) 18 *Topoi* 117, 124.

[51] See H Kelsen, *Pure Theory of Law* (Max Knight trans, Berkeley, University of California Press, 1967) 240: 'the legal rule does not say: "If a certain individual has committed murder, then a punishment ought to be imposed upon him". The legal rule says: "If the authorized court in a procedure determined by the legal order has ascertained, with the force of law, that a certain individual has committed a murder, then the court ought to impose a punishment upon that individual"'.

[52] LI Katzner, 'Presumptivist and Nonpresumptivist Principles of Justice' (1971) 81 *Ethics* 253, 255: 'The real force of establishing a "burden of proof" is to make the point at issue primarily one of "showing". When there is a burden of proof on one side in an argument, this means that the other side will be believed *until* it can be *shown* to be wrong; and hence which side is actually right is in a sense a question of secondary importance'. Since the principle as it operates in law is one of practical deliberation, it is more accurate for our purposes to replace 'believed' with 'accepted' in this quotation.

is guilty of the crime with which she is charged presupposes that, on the whole and for the most part, the police and the prosecutorial authority can be trusted. They may well be trustworthy, on the whole and for the most part. But that is beside the point. The distrust that motivates the presumption of innocence is not directed at the personal integrity of police officers and public prosecutors. It is motivated by the belief that a system that is designed out of fear for the worst is best equipped to prevent the worst from happening.

Contrary to the suggestion of some US scholars, it is an error to read the *presumption* of innocence as an *assumption* of innocence.[53] There is a critical difference. We assume something is the case when we are inclined to believe it to be the case or think that it is likely the case. We presume something is the case when we commit ourselves to act as if something is the case without believing it categorically. 'The main point of using "presume"... is to leave open explicitly the important possibility of being wrong'.[54] If a person is acquitted by the court, the executive is bound to treat that person as if he did not commit the crime. In this sense, the presumption does not end when the court acquits a person. As Rajah JA said, it 'stands unrebutted': the presumption binds the state to accept an acquittal as a declaration of innocence.[55] This must mean, if it is to mean anything at all, that the state and its officials are bound to respect the person's declared status as innocent, whatever their personal belief may be on the matter. But to what extent and for what purposes are they so bound?[56] Clearly, it cannot mean only that the state must release the accused forthwith.[57] According to Rajah JA,

[53] See eg American Law Institute, *Model Penal Code and Commentaries* (Philadelphia, American Law Institute, 1985) Part I, 190; HA Ashford and DM Risinger, 'Presumptions, Assumptions, and Due Process in Criminal Cases: A Theoretical Overview' (1969) 79 *Yale Law Journal* 165, 173. A rebuttable presumption of law takes this standard form: upon proof of A (basic fact), the court must presume B (presumed fact) unless B is disproved by other evidence. The presumption of innocence does not bear this structure and hence I agree that it is not a presumption *of the standard legal form*. But it does not therefore follow that it is not a presumption at all or that 'assumption' is the correct term to use.

[54] R Hall, 'Presuming' (1961) 11 *Philosophical Quarterly* 10. He added: 'Although "assume" too recognises this possibility [of being wrong]... its appearance in a sentence shows that the possibility of refutation is regarded as somehow negligible, even sometimes even unimportant'.

[55] Similarly, G Maher, 'Jury Verdicts and the Presumption of Innocence' (1983) 3 *Legal Studies* 146, 154 takes the view that 'it is impossible to apply the presumption of innocence to a criminal charge and at the end of the case leave the issue of guilt or innocence undetermined'.

[56] The state is not bound for all purposes. Thus, an acquittal does not prevent the court from finding the person liable in a later civil action brought on the same incident, and a matter relating to which a person has been acquitted may still be used as similar fact evidence against her: *R v Z* [2000] 3 WLR 117; P Roberts, 'Acquitted Misconduct Evidence and Double Jeopardy Principles, From *Sambasivam* to *Z*' [2000] *Criminal Law Review* 952.

[57] For one, the doctrine of *autrefois acquit* prevents a second prosecution for the same crime. But apart from this, the law in the United States allows an acquitted person to be treated as less than innocent in a variety of contexts: there, according to Larry Laudan, 'acquitted

state officials are bound in another respect: they may not publicly challenge or impugn the innocence of a person in relation to a charge of which she has already been acquitted. Underlying the controversy in Singapore was the impression (rightly or wrongly perceived) that this was happening in the Ding affair. The government had to explain repeatedly that it was not commenting specifically on his case in order to correct what it thought was a false impression.[58] This controversy had little to do with the presumption understood in the narrow *Woolmington* sense.

3. THE RIGHT TO BE PRESUMED INNOCENT AND THE RIGHT TO A FAIR TRIAL

In a 'heavily satirical piece' co-written with a lawyer in 1972,[59] the indomitable Cambridge philosopher Elizabeth Anscombe suggested changes to the law of evidence that were even more radical than those which had then recently been proposed by the Criminal Law Revision Committee. In a passage as amusing as it is illuminating, they wrote:

> the justice of a trial involves something deeper than procedures designed to procure... accurate results.... [E]ven a man who in fact committed a serious crime... ought only to be convicted in a certain (fair) way, where fairness means not just an accurate finding of all the facts. It means that the trial meet a number of other standards, not meeting which the authorities are a set of top bullies who, for the time being, are especially interested in the punishment of criminals.... That is, 'court of justice' is not the same thing as 'committee for nailing criminals'. Similarly, 'convicting' means more than a group in power being satisfied on good evidence of the guilt of somebody, and using the powers of the state to clobber him.[60]

If a trial is truly to count as a trial, and to amount to something to which an accused can intelligibly claim a cherished right, it must be of value to her;

defendants can ... be legally denied credit by credit agencies, can be disqualified from adopting children, can discover that their prior trial, even if an acquittal, counts against them in child custody hearings, and can be obliged to report their prior arrest(s) to prospective employers, if asked': 'Need Verdicts Come in Pairs?' (2010) 14 *International Journal of Evidence and Proof* 1, 6.

[58] In a letter published in *The Straits Times*, dated 14 May 2008, the spokesperson for the Attorney-General's Chambers 'emphatically denied' that it was 'commenting specifically on Mr William Ding's case'. The Law Minister stressed the same in Parliament: above n 17.

[59] M Geach and L Gormally (eds), *Human Life, Action and Ethics: Essays by GEM Anscombe* (Exeter, Imprint Academic, 2005) xvii.

[60] GEM Anscombe and J Feldman, 'On the Nature of Justice in a Trial' (1972) 33 *Analysis* 33, 35. Lord Denning described the trial of Sir Walter Raleigh as 'outrageous' and 'a travesty of justice' for breaking almost every modern common law rule of evidence. His sense of outrage was undiminished by his belief that Sir Walter was probably guilty of treason: *Landmarks in the Law* (London, Butterworths, 1984) 14–15.

and to qualify as such, it must meet certain minimum standards. An intrinsic part of the rule of law is the right to be treated by the state as innocent unless and until one's guilt is established 'in accordance with law'. If the state is not merely 'a set of top bullies', it must establish by law a system of criminal trial. And a trial system is not deserving of the name if it is run as a 'committee for nailing criminals' bent on 'clobbering' such citizens as it considers to be guilty.

Anscombe's satire brings us back to my earlier contention that, conceived as a human right, the presumption of innocence is about much more than the incidence and standard of proof. It does not only enjoin the prosecution to produce sufficient evidence of guilt whenever it wants a person to be convicted of a crime and for the court to resolve any doubt it may have in favour of the accused. Recall the fundamental rule emphasised by Lord Dipock in *Ong Ah Chuan*. Natural justice, according to him, demands that 'a person should not be punished for an offence unless it has been established to the satisfaction of *an independent and unbiased tribunal* that he committed it'. 'An independent and unbiased tribunal' is not a discrete fair trial standard to be placed alongside the presumption of innocence; it is itself an aspect of the presumption. Innocence is presumed by withholding any initial weight to the prosecutor's assertion that the accused has committed the alleged crime.[61] To the extent that the court is inclined to take the prosecution's case at face value, it has *pro tanto* failed in its duty to hold the state to account on the criminal charge. The accused has not had the full benefit of a trial if the judge is not 'independent and unbiased' but defers instead to the judgement of the executive. Fletcher endorses this conception of the presumption of innocence. He observed of the Soviet system that the courts tended to be deferential to the procuracy in their assessment of guilt. This lack of a critical attitude towards the case prepared by the investigative agencies caused Fletcher to be sceptical of the existence of the presumption in the Soviet Union.[62]

Other basic procedural standards can similarly be deduced from the proposed theory of the criminal trial. Suppose you see it as I do: that the

[61] See above n 48.

[62] GP Fletcher, 'The Presumption of Innocence in the Soviet Union' (1968) 15 *UCLA Law Review* 1203, challenging views expressed by HJ Berman, *Soviet Criminal Law and Procedure—The RSFSR Code* (Cambridge, MA, Harvard UP, 1972) 57–62. See further: HJ Berman and JB Quigley Jr, 'Comment on the Presumption of Innocence under Soviet Law' 1968) 15 *UCLA Law Review* 1230; J Gorgone, 'Soviet Criminal Procedure Legislation: A Dissenting Perspective' (1980) 28 *American Journal of Comparative Law* 577; HJ Berman, 'The Presumption of Innocence: Another Reply' (1980) 28 *American Journal of Comparative Law* 615; J Quigley, 'The Soviet Conception of the Presumption of Innocence' (1989) 29 *Santa Clara Law Review* 301; GP Fletcher, 'The Ongoing Soviet Debate About the Presumption of Innocence' (1984) 3 *Criminal Justice Ethics* 69 and 'In Gorbachev's Courts' (1989) 36(8) *New York Review of Books* 13; the last was criticised by S Sterett and J Waldron in a joint letter to which Fletcher replied: (1989) 36(14) *New York Review of Books* 76.

criminal court is an independent and unbiased tribunal that exists as a check on the executive, requiring the prosecution to justify and defend any call it makes for a person to be convicted and punished. The question then arises: to whom is the justification offered? First, it is offered to the accused, in recognition of her responsible status, as a human being responsive to reasons. Conviction and punishment are harmful and it is oppressive to inflict such harm on a person without telling her the reason for it; hence, the accused has the right 'to be informed'. She is not a mere object to be acted upon by the state, to be condemned and punished as it sees fit. If we are to be duly respectful of her personal dignity, we must accord her the equal status of subject in the proceedings. This we do, in part, by seeking to engage her in a dialogue concerning the truth and soundness of the court's reasons, over the adequacy of the evidence adduced to support the accusations made against her. Hence, the accused is given various rights of participation, such as the right to challenge the witnesses called by the prosecution.

Secondly, the justification is offered to the community. The trial is the central medium that communicates the norms of criminal law generally. Given that purpose, its operation must be made visible to the public, and accordingly we demand an open trial process and transparent adjudication. Many of the familiar standards of fair trial, which are often conceived as discrete if related normative requirements, are internal to our conception of a criminal trial.

4. LIBERTY AND THE PRESUMPTION OF INNOCENCE

No legal system can protect us completely from the harm of wrongful conviction and punishment. But a legal system cannot exist without a commitment by the state to protect its citizens from being arbitrarily subjected to these harms. There is no rule of law where the state offers no assurance for our security and asks simply for our trust in the virtues of its officials, faith in their infallibility, and belief in the soundness of their judgements.

Underlying the presumption of innocence is the demand for government accountability in its enforcement of the criminal law. Illiberal regimes do not like to be held to account. They dislike having their powers curtailed by human rights.[63] Not surprisingly, the presumption of innocence is disparaged by such regimes. It was denounced in 1958 by the Deputy to the

[63] As S Waltoś, *Code of Criminal Procedure of the Polish People's Republic* (Warszawa, Wydawnictwo Prawnicze, 1979) 6 aptly observes: 'Criminal procedure is ... always a highly responsive barometer of the current social and political relationships. Even a superficial glimpse at the history of law in any state must lead to the conclusion that the reform in the system of government, the passing of power from one social class to another, a change of policy to a more democratic, liberal one or in the opposite direction, as a rule is reflected on the provisions of criminal procedure'.

Supreme Soviet as a 'worm-eaten dogma of bourgeois doctrine'. During the anti-rightist campaign of the 1950s in the People's Republic of China it was similarly branded as a 'reactionary bourgeois doctrine' that was incompatible with the socialist judicial system.

A court that respects the presumption of innocence sees its role as a check on government, and it is a distortion of this role to have the court stand in solidarity with the executive in a concerted 'fight against crime'. Some may question the wisdom in institutionalising what they see as inter-branch antagonism, preferring to have all organs of state, including the judiciary, collaborate in the joint pursuit of a shared vision of social order.[64] Instead of presuming a citizen innocent, why not stress her civic responsibility to co-operate fully with the police and the prosecutor?[65] And why should the court not translate this civic responsibility into a presumption of guilt in some situations? Let the accused bear the legal obligation of proving exculpatory facts so long as suspicion hangs over her head. Good citizens work with the state in realising the greater good. 'Liberal' doctrines such as the presumption were once disparaged by communist party spokesmen in China on the ground that '[t]o apply such principles of justice ... would be putting the interest of the accused above the interest of the people'.[66]

The dangers of such sentiments exist not only in authoritarian regimes. They are all around us. Notice the beguiling nature of the 'relative ease of proof' argument: where it is much easier for the accused to show her

[64] One commentator finds a lack of judicial independence in the People's Republic of China because 'the courts are seen as part of the bureaucracy rather than as an entity constituted outside of the executive. Within this framework, the task of the Chinese judiciary is to consult and co-operate with other agencies': K Jayasuriya, 'Corporatism and Judicial Independence within Statist Legal Institutions in East Asia' in Jayasuriya (ed), *Law, Capitalism and Power in Asia* (London, Routledge, 1999) 173, 195.

[65] There is at common law no legal duty to co-operate. As Lord Parker CJ puts it in *Rice v Connolly* [1966] 2 QB 414, 419: 'though every citizen has a moral duty or, if you like, a social duty to assist the police, there is no legal duty to that effect, and indeed the whole basis of the common law is the right of the individual to refuse to answer questions put to him by persons in authority, and to refuse to accompany those in authority to any particular place; short, of course, of arrest'.

[66] 'This in effect would mean "the protection of guilty persons from punishment" and "the restriction of the freedom of judicial organs and the masses in their fight against counterrevolutionary and other criminal elements"': SC Leng, *Justice in Communist China* (New York, Oceana, 1967) 63 and ibid 165: 'To assume the accused innocent in penal prosecution would only protect the interest of the criminal and tie the hands of the judicial and procuratorial organs'. Generally, see TA Gelatt, 'The People's Republic of China and the Presumption of Innocence' (1982) 73 *Journal of Criminal Law and Criminology* 259, 274–78; SC Leng and HD Chiu, *Criminal Justice in Post-Mao China—Analysis and Documents* (Albany, NY, State University of New York Press, 1985) 96–98; GV Thieme, 'The Debate on the Presumption of Innocence in the Republic of China' (1984) 10 *Review of Socialist Law* 277. While the presumption is still not explicitly recognised today, there is arguably room for its recognition in the current Criminal Procedure Law: Albert HY Chen, *An Introduction to the Legal System of the People's Republic of China*, 3rd edn (Hong Kong, Lexis Nexis, 2004) 212–13; HL Fu, 'Comparative Criminal Law and Enforcement: China' in J Dressler (ed), *Encyclopedia of Crime and Justice*, 2nd edn (NY, Macmillan, 2002) 172, 179.

innocence with respect to an element of a crime than it is for the prosecution to prove it beyond reasonable doubt, it is only fair to place the burden of proof on her. If you object, you must be one of those who think that 'the interests of justice means only the interests of the prisoners'.[67] Apparently, legal rights must give way to executive convenience. Witness also how, in defending the reversal of the burden of proof, there is inevitably a reminder that the rights of individuals must be balanced against the interests of society as a whole.[68] But surely the 'society as a whole', even an Asian society, has an interest in the state respecting all of our rights and in protecting each of us from falling victim to a miscarriage of justice.[69]

Greater clarity is required in this debate. We do better to speak of liberty than of truth. The presumption of innocence protects our freedoms. At one level, this is obvious enough. The executive cannot throw us in jail or extract fines from us without first defending before an 'independent and unbiased tribunal' the case for depriving us of our freedoms, to person or property. Liberty is not only protective, it is also empowering.[70] In a police state where the executive governs without any fetters, subjects are fortunate if the rulers, for the time being, happen to be competent and benevolent. While the subjects are fortunate, they are not free. They still live at the mercy of an all-powerful master. The presumption of innocence gives citizens the right to challenge the executive, to hold it to account before the court when it seeks to infringe their liberty. It offers assurance of security from arbitrary and unjust interference by the state.[71]

Those who seek to qualify or limit the scope of the presumption of innocence are also concerned about liberty. But their argument takes a different form. For them, rules that express standards of fair trial serve as side constraints on the main aim of convicting criminal offenders. While we want the guilty to be convicted, it pains us more to convict an innocent person. Hence, we presume the accused innocent, and deliver an acquittal

[67] *R v Grondkowski and Malinowski* [1946] KB 369, 372.

[68] Cf SK Chan CJ, 'From Justice Model to Crime Control Model', unpublished speech delivered at a conference held to celebrate the golden jubilee of the Indian Law Institute in New Delhi on 24 November 2006.

[69] Addressing the Singapore Academy of Law, then Prime Minister Lee Kuan Yew said this of Singapore's criminal justice system: 'The basic difference in our approach springs from our traditional Asian value system which places the interests of the community over and above that of the individual. In English doctrine, the rights of the individual must be the paramount consideration. We shook ourselves free from the confines of the English norms which did not accord with customs and values of Singapore society': (1990) 2 *Singapore Academy of Law Journal* 155, 155.

[70] See P Pettit's discussion of liberty as non-domination in *Republicanism—A Theory of Freedom and Government* (Oxford, Clarendon, 1997) and his earlier work with J Braithwaite, *Not Just Deserts—A Republican Theory of Criminal Justice* (Oxford, Clarendon Press, 1990).

[71] Hence, A Hamilton lauded the presumption as 'one great principle of social security', quoted in *Cummings v Missouri*, 71 US 277, 330 (1866); *Speiser v Randall*, 357 US 513, 534 (1958).

so long as guilt is not established beyond reasonable doubt. It is better to let 10 guilty persons go free than to convict someone who is innocent. But we are caught in a tragic dilemma. If the trial system displays too much 'tenderness' to the accused person, there will be too many criminals left roaming the streets. And as the Singapore Law Minister told a gathering of the New York State Bar Association, this too affects our freedom—the freedom, for example, to 'walk downtown, to any area, at any time, without fear or concern' and the freedom to let our 'children … . move about freely'.[72] Freedom comes from security; it gains strength from the assurance against interference by criminals.

No one can seriously deny that the state may qualify or circumscribe the scope of the presumption of innocence. But where this is done, the burden of proof must be 'shifted' in circumstances and on grounds that are consistent with respect for the inherent dignity of our fellow beings and their right to equal citizenship.[73] Guidance on this matter is to be found, I think, in some notion of what we morally owe each other in a political community. The accused's conduct as established by the prosecution might place her under some moral obligation to answer the charge. Where the prosecution has established that the accused is responsible for a criminal wrong, why should we not call on her to offer some explanation for her action? Indeed, is this not an implicit recognition of her rational capacity? And if she fails to give us an adequate answer, to show either an excuse or a justification for her action, why would it be objectionable to hold her criminally liable?[74] Although the imposition of a persuasive burden grates against the *Woolmington* principle, the accused in Singapore has to prove any defence on which she wishes to rely[75] and, in the United States, it is constitutionally permissible to place on the accused the burden of proving 'affirmative defences'. But does this go too far? Why is it not enough to make the accused carry an evidential burden or to subject her to the risk of an adverse inference if she chooses to remain silent?

A potentially more direct threat to the presumption of innocence is posed by reverse onus provisions and presumptions of law, devices which relieve

[72] 'Fundamentals to Singapore's Progress', *The Straits Times*, 29 October 2009. SK Chan CJ has similarly claimed that most 'Singaporeans … appreciate the safe environment they live in and support a criminal justice system that is responsible for it': 'The Criminal Process—The Singapore Model' (1996) 17 *Singapore Law Review* 433, 434.

[73] See generally A Brudner, 'Guilt Under the Charter: The Lure of Parliamentary Supremacy' (1998) 40 *Criminal Law Quarterly* 287 and 'What Theory of Rights Best Explains the *Oakes* Test?' in LB Tremblay and GCN Webber (eds), *The Limitation of Charter Rights: Critical Essays on R v Oakes* (Montreal, Éditions Thémis, 2009) 59.

[74] See RA Duff, *Answering for Crime—Responsibility and Liability in the Criminal Law* (Oxford, Hart Publishing, 2007) esp ch 9; and J Gardner, 'The Mark of Responsibility' and 'In Defence of Defences' in his *Offences and Defences—Selected Essays in the Philosophy of Criminal Law* (Oxford, OUP, 2007).

[75] Evidence Act 1997, s 107.

the state from proving, or which assist it to prove, the elements of the crime. It is widely accepted that the presumption must concede some ground. The state should be allowed to allocate the legal burden of proof to the accused on some facts and in certain circumstances. But where is the line to be drawn? This raises difficult issues, which cannot even be addressed sensibly unless and until we are clear about the concept and normative foundations of the presumption of innocence. This chapter has undertaken foundational work on the core idea. Difficulties relating to the limits of the presumption, or its qualifications, must be left for another day.

12

Confronting Confrontation

MIKE REDMAYNE

INTRODUCTION

THE RIGHT TO confrontation has precipitated a showdown between the English courts and the European Court of Human Rights. Article 6(3) of the ECHR provides that 'everyone charged with a criminal offence' has the right to 'examine or have examined witnesses against him'. This basically means that the accused, or his lawyer, should have a chance to put questions to adverse witnesses.

In the combined applications of *Al-Khawaja and Tahery v United Kingdom*,[1] the prosecution had introduced witness statements from witnesses who were not present at the defendants' trials. Strasbourg held that there was a breach of the confrontation right because the convictions were based 'solely or to a decisive extent' on the evidence of absent witnesses, even if the witnesses were absent for good reason: in *Al-Khawaja* the witness (the complainant in a sexual assault trial) was dead; in *Tahery* the witness was too frightened to testify. The English courts found this position hard to accept. In *Horncastle* the UK Supreme Court and the Court of Appeal agreed that the ECtHR jurisprudence on confrontation should not be followed.[2] So English hearsay law was in apparent conflict with the Convention: defendants could be convicted on hearsay evidence, seemingly in breach of Article 6.[3] *Al-Khawaja* has now had a rehearing before the ECtHR's Grand Chamber,[4] and the second judgment makes some concessions to the English position by allowing exceptions to the 'sole or decisive' rule. Many commentators will be critical of Strasbourg's abandonment of its hard line.[5]

1 (2009) 49 EHRR 1.

2 *R v Horncastle* [2010] 2 AC 373, [2009] UKSC 14.

3 See W O'Brian, 'Confrontation: The Defiance of the English Courts' (2011) 15 E & P 93.

4 ECtHR (Grand Chamber) 15 December 2011. This chapter was written before the Grand Chamber's judgment was handed down, so only minor changes have been made to reflect it. For detailed analysis, see Mike Redmayne, 'Hearsay and Human Rights: *Al-Khawaja* in the Grand Chamber' (2012) *Modern Law Review* (forthcoming).

5 See, eg, S Trechsel, *Human Rights in Criminal Proceedings* (Oxford, OUP, 2005) ch 11.

Confrontation rights also have a lively recent history in the United States. The Sixth Amendment to the US Constitution provides that 'in all criminal prosecutions, the accused shall enjoy the right ... to be confronted with the witnesses against him'. In a 2004 decision, *Crawford v Washington*,[6] the Supreme Court reinvigorated this clause. Departing from its previous case law,[7] the Court held that even if there are indications that a statement of an absent witness is reliable, the statement would not usually be admissible under the Confrontation Clause. The *Crawford* approach is somewhat stricter than the European one—there is no exception, for example, for evidence which is not the 'sole or decisive' basis on which the accused is convicted.

There is plainly much at stake in debates about confrontation. Complete compliance with the confrontation right means that where a witness makes a statement to the police incriminating the accused and then dies, or cannot be found, or is no longer fit to testify, or, perhaps, is too scared to come to court, then her statement cannot be introduced at trial. While under the European approach there is the caveat that the evidence can be admitted if it is not 'sole or decisive', the practical effect is that the prosecution must fail where it depends on the evidence of an absent witness, even if a court provided with the evidence would consider the case to be proved beyond reasonable doubt. This chapter takes a close look at confrontation in order to see whether this result can be justified. The discussion is confined to absent witnesses, although in Europe the confrontation right has also generated a significant case law on anonymous witnesses.[8] While concentrating on Article 6(3) of the ECHR, I refer to US doctrine to illuminate the scope and rationale of the right in Europe.

1. SPECIFYING THE CONFRONTATION RIGHT

The confrontation right overlaps with, but is narrower than, the hearsay rule. A succinct definition of the hearsay rule is that 'a statement other than one made by a person while giving oral evidence in the proceedings is inadmissible as evidence of any fact stated'.[9] While the hearsay prohibition has been narrowed slightly by the Criminal Justice Act 2003, the rule still applies to a wide range of statements. Statements made to the police are covered, but so are statements made in informal conversations between friends and statements made in business records. In the United States it is clear that the confrontation right does not extend this far. Under *Crawford*, it applies only to

6 541 US 36 (2004).
7 *Ohio v Roberts*, 448 US 56 (1980).
8 See, eg, *Doorson v The Netherlands* (1996) 22 EHRR 330.
9 R Cross, *Cross on Evidence*, 5th edn (London, Butterworths, 1979) 6.

'testimonial' statements. While 'testimonial' has not been definitively defined, the broadest definition mooted in *Crawford* was 'statements ... made under circumstances which would lead an objective witness to believe that the statement would be available for use at a later trial'.[10] Post-*Crawford*, the Court has held that laboratory reports by forensic scientists are testimonial,[11] as are statements made by a complainant to the police shortly after an alleged incident of domestic violence.[12] Statements made in an emergency telephone call to the police, however, were not classified as testimonial, because the operator would have been concentrating on dealing with the emergency rather than producing evidence for trial.[13]

Under the ECHR, things are less clear, but one important element to note is that in all of the cases where a violation has been found, the problematic evidence seems to have been statements made to investigative authorities—police officers or examining judges.[14] Indeed, the Court commonly uses the word 'deposition' to describe the type of evidence to which the confrontation right attaches.[15] Thus where a witness gives what a common lawyer regards as hearsay evidence, there may not be an issue under the Convention so long as the hearsay does not take the form of a witness statement. In *AM v Italy*, a child had complained to his parents that during a holiday in Italy he had been indecently assaulted by the applicant.[16] Statements were taken from the child's parents and from a psychotherapist who was treating him. The arguments before the ECtHR focused on the absence of confrontation of these witnesses, with the Court finding a breach of Article 6(3) because the applicant 'did not have a chance to examine the witness statements [sic] that formed the basis of his conviction'.[17] This suggests that had these witnesses been confronted, proceedings would have been Convention compliant, even though the witnesses would have been relating hearsay, ie what the child had told them.[18]

[10] *Crawford v Washington*, 541 US 36 (2004), 52.

[11] *Melendez-Diaz v Massachusetts*, 129 S Ct 2527 (2009).

[12] *Davis v Washington*, 547 US 813 (2006).

[13] Ibid 822. See also *Michigan v Bryant*, 131 S Ct 1143 (2011).

[14] See J Spencer, *Hearsay Evidence in Criminal Proceedings* (Oxford, Hart Publishing, 2008) 43–44.

[15] See, eg, *AM v Italy* Appln No 37019/97 (1999), [25]; *Luca v Italy* (2003) 36 EHRR 46, [40]; *PS v Germany* (2003) 36 EHRR 61, [24]. Another common formulation is 'statements made at the investigative stage', eg *Gossa v Poland* Appln No 47986/99 (2007). On the other hand, the text of Article 6(3) refers to 'witnesses' which, in some cases, has been given a reasonably wide interpretation, to include anyone whose statements are relied on by the court, eg *Kostovski v Netherlands* (1990) 12 EHRR 434, [40].

[16] *AM v Italy* Appln No 37019/97 (1999).

[17] Ibid [28].

[18] Cf S Summers, 'The Right to Confrontation After *Crawford* v *Washington*: A "Continental European" Perspective' (2004) 2 *International Commentary on Evidence* 8, who claims that the ECHR would apply in this situation, though she cites no evidence in support. See also S Maffei, *The European Right to Confrontation in Criminal Proceedings: Absent, Anonymous and Vulnerable Witnesses* (Groningen, Europa, 2006) 74.

Some witnesses may make statements to the police that while helpful to the prosecution, do not directly incriminate the accused. An example would be a statement such as 'I heard a gunshot at 11 o'clock'. In contrast, all of the cases in which the ECtHR has found a violation seem to have involved 'accusatory' statements, where the defendant accuses a specific person of a crime.[19] In *X v United Kingdom*, various people who had filmed an incident in Northern Ireland at which the killing of two soldiers took place were allowed to give evidence in court anonymously.[20] The evidence apparently involved the witnesses describing the making of their films and photos of the incident; they did not identify the applicant themselves. Among the reasons why the European Commission found that witness anonymity did not infringe the confrontation right in this case was that the evidence 'did not implicate the applicant'.[21] With so little to go on, it is impossible to say how significant this observation is, or how accusatory a statement would have to be before it required confrontation under the ECHR. To give but one example, an eyewitness who provides a description to the police of the person who attacked her might be said to implicate a defendant without accusing him.[22] But while one can only speculate as to what the scope of the ECHR's confrontation right is, there must surely be some limit to it. Otherwise the prosecution would not be able to rely on business records in a case where the original maker of the record was dead or could no longer be identified.

There are various reasons why the restricted scope of the confrontation right is significant. One is that it undermines the British courts' principal argument in *Horncastle*. The courts noted that hearsay can sometimes be perfectly reliable, and thus a rule that it can never be the 'sole or decisive' element in a conviction is unnecessarily strict. But, if the Strasbourg Court sees confrontation as confined to statements made to the authorities, the English courts, by framing the argument in terms of hearsay, may be talking past Strasbourg.[23] This is most evident when we consider a series of examples given by the Court of Appeal, and endorsed by the UK Supreme Court, which are intended to demonstrate that Strasbourg is being unreasonable.[24] In one example a woman makes an emergency telephone call to the police and identifies the person who is attacking her. But this is not really a statement made in response to police questioning, and so might not be seen

[19] See W O'Brian, 'The Right of Confrontation: US and European Perspectives' (2005) 121 *Law Quarterly Review* 481, 494.

[20] (1993) 15 EHRR (CD) 113.

[21] Ibid [1]. The now defunct Commission played a screening role in ECHR applications until 1998.

[22] This sort of distinction was explicitly rejected by a majority of the US Supreme Court in *Melendez-Diaz*, 129 S Ct 2527 (2009), 2533–4.

[23] The conflation of hearsay and confrontation is especially puzzling because the distinction was discussed by the Court of Appeal in *R v Owen* [2001] EWCA Crim 1018. The point is also clearly made by Spencer, above n 14, 43–44.

[24] *R v Horncastle* [2010] 2 AC 373, [61]–[63].

as a 'statement' or 'deposition' in the ECtHR's terms. Nor, in all likelihood, would it be regarded as testimonial in the United States.[25] Another example involves bank records in a fraud case; here it is even clearer that the records would not be regarded as requiring confrontation in either jurisdiction.[26] The example that comes closest to raising a confrontation issue[27] involves a witness who writes down the registration number of a car involved in a drive-by shooting, there being sufficient corroborating evidence (gunshot residue found in the car) to rule out the possibility of mistake. If the witness reports the number to the police, there is a good chance that the confrontation right under the ECHR and the Sixth Amendment would be engaged. But Strasbourg's answer cannot quite be predicted with confidence, for in the terms introduced above the report of the number plate implicates but does not accuse. The example would be more on point if the witness claimed to recognise the car's driver, and gave the police a specific person's name. This is plainly accusatorial and does not quite deliver the intuition that the Court of Appeal wanted: that there is no value in confrontation when evidence is well corroborated.

Paradigmatically, confrontation involves the relevant witness testifying in the accused's physical presence at trial, in full view of the accused and the fact-finders and with the accused being able to put questions.[28] But departures from this paradigm may be permissible.[29] The core of the right under the ECHR seems to be that the accused should have some opportunity to put questions to the witness: procedures whereby the witness is questioned pre-trial, outside the presence of the accused or his lawyer, but where the defence has the ability to influence the questions put to the witness, may comply with Article 6(3).[30] Witness anonymity is permitted, so long as 'counter-balancing' measures are in place.[31] Testimony via video-link would not raise an issue under the Convention.[32]

[25] Cf *Davis v Washington*, 547 US 813 (2006).

[26] But note *Papageorgiou v Greece* Appln No 59506/00 (2003), where the rest of the right specified in Article 6(3)(d) ('to obtain the attendance and examination of witnesses on his behalf') was used to criticise a failure to provide the originals of various documents.

[27] Ignoring an—unhelpfully opaque—example, in which a defendant signals willingness to plead guilty to a drug possession charge.

[28] While it is arguable that true confrontation involves the ability to cross-examine the witness in person, it is clear that under the ECHR there is no such right: eg *SN v Sweden* (2004) EHRR 13.

[29] For the US, see *Maryland v Craig*, 497 US 836 (1990), allowing testimony via video-link. *Crawford* does not address courtroom video-links, but does allow pre-trial confrontation where a witness is unavailable at trial.

[30] *SN v Sweden* (2004) EHRR 13. It is important that the accused is legally advised at any pre-trial confrontation: *Melnikov v Russia* Appln No 23610/03 (2010).

[31] *Doorson v Netherlands* (1996) 22 EHRR 330.

[32] In *Accardi v Italy* Appln No 30598/02 (admissibility decision, 2005), a procedure whereby the complainants were questioned prior to trial, outside the defendant's presence (but where the defendant had an opportunity to put questions), and a video tape of the questioning was presented at trial, was found not to infringe Art 6.

(a) Exceptions

Other than forfeiture (which is considered separately below), the confrontation right in the United States may be without exception.[33] In particular, the *Al-Khawaja* situation, where confrontation is not possible because the witness died unexpectedly before trial, does not give rise to an exception. The position under the ECHR is similar.

However, in one important respect Strasbourg does take a more flexible approach than the US Supreme Court, because a statement made by a justifiably absent witness will be admissible under Strasbourg jurisprudence if it is not the 'sole or decisive' basis of conviction. This is a vague criterion—almost any evidence relied on by the prosecution might turn out to be the decisive 'feather that tips the scales'—and it has not always been consistently applied by the ECtHR.[34] In recent cases, however, the notion seems to be applied quite strictly. In *Al-Khawaja* the witness statement was reasonably well corroborated: another complainant had made a similar allegation against the defendant, and the absent witness had initially made her allegations to friends. But the statement was still considered to be decisive. In other recent cases, the Court glosses the sole or decisive test in terms of whether the statement was the only 'direct' evidence of guilt[35] (as it was in *Al-Khawaja*). There remains some ambiguity, however, as to whether use of a decisive statement from an absent witness will inevitably make the trial unfair. In *Al-Khawaja* the UK Government argued that, because the applicant had had alternative means of challenging the witness statement, there were measures in place to 'counter-balance' the lack of confrontation of the sole and decisive witness statement. The ECtHR disagreed on the facts, but did not quite rule out the possibility of counter-balancing in appropriate cases.[36]

(b) Forfeiture

In the United States the only significant exception to the confrontation right is forfeiture: the defendant can lose the confrontation right through his own wrongful behaviour. This exception was considered in detail in *Giles v*

[33] *Crawford v Washington*, 541 US 36 (2004), 56 fn 6, notes the possibility that dying declarations may be admissible.

[34] Cf *Unterprertinger v Austria* (1991) 13 EHRR 175 and *Asch v Austria* (1993) 15 EHRR 597. Occasionally the test is restricted to 'sole', eg *Gossa v Poland* Appln No 47986/99 (2007), [55] (but cf [63]); *Rachdad v France* Appln No 71846/01 (2003), [24].

[35] Eg *D v Finland* Appln No 30542/04 (2009), [51]; *Demski v Poland* Appln No 22695/03 (2008), [41].

[36] *Al-Khawaja v United Kingdom* (2009) 49 EHRR 1, [37], [41]–[48]. See now the Grand Chamber judgment, above n 4 at [123].

California.[37] While recognising a forfeiture exception, a majority of the US Supreme Court held that the mere fact that the victim had died at Giles's hands was not enough to engage it. Forfeiture was construed narrowly, as applying only to conduct designed to prevent the victim from testifying.

It is not entirely clear how the ECtHR would deal with a case where the absence of a witness whose statement is 'sole or decisive' had been caused by a defendant. In *Rachdad*,[38] the Court noted that the applicant had contributed to the difficulty in securing confrontation: he had apparently been abroad (allegedly to avoid arrest) when his trial took place, and by the time he appealed against his convictions, some five years later, only one witness attended court. A breach of Article 6 was still found. In *Al-Khawaja and Tahery*, the Court distinguished the English Court of Appeal's judgment in *Sellick*,[39] noting that lack of confrontation may have been justified in that case because the witnesses 'were being kept from giving evidence through fear induced by the defendants'.[40] This implies that forfeiture would be recognised in a strong case. However, the indications are that, like the US Supreme Court, Strasbourg would take a restrictive view of the doctrine. The Strasbourg Court recently ventured the following general observations on 'waiver':

> [A] waiver must, if it is to be effective for Convention purposes, be established in an unequivocal manner, be attended by minimum safeguards commensurate with its importance, and should not run counter to any important public interest … . Moreover, before an accused can be said to have implicitly, through his conduct, waived an important right under Article 6, it must be shown that he could reasonably have foreseen what the consequences of his conduct would be.[41]

2. THEORISING CONFRONTATION

Neither the ECtHR nor the US Supreme Court has gone very far in developing an explicit theory of confrontation. Nevertheless, there is value in exploring what these courts have said about the confrontation right, before turning to the rather better developed accounts in the academic literature. At the outset, it is worth noting that there are two main ways in which confrontation—and indeed most procedural rights—can be theorised.

Confrontation might be seen as a right that is instrumental to fact-finding, because it promotes accurate verdicts. We can refer to such accounts of confrontation as 'epistemic'. Alternatively, confrontation might be thought

[37] 554 US 353 (2008).
[38] *Rachdad v France* Appln No 71846/01 (2003).
[39] *R v Sellick* [2005] 1 WLR 3257, [2005] EWCA Crim 651.
[40] *Al-Khawaja v United Kingdom* (2009) 49 EHRR 1, [37].
[41] *Khametshin v Russia* Appln No 18487/03 (2010), [37].

of as a 'non-epistemic right'. On this view, there is value in confrontation even if it would not promote accuracy, perhaps as a way of respecting the defendant's dignity. These are not mutually exclusive ways of thinking about confrontation: one may value confrontation for a mixture of epistemic and non-epistemic reasons. Nevertheless, the distinction is a useful way of analysing arguments about confrontation.

(a) Strasbourg's Human Right

To date, most of the indications are that the ECtHR understands the value of confrontation in purely epistemic terms. Its only explicit statements about the importance of confrontation stress two considerations. First, where confrontation is lacking, a defendant is deprived of 'any opportunity of observing the demeanour of [the] witness when under direct questioning, and thus of testing her reliability'.[42] Secondly, in the case of an anonymous witness:

> If the defence is unaware of the identity of the person it seeks to question, it may be deprived of the very particulars enabling it to demonstrate that he or she is prejudiced, hostile or unreliable. Testimony or other declarations inculpating an accused may well be designedly untruthful or simply erroneous and the defence will scarcely be able to bring this to light if it lacks the information permitting it to test the author's reliability or cast doubt on his credibility. The dangers inherent in such a situation are obvious. Furthermore ... [a trial court is] precluded by the absence of the said anonymous persons from observing their demeanour under questioning and thus forming its own impression of their reliability.[43]

An emphasis on reliability is also reflected in the observation that the evidence of an absent witness should be treated with 'extreme care'.[44] In cases where confrontation does not occur, the 'sole or decisive' test also indicates that unreliability is the key concern.

The only element of the Strasbourg case-law that might be hard to square with an emphasis on reliability is the apparent restriction of the confrontation right to some sort of testimonial evidence—statements made to the authorities, or perhaps a narrower class of 'accusatorial' statements. To the common lawyer familiar with the concept of hearsay, this focus might seem odd. The (epistemic) 'hearsay dangers' of veracity, perceptual ability, memory and ambiguity can affect any hearsay evidence and can be best explored through cross-examination of the declarant. Under a non-epistemic

[42] *PS v Germany* (2003) 36 EHRR 61, [26].
[43] *Kostovski v Netherlands* (1990) 12 EHRR 434, [42]–[43].
[44] See eg *Gossa v Poland* Appln No 47986/99 (2007), [55]. Also *Doorson v Netherlands* (1996) 22 EHRR 330, [76]; *Melnikov v Russia* Appln No 23610/03 (2010), [75] (statements of co-accused require particular care).

conception of the confrontation right, however, it might be thought that the defendant's ability to challenge his accusers—those who denounce him to the authorities—is a way of respecting his dignity. However, the restricted scope of the right might also be explained on epistemic grounds. A rule that all testimony should be subject to direct challenge by the defendant risks being so broad as to be unworkable, encompassing even such things as business records. A focus on accusatorial statements to the authorities might then be a way of marking out a particular category of statement that is potentially outcome-determinative and where the risks of the witness having an axe to grind are pronounced (as in the earlier example where the witness to the drive-by shooting gives a name to the police). Like any rule,[45] this specification will be imperfect, sometimes being over- and sometimes under-inclusive with regards to its rationale of admitting reliable evidence. But it might still draw the line in a sensible place.[46]

This rule-based defence of the confrontation right provides a response to the English courts' claim in *Horncastle* that evidence subject to the confrontation right can nevertheless be reliable enough to be properly decisive. A strict rule might be seen as the most appropriate way of protecting the right from abuse by judicial discretion. From one perspective, it is not surprising that the ECtHR should approach confrontation in this rule-based way. Given that the Court generally defers to national judges' assessments of evidence,[47] it would have little influence over domestic courts' application of the confrontation right were it to allow an exception for reliable evidence. The 'sole or decisive' test is probably the closest it can come to incorporating a reliability rationale in its confrontation jurisprudence. From another perspective, however, the adoption of a hard and fast rule sits less comfortably with the way the ECtHR relates to Member States. While the US Supreme Court justifies its own strict confrontation rule partly on the basis of distrust of judicial discretion,[48] it is hard to imagine Strasbourg explicitly making such an argument. The European Convention on Human Rights is part of a very different political order to the US Constitution. Expressions of lack of faith in domestic judicial decision-making could undermine the ECtHR's authority.[49] This presents something of a dilemma

[45] See F Schauer, *Playing by the Rules: A Philosophical Examination of Rule-Based Decision-Making in Law and Life* (Oxford, OUP, 1991) esp ch 7; and Schauer, 'In Defense of Rule-Based Evidence Law—And Epistemology Too' (2008) 5 *Episteme* 295.

[46] Note that just because a statement does not fall within the domain of an absolute exclusionary rule does not mean that it will be admitted. There might be other reasons for exclusion. In England and Wales, the issue would fall to be decided under the general rules for admitting hearsay.

[47] See B Emmerson, A Ashworth and A Macdonald, *Human Rights and Criminal Justice*, 2nd edn (London, Sweet & Maxwell, 2007) 579–81.

[48] See eg *Crawford v Washington*, 541 US 36 (2004), 67–68.

[49] See N Krisch, 'The Open Architecture of European Human Rights Law' (2008) 71 *Modern Law Review* 183.

for the Strasbourg Court. Its institutional position means that, insofar as the confrontation right is based on an epistemic rationale, it is pushed towards adopting a strict rule that is not entirely responsive to reliability concerns. Yet it is simultaneously pulled away from imposing a rule so strict—as an absolute rule of inadmissibility might be—that the rule's discretion-limiting functions would be obvious.

(b) *Crawford's* Confrontation Clause

The US Constitution is a foundational political document in a way that the ECHR is not. Because the US Supreme Court's recent interpretations of the Confrontation Clause are heavily influenced by this broader context, its pronouncements are not very useful for understanding confrontation in England and Europe. The discussion in this Section can therefore be brief.

In its recent case-law, the US Supreme Court has veered towards an 'originalist' interpretation of the Sixth Amendment Confrontation Clause. Its concern has been largely with how the clause would have been understood at the time of the founding. From this perspective, the Court has felt little need to justify the confrontation requirement, giving the impression that the 'purpose of confrontation is confrontation'.[50] While the Court has suggested that the ultimate goal of confrontation 'is to ensure reliability of evidence',[51] this rationale plays little role in the recent case-law. The reason for this is partly distrust of the judicial discretion that would be involved in creating exceptions for reliable evidence.[52] It is also because, even if the right was originally written into the Constitution because of concerns about the reliability of un-confronted testimony, now that it is in the Constitution it should be honoured for its own sake.

(c) Police Tactics

When we move beyond judicial pronouncements, we find a richer set of theories of confrontation. One theme in the literature is that police interviewing tactics give us reason to distrust witness statements. As William O'Brian puts it: 'statements that are created once litigation is anticipated or underway are inherently suspect'.[53] Even where a witness has no axe to grind—recall the Court of Appeal's number plate example in *Horncastle*—

[50] RC Park, 'Is Confrontation the Bottom Line?' (2006) 19 *Regent University Law Review* 459, 467 (Park attributes the phrase to Peter Tillers).

[51] *Crawford v Washington*, 54 US 36 (2004), 61.

[52] See ibid 67–68.

[53] O'Brian, n 19 above, 500–1.

police questioning can be suggestive and manipulative. Margaret Berger, emphasising deterrence of police misconduct, has made a similar argument.[54]

There is certainly good reason to be concerned about police interviews with witnesses. Research in England and Wales found that 'interviews were... highly interviewer driven, with a confirmatory bias'.[55] One assessment concludes that '[o]fficers are apt to interview witnesses in ways that are wholly improper and ineffective'.[56] However, a strong confrontation right may not be the best way to deal with the problem. To the extent that improper suggestion is the culprit, cross-examination may be ineffective if the police version of events has been internalised by the witness, especially as trials take place months or even years after the alleged crime, requiring witnesses to 'refresh their memories' from their police statements. Berger's hope is that confrontation will encourage better police performance, but even if cross-examination is good at rooting out police malpractice, its influence on police conduct generally is likely to be limited, especially given the high rate of guilty pleas.[57] Electronically recording witness interviews may be a more effective way of regulating police tactics, enabling an assessment of what transpired during interviews irrespective of the witness's availability for cross-examination.[58] By focusing on the dangers of presenting the fact-finder with unreliable evidence, O'Brian side-steps these particular criticisms. It is, however, not obvious that the product of police questioning is so unreliable that we are better off not admitting it at all unless there is confrontation—especially if electronically recorded evidence of an interview is available. I return to this point in the more detailed analysis of reliability below.

By drawing attention to the possibility of police abuse of the questioning process, O'Brian and Berger gesture at a slightly different value inherent in confrontation. The trial of Sir Walter Raleigh is often taken to be paradigmatic of the possibility of abuse in a system without confrontation.

[54] M Berger, 'The Deconstitutionalization of the Confrontation Clause: A Proposal for a Prosecutorial Restraint Model' (1992) 76 *Minnesota Law Review* 557.

[55] C Clarke and R Milne, *National Evaluation of the PEACE Investigative Interviewing Course* (London, Home Office, 2001) 58–59.

[56] E Shepherd and R Milne, '"Have you Told Management About This?" Bringing Witness Interviewing into the Twenty-First Century' in A Heaton-Armstrong *et al* (eds), *Witness Testimony: Psychological, Investigative and Evidential Perspectives* (Oxford, OUP, 2006) 145.

[57] There are parallels with the debates about deterrence of police misconduct as a rationale for excluding improperly obtained evidence. The literature is massive, but a good sceptical account is C Slobogin, 'Why Liberals Should Chuck the Exclusionary Rule' [1999] *Illinois Law Review* 363. While my own view is that the sceptical arguments are a bit overdone, we may have less reason to believe in deterrence where confrontation is concerned. For one thing, we are relying on the ability of cross-examination to bring out manipulation of the declarant, and it must be doubtful whether it often does so.

[58] The ECtHR has used electronic recording of witness interviews as one factor in its assessment of whether the confrontation right has been breached: *Melnikov v Russia* Appln No 23610/03 (2010), [76].

Raleigh was convicted of treason, largely on the basis of the testimony of Sir Thomas Cobham, who had apparently told his questioners that Raleigh had been part of a plot to overthrow James I.[59] Cobham did not testify at the trial. Despite Raleigh's pleas and Cobham's availability, the court refused to order that he be produced in person to repeat his accusation. While Raleigh is the best known historical example, those involved in drafting the US Constitution would have been aware of a catalogue of similar abuses, including the use of 'ex parte' procedures by the British to try colonists.[60] One way of understanding fair trial rights is that they exist to protect us from a state that cannot always be trusted. With authoritarian government being part of recent European history, we can appreciate that a 'liberalism of fear'[61] may be one reason why the ECtHR has taken to upholding a strong confrontation right—and also why British judges, coming from legal jurisdictions with more stable political histories, might react with bemusement. While it is worth highlighting this aspect of confrontation, arguments grounded in concern over police or prosecutorial misconduct are basically epistemic ones, raising issues about the reliability of un-confronted evidence.

(d) Ignobility

Most commentators see confrontation as a right which exists for the benefit of defendants. Sherman Clark has sketched a different way in which we might rationalise the right.[62] Clark labels his theory an 'accuser obligation' account, whereby confrontation is seen as a duty placed on citizens to testify in an appropriate manner. On this view, the confrontation right is rooted in:

> a deep, if inchoate, feeling that it is somehow beneath us—inconsistent with our sense of who we want to be as a community—to allow witnesses against criminal defendants to 'hide behind the shadow' when making an accusation. On this interpretation, requiring confrontation is a way of reminding ourselves that we are, or at least want to see ourselves as, the kind of people who decline to countenance or abet what we see as the cowardly and ignoble practice of hidden accusation.[63]

[59] *Raleigh's Case* 2 How St Tr 1 (1603).

[60] See *Crawford v Washington*, 541 US 36 (2004), 47–48.

[61] J Shklar, 'The Liberalism of Fear' in S Young, *Political Liberalism: Variations on a Theme* (Albany NY, SUNY Press, 2004).

[62] S Clark, 'An Accuser-Obligation Approach to the Confrontation Clause' (2003) 81 *Nebraska Law Review* 1258.

[63] Ibid 1258.

The central idea is that in some circumstances a witness may behave 'ignobly' by making an accusation and then avoiding confrontation. One significant point about Clark's account, however, is that it presumably would not justify excluding the complainant's police statement in *Al-Khawaja*, because Clark treats a declarant's inability to testify as not necessarily displaying the sort of ignobility that the right is intended to guard against. Thus, in *Al-Khawaja* the complainant's death makes a good case for admissibility. Contrast O'Brian's approach, where a statement to the police is the paradigmatic example of evidence that should be excluded. For him, a declarant's inability to testify cannot justify admissibility.

(e) Something Deep in Human Nature

Clark's analysis of confrontation suggests one way of developing a non-epistemic theory, removing the focus from reliability. There are other possibilities. Some years before *Crawford*, the US Supreme Court in *Coy v Iowa*[64] considered the importance of face-to-face confrontation in a case involving testimony given by video-link. Having cited from various non-legal sources, the majority explained:

> This opinion is embellished with references to and quotations from antiquity in part to convey that there is something deep in human nature that regards face-to-face confrontation between accused and accuser as 'essential to a fair trial in a criminal prosecution'. *Pointer v Texas*, 380 US 400, 380 US 404 (1965). What was true of old is no less true in modern times. President Eisenhower once described face-to-face confrontation as part of the code of his home town of Abilene, Kansas. In Abilene, he said, it was necessary to '[m]eet anyone face to face with whom you disagree. You could not sneak up on him from behind, or do any damage to him, without suffering the penalty of an outraged citizenry... In this country, if someone dislikes you, or accuses you, he must come up in front. He cannot hide behind the shadow' ... . The phrase still persists, 'Look me in the eye and say that'.[65]

However, the *Coy* majority ultimately seems to have favoured an epistemic interpretation of the historical importance of confrontation. Thus 'the perception that confrontation is essential to fairness has persisted over the centuries because there is much truth to it'[66]—the point being that confrontation may help deter and detect lies. Face-to-face confrontation was also said to have 'much the same purpose' as the right to cross-examine, ensuring the integrity of the fact-finding process.[67]

64 *Coy v Iowa*, 487 US 1012 (1988).
65 Ibid 1017–18.
66 Ibid 1019.
67 Ibid.

Of course, 'something deep in human nature' can also be given a non-epistemic interpretation, and some commentators have tried to unpack the idea in this way. For example, Toni Massaro argues that there is more to confrontation than enhancing fact-finding.[68] Linking her analysis to the 'dignitarian' strand in due process theorising, the high-point of her argument is that:

> Commonly-held notions about 'fair play' and 'decent treatment' of others in social and business relationships indicate that most people accord intrinsic value to face-to-face encounters … . The United States military acknowledges this intrinsic value of face-to-face encounters by its practice of delivering the news of the death of a serviceman or woman in person. Likewise, in the business world it is 'indecent' to terminate an employee with a letter, instead of in a face-to-face exchange. To use a letter demonstrates a lack of respect for the affected person, and implies he or she is of low status. People in our culture thus regard the delivery of significant bad news through a letter, a telephone call, or other impersonal devices as the choice of a messenger who is cowardly, or who lacks respect for the equality, humanity, and dignity of the recipient.[69]

Massaro's examples are plausible in their own terms, but the analogy to the criminal trial is questionable. If the state introduces the evidence of an absent witness, is it really violating the accused's dignity by treating him in an impersonal manner? The trial itself remains a face-to-face proceeding, and the accused will hear any bad news—a guilty verdict—delivered personally. At its strongest, Massaro's argument seems to collapse into Clark's: the accuser has an obligation to face the accused.

Eileen Scallen has also tried to tease out reasons why confrontation may be valued, apart from its contribution to fact-finding.[70] She argues that confrontation is necessary 'as part of the social relationship between the individual defendant and the accusing witness',[71] and refers to social science research on the reasons why people confront each other in everyday life. Many of these reasons do not map easily onto the criminal trial; the strongest point seems to be that confrontation has cathartic functions.[72] In everyday life confrontation may allow us to vent our frustrations; in a criminal trial perhaps it is important that the defendant should have the satisfaction of seeing his accuser repeat the accusation to his face, even if the witness is an impressive one and her presence actually damages his case.

[68] T Massaro, 'The Dignity Value of Face-to-Face Confrontations' (1988) 40 *University of Florida Law Review* 863.

[69] Ibid 904.

[70] E Scallen, 'Constitutional Dimensions of Hearsay Reform: Toward a Three-Dimensional Confrontation Clause' (1992) 76 *Minnesota Law Review* 623.

[71] Ibid 642.

[72] Ibid 646.

Ian Dennis has argued that non-epistemic arguments of this sort cannot justify a strong confrontation right.[73] This is because the non-epistemic arguments tend to rest on respect for the accused's dignity, but victims and witnesses also have dignity-based interests and rights. This commonality of value allows balancing. If, for example, a witness will find testifying extremely stressful, then we might want to excuse her from appearing in court, or from testifying in the accused's presence, for the loss to the accused's dignity will be offset by the gain to the witness's. There are reasons to be cautious about endorsing this argument. One is that any of the defendant's trial-related rights, including the presumption of innocence, might be traced back to some foundational value such as respect for human dignity that also underlies the rights of victims and witnesses. But that does not mean that the defendant's rights do not deserve special protection, or even that they are open to balancing against other rights. Another reason is that in cases such as *Al-Khawaja*, where the victim is dead, the victim's rights do not seem to be engaged at all, so there would be no reason to undermine the accused's dignity. Further, even in cases where the dignity of a witness will be undermined by requiring her to testify, the state has the option of simply stopping the prosecution, thus protecting the dignity of all parties.

These last two points obviously raise questions about whether other interests—such as those of the community in seeing offenders punished—might be balanced against the accused's dignity-based rights. I will not attempt to resolve those issues here. But while the finer points of Dennis's argument are debatable, his basic point is sound. It is telling that neither Massaro nor Scallen argues for a right as strong as the one now supported by the US Supreme Court and the ECtHR, which excludes a witness statement even when its maker has suddenly died. Whether or not balancing is appropriate, arguments from dignity do not seem weighty enough to justify a strong confrontation right.

(f) Tradition

A further argument for confrontation is that the right—perhaps like jury trial, or the adversarial system[74]—is historically embedded. Confrontation is just the way we do things: testimony must be given in court, and we

[73] I Dennis, 'The Right to Confront Witnesses: Meanings, Myths and Human Rights' [2010] *Criminal Law Review* 255.

[74] On this justification for the adversary system, see D Luban, *Lawyers and Justice: An Ethical Study* (Princeton, NJ, Princeton UP, 1988) 87–92. Luban is sceptical of the argument.

should not tolerate a system that allows it to be given otherwise.[75] This way of seeing things may carry more weight in the US context where, as noted above, the right forms part of a foundational political document. Then again, supporters of confrontation often point to references to the right that long pre-date the US Constitution,[76] and urge its adoption outside the United States.[77] But while this may indicate that confrontation is valuable, the argument from tradition cannot be definitive. The Canadian Supreme Court has interpreted the history as showing that 'the optimal way of testing evidence adopted by our adversarial system is to have the declarant state the evidence in court, under oath, and under the scrutiny of contemporaneous cross-examination'.[78] However, the optimal position does not preclude exceptions.[79] In the same way, though jury trial has ancient roots we have been prepared to introduce new exceptions to the established expectation that serious cases are tried by a jury.[80]

3. THE FORFEITURE PROBLEM

The previous Section's survey of confrontation theory suggests that confrontation is valuable. That is not surprising. But, as should now be obvious, the important question is whether the values underlying the confrontation right justify a right which has roughly the scope and force of the one we find under Strasbourg's current interpretation of the ECHR. Situations where the evidence is not 'sole or decisive' excepted, the right is a strong one, with no allowance made for cases such as *Al-Khawaja* where the declarant is plainly unable to testify. However, the ECtHR does recognise a forfeiture exception where the witness's unavailability is attributable to the accused himself.

Forfeiture is a very significant exception to the right, because it is a useful way of testing the coherence of confrontation theory. If the confrontation right is strong and justified by epistemic concerns, it seems hard to justify forfeiture. Does the defendant who kills the witness forfeit his right to be convicted only on reliable evidence? Consider an analogous situation, where a defendant burns down the forensic science laboratory

[75] See R Friedman, '"Face to Face": Rediscovering the Right to Confront Prosecution Witnesses' (2004) 8 E & P 1, 17. Note that this way of putting the argument depends on classifying the declarant as 'testifying' during police questioning; this might be disputed.

[76] See F Herrmann and B Speer, 'Facing the Accuser: Ancient and Medieval Precursors of the Confrontation Clause' (1994) 34 *Virginia Journal of International Law* 481.

[77] Eg R Friedman, 'Thoughts From Across the Water on Hearsay and Confrontation' [1998] *Criminal Law Review* 697.

[78] *R v Khelawon* [2006] 2 SCR 787, [63].

[79] See D Paciocco and L Stuesser, *The Law of Evidence*, 5th edn (Toronto, Irwin Law, 2008) ch 5; *R v Goodstoney* (2007) 404 AR 60, [2007] 6 WWR 35.

[80] Criminal Justice Act 2003, s 44.

where important evidence in his case is waiting to be tested.[81] That might stymie the prosecution in its efforts to prove its case, but we would surely be reluctant to say that the defendant had forfeited the right to proof beyond reasonable doubt and that we should be satisfied instead with a lower standard of proof.

The analogy with proof beyond reasonable doubt is not perfect—that right is foundational to the criminal trial, and it may be correct to view any attempt to undercut it as unacceptable. It is also true that forfeiture has strong intuitive appeal in the confrontation context. As the UK Supreme Court put it in *Horncastle*, '[a] defendant can never be heard to complain of the absence of a witness if he has been responsible for that absence'.[82] But forfeiture remains a problematic doctrine as long as confrontation is justified in terms of protecting the accused from false conviction, for that just does not look to be the sort of protection that is capable of being forfeited. A criminal defendant *can* be heard to complain about losing the right to demonstrate unreliability by means of confrontation, even where his own wrongdoing caused the loss. To respond that in this situation the accused will still have the right to show the unreliability of the statement by other means is tantamount to undermining the confrontation right completely—at least to the extent of conceding a counter-balancing exception in all cases.

It may well be that non-epistemic theories of confrontation will fare better at justifying forfeiture. However, as we saw in the previous Section, these theories have their own problems. Typically, the normative justifications for the right are not sufficient to explain its doctrinal strength: Al-Khawaja's inability to attain catharsis is not a good reason to acquit him. Theories mixing epistemic and non-epistemic considerations will not fare any better, because they all suffer from the weaknesses of their component parts.

4. RELIABILITY AND THE EXCLUSION OF EVIDENCE

To this point, my arguments have been largely negative, highlighting weaknesses in possible justifications for the sort of confrontation right found under the ECHR. This critical thrust should not be mistaken for scepticism about all forms of confrontation right. In this Section, as the focus turns to

[81] An inculpatory inference might obviously be drawn from the accused's behaviour. But unless it can be argued that by killing the prosecution witness the accused accepts that her statement is true—thus perhaps even losing the right to challenge the witness statement at trial, or losing the confrontation right if an attempt to kill the witness is unsuccessful—this does not explain why the accused loses the right to confrontation.

[82] *R v Horncastle* [2010] 2 AC 373, [104]. See further, R Friedman, 'Confrontation and the Definition of Chutzpa' (1997) 31 *Israel Law Review* 506; R Friedman, '*Giles* v *California*: A Personal Reflection' (2009) 13 *Lewis & Clark Law Review* 733.

the relationship between confrontation and the reliability of verdicts, the argument becomes more constructive.

Astute commentators on confrontation have recognised that reliability is a problematic concept in evidence law.[83] If we took an admonition to exclude unreliable evidence seriously, we might end up excluding all evidence. Eye-witness evidence is an obvious example, but so is confession evidence. Even DNA evidence might be based on a contaminated sample,[84] or be given too much weight by the fact-finder. Moreover, in the context of confrontation, an emphasis on reliability is potentially very unruly. It cannot easily justify the focus on testimonial statements (business records can be unreliable), nor even on prosecution evidence. And unreliability is not even a very realistic concern when it comes to hearsay. Even if much hearsay evidence is suspect, that does not give us any reason to exclude it unless we think that the fact-finder will give it too much weight. Empirical research lends little support to this concern.[85]

But if reliability is not decisive, does that leave us with no objection to make when the prosecution presents a statement from an absent witness? There appears to be something very problematic about relying on such evidence when the witness is in fact available to testify. However, this is most convincingly explained, not as an objection to unreliable evidence, but in terms of there being better evidence available: the declarant's testimony in court. This reflects the 'best evidence principle'.[86] In this specific context, though, the claim is not that testimony in court is necessarily preferable to an out-of-court statement. The witness may lie in court, or offer confusing credibility cues. A preferable way to put it is that bringing the witness to court gives us more evidence—the witness's demeanour as well as her answers to questions on examination and cross-examination. This can be set alongside any out-of-court statement, providing the most complete picture possible.

There is a connection here with reliability, in that more evidence is generally better than less if we are trying to find the truth. This is why it is desirable to present any available evidence.[87] Additionally, when the prosecution fails to produce easily available evidence, our suspicions will be raised, as in the Raleigh trial. The desirability of basing a decision on as

[83] See R Friedman, 'Confrontation: The Search for Basic Principles' (1998) 86 *Georgetown Law Journal* 1011; D Nance, 'Rethinking Confrontation After *Crawford*' (2004) 2(1) *International Commentary on Evidence*; P Westen, 'Confrontation and Compulsory Process: A Unified Theory of Evidence for Criminal Cases' (1978) 91 *Harvard Law Review* 567.

[84] See Gans, Chapter 8 in this volume.

[85] R Park, 'Visions of Applying the Scientific Method to the Hearsay Rule' [2003] *Michigan State Law Review* 1149.

[86] D Nance, 'The Best Evidence Principle' (1987) 73 *Iowa Law Review* 227.

[87] Alex Stein denies this: see *Foundations of Evidence Law* (Oxford, OUP, 2005); cf M Redmayne, 'The Structure of Evidence Law' (2006) 26 *Oxford Journal of Legal Studies* 805, esp 814–15.

much evidence as possible may give us a reason to exclude some hearsay evidence. If the declarant is easily available, we might want to exclude the witness statement in order to provide the prosecution with an incentive to produce the declarant. However, the fact that the amount of evidence we have is connected to the reliability of the decisions we make gives us no reason to exclude the statement of a justifiably absent prosecution witness.

Defendants do not have a right to have a particular amount of evidence admitted against them. They have no legitimate complaint if certain evidence, that might be helpful to their case, is missing (so long as it is not the prosecution's fault that it is missing—a point taken up below). We would not stop a trial just because a key defence witness has dropped dead.[88] What defendants do have is a right to proof beyond reasonable doubt. But that is an issue of sufficiency of evidence, a concern about when a case is too weak to justify a guilty verdict; it is not a doctrine of admissibility. To be sure, concerns about sufficiency of evidence may be germane in prosecutions based on the evidence of an absent witness, but that is a reason for withdrawing some cases from the jury, not for a rigid rule making all testimonial hearsay inadmissible.

5. DELAY AND A RIGHT TO TEST EVIDENCE

Despite the foregoing arguments, it is hard to shake off a feeling that admitting testimonial hearsay affects trial fairness, even when the witness is unavailable. Examining an analogous situation, this Section briefly reviews English case-law on delayed prosecutions, an area of doctrine that might suggest that defendants have a right to test the evidence against them.[89]

In some cases where delay has led to the loss of potentially exculpatory evidence—such as documents, or evidence to support an alibi—courts have stayed proceedings. For example, in *R v B*[90] the defendant was convicted of sexual offences allegedly committed some 30 years earlier. Without criticising the conduct of the trial, the Court of Appeal found B's conviction unsafe:

> All that the defendant could do was to say that he had not committed the acts alleged against him … . [W]hen faced with allegations of the sort that were made here, 'I have not done it' is virtually no defence at all.[91]

[88] See Westen, above n 83, 595.

[89] Along similar lines, see D Hamer, 'Trying Delays: Forensic Disadvantage in Child Sexual Assault Trials' [2010] *Criminal Law Review* 671; and Hamer, Chapter 9 in this volume.

[90] [2003] EWCA Crim 319.

[91] Ibid [28].

The Court in *R v E*[92] subsequently expressed some reservations about its decision in *R v B*, but was able to distinguish the later appeal on the basis that there was material that could be used in cross-examination of the complainant. In *Ali*,[93] the Court of Appeal reflected further on the issues: 'The mere fact that missing material might have assisted the defence will not necessarily lead to a stay'. There should, however, be 'sufficiently credible evidence, *apart from the missing evidence*, leaving the defence to exploit the gaps left by the missing evidence. The rationale for refusing a stay is the existence of credible evidence, itself untainted by what has gone missing'.[94]

These decisions betray considerable unease about the fairness of a trial in which a defendant is not able to challenge the evidence against him. This chimes quite well with the ECtHR's approach to confrontation. As we have seen, the Strasbourg Court does not insist that defendants have a right of face-to-face confrontation even with accusatorial witnesses; instead, defendants have a right to challenge such witnesses. But while the case-law usually equates challenge with the opportunity to put questions to a witness, in *Al-Khawaja* the Court did not quite rule out the possibility that some less direct means of challenge could be acceptable. The Court engaged with the UK Government's argument that the presence of two 'recent complaint' witnesses at the trial, to whom the complainant had made allegations about the applicant, counter-balanced Al-Khawaja's lack of direct confrontation by allowing him to explore inconsistencies between the complainants' accounts. The Court, however, was unimpressed by this argument, because the inconsistencies between the accounts were minor.[95] This is a painfully bad response, rather like saying that a defendant had an unfair trial because he was caught red-handed and could advance no credible defence. What surely matters, and helps to make the trial fair, is that Al-Khawaja had access to evidence that could potentially have undermined the case against him, as opposed to evidence directly contradicting the complainant's allegations.

This suggests that in thinking about a right to test evidence it is the overall strength of the prosecution case that is key. A robust response to the problem of delayed proceedings is therefore possible: so long as the prosecution case is strong enough to go to the jury—ie there is sufficient evidence for proof beyond reasonable doubt—then the fact that the accused no longer has access to evidence that might have helped his case is immaterial. The best analysis of the problem in *B*, then, may be that the prosecution case was not strong enough. Although English courts might be reluctant to put

92 *R v E* [2004] 2 Cr App R 36.
93 [2007] EWCA Crim 691.
94 Ibid [29]–[30].
95 (2009) 49 EHRR 1, [42].

it this way,[96] evidential insufficiency is surely an apt diagnosis when the prosecution case rests on a 30-year-old allegation with no corroboration. We might say that the problem is that the fact-finder cannot rationally test the evidence, and that untested evidence is weaker—so long as 'testing' is understood to encompass not only direct challenge to an item of evidence, but also whether the evidence coheres with any other prosecution evidence. In this way, cross-examination is not significant in itself, but only one means of resolving (or not) questions about the evidential sufficiency of the prosecution's case.

In *Al-Khawaja* the supporting evidence spoke to certain doubts about the complainant, making the case a reasonably strong one to leave to the jury. But *Al-Khawaja*'s sibling case before the ECtHR, *Tahery*,[97] is a different matter. Here the victim was unable to say for certain who his attacker was, whilst the key prosecution witness, who was absent, had made a statement that was in certain respects inconsistent with the victim's evidence.[98] This was a weak case, and there is a good argument that it should never have been left to the jury.[99]

CONCLUSIONS: RETHINKING CONFRONTATION

If the principle underlying confrontation is that it is problematic for the prosecution not to present its best available evidence at trial, confrontation should be conceptualised as a right to cross-examine available witnesses. As we have seen, advocates of a strong confrontation right have tended to restrict the scope of the right to a certain class of witnesses: roughly, those who make accusations. Having rejected arguments for a strong right we are left with little reason to restrict the right in this way. But what if a witness has moved abroad, or can no longer remember much about the event in question?

A framework for answering these questions is provided by the best evidence principle. To forestall unreasonable demands, 'best' must be understood in terms of what is reasonably practicable, as should availability for the purposes of confrontation. A witness is not 'available' in the pertinent

96 Because *R v Galbraith* [1981] 2 All ER 1060 (CA) establishes that issues of credibility are for the jury, so that if the complainant makes a coherent allegation the accused generally has a case to answer.

97 *Al-Khawaja and Tahery v United Kingdom* (2009) 49 EHRR 1.

98 The facts are clearer in the Court of Appeal's decision: *R v Tahery* [2006] EWCA Crim 529.

99 In theory, s 125 of the Criminal Justice Act 2003 provides some protection here. This gives a court the power to direct an acquittal where the prosecution case depends on hearsay evidence which is so unconvincing that a conviction would be unsafe. But it is not clear how much of a safeguard this provides in practice. In *R v Joyce* [2005] EWCA Crim 1785, [19], the section is said not to set a higher standard than *Galbraith*, which is troubling. See also *R v Bennett* [2008] EWCA Crim 248.

sense if, like the factory workers in *Myers*,[100] it is unlikely that she can remember much about the relevant facts. Nor should availability be applied to a witness who has moved abroad if her testimony is not expected to add much of significance.

While the criterion of practical availability is intended to rebuff unreasonable demands, it must not sanction unreasonable complacency. Even if better evidence is not available for production at trial, it might still be appropriate to exclude a pre-trial witness statement if the prosecution ought to have done better. In *Cole*,[101] for example, where a pregnant witness was unavailable at trial, one might have expected the prosecution to have rescheduled the trial to avoid her expected birth date. In *Keet* two elderly witnesses were too frail to give evidence by the time of trial—one even had dementia.[102] In this situation a solution might have been to arrange confrontation prior to trial, a procedure that complies with both the ECHR and the US Sixth Amendment. Yet, as John Spencer notes, English law simply has no provision to facilitate pre-trial confrontation.[103] This is, ultimately, the fault of the state, and there might be an argument for excluding the evidence in order to provide an incentive to develop better procedures for prosecuting crime. Similarly, arguments based on a 'best evidence' view of confrontation rights might be used to press the state to electronically record witness statements, thereby enhancing the ability of defendants to challenge witness accounts, whether or not the witness testifies at trial.[104]

In *Al-Khawaja*, the witness's unavailability at trial was unpredictable. Proponents of a strong confrontation right might still argue that her statement should be excluded because 'the prosecution can greatly reduce, if not eliminate, this risk [of unavailability] by affording the defendant an early opportunity to confront the witnesses'.[105] The prosecution can always insure against the risk of a significant witness becoming absent by offering pre-trial confrontation. But if confrontation is as valuable as proponents of a strong right maintain, this is probably not an effective solution. Just as defendants preferred to keep their powder dry rather than cross-examine witnesses when 'live' committal proceedings existed,[106] it seems unlikely that many defendants would avail themselves of the opportunity to question a witness long before trial when there was no hint that the witness might

[100] *Myers v DPP* [1965] AC 1001.

[101] *R v Cole and Keet* [2007] 1 WLR 2716.

[102] Ibid.

[103] Spencer, above n 14, 57–60; J Spencer, 'Squaring up to Strasbourg: *Horncastle* in the Supreme Court' [2010] 1 *Archbold News* 6.

[104] ECtHR case-law offers some purchase here. In *Gossa v Poland* Appln No 47986/99 (2007), [55], it was observed that Article 6 'requires the contracting states to take positive steps so as to enable the accused to examine or have examined witnesses against him'. On electronic recording, see also *Melnikov v Russia* Appln No 23610/03 (2010), [76].

[105] O'Brian, above n 19. O'Brian here echoes Friedman, see eg above n 83, 1035.

[106] See A Ashworth and M Redmayne, *The Criminal Process*, 4th edn (Oxford, OUP, 2010) 9.1.

become unavailable. Significantly, a defendant's failure to take up such an opportunity would not necessarily satisfy the ECtHR's potentially demanding standard for waiver of the confrontation right.[107] Confrontation would be a rather hollow right in cases of unpredictable absence if the right was fulfilled by a routinely spurned opportunity to confront witnesses before trial.

(a) Judicial Discretion

The 'weak' confrontation right advocated here gives significant scope to judicial discretion in deciding questions of practical availability. And here proponents of a strong right have one further argument to draw upon. Critics might concede many of the specific points made in this chapter, but still argue for a strong right on the grounds that a strict rule is preferable to judicial discretion. This, though, is an argument for clear rules, not for those rules to take a particular shape. The *Al-Khawaja* situation (obvious inability to testify through no fault of the prosecution) could still be carved out as a clear exception to a rigidly-defined confrontation right. Of course, once an exception like this is recognised we must trust judges to make appropriate sufficiency determinations in individual cases, and my criticism of *Tahery* suggests that sometimes this trust may be misplaced. However, if advocates of a strong right are not prepared to concede this much to judicial discretion, they should also abandon a forfeiture exception, since some cases in which the accused has forfeited confrontation will nevertheless be too evidentially weak to go to the jury.[108]

A weak confrontation right obviously extends judicial discretion beyond *Al-Khawaja*-type absences, to include wider questions of practical availability. Should the prosecution, for example, be permitted to rely on the statement of a witness who has moved abroad? What if the witness, as in *Tahery*, claims to be scared of testifying but there is no suggestion that the defendant is responsible? In the English context, these are questions for judges under the structured discretions provided by the Criminal Justice Act 2003. No doubt there is room for disagreement about how well these provisions are working. Given the complexity of the issues—encompassing judgements about how much value confrontation would add in particular cases—and the relative immaturity of Criminal Justice Act 2003 jurisprudence, we are a long way from being able to conclude that we would be better off with a strong confrontation right. Nevertheless, this is the ground on which debates about confrontation properly belong.

[107] See above n 41.
[108] See, eg, *R v M* [2003] 2 Cr App R 357.

(b) Confrontation and Human Rights

This chapter has argued that a strong confrontation right of the type found under the ECHR cannot be justified. Epistemic justifications have intrinsic problems and struggle to account for a forfeiture exception that would keep the right within acceptable limits. Non-epistemic justifications are not sufficiently compelling to support a strong right. Drawing on the best evidence principle, I have argued that confrontation should be seen as a positive right to examine available prosecution witnesses, not as a negative right excluding the evidence of absent witnesses.

In closing, it is worth reflecting on what this analysis implies for the central theme of this book, the role of human rights in evidence law. Readers might suspect that my critique of a strong confrontation right is motivated by scepticism about rights in evidence law more generally. What good, after all, are rights if they are not strong rights, if they crumble under any countervailing pressure or are subject to being balanced away? To believe in rights, according to Jeremy Waldron,

> is to believe that certain key interests of individuals … deserve special protection, and that they should not be sacrificed for the sake of greater efficiency or prosperity or for any aggregate of lesser interests under the heading of the public good.[109]

My argument, however, has not been that the confrontation right should be traded off against other interests. Rather, it has been about the scope of the right.[110] To this extent, the strong/weak terminology is potentially misleading—but terminology more apt to mark this point (broad/narrow) would mislead in other respects. Simply put, I have argued that the scope of the confrontation right should be limited by the practical availability of witnesses. But when a witness is deemed available the right should be seen as absolute. In this way, the confrontation right defended here is as 'strong' as the post-*Crawford*, US Sixth Amendment's, though it does have a different scope.

Nevertheless, the confrontation right advocated here can intelligibly be described as 'weak' in some respects. If the ECtHR were to adopt my analysis it would surrender much of its ability to police Member States' adherence to the right. The test of practical availability is sufficiently nuanced and dependent on factual determinations that, egregious failures to call available witnesses aside, the Strasbourg Court would probably have to defer to state courts' rulings.

[109] J Waldron, 'A Right-Based Critique of Constitutional Rights' (1993) 13 *Oxford Journal of Legal Studies* 18, 30.

[110] See G Webber, *The Negotiable Constitution: On the Limitation of Rights* (Cambridge, CUP, 2010) ch 4.

The importance of fine-grained factual analysis has wider implications for trial rights that are justified on epistemic grounds. For example, defendants have a right to proof beyond reasonable doubt—surely the most valuable of trial rights, and one that assumes even greater importance if the evidence of absent witnesses becomes admissible. In English criminal trials, this right is largely protected through the trial judge's determination of whether there is a case to answer, which is not something Strasbourg would be well placed to review. The judge's instructions to the jury also play a role in protecting the right to proof beyond reasonable doubt. Here Strasbourg has had some influence: in its case-law on inferences from silence, the Court has insisted that juries be carefully instructed.[111] However, so long as judges respect a few simple rules and use a particular form of words when directing juries on inferences from silence, there is little chance of Strasbourg intervening. It is only in relation to a third aspect of the right to proof beyond reasonable doubt that the ECtHR might exert real influence over English courts. Allocation of the burden of proof is usually regarded as being determined by the characteristics of the offence rather than by the circumstances of individual cases. This exercise is sufficiently far removed from complex factual determinations that the ECtHR could justifiably interfere with the decisions of state courts. Rather ironically, the Strasbourg Court has been far less interventionist on this issue than in relation to confrontation.[112]

Extrapolating more broadly from this chapter's analysis, it seems that epistemically-based trial rights are often poor candidates for becoming the sort of human rights that are enshrined in legal documents enforceable at the supra-national level. This implies that human rights are largely useless as a protection against false conviction—an unsettling thought for those who place significant store in human rights. But perhaps this points to one final consideration in favour of a strong right to confrontation: that however misguided conceptually, such a right is the only one worth anything at all.

[111] See, eg, *Condron v United Kingdom* (2001) 31 EHRR 1; *Beckles v United Kingdom* (2003) 36 EHRR 13.

[112] See A Stumer, *The Presumption of Innocence: Evidential and Human Rights Perspectives* (Oxford, Hart Publishing, 2010) ch 4.

13

Human Deliberation in Fact-Finding and Human Rights in the Law of Evidence

CRAIG R CALLEN

INTRODUCTION

US LAW OF Evidence scholars concern themselves with constitutional protections associated with evidentiary rules. They do not generally pose the question whether a particular procedural rule establishes a legally-cognisable 'human' right, as opposed to a moral or political right. Analysis of rights is more familiar territory to legal theorists. In *Justice for Hedgehogs*[1] Ronald Dworkin considers and rejects various standards for distinguishing human rights from political rights, including the arguments that human rights trump national sovereignty and that certain rights are especially important.[2] On Dworkin's account, human rights can be boiled down to just one basic abstract right, 'a right to be treated *as* a human being whose dignity fundamentally matters'.[3] Whilst breaches of political rights may involve injustice and moral error, violations of human rights imply nothing less than disdain for human dignity.

Hock Lai Ho, in his contribution to this collection, likewise depicts human rights as establishing fundamental minima, in the sense that they set the baseline for tolerable human conduct, not standards of excellence.[4] He characterises the presumption of innocence as a human right, since it is not merely a default rule of criminal procedure, but also a check on the executive requiring production of evidence and proof of criminal charges. In the subsequent chapter, Mike Redmayne discusses the relationship between evidence law and human rights at its most practical.[5] He argues

[1] R Dworkin, *Justice for Hedgehogs* (Cambridge, MA, Harvard UP, 2011).
[2] Ibid ch 15.
[3] Ibid 335.
[4] Chapter 11, above.
[5] Chapter 12, above.

that recognition of stronger confrontation rights in the United States and in the case-law of the European Court of Human Rights should not prompt English law to follow suit. Specifically, Redmayne argues that the right to confrontation does not require the exclusion of hearsay statements made by declarants who are genuinely unavailable at trial.

This chapter's method is exploratory and interdisciplinary. It showcases behavioural science research on human cognition and draws out the implications of this neglected perspective for legal adjudication. The analyses of Ho and Redmayne will serve as a springboard for developing my central thesis, that better understanding of human cognition would promote improved trial outcomes. We assume that courts and lay fact-finders must resolve disputed questions of fact under conditions of infinite uncertainty, and where deductive entailment is an inadequate resource for enabling them to sort and evaluate the evidence. Predictable errors occur because the law of evidence fails to recognise that common cognitive strategies used by human beings in daily life do not map well onto trials.[6] One example is systematic over-estimation of the weight of expert evidence.[7] These types of considerations are pertinent to the success of legal fact-finding regardless of a particular procedural environment's significant design features (eg whether the legal system is 'adversarial' or 'inquisitorial'; whether or not criminal procedure is (partly) constitutionalised; whether or not there is a formal hearsay rule, etc).

1. COGNITIVE REALITY OF DECISION-MAKING

Studies of human cognition offer distinctive and unique benefits for comparative or theoretical research. Some cultures have adversarial procedural systems; others do not. Some systems rely heavily on oral evidence, or on presentation of evidence and arguments within a relatively constrained time period. Others may consider adversarialism a mixed blessing at best, and juror participation in trials as misplaced amateurism. And, as comparative legal scholars know, the degree to which cultures differ in their views of authority is profound.[8] However, as this volume indicates, comparative study

[6] See eg CR Callen, 'Simpson, Fuhrman, Grice, and Character Evidence' (1996) 67 *University of Colorado Law Review* 777, 784–87; CR Callen, 'Rationality and Relevancy: Conditional Relevancy and Constrained Resources' [2003] *Michigan State Law Review* 1243, 1272–73; CR Callen, 'Hearsay and Informal Reasoning' (1994) 47 *Vanderbilt Law Review* 43, 86–89.

[7] See eg J Sanders, 'From Science to Evidence: The Testimony on Causation in the Bendectin Cases' (1993) 46 *Stanford Law Review* 1, 39–41, fn 199; E Beecher-Monas, 'Heuristics, Biases and the Importance of Gatekeeping' [2003] *Michigan State Law Review* 987, 1004–7.

[8] M Damaška, *The Faces of Justice and State Authority: A Comparative Approach to the Legal Process* (New Haven, CT, Yale UP, 1991).

may yield other insights when it operates from standpoints of commonality. Human cognitive abilities are one such source of commonality.

My focus is the extent to which the cognitive reality of decision-making (as opposed to arguments from process values or some other normative basis) may ground a right to require the adjudicator to gather or evaluate information in a particular way.[9] The argument presupposes that human cognition is basic to any fact-finding or dispute resolution process and has important ramifications for substantive as well as procedural rights. In particular, what I call the 'right to due deliberation' in criminal adjudication requires that the prosecution gather and produce sufficient evidence, and that triers of fact consider the evidence before them diligently, relative to what is at stake for the accused. To the extent that particular items of evidence could lead to error through the application of commonplace cognitive strategies, the defendant may have a right to have the adjudicator subject that evidence to special processes or even exclude the evidence on the ground that any positive contribution the evidence might make to fact-finding would probably be outweighed by its cost in terms of increased risk of inaccuracy.

The point of adjudication is to determine which parties have the substantive rights they claim, or the extent to which one party's rights should prevail. The strengths and weaknesses of the parties' claims are normally initially uncertain: no party has a right that is clearly superior to any competing claim. Prior to the point of decision-making, adjudicators *at most* can perceive the values at stake in a particular party's contentions, and the importance of the issues in light of those values and the likelihood that any facts the party alleges are true.[10] To depict the cognitive reality of adjudication we must therefore speak of the values or importance of the issues at stake in particular legal proceedings, rather than trying to specify substantive rights.

For adjudicators to treat the defendant as one whose dignity fundamentally matters[11] regard must be had to the possible importance of the claims and defences being adjudicated. Similarly, adjudicators should not use decision-making shortcuts that create unwarranted risks of error.

[9] Whether these adjudicative functions are characterised at law as 'questions of fact' or 'questions of law' raises further juridical complexities: see eg EA Scallen and AE Taslitz, 'Reading the Federal Rules of Evidence Realistically: A Response to Professor Imwinkelried' (1996) 75 *Oregon Law Review* 429, fn 54; AAS Zuckerman, 'Law, Fact or Justice?' (1986) 66 *Boston University Law Review* 487.

[10] For a related notion of cognitive importance, see N Rescher, *Cognitive Economy* (Pittsburgh, PA, University of Pittsburgh Press, 1989) 69–81. No strong claims to calculability are implied, for the reasons elucidated by G Harman, *Change in View: Principles of Reasoning* (Cambridge, MA, MIT Press, 1986) 25–27.

[11] Dworkin, above n 1, 335.

2. COGNITIVE CONSTRAINTS ON THE RATIONALITY OF DECISION-MAKERS

The most subtle, but also most powerful, constraints on human decision-makers are not limitations on their time, or material resources, but limitations on people's abilities to process information and to maintain coherent belief systems. In light of these constraints, the use of strategies to allocate cognitive resources effectively is necessary for the integrity of all human dispute resolution. Decision-makers must allocate their resources among multiple tasks and problems. Accordingly, to enhance the likelihood of accurate fact-finding, legal rules should encourage decision-makers to allocate their cognitive resources relative to the problem-solving task or tasks at hand and so that criminal verdicts are not bought at the price of prejudice to the defendant, or recklessness in regard to her interests. This responds to Dworkin's indispensible human rights criterion, that people must be treated in a manner consistent with their fundamental dignity.

Fact-finders are in a finitary predicament,[12] a situation resulting from limitations on time, information, access to further information, and cognitive resources. Constraints on the ability of the adjudicator to process and evaluate information are of critical importance. They necessarily affect decisions regarding both historical facts and interpretation of legal criteria.[13] These constraints put a premium on efficient use of scarce decision-making capacity and time. Research in cognitive psychology and related disciplines[14] reveals limits on individuals' mental ability to organise masses of data and to deploy those data to solve problems. Potential data overload constrains short-term or working memory.[15] Although one's working-memory capacity may vary according to the nature of the problem[16] and between individuals,[17] the limitations of human memory help shape the manner in which people perform any inferential task, including the interpretation of language.[18] These constraints put a premium on efficient use of scarce

[12] E Stein, *Without Good Reason: The Rationality Debate in Philosophy and Cognitive Science* (New York, OUP, 1996) 234–35.

[13] See eg JN Rakove, *Original Meanings: Politics and Ideas in the Making of the Constitution* (New York, Alfred A Knopf & Co, 1996) 8–11 (showing how differences in cognitive tasks and goals affect originalists' and historians' views of the original meaning of the US Constitution).

[14] P Thagard, *Conceptual Revolutions* (Princeton, NJ, Princeton UP, 1992).

[15] HA Simon, 'The Information Storage System Called "Human Memory"' in HA Simon (ed), *Models of Thought* (New Haven, CT, Yale UP, 1979) 62, 68.

[16] HA Simon, 'How Big is a Chunk?' in Simon (ed), ibid 50, 52.

[17] See HA Simon and WG Chase, 'The Mind's Eye in Chess' in Simon (ed), above n 15, 404, 413; H Gardner, *The Mind's New Science* (New York, Basic Books, 1985) 122; Kevin M Clermont, 'Procedure's Magic Number Three: Psychological Bases of Standards of Decision' (1987) 72 *Cornell Law Review* 1115, 1134–38.

[18] G Lakoff, *Women, Fire and Dangerous Things: What Categories Reveal about the Mind* (Chicago, University of Chicago Press, 1987) 68–78.

decision-making capacity and time, and pose the danger of inappropriate decision-making strategies. At worst these can include guesswork.

Developing strategies to deploy decision-makers' intellectual capacity most effectively should reduce inappropriate decision-making.[19] For any given task, there may, in fact, be a repertoire of suitable strategies from which decision-makers can select one or more through modification or by combination. These strategies, including the revision of failed strategies,[20] can be learnt from experience,[21] or from others.[22] For example, the cognitive trait that distinguishes chess masters[23] and physics teachers[24] from novices in their respective fields is their ability to perceive familiar patterns and use critical data to solve task-related problems. The possible lines of play on a chessboard, anticipating just the next two moves for each number on average one million; for three moves, one billion.[25] Assuming that a chess master would take 10 seconds to consider each possibility afresh, and to consider that move's effect on the opponent's next two moves, comprehensive examination of alternatives would take approximately four months.[26] Or to give an example more proximate to legal decision-making, simply checking 138 independent beliefs for logical consistency (without even attempting to use them to draw any new conclusions) would take the fastest serial computer longer than the history of the universe.[27] The ability to seize upon the critical aspect of a problem and respond effectively to

[19] C Cherniak, *Minimal Rationality* (Cambridge, MA, MIT Press, 1986) 8–12; Harman, above n 10, 5–6, 10, 26.

[20] RC Schank, *The Connoisseur's Guide to the Mind* (New York, Summit Books, 1991) 108–09; MTH Chi and R Glaser, 'Problem-Solving Ability' in RJ Sternberg (ed), *Human Abilities: An Information-Processing Approach* (New York, Freeman & Co, 1985) 227, 241; CA Perfetti, *Reading Ability* (New York, OUP, 1985) 70.

[21] See eg M Johnson, *The Body in the Mind: The Bodily Basis of Memory, Imagination and Reasoning* (Chicago, University of Chicago Press, 1987).

[22] E Goffman, *Frame Analysis: An Essay on the Organization of Experience* (London, Harper & Row, 1974) 21–39.

[23] Simon and Chase, above n 17, 404, 420.

[24] Chi and Glaser, above n 20, 243–46.

[25] HA Simon and PA Simon, 'Trial and Error Search in Solving Difficult Problems' in Simon (ed), above n 15, 175.

[26] Ibid 178. More precisely, 115.74 days of continuous analysis with no breaks whatsoever.

[27] Checking the beliefs for tautological consistency, performing each step in the time it takes a light ray to cross a proton, would take more than 20 billion years: Cherniak, above n 19, 93, 143 (fn 113). One might, of course, say that we can assume that decision-makers approximate consistency, much as one might estimate the distance to the basket when attempting to shoot a basketball into a basket. This argument would assume, though, that we must experience our decisions as sufficiently routine to be essentially self-classifying. Commodities traders or bookmakers might suffer significant losses if their quantifications of inferences related to their business were conflicting or inconsistent. It hardly follows that they would expend the effort necessary to make all their inferences pertaining to other portions of their lives consistent. CR Callen, 'Cognitive Science, Bayesian Norms and Rules of Evidence' (1991) 154 *Journal of the Royal Statistical Society (Series A)* 129.

familiar patterns is indispensable to consistent success in dealing with large amounts of data.

3. SCHEMATIC APPROACHES TO DECISION-MAKING

In assessing the efficacy of decision-makers' allocation of their decision-making resources, it is important to appreciate that they must consider not only possible inferences or inclinations but also counter-possibilities to inferences or inclinations in reaching a particular decision. Further, it is tolerably clear that decision-makers cannot, without employing appropriate strategies, consider all counter-possibilities. Even if a decision-maker had the cognitive resources to consider an infinite number of counter-possibilities,[28] practical limitations mean that he or she, like the chess master, is unlikely to do so thoroughly.

The theoretical construct of a 'schema' (plural, 'schemata') is useful for understanding how we organise knowledge in our memory into strategies for solving problems, given the evident constraints on our ability to evaluate empirical data and maintain a completely coherent belief system.[29] Schemata supply an index to our problem-solving procedures, and help us work out new protocols when necessary.[30] We employ schemata to identify permissible inferences or conclusions on given information, to discern when more information is required before reaching a decision, and to diagnose incoherence in our thought processes.[31] Schemata might be conceptualised as providing slots into which information can be fitted.[32] If enough slots are filled (or preconditions are satisfied), a particular schema becomes operative. If it is well-adapted to the problem, the applicable schema may contain or refer to a procedure for solving it. More generic schemata might simply help us to determine that we should search for certain sorts of information,[33] or that we should consider whether to employ one of a limited number of more specific cognitive strategies.

For a self-aware decision-maker, the availability of decision-making strategies is a two-edged sword. Without them, many decisions are made

[28] On the number of alternatives, see RD Friedman, 'Infinite Strands, Infinitesimally Thin: Storytelling, Bayesianism, Hearsay and Other Evidence' (1992) 14 *Cardozo Law Review* 79, 84–89.

[29] Chi and Glaser, above n 20, 241; CR Callen, 'Second-Order Considerations, Weight, Sufficiency and Schema Theory: A Comment on Professor Brilmayer's Theory' (1986) 66 *Boston University Law Review* 715, 718–22; P Thagard, *Computational Philosophy of Science* (Cambridge, MA, MIT Press, 1988) 41–42, 198–200; M Turner, *The Literary Mind* (New York, OUP, 1996).

[30] Chi and Glaser, above n 20, 241–42.

[31] Ibid 242.

[32] Perfetti, above n 20, 41–45.

[33] Chi and Glaser, above n 20, 244.

more difficult and in some contexts the resolution of complex issues with complete integrity can be impossible.[34] However, schematic short-cuts are effective, but far from fool-proof. If a decision-maker selects the wrong schema from her personalised inventory, and is determined to stick with it, then a correct decision will either be impossible or, at best, a matter of good fortune. In addition, a decision-maker relying on schemata and other cognitive short-cuts must be alert to the potential fallibility of her understanding of relevant events and of relying upon analogical reasoning to extend a strategy to a new situation.[35]

4. DUE DELIBERATION AND ADJUDICATIVE CONSTRAINTS

Having been presented with significant information, the legal fact-finder acts rationally and in accordance with a defendant's right to due deliberation if she explores counter-possibilities to the inferences the prosecution urges, to the extent that this approach is warranted by the interests at stake.[36] Those counter-possibilities may be functions of new data, or of strategies the fact-finder has not previously considered, or combinations of the two. If the fact-finder fails to explore counter-possibilities appropriately—perhaps in reliance on the wrong cognitive strategy—she violates the right to due deliberation. She may act irrationally if she fails to allocate her resources in accordance with the relative importance of the tasks at hand. Finally, in the context of an episodic trial on the civilian procedural model, a decision-maker might reasonably conclude that the best use of her resources is to suspend judgment pending the acquisition of further information.[37]

It is one thing to say that people who use the sorts of reasoning strategies sketched above succeed in solving problems in their daily life. It is quite another to say that the same approach would be appropriate to decision-making that: (i) involves the rights and interests of other people and is determined according to criteria that may be subject to competing interpretations; (ii) must be based on incomplete information; and (iii) dramatically affects third parties if the decision-maker chooses to employ more thorough, elaborate or time-consuming processes.

Dworkin argues that denial of substantive rights through procedural failings constitutes moral harm; or at the least, failure by the adjudicator to accord the claimant equal treatment in the application of a particular legal

[34] Cf E Kades, 'The Laws of Complexity and the Complexity of Laws: The Implications of Computational Complexity Theory for the Law' (1997) 40 *Rutgers Law Review* 403, 481–84.

[35] R Sunstein, *Legal Reasoning and Political Conflict* (New York, OUP, 1996) 72–74.

[36] Ibid 102–03.

[37] P Thagard, 'Defending Explanatory Coherence' (1991) 14 *Behavioral & Brain Science* 745, 746.

standard.[38] One might, of course, disagree with Dworkin's notions about moral harm, but they usefully illustrate an important point. In the absence of any rule or determinate norms to guide or regulate cognitive processes in fact-finding, adjudicators would be free to utilise reasoning procedures that give short shrift to whatever values particular substantive rights entail. And that would be contrary to Dworkin's conception of the basic human right to dignity. In a context where some form of harm might follow from incorrect adjudication of a claim of right, an adjudicator's failure to conduct her decision-making process in light of the possible harm that might flow from incorrectly deciding the claim would, in effect, permit her to disregard that harm, or to employ some idiosyncratic reasoning strategy that was inappropriate in light of the stakes.[39]

Even so, there are limits on the resources we can expend on a particular trial. When there are competing claims on our cognitive resources, we must seek strategies not only for solving individual problems taken in isolation, but also for apportioning resources among multiple problems. It is unlikely that we can even state the expected utility of various decisions or resources with precision.[40] Be that as it may, the limits and conflicting demands upon our resources still imply that judges should employ those resources (and guide jurors' allocation of them) in light of the importance of the issues to be determined in the instant case and with attention to conserving resources for competing claims still awaiting adjudication.

5. A LEGAL RIGHT TO DUE DELIBERATION

Once proffered evidence or inferences satisfy threshold requirements of value or importance, the right to due deliberation entitles one to expect that an adjudicator will consider them to the extent warranted by the importance of the question on which they bear. One should be entitled to expect more thorough evidence-gathering and deliberation when more significant rights or interests are at stake, and somewhat less in other contexts.

Under the right to due deliberation, a criminal defendant is entitled to have the adjudicator consider whether the arguments and evidence advanced by the prosecution warrant a conviction in light of pertinent counter-possibilities consistent with innocence, and with scrutiny reflecting the importance of the claim or defence in question. This specification of the right to due deliberation is consistent with Dworkin's contention

[38] R Dworkin, *A Matter of Principle* (Cambridge, MA, Harvard UP, 1985) 80.

[39] A Stein, 'The Refoundation of Evidence Law' (1996) 9 *Canadian Journal of Law & Jurisprudence* 279, 287.

[40] Cf JL Mashaw, 'The Supreme Court's Due Process Calculus for Administrative Adjudication in *Mathews v Eldridge*: Three Factors in Search of a Theory of Value' (1976) 44 *University of Chicago Law Review* 28, 47–49.

that human rights require that people not be punished 'except through procedures reasonably well calculated to protect the innocent'.[41]

Any number of evidentiary rules in adversarial jurisdictions reflect a desire that fact-finders be as completely well-informed as reasonably possible, not only in the sense that they should be provided with all worthwhile information, but also that they should receive second-order information about the probative worth of at least some of the evidence adduced in the trial.[42] Factual pre-conditions for the admission of evidence normally require proof that proffered evidence has sufficient probative value to make its reception worthwhile, that it will assist in the evaluation of other evidence, or both.[43] To similar effect, the best evidence or original document rule creates an incentive for production of an original or authentic duplicate,[44] which makes accurate evaluation of the document less complex[45] and corroborates the proffering party's claims for its provenance, which in turn serve to reassure the court that evaluation of the document is warranted by its importance for one or more issues at trial.

However, the right to due deliberation does not rest entirely or even predominantly on its implicit grounding in conventional evidentiary doctrine. Regard should also be had to the incentive structures created by particular legal systems. The parties likely to be most directly and seriously affected by the outcome of litigation have the strongest incentives to provide relevant information to the court.[46] Unless restrained by procedural requirements, adjudicators might rely on their own assessments of competing interests in deciding how thoroughly to consider a particular outcome, and its alternatives. However, as Judge Posner pointed out, when the value of additional evidence to the litigants is not equal to its value for society, over- or under-investment in litigation is the predictable result, with consequential impacts on accuracy and deterrence. In party-driven jury systems, rules of evidence can mitigate incentives to over- or under-invest in evidence gathering and evaluation,[47] as do requirements for special findings in judge-driven systems.[48]

Further support for the right to due deliberation comes from research concluding that fact-finders appraise the significance of evidence, and decide

[41] Dworkin, above n 1, 337.

[42] See eg DA Nance, 'The Best Evidence Principle' (1998) 73 *Iowa Law Review* 227; CR Callen, 'Hearsay and Informal Reasoning', above n 6, 96–97.

[43] CR Callen, 'Rationality and Relevancy', above n 6, 1282.

[44] For example, Federal Rules of Evidence 1001–2.

[45] If the document is the original, evidence to undermine its authenticity is unlikely to exist, making the trier's evaluation simpler on that ground, if for no other.

[46] HA Simon, *Reason in Human Affairs* (Stanford, CA, Stanford UP, 1983) 90–91.

[47] See RA Posner, *Frontiers of Legal Theory* (Cambridge, MA, Harvard UP, 2001) 386–408.

[48] CR Callen, 'Cognitive Strategies and Models of Fact-Finding' in J Jackson, M Langer and P Tillers (eds), *Crime, Procedure and Evidence in a Comparative and International Context* (Oxford, Hart Publishing, 2008) 165, 172–73.

questions of fact, by forming stories. Story formation is an appealing explanation of how jurors find facts—empirical data, anecdote and intuition all seem to support the idea that jurors generally find in favour of the party advancing what jurors take to be the best story.[49] Jurors assess evidentiary completeness,[50] amongst other things, in deciding whether to rely on a particular story, drawing on their common sense notions of causation and motivation.[51]

Judge-driven systems of legal adjudication typically do not rule evidence inadmissible, in the sense of precluding access to it by the fact-finder. Instead, they preclude the court from relying on suspect categories of evidence in preparing written findings of fact,[52] or require special justifications for reliance on the evidence.[53] To the extent that evidence law authorises the use of evidence which is insufficiently probative to justify its cost to the court in terms of its expenditure of decision-makers' cognitive resources,[54] it is in tension with the right to due deliberation. Where professional judges are required to make written findings of fact subject to *de novo* review,[55] these safeguards may ameliorate the problem such that a reasonable observer could still say that the system as a whole satisfied Dworkin's standard for compliance with human rights. For special problems associated with particular kinds of evidence, such as hearsay, reviewing courts in judge-driven systems may apply stricter standards, eg a German judge who relies on hearsay without examining the original declarant faces an uphill battle to prepare findings that will satisfy a higher court that such reliance was justified.[56] Party-driven common law adjudication, by contrast, has typically employed exclusionary rules to deal with problematic evidence. Accordingly, we can usefully refer generically to 'special evidentiary measures' to cover a range of legal techniques that have been devised to handle suspect forms of evidence in different legal systems.

[49] See eg Turner, above n 29; RJ Allen, 'A Reconceptualization of Civil Trials' (1986) 66 *Boston University Law Review* 401, 425–34; RJ Allen, 'The Nature of Juridical Proof' (1991) 13 *Cardozo Law Review* 373, 409–10; A Stein, 'The Refoundation of Evidence Law', above n 39.

[50] N Pennington and R Hastie, 'Explanation-Based Decision Making: Effects of Memory Structure on Judgment' (1988) 14 *Journal of Experimental Psychology: Learning, Memory and Cognition* 521, 522.

[51] N Pennington and R Hastie, 'Evidence Evaluation in Complex Decision Making' (1986) 51 *Journal of Personality and Social Psychology* 242, 244–45. For a practical legal illustration, see *St Mary's Honor Center v Hicks*, 509 US 502 (1993).

[52] See eg JF Nijboer, 'The Law of Evidence in Criminal Cases (Netherlands)' in JF Nijboer, CR Callen and N Kwak (eds), *Forensic Expertise and the Law of Evidence* (Amsterdam, Elsevier Science & Technology, 1993) 63, 64–65.

[53] M Damaška, 'Of Hearsay and its Analogues' (1992) 76 *Minnesota Law Review* 425, 454.

[54] Evidence may adversely affect fact-finding if it wastes resources, confuses or prejudices the fact finder, or unduly complicates her task—all of which may impair accuracy: see RA Posner, *Frontiers of Legal Theory* (Cambridge, MA, Harvard UP, 2001) 340–43, 386–408.

[55] See MR Damaška, *Evidence Law Adrift* (New Haven, CT, Yale UP, 1997) 45, 50, 64.

[56] Damaška, above n 53, 454.

6. DUE DELIBERATION AND THE PRESUMPTION OF INNOCENCE

The 'beyond reasonable doubt' standard of proof in Anglo-American criminal law is closely related to the right to deliberation. Of course, a demanding standard of proof is necessary in criminal cases because, for deontological or utilitarian reasons, a wrongful conviction is conventionally regarded as more regrettable than a wrongful acquittal.[57] A requirement that the verdict of guilty be established beyond reasonable doubt requires a finding of innocence not only when the jury or court believes the defendant is actually innocent, but also when it believes that the defendant might well be guilty but the prosecution's evidence is insufficient to prove it to the required legal standard. While the fact-finder's obligation to consider counter-possibilities to the prosecution's case follows directly from the same cognitive concerns animating the right to due deliberation, the 'reasonable doubt' standard is a specific instantiation of the right to deliberation for criminal cases (as is the *conviction intime* standard adopted in the civilian legal tradition).

In his contribution to this volume, Hock Lai Ho argues that the presumption of innocence, embraced in all modern legal systems, is a check on executive action, requiring the prosecution to prove the defendant's guilt of the crime charged, rather than, for example, relying on mere background suspicions, such as the general likelihood that defendants arrested by the police are guilty. Ho's analysis implicitly recognises that fact-finders are active decision-makers, in the sense that they ordinarily employ the indispensable cognitive strategy of bringing information from their everyday experience into play in criminal adjudication. In delineating the effect of the presumption on evidentiary requirements, he invokes the celebrated decision in *Woolmington*[58] and quotes Lord Diplock in *Ong Ah Chuan* for the proposition that,

> [o]ne of the fundamental rules of natural justice in the field of criminal law is that a person should not be punished for an offence unless it has been established to the satisfaction of an independent and unbiased tribunal that he committed it.[59]

The phrase 'established to the satisfaction' is an important link to what studies of cognition tell us about decision-making.

To illustrate, suppose that, having heard all the evidence presented at trial, a juror prone to think in quantities estimated the probability of the prosecution's case being true as 45%, the probability of the defendant's case being true as 4.5%, but the probability of some other explanation for the disputed events being true as 50.5%. Even though this juror regards the prosecution's theory of the case as being 10 times more credible than the defendant's, almost any notion of *proof* would hold that the juror should

[57] Stein, above n 39, 324–25.
[58] [1935] AC 462, HL.
[59] Ho, 267, above.

vote to acquit. Our juror, after all, has concluded that a third possibility supplies a more persuasive explanation of the evidence than the theory of guilt advanced by the prosecution.

Ho's thesis seems to require that, before convicting, the trier of fact must have at least considered and discarded theories inconsistent with guilt to the extent warranted by the rights at stake in the prosecution. Litigants enjoying advantages of wealth and high-quality counsel are obviously better able to generate information—such as expert testimony on the cause of accidents or computerised reconstructions of murder scenes—than their poorer or less advantaged opponents.[60] Hence, a standard simply comparing the strength of each side's evidence and arguments would favour those with greater power or wealth—typically the prosecutor in criminal litigation. And although some scholars assume that parties will not go to the trouble of generating evidence or advancing arguments that are strictly redundant, empirical studies indicate that parties are often motivated to offer redundant evidence in order to 'make certain facts *seem* intuitively more probable, even though [the evidence] does not increase their likelihood'.[61] So, differential access to data, or variable ability to produce data on demand, may well affect the result of adjudication if it is reached without regard to the completeness of evidence, that is, on the relative likelihood of the contentions of the prosecution and defence, without considering whether the prosecution has justified conviction to the requisite normative standard of proof.

Ho's chapter also acknowledges that concepts such as burden of proof do not always cohere as smoothly with judge-driven 'inquisitorial' fact-finding as they do with adjudication in party-driven, 'adversarial' systems. Viewed in the round, Ho's analysis of the presumption of innocence fits well with the concept and rationale of a right to deliberation.

Acceptance of the idea that adjudicators ought to attend to the completeness of evidence and argument in rendering decisions, taken in conjunction with the burden of proof, strongly implies that they ought to refrain from convicting any defendant on the basis of evidence which is recognised to be epistemically deficient. Where the legal system employs episodic proceedings over an extended period of time, it can accommodate the suspension of a decision with relative ease. In adversarial systems, where trials are continuous and generally limited to a few days or weeks, temporary suspension is trickier. In these contexts preliminary determinations of insufficiency of evidence or directed verdicts of acquittal make the continuous trial much more workable.

[60] RJ Allen, 'A Reconceptualization of Civil Trials', above n 49.

[61] MJ Saks and RF Kidd, 'Human Information Processing and Adjudication: Trial by Heuristics' (1980) 15 *Law & Society Review* 123, 136–37.

7. CONFRONTATION AND DELIBERATION

Mike Redmayne's chapter in this volume addresses an issue with a somewhat more uncertain relationship to Dworkin's test of respect for dignity. The right to confrontation is both conceptually indeterminate and, particularly in the United States, subject to rapid doctrinal development, sparked off by the Supreme Court's landmark decision in *Crawford v Washington*.[62] Redmayne falls back on a standard argument in the theory of evidence: that increasing the volume of relevant evidence available to the fact-finder should improve the accuracy of decision-making.[63] Taken at face value, that assumption would imply that whenever the prosecution proffers relevant evidence in good faith to which the defence objects on purely epistemic grounds, its admission could only, at worst, reflect the court's erroneous evaluation of probative value. There could be no question of exhibiting the type of contempt for dignity associated with Dworkinian human rights. But perhaps it might still be said that the epistemic infirmities of certain kinds of evidence necessitate special evidentiary measures, possibly falling short of outright exclusion?

Redmayne is sceptical of the notion that hearsay evidence should be excluded because jurors are likely to over-value it.[64] Yet, empirical research suggests two separate cognitive mechanisms that may incline jurors to be excessively influenced by hearsay if the danger is left unmitigated by special evidentiary measures. In a landmark article, Gilbert (following the Dutch philosopher Spinoza) suggests that there is no firm boundary between comprehension of a proposition and its evaluation.[65] Comprehension of an idea involves the formation of a belief in that idea, if only for a short time. Although an idea might ultimately be rejected, it is cognitively more difficult to reject a belief than to form it in the first place.[66] This asymmetry skews cognitive processes toward confirmation of initial information. Researchers have found that subjects presented with 'mere possibilities' tended to seek out confirmatory information. When experimenters offered subjects a proposition together with its negation, the tendency was eliminated.[67]

Gilbert surmised that cognition developed on the model of perception. Animals do not generally question the accuracy of what they perceive, since perceptions are generally sufficiently accurate most of the time to warrant reliance on their accuracy across the board. Likewise, provided that one is

[62] 541 US 36 (2004). Now also see *Michigan v Bryant*, 131 S Ct 1143, 179 L Ed 2d 93 (2011) (listing hearsay exceptions with pre-conditions indicating presumptive reliability, seemingly at odds with the Court's previous criticisms of such *ex ante* assumptions).

[63] Redmayne, 300–1, above.

[64] Ibid 300.

[65] DT Gilbert, 'How Mental Systems Believe' (1991) 46 *American Psychologist* 107, 108.

[66] Ibid 110–13.

[67] Ibid 115–16.

dealing in ordinary contexts with information that has been pre-vetted or tested in some way, as opposed to merely speculative possibilities, Gilbert proposed that focusing on confirmatory information is 'subjectively more informing' than agnosticism.[68] Confirmatory focus, or 'search', should increase the prospects for an accurate decision. Consider a prosecution for robbery, in which the fact-finder is presented with evidence suggesting that the defendant was 'casing' the store on the day before the robbery. In the light of this initial suspicion, looking for confirmatory information seems to offer the most efficient fact-finding strategy. The fact-finder's attention might now focus on, for example, whether the reported suspicious activity was in fact 'casing' and not innocuous window-shopping; whether the person allegedly casing the store was this defendant now on trial; whether the defendant's protestations of innocence are corroborated by other reliable evidence, and so on. Gilbert concluded that confirmatory search is an efficient cognitive strategy. 'One might even argue', he suggested, 'that the savings of time and energy outweighs the intellectual deficits of inaccurate beliefs'.[69]

Although Gilbert's work does not map seamlessly onto criminal prosecutions, its extrapolation to legal fact-finding does helpfully illuminate how cross-examination might prevent or mitigate confirmatory tendencies in human cognition that might otherwise cause jurors to be prejudiced and to under-invest cognitive resources in finding facts. For example, the confirmation-orientation of ordinary cognitive processing reinforces the importance of cross-examining prosecution witnesses in criminal trials in order to expose jurors to alternative hypotheses and counter-possibilities. Perhaps we should up-date Wigmore's famous assertion that '[c]ross-examination is the greatest legal engine … for the discovery of truth'[70] to add that cross-examination may also serve to pre-empt insufficiently critical reliance on the prosecution's evidence. Of course, the greater part of the evidence and the arguments offered in a trial will obviously be in dispute from the outset. But all admissible evidence imparts new information, and this may be a legitimate cause for concern in relation to hearsay evidence which might evade or frustrate cross-examination. In extreme cases, untested hearsay could be the 'sole or decisive basis' for a conviction, enough to trigger a breach of the European Court of Human Rights' confrontation standards.[71]

Another valuable interdisciplinary perspective on legal problems of hearsay and confrontation is contributed by Wilson and Sperber's simplified

[68] Ibid 115.

[69] Ibid 116.

[70] JH Chadbourn (ed), *Wigmore on Evidence* (Boston, Little, Brown & Co, 1974) vol 5, § 1367, 32.

[71] See *Al-Khawaja and Tahery v United Kingdom* (2009) 49 EHRR 1.

Gricean explanation of the strategies on which we rely in interpreting and evaluating conversations. Communication, on this account, employs not only words, symbols or actions, but also two implicit claims. The first claim is that the information being conveyed is worth the hearer's attention and the effort required to process it.[72] Information benefits the hearer to the extent that it contributes to his existing knowledge or helps him to make decisions with less effort. Even being reminded of something one already knows, such as 'Remember, you have a dental appointment tomorrow', reduces the cognitive effort necessary to recall it.[73] Moreover, to the extent that memory 'recall' is more akin to reconstruction than simple retrieval,[74] an ostensible reminder or implicit assumption may convey information that is, for most practical purposes, new to the hearer, effectively something that the speaker reconstructed for the purpose. It is normally rational to rely on such communications, the assumption being that the speaker would not articulate the reminder unless the benefits of the information merited the hearer's attention.

The second implicit conversational claim proposed by Wilson and Sperber is that the form in which the speaker conveys the information will produce the greatest possible excess of benefits over costs consistent with the hearer's interests.[75] In other words, regardless of whether the speaker expresses herself ironically, loosely, indirectly, or figuratively, she need not specify all the messages that she wishes to convey, so long as what she does say, taken with the implicit claims, would lead the intended hearers to infer the content of her message. Consider the classic hypothetical[76] 'Don't worry, I didn't tell them anything about you', whispered by *D1* to *D2* in the corridors of a police station. The prosecution offers the statement in prosecuting *D2* for masterminding a blackmail scheme in which *D1* also participated. The literal meaning and implications of the statement are evidently ambiguous: *D1* might have been seeking to convey that he did not reveal inculpatory information about *D2*, or *D1* might be seeking to threaten *D2* by hinting at the possibility of later revelations, or thirdly, *D1* might simply be conveying the fact that *D2*'s name hadn't come up during conversation. The prosecution's theory of relevance implicitly relies directly on Wilson and Sperber's second maxim: the most obvious reason for making such a cryptic statement, and the thing that *D2* would most urgently want and need to know if indeed he were guilty of blackmail, is that his

[72] D Wilson and D Sperber, 'Truthfulness and Relevance' (2002) 111 *Mind* 583, 604.

[73] D Wilson and D Sperber, *Relevance: Communication and Cognition*, 2nd edn (Oxford, Blackwell Publishers, 1995) 149–50.

[74] I Rosenfeld, *The Invention of Memory: A New View of the Brain* (New York, Basic Books, 1988) 192–93.

[75] Wilson and Sperber, above n 72, 604: 'Every utterance conveys a presumption of its own optimal relevance'.

[76] Based on *United States v Reynolds*, 715 F 2d 99 (3d Cir 1983).

erstwhile accomplice had not already betrayed him to the police. Notice how this analysis turns on the likelihood that *D2* had reason to be concerned about his implication in the blackmail as a basis for inferring what *D2* most urgently wanted to know. Alternatively, *D1* might have made the statement to reassure an anxious *D2* that *D1* knew nothing harmful or even as ironic mockery of the very idea that *D2* could have been involved.

To weigh hearsay in accordance with the right to due deliberation, one would need to assess not only the degree to which the original declarant (or declarants) complied with the two implicit claims for communication, but also whether the prosecution is doing so when it adduces the evidence in court. Hearers, including fact-finders, will rely on the information they have at their disposal and the speaker's implicit claims in order to interpret and evaluate any of her communications. If evidence law admitted hearsay freely, triers of fact would predictably rely on cognitive strategies, such as Wilson and Sperber's maxims, that save cognitive effort but have serious potential to mislead. This detour into linguistics sheds new light on the law's traditional suspicion of hearsay evidence.

The classic common law exclusionary rule admits hearsay only when it is accompanied by foundational information facilitating its accurate assessment, either by (i) prompting jurors that they must satisfy themselves of the statement's compliance with standard conversational maxims rather than relying on complacent assumptions, or at least (ii) suggesting that hearsay is sufficiently probative to justify the risks inherent in receiving it.[77] The common law's default setting is that the proponent of hearsay must call the declarant to testify directly to the original statement and undergo cross-examination to verify her compliance with the two maxims or expose her non-compliance, as the case may be.

Redmayne concludes that the right to confrontation should not bar admission of hearsay statements where the declarant is genuinely unavailable. He argues that such hearsay statements warrant admission, even if traditional cross-examination is impossible, because the more evidence available to the fact-finder, the better. At first blush, that is reminiscent of the broader contention that fact-finding necessarily improves with increased access to relevant evidence, which is deeply problematic from a cognitive perspective. Trying to take account of all evidence potentially relevant under a minimal standard, such as US Federal Rule of Evidence 401, would so far exceed human cognitive capacity as to be utterly impractical. Risinger ridicules the cognitive gluttony implicit in such arguments as presupposing the 'god perspective'.[78] Redmayne may be thinking in terms of hearsay evidence

[77] Callen, 'Hearsay and Informal Reasoning', above n 6, 96–100.

[78] DM Risinger, 'Inquiry, Relevance, Rules of Admission, and Evidentiary Reform' (2010) 75 *Brooklyn Law Review* 1349, 1353-4. Also see Callen, 'Rationality and Relevancy', above n 6, 1262–63, 1274–78.

with more than minimal probative value, an assumption which ameliorates the objection but does not refute it. Cognitive limitations exert subtle and powerful effects on fact-finders, potentially resulting in over-weighing of all kinds of evidence, including evidence with significant probative value. Moreover, evidentiary 'reliability' is a troublesome legal concept. The question of whether witnesses, documents or objects are reliable evidence of facts in issue is determined in the trial process by the fact-finder, not resolved *ex ante* by judicial presumption. US experience is that courts exploit the concept of 'reliability' to expand hearsay exceptions and thereby erode the exclusionary rule.[79]

Redmayne still maintains that any reasonably available witness should be produced when their statements fall within the scope of the confrontation right, eg the maker of a 'testimonial' statement under *Crawford*.[80] He analyses the right in epistemic terms.[81] Translated into my conceptual language, Redmayne's argument is basically that the benefits of live testimony and cross-examination at trial in comparison to hearsay outweigh the costs of producing an available witness. When it comes to carving out exceptions for unavailable declarants, Redmayne is somewhat sceptical of the importance attached to cross-examination in confrontation case-law. Invoking an analogy to delayed prosecutions, he asserts that 'cross-examination is not significant in itself, but only one means of resolving (or not) questions about the evidential sufficiency of the prosecution's case'.[82]

This line of reasoning might be counter-posed to Justice Scalia's assertion in *Crawford*, that the Sixth Amendment Confrontation Clause 'commands, not that evidence be reliable, but that reliability be assessed in a particular manner: by testing in the crucible of cross-examination'.[83] One might readily infer from this passage that the Court is unwilling to assume that 'testimonial' hearsay within *Crawford* merits admission in the absence of cross-examination. This approach derives epistemological support both from Gilbert's suggestion that comprehension implies acceptance,[84] and also from the propensity of the cognitive strategies described by Wilson and Sperber to mislead fact-finders into drawing mistaken inferences about the meaning and value of out-of-court statements adduced as hearsay.

[79] E Swift, 'The Hearsay Rule at Work: Has It Been Abolished De Facto by Judicial Decision?' (1992) 76 *Minnesota Law Review* 473.

[80] *Crawford v Washington*, 541 US 36 (2004).

[81] Redmayne, 303–4, 306, above.

[82] Ibid 303.

[83] *Crawford v Washington*, 541 US 36, 61 (2004). However, *Michigan v Bryant*, 131 S Ct 1143, 179 L Ed 2d 93 (2011) seems to say that excited utterances are *ex ante* reliable.

[84] See above nn 65–69 and accompanying text.

CONCLUSION

The process of decision-making in adjudication is fundamentally a cognitive process. If legal rights, including human rights, are to be more than mere abstractions, they must be enforced by humans. Decision-making in adjudication is constrained in various ways. In this chapter I have concentrated on the notable limitations imposed by people's cognitive capacities for organising and processing information. Knowledge of how humans make decisions can help us to determine the nature and extent of human rights in the adjudicative process. Failure to utilise that knowledge represents a missed opportunity to develop legal procedures that are well-calibrated to protect human rights, and indeed all substantive legal rights, effectively. Legal processes insensitive to the epistemic and cognitive realities of adjudication will probably either allocate too few resources to litigating particular rights claims, or allocate so many resources to some claims that other rights are consequently in danger of being deprived of effective enforcement.

The right to due deliberation championed in this chapter is grounded in what we have learned so far from the behavioural and cognitive sciences, linguistics and related disciplines about human information processing, inferential reasoning, and decision-making. The right to due deliberation, requiring cognitive effort on the part of the fact-finder to analyse evidence bearing on disputed factual issues commensurate with what is at stake in the litigation, is a necessary precondition of treating defendants as persons whose dignity is worthy of respect. Conceived in that way, it is a human right as Dworkin sees human rights. But in any event, the right to due deliberation should be recognised and enforced as an essential procedural right in all systems of adjudication.

Developing, by way of illustration, discussions of the presumption of innocence and the right to confrontation begun by other contributors to this volume, we have seen how the concept of a right to due deliberation can enrich conventional understandings of legal process, evidence law, fact-finding and proof.

14

Reliability, Hearsay and the Right to a Fair Trial in New Zealand

CHRIS GALLAVIN

INTRODUCTION

THE ADMISSION OF statements of absent witnesses in criminal trials has long posed difficult questions of relevance, reliability, probative value, illegitimate prejudice and fairness. This chapter will focus, in particular, on New Zealand's reliability-based exception to the hearsay exclusionary rule, which is now contained in the Evidence Act 2006 (NZ). New Zealand's reformed law will be reconsidered in the light of underlying rationales for the common law's traditional hearsay prohibition and comparative approaches to admitting 'reliable' hearsay. It will be argued that the approach to admissibility developed by the Canadian courts, in particular, provides a promising model for statutory interpretation in New Zealand.

The law of hearsay in New Zealand diverges from other common law jurisdictions not only in its doctrinal details, but also owing to the potential significance of a defendant's right to cross-examine witnesses under section 25(f) of the New Zealand Bill of Rights Act 1990. If any reliability-based exception to the hearsay prohibition is too lax, evidence may be admitted in breach of the defendant's right to a fair trial. The remedy lies in adopting an approach to the reliability provision, section 18, ensuring *actual* reliability rather than merely rudimentary circumstantial reliability or in enabling the fact-finder to assess reliability independently of cross-examination. This approach emphasises the primary importance of reliability as the test for the admission of hearsay and limits the role of judicial discretion to admit evidence on a nebulous balancing of probative value and unfair prejudice. It also assists in the identification of a clear burden and standard of proof to be applied to the test of reliability.

1. HEARSAY EXCEPTIONS AND FAIR TRIAL RIGHTS IN NEW ZEALAND

The New Zealand Bill of Rights Act 1990 (NZBORA) was passed in fulfilment of New Zealand's obligations as a state party to the International Covenant on Civil and Political Rights (ICCPR), and after extensive local discussion and debate. The operational provisions of NZBORA juggle ultimately irreconcilable notions of supreme law and neo-Diceyan subservience to parliamentary sovereignty. The NZBORA is not supreme law, since legislation inconsistent with protected rights remains in force and must still be applied by the courts.[1] Unlike its UK counterpart, there is no express provision for a 'declaration of incompatibility' under NZBORA. However, section 5 provides that the rights and freedoms contained within NZBORA are subject 'only to such reasonable limits prescribed by law as can be demonstrably justified in a free and democratic society'.[2] Section 6 additionally requires that legislation, wherever possible, should be read consistently with the rights guaranteed by NZBORA.

A criminal defendant's right to fair trial is set out in section 25 of NZBORA, which replicates Article 14 of the ICCPR. The particular aspect of the right to a fair trial which directly overlaps with the hearsay prohibition is contained in section 25(f), providing that:

> Everyone who is charged with an offence has, in relation to the determination of the charge, the following minimum rights:
>
> ...
>
> (f) The right to examine the witnesses for the prosecution and to obtain the attendance and examination of witnesses for the defence under the same conditions as the prosecution.

This wording plainly echoes Article 6(3)(d) of the ECHR, which is extensively canvassed by other contributors to this volume.[3] And like its international counterparts, section 25(f) does not confer an absolute right to cross-examine all prosecution witnesses.[4] However, any admission of the

[1] NZBORA 1990, s 4 'anticipates the lawful passage and dutiful application of legislation which is not reasonable in a free and democratic society': P Rishworth, 'Lord Cooke and the Bill of Rights' in P Rishworth (ed), *The Struggle for Simplicity in the Law: Essays for Lord Cooke of Thorndon* (Wellington, Butterworths, 1997) 296.

[2] For further discussion of the controversial relationship between ss 4, 5 and 6, see P Rishworth, 'Reflections on the Bill of Rights after *Quilter v Attorney-General*' [1988] *New Zealand Law Review* 683, 691; F Brookfield, 'Parliament, the Treaty, and Freedom. Millennial Hopes and Speculations' in P Joseph (ed), *Essays on the Constitution* (Wellington, Brookers, 1995) 42; F Brookfield, 'Constitutional Law' [1993] NZRLR 278; and the leading Supreme Court decision of *R v Hansen* [2007] 3 NZLR 1.

[3] See, in particular, the essays by Ashworth (Chapter 6), Redmayne (Chapter 12), Callen (Chapter 13) and Henning and Hunter (Chapter 15).

[4] NZBORA 1990, s 5.

hearsay statement of an absent witness potentially engages section 25(f), including the reliability-based exception to the hearsay prohibition now contained in the New Zealand Evidence Act 2006. Limitations on the rule against hearsay are limitations on the right to cross-examine. The reliability exception under section 18 is one such limitation.

2. HEARSAY REFORM IN NEW ZEALAND

In 1989 the New Zealand Law Commission concluded that the hearsay rule and its exceptions were 'unclear, inconsistent, and lacking in coherence'.[5] Reform of the hearsay rule in New Zealand was undertaken as a part of a wide-ranging 17-year review of all aspects of evidence law. Rationalisation in pursuit of more extensive admissibility of relevant and probative material was the guiding principle. Rules of inadmissibility were to be retained only where strictly justified by clearly articulated public policy considerations. Against this backdrop, section 17 of the Evidence Act 2006 retained the traditional common law exclusionary rule as a mechanism for protecting a criminal defendant's right to cross-examine witnesses, but only in a depleted form, subject to new and potentially sweeping inclusionary exceptions.

The Evidence Act 2006 takes prior statements of witnesses appearing at trial[6] and implied assertions[7] entirely outside the scope of the hearsay prohibition. Moreover, in addition to retaining established hearsay exceptions,[8] section 18 of the 2006 Act created a new general reliability exception applicable where the circumstances indicate a 'reasonable assurance' that the statement is reliable and the originating witness is unavailable.[9] Apart from the use of the word 'reasonable', no indication is given of the standard of proof to be applied to the test of reliability. The exception is seemingly drafted to apply to all forms of hearsay evidence and is not merely an inclusionary remedy of last resort.[10] Pursuant to section 16, the

[5] New Zealand Law Commission, *Hearsay Evidence: An Options Paper*, PP10 (Wellington, 1989) vi.

[6] 'Hearsay Statement' is defined under s 4 as a statement; '(a) … made by a person other than a witness…' (emphasis added).

[7] 'Statement' is defined under s 4 as meaning '(a) a spoken or written assertion by a person of any matter; or (b) non-verbal conduct of a person that is intended by that person as an assertion of any matter'. Cf uniform Evidence Acts (Australia), s 59(1).

[8] Covering, eg, business records (s 19), proof of convictions, acquittals, and other judicial proceedings (s 139), and proof of conviction by fingerprints (s 140).

[9] A reform first suggested in NZLC *Evidence Law: Hearsay: A Discussion Paper*, PP15 (Wellington, 1991) 17.

[10] The marginal note to s 18 reads, 'General Admission of Hearsay Evidence'. Section 18 also subsumes the previous *res gestae* exception, see *Carr v Amber Homes Ltd* (2009) 19 PRNZ 422, [23] per Duffy J.

'circumstances' capable of constituting 'reasonable assurance of reliability' include:[11]

(a) the nature of the statement; and
(b) the contents of the statement; and
(c) the circumstances that relate to the making of the statement; and
(d) any circumstances that relate to the veracity of the person; and
(e) any circumstances that relate to the accuracy of the observation of the person.

Section 18's dedicated reliability-based hearsay exception is buttressed by a general probative value/prejudicial effect admissibility standard, contained in section 8, which—alongside the threshold test of relevance[12]—underpins the entire Act. In determining whether probative value outweighs potential unfair prejudice in the instant case, the attention of the court is specifically drawn to whether a criminal defendant will be able to offer an effective defence at trial.[13]

In summary, the admissibility in New Zealand criminal trials of ostensibly reliable hearsay evidence is determined in the following way. First, the evidence must necessarily be relevant pursuant to section 7. Secondly, assuming that relevant evidence fits the definition of hearsay and no dedicated inclusionary exceptions apply, one must then consider whether the circumstances of the case provide a reasonable assurance of reliability, in satisfaction of section 18. Thirdly, either the statement-maker must be unavailable, or requiring live testimony would occasion undue expense and delay.[14] Finally, section 8's general exclusionary test of probative value versus illegitimate prejudice must be satisfied, including explicit consideration of the defendant's ability to offer an effective defence.

Two additional procedural rules apply to such evidence. First, pre-trial notice of an intention to adduce a hearsay statement must be served on all the parties.[15] Secondly, when adduced at trial under section 18 'reliable hearsay' may be subject to a judicial warning expressly inviting the jury to consider whether to accept the evidence and, if they do accept it, the weight it should be given.[16]

[11] 'Unavailable witness' is also defined under s 16, and notably excludes fearful, but otherwise available, witnesses: cf the corresponding English provision, Criminal Justice Act 2003, s 116(2), paragraph (e) of which covers fearful witnesses.

[12] Section 7 provides that all relevant evidence is presumptively admissible, subject to statutory exclusionary rules.

[13] Evidence Act 2006, s 8(2).

[14] Evidence Act 2006, s 18(1)(b)(i) and (ii).

[15] Unless waived by agreement of all the parties or dispensed with by the judge: Evidence Act 2006, s 22.

[16] Evidence Act 2006, s 122.

3. TRADITIONAL RATIONALES FOR EXCLUDING HEARSAY

The common law's traditional hearsay prohibition can be rationalised as an attempt to ensure that adversarial process honours several underlying or 'foundational' principles. At a general level of abstraction these principles are: truth, the protection of the innocent, the importance of liberty, ensuring humane treatment and maintaining procedural integrity.[17] If evidence incapable of being tested were routinely admitted a defendant's ability to offer an effective defence could be unjustly limited, as a defendant's primary method of challenge would have been removed.[18] The fact-finder's ability to assess reliability and assign weight would also be compromised. A general rule of hearsay exclusion is therefore one way in which the rights of a defendant may be protected and the normative foundations of a common law criminal justice system upheld. However, hearsay exclusion is not synonymous with the right to fair trial, and general appeals to fair trial rights will not succeed in grounding an absolute rule of exclusion.

At a more detailed level of analysis the adoption of a hearsay prohibition may be justified on various grounds. However, it is here that the need for a flexible rather than an absolute rule becomes self-evident. Perhaps the weakest justification is the contention that hearsay evidence is irrelevant. As the Canadian Supreme Court has stated, '[h]earsay evidence is not excluded because it is irrelevant—there is no need for a special rule to exclude irrelevant evidence'.[19] As a matter of logic, hearsay evidence is clearly capable of being relevant—and indeed, highly probative—to a fact in issue.[20] Rather than relevance per se, the issue is more appropriately conceptualised as a question of reliability. Manifestly unreliable evidence cannot be said to establish a fact in the way presupposed by the legal test of logical relevance.[21] However, reliability is case-specific and consequently incapable of justifying a rigid and categorical rule of exclusion.

The irrelevancy rationale is closely related to the premise that hearsay evidence contravenes the best evidence rule. New Zealand's strict requirement that a witness be unavailable means that any hearsay evidence adduced at trial will, in fact, be the best evidence available.[22] At the core

[17] Roberts and Zuckerman elucidate these 'five foundational principles underlying criminal evidence', which might equally apply to the common law criminal justice system more generally: P Roberts and A Zuckerman, *Criminal Evidence*, 2nd edn (Oxford, OUP, 2010) 18–22.

[18] Evidence Act 2006, s 8(2). In Canada the right to make full answer and defence in criminal proceedings is constitutionally protected by s 7 of the Canadian Charter of Rights and Freedoms.

[19] *R v Khelawon* [2006] 2 SCR 787, [34].

[20] Evidence Act 2006, s 7(3), defines logical relevance broadly, to encompass 'anything that is of consequence to the determination of the proceedings'.

[21] There is an analogy to establishing the authenticity of real evidence: see *R v Bain* [2009] NZSC 16; *R v Gwaze* [2010] NZSC 52.

[22] Unavailability is defined by Evidence Act 2006, s16.

of this justification is the acknowledgment that as information moves away from its original source the danger of unreliability increases.[23] Again, issues of reliability are best considered on a case-by-case basis.[24] Automatic exclusion of all hearsay testimony simply because it is not the 'best' evidence would be, as Spencer contends, 'perverse'.[25]

A further justification for a general exclusionary rule is that the admission of hearsay evidence gives rise to an unwarranted element of surprise. Although valid, this concern is not insurmountable. There are two principal sources of mischief in unwarranted surprise: potential unfair prejudice to the accused and undue delay. In New Zealand, the first of these concerns is addressed by the statutory requirement of pre-trial notice to adduce hearsay evidence.[26] As to the second concern, it is doubtful whether the existence of a hearsay rule of exclusion actually avoids delay;[27] and in any event, delay is expressly factored into the probative value/unfair prejudice test under section 8 of the Evidence Act 2006.[28]

The strongest justification for a general hearsay prohibition is that hearsay evidence is not given by the statement-maker under oath in open court, and is not subject to cross-examination.[29] It is through these pillars of the adversarial process that reliability is primarily tested. In *R v L* the New Zealand Court of Appeal recognised the right to cross-examine as fundamental to our system and, endorsing Wigmore's dictum, declared that cross-examination is 'the greatest legal engine ever invented for the discovery of truth where credibility is in issue'.[30] The witness oath and cross-examination enable a fact-finder to assess character and credibility by observing the witness's demeanour and to evaluate the accuracy and weight of the evidence through direct and indirect forensic challenge in the courtroom. In addition to these outward manifestations of reliability, being required to testify in open court is presumed to have a sobering effect upon the witness and, in conjunction with the threat of prosecution for perjury, supplies an additional incentive for veracity.

[23] Roberts and Zuckerman, above n 17, 366.

[24] Cf *R v Horncastle* [2010] 2 AC 373, [2009] UKSC 14, [20].

[25] JR Spencer, *Hearsay Evidence in Criminal Proceedings* (Oxford, Hart Publishing, 2008) 9.

[26] Evidence Act 2006, s 22.

[27] See Law Commission Consultation Paper No 138, *Evidence in Criminal Proceedings and Related Matters* (London, HMSO, 1995), 6.97.

[28] See Evidence Act 2006, s 8(1)(b).

[29] 'The basic rationale of the hearsay rule', according to J Allan, 'The Working Rationale of the Hearsay Rule and the Implications of Modern Psychological Knowledge' [1991] *Current Legal Problems* 217.

[30] *R v L* [1994] 2 NZLR 54, 61 Also see Blackstone, *Commentaries*, 13th edn, Book 3 (London, A Strahan, 1800) 372 ('open examination of witnesses ... is much more conducive to the clearing up of truth'); M Hale, *History and Analysis of the Common Law of England* (Stafford, J Nutt, 1713) 258 (cross-examination 'beats and bolts out the Truth much better'); *R v Khelawon* [2006] 2 SCR 787, [35] (cross-examination is 'the optimal way of testing testimonial evidence').

The difficulty of testing evidence without the benefit of cross-examination has prompted all common law jurisdictions to subject hearsay evidence to additional tests of admissibility, either in the form of categorical exclusionary rules or context-sensitive balancing. Provision for a reliability-based exception acknowledges that, notwithstanding the absence of cross-examination in open court, the dangers associated with admitting untested—and possibly untestable—evidence can sometimes be avoided. The question is whether the evidence has been or can be tested independently of direct cross-examination in open court.

No discussion of the rationales for excluding hearsay would be complete without brief mention of the issue of confrontation. Whilst the justifications discussed so far share a foundation in considerations of reliability, they also allude to non-epistemic factors. For example, principles of humane treatment and procedural integrity intuitively *feel* imperilled by the admission of hearsay evidence. As elucidated by Redmayne in his contribution to this book,[31] the justification for such a feeling may be rooted in notions as varied as entrenched common law traditions and habits of mind, through to the ignominy of failing to accuse a defendant to their face. Adoption of an explicit right to confront under the Sixth Amendment to the US Constitution implies that nothing short of direct cross-examination will be adequate to alleviate the dangers of unreliability and to provide a fact-finder with the tools needed to assess the weight of testimonial evidence. However, the discourse of an absolute right of confrontation has found little judicial favour in New Zealand, where cross-examination is linked instead to the defendant's right to an effective defence and the associated idea of the testability of prosecution evidence.[32]

4. COMPARATIVE APPROACHES TO 'RELIABLE' HEARSAY

It is apparent that a general presumption of unreliability is difficult to sustain for all hearsay evidence. But different common law systems have improvised their own distinctive local solutions to the challenge of sifting reliable from unreliable hearsay. This Section explores the development, or rejection, of a reliability-based exception to the hearsay rule in Canada, England and Wales, Australia, the United States, and in the jurisprudence of the European Court of Human Rights, with a view to shedding comparative light on the current position in New Zealand.

[31] Chapter 12, above.

[32] See *R v Clode* CA478/07 17 October 2007; *R v J* [1998] 1 NZLR 20 (CA); and *R v L* [1994] 2 NZLR 54 (CA).

(a) Canada

The Canadian reliability exception to the hearsay prohibition was developed through a series of Canadian Supreme Court decisions.[33] The basic test may be satisfied in either one of two ways, as summarised by the Canadian Supreme Court in *Khelawon*:[34]

> When it is necessary to resort to evidence in this form, a hearsay statement may be admitted if, because of the way in which it came about, its contents are trustworthy, or if circumstances permit the ultimate trier of fact to sufficiently assess its worth.

Hearsay evidence is admissible, in other words, if (i) its reliability is confirmed by circumstantial guarantees of trustworthiness (CGT); or (ii) the evidence has been subject to prior testing or is capable of future testing by the fact-finder, ie a criterion of 'testability'.

Canadian case law has consistently emphasised that the reliability exception involves a question of admissibility and not weight. In *Khelawon* Charron J remarked:[35]

> I stress the nature of the hearsay rule as a general exclusionary rule because the increased flexibility introduced in the Canadian law of evidence in the past few decades has sometimes tended to blur the distinction between admissibility and weight.

Admissibility concerns threshold reliability, whereas the final disposition of the case involves an assessment of ultimate reliability by the trier of fact. In determining whether evidence can be introduced into the trial, the judge fulfils a 'gate-keeper' screening role.[36] In *Starr* the relationship between threshold and ultimate reliability was spelt out in the following terms:[37]

> Threshold reliability is concerned not with whether the statement is true or not; that is a question of ultimate reliability. Instead, it is concerned with whether or not the circumstances surrounding the statement itself provide circumstantial guarantees of trustworthiness.

In *Khelawon* the Canadian Supreme Court went so far as to state that, 'failure to respect this distinction would not only result in the undue

[33] *R v Khan* [1990] 2 SCR 531; *R v Smith* [1992] 2 SCR 915; *R v B (KG)* [1993] 1 SCR 740; *R v U (FJ)* [1995] 3 SCR 764; *R v Starr* [2000] 2 SCR 144, *R v Mapara* [2005] 1 SCR 358; and *R v Khelawon* [2006] 2 SCR 787.

[34] *R v Khelawon* [2006] 2 SCR 787, [2]. Strikingly similar terminology was employed by the English Court of Appeal in *R v Horncastle* [57].

[35] *R v Khelawon* [2006] 2 SCR 787, [59]. See also *R v Starr* [2000] 2 SCR 144, [2009] 2 Cr App Rep 15, [199]–[200].

[36] *R v Khelawon* [2006] 2 SCR 787, [2]–[3]. And see *R v B (KG)* [1993] 1 SCR 740; *R v Hawkins*, [1996] 3 SCR 1043. Similar wording was used in the New Zealand case of *R v Manase* [2001] 2 NZLR 197.

[37] *R v Starr* [2000] 2 SCR 144, [215]. Also *R v Khelawon* [2006] 2 SCR 787, [3].

prolongation of admissibility hearings, it would distort the fact-finding process'.[38] Pragmatically speaking, admissibility hearings are often conducted pre-trial. Without having heard all the evidence to be presented at trial, a judge would find it difficult if not impossible to determine the ultimate reliability of any particular item of evidence. Threshold reliability merely requires a conclusion on whether there are sufficient indications of truthfulness for the fact-finder to complete its assessment of reliability, including deciding what weight (if any) to be given to the evidence.

Indicators of ultimate truth, fabrication or inaccuracy do not become irrelevant when assessing threshold reliability. Rather, the test requires a judge to proceed some distance along the road of determining truth, stopping only at the point at which the judge concludes that there are sufficient indicators of reliability (CGT) for the evidence to be possibly considered reliable by the fact-finder, or alternatively, that the evidence is irremediably unreliable and inadmissible. The point on the continuum where such an assurance is met relates to the question of the standard of proof borne by the party seeking to adduce the evidence.

Calibrating and implementing the test of threshold reliability has caused some difficulty in Canada. In *Starr*,[39] the Supreme Court of Canada attempted to distinguish, on a 'principled' basis, between questions seeking to establish the truth of the evidence (ultimate reliability) and those going to the issue of threshold reliability. The majority stated:[40]

> At the stage of hearsay admissibility the trial judge should not consider the declarant's general reputation for truthfulness, nor any prior or subsequent statements, consistent or not. These factors do not concern the circumstances of the statement itself. Similarly, I would not consider the presence of corroborating or conflicting evidence.... In summary, under the principled approach a court must not invade the province of the trier of fact and condition admissibility of hearsay on whether the evidence is ultimately reliable. However, it will need to examine whether the circumstances in which the statement was made lend sufficient credibility to allow a finding of threshold reliability.

In this way, the Court attempted to narrow the scope of the reliability exception by excluding extraneous considerations, including logically relevant indications of credibility and corroborating circumstances. However, the approach taken in *Starr* was later modified by the Canadian Supreme Court in *Khelawon*, where the Court stated that 'the relevance of any particular factor will depend on the particular dangers arising from the hearsay nature of the statement and the available means, if any, of overcoming them'.[41] The Court conceded that its earlier elimination of truth-conducive information

[38] *R v Khelawon* [2006] 2 SCR 787, [3].
[39] *R v Starr* [2000] 2 SCR 144.
[40] *R v Starr* [2000] 2 SCR 144, [217] per Iacobucci J for the majority.
[41] *R v Khelawon* [2006] 2 SCR 787, [55].

from the test of threshold reliability was unhelpful. The Canadian position now envisages that evidence corroborating the reliability of the statement is a valid consideration in determining threshold reliability. Rigid categories of relevance have given way to a more flexible, context-specific approach.

(b) England and Wales

The law of hearsay in England and Wales is now governed by the complex legislative framework introduced by the Criminal Justice Act 2003, which contains an array of inclusionary and exclusionary principles. The starting point is section 114(1), which provides that statements not made in oral evidence are admissible at trial only if one of four criteria is satisfied. First, admission may be authorised directly by legislation (including provisions of the CJA 2003 itself). Secondly, admission may be warranted by common law doctrines (including *res gestae*) expressly preserved by section 118 of the Act.[42] Thirdly, evidence may be adduced by agreement between all parties to the proceedings.[43] Finally, the court may determine admission to be in the interests of justice.[44]

This final, residual judicial discretion to admit hearsay in the interests of justice provides the English judiciary with greater flexibility than their New Zealand counterparts. There is no equivalent provision in New Zealand, or generally at common law. However, the English judiciary were not left without additional guidance in applying this novel provision. Section 114(2) of the CJA 2003 stipulates the following non-exhaustive list of factors that must be weighed by a judge when deciding whether to admit or exclude proffered hearsay:

(a) how much probative value the statement has (assuming it to be true) in relation to a matter in issue in the proceedings, or how valuable it is for the understanding of other evidence in the case;
(b) what other evidence has been, or can be, given on the matter or evidence mentioned in paragraph (a);
(c) how important the matter or evidence mentioned in paragraph (a) is in the context of the case as a whole;
(d) the circumstances in which the statement was made;
(e) how reliable the maker of the statement appears to be;
(f) how reliable the evidence of the making of the statement appears to be;
(g) whether oral evidence of the matter stated can be given and, if not, why it cannot;

[42] Numerous commentators have expressed disappointment at the retention of these, largely outmoded common law doctrines. Roberts and Zuckerman, above n 17, 415, describe s 118 as a 'rag-bag list' of exceptions.

[43] Cf Evidence Act 2006 (NZ), s 9.

[44] Criminal Justice Act 2003, s 114(1)(d).

(h) the amount of difficulty involved in challenging the statement;
(i) the extent to which that difficulty would be likely to prejudice the party facing it.

This statutory articulation of a 'structured discretion' helpfully pre-empts the controversy generated in Canada over the types of considerations that may go to threshold, but not to ultimate, reliability.[45] Of course, any provision designed to expand judicial discretion may generate its own difficulties.[46]

The factors which in England and Wales receive judicial consideration under section 114(2) are in New Zealand distributed between sections 18 and 8 of the Evidence Act 2006. Thus, the criteria specified by paragraphs (a), (b), (c), (h) and (i) would fall for consideration under section 8 in New Zealand and do not therefore form part of section 18's dedicated reliability exception.[47] This tends to narrow down the reliability inquiry and broaden the scope of admissibility, particularly since section 18 is the controlling provision. If it could be shown that cross-examination would serve no purpose then hearsay evidence might be deemed admissible under section 114(1)(d). This brings English law into line with the Canadian approach, recognising a two-pronged approach to reliability based on CGT *and* testability, whereas New Zealand law concentrates more narrowly on threshold reliability.

Testability as a criterion of admissibility in England and Wales finds further echoes in section 124 of the CJA 2003, which empowers the court to admit evidence going to the credibility of the absent statement-maker. Additionally, with the leave of the court, evidence bearing on credibility may be given that could have been put to the witness under cross-examination, if the witness had appeared at trial, but which would not ordinarily be admissible in-chief.[48] Finally, evidence of inconsistent statements may also be adduced to demonstrate self-contradiction.[49] For our purposes, section 124 is revealing for two reasons. First, it is suggestive of a testability exception to the hearsay rule in England and Wales. Secondly, it implies that the operative standard of reliability is not especially demanding, since the section clearly contemplates the admission of hearsay statements where there are tangible doubts about the declarant's credibility, possibly including prior inconsistent statements.

[45] Also see the US case of *Idaho v Wright*, 497 US 805 (1990).

[46] For critical discussion, see D Birch, 'Same Old Story, Same Old Song?' [2004] *Criminal Law Review* 556; R Munday, 'The Judicial Discretion to Admit Hearsay Evidence' (2007) 171 *Justice of the Peace* 276.

[47] Paragraph (g) is the odd one out, since the possibility of oral evidence is not formally part of New Zealand's test of admission—although it could be subsumed within the defendant's right to present an effective defence under s 8.

[48] CJA 2003, s 124(2)(b).

[49] CJA 2003, s 124(2)(c).

(c) Australia

In contrast to the position in New Zealand, Canada, and England and Wales, Australian law[50] does not contain a general judicial discretion to admit reliable hearsay. The closest analogue is section 65 of the Australian Evidence Act 1995 (Cth)[51] and its State counterparts,[52] which are restricted to first-hand hearsay. In other common law jurisdictions (including New Zealand)[53] consideration of the number of links in the chain between the original declarant and the eventual statement adduced in court is subsumed within some local version of a generic CGT test. In addition to being first-hand hearsay, section 65 also requires that (a) the statement-maker was under a duty to make the representation;[54] or (b) the hearsay statement was made soon after the asserted fact in circumstances indicating that fabrication is 'unlikely';[55] or (c) the statement was made in circumstances indicating that its reliability is 'highly probable';[56] or (d) it is a statement against interest[57] and was made in circumstances indicating that it is 'likely' to be reliable.[58] These expressions of probability have been interpreted by the courts sympathetically to their CGT functions,[59] although not always are the accepted tests applied with rigour across all contexts.[60]

A form of testability appears under section 65(3), which establishes an exception where a defendant has previously cross-examined or had the opportunity to cross-examine the maker of the statement.[61] As Henning and Hunter indicate,[62] Australia facilitates fact-finder assessment of hearsay evidence from unavailable declarants in a similar way to the United Kingdom. There are notice requirements for the 'key witness unavailable'

[50] In Australia, the law of evidence varies across States, but the uniform Evidence Acts reflect the legislation flowing from the major modernisation initiatives begun in the mid-1980s and adopted first federally and in New South Wales, both in 1995. Other jurisdictions have followed suit: Tasmania in 2001, Victoria in 2008 and the ACT in 2011. See further Henning and Hunter, Chapter 15 in this volume, fns 6 and 35.

[51] But the Act does contain specific hearsay exceptions covering *res gestae* (ss 65(2)(b) and 66A), business records (s 69), tags, labels or writing attached to an object (s 70), electronic communications (s 71), and Aboriginal and Torres Strait Islander customs (s 72).

[52] Above n 50.

[53] Evidence Act 2006, s 16: see NZLC, *Evidence*, R55 (Wellington, 1999) vol 2, C76.

[54] Or representations of that nature: Evidence Act 1995 (Cth), s 65(2)(a).

[55] Uniform Evidence Acts, s 65(2)(b).

[56] Uniform Evidence Acts, s 65(2)(c).

[57] As defined by uniform Evidence Acts, s 65(7).

[58] Uniform Evidence Acts s 65(2)(d)(i) and (ii).

[59] See for example, *R v Mankotia* [1998] NSWSC 295; *Conway v R* (2002) 209 CLR 203.

[60] For example, see *R v Suteski (No 4)* (2002) 128 A Crim R 275 (NSW SC) and more generally Henning and Hunter, Chapter 15 in this volume.

[61] Uniform Evidence Acts, s 65(3)(a) and (b) and (5). Section 65(3)(b) provides an exception if the defendant has 'had a reasonable opportunity to cross-examine the person who made the representation about it'.

[62] Chapter 14, nn 110–12 and associated text.

exceptions and there is generous scope for adducing evidence of the absent declarant's credibility. In addition, if requested by a party a trial judge may be required to warn the jury of elements of potential unreliability in the evidence.[63]

(d) US Federal and Constitutional Law

Rule 807 of the US Federal Rules of Evidence, titled 'residual exception', is one of the best-known examples of a generic hearsay exception expressly drafted in terms of 'circumstantial guarantees of trustworthiness'. Numerous State jurisdictions have also adopted local variants of Rule 807. Whilst admission of a hearsay statement under this provision primarily turns on there being sufficient circumstantial guarantees of trustworthiness, there are four additional preconditions that must also be satisfied. First, the statement must be offered as evidence of a material fact. Secondly, the probative value of the statement in terms of the fact for which it is tendered must be greater than any other evidence reasonably obtainable. Thirdly, admission must best serve the purposes of the rules of evidence and the interests of justice. Fourthly, and finally, notice of an intention to adduce the statement must be given in order to give the adverse party 'a fair opportunity to prepare to meet it'.

State law, naturally including the law of hearsay, also needs to comply with the dictates of the US federal Constitution. A striking feature of the US Supreme Court's reinvigoration of the Sixth Amendment Confrontation Clause in *Crawford v Washington*[64] was its disdain for any 'amorphous, if not entirely subjective'[65] reliability-based exception to the hearsay prohibition. The Court cited cases in which diametrically opposed factors had been invoked to justify the admissibility of supposedly 'reliable' hearsay.[66] In this way, the constitutional right to confront underscores the importance of in-person examination of witnesses as an integral component of the US adversarial system.

[63] Uniform Evidence Acts, ss 67, 108A, 108B and 165 respectively.

[64] *Crawford v Washington*, 541 US 36 (2004). Also see the contributions to this volume by Redmayne (Chapter 12) and Callen (Chapter 13).

[65] *Crawford v Washington*, 541 US 36 (2004).

[66] For example, 'detailed' versus 'fleeting' statements: *People v Farrell*, 34 P 3d 401, 407 (Colo 2001) vis-à-vis *US v Photogrammetric Data Servs, Inc*, 259 F 3d 229, 245 (2001); custodial statements by suspects versus informal statements: *Nowlin v Commonwealth*, 40 Va App 327, 335–38, 579 SE 2d 367, 371–72 (2003) vis-à-vis *State v Bintz*, 2002 WI App 204, 13, 650 NW 2d 913, 918; and prompt versus long-delayed statements: *People v Farrell*, 34 P 3d 401, 407 (Colo. 2001) vis-à-vis *Stevens v People*, 29 P 3d 305, 316 (2001).

(e) European Convention on Human Rights

Turning finally to Europe, significant pressure has been placed upon English approaches to hearsay, following the passage of the UK Human Rights Act 1998, by the European Court of Human Rights. In *Al-Khawaja and Tahery v UK*[67] the Court was presented with two cases in which a breach of fair trial rights was claimed as a result of the admission of hearsay statements from absent witnesses. In both cases the respective trial judges had directed the jury to assess the evidence bearing in mind that these statements had not been subjected to cross-examination in open court. Despite unambiguous statutory authority for admitting the statements, the Strasbourg Court concluded that the domestic trial proceedings had failed to comply with the requirements of ECHR Article 6, as previously elucidated by the Court in *Lucà v Italy*:[68]

> [W]here a conviction is based solely or to a decisive degree on depositions that have been made by a person whom the accused has had no opportunity to examine or to have examined, whether during the investigation or at the trial, the rights of the defence are restricted to an extent that is incompatible with the guarantees provided by Article 6.

The UK government argued that there were sufficient 'counterbalancing factors' to justify the admission of un-cross-examined hearsay statements in the trials of both Al-Khawaja and Tahery.[69] It was pointed out that these statements did not in themselves compel the applicants to testify in their own defence; there was no suggestion of collusion between complainants; inconsistencies in the absent witnesses' statements could have been explored before the jury, and their general credibility challenged; and in each trial the jury had been warned by the judge to bear in mind that they had neither seen nor heard the absent witness's evidence and that it had not been tested in cross-examination. None of these considerations, taken singly or in combination, was sufficient to persuade the Strasbourg Court that the applicants had received fair trials in accordance with Article 6. In the absence of special circumstances,[70] the Court doubted whether there could be any counterbalancing factors sufficient to justify the admission of an untested statement which amounted to the 'sole or decisive basis' for a criminal conviction.[71] However, whilst the US right to confrontation under

[67] *Al-Khawaja and Tahery v UK* (2009) 49 EHRR 1. Now also see the Grand Chamber Judgment of 15 December 2011, noted by Mike Redmayne in Chapter 12, in which the UK Government successfully argued that Al-Khawaja had received a fair trial. The Chamber ruling in Tahery was upheld.

[68] *Lucà v Italy* (2003) 36 EHRR 46, [40].

[69] See *Al-Khawaja and Tahery v UK* (2009) 49 EHRR 1, [41]–[42].

[70] Such as the witness's absence being a direct result of the defendant's actions: cf *R v Sellick* [2005] 1 WLR 3257, [2005] EWCA Crim 651.

[71] *Al-Khawaja and Tahery v UK* (2009) 49 EHRR 1, [37].

Crawford equates to a 'right to eyeball' the witness in court, Article 6 of the ECHR can be satisfied by indirect pre-trial opportunities to examine a witness or have questions put to them.[72]

Most of the contextual considerations identified by the UK government as potential counterbalancing factors (except possible collusion between witnesses) relate to the testability of the statement. Their flat rejection by the Strasbourg Court as a justification for admitting hearsay seemed to rule out the possibility of a general reliability-based exception to the hearsay prohibition under the Convention. In the meantime, *Al-Khawaja*'s potential impact on English trial judges' application of their discretionary power to admit hearsay under section 114(1)(d) of the Criminal Justice Act 2003 has been neutralised by the UK Supreme Court's robust decision in *Horncastle*.[73] New Zealand judges, however, might draw inspiration from both the European Court in *Al-Khawaja* and the US Supreme Court in *Crawford*. Section 6 of the NZBORA could be invoked to demand an exacting standard of proof when the prosecution seeks to establish a 'reasonable assurance' of reliability under section 18 of the Evidence Act 2006.

5. DEVELOPING THE RELIABILITY EXCEPTION IN NEW ZEALAND

We have seen that neither the 'reasonable assurance of reliability' standard established by section 18 of the Evidence Act 2006, nor section 8's general probative value/prejudicial effect balancing test, provides much concrete legislative guidance on the particular factors that must be considered in each case or the burden and standard of proof to be applied. What have the courts made of these provisions in practice?

The District Court, the workhorse of the New Zealand justice system, is charged with applying these provisions on a daily basis. In contrast to the Canadian example, there has been little or no consideration of the principles underlying the existence of a hearsay rule of exclusion.[74] Perhaps this goes some way towards explaining the apparent lack of consistency in decision-making. Section 18 has on occasion been deemed satisfied by the merest indication of formality in making the statement, with little regard for the significance of cross-examination in promoting reliability. Yet on other occasions a fairly rigorous test has been applied.[75] Where a reasonable assurance of reliability has been established, section 8 factors have included

[72] *Doorson v Netherlands* (1996) 22 EHRR 330; *SN v Sweden* (2004) EHRR 13.

[73] *R v Horncastle* [2010] 2 AC 373, [2009] UKSC 14, discussed by Redmayne, Chapter 12 in this volume.

[74] See eg *Police v Bell* [2008] DCR 681 (DC).

[75] *Police v Rahman* CIR 2009-090-00011, 12 May 2009, Waitakere District Court (Judge Tremewan); *Police v Whiu* 2007-090-011345, Waitakere District Court (Judge Taumaunu).

consideration of the possibility that the witness may recant or change their story,[76] the nature and quality of the evidence,[77] and the possibility that the witness's oral testimony might independently support the defence case.[78] It has also been suggested that many of the factors to be considered under the threshold test of relevance (section 7) will be replicated under sections 18 and 8.[79] Therefore even if reliability under section 18 is satisfied, the evidence may nonetheless still be excluded if cross-examination might have had a material bearing on reliability.[80] The division of reliability across these sections is untenable. It contributes to the dilution of the test of reliability and may give rise to difficulties in the application of the burden and standard of proof.

Further judicial guidance may be derived from pre-2006 Act cases, especially *R v Manase*, which expressly considered the Evidence Act proposals, then in draft. Referring to a reliability exception substantially similar to what became section 18, the Court of Appeal stated:[81] 'The hearsay evidence must have sufficient apparent reliability, either inherent or circumstantial, or both, to justify its admission in spite of the dangers against which the hearsay rule is designed to guard'. Section 18 was regarded as specifying reliability as the main ground of admissibility, with section 8 operating as an incidental 'final check'.[82] This is consistent with the Court of Appeal's approach in *R v L*, where the defendant's right to cross-examine witnesses was circumscribed by an overriding criterion of contextual reliability:[83]

> In harmony with the justified limitations on the specified rights and freedoms recognised by section 5 [of the NZBORA], the Court may properly assess the practical implications of the absence of an opportunity for cross-examination in the particular case. It is not enough for an accused to assert a defence and a desire to cross-examine to support the defence. The likely veracity of the complainant's statement is a crucial consideration.

For the Court in *R v L*, assessing the significance of the defendant's lost opportunity to cross-examine was an exercise intrinsically linked to the reliability of the evidence. In *R v J*,[84] where a proffered hearsay statement

[76] *Bishop v Police* CIR 2008-416-000003, 28 February 2008, Gisborne High Court, [35], per Lang J.

[77] Ibid [36].

[78] Ibid [35].

[79] *R v Key* 2006-096-12705, Auckland High Court, 19 February 2009, [19], per Winklemann J.

[80] *R v Aekins* CIR 2006-004-013245, 16 August 2007, Auckland District Court (Judge Wilson QC).

[81] *R v Manase* [2001] 2 NZLR 197, [30] (CA).

[82] Ibid [31].

[83] *R v L* [1994] 2 NZLR 54, 63. The Court also noted the opinion of the Privy Council in *Scott v R* [1989] AC 1242, 1249, where it was stated that the quality of the evidence was of central importance.

[84] *R v J* [1998] 1 NZLR 20.

was in fact the only evidence against the accused, it was said that, '[i]n such a situation a Court would need to exercise extreme care before concluding that cross-examination would not make any relevant difference to the result of the trial'.[85] These cases forged a direct (epistemic) connection between reliability and cross-examination, which ought to have been carried over to the application of section 18 of the 2006 Act. Unfortunately, this interpretation is not supported by the post-Act case-law, which tends to associate the dicta of *R v L* and *R v J* with section 8's residual balancing test. Thus, in *Bishop*[86] Lang J noted that the nature and quality of the evidence was 'to a large extent' recognised under section 18's reliability test, but added that this consideration still had some force under section 8, particularly when, as in *R v J*, the hearsay statement was the only evidence against the defendant.

This line of cases illustrates the inherent structural weakness of New Zealand's reliability-based hearsay exception. Under the Canadian approach, either the evidence commands a reasonable assurance of reliability (on CGT or testability grounds) and is admissible, or the unmitigated risk of unreliability mandates exclusion. In New Zealand, a finding of reliability under section 18 could be followed by exclusion under section 8 on the basis that cross-examination may well be successful. This seems self-contradictory, or possibly appeals to—largely unarticulated—non-epistemic considerations favouring live confrontation or cross-examination at trial. More generally, it is awkward and confusing to parcel out different aspects of reliability between section 18 and section 8. The lesson of the Canadian Supreme Court's flirtation with a narrow conception of reliability in *Starr*[87] is that this bifurcation cannot be achieved on any neat, justifiable or sustainable basis.

Not only does a bifurcated test of reliability appear illogical, it also creates difficulty when assigning the burden and standard of proof. The party seeking to adduce the evidence bears the burden of establishing reliability under section 18. We have seen that this standard is not necessarily particularly demanding. It then falls upon the opposing party to establish insufficient probative value, including consideration of the unreliability of the evidence under section 8. In effect, a statutory exception to a rule of exclusion favouring one party may de facto become a judicial discretion favouring the other party. This is particularly worrying where the proponent of hearsay evidence is the Crown. Entire statements made, for example, by the complainant could easily satisfy a narrow reliability test under section 18 in which issues of corroborating evidence, witness credibility and the value of cross-examination are, at best, deferred for consideration under section 8.

[85] *R v J* [1998] 1 NZLR 20, 25.
[86] *Bishop v Police* CIR 2008-416-000003, 28 February 2008, Gisborne High Court.
[87] Above nn 37–40, and accompanying text.

A final difficulty concerns the testability component of the reliability test. Serious questions over the reliability of a statement should not warrant exclusion if the fact-finder would be well able to assess reliability for itself. Therefore, admission is justified where the evidence is clearly reliable or it is capable of reliable testing by the fact-finder despite the absence of cross-examination. The pre-Act case of *R v Hovell*[88] provides a telling illustration of the notion of testability. This case involved an elderly rape complainant who made a statement to the police but died before trial. The only issue at trial was identification. In her notably frank statement, the complainant described her attacker but added that she would not be able to identify the offender if he was standing right in front of her. This statement was admitted on the basis that cross-examination would have served no useful purpose and its reliability could therefore be assessed without hearing from the witness in person. Yet if this scenario recurred today, the complainant's statement would probably be excluded, since there would be no 'reasonable assurance of reliability' capable of satisfying section 18 of the Evidence Act 2006.

In my view, section 8 ought not to be seen as encompassing issues of reliability or testability, which—in relation to reliability—is the rightful realm of section 18. Section 8 (encompassing the accused's right 'to offer an effective defence') should instead be restricted to evaluations of probative value[89] and the prejudice that would accrue if an evidential foundation for a defence could not be established due to the non-appearance of the statement-maker.[90] Testability on the other hand is currently without a home. If it is a component of section 8 then it is unnecessarily encumbered by section 18's reliability threshold, which is incapable of satisfaction in cases such as *Hovell*. Section 18 achieves the worst of both worlds. Not only does it apply a narrow view of reliability which the New Zealand courts have treated as undemanding, but it also operates to exclude evidence that ought to be admitted on the basis of testability.

CONCLUSION

The hearsay prohibition is often regarded as a peculiarly characteristic, and idiosyncratic, feature of common law systems of criminal evidence. However, recent years have witnessed systematic reform of the hearsay rule in many common law jurisdictions, including New Zealand, typically

[88] *R v Hovell* [1987] 1 NZLR 610 (CA).

[89] Consistent with the reasoning of the minority in *R v Bain* [2009] NZSC 16.

[90] In *Police v Bell* [2008] DCR 681 (DC) the fact that admitting the complainant's hearsay statement would force the accused to testify was not regarded as preventing him from offering an effective defence.

with the accent on achieving greater admissibility of relevant and reliable evidence. But this reform objective begs the question how reliability is to be assessed and guaranteed, consistently with the accused's right to a fair trial. Constitutional law and human rights law—in New Zealand, section 25 of the NZBORA—add further levels of complexity to the law reformer's aspirations.

Having briefly reviewed the traditional rationales for the hearsay prohibition, this chapter explored the development, or rejection, of reliability-based exceptions to hearsay exclusion in Canada, England and Wales, Australia, US federal and Constitutional law, and in the jurisprudence of the European Court of Human Rights. A diversity of approaches is apparent. Viewed against this comparative backdrop, New Zealand's narrow approach to testing reliability combined with a broadly unfettered judicial discretion represents perhaps the weakest protection of the hearsay exclusionary rule and the associated right of the defendant to cross-examine witnesses. In this regard, New Zealand courts might draw inspiration from the more rights-orientated approaches of the US Supreme Court in *Crawford*[91] and the European Court in *Al-Khawaja*,[92] and the institutional authority to do so, in the form of the interpretative obligation imposed by section 6 of the NZBORA, is readily at hand. In more conventional doctrinal terms, the experiences and precedents of the Canadian Supreme Court point the way to developing a more principled and coherent reliability-based exception to the hearsay prohibition in New Zealand.

[91] Above n 64, and associated text.
[92] Above n 67, and associated text.

15

Finessing the Fair Trial for Complainants and the Accused: Mansions of Justice or Castles in the Air?

TERESE HENNING AND JILL HUNTER*

INTRODUCTION

HEARSAY REFORM AND the related right to confrontation have recently attracted the attention of apex courts in Strasbourg,[1] North America[2] and England and Wales,[3] and sparked renewed debates amongst commentators about the procedural requirements of a fair criminal trial. The major focus[4] concerns courts' attempts to reconcile the goals of ensuring trials are both fair and well-informed when faced with unavailable witnesses and, in their stead, rely upon available hearsay statements. It is fertile ground for deliberation, as illustrated in the search for sweet compromise by courts and legislatures discussed in this chapter. Singly and collectively these attempts reveal the massive challenge in identifying an apparently elusive formula to satisfy the fair trial right to confront one's accusers in the face of key witnesses who have died, fled or refused to testify. There are vastly differing philosophies underpinning responses to these issues. One commonality however is that, in recent years, many common law systems have introduced sweeping legislative reforms in an effort to fashion their own local regimes for regulating the admission of reliable hearsay. Australia's legislature and courts have followed the common

* Special thanks to Candida Saunders and Christine Boyle for their comments and suggestions.

[1] *Al-Khawaja and Tahery v United Kingdom* (2009) 49 EHRR 1; Grand Chamber Judgment, 15 December 2011.

[2] *Crawford v Washington*, 541 US 36 (2004); *R v Khelawon* [2006] 2 SCR 787.

[3] *R v Horncastle* [2010] 2 AC 373, [36].

[4] See, eg, the contributions to this volume by Redmayne, Callen and Gallavin.

law trend of shifting the traditional exclusionary rule in a markedly pro-admissibility direction.

This chapter throws up new issues by addressing the *application* of doctrine, not its boundaries. Its locus is Australian hearsay law and its focus is upon the accused and upon the complainant of domestic or sexual violence[5]—both beneficiaries of unique (though different) special testimonial protections. A snapshot of reported Australian cases dealing with unavailable witness hearsay since 1995[6] is revealing. It shows, first, that the accused, defence witnesses and vulnerable victims[7] fare poorly when they[8] seek access equal to other claimants to a hearsay 'voice' in the courtroom. Secondly, it reveals numerous apparent contradictions in Australian courts' approaches to these key criminal trial protagonists and, in particular, the lack of availability to them of Australia's 'witness unavailable' hearsay exception, section 65 of the uniform Evidence Acts. The scenario, we say, is reminiscent of sceptical attitudes towards complainants and defendants which had supposedly been purged from the modern law. In contrast to earlier manifestations of judicial mistrust, twenty-first-century doubts are not etched in legal doctrine. They pass under the radar, in the selective application of Australia's expansive hearsay exceptions. This selectivity is revealed through the notably uneven application of hearsay exceptions with respect to our two groups of trial participants who are seemingly being left behind by Australian courts' new-found enthusiasm for hearsay evidence.

There is an apparent incongruity in the complainant and the accused sharing in common this differentiated and parsimonious treatment under the unavailable witness hearsay exceptions. They are, after all, placed inevitably on opposite sides of the adversarial battle and generally perceived to possess diametrically opposed fair trial interests. It is our conclusion that it is neither coincidental nor is it necessarily a quirk of Australian practice that the accused and the complainant of sexual or domestic violence are invisible in the list of those trusted by courts to be heard without entering the witness box. In our view it reflects the de facto retention of age-old and unreconstructed suspicions of the testimonial veracity of the accused and

[5] On occasion we interchange 'vulnerable witnesses' with these other descriptors.

[6] That is, when the earliest of the Acts became operative in three Australian jurisdictions (Commonwealth, ACT and New South Wales), with other (but not all) Australian States and territories following in dribs and drabs subsequently: see n 35 below.

[7] The term 'vulnerable witnesses' is used in this chapter to encapsulate witnesses who because of their age or other personal characteristics such as cognitive impairment, their relationship to the defendant or because the offences they allege involve intimate or distressing and, to many, shameful, personal experiences, are recognised through special measures and socio-legal research as likely to experience heightened stress in the trial process.

[8] Or, in the case of the accused, defence witnesses.

domestic and sexual violence complainants within the context of Australia's modernised law of hearsay.

The statutory provisions are not the root of the problem. Rather, the fault lies elsewhere. First, there appears to be an issue regarding prosecutors' unwillingness to exploit hearsay exceptions for complainants and second, there is an issue with judges' unwillingness to utilise hearsay exceptions for the accused. This state of affairs raises serious concerns as to whether Australian legal practice is recreating its historical past. In doing so, it provides food for thought for other similar jurisdictions.[9]

Finally, this chapter illustrates important differences between human rights and common law criteria of a pre-eminently oral trial process. Most prominently, human rights instruments treat the right to confrontation as a mechanism of *defence* (not *party*) empowerment. They emphasise the defendants' rights to due process as an important part of the fair trial and oral process package. In contrast, the common law does not seek to embed defendant-focused protections through its traditional hearsay exceptions. Instead it traditionally treats the right to cross-examination as the pre-eminent test of all witnesses' testimony.

1. THE HUMAN RIGHTS FRAMEWORK

Human rights legislation remains a work-in-progress in Australia. Victoria and the Australian Capital Territory are the only Australian jurisdictions to have legislated comprehensive human rights protection. Both these jurisdictions also apply Australia's uniform Evidence Acts.

Because Australia has no comprehensive national human rights legislation encompassing criminal process rights the international human rights treaties to which Australia is a signatory, and decisions of the United Nations Human

[9] For example, in relation to modern case-law regarding defendants' access to hearsay exceptions for exculpatory hearsay, see United Kingdom: *R v Y* [2008] 1 WLR 1683, [2008] EWCA Crim 10, [37]–[38]; *R v Gorski* [2009] NICC 66, [19] ('the courts place very strict conditions on whether or not extrajudicial confessions by third parties should be admitted in evidence. I consider that [the words spoken by phone call inferring guilt of the caller] fall very far short of amounting to any form of credible evidence that could be put before the jury and for those reasons I refuse the application'); Ireland: see L Heffernan and EJ Imwinkelried, 'The Accused's Constitutional Right to Introduce Critical, Demonstrably Reliable Exculpatory Evidence (2005) 40 *Irish Jurist* 111; Canada: *R v Edgar* [2010] ONCA 529 (leave to appeal to SC dismissed, 31 March 2011); cf Strasbourg and United States: *Mirilashvili v Russia*, Appln No 6293/04, 11 December 2008 (relying on the defendant's right to produce evidence under the same conditions as the prosecution); *Washington v Texas*, 388 US 14 (1967); *Chambers v Mississippi*, 410 US 284 (1973); *Davis v Alaska*, 415 US 308 (1974); *Holmes v South Carolina*, 547 US 319 (2006) (relying on either the due process clause (Fourteenth Amendment) or the compulsory process clause (Sixth Amendment)).

Rights Committee under those treaties, constitute the most significant human rights reference points for most Australian courts.[10] For present purposes, we may note that Australia is a party to the International Covenant on Civil and Political Rights (ICCPR);[11] the International Convention on the Elimination of All Forms of Racial Discrimination (ICERD);[12] the Convention on the Elimination of Discrimination Against Women (CEDAW);[13] the Convention on the Rights of the Child (CRC);[14] and the Convention Against Torture and Other Cruel, Inhuman or Degrading Treatment or Punishment (CAT).[15] Dedicated criminal process rights sit within a broader human rights framework comprising dignitarian rights given general expression in the Preamble to the ICCPR, defendants' rights to equality of treatment before the courts, the right to minimum fair trial guarantees, the right to the presumption of innocence, and the right to remain silent. A representative expression of the rights of most immediate concern for our discussion can be found in the following parts of Articles 7 and 14 of the ICCPR:[16]

> 7. No one shall be subjected to torture or to cruel, inhuman or degrading treatment or punishment ...
>
> 14.1. All persons shall be equal before the courts and tribunals.
>
> 14.2. Everyone charged with a criminal offence shall have the right to be presumed innocent until proved guilty according to law.
>
> 14.3. In the determination of any criminal charge against him, everyone shall be entitled to the following minimum guarantees, in full equality ...
>
> (e) To examine, or have examined, the witnesses against him and to obtain the attendance and examination of witnesses on his behalf under the same conditions as witnesses against him.... [and]
>
> (g) Not to be compelled to testify against himself or to confess guilt.

[10] As does the Universal Declaration of Human Rights 1948. See *Chow Hung Ching v R* (1948) 77 CLR 449, 477, per Dixon J; J Gans et al, *Criminal Process and Human Rights* (Sydney, Federation Press, 2011) ch 2.

[11] Signed 18 December 1972; ratified 13 August 1980; entered into force for Australia, 13 November 1980; acceded to the First Optional Protocol, 25 September 1991, ratified 25 December 1991; acceded to the second Optional Protocol aiming at the elimination of the death penalty, 2 October 1990, ratified 11 July 1991.

[12] Signed 13 October 1966; ratified 30 September 1975; entered into force for Australia 30 October 1975.

[13] Signed 17 July 1980; ratified 28 July 1983; entered into force for Australia 27 August 1983. Acceded to the Optional Protocol, 4 December 2008; ratified 4 March 2009.

[14] Signed 22 August 1990; ratified, 17 December 1990; entered into force for Australia, 16 January 1991; signed Optional Protocol on the Sale of Children, Child Prostitution and Child Pornography, 18 December 2001, acceded 8 January 2007; signed Optional Protocol on the Involvement of Children in Armed Conflict, 21 October 2002, ratified 26 September 2006.

[15] Signed 10 December 1985; ratified 8 August 1989; entered into force for Australia, 7 September 1989; signed the Optional Protocol, 19 May 2009.

[16] See the Charter of Human Rights and Responsibilities Act 2006 (Vic), ss 10, 25(2)(g), (h) and (k); Human Rights Act 2004 (ACT) ss 10, 22(2)(g) and (i). In like terms, see ECHR, Art 6(3)(d); Bill of Rights Act 1990 (NZ), s 25(f); and Constitution of the United States of America, Bill of Rights, Sixth and Fourteenth Amendments.

Our conception of a fair trial incorporates a triangulation of the interests of the accused, the victim, and the rather more protean notion of community interests. This has become a fairly orthodox view in human rights adjudication,[17] marking a shift away from the traditional defendant-centric fair trial guarantees articulated in Article 14 of the ICCPR.[18] It recognises and adopts human rights jurisprudence promoting recognition of victims' and witnesses' fair trial rights,[19] building on the right to dignified treatment,[20] the right to be protected from degrading treatment, the right to security of the person,[21] the right to life and the right to privacy.[22]

Acknowledging and respecting the fair trial rights of victims and witnesses does not detract from the traditional fair trials rights of the accused or diminish their need for special treatment. It does not alter the fact that defendants face the might of the State, possibly at peril of their liberty. Yet global models of fair trial rights, such as Article 14 of the ICCPR and Article 6 of the ECHR, are creatures of the 1950s and 1960s. Today these need to accommodate the legitimate expectations of vulnerable witnesses to be protected from degrading questioning and from the trauma associated with reliving the crime and confronting the accused in court.[23]

2. AUSTRALIAN HEARSAY REFORM IN COMPARATIVE PERSPECTIVE

For the persuasive reasons rehearsed by Mike Redmayne in Chapter 12 of this book, the default mode of evidence presentation in criminal trials should be the oral presentation of evidence in a public forum. This default setting should alter only where there are convincing reasons to favour a non-oral or a non-public presentation of certain evidence. One consideration with respect to the assumption of orality is electronic recording technology. Electronic recording of pre-trial statements is both easy and inexpensive

[17] See eg *R v A (No 2)* [2002] 1 AC 45, [38] per Lord Steyn (referring to 'the familiar triangulation of interests of the accused, the victim and society'); *Attorney General's Reference No 3 of 1999* [2001] 2 AC 91, 118, per Lord Steyn; *R v H* [2004] 2 AC 134, [12]. *R v Grant* [2007] 1 AC 1, [17] per Lord Bingham; *R v Mayers* [2009] 1 Cr App R 3.

[18] Cf *Albert and Le Compte v Belgium* (1983) EHRR 533, [39]; *Dombo Beheer v Netherlands* (1994) 18 EHRR 213, [32]. For detailed exploration, see Gans et al above n 10.

[19] *Doorson v Netherlands* (1996) 22 EHRR 330, [70]; *Van Mechelen v Netherlands* (1998) 25 EHRR 647, [53].

[20] See Charter (Vic), s 7; Human Rights Act 2004 (ACT), Preamble. See Gans et al, above n 10, ch 9.

[21] *Doorson v Netherlands* (1996) 22 EHRR 330, [70]; *Van Mechelen v Netherlands* (1998) 25 EHRR 647, [53] and see Charter (Vic), s 21; Human Rights Act 2004 (ACT), s 18.

[22] *Doorson v Netherlands* (1996) 22 EHRR 330, [70]; *Van Mechelen v Netherlands* (1998) 25 EHRR 647, [53] and see Charter (Vic), s 13; Human Rights Act 2004 (ACT), s 12.

[23] Also see J Hunter, 'Battling a Good Story: Cross-examining the Failure of the Law of Evidence' in P Roberts and M Redmayne (eds), *Innovations in Evidence and Proof* (Oxford, Hart Publishing, 2007).

and in Australia audio-visual recording is common for suspects' and complainants' statements made during police interviews. As discussed further below, compared to traditional forms of reporting, electronic technology greatly enhances the reliability and probative value of out-of-court speech and writing, many kinds of which would formerly have been inadmissible hearsay at common law.

It is generally recognised that criminal proceedings would grind to a standstill if courts were precluded from relying on hearsay statements in appropriate cases, and it has always been recognised by the common law that justice is enhanced by the existence of some hearsay exceptions.[24] More recently, Victoria's Charter of Rights and Responsibilities 2006 affirms that the accused's right to confront witnesses is not absolute.[25] As Charron J observed in the Canadian Supreme Court case of *R v Khelawon*:[26]

> [T]he extent to which hearsay evidence will present difficulties in assessing its worth obviously varies with the context. In some circumstances, the evidence presents minimal dangers and its *exclusion*, rather than its admission, would impede accurate fact finding. Hence, over time a number of exceptions to the rule were created by the courts.... [T]raditional exceptions to the exclusionary rule were largely crafted around those circumstances where the dangers of receiving the evidence were sufficiently alleviated.... When it is necessary to resort to evidence in this form, a hearsay statement may be admitted if, because of the way in which it came about, its contents are trustworthy, or if circumstances permit the ultimate trier of fact to sufficiently assess its worth. If the proponent of the evidence cannot meet the twin criteria of necessity and reliability, the general exclusionary rule prevails.

(a) Comparative Jurisprudence

As mentioned, the prevailing trend across the common law world is towards greater liberality in the admission of hearsay statements from unavailable witnesses. In New Zealand, for example, hearsay from unavailable witnesses (other than the accused) is admissible where 'the circumstances relating to the statement provide reasonable assurance that the statement is reliable'.[27] Under the admissibility framework introduced by the Criminal Justice Act 2003, hearsay evidence in England and Wales is now subject to a general inclusionary exception in the 'interests of justice'[28] and there is also fairly

[24] See J Stone and WAN Wells, *Evidence: Its History and Policies* (Sydney, Butterworths, 1991) 318.

[25] Charter (Vic), s 25(2)(g) provides that a 'person charged with a criminal offence is entitled without discrimination ... to examine, or have examined, witnesses against him or her, unless otherwise provided for by law'.

[26] *R v Khelawon* [2006] 2 SCR 787, [2].

[27] Evidence Act 2006 (NZ), s 18 (general admissibility) and s 22 (notice).

[28] Criminal Justice Act 2003 (UK) (CJA), s 114(1)(d).

comprehensive provision for admitting the first-hand hearsay statements of absent witnesses,[29] including those who do not give—or cannot continue giving—evidence through fear.[30] As the above quotation from Charron J in *R v Khelawon* indicates, the Supreme Court of Canada has innovated a flexible inclusionary exception for presumptively reliable hearsay at common law.[31]

Viewed against this backdrop, the US position represents something of a counter-trend, in which the constitutional right of confrontation places tangible constraints on any liberalisation of the hearsay prohibition. The US Supreme Court's interpretation of the Sixth Amendment Confrontation Clause permits the admission of a declarant's 'testimonial' statements only if the declarant testifies.[32] An obvious parallel can be drawn with the European Court of Human Rights' interpretation of the requirements of Article 6(3) of the ECHR. This appears to imply a blunt corroboration-like requirement if a conviction might otherwise be based 'solely or to a decisive extent' on an untested hearsay statement.[33] Where there is little other incriminating evidence, such as in a typical rape or domestic violence prosecution, Strasbourg's requirements for confrontational fairness operate from an initial standpoint that is far more exacting than those stipulated by legislatures and courts in England and Wales,[34] Australia, New Zealand and Canada.

In broad terms, human rights principles are infiltrating common law jurisdictions at a varying pace and they hold out some promise for significant positive change. However, in the context of concern for vulnerable witnesses the jurisprudence of the European Court of Human Rights and post-*Crawford* decisions in the US both demonstrate that the 'right of confrontation' is something of a double-edged sword.

(b) Australian Uniform Evidence Acts

Criminal justice in Australia is largely state-based, as in other federated jurisdictions, like the United States. Australian evidence law, including the law of hearsay, is governed by a systematic modernisation of common law principles known collectively as the uniform Evidence Acts.[35] Business

[29] CJA, s 116.

[30] CJA, s 116(2)(e).

[31] *R v Khelawon* [2006] 2 SCR 787.

[32] *Crawford v Washington*, 541 US 36 (2004). See also *Davis v Washington*, 547 US 813 (2006) *Melendez-Diaz v Massachusetts*, 129 S Ct 2527 (2009): *Michigan v Bryant*, 131 S Ct 1143 (2011).

[33] As confirmed in *Al-Khawaja and Tahery v United Kingdom* (2009) 49 EHRR 1 albeit with some increased flexibility in the Grand Chamber's Judgment of 15 December 2011. Notice, however, that pre-trial testing may be sufficient: *SN v Sweden* (2004) 39 EHRR 13; *Doorson v The Netherlands* (1996) 22 EHRR 330.

[34] *R v Horncastle* [2010] 2 AC 373, [36].

[35] Evidence Act 1995 (Cth); Evidence Act 1995 (NSW); Evidence Act 2001 (Tas); Evidence Act 2004 (Norfolk Island); Evidence Act 2008 (Vic); Evidence Act 2011 (ACT).

records and related exceptions aside, the main absent witness exception under the Australian uniform Evidence Acts is contained in section 65, which provides in material part:

> 65(1) This section applies in a criminal proceeding if a person who made a previous representation is not available to give evidence about an asserted fact.
>
> (2) The hearsay rule does not apply to evidence of a previous representation that is given by a person who saw, heard or otherwise perceived the representation being made, if the representation:
> (a) was made under a duty to make that representation or to make representations of that kind, or
> (b) was made when or shortly after the asserted fact occurred and in circumstances that make it unlikely that the representation is a fabrication, or
> (c) was made in circumstances that make it highly probable that the representation is reliable, or
> (d) was:
> (i) against the interests of the person who made it at the time it was made, and
> (ii) made in circumstances that make it likely that the representation is reliable....
>
> (8) The hearsay rule does not apply to:
> (a) evidence of a previous representation adduced by a defendant if the evidence is given by a person who saw, heard or otherwise perceived the representation being made, or
> (b) a document tendered as evidence by a defendant so far as it contains a previous representation, or another representation to which it is reasonably necessary to refer in order to understand the representation.

By section 62 of the uniform Evidence Acts, the declarant must have seen or heard (or otherwise perceived) those matters asserted in their out-of-court statement. This limits the scope of the section 65 exceptions to first-hand hearsay. Except in relation to court transcripts,[36] section 65 requires that the testifying witness must have perceived the absent declarant's hearsay statement directly. The further conditions imposed by subsection (2) mirror well-established common law hearsay exceptions for statements against interest, *res gestae*, and statements made in furtherance of a duty. In addition, section 65(2)(c) introduces a broad exception for representations 'made in circumstances that make it highly probable that the representation is reliable'. Finally, the broadest exception of all in terms of reliability preconditions is section 65(8). It is restricted to defence evidence only and it permits the admission of first-hand hearsay evidence adduced by the

[36] Uniform Evidence Acts (UEA), s 65(3)–(6). See also the statutory definition of 'unavailability of persons', Dictionary, UEA, discussed below.

accused, as long as it is given by a person who directly saw or heard the making of the representation. Its terms permit the admission of previously inadmissible, but potentially exculpatory proof of innocence, such as third party confessions (as in *R v Blastland*)[37] or, as in *Sparks v R*,[38] a victim's description of a perpetrator that bears no resemblance to the accused.

There are no express inclusionary discretions in the uniform Evidence Acts, but there are two general exclusionary discretions. The first is a statutory version of the familiar *Christie*-style[39] exclusionary 'discretion'[40] applicable to unfairly prejudicial *prosecution* evidence. The second is contained in a statutory formulation of legal relevance that permits the exclusion of relevant but distracting, time-wasting or unfairly prejudicial evidence.[41] Although the hearsay exceptions are broad in scope, the comparatively prescriptive style of drafting adopted in the uniform Evidence Acts fosters a relatively mechanical judicial approach to determining the admissibility of hearsay statements. At the same time however, it promotes transparency in admissibility determinations, and this facilitates assessing how the provisions are applied in particular contexts.

R v Suteski (No 4)[42] represents the high-water mark of Australian courts' willingness to receive hearsay from 'unavailable' witnesses. The key evidence was from Witness B who was in gaol for his part in the contract killing allegedly perpetrated by Sneza Suteski. Previously, Witness B had given a video-recorded police interview in which he claimed that Suteski had instructed him to 'stab' the deceased, to 'bash him, kill him if you want', with 'words to the effect of break his knees or his legs'. However, when Witness B was brought to court, he refused to testify in accordance with his police statement, apparently because he no longer wished to cooperate with the authorities, or at any rate did not wish to be seen to be doing so. The judge ruled that Witness B's statement could be admitted under section 65 of the uniform Evidence Act, since 'all reasonable steps have been taken, by the party seeking to prove the person is not available, to compel the person to give the evidence, but without success'.[43] This ruling was upheld on appeal. It did not seem to matter that, in traditional currency, Witness B looked more like an unwilling than an unavailable witness. This decision has been widely cited and applied.[44] The Australian High Court's refusal of special leave to appeal, on the basis of insufficient

37 [1986] AC 41.
38 [1964] AC 964.
39 [1914] AC 545.
40 UEA, s 137.
41 UEA, s 135.
42 *R v Suteski (No 4)* (2002) 128 A Crim R 275 (NSW SC).
43 Dictionary, UEA, 'unavailability of persons'.
44 *R v Alchin* (2006) 200 FLR 204 (ACT SC); *R v Darmody* (2010) 25 VR 209; *Director of Public Prosecutions v BB* [2010] VSCA 211.

prospects of success, in a hearing lasting less than 20 minutes, suggests that there is little likelihood of the *Suteski* precedent being displaced for the foreseeable future.[45]

The ruling in *Suteski* has fuelled a lack of timidity in applying section 65. Its endorsement by other courts is grounded in the view expressed often by Australian appellate courts that they must respect the legislative intention evinced by section 65 and the Acts' formula of reliability assurances. They must therefore admit evidence falling expressly within the unavailable witness exception, even if the evidence is sole or decisive in sustaining a guilty verdict. Courts have reiterated that the Acts' intention to admit hearsay evidence from absent witnesses is to be respected[46] and they have cautioned against exercising the exclusionary discretions 'to emasculate provisions in the Act'[47] in the face of Parliament's clear intentions to provide exceptions to the hearsay rule. Deceased,[48] demented[49] or seriously ill[50] prosecution witnesses are the most common categories of unavailable witness. Their evidence has been admitted in the most serious of crimes and with respect to the most contentious of issues. In murder and manslaughter trials, for example, section 65 has permitted admission of statements of deceased declarants detailing the incident giving rise to the charge,[51] identifying the perpetrator,[52] previous episodes of violence by the accused, the injuries sustained,[53] the nature of the relationships between the accused and the deceased, and the deceased's fear of the accused and his threats.[54] In a sentencing case, the court admitted previous statements of a murder victim that the accused had threatened and acted violently towards her.[55]

Australian courts have been generous in classifying a prosecution witness who is untraceable or has disappeared (possibly out of fear) as 'unavailable' under the uniform Evidence Acts. If the witness's testimony forms part of a transcript of committal proceedings, confrontation opportunities have

45 *Suteski v R* [2003] HCA Trans 493.

46 *R v Suteski* (2002) 56 NSWLR 182, [126] per Wood CJ at CL; *R v Clark* [2001] NSWCCA 494, [164] per Heydon J.

47 *Papakosmas v R* (1999) 196 CLR 297, [97] per McHugh J.

48 Eg, *R v Gover* (2000) 118 A Crim R 8 (NSWCCA), a credit card fraud case, where the deceased owner of a credit card had made a statement indicating he had not authorised its use by the defendant.

49 In *R v Anyang (Ruling No 2)* [2011] VSC 38 (the elderly witness had suffered cognitive loss such that she was mentally incapable of giving evidence). The transcript of her evidence at the committal proceedings and a written statement made shortly after the incident was admitted.

50 *Easwaralingam v DPP* [2010] VSCA 353.

51 *R v Harris* (2005) 158 A Crim R 454 (NSWCCA).

52 *Conway v R* (2000) 172 ALR 185; *R v Polkingthorne* (1999) 108 A Crim R 189; *R v Kuzmanovic* [2005] NSWSC 771; *R v Dean* (Unreported NSWSC, Dunford J, 12 March 1997).

53 *R v Toki* (2000) 116 A Crim R 536.

54 *R v Mankotia* [1998] NSWSC 295; *R v Dean* (Unreported NSWSC, Dunford J, 12 March 1997); *R v Lubik (No 1)* [2010] VSC 465; *DPP v Curran* [2011] VSC 279.

55 *R v Jang* [1999] NSWSC 1040.

been satisfied and the admission of the (hearsay) transcript is relatively unremarkable.[56] In *R v Kazzi*[57] and in *R v Morton*[58] victims of armed robberies had made police statements, but had subsequently travelled overseas. Their statements were successfully tendered under section 65. This general trend towards receiving more hearsay in criminal trials, which Australia shares with most of the common law world, is very much in sympathy with the modern zeitgeist.

However, as we will see, the Australian courts' approach to admitting hearsay statements under section 65 has not been uniformly so receptive.

3. VICTIMS OF DOMESTIC AND SEXUAL VIOLENCE

It is a historical and a contemporary fact that victims of violent crime and most particularly victims of intimate and domestic violence, fear court proceedings. They may be fearful of suffering social, economic or physical harm when the proceedings are completed, or they may fear the actual process of confrontation with the accused and his family in court or in the court precinct. As one prosecutor interviewed in Lievore's study of adult sexual assault cases summarised the position, '[t]hey're more traumatised, there's usually less physical evidence, and it's more emotionally and socially difficult to recount the events in front of strangers'.[59] High rates of discontinuance for prosecutions of sexual assault and domestic violence are notorious.[60] They have resulted in the introduction of 'special measures' to assist vulnerable complainants and witnesses, such as testimony through closed circuit televised (CCTV), pre-recorded video statements and, at a more low-tech level, in-court screening.[61]

It is now common in most Australian States for sexual assault complainants to make pre-trial video-recorded statements, popularly known as VATE tapes—video and audio taped evidence. A patchwork of State legislative provisions governs the admissibility of these pre-trial statements. In New South

[56] *R v Rossi (Ruling No 1)* [2010] VSC 459; *Director of Public Prosecutions v BB* [2010] VSCA 211; *Puchalski v R* [2007] NSWCCA 220.

[57] *R v Kazzi; Williams; Murchie* (2003) 140 A Crim R 545 (NSWCCA).

[58] *R v Morton* [2008] NSWCCA 196. See also *Vickers v R* [2006] 160 A Crim R 195 (NSW CCA), where the reason for the unavailability of an eye-witness to a serious assault in a nightclub was unclear, but still accepted by the court. His police statement was ruled partially admissible under s 65.

[59] D Lievore, *Prosecutorial Decisions in Adult Sexual Assault Cases: An Australian Study* (Canberra, AIC for the Office of the Status of Women, 2004) 46.

[60] See for example, the study by M Heenan and S Murray, reported in *Study of Reported Rapes in Victoria 2000–2003: Summary Research Report* (Melbourne, Office of Women's Policy, Department for Victorian Communities, 2006).

[61] For example, Evidence (Children and Special Witnesses) Act 2001 (Tas) s 5; Evidence Act 1906 (WA) s 106H; Criminal Procedure Act 1986 (NSW) s 306U; Criminal Procedure Act 2009 (Vic) ss 366 and 369.

Wales and Victoria, for example, only children under 16 and cognitively impaired adults may give evidence by pre-recorded statement as their examination-in-chief.[62] But all vulnerable witnesses must still be available for cross-examination. Given that two of the major disincentives to testifying for vulnerable witnesses are fear of intimate details being raked over in public and fear of confrontation with the accused and his family, these special measures, well-intentioned though they are, do not necessarily encourage vulnerable and fearful witnesses to come to court. However, hearsay exceptions, including section 65 of the uniform Evidence Acts, offer prosecutors an alternative means of adducing the testimony of fearful witnesses.

Victoria, the latest State to enact uniform evidence legislation has come closest to extending unavailability to include the fearful witness. It has specifically incorporated the Australian Law Reform Commission's recommendation that 'unavailability' should expressly extend to witnesses who are mentally … unable to testify.[63] But even in the absence of any explicit reference to fear (comparable to section 116(2)(a) of the Criminal Justice Act 2003 in the England and Wales), the liberal approach to 'unavailability' endorsed by *R v Suteski (No 4)*[64] ought in principle encompass vulnerable witnesses who are too fearful to testify, and for whom the very threat of compelled testimony might be enough to drive them into hiding.

In fact, despite the large cohort of fearful complainants and witnesses and the many cases applying the modest unavailability requirements set by *Suteski (No 4)* in other contexts, there is only one reported Australian case in which section 65 has been utilised to admit a living complainant's out-of-court statement. In *DPP v Nicholls*,[65] the magistrate refused to admit the hearsay statement of a domestic violence complainant. Without it, the case would collapse. The magistrate rejected the contention that the complainant was 'unavailable' under section 65 even though her unavailability was founded upon the magistrate's earlier ruling that the complainant could not be compelled to testify under the Acts' spousal non-compellability provision.[66] On the prosecutor's appeal from the section 65 ruling and against dismissal of the charges, Beach J applied *Suteski*'s broader interpretation of unavailability, allowed the appeal and remitted the case to the Magistrates Court for determination.

This single reported decision testifies to the largely untapped potential of section 65 in domestic violence prosecutions. We suggest that the elaborate legislative provision for vulnerable witnesses may distract courts' and prosecutors' attention from the possibilities opened up by the uniform

[62] Criminal Procedure Act 1986 (NSW), s 306U; Criminal Procedure Act 2009 (Vic), s 366.
[63] ALRC, *Uniform Evidence Law*, Report 102 (Canberra, 2006) 8.33–8.37.
[64] *R v Suteski (No 4)* (2002) 128 A Crim R 275 (NSW SC).
[65] [2010] VSC 397.
[66] UEA, s 18(6).

Evidence Acts' generous hearsay exceptions. This distraction is further complicated by prosecutors' need to establish a reasonable prospect of conviction to proceed. This may be perceived as difficult where the complainant is unwilling to testify.

Reluctance to testify was a determinative factor in almost half of the 53 discontinued cases in Lievore's sexual assault prosecution study,[67] and the prosecution proceeded to trial in only one of the 25 cases in which the complainant did not wish to proceed.[68] In that case the unwilling complainant was subpoenaed. The link between continuance of domestic violence prosecutions and the admissibility of complainants' hearsay statements is further illustrated by Lininger's study of 60 US prosecutors' offices in California, Oregon and Washington:

> Sixty three percent of respondents reported the *Crawford* decision has significantly impeded prosecutions of domestic violence. Seventy-six percent indicated that after *Crawford*, their offices are more likely to drop domestic violence charges when the victims recant or refuse to cooperate. Alarmingly, 65 percent of respondents reported that victims of domestic violence are less safe in their jurisdictions than during the era preceding the *Crawford* decision.[69]

In the United States there is much interest in the impact of the hearsay rule on the success, or otherwise, of prosecutions for domestic and sexual violence.[70] This scholarship sits within a vibrant (and apparently thankless) tradition of critiquing the US Supreme Court's interpretation of the 6th Amendment's Confrontation Clause, highlighting the increased burden of a strong right to confrontation, defined without any consideration for competing public policies. On current interpretations of the Sixth Amendment Confrontation Clause, if the victim is unavailable to enter the witness-box only evidence of calls for assistance that convey a plea for help, typically in the face of fear, are admissible. If the call for assistance is classified not as a plea for help but as a report of the offence (or the culprit's identity) it will be characterised as 'testimonial' and cannot be adduced as an out-of-court statement unless the victim testifies in person.[71] If the victim is dead her

[67] Lievore, above n 59, 55. Orenstein catalogues largely identical problems arising from victim reluctance to testify in the United States along with the amplification of their impact on the prosecution of domestic violence offences as a result of the US Supreme Court decision in *Crawford v Washington*: AA Orenstein, 'Sex, Threats, and Absent Victims: The Lessons of *R v Bedingfield* for Modern Confrontation and Domestic Violence cases' (2010) 79 *Fordham Law Review* 115.

[68] Lievore, above n 59, 40.

[69] T Lininger, 'Prosecuting Batterers after *Crawford*' (2005) 91 *Virginia Law Review* 747, 750 (footnotes omitted), quoted in Orenstein, above n 67.

[70] For some recent contributors, see AA Orenstein, above n 67; M Raeder, 'Being Heard after *Giles*: Comments on the Sound of Silence' (2010) 87 *Texas Law Review* 105; M Raeder, 'History Redux: The Unheard Voices of Domestic Violence Victims, A Comment on Aviva Orenstein's *Sex, Threats, and Absent Victims*' (2011) 79 *Fordham Law Review Res Gestae* 21.

[71] *Davis v Washington*, 547 US 813 (2006), 827.

statement cannot be used and, according to US commentators, prosecutions fail as a result.[72]

4. THE ACCUSED, THE RIGHT TO SILENCE AND HEARSAY

The impact of trial dynamics upon defendants is inevitably unique, represented in part by their rights to silence and to the presumption of innocence. From a historical perspective, until defendants gained the right to counsel and to testify, there could be no right to silence because silence was imposed.[73] However, one should pause before jumping to the conclusion that previously excluded defendants' voices are now being heard in full in contemporary Australian criminal trials.

It was not until 1891 (in New South Wales)[74] that the accused gained the right to give sworn evidence. This right stood side by side with the right to give an unsworn (or dock) statement, a right that meant the accused was not exposed to cross-examination. With the dock statement juries could hear defendants' explanations, sometimes unvarnished and rambling and not always to their advantage, but at least it was at their option. We need to look to the past, to the century following 1891, to find the period when defendants' formal rights to be heard at trial were at their climax. Progress has not been linear.

The defendant's right to make an unsworn statement from the dock disappeared decades ago,[75] partly because it gave defendants a platform to make baseless allegations against witnesses, including victims of sexual assault. Tapping into familiar reservoirs of mistrust, the problem was perceived to be that 'an accused person who is well-educated and articulate, or a recidivist who knows the criminal justice system well, can manipulate the dock statement to his or her advantage'.[76] Concerns that its abolition would disadvantage socially and economically deprived defendants went unheeded. Most defendants, it was said,[77] would be represented by lawyers, and those that were not would be protected by the trial judge in discharging the general duty to ensure a fair trial.[78] But the reality is that, especially if the admissibility of pre-trial statements is restricted, many accused are

[72] See *Giles v California*, 554 US 353 (2008) per Scalia J and Orenstein, above n 67.

[73] J Langbein, *The Origins of the Adversary Criminal Trial* (Oxford, OUP, 2003) 48, 61.

[74] CR Williams, 'Silence and the Unsworn Statement: An Accused's Alternatives to Giving Sworn Evidence' (1976) 10 *Melbourne University Law Review* 481.

[75] The right to make an unsworn statement was abolished in Queensland in 1975, Western Australia in 1976, the Northern Territory in 1983, South Australia in 1985 and Victoria and Tasmania in 1983.

[76] C Hartcher, Second Reading speech for the Crimes Legislation (Unsworn Evidence) Amendment Bill 1994 (NSW), Legislative Assembly, Hansard 1547 (20 April 1994).

[77] Ibid.

[78] Cf *Dietrich v R* (1992) 177 CLR 292, regarding the challenges facing the trial judge protecting an unrepresented defendant's trial rights.

forced to testify in their own defence or risk almost certain conviction, and this is likely to mean that defendants who are 'illiterate, poorly educated … or those from different cultural backgrounds, particularly Aborigines, may be seriously disadvantaged'.[79]

Even though there is obviously no human rights objection to receiving out-of-court statements tendered by the defence, common law jurisdictions like Australia have always regarded exculpatory out-of-court statements whether by the accused or by someone else as the epitome of inadmissible hearsay. Prior to the uniform Evidence Acts, Australia followed common law orthodoxy in this regard. By well-established concession, mixed exculpatory and inculpatory statements could be adduced in their entirety to allow the jury to contextualise incriminating remarks,[80] but entirely exculpatory statements were always inadmissible. Some prosecutors adopted the fair-minded practice of routinely placing defendants' out-of-court statements before the jury, even if entirely exculpatory. This indulgence has garnered judicial approval,[81] but its discretionary nature makes it quite unsatisfactory as a guarantor of trial fairness.

In 1995 section 65(8) of the uniform Evidence Acts became the law in New South Wales and federally. It now applies in all uniform Evidence Act jurisdictions. As noted earlier in this chapter, this hearsay exception for *defence* (only) evidence from unavailable witnesses is notably broad. Apart from the personal knowledge requirement, it contains none of the additional assurances of trustworthiness and prior testing embedded elsewhere in section 65. Has this broad exception been widely utilised in accordance with the generally liberal approach to section 65 endorsed in *R v Suteski*? The trio of reported cases to-date, discussed below, would indicate otherwise. Thus, instead of utilising a dedicated and broad hearsay exception for defence evidence, defendants have two second-best alternatives. They either remain reliant on the discretion of the prosecutor or they are obligated to testify and submit to cross-examination.[82]

R v Parkes[83] actually concerned the evidence of a hostile[84] prosecution witness, who testified to an exculpatory remark by the accused. The question then arose as to whether the defendant's out-of-court statements would have been admissible for the defence. A majority of the New South Wales Court of Criminal Appeal noted that the accused was not available

[79] C Hartcher, above n 76.

[80] *Mahmood v Western Australia* (2008) 232 CLR 397; *R v Su* [1997] 1 VR 1, 64; *R v Rudd* [2009] VSCA 213 and see also *R v McCarthy* (1980) 71 Cr App R 142; *R v Storey and Anwar* (1968) 52 Cr App R 334 (admissibility of spontaneous exculpatory responses to accusations).

[81] Eg *R v Sidhu* (1994) 98 Cr App R 59.

[82] Cf *R v Rymer* [2005] NSW CCA 310.

[83] (2003) 147 A Crim R 450.

[84] Or, as it is known in Australia, unfavourable witness: UEA, s 38.

in the prosecution case[85] but that he would be available in his own case to confirm the out-of-court statement. *Parkes* is an ambiguous precedent. The question of the defendant's availability was not well-ventilated, and section 65(8) was not discussed at all. It does suggest that when there is exculpatory hearsay evidence, a defendant's notional availability in his or her own case will preclude its admission unless he or she testifies (a requirement under the 'witness *available*' hearsay exception in the Acts).[86]

If *Parkes* suggests defendants' exculpatory out-of-court statements may fit unhappily in the modern regime of first-hand hearsay exceptions, *R v O'Connor*[87] suggests judicial bloody mindedness regarding section 65(8)'s clear intention that defendants benefit by the loosening of hearsay exceptions. This case concerned a bottle shop robbery in which the only issue in dispute was the perpetrator's identity. On appeal, the accused wished to rely on two forms of documentary evidence indicating that a co-accused, Makhoul (who was still at large during O'Connor's trial), had on two separate occasions indicated that O'Connor was not involved. Makhoul's first statement to the police included the passage 'and why is Linda [O'Connor] here anyway, she had nothing to do with it'. Secondly, at Makhoul's own trial (which post-dated O'Connor's) he adhered to his earlier account to police, namely, that 'a girl named Nicky' had followed him into the bottle shop. Makhoul denied under cross-examination that Linda O'Connor was with him. The appeal court held that Makhoul's own trial testimony, subjected to cross-examination and resulting in a hung jury, lacked credibility—apparently because the justices themselves did not believe it. The court further observed that Makhoul had not been made available for cross-examination on appeal—even though section 65(8) does not invoke reliability as a further condition of admissibility. Dismissing the appeal, the court concluded that, whilst Makhoul's evidence was prima facie admissible for the defence under section 65(8):

> it may be unfairly prejudicial to the Crown for an accused person to adduce evidence of out-of-court statements of absent co-offenders exculpatory of the accused. Such persons may have a motive to lie. The probative value of such evidence is likely to be slight. The inability of counsel to test the evidence by cross-examining the maker of the statement may prejudice the Crown. Such prejudice may outweigh the probative value of the evidence.[88]

The decision in *O'Connor* seems clearly at odds with *Suteski (No 4)* where, it will be remembered, an 'unavailable' accomplice's hearsay evidence of how he relayed the contract killer's instructions to the hitman was deemed

[85] UEA, s 17.
[86] UEA, s 66.
[87] *R v O'Connor* [2003] NSWCCA 335.
[88] *R v O'Connor* [2003] NSWCCA 335, [13] per Barr J.

sufficient to satisfy section 65's more demanding requirements. The tone of the *O'Connor* judgment and its reliance on discretionary exclusion runs counter to the general pro-admissibility philosophy animating the uniform Evidence Acts' hearsay exceptions.[89]

The final case in the trio of reported decisions is *R v Rymer*.[90] The accused wished to rely on his pre-trial denials without testifying at trial. Applying section 66 (the *available* witness hearsay exception limited to matters fresh in the declarant's mind), the trial judge indicated that the defendant's out-of-court denial would be admissible only if he gave evidence. Rymer then testified and his pre-trial denial was admitted. On appeal, Rymer contended that the judge's ruling had deprived him of his right to remain silent. The appeal court indicated that the four-year delay between the alleged crime and Rymer's out-of-court denial made his recollection stale and, under the terms of section 66, inadmissible. Neither judge nor counsel expressly considered the potential applicability of section 65(8). The NSW Court of Criminal Appeal suggested instead that the denial could have been admitted as a prior consistent statement—consistent with Rymer's plea of not guilty—without requiring the accused to testify in his own defence. Once admitted in the trial, section 60 would permit the statement to be utilised to prove the facts asserted. This resort to the prior consistent statement artifice was a contorted technical fix. However, the Court did at least expressly reject the old common law position summarised by Baron Parke in *R v Higgins*[91] (and quoted by Justice Grove in *Rymer*):

> What a prisoner says is not evidence, unless the prosecutor chooses to make it so, by using it as part of his case against the prisoner; however, if the prosecutor makes the prisoner's declaration evidence, it then becomes evidence for the prisoner, as well as against him.

In sum, the current Australian case law suggests that despite clearly permissive statutory language sub-section (8) appears to be no more than an illusory indulgence towards defendants. The Australian courts' conservative approach to section 65(8) of the uniform Evidence Acts indicates that old habits die hard, at least when they concern the common law's inherent suspicion of the out-of-court exculpatory statement.

[89] See *Papakosmas v R* (1999) 196 CLR 297, esp [23]–[42] and [90]–[97]; *Roach v Page (No 11)* [2003] NSWSC 907, [74]: '[W]here hearsay evidence is admissible under an exception to the hearsay rule because of the unavailability of the maker of the representation, there is a special reason for not disallowing the evidence or limiting its use on the ground that the evidence cannot be tested by cross-examination. That is because the legislature has made the evidence admissible notwithstanding that consideration'.

[90] (2005) 156 A Crim R 84 (NSW CCA).

[91] (1829) 3 C & P 603.

This is clearly not an exclusively Australian conceit.[92] New Zealand's modernised evidence statute specifically prohibits an accused from relying on his or her hearsay statements without also testifying.[93] This extraordinary limitation on defendants' access to New Zealand's otherwise generous hearsay exceptions applies notwithstanding section 25 of the New Zealand Bill of Rights Act 1990 (NZBORA) expressly guaranteeing defendants' rights to the presumption of innocence, to present a defence and to non-compellability.[94] The decision appears to ignore the New Zealand Law Commission's contrary recommendation.[95] Indeed, it appears to be a matter of political calculation: Cabinet records, quoted in the New Zealand Court of Appeal case of *R v Frost*,[96] indicate no deeper rationale than the peremptory stipulation that 'a defendant is not, in reality, "unavailable" to him or herself'.

5. MANSIONS OF JUSTICE?

In the mid-1960s the US legal scholar Yale Kamisar evoked a striking contrast between the 'gatehouse' of the police interview room and the courtroom 'mansion'.[97] Kamisar's metaphors underscored the flimsiness of pre-trial protections for suspects in the 'gatehouse', compared with the relative grandeur of the US Constitution's in-court protections for criminal defendants. This theme struck a chord beyond US shores because it encapsulated a major focus of criminal justice policy in the second half of the twentieth century, namely, the prevention of police abuse of *suspects*' rights in a gatehouse that was closed to public scrutiny and bereft of real protections. The courtroom, however, was by comparison *relatively* rich in its protections for defendants. It was a mansion of rights.

However, for vulnerable witnesses in Kamisar's time, no part of the criminal justice system was a mansion. During the investigation of sexual assault and domestic violence crimes complainants were as suspicious to investigators as the accused. In the name of eliminating false complaints they were (in the words of Kemisar describing police treatmeant of suspects) '"sized up" and subjected to "interrogation tactics and techniques most

[92] See eg *R v Y* [2008] 2 All ER 484; *R v Gorski* [2009] NICC 66 (usefully summarising the debate); *R v McCarthy* (1980) 71 Cr App R 142; *R v Edgar* [2010] ONCA 529; L Heffernan and EJ Imwinkelried, 'The Accused's Constitutional Right to Introduce Critical, Demonstrably Reliable Exculpatory Evidence (2005) 40 *Irish Jurist* 111.

[93] Evidence Act 2006 (NZ), s 21(1), 'If a defendant in a criminal proceeding does not give evidence, the defendant may not offer his or her own hearsay statement in evidence in the proceeding'.

[94] Evidence Act 2006 (NZ), s 25(c)–(e).

[95] See discussion in *R v Frost* [2008] NZCA 406, [39].

[96] *R v Frost* [2008] NZCA 406, [39].

[97] Y Kamisar, 'Equal Justice in the Gatehouse and Mansions of American Criminal Procedure' in A Howard (ed), *Criminal Justice in Our Time* (Charlottesville, VA, Virginia UP, 1965).

appropriate for the occasion"',[98] the objects of curiosity, suspicion and humiliating investigative practices. They fared no better at trial. Here they were '"game" to be stalked and cornered',[99] harried, bullied and hemmed in, their credibility, integrity and morality attacked. It is hardly a matter of surprise that for such witnesses the trial process was 'ritualised degradation dressed up as court process' and their treatment, 'state sanctioned victimisation'.[100] For vulnerable witnesses the criminal justice process resembled the Roman Circus.

Further, the voices of victims of sexual assault were excluded or devalued in court by competence and corroboration rules. Young children, often victims or eyewitnesses to sexual assault, were silenced completely. Like the accused, they were not competent to testify. Corroboration rules dictated that the voices of older children and the voices of complainants in sexual offences cases were insufficient to sustain a conviction. Even though competency and corroboration rules were in their time perceived as enhancing accurate fact-finding, it is now commonly recognised that in reality they diminished the opportunity for its achievement. Sexual assault complainants' evidence was also confined by rules relating to complaint evidence. While the complaint rules were touted as a concession to sexual offence complainants, they were a distorted concession. Only evidence of *recent* complaint was admissible and then only if the cross-examiner asserted its absence. If admitted it was merely evidence of complainants' consistency. It could not be used as evidence of the facts asserted. Unlike a confession which despite its suspicious integrity (at least prior to mandatory electronic recording), has always been admissible as evidence of its truth. Further, a delayed complaint was and remains a source of complainant discredit. And so the traditional conception of the law of evidence joined trial process and the myriad of social, psychological and economic pressures to silence victims of intimate and domestic violence.

But, during the course of the last half-century, Australian law—like most other common law systems—has witnessed major doctrinal and institutional reform aimed at improving the lot of vulnerable complainants and witnesses. Indefensible restrictions on witness and defendant competency have been lifted and sexist corroboration rules abandoned. A raft of 'special measures' has been introduced to assist vulnerable witnesses to give their best evidence. In addition, in Australia since the early 1990s mandatory electronic recording of interviews with suspect persons (ERISP) in the police station has sat alongside routine recording of other investigative activities like executing search warrants and conducting identification parades.

[98] Ibid 19–21.
[99] Ibid.
[100] P van de Zandt, 'Heroines of Fortitude' in P Easteal (ed), *Balancing the Scales: Rape Law Reform and Australian Culture* (Sydney, The Federation Press, 1998) 125.

These electronic recordings present the court with a far superior view of the defendant's situation under police questioning than their paper-based predecessors. As a consequence, the expansion of electronic recording of police questioning and its impetus towards professionalising police interviewing[101] have reduced the contrast between trial testimony and pre-trial statements.

These changes underscore the fact that the mansion and gatehouse dichotomy reflects a time when witnesses came into the courtroom and there was no evidence in the form of surveillance tapes, closed-circuit TV testimony or electronically recorded interviews. There were just some limited documentary hearsay alternatives to viva voce evidence. Now, over 50 years later, when (outside the mansion) suspects and complainants speak to camera, there are fewer points of forensic contrast between inside and outside the mansion. In a world of ERISPs and VATEs, the formal distinction between evidence gathering in the gatehouse and testimony in the mansion is not nearly so stark as Kamisar first drew it.

Electronic recording in police station interviews has upgraded the gatehouse to approach mansion proportions. In addition, it has captured, made immediate and de-mystified the complainant's early reporting of assault. Electronically-recorded interviews provide an unlaundered view of events, incriminations and exculpations that can (all but) equal courtroom testimony. Electronic recording may even surpass live testimony by preempting the gamesmanship of cross-examination at trial. Jurors can evaluate the declarant's veracity with reference to the actual words and cadence of the moment; context, language, demeanour, inebriation and emotions are laid bare to the court. All these factors suggest that section 65(2)(c)'s admissibility test, 'that the previous representation be made in circumstances that make it highly probable that it is reliable', will often be satisfied. Of course, section 65(8) sets even lower admission standards for defence hearsay evidence.

We saw earlier the impact of law reform on defendants' ability to speak in court. On the vulnerable complainants' side of the equation, the swag of legislated protective measures has been met with some judicial resistance[102] and in Australia new procedural rules have tenaciously preserved historical approaches in alternative guises.[103] Moreover, practical compliance with legislated witness protections can be patchy. For example, Oliver found that

[101] D Dixon, '"A Window into the Interviewing Process"? The Audio-visual Recording of Police Interrogation in NSW Australia' (2006) 16 *Policing & Society* 328.

[102] Eg *Crofts v R* (1996) 186 CLR 427 (mandating judicial directions reflecting on the credibility of the complainant where there is no evidence of recent complaint); *Conway v R* (2002) 209 CLR 203, 223 (resisting the abolition of corroboration laws).

[103] Eg *Crofts v R* (1996) 186 CLR 427 (the resurrection of the recent complaint doctrine); (*Longman v R* (1989) 168 CLR 79; *Crampton v R* (2000) 206 CLR 161 and *Doggett v R* (2001) 208 CLR 343 (the establishment of new warnings about the dangers of convicting on

one Brisbane judge refused to allow a screen between a child witness and the accused 'under any circumstances'.[104] In a similar vein, a recent overview of research on child complainants shows that the legislation has failed in significant ways to achieve its legislative intent.[105] Additionally, courts have constrained the operation of the VATE provisions by requiring judicial warnings accompany its use[106] and elaborating a raft of rules stipulating how juries may use pre-recorded testimony, for example that they must not have unsupervised or unrestricted access to it.[107] The courts' fundamental concern is that juries will give pre-recorded evidence 'undue weight'—that they will amplify the value of the recorded witness's voice too greatly. This fear fits squarely with the historical distrust of sexual assault complainants' and children's testimony. So, whilst vulnerable witness reforms represent a massive ideological shift in the conception of a fair trial, they can be stymied in their application. Taking the protections to ameliorate the ordeal of confrontation for vulnerable witnesses at their highest, they still require complainants to be available for cross-examination[108] and therefore vulnerable witnesses remain potential quarry for counsel.

CONCLUSION

The case law surveyed in this chapter indicates that defendants (and defence witnesses) and vulnerable witnesses miss out in the application of general hearsay law reform apparently because the common law's traditional mistrust of them remains essentially undiminished. The sticking point is not the scope of legislative hearsay exceptions, which are generously drafted, but professional attitudes and culture. This cold front languishes in a microclimate of Australian legal practice where all around it courts embrace the relaxation of the hearsay rule.

complainants' uncorroborated evidence in cases of delayed complaint/prosecution, applied exceptionally rarely in cases other than those involving sexual assault).

[104] J Oliver, 'The Legislation Changed What about the Reality?' (2006) 6 *Queensland University of Technology Law & Justice Journal* 55, 59.

[105] K Richards, *Child Complainants and the Court Process in Australia*, Trends and Issues in Criminal Justice No 380 (Canberra, AIC, 2009).

[106] *R v NRC* [1999] 3 VR 537, [34] per Winneke P; *R v BAH* (2002) 5 VR 517; *R v Lewis* (2002) 137 A Crim R 83, [11]; *R v MAG* [2005] VSCA 47, [20]; *R v NZ* (2005) 63 NSWLR 628, [169]; *R v Lyne* (2003) 140 A Crim R 522; *R v Knigge* (2003) 6 VR 181, [30].

[107] *Gately v R* (2007) 241 ALR 1, [93]–[96] (Hayne J) and [28] (Gleeson CJ).

[108] Evidence Act 1977 (Qd), s 93A; Evidence Act 1929 (SA), s 34C; Evidence (Children and Special Witnesses) Act 2001 (Tas), s 5; Evidence Act 1906 (WA), s 106H. In some jurisdictions the whole or part of vulnerable witnesses' evidence may be pre-recorded on video-tape and shown at trial: Criminal Procedure Act 1986 (NSW), s 306U; Criminal Procedure Act 2009 (Vic), ss 366 and 369; Evidence Act 1929 (SA), ss 13A(2)(b) and 13C; Evidence Act 1977 (Qld), ss 21AK–AM; ss 93A and 93C; Evidence Act 1906 (WA) ss 106HB and 106I.

The first step in more fully realising fair trial rights, we suggest, is to recognise that cross-examination is not the only confrontation tool in town. Australia, like the United Kingdom, Canada and New Zealand, prioritises assurances of reliability and necessity in permitting hearsay evidence despite the lack of in-court confrontation of the declarant. A witness to the making of the statements must testify and can be cross-examined about elements of circumstantial unreliability.[109] Opposing parties are put on notice[110] and can respond to hearsay evidence by adducing credibility evidence of the absent declarant[111] and by requesting a judicial warning reminding the jury of the potential unreliability of hearsay evidence.[112] Where prosecutors tender hearsay from an absent witness they are obliged to disclose any related material in their possession, including other relevant statements that might impact on the declarant's credibility. Further, a specific check on the impact of defence hearsay admitted under s 65(8) is provided by section 65(9), which facilitates the admission of rebuttal hearsay evidence from another party.

If the out-of-court statements of frightened accomplices like Witness B in *Suteski* are capable of satisfying these admissibility criteria, why are complainants and the accused stubbornly excluded from the benefits of section 65? Behind the doctrinal façade of progressive reforms, this chapter suggests, lurk traditional—but now largely unarticulated—suspicions of non-testimonial credibility which are inhibiting truly fair trials in the courtroom mansion.

109 UEA, s 65. And see *R v Dean*, NSWSC (Dunford J) 12 March 1997.
110 UEA, s 67.
111 UEA, ss 108A and 108B.
112 UEA, s 165(1)(a).

16

*Human Rights, Cosmopolitanism and the Scottish 'Rape Shield'**

PETER DUFF

INTRODUCTION

OVER THE LAST 30 years, many common law jurisdictions have implemented statutory provisions designed, broadly speaking, to restrict the questioning of the victims of alleged sexual offences about their sexual history or bad character in criminal trials. The purpose of enacting 'rape shield' legislation, as it is commonly known,[1] was to dispel the 'twin myths' that, first, 'unchaste women were more likely to consent to intercourse' and, secondly, they 'were less worthy of belief'.[2] With the advent of the Human Rights Act 1998, human rights jurisprudence has become increasingly important in Scotland.[3] This chapter examines the development of the Scottish rape shield against this backdrop, without, I hope, descending to a level of doctrinal detail which would interest only a Scottish reader.[4] I will however suggest a way in which the implementation of the current legislation might be improved while remaining compatible with human rights requirements.

* I am grateful to my fellow participants in this project for comments on earlier drafts of this essay and to the Carnegie Trust for funding my trip to the Sydney workshop.

1 I am going to use this phrase as useful shorthand despite the fact that it has been judicially disapproved in Scotland: see *M(M) v HMA* 2004 SCCR 658, [13], per Lord Macfadyen, citing McLachlin J's view in the extremely influential Canadian case of *R v Seaboyer* [1991] 3 DCR 193, 258.

2 These *dicta* of McLachin J in *Seaboyer* [1991] 3 DCR 193, 258–59, have been widely quoted by both academics and judges in various jurisdictions. Regarding Scotland, see *M(M) v HMA* 2004 SCCR 658, [13]–[16] (Lord MacFadyen), [7] (Lord Gill).

3 Scotland has a separate legal system from that of England and Wales. For detailed analysis of ECHR influence on Scots law, see R Reed and J Murdoch, *A Guide to Human Rights Law in Scotland*, 2nd edn (Edinburgh, Butterworths, 2008) chs 1–3.

4 See P Duff, 'The Scottish "Rape Shield": As Good as it Gets?' (2011) 15 *Edinburgh Law Review* 218.

1. THE IMPACT OF HUMAN RIGHTS JURISPRUDENCE IN SCOTLAND

The original Scottish rape shield[5] was brought into force by the Law Reform (Miscellaneous Provisions) (Scotland) Act 1985, section 36, following a report by the Scottish Law Commission (SLC) in 1983.[6] At that time, the attitude of the Scots legal establishment towards the ECHR was (in) famously summarised by the Lord Justice Clerk, Scotland's second most senior judge, when he observed in *Kaur* that a Scottish court was *not* entitled to have regard to the ECHR, either as an aid to construction or for any other reason.[7] These *dicta* came only three years before publication of the SLC report and were approved a further two years later, and were in marked contrast to the approach then being adopted in the England.[8] Consequently, in discussing both the importance of maintaining adequate safeguards for accused and the need to protect complainers from distressing questioning, it is not surprising that the SLC's report made no reference to the ECHR nor uses any terminology from the associated discourse, not even the phrases 'human rights' or 'fair trial'.[9] There was, however, some discussion of equivalent provisions in other jurisdictions, most notably England and Canada.[10] Therefore, the SLC did not adopt an entirely parochial approach. The initial 1985 legislation was subsequently consolidated into the Criminal Procedure (Scotland) Act 1995.

A major research study published in 1992 by Brown et al[11] demonstrated that, as was common elsewhere, the Scottish rape shield was not particularly effective in preventing complainers from being subjected to often embarrassing and distressing questioning. As a result, the Scottish Executive undertook further work in this area, culminating in 2000 with the publication of *Redressing the Balance*,[12] a consultation document which canvassed options for strengthening the rape shield, as well as considering measures to prevent sexual offenders from cross-examining their victims in person.[13] By this time, the Scottish legal landscape had changed dramatically. First, a new generation of Scottish judges who were much more sympathetic

[5] For a full history, see B Brown, M Burman and L Jamieson, *Sex Crimes on Trial* (Edinburgh, Edinburgh UP, 1993) ch 1, and M Burman et al, *Impact of Aspects of the Law of Evidence in Sexual Offence Trials: An Evaluation Study* (Edinburgh, Scottish Government Social Research, 2007) ch 1.

[6] Scottish Law Commission, *Evidence: Report on Evidence in Cases of Rape and Other Sexual Offences* (Edinburgh, Scot Law Com No 78, 1983).

[7] *Surjit Kaur v Lord Advocate* 1980 SC 319, 324, 328–29.

[8] See Reed and Murdoch, above n 3, 1.11.

[9] SLC, above n 6, 5.1–5.28.

[10] Ibid 4.7–4.8.

[11] B Brown, M Burman and L Jamieson, *Sexual History and Sexual Character Evidence in Scottish Criminal Trials* (Edinburgh, Scottish Office Central Research Unit Papers, 1992).

[12] Scottish Executive, *Redressing the Balance: Cross Examination in Rape and Sexual Offences Trials* (Edinburgh, Scottish Executive, 2002).

[13] Ibid [2]–[5] recount its genesis.

to the ECHR had emerged. In *T, Petitioner*, Lord Justice General Hope, then Scotland's most senior judge, disapproved Lord Ross's 'increasingly outdated' view in *Kaur* and brought the Scottish approach to the ECHR into line with that adopted in England and Wales.[14] Lord Hope stated that henceforth when legislation was ambiguous, it should be interpreted in conformity with the ECHR rather than in conflict with it. After this decision, the ECHR and the jurisprudence of the European Court of Human Rights began to be cited frequently in the Scottish courts, particularly in criminal cases.[15] Very soon afterwards came the Scotland Act 1998, which created a devolved Scottish Parliament and Executive (the latter now styling itself 'Government') and also in some respects rendered Scots law consistent with the ECHR. It was followed by the Human Rights Act 1998 (HRA) which, when fully in force, demanded ECHR compliance right across the United Kingdom. It is significant that in Scotland, the former Act has been far more significant for Scottish criminal procedure than human rights legislation.

In essence,[16] it is *ultra vires* under the Scotland Act for the Scottish Parliament to legislate or the Scottish Executive to act in breach of the ECHR.[17] Any claim that either body has done so raises what has become known as a 'devolution issue'. There have been 'only a handful of challenges' to Scottish parliamentary legislation,[18] two of which concerned the legality of the rape shield provisions.[19] In contrast, challenges to acts of the Scottish Executive have been plentiful and, in a largely unanticipated development, many of these have been directed at ordinary, day-to-day decisions of Scottish prosecutors. This has resulted from the fact that the Lord Advocate, who is head of the prosecution service in Scotland, is a member of the Scottish Executive. Thus she, and all her subordinates within the Scottish prosecution service, must act in conformity with the ECHR at all times in the exercise of their function as prosecutors. Indeed, any human rights challenge to the actions of the Lord Advocate must be raised under the Scotland Act rather than the HRA.[20] As a result, a large number of such claims have been raised in the Scottish criminal courts by accused who have argued that the prosecution has, or is about to, breach their Article 6 rights—for example, the right to silence[21] or the presumption of innocence.[22]

[14] *T, Petitioner* 1997 SLT 724, 733.

[15] See Reed and Murdoch, above n 3, 1.13–1.14.

[16] For a full account, see Reed and Murdoch, above n 3, 1.18–1.45. See also N Walker, *Final Appellate Jurisdiction in the Scottish Legal System* (Edinburgh, Scottish Government and Edinburgh University, 2010), available at www.scotland.gov.uk/publications.

[17] Sections 29 and 57, respectively.

[18] Reed and Murdoch, above n 3, 1.22.

[19] *DS v HMA* 2007 SCCR 222 and *M(M) v HMA* 2004 SCCR 658.

[20] See Reed and Murdoch, above n 3, 1.25–1.27.

[21] *Stott v Brown* 2001 SCCR 62.

[22] *HMA v McIntosh* 2001 SCCR 191.

Obviously, the jurisprudence of the Strasbourg-based European Court of Human Rights is critical in determining whether there has been a breach of Article 6 in such cases. Under section 2(1) of the HRA, the domestic courts in the UK must 'take into account' any decision of the Strasbourg Court. Scottish courts have followed the English lead and 'will not without good reason depart from the principles laid down in a carefully considered judgment' of the Strasbourg Court.[23] In this regard, the Scottish courts do not differentiate between 'devolution issues' raised under the Scotland Act and HRA-based claims. Consequently, in the last 20 years the ECHR and its associated human rights jurisprudence has gone from having virtually no impact on Scottish criminal procedure to becoming the single most influential factor in the development of the law in this area. As Reed and Murdoch state in the opening sentence of their 800-page *Guide to Human Rights Law in Scotland*, '[u]ntil comparatively recently, the concept of "human rights" did not form a recognised part of the Scottish legal system'.[24] It is worth noting that, in contrast to its effect on criminal procedure and evidence, the ECHR has had very little impact on substantive criminal law, which rarely gives rise to a devolution or human rights issue.[25]

The impact of the ECHR and associated human rights concepts on Scottish criminal procedure has been strengthened by what is viewed by many as an anomaly,[26] namely, that while Scottish criminal appeals have always been determined domestically by the High Court of Justiciary, sitting in appellate mode in Edinburgh ('the appeal court'),[27] the ultimate appeal on devolution issues was originally to the Judicial Committee of the Privy Council (JCPC) in London. It now lies with the new UK Supreme Court (UKSC).[28] At the time of the Scotland Act, it was anticipated that most devolution issues would revolve around disputes between the Scottish and UK Parliaments about their respective powers and other constitutional matters. The JCPC provided the most convenient vehicle for resolving this constitutional issue because, with its long-standing commonwealth jurisdiction, it was not perceived primarily as an 'English' (in contrast to UK) domestic court, unlike the House of Lords. In the event, however, most Scottish cases going to the JCPC (and now the UKSC) have concerned criminal procedure arising from the appeal court rather than civil matters.

[23] *Maclean v HMA* [2009] HCJAC 97, [29] (Lord Hamilton).

[24] Reed and Murdoch, above n 3, 1.1.

[25] See ibid 1.4–1.5 for a list of the issues which have gone to the Strasbourg Court.

[26] See Walker, above n 16, 3.4, which contains further references; and A Page, 'Final Appellate Jurisdiction in the Scottish Legal System: The End of the Anomaly?' (2010) 14 *Edinburgh Law Review* 269.

[27] In contrast, the House of Lords in London hears final appeals in Scottish civil cases.

[28] Under s 40 of the Constitutional Reform Act 2005, a new United Kingdom Supreme Court took over the jurisdiction of both the House of Lords and, as regards United Kingdom matters, the Judicial Committee of the Privy Council on 1 October 2009.

This was unexpected, and has aroused some resentment in Scotland because of a perception that domestic criminal law issues are now being decided by an alien court rather than domestically, upsetting settled practice since the Act of Union in 1707.[29]

The loss of the appeal court's exclusive jurisdiction over Scottish criminal cases has been mitigated by the presence of two Scottish judges, Lords Hope and Rodger, on the bench of the JCPC and subsequently as members of the UKSC. Both previously held office as Lord Justice General, Scotland's most senior judge. In the great majority of Scottish appeals which have been heard by the JCPC, the Scottish judges have given the leading opinions and their non-Scottish colleagues have concurred. Nevertheless, it is apparent even from casual scrutiny that JCPC decisions pay closer attention to the ECHR jurisprudence than decisions of the native Scottish appeal court. Lords Hope and Rodger in particular seem to have been influenced by the human rights discourse, both in Europe and further afield, to a greater extent than many of their judicial colleagues back in Scotland,[30] although there are some notable exceptions.[31] Thus, the impact of human rights jurisprudence on the development of Scottish criminal procedure since the turn of the century has been considerably strengthened by the largely unexpected—and, to some, unwelcome—arrival of the JCPC and, subsequently, the UKSC in this domestic arena.

In light of these institutional developments, it is not surprising that the Scottish Executive's 2000 consultation paper *Redressing the Balance* addressed the human rights implications of proposed reforms of the rape shield, something the earlier SLC paper did not attempt. At the outset, the authors acknowledged the imperative of ensuring compatibility with the ECHR and then set out a series of 'principles ... intended to reflect the rights' of the accused under Article 6 as well as those of witnesses under Article 8.[32] *Redressing the Balance* noted that the original Canadian rape shield legislation was found to be contrary to the Canadian Charter of Rights and Freedoms by the Canadian Supreme Court in *Seaboyer*,[33] and that this defect was addressed by granting trial judges a discretion to admit evidence of sexual history where its probative value outweighs its prejudicial

[29] For further discussion, see Walker, above n 16, 25–27, 32–33; and J Chalmers, 'Scottish Appeals and the Proposed Supreme Court' (2004) 8 *Edinburgh Law Review* 4.

[30] This was also true while they were still serving as Scottish judges. See for example, Lord Rodger's leading opinions in the appeal court in *Brown v Stott* 2000 SCCR 314 and *Mcleod v HMA* 1998 SCCR 77 and, as noted above, it was Lord Hope in *T, Petitioner* 1997 SLT 724, 733 who dispensed with the rule that the Scottish courts could not even refer to the ECHR cases.

[31] Lord Reed, co-author of the major Scottish textbook on human rights, above n 3, is perhaps the most prominent. See also Lord Cullen's opinion in *Starrs v Ruxton* 1999 SCCR 1052 for early and copious citation of the European and other human rights jurisprudence in the Scottish appeal court.

[32] Above n 12, [19]–[22].

[33] [1991] 3 DCR 193.

effect. Observing that the Canadian Charter is very similar to the ECHR,[34] the consultation paper recommended that a modified version of the revised Canadian legislation should be adopted in Scotland.[35] More generally, the influence of the new human rights discourse might also be inferred from the use of the term 'fair trial',[36] a phrase absent from the earlier SLC paper which referred instead to 'the interests of justice'.[37]

This consultation exercise resulted in the Sexual Offences (Criminal Procedure) (Scotland) Act 2002, which replaced the earlier versions of sections 274 and 275 of the Criminal Procedure (Scotland) Act 1995. The new provisions were part of a 'second wave' of rape shield legislation sweeping the world, in response to the perceived failure of most initial attempts to operate as intended.[38] The Scottish Executive deliberately opted not to follow the English model,[39] essentially because it was thought to be too inflexible, preferring the Canadian Criminal Code-inspired model endorsed by *Redressing the Balance*.[40] Human rights jurisprudence has continued to influence the way in which the new legislation has been interpreted by the courts.

DS v HMA is the only rape shield case so far to have been appealed to either the JCPC or the UKSC.[41] At issue here was section 275A of the 1995 Act which provides that, where a defence application to raise the complainer's sexual history or bad character is successful, if the accused has any previous convictions for sexual offences, these will be revealed to the jury unless this would be contrary to the interests of justice. The accused claimed that section 275A was incompatible with his right to fair trial under the ECHR, and thus *ultra vires* the Scottish Parliament, because it unfairly hindered his ability to defend himself. The judgments of Lords Hope and Rodger are peppered with references to the leading European cases,[42] and *Seaboyer* was also cited. The appeal was dismissed because the JCPC took the view that previous convictions for sexual offences were potentially relevant and the discretion granted to the trial judge to refuse 'in the interests of justice' to allow the conviction to be revealed ensured that the trial would

[34] *Redressing the Balance*, above n 12, [106].

[35] Ibid [107]–[116].

[36] For example, in the *Foreword* by the Minister for Justice, and [14] and [17].

[37] Above n 6.

[38] See J Temkin, *Rape and the Legal Process*, 2nd edn (Oxford, OUP, 2002) 236 and, more generally, 196–245; and L Ellison, *The Adversarial Process and the Vulnerable Witness* (Oxford, OUP, 2001) 88–93.

[39] Youth Justice and Criminal Evidence Act 1999, s 41.

[40] *Sexual Offences (Procedure and Evidence) (Scotland) Bill, Policy Memorandum* (Edinburgh, SP Bill 31-PM, Session 1, 2001), [35]. The paper noted that fears of inflexibility were borne out by *R v A (No 2)* [2002] 1 AC 45, [2001] UKHL 25.

[41] *DS v HMA* 2007 SCCR 222.

[42] Including *Doorson v Netherlands* (1996) 22 EHRR 330; *Kostovski v Nethelands* (1989) 12 EHRR 434; and *Salabiaku v France* (1988) 13 EHRR 379.

be fair. The influence of the ECHR can be seen from the fact that, while the legislation expressly placed an onus on the accused to rebut the presumption that previous convictions should go to the jury, the JCPC utilised section 3(1) of the HRA to 'read down' this requirement so that the accused need only object to disclosure and the court must then consider the matter on its merits.[43]

In the proceedings before the Scottish appeal court in *DS*, the defence placed much reliance on the European cases[44] and also cited the leading Canadian case of *Darrach*[45] and the English decision in *A*.[46] However, in giving the decision, Lord Cullen barely mentioned the European jurisprudence,[47] bearing out the general impression that the JCPC appears to be more enthusiastic about Strasbourg jurisprudence than the Scottish appeal court. On the other hand, in the other leading rape shield case, *M*,[48] both the trial judge and the appeal court made extensive reference to the European jurisprudence as well as the leading Canadian authorities. Notably, as in *DS*, the accused was arguing that the Scottish Parliament had exceeded its powers because the rape shield legislation breached his Article 6 rights by restricting his right to cross-examine the complainer. This was not a routine challenge to prosecutorial decision-making, where the courts would be less inclined to embark upon systematic review of the legislation in order to assess its conformity with the ECHR. It may be significant that the same defence counsel appeared in both cases and on each occasion his arguments were rooted in the European jurisprudence.

2. THE SCOTTISH RAPE SHIELD

Before examining the shield itself, it is necessary to mention three other changes brought about by the new legislation. First, as alluded to above, the accused's previous convictions for sexual offences may be disclosed if there is a successful application to lead sexual history evidence. Obviously, this is a major innovation, particularly since Scotland has never embraced the common law 'similar fact evidence' doctrine.[49] Secondly, the Crown, too, must now seek the permission of the court if it wishes to lead evidence or

[43] *DS v HMA* 2007 SCCR 222, [48] (Lord Hope). See also G Gordon, *Commentary*, *DS* 2007 SCCR 222, 257.

[44] A summary of the defence submissions is provided in Lord Cullen's judgment in *HMA v DS* 2005 SCCR 655, [13]–[18].

[45] *Darrach v R* [2002] 2 SCR 443.

[46] *R v A (No 2)* [2002] 1 AC 45, [2001] UKHL 25.

[47] *HMA v DS* 2005 SCCR 655, [19]–[26].

[48] *M(M) v HMA* 2004 SCCR 658.

[49] See P Duff, 'Similar Facts Evidence in Scots Law?' (2008) 12 *Edinburgh Law Review* 121. For discussion of the English position, see P Roberts and A Zuckerman, *Criminal Evidence*, 2nd edn (Oxford, OUP, 2010) ch 14.

question the victim about her sexual history or bad character.[50] The 1992 Brown et al study had indicated that the Crown sometimes thwarted the purpose of the old rape shield by opening up this issue.[51] Additionally, the Scottish Government thought that applying the same rules to the prosecution and defence was 'likely to look fairer'.[52] Thirdly, where previously a verbal application to introduce sexual history evidence could be made to the trial judge, a written application must now be submitted in advance of the pre-trial hearing, indicating the nature of the evidence and why it is relevant to the issues at trial.[53] The intention was both to force the party making the application to spell out precisely why the evidence is relevant and to focus the minds of trial judges upon the purpose of the rape shield. Applications are now considered and determined at a pre-trial hearing, although it is still open to either party to renew such an application at trial on 'special cause shown'.[54]

(a) The Restriction—Section 274

The amended section 274 of the 1995 Act renders inadmissible four categories of evidence relating to the complainer's sexual history or bad character, subject to the exception set out in section 275. First, section 274(1)(a) bans evidence that the complainer is not of 'good character (whether in relation to sexual matters or otherwise)'. The previous rape shield had applied only to attacks on the complainer's character 'in relation to sexual matters', which phrasing had failed to prevent 'subtle character attacks' which were designed to suggest that the complainer was of 'easy virtue' and thus undermine her credibility.[55] In this respect, the new provision is more extensive than its Canadian counterpart which covers only 'sexual activity'.[56] Secondly, section 274(1)(b) prevents questioning about any 'sexual behaviour not forming part of the subject matter of the charge'; this remains unchanged from its previous incarnation. In an early case, the appeal court ruled that prior cohabitation is not primarily 'sexual' behaviour. Further, if there were

[50] In England only the defence need seek leave: see D Birch, 'Rethinking Sexual History Evidence: Proposals for Fairer Trials' [2002] *Criminal Law Review* 531, 534.

[51] Above n 11, 71–72.

[52] *Policy Memorandum*, above n 40, [37].

[53] The 1995 Act, s 275(3) lists 6 subjects which must be covered in such an application. This provision seems to have worked (Burman et al, above n 5, Table 3.2) unlike its English counterpart where most applications are still made at trial: L Kelly, J Temkin and S Griffiths, *Section 41: An Evaluation of New Legislation Limiting Sexual History Evidence in Rape Trials*, Online Report 20/06 (London, Home Office, 2006) 23.

[54] The 1995 Act, s 275B(1). The 2007 research indicates that this happens in 'few instances': above n 5, 5.39.

[55] *Redressing the Balance*, above n 12, [104].

[56] Canadian Criminal Code, 276(2).

any doubt about that, it would be removed by invoking section 3 of the Human Rights Act 1998.[57] In *DS*, the JCPC agreed with this earlier view.[58] A second point is that, after some debate, the courts have determined that statements or comments made by the complainer about her sexual activities do not fall within the definition of 'sexual behaviour'. Initially, the appeal court took the view that, in order to comply with the spirit of the legislation, such evidence should be construed as falling under section 274's general ban.[59] Shortly afterwards, the JCPC observed that the appeal court had given too wide a meaning to the word 'behaviour'. It would be incompatible with the accused's Article 6 right to a fair trial to prevent him from, for instance, leading evidence that the complainer had told a third party that she had consented to intercourse.[60] In a subsequent case, the appeal court followed the JCPC and the law now appears settled.[61] In resolving both of the above issues of interpretation, the ECHR proved a useful resource for the Scottish courts.

Thirdly, section 274(1)(c) presumptively prohibits evidence that the complainer has at any time 'other than shortly before, at the same time as, or shortly after' the alleged offence, 'engaged in behaviour, not being sexual behaviour' which might found an inference that she consented or is not a credible or reliable witness. Again, this was designed to prevent the type of backdoor character attacks which had been commonplace under the previous regime. Finally, section 274(1)(d) restricts evidence of 'any condition or predisposition' of the complainer which might lead to inferences of consent or lack of credibility. The intention was to cover the use of medical evidence about the complainer which does not relate directly to the alleged sexual assault.[62] The meaning attached to this phrase by the courts is discussed below.

(b) The Exception—Section 275

Section 275 creates a structured discretion. Its predecessor, like the first attempts at rape shield legislation in other jurisdictions, was expressed in wide terms, allowing questioning about previous sexual history *inter alia* 'to explain or rebut evidence led by the prosecution' or where 'it would

57 *M(M) v HMA* 2004 SCCR 658, [27] (Lord Gill, citing Lord Steyn's opinion in *R v A (No 2)* [2002] 1 AC 45).

58 *DS v HMA* 2007 SCCR 222.

59 *M v HMA* 2007 SCCR 159, [20]–[22] (Lord Johnston), [43] and (Lord Eassie), and [48] (Lord Marnoch dissenting). An application could be made to lead it under the exception set out in s 275 however.

60 *DS v HMA* 2007 SCCR 222, [46] (Lord Hope), and [76]–[77] (Lord Rodger).

61 *Judge v HMA* 2010 SCCR 135.

62 *Policy Memorandum*, above n 40, [21].

be contrary to the interests of justice to exclude it'. Many commentators concluded that the effect of this was 'almost to render the basic prohibition ineffective'.[63] The replacement section 275 sets out a three-stage cumulative test to be applied before allowing questioning about sexual history or bad character.

First, under section 275(1)(a) the evidence must relate 'only to a specific occurrence or occurrences of sexual or other behaviour or to specific facts demonstrating (i) the complainer's character or (ii) any condition or predisposition to which the complainer is or has been subject'. Although never explicitly stated during the legislative process, this precondition was obviously designed to ensure that any questioning by the defence has a firm evidential base. It prevents 'fishing expeditions' by the defence and wide-ranging attempts to blacken the general character of the complainer which were so typical under the previous regime.[64] Gotell observes that the equivalent provision in Canada has been the most effective barrier to defence requests for the complainer's medical and similar records because such demands usually have little or no evidential basis.[65] The courts were forced to insert what is now known as the 'invisible comma' between the words 'other behaviour' and 'or specific facts' in the statutory formula. Otherwise it would prohibit questioning the complainer about, for instance, the fact that she had consensual sexual intercourse with the accused a couple of hours before the alleged assault (unless this sheds light on her character or a condition or predisposition from which she suffers). In approving this interpretational refinement, first adopted by Lord Macfadyen in *M(M)*,[66] Lord Hope in *DS* observed that the 'invisible comma' was necessary to ensure compliance with Article 6.[67]

In *M(M)* defence counsel argued that section 275(1)(a) was contrary to the accused's Article 6 rights because it was too restrictive. The appeal court disagreed, stating that 'if there were to be an attack on the complainer's character, the prejudice to her should be minimised by the exclusion of vague and general allegations'. In Lord Gill's view, the court would in any event require the evidence to be specific under the ordinary rules of evidence.[68] A more problematic issue has been the phrase 'condition or predisposition', which was interpreted in *M* as requiring something akin

[63] *Redressing the Balance*, above n 12, [97].

[64] Ibid [115]–[116]; *Policy Memorandum*, above n 40, [23].

[65] L Gotell, 'When Privacy is Not Enough: Sexual Assault Complainants, Sexual History Evidence and the Disclosure of Personal Records' (2006) 43 *Alberta Law Review* 743, 761–62.

[66] *M(M) v HMA* 2004 SCCR 658, [40].

[67] *DS v HMA* 2007 SCCR 222 [47].

[68] *M(M) v HMA* 2004 SCCR 658, [37]. See also the pre-reform case of *Thomson v HMA* 2001 SCCR 162 and in particular Lord Bonomy's observations at 167. See *Dunnigan v HMA* 2006 SCCR 398 for an example of the appeal court approving a sheriff's quite strict approach to this requirement.

to a medical condition in order to be admissible.[69] Subsequently, in *Ronald*, Lord Hodge concluded that this did not mean that psychiatric evidence is to be 'confined' to diagnoses meeting the 'criteria of a disorder or syndrome and nothing else'. Medical evidence of a borderline condition not quite amounting to a 'separate disorder' and information about other aspects of a person's behaviour would also be relevant to the existence of a 'predisposition' because a psychiatrist in making a 'clinical judgement' looks at all the behaviour of a mentally disordered person.[70]

Pursuant to section 275(1)(b), admissible behaviour or facts must be 'relevant to establishing whether the accused is guilty of the offence with which he is charged'. This was designed to focus the mind of the court on the 'real issue' in determining whether to allow evidence about the complainer's sexual history or character to be admitted.[71] *Redressing the Balance* cited McLachlin J's identification in *Seaboyer*[72] of two basic flaws in legislative attempts to ensure relevance by banning particular categories of evidence, namely: the failure to distinguish between the different purposes to which evidence might be put; and the 'pigeonhole' approach, whereby if the evidence fits into a permitted category, the courts tend to admit it without adequately addressing its possible relevance.[73] Hence, the emphasis was put squarely on relevance itself. When interpreting section 275(1)(b), the courts have held, entirely logically, that it does not provide a gateway whereby evidence which would not be relevant at common law may now be admitted.[74] Secondly, it has also been observed that sexual history cannot be admitted 'simply for its bearing on the credibility of the complainer' because one of the purposes of the legislation was 'precisely to counteract' the idea that such evidence can indicate that the complainer is not a credible witness. Instead, if admitted, the jury must simply take it 'into account' when deciding if the Crown has proved the accused's guilt. For instance, if the complainer has previously had sexual relations with the accused, does this 'cast light' on whether she would have consented to the sexual act forming the subject matter of the charge on this occasion?[75] I will return to the threshold question of relevance in the final Section of the chapter.

The third stage of the test, framed by section 275(1)(c), demands that 'the probative value of the evidence ... is significant and is likely to outweigh any risk or prejudice to the proper administration of justice'. A shortcoming of the previous legislation was that it contained no 'guiding principles'

[69] *M v HMA* 2007 SCCR 159, [24] (Lord Johnston).
[70] *HMA v Ronald* 2007 SCCR 451, [26]. See also *HMA v A* 2005 SCCR 593.
[71] *Redressing the Balance*, above n 12, [100].
[72] [1991] 3 DCR 193.
[73] *Redressing the Balance*, above n 12, [106]–[116].
[74] *DS v HMA* 2007 SCCR 222 [27] (Lord Johnston) and [41] (Lord Eassie).
[75] Ibid [78] (Lord Rodger).

to structure judicial discretion to admit relevant evidence or questioning about the complainer's sexual history or character. This prompted concern, borne out by the 1992 Brown research study, that judges were 'unwilling to exclude any evidence which may even be slightly relevant, even though its prejudicial effect may be identifiable'.[76] Following the Canadian example,[77] section 275(2)(b) now specifically identifies 'appropriate protection of a complainer's dignity and privacy' as a factor in 'the proper administration of justice'.

This third criterion has not been discussed in any detail by the Scottish courts. There has been no reported case where it has been the decisive factor, but several *obiter dicta* pronouncements. In *Cumming*, for instance, Lord Carloway refused to allow evidence in a historic sexual abuse case about a social occasion many years later when the complainer allegedly sat on the accused's knee. In his view, this was not relevant but he added that, even if it were, the probable 'affront to the complainer's dignity' outweighed its probative value.[78] The priority remains, quite correctly, ensuring that the accused receives a fair trial and, of necessity, this means the protection that can be given to the complainer's interests under section 275(1)(c) is not unlimited. In *Ronald*, for instance, Lord Hodge thought that the 'paramount consideration of a fair trial' meant that the defence should be allowed to explore a variety of issues, subject to a partial restriction on one avenue of questioning, and to this extent it was permissible to 'compromise' the complainer's privacy.[79]

3. THE FUTURE

A 2007 large-scale evaluation of the revised Scottish rape shield regime[80] was carried out by the core team which undertook the 1992 study by Brown et al.[81] In a nutshell, the researchers found that the new legislation has had very little practical effect in terms of protecting the victims of sexual offences from embarrassing or harrowing cross-examination about their sexual history or general character. Indeed, the main conclusion was that, perversely, the 2002 Act 'has had the largely unanticipated and unintended consequences of the introduction of *more* sexual history and character

[76] *Redressing the Balance*, above n 12, [109]. See Brown et al, above n 11, 68.

[77] *Redressing the Balance*, above n 12, [110]–[112].

[78] *Cumming v HMA* 2003 SCCR 261, 265, although the appeal court did not share his view and thought the evidence both relevant and not unduly prejudicial. See also *Dunnigan v HMA* 2006 SCCR 398.

[79] *HMA v Ronald* 2007 SCCR 451 [29]–[32].

[80] Burman et al, above n 5.

[81] Brown et al, above n 11.

evidence than occurred under the 1995 legislation'.[82] The bald figures are revealing.[83] Of the 123 sexual offence cases that went to trial, 72% involved an application to lead sexual history and/or character evidence[84] and only 7% of these were refused, although in some further cases, questioning was restricted.[85] Therefore, almost three-quarters of sexual offence trials involved an application, compared with one-fifth under the previous regime.[86] The most common issues raised by applicants were: the complainer's character (24%); her sexual history with someone other than the accused (20%); and her sexual history with the accused (16%).[87] It is also significant that in 14 out of the 32 trials observed by the researchers, evidence or questioning went beyond what had been allowed under the application. Objections by the Crown or interventions by the judge in such cases were rare. In this respect, there was again no improvement on the previous regime.

Criminal practitioners offered various explanations for the dramatic increase in applications to raise the complainer's sexual history in evidence. First, part of the rise might be more apparent than real, because: (1) a greater range of evidence now falls under the general ban in section 274; (2) the Crown also is now required to make an application; and (3) the number of multiple applications in a single case has doubled.[88] It was further suggested that a range of other procedural changes had concentrated counsels' minds at an early stage on what sexual history evidence might be adduced:[89] the introduction of preliminary hearings to the High Court with an emphasis on early case preparation; the requirement that counsel submit a detailed written application before the preliminary hearing to raise sexual history; and the impact of the case of *Anderson* which established that negligent representation by defence counsel is a valid ground of appeal.[90] This has prompted counsel to adopt a 'scatter gun' or 'belt and braces' strategy, submitting applications where previously they might not have done so.[91] In any event, it is abundantly clear that the revised Scottish rape shield has proved no more successful than its predecessor. This, I think, is the result of two

[82] Burman et al, above n 5, ' Executive Summary', 7.

[83] Ibid 'Executive Summary', 1–7 and ch 3.

[84] The Crown was responsible for around one-quarter of applications, usually where the defence was making one as well: ibid 3.39.

[85] Ibid 3.42.

[86] Ibid 3.29.

[87] Ibid 4.39–4.41.

[88] Ibid 3.37–3.41, 4.45.

[89] Ibid 3.55–3.68.

[90] *Anderson v HMA* 1996 SCCR 487. This has led to the criminal bar raising all sorts of issues they would previously have ignored as unimportant in order to forestall an appeal based on their incompetence. See the 2007 study, ibid 3.57–3.60 and also J Chalmers et al, *An Evaluation of the High Court Reforms Arising from the Criminal Procedure (Amendment) (Scotland) Act* (Edinburgh, Scottish Executive Social Research, 2007) 5.14.

[91] Burman et al, above n 5, 10.19.

fundamental problems which I shall now explore in more detail. First, there is the wide definition given to relevance. The second problem is judges' reluctance to use the third stage of the cumulative test which allows them to deem that the prejudicial effect of the proposed evidence outweighs its probative value.

(a) Relevance

The legal concept of relevance is not an objective, analytically-derived creation of pure logic but instead is socially constructed, nebulous and shifting. Relevance is politically and morally charged and means different things to different audiences. Dennis has observed that English law has 'no authoritative statutory or common law definition of the core concept of relevance' and, while this permits 'flexibility in the application of the concept', it is 'purchased at the cost of some obscurity and inconsistency'.[92] For present purposes, it can be assumed that the Scottish definition of relevance is the same as its English counterpart.[93] With regard to sexual assaults in particular, as many commentators have observed, what one regards as relevant is bound up with moral values and associated social attitudes towards sexual behaviour.[94] As Kelly et al rather gloomily observe in their recent research on the English rape shield, '[r]elevance… is in the mind of the beholder'.[95] Put somewhat simplistically, supporters of a strong rape shield tend to claim that a victim's sexual history or general character is irrelevant when determining whether she consented to the sexual activity which is the subject of the prosecution, whereas many legal practitioners would disagree.

For instance, Brindley, a spokesperson for Rape Crisis in Scotland, has claimed: 'Questioning about how a woman was dressed or *her previous sexual history* should have no place in our courts' (emphasis added).[96] Similarly, Caringella, an American academic, claims that the admission of sexual history evidence to establish consent is 'ridiculous' and that its only

[92] I Dennis, *The Law of Evidence*, 3rd edn (London, Sweet and Maxwell, 2007) 60. For detailed discussion of the English concept, see ibid 60–84; and Roberts and Zuckerman, above n 49, 99–109.

[93] See Ross and Chalmers, *Walker and Walker: The Law of Evidence in Scotland*, 3rd edn (West Sussex, Tottel, 2009) 1.3 (which has attained authoritative status in the Scottish courts). See also F Davidson, *Evidence* (Edinburgh, Thomson/W Green, 2007) 2.05–2.06.

[94] A McColgan, 'Common Law and the Relevance of Sexual History Evidence' (1996) 16 *Oxford Journal of Legal Studies* 275; Temkin, above n 38, 196–225.

[95] Kelly et al, above n 53, 12.

[96] S Brindley, 'A Line Too Often Crossed', 2008 (April) *The Journal (Law Society of Scotland)* 9. In fairness, it is not clear from the rest of the article that she would actually argue that previous sexual history is always irrelevant.

relevance is 'to determine the origin of semen, pregnancy or disease'.[97] Not quite so starkly, Lees argues in her influential book that 'a woman's sexual character and past sexual history are rarely, if at all, relevant'.[98] Similarly, McColgan in a much-cited article claims that 'sexual history evidence will be irrelevant, in all but the most exceptional cases, to the issue of the defendant's guilt'.[99] I have a great deal of sympathy with the motive underlying such claims because the research studies cited by those making them demonstrate emphatically that, despite the advent of rape shield legislation, it is still very common for all sorts of completely irrelevant, embarrassing and demeaning questions to be put to complainers in cross-examination about their sexual and other behaviour.[100] Nevertheless, one wonders if such commentators tend, in an understandable over-reaction, to over-state their case by underestimating the extent to which sexual history or character evidence may sometimes be relevant.[101]

In contrast, it is apparent, both from the empirical research and the reported cases that most Scottish lawyers and judges think that a complainer's previous sexual activity or behaviour quite often has some bearing on the issue of consent.[102] Unsurprisingly, given the cultural similarities, the mindset of lawyers and judges in both Canada and England appears to be similar.[103] Indeed, most Scottish legal professionals saw little need for the 2002 reforms and gave evidence to this effect to the Scottish Parliament.[104] Raitt, somewhat despairingly, talks of the 'stark contrast' between the perceptions of relevance held by the Scottish legal profession and their critics.[105] In this context, it is illuminating to mention briefly the first two appeals to be decided under the new legislation. In *Cumming*, as we saw above, the appeal court did not agree with the trial judge that the proposed

[97] S Caringella, *Addressing Rape Reform in Law and Practice* (New York, Columbia UP, 2009) 182–83.

[98] S Lees, *Carnal Knowledge: Rape on Trial*, 2nd edn (London, Women's Press, 2002) 57.

[99] McColgan, above n 94, 302. See also Temkin, above n 38, ch 4.

[100] These include the Scottish studies in 1992, above n 11, and 2007, above n 5. For similar English research, see Z Adler, *Rape on Trial* (London, Routledge, 1987); Lees, above n 98; and Kelly et al, above n 53.

[101] See M Redmayne, 'Myths, Relationships and Coincidences: The New Problems of Sexual History Evidence' (2003) 7 *International Journal of Evidence & Proof* 75 for a convincing argument that a previous sexual relationship with the accused may well be relevant on occasion.

[102] See the 2007 study which shows, for example, that most judges and practitioners think that evidence of past sexual relations with the accused is virtually always relevant: above n 5, 5.66–5.71.

[103] Gotell, above n 65, 755–56, argues that the attitude of the legal profession has undermined the Canadian rape shield. For similar views about English lawyers, see J Temkin, 'Prosecuting and Defending Rape: Perspectives from the Bar' (2000) 27 *Journal of Law and Society* 219; and Kelly et al, above n 53, ch 7.

[104] Justice 2 Committee, *13th Report 2001: Stage 1 Report on the Sexual Offences (Procedure and Evidence) (Scotland) Bill* (Edinburgh, Scottish Parliament Paper 446, 2001) 51–2.

[105] F Raitt, *Evidence: Principles, Policy and Practice* (Edinburgh, Thomson/W Green, 2008) 247.

line of questioning was irrelevant.[106] This prompted Gordon to comment that the Act 'may not be quite as restrictive as one might have expected, or as perhaps its supporters wished'.[107]

The second case, *Kinnin v HMA*[108] was even more disappointing for supporters of the strengthened rape shield. *Kinnin* involved a defence of consent to a charge of attempted rape. The defence wished to ask the complainer about a couple of occasions during the month prior to the events in question when she had allegedly indicated to the accused's son that she wished to have a sexual relationship with him (ie the son). This, it was claimed, would allow the jury to infer that she 'was a person willing to engage in adulterous liaisons', a conclusion which would 'assist' the defence.[109] At a preliminary hearing the sheriff, not surprisingly, held that this evidence was not relevant under section 275(1)(b) because it was too 'remote' from the events at issue.[110] On appeal, the sheriff was criticised by the defence for failing to explain his reasoning but one would have thought it obvious, at least from a common-sense viewpoint, that the fact that the complainer might have indicated a willingness to have sex with the accused's son had no bearing on whether she was prepared to have sex with the father.

In a lamentable decision,[111] the appeal court simply stated that it supported the defence submissions and allowed the appeal without any further explanation.[112] Fears were now voiced that the legislation was going to have no impact at all in the face of the entrenched view of legal practitioners that virtually all the recent sexual history of a complainer was relevant.[113] It is particularly disappointing that the court's opinion was delivered by the Lord Justice General, Scotland's most senior judge. Nevertheless, it is fair to say that some of the more recent decisions indicate that the appeal court is now taking a more restrictive approach to the definition of relevance, as demonstrated by *M*, where questioning regarding allegations of sexual fantasising and habitual lying was not permitted.[114] Similarly in *Wright v HMA*[115] the defence, arguing consent, was not allowed to question the complainer in

[106] *Cumming v HMA* 2003 SCCR 261 (complainer in historic sexual abuse case allegedly sitting on accused's knee as an adult at a social occasion).

[107] Ibid 269.

[108] *Kinnin v HMA* 2003 SCCR 294.

[109] The defence application is quoted, ibid 296.

[110] The sheriff's decision is quoted by the appeal court, ibid [5].

[111] See F Raitt, above n 105, 12.43; G Gordon's *Commentary* on *Kinnin*, 2005 SCCR 298 (observing diplomatically, 'I doubt whether it would be generally thought that willingness to have sexual relations with a man was something from which one could infer willingness to have them with his father').

[112] *Kinnin v HMA* 2003 SCCR 294, [8].

[113] See Raitt, above n 105, 12.41–12.46; Davidson, above n 93, 10.72–10.73; Gordon's *Commentary*, above n 111, 298.

[114] *M v HMA* 2007 SCCR 159.

[115] *Wright v HMA* 2005 SCCR 780. See also *Cassels v HMA* 2006 SCCR 327 and *Dunnigan v HMA* 2006 SCCR 398.

a rape trial about two occasions when she had allegedly attempted to kiss the accused on the lips. Both the trial judge and the appeal court refused the application *inter alia* on grounds of relevance, because of the difference between the types of behaviour and the lapse of time (the alleged incidents were respectively nine months and over two years earlier).[116]

It is significant that the Crown in *Kinnin* did not support the sheriff's decision on appeal, and even went as far as to submit, in agreement with the defence, that the evidence was relevant and ought to be admitted.[117] This chimes with Burman et al's 2007 study's finding[118] that the prosecution frequently does not oppose defence applications and that most section 275 hearings were 'characterised by a lack of discussion of relevance'.[119] Defence and Crown counsel had often reached prior agreement on the application, and judges tended not to intervene.[120] It is worth noting that recent research in England and Wales produced similar results.[121] One might call upon the Scottish judiciary to adopt a more interventionist stance, as many supporters of rape shield legislation do. Yet this strategy implicitly assumes that the line between relevant and irrelevant sexual history is clear. Unfortunately, the judicial decisions in *Seaboyer* and *A*, and copious academic literature refute this assumption.[122]

Redmayne demonstrates that relevance is always context-specific,[123] a point nicely captured by one of the judges interviewed for the 2007 study, referring to the requirement to determine section 275 applications in advance of trial: 'We're asking to decide matters of relevancy ... in a vacuum; that's a problem for us'.[124] However, the fundamental problem is that a radical feminist or a liberal male academic or a traditionalist Catholic bishop or a reader of 'lads' mags' may have conflicting views about the relevance of a specific piece of sexual history evidence, in the context of a particular case, because of their very different moral values and social attitudes. A much more critical and reflective approach by the judiciary, taking account of feminist arguments, may resolve some of the difficulties

[116] *Wright v HMA* 2005 SCCR 780, [6]–[8].

[117] *Kinnin v HMA* 2003 SCCR 294, [7].

[118] Above, n 5, 5.5–5.18 revealing that the Crown opposed only 10 out of 32 defence applications and these tended to involve character evidence rather than sexual history.

[119] Ibid 10.15.

[120] Ibid 10.10–10.16.

[121] Kelly *et al*, above n 53, 54–55.

[122] Redmayne, above n 101. See also the disagreement between two other eminent English scholars: Birch, above n 50; J Temkin 'Sexual History Evidence—Beware the Backlash' [2003] *Criminal Law Review* 217; and D Birch, 'Untangling Sexual History Evidence: A Rejoinder to Professor Temkin' [2003] *Criminal Law Review* 370.

[123] Redmayne, above n 101. This point is also stressed by Roberts and Zuckerman, above n 49, 274.

[124] Burman et al, above n 5, 5.53.

but there is always going to be a large grey area where the question of relevance remains highly controversial.[125]

(b) Prejudice to the Administration of Justice Outweighs Probative Value[126]

As noted above, the Scottish judiciary has rarely invoked prejudice to the administration of justice as a basis for protecting rape victims from offensive or upsetting questioning. It will be remembered that section 275(2)(b) states that this includes the 'appropriate protection of a complainer's dignity and privacy'. The 2007 Burman research indicated that judges have difficulty imagining circumstances where they would rule out otherwise relevant evidence for this reason.[127] In my view, however, a more robust judicial approach would be perfectly possible without giving rise to appeals based on asserted breaches of the ECHR. The 'landmark ruling'[128] here is *Doorson*, one of a number of anonymous witness cases heard by the Strasbourg Court, where the court stated that, while not explicitly mentioned in the Convention text, the rights of witnesses must also be taken into account under Article 6: '[P]rinciples of fair trial also require that in appropriate cases the interests of the defence are balanced against those of witnesses or victims called upon to testify'.[129]

It further observed that Article 6 would not be breached as long as the 'handicaps' faced by the defence, as a result of the need to protect witnesses' rights, were 'sufficiently counterbalanced by the procedures followed by the judicial authorities'.[130] Following *Doorson*, there have been several more cases involving the rights of victims of sexual offences but, as far as I can ascertain, only one concerning rape shield provisions.[131]

Oyston v UK[132] concerned a decision by the Court of Appeal, in relation to the original English rape shield contained in section 2 of the Sexual Offences (Amendment) Act 1976, to reject fresh evidence that the

[125] For instance, the Burman study, above n 5, 7.30–7.34, indicates that judges and practitioners had considerable difficulty in determining whether the complainer's consumption of alcohol at the time of the alleged offence was relevant.

[126] I am grateful to Terese Henning for emphasising to me the potential of this ground of exclusion.

[127] Burman et al, above n 5, 5.62.

[128] Ellison, above n 38, 78.

[129] *Doorson v Netherlands* (1996) 22 EHHR 330, [70]. These *dicta* were repeated in another anonymous witness case, *Van Mechelen v Netherlands* (1997) 25 EHHR 647, [53].

[130] *Doorson v Netherlands* (1996) 22 EHHR 330, [72].

[131] For discussion of the European jurisprudence on the Article 6 right to have witnesses questioned, see SJ Summers, *Fair Trials: The European Criminal Procedural Tradition And the European Court of Human Rights* (Oxford, Hart Publishing, 2007) 132–55.

[132] App No 42011/98, ECtHR Admissability Decision of 22 January 2002, noted at [2002] Crim LR 497. The domestic appeal is unreported.

complainant had, while on holiday, had a brief sexual relationship with a young man, either shortly before or after the alleged rape by the applicant who was nearly four times her age. Phillips CJ, giving the court's judgment, stated that the evidence would not have been admissible at trial, observing that this was a 'paradigm example' of what the rape shield was designed to exclude. The applicant went to the Strasbourg Court, arguing that section 2 afforded special treatment to complainants which amounted to 'inequality of arms', because an important defence witness had been subject to extensive questioning about *her* sexual history. The Strasbourg Court found the application 'manifestly unfounded' and inadmissible.[133] Citing *Doorson*, the Court stated that the distinction created by the rape shield between rape victims and other female witnesses was not incompatible with Article 6. It further observed that, while section 2 did place certain restrictions on the questions which could be asked of the complainant in cross-examination, the trial judge had permitted the defence to raise one aspect of her sexual history which was clearly relevant.

The more recent Strasbourg case of *SN v Sweden*[134] is also informative. The accused was convicted of sexually abusing an 11-year-old child on the basis of two taped (one video and one audio) police interviews which were the decisive evidence in the case. Swedish legislation allowed the use of such evidence in cases involving child witnesses in order to prevent them from the harm which might be caused by having to give evidence at trial. In determining that there had been no breach of the Article 6 rights to fair trial and to examine witnesses, the European Court reiterated its view that the accused does not have 'an unlimited right' to demand the attendance of witnesses at court. Moreover, it is normally for the domestic courts to decide 'whether it is necessary or advisable to hear a witness'.[135] The Court took into account the 'special features of criminal proceedings concerning sexual offences' which are 'often conceived of as an ordeal by the victim' and emphasised the importance of 'respect for the private life' of victims of crime. Consequently, in sexual offence cases 'measures may be taken for the purpose of protecting the victim, provided that such measures can be reconciled with an adequate and effective exercise of the right of the defence'.[136] In order to ensure the latter, the courts may need 'to take measures which counterbalance the handicaps under which the defence labours'.[137] In the view of the Strasbourg Court, there had been adequate protection for the

[133] In theory, therefore, this was not technically a substantive 'decision' on the merits of the case but the Strasbourg Court, as it often does, gave some indication of its thinking.

[134] (2004) 39 EHHR 13.

[135] See *Baegen v Netherlands* (1995, App No 16696/90) and *Finkensieper v Netherlands* (1995, App No 19525/92) which also involved children who had been sexually abused. These cases, which did not go the full European Court, are discussed by Ellison, above n 38, 78–80.

[136] *SN v Sweden* (2004) 39 EHHR 304 [49]–[51]

[137] Ibid [44]–[47]. This echoes *Doorson v Netherlands* (1996) 22 EHHR 330, [72].

accused in *SN v Sweden* because the second interview had taken place following a defence request to obtain further information and defence counsel had been given the opportunity to attend the interview and have questions put to the victim.[138]

In the context of the Scottish rape shield, we are not of course dealing with the extreme situation where the defence is unable to cross-examine the victim in court at all, but simply with relatively narrow restrictions upon the type of questions which may be asked. In my view, there is little doubt that the Strasbourg Court would hold, in line with *Oyston*, that the limitations on cross-examination set out in section 274 are legitimate and that the safeguard of the exception in section 275 provides the defence with an adequate counterbalance. In particular, the fact that it is a judge who decides upon relevance and whether the probative value of the evidence outweighs its prejudicial effect would be regarded as important. These were precisely the arguments advanced by Lord Macfadyen in the appeal court's decision in *M(M)*, which held that the Scottish rape shield was compliant with Article 6 after a review of the European cases.[139] Indeed, the defence has the further safeguard of an immediate right of appeal against the judge's decision. Further, the European Court has stressed on repeated occasions that the admissibility of evidence is primarily governed by domestic law and is a matter for national courts, its own role being limited to ascertaining that the proceedings as a whole are fair.[140] Thus, it will intervene only where the effect of a domestic ruling has been to deprive the accused of a 'fair trial' overall.[141] With this track-record, it is unlikely that the Strasbourg Court would hold that any specific decision reasonably made by a Scottish court not to allow a particular line of cross-examination in order to protect the complainer's mental health, privacy or dignity was a breach of Article 6.

Further support for this view might be derived from the Canadian case of *Darrach*, in which the post-*Seaboyer* rape shield was held by the Canadian Supreme Court not to be contrary to the Canadian Charter.[142] In delivering the Court's opinion, Gonthier J emphasised that the Canadian shield successfully balances the 'divergent interests' of the accused to a fair trial, of the complainant to privacy, and of the court to procedural integrity

[138] See also the more recent case of *Bocos-Cuesta v Netherlands* (2005, App No 54789/00) where the European Court held there was a breach of Article 6 because *inter alia* the accused was given no opportunity to have questions put to witnesses.

[139] *M(M)* 2004 SCCR 658, [33]–[44].

[140] *Doorson v Netherlands* (1996) 22 EHHR 330, [67], *SN v Sweden* (2004) 39 EHHR 304, [43]. See also Summers, above n 131, 132–34.

[141] Cf *PS v Germany* (2003) 36 EHHR 61 (ruling criminal proceedings unfair because the accused had no opportunity to have questioned an 8-year-old girl he had allegedly abused sexually and whose accusations, relayed to her mother and the police, comprised the 'sole and decisive' evidence).

[142] *R v Darrach* [2002] SCR 443.

(by excluding misleading evidence).[143] The accused is not entitled to 'the most favourable procedures that could possibly be imagined'.[144] The judicial discretion to admit relevant evidence ensures that the Canadian shield is constitutional, and the requirement that the evidence has 'significant probative value' does not 'raise the threshold to the point that it is unfair to the accused'. Gonthier J further observed that, once the accused has established that the evidence does meet the significance test, it will be excluded only if its probative value is 'substantially' outweighed by the risk of prejudice to the administration of justice.[145] Finally, given that competing interests are involved, the accused's right to a fair trial is not 'necessarily breached' when he is 'not permitted to adduce relevant evidence which is not "significantly" probative, under a rule of evidence that protects the trial from the distorting effect of evidence of prior sexual history'.[146] It seems highly likely that, against the background of *Doorson* and similar cases, the European Court would adopt a similar approach.

CONCLUSION

This essay has shown that over the last decade Scottish legal institutions have increasingly adopted a more cosmopolitan approach, to a large extent as a result of the arrival of the ECHR through the Scotland Act 1998. Frequent references are now made in the Scottish criminal courts to Article 6 rights and 'foreign' cases, something which simply would not have happened a few years ago. We have seen the way in which the ECHR and its associated jurisprudence have shaped the development of the Scottish rape shield and could continue to do so.

Secondly, it has provided a brief description of the rape shield itself, indicating where its operation could be improved. I have suggested that there is little further that can be done to improve the statutory provisions[147] but that there is some scope for improving their implementation. In particular, judges could adopt a stricter approach to relevance and make more use of their power to exclude evidence which damages the interests of the complainer and is of little probative value.

143 Ibid [31]. See also [19] and [25].

144 Ibid [24], citing *R v Lyons* [1987] 2 SCR 309.

145 Ibid [39]–[40].

146 Ibid [24].

147 Jenny McEwan likewise doubts 'the endless quest for the perfect rape shield': see J McEwan, 'Proving Consent in Sexual Cases: Legislative Change and Cultural Evolution' (2005) 9 *International Journal of Evidence & Proof* 1.

Index